Understanding the Implications of Trade and Financial Market Integration for Business Cycles

World Scientific Studies in International Economics
(ISSN: 1793-3641)

World Scientific Studies in International Economics includes works dealing with the theory, empirical analysis, and evaluation of international economic policies and institutions, with topics covering international macroeconomics and finance, international trade theory and policy, as well as international legal and political economy. Monographs and edited volumes will comprise the core of the publications.

Vol. 74 *Understanding the Implications of Trade and Financial Market Integration for Business Cycles*
by Mario J. Crucini (Vanderbilt University, USA)

Vol. 73 *The International Economics of Wine*
edited by Kym Anderson (University of Adelaide, Australia & Australian National University, Australia)

Vol. 72 *Foreign Direct Investment*
by Bruce A. Blonigen (University of Oregon, USA & National Bureau of Economic Research, USA)

Vol. 71 *Offshoring: Causes and Consequences at the Firm and Worker Level*
edited by Holger Görg (Kiel Institute for the World Economy, Germany) & Aoife Hanley (Kiel Institute for the World Economy, Germany)

Vol. 70 *Policy Externalities and International Trade Agreements*
by Nuno Limão (University of Maryland, USA)

Vol. 69 *Economic Analysis of the Rules and Regulations of the World Trade Organization*
edited by Kamal Saggi (Vanderbilt University, USA)

Vol. 68 *International Trade, Capital Flows and Economic Development*
edited by Francisco L. Rivera-Batiz (Columbia University, USA) & Luis A. Rivera-Batiz (University of Puerto Rico, USA)

Vol. 67 *Megaregionalism 2.0: Trade and Innovation within Global Networks*
edited by Dieter Ernst (East-West Center, USA & The Centre for International Governance Innovation/CIGI, Canada) & Michael G. Plummer (The Johns Hopkins University, SAIS, Italy)

Vol. 66 *International and Interregional Migration: Theory and Evidence*
edited by Francisco L. Rivera-Batiz (Columbia University, USA)

The complete list of the published volumes in the series can be found at
https://www.worldscientific.com/series/wssie

74 World Scientific Studies in International Economics

Understanding the Implications of Trade and Financial Market Integration for Business Cycles

MARIO J CRUCINI
Vanderbilt University, USA

World Scientific

NEW JERSEY • LONDON • SINGAPORE • BEIJING • SHANGHAI • HONG KONG • TAIPEI • CHENNAI • TOKYO

Published by

World Scientific Publishing Co. Pte. Ltd.
5 Toh Tuck Link, Singapore 596224
USA office: 27 Warren Street, Suite 401-402, Hackensack, NJ 07601
UK office: 57 Shelton Street, Covent Garden, London WC2H 9HE

Library of Congress Cataloging-in-Publication Data
Names: Crucini, Mario J. (Mario John), 1962– author.
Title: Understanding the implications of trade and financial market integration for business cycles / Mario J. Crucini, Vanderbilt University, USA.
Description: New Jersey : World scientific, 2020. | Series: World scientific studies in international economics ; vol 74 | Includes bibliographical references and index.
Identifiers: LCCN 2019053523 | ISBN 9789811208232 (hardcover)
Subjects: LCSH: Business cycles. | Commerce. | Monetary policy. | Tariff preferences.
Classification: LCC HB3711 .C78 2020 | DDC 338.5/42--dc23
LC record available at https://lccn.loc.gov/2019053523

British Library Cataloguing-in-Publication Data
A catalogue record for this book is available from the British Library.

For any available supplementary material, please visit
https://www.worldscientific.com/worldscibooks/10.1142/11498#t=suppl

Desk Editors: Balasubramanian/Shreya Gopi

Typeset by Stallion Press
Email: enquiries@stallionpress.com

Preface

This book is a collection of the editor's scholarly work spanning a quarter century of inquiry into the causes of international business cycles. Part I reviews salient business cycle facts relating to quantities, prices, and the driving forces of international business cycles. Part II focuses on the role of risk sharing and asset market structure in shaping business cycles and welfare. Part III deals with economic models of relative price determination and the terms of trade; it stresses the roles of retail distribution, information frictions, and the need to tie commodity-specific shocks to particular nations or world regions that specialize in their production and trade. Part IV is a collection of work focusing on the trade collapse and aggregate inefficiencies brought about by the Hawley-Smoot Tariff Act of 1930 and foreign retaliation.

The research topics of this book are explored using varied research methodologies: gathering new facts from historical archives; estimating reduced-form models of economic dynamics; and developing, solving, and simulating multicountry Dynamic Stochastic General Equilibrium (DSGE) models.

Part I focuses on the facts. Chapter 1 studies the business cycles of large industrialized countries using Bayesian Factor models. Among the most important features of international business cycles is the tendency for output to rise and fall in a reasonably synchronous fashion across countries. The Bayesian Factor model captures this by positing a three-factor model of stochastic variation in the NIPA components. The world business-cycle factor is common to all countries and all NIPA components. The national factor is common to all NIPA components in a particular country. The idiosyncratic factor is specific to a particular NIPA component and country. The three sets of factors are also mutually uncorrelated with each other.

The relative importance of the three factors influences the extent to which economic growth rates are correlated across countries and components of aggregate demand (consumption, investment, and government spending). For example, if the world factor accounted for all of the variation in the international macroeconomic data, there would be perfect collinearity of national business cycles. Among large industrialized countries, it turns out that world (common) and national components each account for about half of GDP growth variation.[1] In contrast, the national component of total factor productivity is twice as large as the common or world component. This poses a challenge for models that rely heavily on productivity-driven business cycles: in these models, the international correlation of productivity tends to lie strictly above the international correlation of output. It could be financial market integration and monetary policy that elevate international business-cycle correlations since the world component of the *ex post* short-term real interest rate, which follows the policy rate closely, is mostly driven by a common world factor. Fiscal policy measures, in contrast, are mostly idiosyncratic and not correlated across nations or with the national GDP.

The remaining three chapters of Part I focus on international relative prices. The disproportionate attention to prices in this book is typical of the international finance literature. It reflects deeply puzzling behavior of local currency prices within and across countries. This literature focuses on two properties of relative price behavior.

The first property of relative price behavior is the extent to which international prices obey the Law-of-One-Price (LOP). To be clear, there are two versions of the LOP. The first version is literal: the price of a good in two locations will be equal once converted

[1]Perhaps coincidently, Crucini and Vu (2019) find that national and county-specific wage shocks contribute about equally to the variance of quarterly US county-level real wage growth.

into common currency units. Rogoff (1996) correctly observes that based on existing research, this version of the LOP holds mainly in the breach. The second version of the LOP is that common currency prices should differ by the magnitude of official and natural barriers to trade. Official barriers to trade include tariff and non-tariff barriers as well as more subtle regulatory policies that impair international arbitrage. Natural barriers to trade include shipping costs and, in the case of consumer goods, rent and wages associated with retail trade. Notice that the second, more realistic, version of the proposition requires the rather daunting empirical exercise of measuring all natural and official barriers to trade for all the goods and services that make up the modern consumption basket. The contents of the consumption basket run into the tens of thousands of items in most countries. Ideally, one would want items of comparison to match down to the exact make and model (as captured by barcode-level comparisons in contemporary markets), but this is infeasible. Instead, economists have relied on large, representative, samples of goods and services of varying degrees of comparability. Chapters 2 and 3 fall into this subset of the empirical literature on international relative prices.

The second property of relative price behavior is the apparent disconnect between retail price changes in US and those in our major trading partners, such as Canada. In common currency units, a change in price of a box of cereal at a grocer in Toronto should be equal to the change in the price of the same box of cereal in Buffalo. The most obvious violation of this property of relative price behavior is the fact that the bilateral nominal exchange rate often changes by a few percentage points in a week while retail prices remain fixed in local currency units for at least that long. Chapter 4 falls into this subset of the empirical international price literature.

Turning to the details, Chapter 2 studies retail prices across 13 European cities at 5-year intervals between 1975 and 1990. A key attribute of these retail prices is that Eurostat, the statistical agency of the European Union, asked the national statistical agencies to obtain price quotes on the same items across cities. This is far superior to national consumer price surveys designed to match the individual goods and services that are typical of the local consumption basket. As such, the Eurostat survey follows the protocol of the LOP requirement of identical items across locations.

Remarkably, the average price of the items in the retail basket was close to equality except across cities with very different levels of real income (Lisbon compared to Paris, for example). What was also true is that the deviations of prices of individual goods often exceeded more than 50%. Essentially, the deviations of prices from equality in common currency units tend to average out across items in the consumption basket. One might be tempted to conclude that the underlying microeconomic price dispersion is somehow irrelevant for macroeconomics, given the focus on aggregate consumption and aggregate price levels. This is not the case since if individuals purchase each item in the city where its price is the lowest, they could save a huge fraction of their aggregate expenditure. Essentially, the price distributions point to massive consumption inefficiencies as would arise, for example, if the price deviations were the result of high and heterogeneous tariff rates across goods within the European Union. That large consumption distortions exist within a customs union poses a genuine puzzle, which some of the subsequent chapters aim to resolve.

Chapter 3 undertakes the complex task of parsing long-run international price differences into four basic frictions: (i) traditional trade costs, (ii) national barriers to trade, (iii) retail and distribution costs, and (iv) markups. To help identify all these margins, this study uses the Economist Intelligence Unit worldwide retail price survey. This survey covers a much broader sample of cities than Eurostat — 123 cities spanning 79 nations. The larger scope of the geographic coverage comes at the expense of exact matching of items across locations. For the world as a whole, about 24% of LOP variance is due to national borders, 30% is due to distance, and the remaining 44% is accounted for by retail costs and markups. Following the literature, the border effect should capture mostly official barriers to trade while the distance effects are due to traditional trade costs. The retail portion combines traditional retailing costs (rent and wages to workers in that sector) and markups that retailers may charge when they can segment national (and possibly sub-national and city-level) markets. Effectively this means that most of the apparent inefficiency in consumption arising from international relative price differences is the inescapable implication of brick-and-mortar retail and economic geography (distance). The former cost is now falling with the advent of e-commerce just as the latter costs fell long ago, during transportation revolutions.

Chapter 4 deals with the persistence of international relative prices from the long-run averages studied in Chapter 3. The metric typically used in this literature is the half-life of a relative price deviation. Imagine the price of toothpaste has risen by 10% in Toronto relative to Buffalo and the long-run price difference is 0% (i.e., citizens in both cities spend the same amount of USD on toothpaste per tube purchased, on average over time or in the "long run"). If the half-life is 1 year, the relative price difference will be 5% at that point in the transition back to price parity. We find the median half-life is about 2 years for non-traded goods (or services) and 1.5 years for goods. This is consistent with the view that good markets are less segmented than are the markets for services. These transition rates are considerably faster than what an earlier literature using CPI indices found. In that literature, the consensus half-lives were 3–5 years.

Understandably, the fact that the microdata indicate faster relative price convergence than macrodata has attracted considerable attention in the academic literature. Imbs *et al.* (2005) claim that the elevated persistence in the CPI indices is due to aggregate bias. Aggregation bias is an analytical feature whereby the aggregation of individual series with different levels of persistence will skew aggregate persistence toward the more persistence components of the aggregate. Another plausible and largely unexplored possibility is that the conflicting microeconomic and macroeconomic evidence reflects the inherent heterogeneity of goods and services in the consumption baskets of different nations. That is, the CPI-based comparisons violate the requirement that we examine the relative prices of identical or at least highly comparable goods across locations. If one country's food expenditure share is higher than that of another, changes in the relative price of food will alter the aggregate real exchange rate between them, even if the LOP holds for all goods and services, including food.

Part II of the book focuses on the second generation of real business-cycle models that extended Kydland and Prescott (1982) to open economy settings. By way of background, what Kydland and Prescott demonstrated was that one could construct a theoretical representative agent economy, featuring perfect competition and full utilization of labor and capital inputs that produced both growth and business-cycle fluctuations. Moreover, the time paths of macroeconomic aggregates implied by the choices the representative agent makes in this setting strongly resemble those of the actual economies, even when the only source of economic impulse is a highly persistence and uncertain path of total factor productivity.

The second generation of real business-cycle models started by effectively cloning the model structure of Kydland and Prescott and allowing the US economy to trade with the rest of the world. Unlike the KP model, which has one agent and one good and thus no trade among agents, the two-country version retains the one-good assumption, but allows agents to consume and/or investment more than their current level of production. Essentially, these models extend the intertemporal approach to the current account to a general equilibrium setting in which both savings and investment decisions by the US and the foreign country are fully endogenous. Following KP, productivity in each economy is uncertain and highly persistent. In the model developed in Crucini (1997), when productivity shocks are perfectly correlated, as would be the case in which technology diffuses symmetrically over time and across borders, domestic and foreign macroeconomic aggregates will be perfectly correlated, business-cycle fluctuations will be identical across countries, and there would be no gains from intertemporal trade across nations. Effectively, the equilibrium paths revert to the closed economy equilibrium in both countries. Conversely, the gains from trade in this theoretical setting arise from changes in productivity in one country relative to another.

This transformation from a focus on a country's absolute level of productivity to international relative productivity has the same conceptual origins as the notion of absolute and comparative advantage in international trade theory. The theory of comparative advantage predicts countries will specialize in the production of goods and services in which they have a relative productivity advantage. The business-cycle counterpart is the theory of intertemporal comparative advantage — when the US gains a persistent relative productivity advantage, it attracts a higher share of the world physical capital stock and produces more than its less productive trading partners produce. The quantitative adjustments that occur depend on the persistence of the productivity gain, the extent to which individuals and nations pool risk, and the cost of moving physical capital across nations, among other factor as the chapters in this part of the book show.

The efficacy of macroeconomic policy aimed at reducing income inequality depends upon the extent of risk sharing undertaken by individuals and firms in the private sector. It also depends on the extent to which underlying economic risks are common or idiosyncratic, the notion of relative movements in relation to aggregate movements in productivity, rates of return, and so forth. Chapter 5 explores the covariance properties of income and consumption across political jurisdictions within countries and across nations. The extent of risk sharing is estimated, nesting both strawman null hypotheses of complete or non-existent risk sharing. The estimated parameter is intended to emulate a situation in which agents pool a fraction of their income in a common "mutual fund" from which all agents draw equally with the remaining income being the non-pooled fraction. The estimated risk-sharing parameter is in the range of 0.84–0.94 for Canadian provinces and US states, compared to the much lower range of 0.37–0.60 for the G-7 nations (Canada, France, Germany, Italy, Japan, the United Kingdom, and the United States). This indicates that direct and indirect mechanisms for pooling risk are much more evident across regions residing in the same country than across nations of the world.[2]

[2]It is important to recognize that risks at the level of the individual will be much larger and often of a different source than the shocks identified in

The incompleteness of risk sharing and the resultant consumption inequality motivate Chapter 6: an exploration of the consequences of asset market structure for the properties of international business cycles and national economic welfare. The approach taken in this chapter is to contrast the response of the economy to a national productivity shock when agents pool all risk with an environment in which agents trade one-period, non-contingent, bonds. This particular asset market restriction is standard in the macroeconomics literature that focuses on business cycles in small open economies [see, for example, Mendoza (1991)]. As it turns out, when international productivity gaps are highly persistent, both the stochastic properties of international business cycles and their welfare implications contrast sharply with the complete markets case. Applying Hicksian decompositions of consumption and effort into wealth and substitution effects allows for a clear identification of the channels through which these differences arise. Intuitively, the persistence of the productivity gap maps directly into relative wealth effects associated with domestic and foreign productivity changes; these wealth effects are shared perfectly under complete markets, but not in the bond economy. The best an agent can do in the bond economy — after observing the productivity advance abroad — is to lend to that economy and thereby effectively acquire an *ex post* claim to the more productive firms in the foreign country. Had we allowed *ex ante* trade in equity claims, the asymmetry of the wealth effects would be mitigated and the model would more closely match the complete markets case. That said, in actual economies, the combination of low international consumption growth correlations combined with a strong home bias in national equity portfolios appears to support the model with only bond and goods trade. Moreover, even in advanced economies with deep financial markets, the median household holds little in the way of equity claims beyond those associated with their own homes.

---

aggregated provincial-, state-, and national-level macroeconomic data. The risk-sharing parameter estimates in Crucini (1999) have nothing to say about these microeconomic risks (health, localized unemployment risks, and so forth).

Chapter 7 substantively extends the work of Chapter 6 from the highly stylized case of two large economies to an extensive cross-section of small open economies. The exercise is motivated by an intriguing study by Aguiar and Gopinath (2007), who estimate that the random walk component of TFP accounts for 84% of the total TFP growth variation for emerging markets and only about 61% for developed countries. Their analysis was undertaken in the context of a small open economy model with no accounting for the correlation of shocks across countries and with the world interest rate essentially held constant over time in all countries. Since Crucini (1997) demonstrates that as productivity shocks become more correlated across countries, the world moves toward a no-trade equilibrium in which the consumption and output of all countries have equal variability; the assumptions made by AG are not innocuous. The general equilibrium approach reverses the AG result: in developed (emerging) economies, permanent shocks account for about 51% (48%) of the output growth variability. Thus, from the point of view of quantitative analysis of international business cycles, the general equilibrium approach gives a very different answer to a central question in macroeconomics: the extent to which transitory or permanent shocks drive national business cycles. The answer clearly depends on the extent to which those shocks are common or idiosyncratic to the nation.

An important limitation of much of the existing macroeconomics literature is the lack of attention to variation in the terms of trade. This contrasts sharply with the emphasis placed on the terms of trade in studies of economic development and business cycles in small, open, commodity-dependent nations. Part of the intellectual disconnect of the closed and open economy sub-literatures in macroeconomics is the fact that macroeconomists have tended to concentrate on large industrial countries, particularly the US and members of the EU; these nations are both highly diversified in their export profiles and have production and consumption dominated by non-traded services (e.g., retail services, education, and health). Chapter 8 studies the role of commodity specialization in the export income and consumption variability of 66, mostly emerging markets.

The variation of export growth earnings is decomposed into the terms of trade effect at fixed production levels, a common world supply response (weighted to reflect an individual nation's export basket), and the deviation of the nation's export supply response relative to the world. Most of the variation in export earnings is attributed to the terms of trade changes, not supply responses. Moreover, the supply responses are as often positive as negative, which indicates that the endogenous risk-sharing mechanism elaborated in the Cole and Obstfeld (1991) provides little, if any, offset to domestic export income variation.

Part III contains chapters focusing on economic models of relative price determination across nations and sectors. It includes models where oil prices interact with manufacturing costs through an input–output relationship, models that distinguish prices at the dock from those at the retail level and models with Calvo time-dependent pricing (called "sticky-price" models).

Backus, Kehoe, and Kydland (1994) studied the business-cycle interactions of two large economies that specialize in production. In their quantitative assessment of the model, one region is the US and the other is Europe. The goods produced by the two regions are imperfect substitutes in the production of a final good, which in turn serves to satisfy aggregate private and government consumption as well as private investment demand. Chapter 9 adds to this two-region structure, a third region specializing in the production of oil. Oil, in turn, is an intermediate input to the production in the other two regions. The model is motivated by a striking empirical regularity. The terms of trade (ratio of the import price index to the export price index) are very highly correlated with the relative price of oil (i.e., the spot price of oil on commodity exchanges relative to the US CPI). From 1973 to 1986, the correlation is 0.63 in the United States and −0.47 in Canada. These signs are consistent with the observation that the US is a net oil importer while Canada is a net oil exporter. The strength of the correlation is surprising because oil is a relatively small share of aggregate trade. The reason the relative price of oil plays an exaggerated role in the terms of trade is that it is much more variable than the price of other traded goods, particularly so during the 1970s and 1980s.

The chapter shows that the cyclicality of the US terms of trade changes from strongly procyclical to strongly counter-cyclical when the impulse driving the world business cycle switches from a nation-specific productivity shock to an oil supply shock. An increase in US productivity drives up the relative price of imports (the terms of trade) because the outward supply shift in US production results in a decline in the relative price of US exports in order to clear the world market. Conversely, a negative oil supply shock increases the world relative price of oil and raises the cost of US production, producing a mild recession. So the terms of trade become counter-cyclical. The former mechanism is no different from BKK and the latter mechanism is consistent with that obtained by Hamilton (1983), who shows that spikes in the relative price of oil precede most US recessions. In combining productivity shocks with oil supply shocks, the three-region general equilibrium model helps to flesh out the evolving sources of business-cycle fluctuations arising as a consequence of productivity changes and oil supply disruptions. Since oil is a relatively small share of productive inputs and oil supply disruptions, while often very large and abrupt, are infrequent, most of the variation of output and other macroeconomic aggregates is accounted for by productivity variation.[3]

One of the most robust empirical relationships in economics is the rate of decline in the volume of trade as a function of distance, as demonstrated in the vast empirical literature on the trade gravity equation. Disdier and Head (2008) provide a meta-analysis of this literature. Trade theorists studying these long-run relationships have typically estimated trade elasticities in the neighborhood of four. In contrast, macroeconomic theorists studying business-cycle dynamics

[3]The reader should be aware that the rapid industrialization of China has tended to move the correlation between oil prices and the world business cycle into the positive region, this is presumably because oil demand shifts dominate the oil market, during the 2000s, for example.

have typically estimated trade elasticities closer to one (recall that this is the critical value discussed earlier in reference to the Cole and Obstfeld risk-sharing mechanism). Since the trade elasticity is meant to be a preference parameter in both sub-literatures, it would be more satisfying if one value could be used in both sub-disciplines of economics. Put differently, from a structural modelling perspective, it would be more convincing if the short-run business-cycle models and long-run trade models were internally consistent.

Chapter 10 attempts to reconcile the two empirical estimates by modelling segmentation of retail and distribution across home-produced and imported goods. The basic intuition is that in the short-run, distribution capital is predetermined across these distribution channels and is costly to adjust. In the short term, then, trade is less sensitive to movements in the terms of trade than in the long run when distribution capital is reallocated in response to the change in the terms of trade and relative demand. Since the model has only one elasticity governing the preference for home and foreign goods and yet has some success in generating differential short- and long-run empirical elasticities of relative demand with respect to the terms of trade, it offers a potentially internally consistent mechanism linking the traditional trade and macroeconomic approaches. That said, at present, we know little about the reallocation of capital and labor in the retail and distribution sector. We know even less about how this reallocation relates to changes in domestically produced versus imported goods.

No two economists are more associated with the intellectual debate on real exchange rate determination than Alan Stockman and Michael Mussa. Stockman (1980) developed models in which real shocks (such as productivity and government spending) generated changes in international relative price levels. His work built from an earlier tradition that partitioned the consumption basket into two parts: traded goods and non-traded services. Firms and consumers would source traded goods globally from the lowest cost locations, whereas services were produced in the location of consumption (locally sourced). The implication is that movements in aggregate real exchange rates were expected to be isolated to the service component of the consumption basket, not the traded goods component. Mussa (1986), in contrast, built from a tradition based on the observation that local currency prices of both goods and services adjusted less frequently than the nominal exchange rate. Movements in nominal exchange rates would thus shift the entire distribution of home and foreign prices and differences across traded and non-traded real exchanges rate are small enough to ignore. Real exchange rates movements were a reflection of the nominal stickiness of retail prices in the face of volatility nominal exchange rates. This approach generates monetary non-neutrality and a role for monetary policy in relative price determination.

The debate is certainly not fully resolved: economists employ both models that fail to distinguish traded and non-traded goods in a meaningful way as well as models in which the differences are stark. Chapter 11 helps to place the theoretical debate on a more solid empirical footing by developing a model with both real frictions and nominal rigidities. The real frictions are trade costs, which result in consumption bias toward home varieties and sustain relative price differences in both the short run and the long run. The model features nominal rigidities using Calvo time-dependent pricing, in the New Keynesian tradition. In this setting, the relative prices of consumption items with a greater degree of price stickiness in the Calvo sense are more volatile in the presence of nominal shocks and less volatile in the presence of real shocks. The reverse is true of goods (or services) with a low degree of price stickiness. By looking at the across-sector distribution of exchange rate volatility, it is possible to determine if real or nominal shocks dominate the variance of a sector's real exchange rate and the preponderance of these two sources of variation in the overall macroeconomy. Using European real exchange rates across 66 sectors and four European countries (relative to the US) from 1996 to 2006, real shocks are found to dominate real exchange rate variance in the cross-section.

Chapter 12 examines real exchange rates across US cities. Interest in relative price variation has a long history in economics as it is often used to motivate monetary non-neutrality and to calibrate the impact of monetary policy changes on the real economy. This chapter develops a microfounded model in which trade costs and information frictions sustain price differences across locations and may amplify both the time series volatility and the persistence of deviations from the Law-of-One-Price. As is well known, physical trade costs result in absolute deviations from the LOP and can generate relative price volatility in price indices through a home bias effect. That is, if a trade cost makes the local variety less expensive on average, it will account for a larger share of home consumption than the imported varieties of that good. Consequently, cost shocks to the local variety have a larger impact on the home price index and welfare due to this home bias. Typically, however, the high volatility prediction of the standard real trade mechanism does not also produce greater persistence in the deviations from the LOP. By adding an information friction whereby local retail managers receive noisy signals about the state of aggregate nominal demand, the model also predicts that the persistence of LOP deviations is rising in the distance separating the cities, which is a robust feature of microprice data across cities within the US. Since persistence of relative price changes is part of the calculus of the welfare implications of monetary shocks, the model predicts asymmetric transmission of monetary policy as a function of distance.

Part IV provides both historical documentation of the extent and scope of the tariff war of the 1930s and a number of modelling approaches to assess the quantitative impact of tariffs on trade, aggregate efficiency, and macroeconomic activity.

The world has arrived at a historic point of very low traditional tariff barriers to trade following a series of successful multilateral tariff reductions under the GATT and increasing number of free trade areas and customs unions. The North American Free Trade Agreement and the formation of the European Union being prime examples of the latter. While the recent tariff escalation between the United States and China has attracted considerable attention, it pales in comparison to the tariff war of the interwar period (between World War I and World War II). The extent of the tariff war has been largely forgotten and the implications for macroeconomic activity and international trade remain incompletely understood.

Part of the misunderstanding dates back to the practice of economic historians such as Taussig (1930) comparing nominal levels of protection across distant years without converting the duties to real *ad valorem*-equivalent rates. It is common to read about a tariff increase from 10 cents a pound in 1914 to 12 cents a pound in 1921 being described as a 20% increase. While literally true in nominal terms, the appropriate conversion is to express each nominal duty as a ratio of the market price of the good at the time the tariff is in effect and thus compare ad valorem-equivalent rates. This is a serious deficiency in the interwar period because World War I inflation vastly eroded the nominal rates passed under the Underwood Act of 1914 while the deflation of the early 1930s vastly advanced the *ad valorem*-equivalent rates passed under the Hawley-Smoot Tariff Act of 1930.

Chapter 13 uses an archive of 32 line-item imports into the US from 1914 to 1940 to decompose the variation in the *ad valorem*-equivalent rates into changes due to legislative amendments, changes in the aggregate price level, and changes in the relative prices of individual imports. It finds that, if anything, the legislative adjustments moved average tariff levels toward their long-run mean, rather than advancing liberalization or protectionism as emphasized in most historical accounts. In effect, the price-level variation under the Gold Standard combined with monetary policy decisions is responsible for most of the variation in the tariff levels during this period. Harrison (2018) extends the cross-section to almost 1,000 tariff line items and finds a similar result (his period is shorter however, 1926–1933).

Trade economists have long recognized that most of international trade involves intermediate inputs into production, not final goods. Tariffs imposed on intermediate inputs result in inefficient input choices by firms, reducing production efficiency and lowering both aggregate output and trade (see Rodrigue and Kasahara (2008) for a modern application of this principle using Chilian microdata). Chapter 14 studies the contribution of US tariff increases in terms of generating aggregate inefficiency in terms of the number of units of domestic value added needed to produce a unit of domestic consumption. To accomplish this, the model incorporates a rich input–output structure patterned after Leontief's construction of input–output tables for the US economy in 1929 combined with a novel tariff and import database spanning more than 4,000 products and three cross-sections. We estimate trade elasticities of between 2.5 and 3.5. Incorporating the entire distribution of tariff levels and revisions in tariffs during this period, we find these distortions reduced aggregate productivity by 1.7% relative to free trade and the declines resulting from Hawley-Smoot were about 0.5%. These aggregate effects are considerably larger than estimates arising from the literature that treats imports as final goods as opposed to intermediate inputs.

One limitation of comparative statics exercises comparing efficiency and trade impacts of tariff changes across steady states is that this abstracts from the transitory and uncertain nature that many actual tariff policies take. This is pernicious in the interwar period because of the frequent use of specific duties, which assess a nominal local currency charge per physical unit imported. With this form of duty, absent frequent tariff revisions, the *ad valorem*-equivalent duty varies inversely with the nominal price level. In the context of the gold standard period and the interwar period in particular, this resulted in highly varying tariffs with persistent, but transitory, declines during the rapid inflation during World War I and increases during the rapid deflation of the Great Depression. Chapter 15 employs a multisector, two-region DGSE business-cycle model to account for these features of tariffs. This chapter also employs the Chari, Kehoe, and McGrattan (2007) method of business-cycle accounting by creating a mathematical isomorphism between the two-country, four-sector trade model of Crucini and Kahn (2007) and the standard two-country, one-sector neoclassical model that has served as the workhorse of modern business-cycle research.

It turns out that the symmetry of capital's intensity across sectors and countries in the original model, combined with a near-symmetrical level of foreign tariff retaliation, makes it possible to mimic the tariff war as if the US and its trading partners suffered a simultaneous productivity decline in the early 1930s and a recovery starting in 1934. This cycle arises because the tariffs were rising in the early 1930s and reversed themselves later in the 1930s. The outcome of the global tariff war produces a reasonable-sized recession by modern standards, but certainly not a Great Depression. The exercise also provides us with some perspective on the recent tariff war with China. Tariffs increased in most countries during the interwar period, unlike the recent trade dispute between the US and China. On the other hand, the trade share was considerably lower earlier in US history and while the US levied vastly different tariffs across goods, the tariff on each good applied nearly universally to all nations. Based on the historical context and the model used, it would be difficult to argue that the current tariff war would have a larger impact than Hawley-Smoot and foreign retaliation. That said, there is much more research needed on production structure, international supply chains, and consumer preferences to gain greater confidence in the quantitative predictions of these models for use in policy analysis both then and now.

The good news for budding research economists of this generation: much remains to be done.

References

Aguiar, M., and Gopinath, G. 2007. Emerging market business cycles: The cycle is the trend. *Journal of Political Economy* 115 (1), 69–102.

Backus, David K., Kehoe, P.J., and Kydland, F.E. 1994. Dynamics of the trade balance and the terms of trade: The j-curve? *American Economic Review* 84, 84–103.

Chari, V. V., Kehoe, P. J., and McGrattan, E.R. 2007. Business cycle accounting. *Econometrica* 75 (3), 781–836.

Cole, H., and Obstfeld, M. 1991. Commodity trade and international risk sharing: How much do financial markets matter? *Journal of Monetary Economics* 28, 3–24.

Crucini, M.J. 1997. Country size and economic fluctuations. *Review of International Economics* 5 (2), 204–220.

Crucini, M.J. 1999. On international and national dimensions of risk sharing. *The Review of Economics and Statistics* LXXXI, (1), 73–84.

Crucini, M.J. and Kahn, J. 2007. Tariffs and the Great Depression revisited. In: T. Kehoe and E. Prescott, eds., *Great Depressions of the Twentieth Century* (Federal Reserve Bank of Minneapolis), 305–334.

Crucini, M.J. and Vu, N. 2019. Did the American Recovery and Reinvestment Act help counties most affected by the Great Recession? National Bureau of Economic Research Working Paper No. 24093.

Imbs, J., Mumtaz, H., Ravn, M.O., and Rey, H. 2005. PPP strikes back: Aggregation and the real exchange rate. *The Quarterly Journal of Economics* 120 (1), 1–43.

Disdier, A.-C., and Head, K. 2008. The puzzling persistence of the distance effect on bilateral trade. *The Review of Economics and Statistics* 90 (1), 37–48.

Hamilton, J.D. 1983. Oil and the macroeconomy since World War II. *Journal of Political Economy* 91(2), 228–248.

Harrison, J. 2018. Impacts of the Smoot-Hawley tariff: Evidence from micro-data (Chapter 3). In: *Trade Frictions and Micro-price Behaviors: Historical Applications from the United States*, Ph.D. dissertation, Vanderbilt University.

Kydland, F.E., and Prescott, E.C. 1982. Time to build and aggregate fluctuations. *Econometrica* 50 (6), 1345–1370.

Mendoza, E.G. 1991. Real business cycles in a small open economy. *American Economic Review* 81 (4), 797–818.

Mussa, M. 1986. Nominal exchange rate regimes and the behavior of real exchange rates: Evidence and implications. *Carnegie-Rochester Conference Series on Public Policy* 25, 117–214.

Rodrigue, J., and Kasahara, H. 2008. Does the use of imported intermediates increase productivity? Plant-level evidence. *Journal of Development Economics* 87 (1), 106–118.

Rogoff, K. 1996. The purchasing power parity puzzle. *Journal of Economic Literature* 34 (2), 647–668.

Stockman, A.C. 1980. A theory of exchange rate determination. *Journal of Political Economy* 88 (4), 673–698.

About the Editor

Mario J. Crucini is Professor of Economics at Vanderbilt University, Research Associate at the National Bureau of Economic Research, Senior Fellow at the Globalization and Monetary Policy Institute at the Federal Reserve Bank of Dallas, and Managing Director of the Center for International Price Research. He currently serves as Associate Editor of the *Journal of Monetary Economics.* He served as Co-editor of the *Canadian Journal of Economics* (2010–2013) and Associate Editor of the *Journal of International Economics* (2001–2010), the *Journal of Money, Credit and Banking* (2001–2008), and the *Review of International Economics* (2000–2003). He served as President of the International Economics and Finance Society from 2012 to 2014. He has held faculty appointments at the Wharton School, University of Pennsylvania; Ohio State University; Stern School of Business, New York University; and Melbourne Business School. He received his MA and PhD from the University of Rochester and an honors BA from the University of Western Ontario in Canada. His research focuses on international business-cycle transmission, microeconomic and macroeconomic aspects of international price determination, and the role of commercial policy during the Great Depression. His research appears in the leading peer-reviewed journals of the profession.

About the Editor

Acknowledgments

I dedicate this book to my wife of more than 25 years, Jill Lloyd-Crucini, and my twin sons, Christopher Crucini and Gabriel Crucini. Their love, support, understanding, and encouragement has had an enormous impact on my career as a researcher and as a teacher. Just as important, they have helped me to maintain a balance of work and play that will sustain my passion for both for many more years to come. I thank my parents, Louie Crucini and Ann Smith, my sisters, Sandy Martel and Margie Usitalo, my step parents, Joan Polano and Gerald Smith and my in-laws, John and Mary Ellen Lloyd, for their love and for enduring the increasing geographic distance between us as my education took me from London, Ontario to Rochester, New York and my career took me from Columbus, Ohio to Nashville, Tennessee. Ever southward, from my birthplace of Sudbury, Ontario. I especially want to acknowledge my paternal grandmother, Teresa Mariotti, for being the loving leader of the family. She would not understand or necessarily much care about the contents of this book except insofar that it is important for my happiness and the well-being of those closest to me. This is perhaps the truest source of academic freedom.

Without education, wither shall scholarship head? I benefited by attending two great universities with almost no personal or familial out-of-pocket expenses: the first as an undergraduate honors economics student at the University of Western Ontario, a public university in Canada; the second as a scholarship-funded graduate student at the University of Rochester, a private university in the US.

In the economics departments at both these venerable institutions, the faculty I took instruction from — macroeconomists, international economists, and econometricians — were in significant agreement on the role of economic theory and the need to ground theories in real-world relevance and evidence. Ronald Wonnacott advised my honors thesis in which I studied an early vintage of the Canada–US trade agreement. Marianne Baxter, James Kahn, and Robert King were a dream team of dissertation advisers on the topic "The Transmission of Business Cycles in the Open Economy."

Scholarship is a collaborative effort, building on the work of many scholars, past and present. The work contained in this book is a testimony to the gains from trade in scholarship: the maturation of mentorship into coauthorship and the progress of shared interests into lifelong friendships. Two chapters resulted from collaboration with members of my PhD dissertation committee, Marianne Baxter and James Kahn. Five chapters resulted from collaboration with former PhD advisees: Kan Chen, J. Scott Davis, Chih-Wei Wang, Hakan Yilmazkuday, and Marios Zachariadis. One chapter evolved from advising a former honors economics student, Tristan Potter, who is now on the economics tenure track at Drexel University. I have found common research themes with colleagues in my department: three chapters with my colleague, Mototsugu Shintani, and one jointly with Eric W. Bond and Joel Rodrigue.

Eric and Joel, along with Kamal Saggi, have been instrumental in making the economics department at Vanderbilt University a sought-after destination for international economics speakers and graduate students and a productive home for me. Travel has brought me into contact with many, many, remarkable scholars and this, in turn, led to the peer-reviewed publications co-authored with David K. Backus, Martin Berka, Ayhan Kose, Christopher Otrok, and Christopher I. Telmer.

Much of the research summarized in this book has benefited from the financial support from the National Science Foundation, Social and Economic Sciences, Economics Program (awards #1030164, #0524868, and #0136797). These awards were essential in my research: supporting faculty in collaborative work, providing research assistantships for graduate and (a few) undergraduate students, and contributing resources for me to travel to disseminate the work at conferences worldwide. Specific articles supported by these grants acknowledge that support at the end of the chapters. Acknowledgments of individual scholars and seminar or conferences that helped to improve a chapter's content are also contained there.

Each chapter of this book has been previously published in a peer-reviewed academic journal or book. Each chapter provides an acknowledgment of the relevant press and the exact citation to the original work. I am grateful for the professionalism of these presses and their editors in the process leading to these publications as well as for the permission to collect these works in the current reference book. Last, but not least, I would like to thank Keith Maskus and Zvi Ruder for inviting my contribution to the series, S. Balasubramanian and Shreya Gopi for their patience and efficiency in production and Hanjo Kim for carefully reading and noting corrections on the penultimate version of the proofs.

Contents

Preface v

About the Editor xxiii

Acknowledgments xxv

Part I. Business Cycle Facts **1**

Chapter 1. What Are the Driving Forces of International Business Cycles? **3**

Mario J. Crucini, M. Ayhan Kose and Christopher Otrok

Chapter 2. Understanding European Real Exchange Rates **49**

Mario J. Crucini, Chris I. Telmer and Marios Zachariadis

Chapter 3. Understanding Long-Run Price Dispersion **83**

Mario J. Crucini and Hakan Yilmazkuday

Chapter 4. Persistence in Law of One Price Deviations: Evidence from Micro-Data **117**

Mario J. Crucini and Mototsugu Shintani

Part II. Business Cycles, Risk Sharing and Asset Market Structure **147**

Chapter 5. On International and National Dimensions of Risk Sharing **149**
Mario J. Crucini

Chapter 6. Business Cycles and the Asset Structure of Foreign Trade **185**
Marianne Baxter and Mario J. Crucini

Chapter 7. Trends and Cycles in Small Open Economies: Making the Case for a General Equilibrium Approach **231**
Kan Chen and Mario J. Crucini

Chapter 8. International Risk Sharing and Commodity Prices **253**
Martin Berka, Mario J. Crucini and Chih-Wei Wang

Part III. Models of International Prices **297**

Chapter 9. Oil Prices and the Terms of Trade **299**
David K. Backus and Mario J. Crucini

Chapter 10. Distribution Capital and the Short- and Long-Run Import Demand Elasticity **337**
Mario J. Crucini and J. Scott Davis

Chapter 11. Do Sticky Prices Increase Real Exchange Rate Volatility at the Sector Level? **389**
Mario J. Crucini, Mototsugu Shintani and Takayuki Tsuruga

Chapter 12. Noisy Information, Distance and Law of One Price Dynamics Across US Cities **423**

Mario J. Crucini, Mototsugu Shintani and Takayuki Tsuruga

Part IV. Commercial Policy **457**

Chapter 13. Sources of Variation in Real Tariff Rates: The United States, 1900–1940 **459**

Mario J. Crucini

Chapter 14. Misallocation and Productivity Effects of the Smoot-Hawley Tariff **479**

Eric W. Bond, Mario J. Crucini, Tristan Potter and Joel Rodrigue

Chapter 15. Tariffs and the Great Depression Revisited **515**

Mario J. Crucini and James A. Kahn

Part I

Business Cycle Facts

Chapter 1

What Are the Driving Forces of International Business Cycles?*

Mario J. Crucini

Department of Economics, Vanderbilt University, Nashville, TN, USA and National Bureau of Economic Research, Cambridge, MA, USA
mario.j.crucini@vanderbilt.edu

M. Ayhan Kose

Research Department, International Monetary Fund, Washington, D.C., USA
akose@imf.org

and

Christopher Otrok

Department of Economics, University of Virginia, Charlottesville, VA, USA
cmo3h@virginia.edu

Abstract. We examine the driving forces of G-7 business cycles. We decompose national business cycles into common and nation-specific components using a dynamic factor model. We also do this for driving variables found in business cycle models: productivity; measures of fiscal and monetary policy; the terms of trade and oil prices. We find a large common factor in oil prices, productivity, and the terms of trade.

*This chapter originally appeared in *Review of Economic Dynamics*, 2011, **44**(1), 156–175.

Productivity is the main driving force, with other drivers isolated to particular nations or sub-periods. Along these lines, we document shifts in the correlation of the common component of each driver with the overall G-7 cycle.

Keywords: International business cycles; Productivity shocks; Oil prices; Stochastic dynamic general equilibrium; Bayesian estimation; Factor model

1. Introduction

An extensive literature employs dynamic stochastic general equilibrium (DSGE) modeling to quantify and elucidate the role of particular exogenous variables in driving national business cycles. The median study has included one exogenous driving variable per country. Backus *et al.* (1992), for example, focus on U.S. and European average labor productivity in a one-sector, flexible price model, with the world economy divided into two symmetric countries. Recent work has considered the role of unexpected changes in the money supply in accounting for real exchange rate dynamics in the presence of sticky prices while abstracting entirely from productivity shocks (see, for example, Kehoe and Midrigan, 2007). When studies do consider multiple shocks, rarely is an attempt made to conduct a variance decomposition of each nation's output into the role of home and foreign shocks of various origins.[1]

These studies are typical of existing DSGE models in the sense that both the number of countries and number of stochastic shocks are kept to a minimum. There are two reasons for this. The first is tractability in terms of the ability of the researcher or the researcher's audience to sort out an expanding list of theoretical interactions as the dimension of the model grows. To some extent this is alleviated by tracing out the time profile reaction of the economy to one shock, in one location, at a time. This is the dynamic comparative statics counterpart to an impulse response function in time series econometrics. The second is data limitations. Even

[1]An exception is Backus and Crucini (2000) who examine the separate and combined role of productivity and oil price shocks in a three region, DSGE model.

if the researcher decides to calibrate preferences and technology using existing micro-studies, thereby economizing on the number of parameters to estimate using macroeconomic series, the number of parameters in the dynamic covariance structure of the shocks grows rapidly with the dimension of the model. This is a consequence of the need — in dynamic rational expectations models — to forecast the future evolution of exogenous variables and their interdependence.

As the literature has developed, the list of driving forces has grown to include: total factor productivity shocks, fiscal and monetary policy shocks, oil price shocks, shocks to the terms of trade, shocks to preferences, news and others. While most researchers treat these variables as exogenous to the representative agents and firms inhabiting the model, a growing number of studies allow for at least some endogenous variation either by estimating a policy rule or moving from the partial equilibrium framework of a small open economy to a general equilibrium framework.

The result has been to leave the literature rather fragmented in the sense that a very interesting collection of papers fails to provide an answer to the question: "What are the driving forces of international business cycles?" We provide an answer to this question by conducting a comprehensive analysis of the driving variables found in the literature and their covariance properties with international macroeconomic aggregates: output, consumption and investment. Our study focuses on the G-7 countries over the period 1960–2005 and contributes to the research program on international business cycles in three ways.

First, we mitigate the curse of dimensionality by employing dynamic factor models. This allows us to model the stochastic processes for both endogenous variables and exogenous variables with far fewer parameters than would be true had we employed a VAR.

Second, our methodology helps us to differentiate the domestic and external factors in explaining these variables. We model the endogenous and exogenous variables as the sum of three unobserved factors: a common G-7 factor, a nation-specific factor and an idiosyncratic factor. Aside from parsimony, this approach lends itself to the interpretation of shocks as arising from global or nation-specific sources; a distinction upon which many predictions of international business cycle theory hinge. For example, a class of intertemporal models of the current account has the property that only idiosyncratic movements in exogenous variables lead to current account imbalances. Common factors are obvious candidates for sources of international business cycle comovement and may give rise to beggar-thy-neighbor policy choices, both are enduring topics in the literature.

Third, we have a comprehensive list of driving variables. Our list includes total factor productivity, the monetary base, short-term interest rates targeted by the central bank, government expenditures, tax revenues, the relative price of oil and the terms of trade. Apart from parsing the endogenous and exogenous variables into common, nation-specific and idiosyncratic variation, we also estimate the fraction of variation of output, consumption and investment attributed to each component of each shock. Using multiple macroeconomic aggregates, rather than just output, allows us to derive more robust measures of common and nation-specific business cycles.

Our analysis is carried out using a dynamic factor model. Dynamic factor models have increasingly become a popular econometric tool for quantifying the degree of comovement among macroeconomic time series. While these models are often used to analyze the degree of business cycle comovement in the international business cycle literature, they have also been employed in other contexts such as forecasting and monetary policy analysis. See Otrok and Whiteman (1998) for an application to a forecasting exercise, and Bernanke *et al.* (2005) for an application to the analysis of monetary policy. Kose *et al.* (2008) provide a brief survey of the literature employing these types of models to study the extent of business cycles comovement. However, these methods have yet to be used to examine a large set of driving forces and their relationship to macroeconomic variables. We summarize this economic relationship in terms of a variance decomposition.

Our international business cycle variance decomposition is achieved using a three step procedure. First, we use national data on output, consumption and investment to estimate the common

G-7, nation-specific and idiosyncratic components of each national business cycle. The common component is common across all variables and countries, the national component is common to all variables of a country, and the idiosyncratic component is specific to each variable. In step two, we use the same statistical model to estimate the common G-7, nation-specific and idiosyncratic components of each driving variable. In step three, we project measures of the components of the shocks on components of the endogenous variables. The objective of this exercise is to generate a variance decomposition of the common and nation-specific components of G-7 business cycles into the common and nation-specific components of the driving variables. This allows us to answer the key question we are interested in "what are the driving forces of international business cycles?" We are also able to answer narrower questions such as: "How much of the German business cycle is accounted for by movements in G-7 productivity versus German productivity?"

In all countries, the world business cycle factor is most important for output and least important for investment. Across countries, the world component is least important for macroeconomic fluctuations in the U.S., despite the fact that the U.S. is widely viewed as the driver of the world business cycle. While all the shocks have non-trivial world factors, the contribution of the world factor to variance ranges from a high of 90% for the price of oil relative to the domestic consumption deflator to a low of 5% for the money supply. Productivity is found to be the dominant driving force of the business cycle, typically accounting for more of the variation than all of the other variables combined. Fiscal and monetary policy variation account for much less of the variation in the business cycle than productivity, but more than either oil prices or the terms of trade.

Our work contributes to the literature documenting business cycle facts, dating back to the seminal work of Burns and Mitchell (1946) and Zarnowitz (1992). The goal of this literature is to accumulate historical and cross-country evidence on the time series properties of macroeconomic aggregates to inform business cycle theory and macroeconomic policy.

Recent contributions to historical perspectives on international business cycles include Backus and Kehoe (1992) and Mumtaz *et al.* (2011). Backus and Kehoe (1992) study output, consumption, investment, government spending, net exports, money and price levels across ten industrialized countries (Australia, Denmark, Norway, Sweden and the G-7, excluding France). They document a reduction in output volatility and a striking shift from procyclical to countercyclical prices between the interwar period and the postwar period. Mumtaz *et al.* (2011) study a similar period, but extend the sample of countries dramatically to 36 and narrow the cross-section of variables to output and inflation. They find a growing role for geography in business cycles fluctuations in the sense that the common factor shared by countries in geographic proximity has increased relative to the global component. Building on Backus and Kehoe (1992), they find even stronger evidence of counter-cyclical prices after 1984 (the end point of most series in the study by Backus and Kehoe, 1992).

Two facets of our analysis distinguish our study from these works. First, we subject the variables that business cycle theorists assume to be driving (i.e., causal) variables to similar empirical scrutiny to what the NIPA components, money and price levels receive in existing studies. Second, we relate global and national components of driving and macroeconomic variables in a simple variance decomposition.

The second facet of our work builds on Gregory and Head (1999), who employ dynamic factor analysis and Kalman filtering methods to analyze the sources of fluctuations in productivity, investment and the current account in the G-7 countries. They report that the common component of business cycle fluctuations has a substantial impact on both productivity and investment in these countries, but very little impact on the current account. Empirical work using vector autoregressions to identify structural shocks and infer their contribution to output variance in an international context are few. An important early contribution is Ahmed *et al.* (1993). They allow for home, foreign and world supply shocks, a relative fiscal shock, a relative preference shock and a relative money shock. Their data sample includes the U.S. and an aggregate of five major industrialized countries. They find, as we do, that supply shocks explain most of the variation in output.

It is important to emphasize that the methodological approach we take is driven by the broad-based question that we ask in this paper. We are not advocating an alternative to DSGE modeling. To the contrary, the factor modeling approach to specifying the stochastic properties of the driving variables is motivated by practical econometric challenges faced in DSGE modeling of international business cycles where the dimensionality of the state space is (or should be) large. These are challenges we have encountered in our own DSGE models and our hope is that the results reported here lead to widespread application of the approach within DSGE models. The accuracy, and certainly the structural interpretations, of the second stage of our variance decomposition, where we project components of the driving variables on the components of the macroeconomic aggregates are admittedly more controversial. Clearly it will be of interest in future work to take a large scale DSGE model of the G-7 with the shocks considered here and see what sort of variance decomposition emerges relative to what is reported here.

2. The Model

In this section, we first review how our empirical framework relates to the structure of DSGE models. This serves to highlight the curse of dimensionality which limits the number of countries and number of driving variables in this class of models and how factor models can help overcome this problem. Next, we provide a brief description of how we employ dynamic factor models to deconstruct international and national business cycles.

2.1. *Linear business cycle models*

Dynamic stochastic general equilibrium modeling begins with a mathematical representation of tastes, technology, constraints and asset market structure. The move from qualitative implications to quantitative predictions involves choosing functional forms and parameterizing them with a mix of calibration and estimation. Typically calibration is used in parameterizing tastes, technology and constraints while estimation is used to characterize the time series properties of the exogenous driving variables. The final step is the solution stage, which typically involves a first-order approximation around the steady-state level or along a balanced growth path. The solution is fully described by two sets of linear equations[2]:

$$S_t = MS_{t-1} + e_t, \tag{1}$$

$$Z_t = \Pi S_t. \tag{2}$$

The first set of equations describes the dynamic evolution of the state vector, which contains both predetermined endogenous variables and purely exogenous variables. The second set of equations are the decision rules, the contemporaneous optimal responses of endogenous variables to changes in the state variables. In what follows, the state vector is partitioned into predetermined and exogenous variables:

$$S_t = [P_t \vdots X_t].$$

We focus, as other international business cycle researchers do, on the business cycle properties of output, consumption and investment of the G-7 countries. Thus, the Z_t vector has 21 elements. Where we depart from existing practice is in the list of exogenous variables to include in the state vector. Most studies focus on a single type of shock which evolves somewhat independently across two countries. In the first generation of international real business cycle models, home and foreign total factor productivity followed a first-order vector autoregression with correlated innovations. In the first generation of international monetary models, home and foreign money growth rates followed first-order autoregressions with uncorrelated innovations.

The curse of dimensionality is obvious when one mechanically follows existing practice while expanding the number of countries

[2]Linear here means a set of linear equations describing the equilibrium solution in either the levels of the variables or their logarithms (which one depends on the method of linearization the researcher employs).

and menu of shocks, even under the restrictive assumption that all exogenous variables follow a first-order autoregressive process. We have:

$$X_t = \Gamma X_{t-1} + e_t, \tag{3}$$

with the vector of five exogenous variables spanning seven countries, X_t, consists of seven (i.e., the number of countries) representative subvectors, $X'_{i,t} = [a_{i,t}, m_{i,t}, g_{i,t}, p^o_{i,t}, q_{i,t}]$, containing total factor productivity, a narrow monetary aggregate, government consumption, the relative price of oil and the terms of trade. The coefficient matrix, Γ, contains 1225 parameters and the variance–covariance matrix of the innovations adds another 560 parameters for a total of 1785 parameters. This is where the factor model is irresistible, since it captures most of the covariation in the exogenous variables with far fewer parameters.

The factor model is structured as follows. First, to capture the important distinction between common sources of variation in the world and those specific to a country, we allow for a common G-7 factor, a nation-specific factor and an idiosyncratic component. Second, we use multiple empirical proxies for each variable under examination, with individual proxies indexed by j. We make repeated use of the following factor model structure:

$$\Delta x_{ij,t} = \alpha_{ij} + \beta_{ij} F_{x,t} + \gamma_{ij} f_{x,i,t} + \varepsilon_{x,ij,t}. \tag{4}$$

Here, $x_{ij,t}$ is the jth empirical proxy for variable x in country i. Typically there are 3 or more variables per country in each of these estimated factor models. Then, $F_{x,t}$, is a common factor shared by the G-7 for the set of variables included in the estimation, $f_{x,i,t}$ is a nation-specific factor and $\varepsilon_{x,ij,t}$ is an idiosyncratic component. For example in estimating the world and nation-specific component of business cycles, the vector $x_{ij,t}$ consists of GDP, total private consumption expenditure and investment. The component $F_{x,t}$, then, is the estimated world business cycle factor, common to all countries and National Income and Product Accounts (NIPA) components, $f_{x,i,t}$ is the national business cycle factor common to all NIPA components in country i and $\varepsilon_{x,ij,t}$ is variation specific to NIPA component j in country i. This latter component is viewed as a combination of variable-specific variation and pure measurement error. The term nation-specific factor and national component are used interchangeably as are the terms G-7 factor or component and world factor or component.

Note, that since the endogenous variables are linear functions of the state variables, they inherit the factor structure of the state vector. That is, the decision rules will have five common factors and five nation-specific factors (one for each of productivity, monetary policy, fiscal policy, oil prices and the terms of trade). To the extent that output responds in the same direction to the common factor in all countries, that common factor will be a source of positive international business cycle comovement. It is also possible that countries may respond to a common shock (perhaps oil prices) with opposite signs, in which case the common factor would be a source of negative international business cycle comovement.

We estimate six such factor models, one for the macroeconomic aggregates (output, consumption and investment) and one for each of the five groups of driving variables (consisting of measures of, or proxies for, productivity, oil prices, the terms of trade, fiscal policy and monetary policy). For example, in the case of productivity, the different proxies arise due to the use of different measures of capital and labor inputs or different breadth of the sectors included in these measures (e.g., manufacturing sector versus the entire economy). The common factor is interpreted as world productivity variation, the nation-specific factor is the deviation of a nation's productivity level from this common level and the idiosyncratic factor is assumed to consistent primarily of measurement error. The interpretation of the factors differs somewhat based on the context. We discuss these details in the relevant sections that follow.

These factor models, then, provide a convenient way to decompose the variance of the growth of each variable into the contributions of the G-7 factor, the nation-specific factor and an idiosyncratic component. This is done for the macroeconomic aggregates and each of the driving variables separately. We then take the macroeconomic aggregates, one at a time, and project them onto orthogonalized common and nation-specific factors of the driving variables. Thus, output, for example, is decomposed into ten components, a world and national component of each of the five drivers (productivity, fiscal policy, monetary policy, oil prices and the terms of trade).

Most of the driving variables are non-stationary, so we work with first-differences in our estimation. The error term is assumed to be uncorrelated cross-sectionally at all leads and lags, and follows an autoregressive process of order p_i for each element in the vector. The factor $f_{i,t}$ follows an autoregression of order q_k. The β's and γ's are factor loadings on the common and nation-specific factors. The estimation of the model is Bayesian and follows the procedure in Otrok and Whiteman (1998). The priors on the model parameters are loose enough to be uninformative except for the prior belief that the autoregressive polynomials are stationary, which seems reasonable for data in growth rates. The estimation procedure itself is based on the Gibbs sampler and is outlined in Appendix A.

3. The Data

We use annual data covering the period 1960–2005. Our selection of annual frequency stems from the fact that we include a broad set of measures for driving variables, some of which are not available at higher frequencies. Our macroeconomic aggregate for output is real gross domestic product, consumption is real private consumption expenditure and investment is real gross private capital formation. These series are from the World Development Indicators (WDI) and the World Economic Outlook (WEO) databases.

For the driving variables, we separate them into policy and non-policy variables; all are treated as strictly exogenous. These exogeneity restrictions have been invoked individually in various DSGE models of the past two decades. In reality, all of these variables are to some extent endogenous. Productivity is endogenous to the sector engaged in innovation and may be contaminated with endogenous variation due to various measurement issues. Oil prices are determined in world commodity markets as well as manipulated by dominant producers, such as OPEC. Monetary and fiscal policy functions would allow some of the observed variation in the money supply, interest rates and fiscal variables to be endogenous responses to the state of the economy. Doing justice to the endogeneity issues of the large number of driving variables we study here is left to a sequel paper.

We use multiple measures of driving variables, not simply because the factor model methodology requires it, but because different measures of each driving variable contain different information about the theoretical variable of interest. An important by-product of the factor model is that the size of the idiosyncratic component of a particular measure indicates the extent of independent variation across competing measures of the same economic variable. This could be measurement error or conceptual differences in the variable construction. Consequently, empirical results that use the common factor may be more robust than those that examine only a specific measure, our analysis will help to distinguish these cases.

On the monetary policy side, we use short-term real interest rates and real stocks of money, narrowly defined. The interest rates we employ are call rates and other short-term interest rates, including the T-Bill rates and Discount Rates. These are most closely influenced by interest rates targeted directly by the central banks, such as the Federal Funds rate in the United States. In our empirical work, we use the ex post real interest rate, with inflation measured using the CPI. The real monetary aggregates are represented by the sum of money and quasi money series, also deflated by the CPI. Interest rates and monetary aggregates are from the International Financial Statistics (IFS) of the IMF and the CPI series are from the World Economic Outlook (WEO) database.

On the fiscal policy side, we include total expenditure, government consumption, and total revenue. This list is more extensive than is typically used in the business cycle literature, allowing us to provide a broad fiscal picture. The fiscal series are from the OECD and IFS sources, completed with the help of the WEO database whenever the series are missing. The series are then deflated by the CPI.

The non-policy variables are productivity, the relative price of crude petroleum and the terms of trade. Productivity is the central focus of the international real business cycle literature. We use four different productivity measures. The first two measures are based on the framework developed by Klenow and Rodriuez-Clare (2005). These measures both use capital and labor input measures in the computation of total factor productivity. One of the measures also includes human capital in the decomposition. To construct these productivity series, we employ data from the Penn World Tables 6.2 (Heston *et al.*, 2006). The other two productivity measures use only labor data, not capital, which is consistent with the approach of Backus *et al.* (1992). The first uses gross domestic product and employment (number employed, not hours) from the OECD. The second uses manufacturing output and total hours in manufacturing from the Bureau of Labor Statistics.

We have four prices of crude petroleum in U.S. dollars: (i) the world average price, (ii) the Dubai price, (iii) the Brent price and (iv) the West Texas price. The latter three are the products produced in the markets referenced, the first is an expenditure weighted average of these prices. These U.S. dollar prices are converted to domestic currency and then deflated by the domestic consumer price index. These series are taken from the IFS.

The terms of trade is the price of exports relative to imports. We have two measures, one taken from the WEO and the other from the IFS. In the former, the terms-of-trade is the terms-of-trade of goods and services computed using the trade shares of all trading partners. In the latter, terms-of-trade refers to the ratio of unit value of exports to unit value of imports.

4. International Business Cycles

Following Gregory *et al.* (1997), we start by estimating a factor model for the macroeconomic aggregates:

$$\begin{bmatrix} \Delta y_{i,t} \\ \Delta c_{i,t} \\ \Delta i_{i,t} \end{bmatrix} = \alpha_{ij} + \begin{bmatrix} \beta_{iy} \\ \beta_{ic} \\ \beta_{ii} \end{bmatrix} F_t + \begin{bmatrix} \gamma_{iy} \\ \gamma_{ic} \\ \gamma_{ii} \end{bmatrix} f_{i,t} + \varepsilon_{ij,t}, \tag{5}$$

where the elements of the data vector are the growth rates of real gross domestic product, real private consumption expenditure and real investment for country i, respectively. The factor F_t is a common factor shared by all aggregates across all of the G-7 countries and this is what we will refer to as the G-7 factor. The quantitative impact of the G-7 factor on an individual macroeconomic aggregate is determined by the factor loading β_{ij}. These factor loadings are different across macroeconomic aggregates and across countries.[3] Both the factors and the residual entering the equation follow autoregressive processes. Innovations to both the factors and the residuals are assumed to be contemporaneously uncorrelated.

An important starting point for our analysis is to compare the G-7 factor with a well-known measure of the G-7 business cycle. The measure that we use here is a country-size weighted average of the growth rates of the G-7 macroeconomic aggregates. Following the methodology employed by Crucini (1997), we use Purchasing Power Parity valuations to arrive at the country weights. While the G-7 economies on average constitute about 50 percent of total world output, the United States alone accounts for roughly 46 percent of G-7 output and this number drops dramatically to about 15 percent for Japan, the next largest member. The G-7 share of world output has declined in recent decades as emerging market economies, including China and India, have grown much faster than the G-7. However, the G-7 cycle is still — in a value-weighted sense — a good approximation to the world business cycle.

Figure 1 compares the estimated G-7 factor to a G-7 aggregate growth rate computed as a country-weighted average of national output growth rates and to U.S. output growth.[4] The correlation between U.S. output and the G-7 aggregate is 0.81 and is readily evident in the figure. While this may reflect common disturbances and genuine business cycle propagation across the U.S. and other G-7 countries, it also reflects the large economic weight of the U.S. in the construction of the G-7 aggregate. To a first approximation, the G-7

[3]To save space, we do not report factor loadings, these are available from us upon request.

[4]The G-7 factor is estimated quite precisely evidenced by the tightness of 10 percent and 90 percent posterior quintile bands available from the authors upon request.

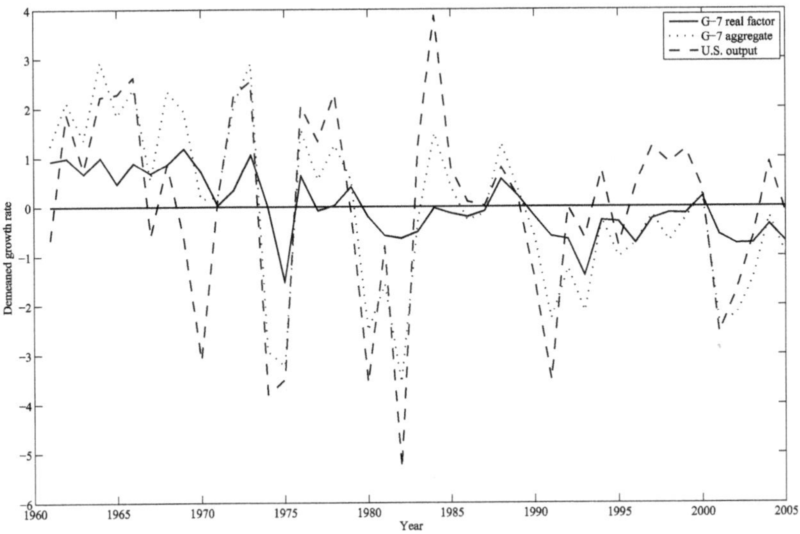

Fig. 1. Three views of the world business cycle.

business cycle looks like a moderated version of the U.S. business cycle. The G-7 common real factor is the smoothest of the three measures; its correlation with G-7 output growth is 0.84 compared to a mere 0.43 in the case of U.S. output. We conclude from this that the simple view that the U.S. business cycle drives the G-7 cycle is not a reasonable description of international business cycles.

Casual inspection of Fig. 1 also indicates that the G-7 factor captures the major economic events of the past four decades: the relatively steady expansion of the 1960s; the rapid boom of the early 1970s; the sharp, but short recession of the mid-1970s associated with the first oil price shock; the more enduring recession of the early 1980s stemming from a variety of forces including the tight monetary policies of major industrialized nations; the mild recession of the early 1990s; the 2001 recession and the subsequent recovery and slowdown.[5]

[5]While not the focus of this paper, we also examine the behavior of nation-specific factors in detail. The results suggest that the nation-specific factors capture most of the major peaks and troughs of business cycles in each of the G-7 countries. The figures of nation-specific factors are available from us upon request.

How important is the G-7 factor in the evolution of national macroeconomic aggregates? After all, if it is not quantitatively important, we should be less concerned about refining our measure of it. To address this question we compute variance decompositions using the estimated factor model (see Appendix B). Table 1 reports our findings. Beginning with output, the usual business cycle reference variable, the world and national components are of equal

Table 1. Variance decompositions for macroeconomic variables.

		Output			Consumption			Investment		
Country	Factor	33%	50%	66%	33%	50%	66%	33%	50%	66%
Canada	Common	33.5	35.9	38.4	17.6	19.6	21.5	5.2	6.6	8.0
	Nation-specific	49.5	52.3	54.9	66.4	68.8	71.4	53.8	56.4	58.9
	Variable-specific	10.2	11.7	13.2	9.6	11.5	13.2	34.8	36.9	38.8
France	Common	77.2	80.0	82.7	51.1	56.2	61.1	51.2	54.3	57.6
	Nation-specific	10.5	13.4	16.3	16.2	22.3	29.7	12.9	16.7	20.8
	Variable-specific	5.3	6.6	7.9	18.2	20.8	23.0	26.4	28.7	30.7
Germany	Common	45.7	49.0	52.3	30.7	33.4	35.7	19.1	21.6	24.3
	Nation-specific	38.7	42.3	46.0	38.6	41.9	45.3	52.0	55.5	59.1
	Variable-specific	6.7	8.3	10.0	22.8	24.9	27.1	20.7	22.8	24.9
Italy	Common	70.1	74.0	77.5	60.3	64.9	69.4	28.2	31.4	34.7
	Nation-specific	10.5	13.8	17.0	13.1	17.7	22.4	28.9	35.1	40.4
	Variable-specific	10.3	12.0	13.7	15.6	17.3	18.9	30.7	33.9	37.3
Japan	Common	54.8	58.0	61.2	48.3	52.0	55.6	51.6	54.8	57.7
	Nation-specific	36.5	39.6	42.8	32.6	36.3	39.8	37.4	40.3	43.6
	Variable-specific	1.8	2.2	2.7	11.0	11.6	12.3	4.3	4.8	5.4
UK	Common	12.0	14.0	16.0	2.5	3.4	4.3	9.6	11.4	13.1
	Nation-specific	69.5	72.9	76.0	64.0	66.9	70.0	40.6	43.3	46.1
	Variable-specific	10.4	12.8	15.8	26.7	29.6	32.3	43.0	45.1	47.3
US	Common	13.9	15.9	17.9	10.0	12.0	14.0	3.6	4.7	6.0
	Nation-specific	77.0	79.4	81.7	61.4	63.8	66.1	80.2	82.0	83.7
	Variable-specific	3.4	4.4	5.4	23.0	24.1	25.2	12.0	13.3	14.5
Average	Common		46.7			34.5			26.4	
	Nation-specific		44.8			45.4			47.0	
	Variable-specific		8.3			20.0			26.5	

Notes: In each cell, the variances share attributable to there relevant factor is reported. 33%, 50%, and 66% correspond to the respective quantiles of posterior shares.

importance in accounting for variation in the typical G-7 country. Based on this statistic, the world cycle merits as much scrutiny as the nation-specific component. From the perspective of individual countries, though, the picture is quite different. The world factor dominates the business cycles of France, Italy and Japan, on average accounting for more than 70 percent of the variation. It is of less importance for the United Kingdom and the United States, where it accounts for less than 15 percent of output variation. There is no obvious correlation between the relative economic size of a country and the importance of the G-7 factor.

Consumption tells a different story in a couple of respects. First, the G-7 factor on average accounts for a lower share of consumption variance than does the nation-specific factor. At first blush this seems consistent with the consumption-risking sharing puzzle, national consumption variance is not shared even among these highly integrated, financial developed nations. Note, however, that the national component of consumption is not significantly different from what we see in output. The difference between income and consumption variance lies mostly in the larger idiosyncratic term in the consumption decomposition. Thus it could be that larger measurement errors in consumption than income measurement skews international consumption correlations toward zero. While this certainly does not solve the correlation or risk-sharing puzzle, it helps to mitigate the puzzle somewhat.

Investment has a slightly more pronounced national component than output or consumption. Averaging across the G-7 the nation-specific component accounts for roughly 50 percent of the variation. Though this is not much higher than was true of output or consumption, the idiosyncratic component is almost as large as the G-7 factor for the typical country. International real business cycle models predict a large nation-specific component in investment fluctuations as capital searches for its highest reward. The small G-7 component for investment is consistent with this prediction.

To summarize, we have found sizable G-7, nation-specific and variable-specific components in macroeconomic aggregates. The common and nation-specific components tend to be larger than the idiosyncratic component with the exception of investment where it is on par with the G-7 component. Most of the heterogeneity we see is across countries, with France, Italy and Japan sharing a large common component and the United Kingdom and the United States business cycles being mostly driven by national factors. Canada and Germany fall between these extremes. The remainder of the paper is devoted to understanding why there is a common cycle in the first place and how these similarities and differences arise across countries. To develop this understanding we begin with an analogous decomposition of our driving variables into G-7, nation-specific and variable-specific components.

5. Properties of the Driving Variables

We ask similar questions regarding the driving variables as were addressed in our analysis of macroeconomic aggregates in the previous section. We first analyze the evolution of each driving variable. We then focus on the relative importance of the G-7, nation-specific and variable-specific components in explaining the volatility of the driving variables.

5.1. *Productivity, oil prices and the terms of trade*

We first examine the properties of driving variables that are not instruments of policy: productivity, oil prices and terms of trade. Policymakers clearly scrutinize these variables to refine their policy actions in light of the evolution of output growth and inflation. Economic growth accompanied by labor productivity advance is viewed as less likely to alter inflation and inflation expectations than situations when productivity growth stagnates. Oil price increases in the absence of broad movements in inflation are appropriately viewed as relative price changes, though unpleasant policy trade-offs may present themselves. Productivity changes have been the dominant driver of quantitative theory on business cycles in closed economy models, with oil prices and the terms of trade playing a supporting role in small open economy models.

To compute our productivity series, we use a standard Solow residual decomposition for country i:

$$a_{i,t} = y_{i,t} - s_i n_{i,t} - (1 - s_i)k_{i,t} \tag{6}$$

where $y_{i,t}$ is the logarithm of output, s_i is the share of labor income in total factor income, and $n_{i,t}$ and $k_{i,t}$ are measures of labor and capital inputs.

We use four different measures of productivity. The construction of the first two measures follows the methodology in Klenow and Rodriuez-Clare (2005), using both capital and labor input measures in the computation of total factor productivity. One of their capital measures includes human capital. Consistent with the approach used by Backus *et al.* (1992), our other pair of measures use only labor data on the input side. The first of these two uses gross domestic product and total civilian employment (number employed, not hours) from the OECD. The second is from the Bureau of Labor Statistics and uses manufacturing output and total hours in manufacturing.

The correlation of the two labor productivity measures in growth rates averages 0.81, but there are important differences across them. First, manufacturing productivity is more volatile than overall productivity. The standard deviation of the growth rate manufacturing productivity is on average roughly 2.5 times higher than the analogous measure using GDP (1.97 compared to 0.81). Second, the bilateral cross-country correlations of manufacturing productivity are higher than those computed for GDP in most cases, but the differences are not statistically significant. This is consistent with a broader literature that documents larger international labor productivity differences in the service sector than the goods sector. The factor model for the four measures of national productivity is identical in structure to what we use elsewhere, except we have four proxies for productivity in each country, the highest number with the exception of oil prices.

The first panel of Table 2 reports the common, nation-specific and variable-specific components of productivity. We see that the nation-specific component tends to dominate when we use the more

Table 2. Variance decompositions for productivity measures.

Country	Factor	KRC1			KRC2			OECD			BLS		
		33%	50%	66%	33%	50%	66%	33%	50%	66%	33%	50%	66%
Canada	Common	34.1	47.2	55.3	33.2	46.6	54.6	61.5	69.3	74.3	62.8	70.6	76.5
	Nation-specific	43.6	51.7	65.0	44.2	52.3	65.6	10.1	14.8	24.2	2.1	4.7	11.9
	Variable-specific	0.7	0.9	1.0	0.8	1.0	1.1	14.2	15.5	16.6	21.1	23.5	26.0
France	Common	25.9	27.9	30.3	27.3	29.4	31.7	35.6	40.9	46.7	35.1	38.9	43.0
	Nation-specific	68.7	71.0	73.1	67.3	69.5	71.7	33.6	37.6	41.5	19.8	22.5	24.9
	Variable-specific	0.7	0.8	0.9	0.7	0.8	0.9	20.0	21.6	22.9	37.2	38.9	40.2
Germany	Common	9.0	10.8	12.9	13.9	16.0	18.6	45.2	49.9	57.4	43.3	47.7	52.8
	Nation-specific	46.2	51.2	56.4	39.6	44.2	48.5	16.2	20.9	25.5	13.9	17.9	22.2
	Variable-specific	32.8	37.2	42.2	35.7	39.1	42.6	22.1	25.4	29.2	29.7	32.4	35.4
Italy	Common	13.8	16.2	18.4	13.3	15.7	17.8	28.0	31.8	35.6	26.0	29.6	33.8
	Nation-specific	81.5	83.6	86.0	82.0	84.1	86.5	49.0	52.2	55.5	36.2	39.3	42.1
	Variable-specific	0.1	0.1	0.2	0.1	0.1	0.2	15.5	16.2	16.7	30.5	31.5	32.2
Japan	Common	13.6	16.1	19.9	13.0	15.6	19.1	16.5	20.7	27.0	12.2	15.0	20.0
	Nation-specific	79.5	83.3	86.0	80.0	83.7	86.4	63.2	69.1	72.8	61.9	66.7	69.6
	Variable-specific	0.3	0.4	0.5	0.4	0.5	0.6	9.8	10.4	10.8	17.9	18.3	18.6
UK	Common	27.4	31.7	35.5	22.0	26.3	29.9	21.0	23.4	25.7	29.1	31.5	33.6
	Nation-specific	63.1	66.8	71.2	68.8	72.4	76.6	44.1	46.4	48.8	19.9	21.9	24.2
	Variable-specific	1.1	1.3	1.5	1.0	1.2	1.4	29.8	30.3	30.8	45.3	46.5	47.5
US	Common	34.0	43.3	49.8	44.6	55.1	61.6	38.2	47.3	52.5	25.1	33.2	39.4
	Nation-specific	43.5	50.3	59.6	34.1	41.0	51.1	34.1	39.7	48.2	20.3	26.5	34.6
	Variable-specific	5.3	6.1	6.9	3.5	4.0	4.6	12.7	13.5	14.2	39.0	40.0	41.0
Average	Common		27.6			29.2			40.5			38.0	
	Nation-specific		65.4			63.9			40.1			28.5	
	Variable-specific		6.7			6.7			19.0			33.0	

elaborate decompositions including physical and human capital than those using basic labor input measures. The nation-specific component accounts for about two thirds of the variance in productivity growth in these cases, the contribution of the G-7 and nation-specific components fall when we move to the simpler measures, but only to the point of equality. The appearance of large idiosyncratic components in the simpler measure is consistent with the omission of capital measures in the computation of the Solow residual in these cases. The fact that the BLS measure has a full third of its variance accounted for by the idiosyncratic component may be due to the fact that this measure includes only manufacturing while the other three span the entire production side of the economy. Taken at face value, the results indicate that while the G-7 countries are not technologically integrated in the literal sense of sharing a common productivity level, there is a large common component.

Figure 2 plots the G-7 business cycle factor against the G-7 productivity factor, their correlation is 0.69. As we shall see in the next section, productivity will be a key driving variable both

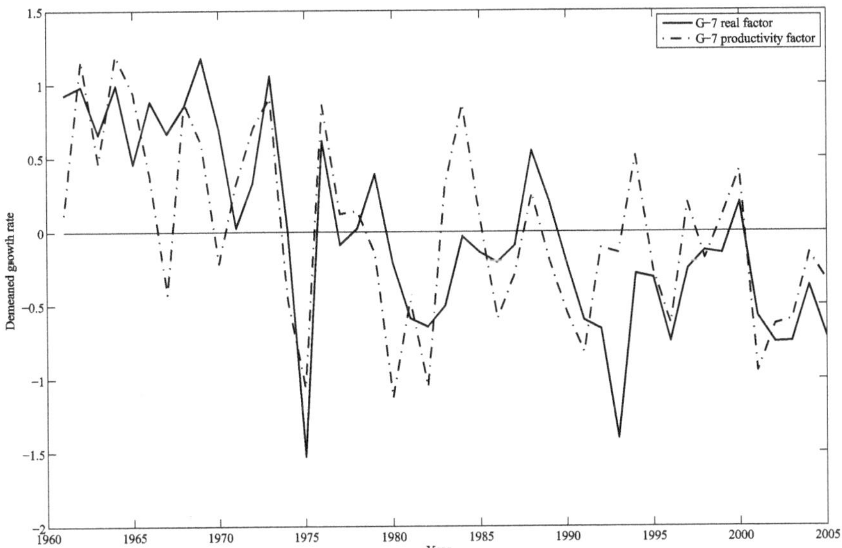

Fig. 2. The G-7 business cycle and G-7 productivity.

at the G-7 and national level. The implication is that business cycle models focusing on productivity shocks will need the nation-specific components of productivity to generate positive international output spillovers. Models with supply-side complementarities such as Ambler *et al.* (2002) fall into this category. Coordinated monetary and fiscal policies that shift world demand are two other candidates.

Turning to the relative price of oil, recall that we use four international benchmark prices for crude petroleum in U.S. dollars: Dubai, Brent, West Texas and a world average price. These are converted to domestic currency at the spot exchange rates between the U.S. and each country and then divided by the domestic CPI and employed in our standard factor model. In Table 3, we see that the G-7 component accounts for virtually all of the variation. While it is well known that various benchmark U.S. dollar prices of crude petroleum correlate very strongly, it is more surprising that this is also true of the relative price of oil in terms of the broader consumer basket in each nation. Basically, this suggests complete pass-through of world oil price movements to domestic relative oil prices. Oil is one of the few driving variables that is literally a common shock to all G-7 nations.

The variance decomposition for the terms of trade is found in Table 4. As noted by Backus and Crucini (2000), the terms of trade and the relative price of oil tend to be highly correlated for the G-7 due to the higher variance of oil prices relative to other goods and services entering into trade flows. Moreover, oil accounts for a non-trivial share of trade even in highly industrialized countries. Figure 3 presents the G-7 common factor for oil and G-7 factor for the terms of trade along with the G-7 business cycle factor. The correlation of the terms of trade and the relative price of oil in terms of the common factors is evident in the figure, particularly at the points of the sharp oil price increases in 1974, 1979, 1999 and 2005 and the drop in 1986. The correlation between the two factors over the entire sample is 0.76.

Backus and Crucini (2000) conclude that exogenous shifts in oil supply from OPEC producers can account for only about 10% of output variance in a sample of countries overlapping significantly with

Table 3. Variance decompositions for oil prices.

		World average			Dubai			Brent			West Texas		
Country	Factor	33%	50%	66%	33%	50%	66%	33%	50%	66%	33%	50%	66%
Canada	Common	88.2	89.3	93.1	89.6	90.5	94.2	86.7	87.9	90.7	85.8	87.0	91.5
	Nation-specific	6.8	10.7	11.7	4.7	8.3	9.2	5.9	8.7	9.9	8.4	13.0	14.2
	Variable-specific	0.0	0.0	0.1	1.1	1.2	1.2	3.4	3.4	3.4	0.0	0.0	0.1
France	Common	89.0	89.8	94.6	89.2	90.1	94.6	87.0	87.7	91.8	86.5	87.4	92.9
	Nation-specific	5.4	10.2	11.0	4.4	8.9	9.7	5.0	9.1	9.9	7.1	12.6	13.4
	Variable-specific	0.0	0.0	0.0	1.0	1.0	1.0	3.1	3.2	3.2	0.0	0.0	0.0
Germany	Common	89.2	90.0	94.7	90.1	90.9	95.2	86.9	87.7	91.6	86.7	87.6	92.9
	Nation-specific	5.3	10.0	10.8	3.8	8.1	8.9	5.2	9.1	9.9	7.0	12.4	13.3
	Variable-specific	0.0	0.0	0.0	1.0	1.0	1.0	3.1	3.2	3.2	0.0	0.0	0.0
Italy	Common	89.3	90.0	94.7	89.7	90.4	94.7	87.2	88.0	91.8	86.9	87.6	92.9
	Nation-specific	5.3	10.0	10.6	4.2	8.5	9.1	4.9	8.7	9.5	7.0	12.4	13.1
	Variable-specific	0.0	0.0	0.0	1.1	1.1	1.2	3.3	3.3	3.3	0.0	0.0	0.0
Japan	Common	85.1	86.3	90.5	87.3	88.4	92.4	81.9	83.1	86.3	82.7	84.0	88.9
	Nation-specific	9.4	13.7	14.9	6.7	10.7	11.8	10.7	13.9	15.0	11.1	16.0	17.2
	Variable-specific	0.0	0.0	0.1	0.9	0.9	1.0	3.0	3.0	3.1	0.0	0.1	0.1
UK	Common	88.6	89.4	94.4	89.4	90.2	94.9	87.2	88.0	92.1	86.0	86.9	92.6
	Nation-specific	5.6	10.5	11.3	4.0	8.6	9.4	4.5	8.6	9.4	7.4	13.0	13.9
	Variable-specific	0.0	0.0	0.0	1.2	1.2	1.2	3.4	3.4	3.4	0.0	0.0	0.1
US	Common	87.0	88.1	92.6	88.5	89.4	93.7	85.2	86.4	90.3	84.3	85.6	90.8
	Nation-specific	7.4	11.9	13.0	5.2	9.4	10.4	6.4	10.2	11.4	9.2	14.4	15.6
	Variable-specific	0.0	0.0	0.1	1.1	1.1	1.2	3.4	3.4	3.4	0.0	0.0	0.1
Average	Common		89.0			90.0			87.0			86.6	
	Nation-specific		11.0			8.9			9.8			13.4	
	Variable-specific		0.0			1.1			3.3			0.0	

Table 4. Variance decompositions for the terms of trade.

		TOT1			TOT2		
Country	Factor	33%	50%	66%	33%	50%	66%
Canada	Common	30.3	32.3	34.3	6.7	7.6	8.7
	Nation-specific	32.9	37.6	43.0	47.1	54.0	60.6
	Variable-specific	24.6	29.7	34.4	31.4	38.2	45.3
France	Common	70.8	73.2	75.8	68.0	70.5	72.9
	Nation-specific	5.7	9.2	12.5	5.8	9.0	12.8
	Variable-specific	14.2	17.5	20.3	16.9	20.5	23.3
Germany	Common	42.5	44.7	47.1	64.6	66.6	68.4
	Nation-specific	22.1	28.4	33.9	6.4	8.7	11.6
	Variable-specific	21.2	26.9	33.0	21.7	24.6	26.9
Italy	Common	37.4	39.8	42.2	75.6	77.8	80.1
	Nation-specific	38.6	43.6	48.3	9.8	11.7	13.8
	Variable-specific	12.4	16.4	20.6	8.2	10.0	11.7
Japan	Common	56.3	58.5	60.7	57.4	59.4	61.6
	Nation-specific	34.4	36.6	39.1	31.9	34.3	36.5
	Variable-specific	3.3	4.5	5.8	5.3	6.6	7.6
UK	Common	8.6	10.0	11.5	15.0	16.4	18.1
	Nation-specific	48.8	54.1	60.2	46.0	51.5	57.1
	Variable-specific	29.5	35.6	41.1	26.4	31.7	37.1
US	Common	36.8	38.9	40.9	49.4	51.3	53.3
	Nation-specific	47.6	50.5	53.3	37.5	40.0	42.5
	Variable-specific	8.6	10.7	12.8	6.6	8.4	10.4
Average	Common		42.5			50.0	
	Nation-specific		37.1			29.9	
	Variable-specific		20.2			20.0	

those include here. Consistent with their findings, the correlation between the G-7 business cycle factor and the G-7 oil price factor (G-7 terms of trade factor) is 0.03 (0.12) for the full sample. One should keep in mind, however, that theory predicts an ambiguous sign: exogenous oil supply shocks generate a negative correlation, while increases in oil demand by the G-7 generate a positive correlation. Since oil supply disruptions tend to be associated with dramatic oil price increases, we tend to see oil prices, the terms of trade and world output behaving consistently with the supply-shock

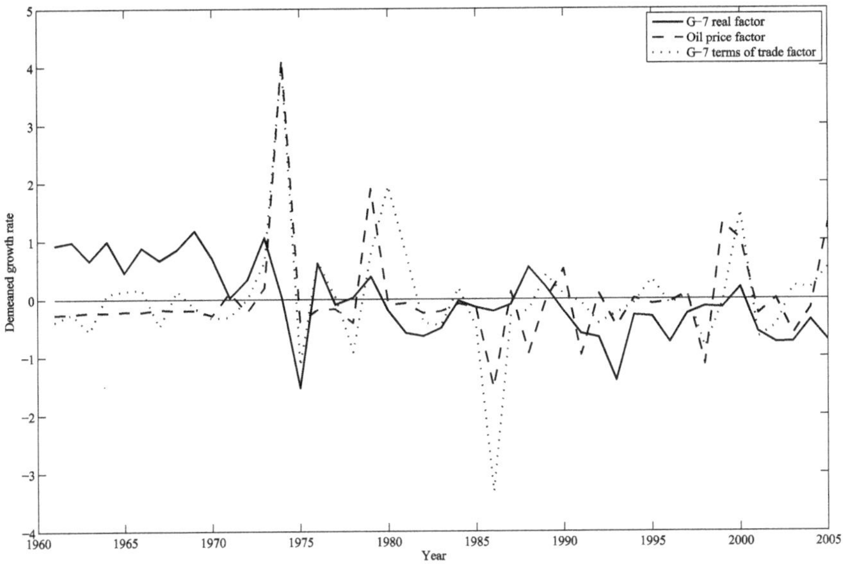

Fig. 3. The G-7 business cycle, the relative price of oil and the terms of trade.

interpretation. In most periods, however, the correlation of the terms of trade, oil and G-7 output is weak and ambiguous.

As one might expect, when the oil prices are less volatile the correlation of the terms of trade and oil prices falls considerably. This is evident when we compare the variance decomposition of the terms of trade to that of the relative price of oil. Table 4 shows that the G-7 terms of trade is not dominated by the world component, though it remains considerable, at between 40 and 50 percent, depending on the terms of trade measure.

5.2. *Monetary and fiscal policy variables*

Our goal is to capture periods of monetary and fiscal expansion and contraction in each country as well as the extent to which these policies are followed concurrently across the G-7. What the dynamic factor model allows us to do is to extract the common dynamic component from multiple observable measures of monetary or fiscal policy.

Formally, the model for fiscal policy variables in country, i, can be written as:

$$\begin{bmatrix} \Delta\tau_{i,t} \\ \Delta e_{i,t} \\ \Delta g_{i,t} \end{bmatrix} = \begin{bmatrix} \beta_{i\tau} \\ \beta_{ie} \\ \beta_{ig} \end{bmatrix} F_{F,t} + \begin{bmatrix} \gamma_{i\tau} \\ \gamma_{ie} \\ \gamma_{ig} \end{bmatrix} f_{i,F,t} + \begin{bmatrix} \varepsilon_{\tau_{i,t}} \\ \varepsilon_{e_{i,t}} \\ \varepsilon_{g_{i,t}} \end{bmatrix} \tag{7}$$

where $\Delta\tau_{i,t}$, $\Delta e_{i,t}$ and $\Delta g_{i,t}$ are the growth rates of total revenue, total expenditure and consumption by the national government of country i.

Thus we have three measures of fiscal policy, each with a different amount of information about the intentions of the fiscal authority. Loosely speaking, if a variable contains a lot of information about fiscal policy its factor loading, β or γ, will be larger in absolute value, indicating that it reacts more to the changes in fiscal policy. For example, it may be the case that a decision to change the thrust of fiscal policy is largely carried out through changes in government revenues, in this case the factor loading associated with revenues will be the highest (our variance decompositions give us more information on this). In the language of the dynamic factor literature we are extracting a signal (here of fiscal policy) from three noisy measures of that signal.

The error terms (ε's) contain two components under this interpretation of the signal extraction problem. One component is the noise component, which may be interpreted as simply measurement error. The second component is the idiosyncratic movement in a particular variable that does not have an interpretation as changes in broadly defined fiscal policy but of targeted, sector specific changes, for example, perhaps changes aimed to lessen income inequality (by lowering labor tax rates and raising capital tax rates). We are unable to distinguish between the two interpretations of the error term.

For monetary policy we include a short-term real interest, $r_{i,t}$, and a narrow monetary aggregate, $m_{i,t}$:

$$\begin{bmatrix} r_{i,t} \\ \Delta m_{i,t} \end{bmatrix} = \begin{bmatrix} \beta_{ir} \\ \beta_{im} \end{bmatrix} F_{M,t} + \begin{bmatrix} \gamma_{ir} \\ \gamma_{im} \end{bmatrix} f_{M,i,t} + \begin{bmatrix} \varepsilon_{ir,t} \\ \varepsilon_{im,t} \end{bmatrix}. \tag{8}$$

The short-term real interest rate is designed to capture changes in a variable targeted by the central bank. Of course, since we use market rates, much of the variation will be due to supply and demand factors in each country and care must be taken when we attempt to interpret movements in the context of monetary policy discussions. The narrow monetary variable is included to incorporate the fact that central banks use money growth as an instrument as well. This may take the form of medium term targeting of money growth with a particular inflation target in mind or some short term interaction of narrow monetary aggregates and the setting of short-term interest rate targets.

Tables 5 and 6 contain the variance decompositions for the policy variables. The most striking feature of these results is how different short-term interest rates and monetary aggregates look through the lens of the factor model. Short term real interest rates are dominated by a common G-7 component, with two-thirds of the variance attributable to the common factor and almost none attributed to the nation-specific component. Money growth, in contrast, is dominated by the idiosyncratic component though a sizable nation-specific variation is also found.

The large world component in short-term real interest rates has a number of possible interpretations. The most obvious interpretation is that financial markets are highly integrated and capital mobility tends to drive the rate of return to capital in the same direction internationally. This is good news for models that feature trade in bonds and physical capital mobility. A policy interpretation is also possible here, namely the desire to avoid either large short-term capital movements or sharp exchange rate responses to uncoordinated movements in the interest rate target across the G-7. Finally, the common factor could be picking up the common factor in the business cycles of the G-7. Since business cycles tend to be positively correlated across countries, it is natural to expect real interest rates to share that correlation pattern too. The latter explanation is of particular interest because the cyclicality of the real interest rate within individual countries have been difficult to establish.

Table 5. Variance decompositions for monetary variables.

		Short interest rates			Money supply		
Country	Factor	33%	50%	66%	33%	50%	66%
Canada	Common	79.2	81.4	83.4	3.9	4.9	5.9
	Nation-specific	0.5	1.3	3.5	11.9	27.7	49.5
	Variable-specific	12.8	15.4	17.8	45.4	66.9	83.4
France	Common	65.5	68.2	70.9	1.0	1.6	2.2
	Nation-specific	2.0	5.4	10.5	3.1	8.8	22.1
	Variable-specific	19.6	23.9	27.5	76.2	89.1	94.8
Germany	Common	32.4	34.5	36.7	1.1	1.6	2.2
	Nation-specific	2.8	6.5	14.7	10.5	27.6	52.9
	Variable-specific	49.5	56.5	61.0	45.0	70.7	87.5
Italy	Common	64.8	67.2	69.5	0.4	0.8	1.3
	Nation-specific	10.6	13.7	17.3	34.7	44.7	56.4
	Variable-specific	15.2	18.4	21.4	42.7	54.3	64.3
Japan	Common	44.2	46.4	48.6	13.9	15.5	17.2
	Nation-specific	9.6	14.0	19.4	22.0	31.0	40.6
	Variable-specific	33.8	38.9	43.4	43.8	53.3	62.2
UK	Common	63.7	66.2	68.5	3.8	4.6	5.6
	Nation-specific	3.4	5.5	9.0	24.7	41.8	58.9
	Variable-specific	23.3	27.0	30.1	36.4	53.6	71.0
US	Common	48.9	51.8	54.7	1.6	2.2	2.8
	Nation-specific	2.8	5.8	10.6	8.5	20.5	35.1
	Variable-specific	35.1	39.9	44.0	62.8	77.5	89.0
Average	Common		59.4			4.5	
	Nation-specific		7.4			28.9	
	Variable-specific		31.4			66.5	

Therefore, to the extent we find one at the level of G-7 countries, it is encouraging.[6]

That money growth lacks a large common component is not surprising given the different inflationary histories of the countries in the cross-section. Somewhat more surprising is the size of the idiosyncratic component. This could be due to shifts in money

[6]Barro and Sali-i-Martin (1990) construct a world interest rate variable using a different methodology and find it depends mostly on world factors.

Table 6. Variance decompositions for measures of fiscal policies.

		Government consumption			Government expenditure			Government revenue		
Country	Factor	33%	50%	66%	33%	50%	66%	33%	50%	66%
Canada	Common	12.3	14.9	18.0	0.3	0.7	1.4	11.6	14.8	18.2
	Nation-specific	10.6	15.3	20.4	41.5	50.4	59.4	21.5	28.0	35.7
	Variable-specific	62.6	68.6	73.8	39.4	48.3	57.0	46.8	55.5	63.2
France	Common	16.7	21.0	25.5	18.5	21.5	24.6	0.8	1.7	2.8
	Nation-specific	16.5	23.4	32.7	20.9	29.4	39.4	0.4	1.0	2.2
	Variable-specific	44.9	54.4	61.5	38.4	49.0	57.4	94.6	96.2	97.4
Germany	Common	4.0	5.8	8.0	16.4	20.2	24.3	3.1	4.4	5.8
	Nation-specific	25.2	34.7	47.5	0.8	2.0	4.6	28.2	39.9	53.7
	Variable-specific	45.3	57.6	67.2	70.5	75.0	79.0	41.0	55.3	67.0
Italy	Common	5.9	8.6	11.8	34.3	38.5	42.7	3.1	4.7	6.8
	Nation-specific	1.6	4.0	9.0	11.1	19.4	28.7	5.6	10.8	17.7
	Variable-specific	78.6	84.9	88.7	31.6	40.4	48.5	77.2	82.8	87.0
Japan	Common	0.9	1.7	2.7	1.4	2.6	4.3	1.2	2.1	3.5
	Nation-specific	2.5	7.2	21.2	4.8	15.3	35.5	0.4	1.0	2.3
	Variable-specific	76.3	89.8	94.8	60.6	80.8	90.7	93.4	95.5	97.3
UK	Common	27.9	32.9	38.1	22.9	27.2	32.2	0.2	0.4	0.7
	Nation-specific	13.6	19.8	26.2	31.3	39.5	47.3	12.3	17.1	23.3
	Variable-specific	41.4	46.2	50.6	25.9	32.4	38.4	76.0	82.3	86.9
US	Common	0.4	0.9	1.9	3.8	6.2	9.2	38.9	44.2	49.6
	Nation-specific	54.7	60.4	66.0	51.6	57.5	63.1	1.7	3.5	5.9
	Variable-specific	32.3	37.9	43.3	29.0	34.5	40.2	44.7	50.7	56.7
Average	Common		12.3			16.7			10.3	
	Nation-specific		23.5			30.5			14.5	
	Variable-specific		62.8			51.5			74.0	

demand across near substitutes within a country and differences in the definitions of money across countries.

Figures 4 and 5 present the G-7 fiscal and monetary factors, respectively, alongside the G-7 business cycle factor. The world fiscal factor is sharply countercyclical in the first part of the sample, most notable in the sharp recession of the early 1970s. Later in the sample, the correlation becomes ambiguous. The countercyclicality is likely due to the normal evolution of tax revenue and non-discretionary spending over the cycle with tax revenue falling and expenditure rising. The later period has some large discretionary changes in tax rates, such as the Reagan and Thatcher tax cuts.

We see a dramatic swing in monetary policy from stimulative in the 1970s to contractionary in the late 1970s and particularly the early 1980s. This is consistent with the broad brush view that monetary growth and low nominal and real interest rates set the world economy into a boom and inflationary spiral, followed by a concerted effort by the U.S. Federal Reserve and other central bankers to tame inflation. The very gradual down-slope of the world monetary factor in the 1980s and 1990s is consistent with the gradual disinflation and

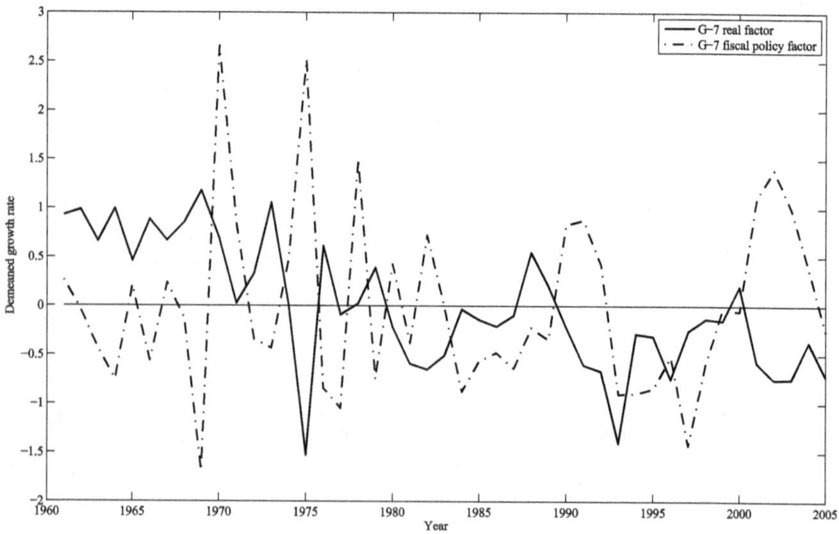

Fig. 4. The G-7 business cycle and the G-7 fiscal factor.

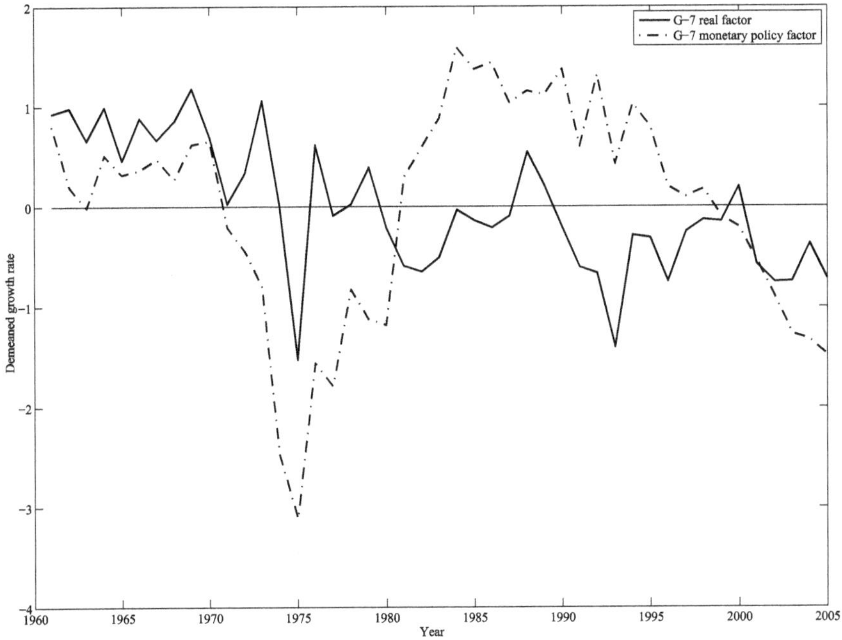

Fig. 5. The G-7 business cycle and the G-7 monetary factor.

moderating real interest rate levels that were at least partly a result of establishing central bank credibility on the inflation front.

6. What Drives International Business Cycles?

Up to now we have described the common and nation-specific components of national business cycles and the variables that business cycle theorists have proposed as driving variables. What we would like to know is how much of a nation's output variation is generated by common and nation-specific sources of variation in each of the driving variables.

6.1. *Deconstructing the G-7 and national business cycle*

The first step in undertaking this exercise, is to regress the common component of the G-7 business cycle on the common G-7 components of each of the driving factors:

$$F_{Y,t} = \beta_M F_{M,t} + \beta_F F_{F,t} + \beta_O F_{O,t} + \beta_A F_{A,t} + \beta_T F_{T,t} + \varepsilon_{Y,t}. \quad (9)$$

By applying the variance operator to the both sides of this equation, we can decompose the variance of the estimated G-7 real business cycle into the parts due to the common G-7 component of each of the driving variables plus an idiosyncratic component.[7] In order to ensure that the variance sums to one hundred, we first orthogonalize the factors for each of the driving variables. Specifically, we orthogonalize the regressors by first regressing the second factor on the first factor, and retaining the residual as the orthogonalized second factor. We proceed sequentially projecting factors onto the orthogonalized factors until we have a set of 5 orthogonalized factors. The order of orthogonalization we employ is the order the variables appear above: monetary policy, fiscal policy, oil prices, productivity and the terms of trade. This ordering implies that we use the monetary factor as it is estimated by the factor model and the orthogonal terms of trade factor is the part of the estimated factor that is orthogonal to all other factors.

Our decision to order technology next to last is so that it is part of the measured technology that is orthogonal to movements in monetary and fiscal policy to address the common critique that the Solow residual type measures are contaminated with other non-technology shocks. Some authors consider the terms of trade as a proxy measure of relative productivity movements across countries that specialize in traded sectors. Even so, the terms of trade is arguably endogenous in a general equilibrium setting and we include it as the last factor in our orthogonalization of the components for this reason. We checked the robustness of the variance decomposition

[7]Our decomposition is distinct from the question in Bai and Ng (2005). In their work they provide a statistical test to determine if an unobserved factor is a proxy for one observable variable. We explicitly believe, as predicted by our structural model, that the common factors for real variables are in fact linear combinations of the driving forces. It is this combination we wish to disentangle. Note also that the Bai and Ng (2005) test is based on asymptotics that require both N and T to be larger, which does not hold in our case or in most business cycle models.

to alternative orderings of the variables and found the results were virtually unchanged.

The result of this exercise suggests that productivity is the main driving variable for the common component of the business cycles among the G-7. In particular, this factor accounts for 47 percent of the fluctuations in the G-7 real factor over the full sample period. The terms of trade factor accounts for less than 1.5 percent of the movements in the G-7 cycle, while oil, fiscal and monetary factors account for even less than one percent. A caveat to these results is that they represent a decomposition of the unconditional variance over the whole period. It is certainly plausible that some variables, such as oil, play an important role in certain sub-periods, as pointed out in Section 5.1.

To complete our variance decomposition at the level of individual macroeconomic aggregates we need to also include the nation-specific components. To accomplish this, we employ the procedure described above with one of the NIPA aggregates on the left-hand side and *either* the complete list of G-7 common factors (i.e., the common factor driving monetary policy, fiscal policy, productivity, the terms of trade and oil across the G-7) or the complete list of the nation-specific driving variables on the right-hand side. Thus, for, say U.S. output growth we use the following two equations to decompose the output variance by shock and component:

$$\Delta y_{i,t} = \pi_M F_{M,t} + \pi_F F_{F,t} + \pi_o F_{O,t} + \pi_A F_{A,t} + \pi_T F_{T,t} + \epsilon_{y,i,t}, \tag{10}$$

$$\Delta y_{i,t} = \varphi_m f_{M,i,t} + \varphi_F f_{F,i,t} + \varphi_o f_{O,i,t} + \varphi_A f_{A,i,t} + \varphi_T f_{T,i,t} + \nu_{y,i,t}. \tag{11}$$

It is important to note that while the factors on the right-hand side of each equation are orthogonalized with respect to each other, these components need not have a zero covariance across equations. The G-7 component of fiscal policy may be correlated with the nation-specific component of productivity, for example. Thus, when we add up the contributions of the G-7 shocks and the nation-specific shocks, they need not add up to less than 100%. If these two factors are orthogonal, the result is a unique variance decomposition with only the idiosyncratic factors left as a residual. In practice, the G-7 factors and nation-specific factor have non-zero sample correlation so there are instances where some ambiguity arises in assigning, say, the U.S. output fluctuations to the G-7 productivity factor versus the U.S. nation-specific monetary factor. The results suggest that the sum of the two variance decompositions is usually less than one hundred, and rarely much greater than one hundred. We interpret the results as being an upper bound on the variance contribution of the G-7 and nation-specific components.

We begin with the decomposition of output, reported in the first panel of Table 7. Taken together, the driving variables account for a substantial portion of the variation in output growth. The G-7 common factor on average explains a smaller share of the variation than the nation-specific factors. Italy and Japan appear to be the most idiosyncratic with the national components of driving variables accounting for more than 90 percent of the variation. Canada and the United States lie at the other end of the distribution with a very significant role for the common components of the driving variables.

At first glance the results for France, Italy and Japan that the main driving force of output in these countries is the nation-specific component seems at odds with the results in Section 4 that report their output fluctuations have a large G-7 component. However, these results can be reconciled by first noticing that for these three countries productivity has a small G-7 component but a large nation-specific component. The latter component turns out to explain a large amount of output variation. At the same time, our results above show that movements in the G-7 productivity factor explain about 50 percent of the G-7 real factor. The G-7 component of movements in output in France, Italy and Japan are then due to the 50 percent of the G-7 real cycle that remains unexplained.[8]

[8]Recall also that the variance decomposition of the nation-specific and G-7 components come from separate regressions and need not sum to one. It turns out that for France, Italy and Japan the correlation between the country and G-7 factors is the largest, implying that the results for these three countries must be somewhat less than the reported upper bounds.

Table 7. Variance decompositions for macroeconomic variables.

	Common component						Nation-specific component					
	Productivity	Fiscal	Monetary	Oil price	Terms of trade	Total	Productivity	Fiscal	Monetary	Oil price	Terms of trade	Total
Panel A. Variance decomposition of gross domestic product												
Canada	53.84	19.54	0.04	0.15	0.39	73.95	10.42	0.88	0.02	0.28	0.07	11.66
France	40.13	1.34	2.66	0.28	0.12	44.53	78.84	0.46	0.02	0.97	0.45	80.73
Germany	35.69	1.94	8.50	0.00	0.87	47.00	15.87	14.54	0.53	0.01	0.01	30.95
Italy	20.15	4.90	1.11	3.05	1.48	30.69	86.20	0.96	0.00	4.98	0.17	92.32
Japan	25.74	0.00	4.71	1.84	0.24	32.52	80.29	0.91	10.17	0.21	0.00	91.58
UK	18.11	9.44	7.15	3.23	9.45	47.38	43.70	5.12	24.25	0.00	0.27	73.34
US	38.43	25.71	4.06	3.10	2.41	73.71	24.45	2.91	6.38	0.21	1.31	35.25
Average	33.16	8.98	4.03	1.66	2.14	49.97	48.54	3.68	5.91	0.95	0.32	59.40
Median	35.69	4.90	4.06	1.84	0.87	47.00	43.70	0.96	0.53	0.21	0.17	73.34
Panel B. Variance decomposition of total private consumption												
Canada	39.51	12.67	3.33	0.05	2.30	57.86	8.93	1.06	1.52	0.20	1.62	13.32
France	29.74	0.05	0.02	2.56	3.51	35.89	60.25	0.00	0.58	0.48	2.30	63.62
Germany	31.03	1.06	3.72	1.04	1.54	38.39	3.86	14.75	2.60	0.30	5.83	27.35
Italy	11.18	0.67	1.44	0.07	0.29	13.65	67.79	0.66	0.06	0.55	0.01	69.07
Japan	25.31	0.00	4.07	1.26	1.23	31.86	65.02	2.70	9.44	0.04	0.34	77.54
UK	4.23	0.67	7.47	1.85	13.61	27.82	35.24	0.68	29.40	0.32	1.40	67.04
US	42.60	11.26	4.79	8.84	8.77	76.27	12.20	3.90	18.63	0.21	0.30	35.23
Average	26.23	3.77	3.55	2.24	4.46	40.25	36.18	3.39	8.89	0.30	1.69	50.45
Median	29.74	0.67	3.72	1.26	2.30	35.89	35.24	1.06	2.60	0.30	1.40	63.62

(*Continued*)

Table 7. (*Continued*)

	Common component						Nation-specific component					
	Productivity	Fiscal	Monetary	Oil price	Terms of trade	Total	Productivity	Fiscal	Monetary	Oil price	Terms of trade	Total
	Panel C. Variance decomposition of investment											
Canada	7.90	16.45	3.25	0.21	0.43	28.24	29.29	1.66	0.55	1.04	1.61	34.16
France	17.40	3.55	5.76	0.59	0.01	27.30	71.63	1.92	0.74	0.05	3.19	77.54
Germany	17.34	0.26	13.88	1.15	0.06	32.69	12.40	15.00	3.68	0.35	0.40	31.82
Italy	0.50	1.22	1.63	1.69	0.29	5.34	54.05	0.00	0.68	0.24	3.80	58.77
Japan	18.63	0.01	9.95	1.74	0.04	30.36	75.75	1.88	13.84	0.20	0.21	91.89
UK	7.54	2.72	10.17	0.46	1.71	22.60	27.60	3.11	11.47	0.03	0.25	42.47
US	24.29	32.12	2.80	1.35	2.09	62.65	31.68	0.05	5.44	0.04	2.24	39.45
Average	13.37	8.05	6.78	1.03	0.66	29.88	43.20	3.37	5.20	0.28	1.67	53.73
Median	17.34	2.72	5.76	1.15	0.29	28.24	31.68	1.88	3.68	0.20	1.61	42.47

Turning to the individual driving variables, the columns are ordered by the fraction of output variance accounted for by the national component of the driving variable. By this metric the most important driving variable, by far, is productivity, followed by fiscal factors and monetary factors. Oil prices and the terms of trade play a very small role overall. For oil prices, it is the common component that is slightly more important, which makes sense given the significant role of OPEC pricing decisions over the period of study.

To the extent that productivity movements reflect technological shifts, they are not universally shared. The nation-specific component rivals the common G-7 component, each on average accounting for between 30 and 50 percent of output growth. Variation in the contribution of the common factor in productivity in the cross-section of countries is significant, ranging from a low of 18 percent in the United Kingdom to a high of 54 percent in Canada. Thus the importance of the G-7 factors overall for Canada and the United States is a combination of productivity shocks and the fiscal factor.

Comparing monetary and fiscal factors, the nation-specific component plays a slightly more important role in the case of monetary factors while the G-7 factor tends to be more important in a few cases for fiscal factors. We do not want to overstate the differences here because the absolute variances associated with them are small and for most countries neither component plays a large role.

For consumption growth, also reported in Table 7, we see similar patterns to what was found in our examination of output growth. In particular, taken together, the G-7 and national components are both important and the productivity tends to dominate as a driving variable. Again, the nation-specific factors are particularly strong in Italy and Japan while the G-7 factor is more relevant in Canada and the United States. The nation-specific monetary factors and the G-7 common fiscal factor again account for a lower order of magnitude of business cycles in consumption. While the role of oil is still marginal, the terms of trade as a driving variable on average plays a slightly more important role in explaining consumption than it does output. Given that consumption on average constitutes two-thirds of aggregate output, the similarity of the output and consumption results is not altogether unexpected.

Turning to investment, a key difference relative to earlier variables emerges, namely that nation-specific factor plays a much more important role than the G-7 factor does when all of the driving variables are considered together. In particular, the nation-specific productivity factor is much more important than the G-7 productivity factor in explaining the investment growth variation. This is consistent with the view that changes in the marginal productivity of capital across countries is an important facet of investment dynamics in an integrated world economy. In the case of monetary and fiscal policy variables, while the G-7 factor is more important than the nation-specific factors, this result is mostly driven by a small set of countries. Neither oil prices nor the terms of trade factor appears to contribute much to investment fluctuations.

6.2. *Toward a business cycle chronology*

The seminal work by Friedman and Schwartz (1963) is most often associated with the robust correlation between monetary events and the real business cycle. However, part of what distinguishes their work from modern business cycle research is the attention to detail at the level of individual business cycles and even phases of individual business cycles. This allowed them to provide texture to the chronology, high-lighting periods when monetary policy played a crucial role and when it was more passive. Recent analysis typically reduces the business cycle to a set of moment conditions, often without attention to possible shifts in the relationships among endogenous and exogenous variables over time. A recent exception is the Great Moderation literature which focuses on the falling business cycle volatility over the most recent quarter century.

Here we draw inspiration from Friedman and Schwartz, but follow the modern literature by characterizing the chronology of business cycles in terms of time series moments. We focus on the G-7 cycle. To accomplish this we compute ten-year centered moving average correlations between the common G-7 business cycle factor and the

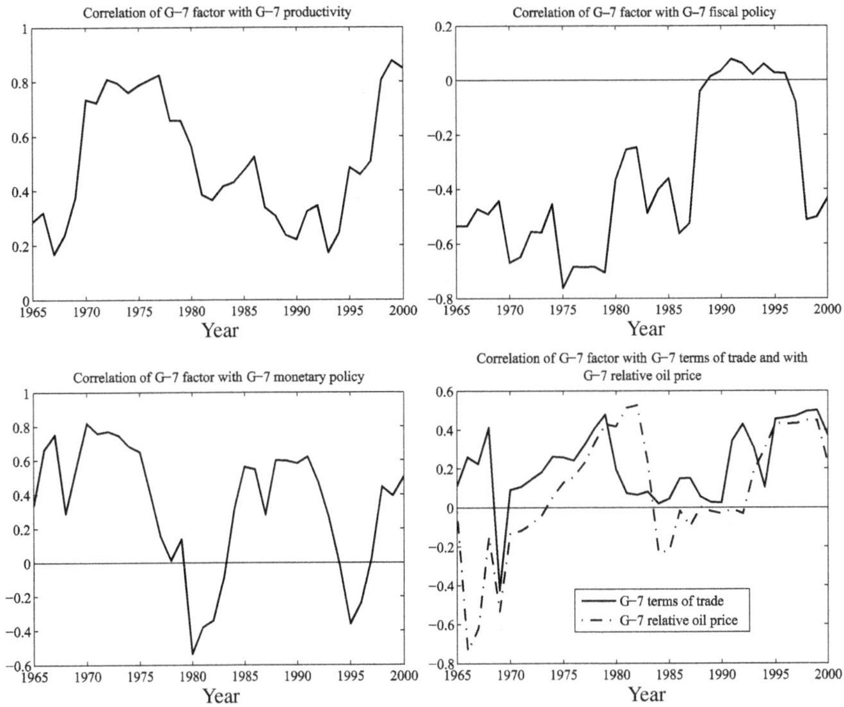

Fig. 6. Ten-year rolling correlations; G-7 business cycle and the G-7 driving factors.

common G-7 components of each of the driving variables. Figure 6 presents the results.

Since we are relating the common components to each other, a good starting point is the correlation of the common real factor with aggregate G-7 output (not shown in Fig. 6), which averages 0.76 over the period. Thus the common real factor we extract from the G-7 NIPA aggregates is strongly correlated with the G-7 business cycle measured as a country-size weighted average of their output series. The correlation is quite stable over time, rising from 0.71 to 0.80 as we move from the first 10 year interval to the last (recall we lose 5 years of data at each end point in the rolling correlation).

From here on we will use the term world business cycle to refer to the G-7 real factor. The correlation of the world business cycle and G-7 productivity is a healthy 0.51, it falls only slightly from 0.56

to 0.46 as we move from about 1970 to 1995. Figure 6 shows the full time path of the rolling correlations. Note that the correlation of the other driving variables with the G-7 business cycle are both lower and less stable over time.

The G-7 fiscal factor, for example, is quite stable and negative over the first part of the sample, it then jumps to about zero from the late 1980s to the late 1990s, before falling back down toward the end of the sample. It is tempting to interpret the earlier period as fiscally passive in the sense of a tendency of tax revenue to fall and expenditures to rise in the absence of legislative actions due to the progressivity of the income tax, procyclicality of capital gains and profit taxes and movements in non-discretionary spending, such as welfare payments and unemployment assistance. The absence of a clear cyclical pattern to fiscal policy reported in many business cycle papers is consistent with what we find toward the end of the sample. The fact that the correlation is strikingly negative across the world in the earlier period is important because it suggests a role for fiscal policy in the past, which may have been overlooked in the existing literature.

Monetary policy oscillates from being strongly positively correlated with the G-7 cycle to strongly negatively correlated. Broadly speaking, monetary policy appears to be accommodating in most periods except the early 1980s, when central bankers made concerted efforts to reduce inflationary trends, and in the mid-1990s which seems to match up with the increases in the discount rate during the productivity and stock market boom.

The correlation of the oil price factor and the world business cycle moves from −0.17 to 0.24 across the decades. While these averages are closer to zero than some of the others, it is instructive to examine Fig. 6 more carefully. We see what appears to be a rising trend in the correlation with reversals at the dates of sharp increases in the relative price of oil. These patterns seem broadly consistent with a recent hypothesis concerning the relationship between the business cycle and the relative price of oil. Some economists have argued that the relative importance of negative oil supply disruptions versus positive demand shifts have changed significantly over time.

The conventional wisdom of sharp exogenous increases due to supply disruption and OPEC pricing decisions seems consistent with the negative correlation, a contractionary oil price increase. Sharply rising demand for energy by newly industrializing countries, India and China prominent among them, would give rise to a positive correlation to the extent the real growth spillovers to the G-7 are positive (which seems very likely).

Examining the contribution of G-7 and nation-specific movements in the driving variables over time and in particular business cycle episodes is an important area for future research. The broad correlations outlined here are suggestive of some of the themes that could emerge from such an examination.

7. Conclusion

There has been much interest in the contribution of the international business cycle to variation in national macroeconomic aggregates such as output, consumption and investment. We confirm previous findings that a world business cycle does indeed exist. We take the next obvious step and find the international business cycle to be primarily driven by productivity, though we are only able to explain roughly half of the variation in the G-7 cycle. A visual inspection of the international cycle and the driving variables shows that the correlation of oil prices and the world business cycle may have changed over time, possibly shifting from a preponderance of negative supply shocks in the 1970s and 1980s to a more significant role for positive demand shocks in recent decades.

Turning to individual countries, our findings suggest that the common G-7 business cycle is important for the evolution of most macroeconomic aggregates and the driving variables of business cycles, including policy variables. Despite the significance of the common G-7 component in many of these variables, most appear to play a relatively minor role in explaining aggregate real business cycle fluctuations, with the exception of productivity.

Our results relating components of the driving variables to endogenous choice variables are subject to the obvious caveat that our approach imposes no restrictions on the stochastic structure with the exception of a partition of variables into endogenous and exogenous. The factor modeling of the exogenous processes could easily be utilized in existing DSGE models. Moreover, our approach suggests it is productive to look beyond unconditional moment matching and examine the contribution of different shocks and different (world and nation-specific) components of the shocks to variation in each endogenous variable under examination.

We further believe that this framework will help rekindle an interest in developing chronologies of national and world business cycles along the lines of Friedman and Schwartz and Burns and Mitchell. Such an exercise would likely bring important nuances to our understanding of individual business cycle episodes as well as policy responses to different causal factors than is possible with the first pass we have attempted here. Much remains to be done.

Acknowledgments

We thank Vivien Yue for insightful comments. The views expressed in this paper are those of the authors, not the International Monetary Fund.

Appendix A. Bayesian Estimation of Dynamic Factor Models

This appendix reviews the methodology used in estimating the dynamic factor model. The model here is a multi-factor extension of the single dynamic unobserved factor model in Otrok and Whiteman (1998). Kose *et al.* (2003) also employ a similar multi-factor model in an exercise studying international business cycles. Since they provide a detailed discussion of the multi-factor model, this section is brief and closely follows the description in that paper.

Our interest in estimating the dynamic factor model is to characterize the joint posterior of the model parameters and latent factors. Since analytic forms for the joint posterior of the factors and parameters are unobtainable, we employ numerical methods to simulate from the posterior. To do so we use a "data augmentation" algorithm to generate draws from the joint posterior of interest (see Tanner and Wong, 1987; Otrok and Whiteman, 1998). Data augmentation in this context builds on the following key observation: if the factors were observable, under a conjugate prior, the factor models we estimate would each constitute a simple set of regressions with Gaussian autoregressive errors. Then, conditional on the regression parameters and the data, one can determine the conditional distribution of the factors. It is straightforward to generate random samples from this conditional distribution, and such samples can be employed as stand-ins for the unobserved factors.

To be more specific, the dynamic factor models can be thought of as consisting of a specification of a Gaussian probability density for the data $\{y_t\}$ conditional on a set of parameters Ψ and a set of latent variables $\{f_t\}$. Call this density function $g_y(Y|\Psi, F)$ where Y denotes the vector of data on the observable data, and F denotes the vector of dynamic factors. In addition, there is a specification of a Gaussian probability density $g_f(F)$ for F itself. Given a prior distribution for Ψ, $\pi(\Psi)$, the joint posterior distribution for the parameters and the latent variables is given by the product of the likelihood and prior, $h(\Psi,\ F|Y) = g_y(Y|\Psi,\ F)g_f(F)\pi(\Psi)$. As is shown in Otrok and Whiteman (1998), although the joint posterior $h(\Psi,\ F|Y)$ is extremely cumbersome, under a conjugate prior for Ψ the two conditional densities $h(\Psi|F,\ Y)$ and $h(F|\Psi,\ Y)$ are quite simple. Moreover, it is possible to use this fact and Markov–Chain Monte Carlo methods (MCMC) to generate an artificial sample $\{\Psi_j,\ F_j\}$ for $j = 1,\ \ldots,\ J$ as follows:

1. Starting from a value F_0 in the support of the posterior distribution for F, generate a random drawing Ψ_1 from the conditional density $h(\Psi|F_0,\ Y)$.
2. Now generate a random drawing F_1 from the conditional density $h(F|\Psi_1,\ Y)$.
3. This process is repeated, generating at each step drawings $\Psi_{\tilde{j}}h(\Psi|F_{j-1},\ Y)$ and $F_{\tilde{j}}h(F|\Psi_{j-1},\ Y)$.

Under regularity conditions satisfied here (see Tanner and Wong, 1987), the sample so produced is a realization of a Markov chain whose invariant distribution is the joint posterior $h(\Psi, F|Y)$. What makes this process feasible is the simplicity of the two conditional distributions. For example, $h(\Psi|F, Y)$ is easily constructed from the linear factor model when F is known. In particular, the linear factor model is just a normal linear regression model for y_i given the factors (albeit a regression that has autocorrelated errors that requires the use of the procedure in Chib and Greenberg, 1994, to simulate from the posterior). The other conditional density, $h(F|\Psi, Y)$ is a little more complicated because it is the solution to a Gaussian signal extraction problem. Otrok and Whiteman (1998) derive this distribution, which turns out to be a Normal distribution.

The prior on all the factor loading coefficients is $N(0, 10)$, which is quite diffuse. For the parameters of autoregressive polynomials, the prior is $N(0, \Sigma)$, where

$$\Sigma = \begin{bmatrix} 1 & 0 & 0 \\ 0 & 0.5 & 0 \\ 0 & 0 & 0.25 \end{bmatrix}.$$

Because the data are growth rates, this prior embodies the notion that growth is not serially correlated though the prior is loose enough to allow for significant serial correlation; also, the probability that lags are zero grows with the length of the lag.[9] Experimentation with tighter and looser priors for both the factor loadings and the autoregressive parameters did not produce qualitatively important changes in the results reported below. The prior on the innovation variances in the observable equations is *Inverted Gamma* (6, 0.001), which is also quite diffuse.

Appendix B. Variance Decompositions

To measure the relative contributions of the G-7, nation-, and variable-specific factors to variations in aggregate variables in each

[9]Otrok and Whiteman (1998) discuss the procedure for ensuring stationarity of the lag polynomial. The method involves drawing from a truncated Normal distribution in the Metropolis–Hastings step.

country, we estimate the share of the variance of each macroeconomic aggregate due to each factor. In particular, we decompose the variance of each observable into the fraction that is due to each of the two factors and the variable-specific component. With orthogonal factors the variance of observable i can be written:

$$var(y_{i,t}) = (b_i^{G\text{-}7})^2 var(f_t^{G\text{-}7}) + (b_i^{nation})^2 var(f_t^{nation}) + var(\varepsilon_{i,t}).$$

The fraction of volatility due to, say, the G-7 factor would be:

$$\frac{(b_i^{G\text{-}7})^2 var(f_t^{G\text{-}7})}{var(y_{i,t})}.$$

These measures are calculated at each pass of the Markov chain; dispersion in their posterior distributions reflects uncertainty regarding their magnitudes.

Appendix C. Supplementary material

The online version of this article contains additional supplementary material.
Please visit doi:10.1016/j.red.2010.09.001.

References

Ahmed, Shagil, Ickes, Barry W., Wang, Ping, Yoo, Byung Sam, 1993. International business cycles. *American Economic Review* 83 (3), 335–359.

Ambler, Steve, Cardia, Emanuela, Zimmermann, Christian, 2002. International transmission of the business cycle in a multi-sector model. *European Economic Review* 46 (2), 273–300.

Backus, David, Crucini, Mario J., 2000. Oil prices and the terms of trade. *Journal of International Economics* 50 (1), 185–212.

Backus, David K., Kehoe, Patrick J., 1992. International evidence on the historical properties of business cycles. *American Economic Review* 82, 864–888.

Backus, David K., Kehoe, Patrick J., Kydland, Finn E., 1992. International real business cycles. *Journal of Political Economy* 100, 745–775.

Bai, Jushan, Ng, Serena, 2005. Evaluating latent observed factors in macroeconomics and finance. *Journal of Econometrics* 131, 507–537.

Barro, Robert, Sali-i-Martin, Xavier, 1990. World real interest rates. National Bureau of Economic Research, Working Paper No. 3317, April.

Bernanke, Ben S., Boivin, Jean, Eliasz, Piotr, 2005. Measuring the effects of monetary policy: a factor-augmented vector autoregressive (FAVAR) approach. *Quarterly Journal of Economics* 120 (1), 387–422.

Burns, A.F., Mitchell, W.C., 1946. *Measuring Business Cycles.* National Bureau of Economic Research, New York.

Chib, Siddhartha, Greenberg, Edward, 1994. Bayes inference in regression models with ARMA (p, q) errors. *Journal of Econometrics* 64, 183–206.

Crucini, Mario J., 1997. Country size and economic fluctuations. *Review of International Economics* 5 (2), 204–220.

Friedman, Milton, Jacobson Schwartz, Anna, 1963. A Monetary History of the United States, 1867–1960. Princeton University Press, Princeton.

Gregory, Allan W., Head, Allen, 1999. Common and country-specific fluctuations in productivity, investment, and the current account. *Journal of Monetary Economics* 44 (3), 423–451.

Gregory, Allan W., Head, Allen, Raynauld, Jean, 1997. Measuring world business cycles. *International Economic Review* 38, 667–702.

Heston, Alan, Summers, Robert, Aten, Bettina, 2006. Penn World Table Version 6.2. Center for International Comparisons of Production, Income and Prices at the University of Pennsylvania, September.

Kehoe, Patrick J., Midrigan, Virgiliu, 2007. Can heterogeneity in price stickiness account for the persistence and volatility of good-level real exchange rates? Federal Reserve Bank of Minneapolis Research Department Staff Report.

Klenow, Peter J., Rodriuez-Clare, Andres, 2005. Externalities and growth. In: Aghion, Philippe, Durlauf, Steven (Eds.), *Handbook of Economic Growth.* Elsevier Science, The Netherlands, pp. 817–861.

Kose, Ayhan, Otrok, Christopher, Whiteman, Charles H., 2003. International business cycles: world, region, and country-specific factors. *American Economic Review* 93 (4), 1216–1239.

Kose, Ayhan, Otrok, Christopher, Whiteman, Charles H., 2008. Understanding the evolution of world business cycles. *Journal of International Economics* 75 (1), 110–130.

Otrok, Christopher, Whiteman, Charles H., 1998. Bayesian leading indicators: measuring and predicting economic conditions in Iowa. *International Economic Review* 39 (4), 997–1014.

Mumtaz, Haroon, Simonelli, Saverio, Surico, Paolo, 2011. International comovements, business cycle and inflation: A historical perspective. *Review of Economic Dynamics* 14 (1), 176–198.

Tanner, A.M., Wong, H.W., 1987. The calculation of posterior distributions by data augmentation. *Journal of the American Statistical Association* 82 (398), 84–88.

Zarnowitz, Victor, 1992. *Business Cycles: Theory, History, Indicators, and Forecasting.* The University of Chicago Press, Chicago.

Chapter 2

Understanding European Real Exchange Rates*

Mario J. Crucini

Department of Economics, Vanderbilt University,
Nashville, TN, USA
mario.j.crucini@vanderbilt.edu

Chris I. Telmer

Carnegie Mellon University Graduate School of Industrial Administration,
Pittsburgh, USA
and Departament d'Economia i Empresa,
Universitat Pompeu Fabra, Barcelona, Spain
chris.telmer@cmu.edu

and

Marios Zachariadis

Department of Economics, University of Cyprus, 1678 Nicosia, Cyprus
and Department of Economics, Louisiana State University,
Baton Rouge, LA, USA
zachariadis@ucy.ac.cy

Abstract. We study good-by-good deviations from the Law-of-One-Price (LOP) for over 1,800 retail goods and services between all European Union (EU) countries for the years 1975, 1980, 1985, and 1990.

*This chapter originally appeared in *American Economic Review*, 2005, **95**(3), 724–738.

We find that for each of these years, after we control for differences in income and value-added tax (VAT) rates, there are roughly as many overpriced goods as there are underpriced goods between any two EU countries. We also find that good-by-good measures of cross-sectional price dispersion are negatively related to the tradeability of the good, and positively related to the share of non-traded inputs required to produce the good. We argue that these observations are consistent with a model in which retail goods are produced by combining a traded input with a non-traded input.

The LOP states that identical goods in different countries should have identical prices, once the prices are expressed in common currency units. Purchasing Power Parity (PPP) is the notion that this should hold on average; similar baskets of goods should cost the same once expressed in common units. Each of these propositions is essentially a statement about the *cross-sectional* distribution of international relative prices. Due to data limitations, however, most empirical work has examined the *time-series* distribution of international relative prices. That is, because most data take the form of index numbers, most of what we know about LOP and PPP deviations involves the volatility and persistence of *changes* in relative prices. We know relatively little about the absolute relative prices themselves. This is particularly troublesome given that economic theory places much starker restrictions on absolute LOP deviations than on their changes.

This paper uses a novel dataset on absolute LOP deviations to bridge this gap. Our data are local-currency retail prices for a broad set of goods and services in all EU countries over five-year intervals between 1975 and 1990. The data are quite comprehensive, covering most CPI categories, and are collected with the explicit goal of generating cross-country comparisons of individual goods and services that are as similar as possible.

We focus on the cross-sectional distribution of the LOP deviations from this dataset. For each good, the deviation is defined relative to that good's intra-European average price. We have two sets of results, the first relating to the mean of the distribution and the second relating to the variance. For the mean, we compute the average LOP deviation across goods for each country. We find that, after controlling for national income and VAT differences, most of the means are close to zero. In only four of 47 cases is a mean greater than 10 percent in absolute value. This phenomenon is quite stable over the time period we study. In simple terms, if we consider most pairs of EU countries with similar incomes and VATs, at any point in time between 1975 and 1990, there are roughly as many overpriced goods as there are underpriced goods.

Our results about the mean go against the grain of many previous studies, which have emphasized large and persistent deviations from PPP. Most of these studies, however, have involved the U.S. dollar and have involved time-series variation over short (i.e., quarterly horizons). Our results, in contrast, apply only to intra-European prices and are characteristic of absolute price dispersion at four different points in time (1975, 1980, 1985, and 1990). They are also consistent with several independent data sources (documented below). Our main point is that one should be wary of extrapolating the "consensus" about real-exchange rate behavior. "Large and persistent deviations from PPP" is not a good description of Europe between 1975 and 1990.

While the mean is across goods for each country, the variance is across countries for each good. That is, we focus on good-by-good dispersion in the absolute LOP deviations. We find that much of this dispersion can be attributed to two classic characteristics of goods: how tradeable they are, and how tradeable the inputs required to produce them are. For example, the average amount of price dispersion in our data is 28 percent. The average is 25 percent versus 40 percent, however, for traded versus non-traded goods. Similarly, the average is 25 percent versus 32 percent for goods requiring a below-average versus an above-average share of non-traded inputs. Combining these effects in a regression framework, we find that if we consider a non-traded good with the maximum share of non-traded inputs, the predicted price dispersion is 43 percent. In contrast, the prediction for the most-traded good, requiring the lowest share of non-traded inputs, is just 12 percent. The difference of 31 percent is large, relative to both the unconditional amount of dispersion in the data, 28 percent, and the range of the good-specific dispersion measures, 2 percent to 82 percent. Interestingly, our estimates suggest that the lion's share of the price dispersion is attributable to the tradeability of inputs, not tradeability of the final good.

Our results stand on their own as empirical facts. In order to provide a tighter link between facts and theory, however, we begin our paper by outlining a simple model of retail price determination. Retail goods are produced by combining a traded input with a non-traded input. LOP deviations are a convex combination of input cost deviations. This simple theory provides a coherent economic context for the motivation and interpretation of our regressions. It also provides functional form restrictions, which we test. We find that, while the explanatory variables suggested by the theory are supported by the data, the functional form restrictions are not. We discuss reasons for the latter and what it suggests about future research directions.

Our work is most closely related to a large body of empirical work on the international comparison of microeconomic prices. Most data either take the form of index numbers across relatively broad sets of goods, or absolute prices across a very narrow sets of goods. Examples of the former are Charles Engel (1993), Engel and John H. Rogers (1996), Alberto Giovannini (1988), Peter Isard (1977), Rogers and Michael Jenkins (1995), and J. David Richardson (1978). Examples of the latter are Robert E. Cumby (1996), Harry Flam (1992), Kenneth Rogoff *et al.* (1995), Atish R. Ghosh and Holger C. Wolf (1994), Jonathan Haskel and Wolf (2000), Michael M. Knetter (1989, 1993), Matthias Lutz (2004), and David C. Parsley and Shang-Jin Wei (2000). Our data, in contrast, are distinguished by absolute prices across a very broad set of goods. This allows us to say something akin to absolute PPP and also to relate absolute price dispersion to the characteristics of goods in the cross section.[1]

[1]Some recent work that has used a broad cross-sectional dataset on absolute prices from the Economist Intelligence Unit includes Crucini and Mototsugu Shintani (2004), Engel and Rogers (2004), Parsley and Wei (2003), and Rogers (2001). These data are quite broad in terms of countries, but lack the detail and, to some extent, the comparability, of the goods in our Eurostat (the Statistical Agency of the European Community) source. It also covers a more recent time period, 1990–present. In addition Collin Crownover *et al.* (1996) use data on price levels

The remainder of the paper is organized as follows. We begin in Section 1 by outlining a conceptual framework, both in terms of data objects and economic theory. Section 2 describes our data. Our analysis is organized around understanding the mean and the variance of the cross-sectional distribution of the LOP deviations from this data. Section 3 examines the mean and Section 4 examines the variance. Section 5 concludes.

1. Conceptual Framework

Before describing our data, it is useful to develop a conceptual framework with which to organize it. The price data we seek to understand are denoted P_{ij}: the price of good i in country j, expressed in units of some numeraire currency. None of our analysis will depend on what this numeraire currency is. We transform the price data into log deviations from the geometric-average European price, which we denote q_{ij}:

$$q_{ij} \equiv \log P_{ij} - \sum_{j=1}^{M} \log P_{ij}/M \tag{1}$$

where M is the number of countries. Note that q_{ij} is independent of the numeraire.

Most of our paper attempts to relate dispersion in q_{ij}, across countries j, to economically meaningful characteristics of the goods i. Following Bela Balassa (1964), William J. Baumol and William G. Bowen (1966), Paul A. Samuelson (1964), Wilfred Ethier (1979), Irving B. Kravis and Robert E. Lipsey (1983), and Alan C. Stockman and Linda L. Tesar (1995), we focus on two characteristics: the international tradeability of the good and the amount of non-traded inputs required to produce the good. To be concrete, consider a typical non-traded good, a taxi ride. As is often asserted, all retail goods involve significant amounts of non-traded inputs, such as

from Internationaler Vergleich der Preise fur die Lebenshaltung, published by the German Statistical Office. The data are annual from 1927 to 1992 and cover six major industrialized countries.

labor. A taxi ride is no exception. Less well appreciated, however, is the fact that all non-traded goods involve traded inputs, in this case the automobile and gasoline. We use the following simple framework to organize this view of what distinguishes goods in different locations.

We view retail goods as being produced by combining a non-traded input with a traded input. With perfect competition, Cobb-Douglas technology and constant returns to scale, we have

$$P_{ij} = W_j^{\alpha_i} T_{ij}^{(1-\alpha_i)} \tag{2}$$

where W_j is the cost of the non-traded input in country j (e.g., the wage rate), α_i is the share of the non-traded good required to produce good i, and T_{ij} is the cost of the traded input for good i in country j. Inherent in the notation are two standard assumptions. The first is that factor mobility is much higher across sectors within a country than across countries; W_j is country-specific, not good-specific. The second is that retailers in all countries produce good i using the same production technology; α_i is good-specific, not country-specific.

Taking logs of Eq. (2) and subtracting the geometric average (across j) gives

$$q_{ij} = \alpha_i w_j + (1 - \alpha_i) t_{ij} \tag{3}$$

where, following Eq. (1), w_j and t_{ij} denote log differences from the cross-country geometric average. Equation (3) says that deviations from LOP should be related to cross-country differences in non-traded and traded factor input costs, as well as differences in the production share attributable to each. Differences in non-traded input costs are the crux of the classic Balassa-Samuelson hypothesis, with w_j being positive for countries with higher productivity in the traded sector relative to the non-traded sector. Differences in traded costs are often thought of as deriving from transport costs, with t_{ij} being positive for an importer of good i and negative for an exporter.

Our empirical work is organized around Eq. (3). In Section 3 we begin by examining the country-specific cross-sectional means, which we denote $E(q_{ij}|j)$. These variables are close cousins of real exchange rates. We find that w_j is important in the sense that the mean is negative for relatively poor countries. We also find that, having controlled for income differences, $E(q_{ij}|j)$, is often quite close to zero for most European countries. The interpretation offered by Eq. (3) is that t_{ij} changes sign a lot across goods. In other words, countries import some goods, export others, and on average the effects on LOP deviations cancel out.

In Section 4 we examine the cross-sectional variances, denoted $Var(q_{ij}|i)$. That is, we examine how cross-country dispersion in LOP deviations varies across goods. According to Eq. (3),

$$\begin{aligned} Var(q_{ij}|i) = {} & \alpha_i^2 Var(w_j) \\ & + (1-\alpha_i)^2 Var(t_{ij}|i) \\ & + 2\alpha_i(1-\alpha_i) Cov(w_j, t_{ij}|i). \end{aligned} \tag{4}$$

We estimate a cross-sectional regression (across i) corresponding to this equation. We use industry-level data on the share of non-traded inputs required for production as a proxy for α_i. We use industry-level data on the tradeability of the final good — as measured by international trade flows divided by total output — to proxy for $Var(t_{ij}|i)$. We find that an economically important portion of the price dispersion across goods can be accounted for by tradeability and non-traded input cost shares.

Having laid out our data requirements, we now describe our data.

2. The Data

Corresponding to Eq. (1), we begin by describing our data on local currency prices, P_{ij}, of goods i in countries j.

Our price data are from a series of publications of Eurostat (1975–1990).[2] The publications contain the results of four surveys of retail prices in the capital cities of EU countries for each of the

[2]The data were not made available to us by Eurostat. We obtained hard-copies of the publications from various libraries and had the data entered into an electronic format by a professional data-entry firm.

years 1975, 1980, 1985, and 1990.[3] For our purposes it is sufficient to treat the surveys as four separate cross sections. It is important to note, however, that the goods in each cross section maintain a high degree of comparability, across both locations and time. Table 1 presents basic information about what these cross sections entail. The 1975 survey covers nine EU countries. Greece, Portugal, and Spain were added in 1980. Austria was added in 1985. The number of goods also grows over time, from 658 items in 1975 to 1,896 items in 1990. Finally, a substantial fraction of goods are labeled as "branded goods." The importance, for our purposes, is in terms of comparability of goods. In many cases we are literally talking about the same automobile, portable radio, or type of cheese.[4]

As Table 1 indicates, there are a great number of missing observations in the price surveys: 13 percent in 1975, an abrupt increase in 1980 to 36 percent, and a similar level in 1985 and 1990. This increase does not reflect a discrete change in the data collection procedure, but instead (we hypothesize) the inclusion of lower-income countries which tend to consume fewer items of the survey's basket of goods. The number of missing observations also differs systematically across countries from a low of about 9 percent to a high of about 55 percent. Belgium is consistently the country with the fewest missing observations, while Ireland is consistently the country with the most missing observations.

Since our main focus is on explaining price dispersion across countries, we eliminate any good that has an insufficient number of cross-country observations, which we define as four in 1975, five in 1980, and six in 1985 and 1990. The increments reflect the fact that the number of countries in the sample increases over time. We also control for gross measurement error by eliminating goods for which the common-currency price differs from the good-specific median by a

[3]Exceptions are the survey data for Germany and the Netherlands in 1980, 1985, and 1990, where the prices are averages across cities within each country.

[4]A comprehensive list of the goods is available at http://www.e-aer.org/data/june05_app_crucini.pdf. The raw data will also be made available at this location in the future.

Table 1. Scope of the price surveys.

	1975	1980	1985	1990
Panel A: Raw survey data				
Number of countries	9	12	13	13
Number of goods	658	1090	1805	1896
Proportion missing	13%	36%	38%	44%
Least missing[a]	9%	23%	25%	32%
Most missing[a]	27%	47%	53%	55%
Proportion of branded goods	31%	42%	48%	54%
Panel B: After eliminating goods with insufficient data and outliers				
Number of countries	9	12	13	13
Number of goods	594	686	1164	1101
Proportion missing	10%	17%	19%	23%
Least missing[a]	4%	3%	7%	9%
Most missing[a]	22%	28%	37%	34%
Proportion of branded goods	31%	28%	33%	38%

Notes: The countries are Belgium, Denmark, France, Germany, Ireland, Italy, Luxembourg, the Netherlands, and United Kingdom (all years), Greece, Portugal, Spain (added in 1980), and Austria (added in 1985). In panel B, we eliminate any observation that has a relative price more than or less than five times that of the EU median. Then we eliminate goods for which there are more than four missing observations in 1975, five in 1980, and six in 1985 and 1990 (this ensures that, for each good, we have data for at least half of the countries). The category "Proportion of branded goods" refers to the proportion of goods for which two or more brands exist in the price survey. Explicit descriptions of the goods are available at http://www.e-aer.org/data/june05_app_crucini.pdf.

[a]Belgium is the country with the least number of missing observations in every year, and Ireland is the country with the greatest number of missing observations in each year, except for 1990, in which case the United Kingdom has the most missing.

factor of five or more. These filters reduce our sample of goods from a total of 5,449 to 3,545, with the details for individual years provided in panel B of Table 1. Of the remaining data, the proportion of missing observations never exceeds 25 percent. Our survey data also contain a large number of brand-name goods, typically accounting for about one-third of the goods that we utilize.

Table 2 reports a number of individual records from the 1985 survey with the goods chosen to represent the various categories of goods and services contained in our dataset. All the surveys have a similar structure involving a Eurostat code, a detailed description of the particular good, the units of measure, and columns of price data. The retail prices are cash prices paid by final consumers and therefore include such taxes as VAT (we control for VAT below). The prices are averages of the surveyed prices across different city-wide sales points.[5]

As is evident from the sample of goods reported in Table 2, the surveys are as comprehensive as those used to construct national consumer price indices. We see food items, clothing, major appliances, automobiles, services, and so on. Although Eurostat reports the prices in local currency units, Table 2 presents prices in Belgian francs to facilitate comparisons. The deviations we see from the LOP are suggestive of what is to come. The rental cost of a television, for example, varies widely across countries, whereas the dispersion in the cost of rice is considerably smaller.

The goods-descriptions published by Eurostat are abbreviated versions of those used by the statistical agency to compile the data. The level of detail in the published version also varies across goods. In particular, goods can be placed into two categories: those indicated as selected brands (s.b. in Table 2) and those without such a designation. The reason provided by Eurostat for the selected brand designation is the need for confidentiality. While we might like to know which automobiles are Mercedes and which are Volvos, the record does not provide us with the necessary details. It is important to note, however, that the survey is explicitly designed to assure comparability of goods across locations.

One last issue is the exact timing of the surveys. While we find it convenient to refer to our cross sections by year, in reality

[5]The procedure for selecting sales points follows the practice used to construct national consumer price indices. Sales points are selected by the national statistical offices so that the sample is representative of the distribution of prices in the city with more observations collected for goods having greater price dispersion within the city.

Table 2. Sample records from price survey.

Code	Good description	Units	AUS	BLG	DEN	FRF	GER	GRC	IRL	ITL	LUX	NET	POR	ESP	UK
11111	Long grain rice, carton	500 g	26	50	48	52	52	42	51	35	52	36		39	32
11251	Chicken-fresh, 70% pres	1.2 kg	107	204	207	203		115	159	163			88		148
11421	Cond. milk 9–10% b.f.	410g		48			56	31				54	56	42	42
11621	Dried almonds	100 g	28	54		61	34	28	43	35	54	49	37	49	50
11911	Ground blended coffee	1 kg	234	439	425	350				586		355	451	437	446
13112	Liqueur — s.b.	0.7 L		579	1294	542	599	589	980	414	502	599	1152	491	910
21112	Man's k-way jacket	1 nb	1584	544	1596	1022	824	1373	1331	872	996	1196	904	713	
22121	Ladies boots, box caf	1 pr	3720	4027	4095	3733	3692	2645	2362		4422	2615	2745	2951	3176
41112	Chest of drawers	1 nb	2834	6988	2192	11400	4889	2904	5078	7186	3990	7742	3529	4630	4065
42111	Spring mattress: s.b.	1 nb	4070		3923	3253	2674					3803			
43121	Dishwasher: s.b.	1 nb		23480						23548			22705	22823	
43161	Iron: steam, s.b.	1 nb	2436		2201	1925	2089	3018		1916	1745	1810	2495	2450	1485
45111	Washing powder: s.b.	700 g	414	299		337	316		310		313				
52211	Hearing aid: s.b.	1 nb				29528	25976					23343	17734	19134	26054
61113	Car: 1200–1700 cc, s.b.	1 nb	357298		524411	341213						346786	356516		
61212	Bicycle: racing, s.b.	1 nb				15147	19314				18000	17788			15238
63111	Bus fare, 6 km, no transf	1 tik	52	30	50	58	43	9	41	12	25	39	17	16	33
71131	Record player, s.b.	1 nb	7091	5190		5158	4172	10955		4719	4848	4861	4194	7828	
71311	Cassette for game: s.b.	1 nb	873	850		1299			948	1072	1066	400			764
72221	Rental of television	1 mo		2296	1340	1631	1191	2962	1382	1285	3136	1490	1670	1795	1487

Notes: Sample of 20 records from the original 1,805 records of the 1985 survey. Currency units are Belgian francs. Countries are Austria (AUS), Belgium (BLG), Denmark (DEN), France (FRF), Germany (GER), Greece (GRC), Ireland (IRL), Italy (ITL), Luxembourg (LUX), the Netherlands (NET), Portugal (POR), Spain (ESP), and the United Kingdom (UK). Branded goods are denoted 's.b.' (selected brand). Prices are rounded to the nearest franc, although the raw data (and our analysis) are in units of francs and centimes. Blank entries denote missing data.

the price data for each cross section are collected in a sequence of surveys. In what we call "1985," for example, the prices of most services were collected in September and October 1985, while prices of most clothing items were collected in December 1984. The nominal exchange rate data, with which we convert prices into a common currency, take explicit account of this timing, taking the form of averages of daily data over the relevant time intervals.

2.1. *Supplemental data*

Following the discussion in Section 1, we supplement our retail price data with data on tradedness and production structure. Because these variables are unavailable at the level of the individual good, we assign each good to an industry and use the industry-level measure in place of the good-specific measure.

The variable α_i in Eq. (4) is the non-traded input share for good i. We measure this as the ratio of non-traded input costs to total cost where both numbers are computed from the 1988 input-output tables of the United Kingdom.[6] Table A1 of the Data Appendix contains the cost shares of non-traded intermediate inputs by industry. The values range from a low of 4.6 percent for tobacco to a high of 31.8 percent for forestry and fisheries.

The other variable in Eq. (4), $Var(t_{ij}|i)$, is the cross-sectional variance (across locations j for each good i) in the traded input cost. We proxy this with the tradeability of the final good, measured as the ratio of the total trade among the countries in our sample, in a particular industry, divided by total output of that industry across the same countries.[7] The (admittedly coarse) idea is that, at the retail level, the intermediate input is often very similar to the final

[6]Non-traded inputs are assumed to include: utilities, construction, distribution, hotels, catering, railways, road transport, sea transport, air transport, transport services, telecommunications, banking, finance, insurance, business services, education, health, and other services.

[7]We use the actual trade share whenever trade data are available and assign an index of zero otherwise. The industries assigned zero trade shares are: restaurants and hotels, transport, storage and communication, inland transport, maritime transport, communication, financing, insurance, real estate, and community, social, and personal services.

good itself. A seller of computers combines labor with computers and sells computers. The same applies to the seller of furniture. Since computers are more tradeable than furniture, however, the cross-sectional dispersion in the "intermediate input cost" for computers should be lower than that for furniture. Table A2 of the Data Appendix reports the trade shares. Among traded goods, average shares for the period 1974 to 1990 range from a low of 13 percent for tobacco products and 15 percent for printing, publishing, and allied industries, to highs of 122 percent for professional goods and 121 percent for office and computing machinery. The average trade share across goods for this period is a substantial 53 percent.

Comparing some of the numbers in Tables A1 and A2 suggests that the distinction between tradeability and trade in "middle products" is important. Leather products, for instance, are highly tradeable in the sense that their trade share is high and their non-traded input share is low. The exact opposite is true of most service-related goods. Forestry products (telecommunications), in contrast, are quite tradeable (non-tradeable), yet they require a large (small) amount of non-traded inputs. From an economic standpoint it is unclear whether a non-traded good with substantial traded inputs will exhibit more or less price dispersion than a traded good with substantial non-traded inputs. Our empirical analysis is designed to identify these two economic effects separately.

The remaining supplemental data we use are data on European nominal exchange rates, national income, and VAT rates. Details are provided in the Data Appendix.

3. LOP Deviations: The Mean of the Distribution

Figure 1 summarizes the empirical distribution of deviations from the LOP, q_{ij} defined in Eq. (1). The figure contains one chart for each country. Each chart reports one kernel estimate of the density of q_{ij} for each available year. We see four striking features. First, and most obviously, LOP deviations can be large, with the support of most of the densities being on the order of ± 100 percent. Second, there is a clear income effect. The densities of the relatively poor countries — Greece, Portugal, and Spain in particular — seem to be located

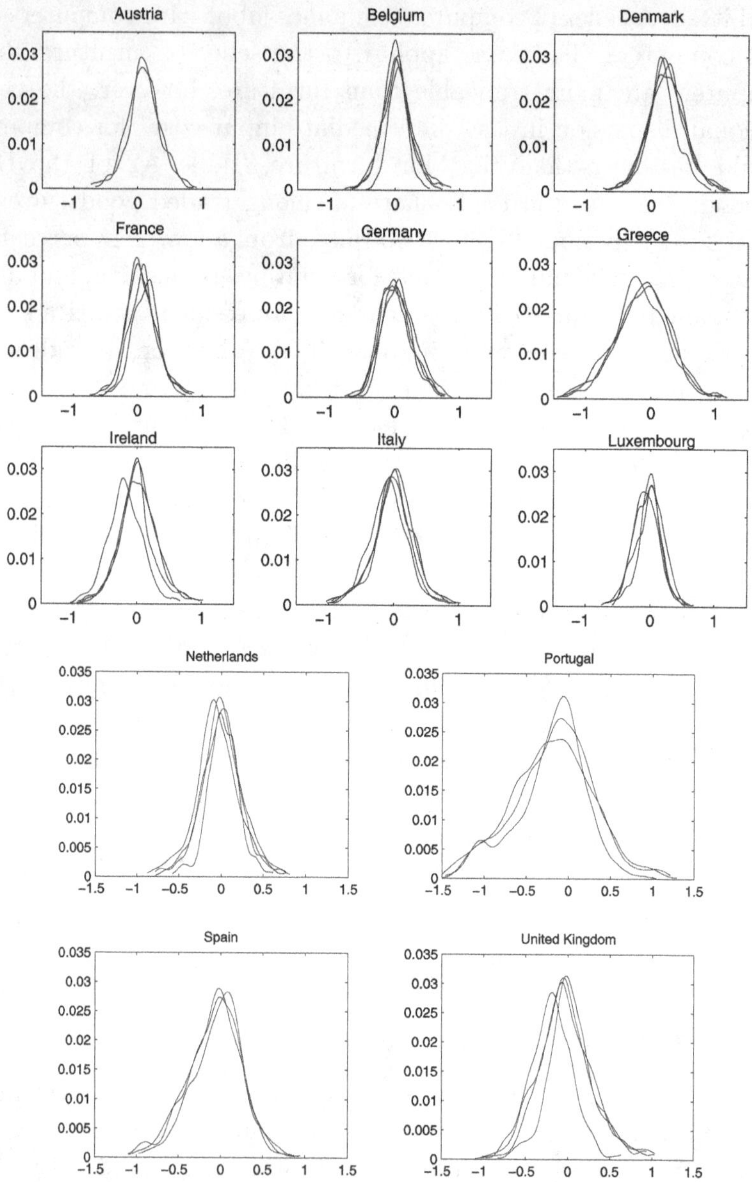

Fig. 1. Empirical distributions of LOP deviations.

Notes: Each line represents an estimate of the density of good-by-good deviations from the LOP, relative to the European average price, for each of the years 1975, 1980, 1985, and 1990. The exceptions are Austria, where we do not have data for 1975 and 1980, and Greece, Spain, and Portugal, where 1975 is missing.

farther to the left. Third, for the other (relatively wealthy) countries, most of the densities seem to be located near zero. That is, there seem to be roughly as many overpriced goods as underpriced goods. Finally, this latter phenomenon seems quite stable over time. In spite of many relatively large nominal exchange rate movements, the location and shape of the densities don't seem to move around much.[8]

To be more precise, Table 3 reports the sample means, $E(q_{ij}|j)$, of the density estimates from Fig. 1. The countries are organized from richest to poorest. The values in the left-most columns of panel A confirm what we see in Fig. 1; many of the means for the relatively rich countries are within the interval ± 10 percent. There are, however, some exceptions, most notably Denmark. With this in mind, the remainder of the table makes the following adjustments.

(a) First, we use industry/year-specific data on VAT rates to reduce each price in our dataset to be a before-VAT rate. The VAT data are described and documented in the Data Appendix. Note that Denmark is by far the highest VAT country. We then recompute the values q_{ij} and their cross-good averages. The results are reported in Table 3, in the left-most columns of panel B.

(b) Second, we adjust the means for relative income differences via the regression

$$E(q_{ij,t}|j,t) = a + bz_{j,t} + \text{residuals} \tag{5}$$

where $z_{j,t}$ denotes the (log) per-capita income difference between country j and the EU average in date t, and (as above), and $\mathrm{E}(q_{ij,t}|j)$ denotes the (cross goods i) average LOP deviation for

[8]There are several glaring exceptions but, interestingly, they go against the notion that movements in the distribution are driven by movements in nominal exchange rates. Between 1975 and 1980, for instance, average prices in Ireland and the United Kingdom increased substantially relative to Europe (see also Table 3), yet their currencies actually *devalued* relative to Europe.

Table 3. Average (across goods) LOP deviation.

		Without income adjustment				With income adjustment			
Country	z_j	1975	1980	1985	1990	1975	1980	1985	1990
Panel A: Without VAT adjustment									
Luxembourg	0.299	−0.009	0.030	−0.043	−0.027	−0.097	−0.045	−0.137	−0.165
Denmark	0.260	0.177	0.215	0.222	0.219	0.081	0.132	0.125	0.155
Netherlands	0.126	0.023	0.018	−0.055	−0.007	−0.031	−0.022	−0.088	−0.030
France	0.126	0.119	0.112	0.075	0.072	0.084	0.072	0.034	0.039
Belgium	0.122	0.042	0.044	0.067	0.053	0.006	0.002	0.032	0.023
Germany	0.105	0.066	0.089	0.013	0.053	0.046	0.055	−0.028	0.028
Austria	0.096			0.096	0.078			0.065	0.049
Italy	0.061	−0.055	−0.087	−0.007	0.034	−0.050	−0.105	−0.030	0.014
U.K.	0.035	−0.200	0.050	−0.001	−0.037	−0.213	0.054	−0.011	−0.038
Spain	−0.192		−0.100	−0.082	−0.067		−0.018	0.013	0.015
Greece	−0.257		−0.170	−0.170	−0.173		−0.098	−0.067	−0.023
Ireland	−0.323	−0.195	−0.029	0.048	0.012	−0.052	0.104	0.170	0.102
Portugal	−0.457		−0.213	−0.174	−0.254		−0.046	0.008	−0.114
Std. Dev.	0.232	0.129	0.123	0.109	0.118	0.094	0.077	0.083	0.083
Panel B: With VAT adjustment									
Luxembourg	0.299	0.029	0.056	−0.020	0.018	−0.035	0.002	−0.089	−0.082
Denmark	0.260	0.143	0.108	0.124	0.144	0.074	0.048	0.053	0.098
Netherlands	0.126	0.024	−0.001	−0.073	−0.012	−0.015	−0.031	−0.097	−0.029
France	0.126	0.074	0.065	0.041	0.056	0.049	0.036	0.011	0.032
Belgium	0.122	0.016	0.015	0.036	0.046	−0.011	−0.016	0.010	0.024
Germany	0.105	0.078	0.077	−0.002	0.060	0.063	0.053	−0.031	0.042
Austria	0.096			0.044	0.050			0.021	0.028
Italy	0.061	−0.042	−0.097	−0.028	0.032	−0.039	−0.110	−0.045	0.017
U.K.	0.035	−0.152	0.056	0.016	0.007	−0.161	0.059	0.009	0.005
Spain	−0.192		−0.018	0.003	−0.048		0.041	0.072	0.012
Greece	−0.257		−0.088	−0.083	−0.169		−0.036	−0.009	−0.061
Ireland	−0.323	−0.200	−0.060	0.035	0.029	−0.096	0.037	0.123	0.094
Portugal	−0.457		−0.134	−0.087	−0.251		−0.013	0.044	−0.150
Std. Dev.	0.232	0.111	0.078	0.060	0.103	0.076	0.050	0.062	0.069

Notes: The variable z_j denotes average log income differences, 1975–1990, relative to the EU average. The remaining data are equally weighted averages of LOP deviations, across goods i, for each country j: $E(q_{ij}|j)$. Standard errors were reported in the previous version of the paper (available at http://www.e-aer.org/data/iune05_app_crucini.pdf) but are omitted here for space considerations. All standard errors are between 0.01 and 0.02 with the exception of those from Greece, Portugal, and Spain which are between 0.015 and 0.025. Income and VAT adjustment are described in the text and the Data Appendix. For these calculations we eliminate multiple brands of the same good.

country j relative to the EU average at date t.[9] The results are reported in the rightmost columns of Table 3.

Net of these adjustments, the average deviations from LOP are substantially reduced and are quite small in magnitude. Out of 47 average LOP deviations, only four are outside the interval ± 10 percent. The standard deviations of the averages (across countries), shown in the final row of each panel, are reduced by almost half. Figure 2 provides emphasis by plotting the average LOP deviations before and after income/VAT adjustment.[10]

What does the simple model of Section 1 have to say about these results? First, the interpretation of the income adjustment is obvious; it represents cross-country variation in w_j in the manner of Balassa-Samuelson. Second, the fact that (net of VAT) the remaining average price differences are small suggests that t_{ij} changes sign a lot across goods. Countries import some goods, export others, and on average the effects on LOP deviations cancel out.

Further evidence is provided in Table 4, where we distinguish the averages $E(q_{ij}|j)$ by the tradedness of the goods across which the average is taken. We see that average prices for traded goods tend to be much closer to zero than for non-traded goods. While this is interesting in and of itself, our model suggests two possibilities. First, cross-sectional variation in the α_i's for non-traded goods could bias our income adjustment, which (in Table 4) is done based on the *average* traded/non-traded LOP deviation. Second, it could be

[9]The time subscript is included here to indicate that, in our relative income adjustments, we incorporate the important changes that occurred during 1975–1990 (e.g., Ireland).

[10]In a previous version of the paper, available at http://www.e-aer.org/data/june05_app_crucini.pdf, we show that CPI expenditure share weighted averages tell very much the same story as the equally weighted averages reported here. In addition, we perform a number of consistency checks on our data using different data sources. We show that (a) before income/VAT adjustment, our estimates of (absolute) average LOP deviations are quite similar to the absolute PPP data available from the OECD and from the Penn World Tables (PWT); and (b) when we first-difference our data (necessarily over five-year intervals), the implications for correlations between changes in real and nominal exchange rates (e.g., Michael Mussa, 1986) are consistent with those from the PWT, the OECD, and the national CPI data contained in the International Financial Statistics (IFS).

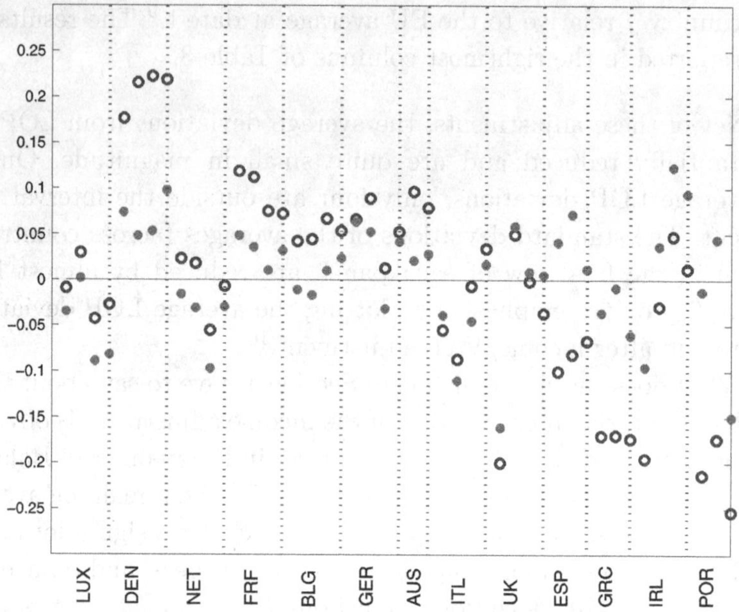

Fig. 2. Average LOP deviations.

Notes: The raw data are open circles and the income-VAT adjusted data are filled circles.

Each point is the average LOP deviation for a particular country/year. Vertical dashed lines delineate countries. Each point between these dashed lines is one particular year for that country. Thus, the first four points represent Luxembourg for 1975, 1980, 1985, and 1990, the next four represent Denmark for the same years, and so on. The countries are organized from lowest to highest income, as in Table 3. Finally, open circles represent unadjusted data (i.e., the means from Table 3 in the left-most columns of panel A), whereas filled circles represent means which have been adjusted for income and VAT differences (i.e., from the right-most columns of panel B in Table 3).

the case that, among the set of non-traded goods for a particular country, there is less "averaging out" associated with some traded inputs being exported and others imported. Our supplementary data are not yet rich enough to distinguish between these possibilities.

4. LOP Deviations: The Variance of the Distribution

We now examine good-by-good price dispersion which, as in Eq. (4), we measure as the variance of q_{ij} across countries j: $\sigma_i^2 \equiv Var(q_{ij}|i)$.

Table 4. Average (across goods) LOP deviation by tradedness.

	1975			1980			1985			1990		
	All	Traded	Non-traded	All	Traded	Non-traded	All	Traded	Non-traded	All	Traded	Non-traded
Luxembourg	−0.035	0.006	−0.273	0.002	0.009	−0.031	−0.089	−0.064	−0.239	−0.082	−0.043	−0.318
Denmark	0.074	0.082	0.020	0.048	0.067	−0.064	0.053	0.063	0.001	0.098	0.101	0.083
Netherlands	−0.015	−0.023	0.016	−0.031	−0.055	0.109	−0.097	−0.108	−0.027	−0.029	−0.049	0.094
France	0.049	0.045	0.063	0.036	0.026	0.098	0.011	0.001	0.068	0.032	0.038	−0.005
Belgium	−0.011	−0.012	−0.003	−0.016	−0.034	0.094	0.010	0.008	0.026	0.024	0.018	0.067
Germany	0.063	0.049	0.137	0.053	0.040	0.128	−0.031	−0.046	0.051	0.042	0.022	0.149
Austria							0.021	0.010	0.083	0.028	0.015	0.124
Italy	−0.039	0.000	−0.247	−0.110	−0.097	−0.186	−0.045	−0.026	−0.165	0.017	0.039	−0.108
U.K.	−0.161	−0.151	−0.222	0.059	0.036	0.184	0.009	−0.026	0.217	0.005	−0.056	0.326
Spain				0.041	0.044	0.028	0.072	0.079	0.017	0.012	0.015	−0.020
Greece				−0.036	−0.010	−0.160	−0.009	0.007	−0.111	−0.061	−0.035	−0.278
Ireland	−0.096	−0.115	0.017	0.037	−0.002	0.261	0.123	0.085	0.351	0.094	0.059	0.298
Portugal				−0.013	0.026	−0.222	0.044	0.076	−0.133	−0.150	−0.117	−0.301
Std. Dev.	0.076	0.076	0.151	0.050	0.047	0.153	0.062	0.059	0.158	0.069	0.058	0.211

Notes: See notes to Table 3. Data here are identical (income/VAT adjusted) except for the distinction between traded and non-traded goods. A non-traded good is defined as having a trade share equal to zero according to Table A2 of the Data Appendix.

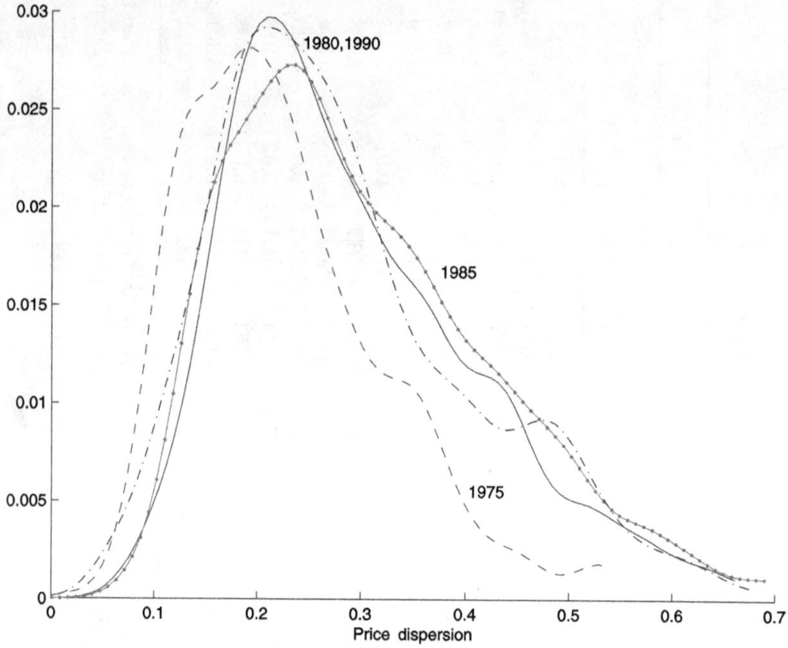

Fig. 3. Empirical distributions of $Var(q_{ij}|i)^{1/2}$.

Notes: Each line represents an estimate (for each year) of the density of $Var(q_{ij}|i)^{1/2}$, the standard deviation of the LOP deviation for good i across countries j.

Figure 3 plots kernel estimates of the density of σ_i for each year. We see that different goods can have substantially different amounts of price dispersion, with the sample standard deviations ranging from 2 percent to 80 percent. While it might seem that price dispersion increased after 1975, this is instead an artifact of the sample of countries expanding in 1980 to include lower-income countries.

Table 5 reports means of the distributions from Fig. 3 broken down by year, tradeability, and the fraction of non-traded inputs required for production. We see strong evidence that these variables are important determinants of good-by-good price dispersion. Average price dispersion across traded goods is 25 percent versus 40 percent for non-traded goods. The average for goods

Table 5. Averages of good-specific measures of price dispersion.

	1975	1980	1985	1990	Average
All goods	0.2290	0.2941	0.3024	0.2855	0.2777
Non-traded goods	0.3138	0.4146	0.4252	0.4537	0.4018
Traded goods	0.2164	0.2750	0.2846	0.2596	0.2589
Above avg. share of services	0.2619	0.3372	0.3464	0.3378	0.3208
Below avg. share of services	0.2116	0.2703	0.2779	0.2551	0.2537

Notes: Values are averages of good-specific measures of price dispersion. Each value is the average (across goods i) of $Var(q_{ij}|i)^{1/2}$, the good-by-good sample standard deviation, where the standard deviation is across countries j.

with above-average share of non-traded inputs is 32 percent versus 25 percent for goods with a below-average share.

Next we consolidate this information in a regression framework.

4.1. *Regressions*

We begin by slightly rewriting our model of price dispersion, Eq. (4), as

$$\sigma_i^2 = \alpha_i^2 Var(w_j) + (1-\alpha_i)^2 x_i \tag{6}$$

where, for notational simplicity, we define $x_i \equiv Var(t_{ij}|i)$. Recall that, as is discussed in Section 2.1, we do not have direct data on t_{ij}. Instead, we proxy x_i itself with a measure of the tradeability of the final good. We also assume that the conditional covariance from Eq. (4) is zero.[11] Based on this, Table 6 reports estimates of the parameters of the following regression:

$$\sigma_i^2 = a + b\alpha_i^2 + c(1-\alpha_i)^2 x_i + \text{residuals}. \tag{7}$$

[11]We do not have data that allow us to identify variation in $Cov(w_j, t_{ij}|i)$ across goods i. Given this, the only alternative is to assume a constant instead of zero. The difference, however, is minor, resulting in only a slightly more complex quadratic function via the inclusion of the term $\alpha_i(1-\alpha_i)$. Moreover, when we do this, we find that (a) the hypothesis that the coefficient on the additional variable is zero cannot be rejected; and (b) the economic implications of the remaining parameter estimates are almost identical to those of Eq. (7).

Table 6. Regression estimates.

$\sigma_i^2 = a + b\alpha_i^2 + c(1-\alpha_i)^2 x_i +$ residuals					
Year	a	b	c	R_a^2	R_d^2
1975	0.083 (0.006)	0.299 (0.115)	0.090 (0.013)	0.433	0.120
1980	0.099 (0.007)	0.921 (0.143)	0.051 (0.012)	0.291	0.107
1985	0.115 (0.006)	0.791 (0.118)	0.059 (0.008)	0.319	0.106
1990	0.122 (0.005)	1.033 (0.106)	0.100 (0.008)	0.537	0.291
Pooled	0.102 (0.003)	0.868 (0.064)	0.062 (0.005)	0.417	0.129

Notes: Estimates of the parameters of the regression are based on Eq. (7) in the text. σ_i^2 denotes our good-specific measure of price dispersion: the sample variance of q_{ij} from Eq. (1) in the text. α_i denotes the non-traded input share for good i and x_i is (the negative of) the trade share of good i (see Section 2.1 for details). standard errors are in parentheses. Because our explanatory variables are averaged across different numbers of goods within industry groups, the residuals will be heteroskedastic. We therefore use a feasible GLS estimator (details are provided in the Data Appendix). R_a^2 denotes the regression R^2 that results in averaging the dependent variable in the same manner as the explanatory variables. R_a^2 denotes the regression R^2 from the "raw regression" where, necessarily we are trying to account for variation in σ_i^2 using variables that have (potentially) had some of their explanatory variation averaged away.

We see that the coefficients are all highly significant and that the regression function explains a significant portion of the cross-sectional variation in our data on price dispersion. Moreover, the coefficients are economically significant. For example, if we consider the good with the smallest share of non-traded inputs α_i, and the smallest x_i (the latter meaning that the good is highly traded), the predicted price dispersion (based on the pooled regression) is 0.12 (in standard deviation). The opposite case — the good requiring the most non-traded inputs with the highest x_i (lowest trade-ability) — gives a value of 0.43. The increase of 0.31 is substantial, both relative to the unconditional (average) dispersion in the data (standard deviation of roughly 0.28), as well as the range of σ_i which is 0.02 to 0.82.

What does theory add here? There are two main differences between the regression (7) and the (obvious) reduced-form regression of σ_i^2 on α_i and x_i. The first is the quadratic functional form. This is a relatively uninteresting artifact of our choice of price-dispersion measure, the variance. Empirically, it turns out to be of little importance. The second difference relates to economics. The essence of the interaction term, $(1-\alpha_i)^2 x_i$, is that the explanatory power of the tradeability variable, x_i, should diminish for goods requiring a high share of non-traded inputs, α_i. If most of the cost of a taxi ride is labor, then the relative price of gasoline shouldn't matter much.

We examined the importance of the interaction term in several ways. All of them indicated that this restriction is inconsistent with our data. For example, if one writes out Eq. (4) as a quadratic function of five variables, two of those will be α_i and x_i. In no case were we able to reject the hypothesis that the coefficients on the remaining variables were equal to zero. Similarly, if we add the interaction term to the simple linear specification involving α_i, and x_i, we cannot reject the hypothesis that its coefficient is zero. Finally, we took a subsample of goods with relatively high non-traded input shares and regressed the price dispersion measures from this subsample on our tradeability measure. We found strong evidence that the opposite is true. That is, the tradeability measure x_i has more explanatory power conditional on high non-tradedness, not low non-tradedness.

Overall, the message is that α_i and x_i have strong explanatory power for cross-sectional price dispersion, but that the functional-form restrictions from our theory are not an important part of this. This could represent a limitation of the theory. It could also represent a limitation of our data on the characteristics of individual goods. One limitation is that we are forced to use industry-level data to try to explain good- specific price dispersion. More important, in our view, is our use of the trade share as a proxy for trade costs. As is well known, the volume of trade depends upon not only trade costs, but also comparative advantage and the elasticity of substitution between domestic and foreign goods. Carolyn L. Evans (2003), for example, shows how a traditional gravity model of trade predicts that bilateral trade flows depend (negatively) upon the trade cost multiplied by the elasticity of substitution. Thus, higher trade shares could reflect lower elasticities of substitution, higher trade costs, or both. Future work should concentrate on developing additional microeconomic data on the characteristics of individual goods, including elasticities of substitution.

5. Concluding Comments

A considerable body of empirical and theoretical work in international economics attempts to answer two basic questions. The first question is: What determines whether a deviation from the LOP will be large or small? The second question is: What determines whether a deviation from the LOP will be enduring or short-lived?

The empirical literature on the first question is very limited due to a paucity of absolute price data on comparable goods across international locations. The theoretical literature, in contrast, is well-developed and offers a number of potential answers. The models of Bernard Dumas (1992) and Piet Sercu *et al.* (1995) emphasize the magnitude of shipping costs in consumption goods and physical capital, respectively. The models of Paul R. Krugman (1987) emphasize imperfect competition. The models of Balassa (1964) and Samuelson (1964) emphasize productivity differences across traded and non-traded goods. The models of Ethier (1979) and Ronald W. Jones and Kalyan K. Sanyal (1982) emphasize that much of international trade takes place in intermediate inputs, not final goods and services. In each case, the first-order restrictions from theory are on absolute LOP deviations. Our paper represents the development of better data to test these restrictions. What we find is encouraging from the perspective of theory. An economically important part of the heterogeneity across goods in LOP deviations is related to the tradeability of the good and the share of non-traded inputs required to produce the good.

The empirical literature on the second question is vast, in part because persistence may be studied using relative versions of the

LOP and PPP, thus eliminating the need for absolute price data. The consensus is that the half-lives of deviations from parity last between three and five years.[12] The theoretical literature, however, has focused almost exclusively on the adjustment (or lack of adjustment) of domestic-currency prices to changes in the nominal exchange rate. In particular, the sticky-price models, which have followed Maurice Obstfeld and Rogoff (1995), are distinguished by assumptions of when firms can change their prices and, therefore, impose first-order restrictions on changes in LOP deviations. Given the persistence of the deviations, most economists believe that sticky prices, in their various forms, cannot account for the observed persistence in real exchange rates.

Is there an important link between these questions? We think so, in spite of the fact that the two bodies of literature addressing them have evolved more or less independently. To understand this, consider the "PPP Puzzle" posed by Rogoff (1996); the persistence and conditional volatility in PPP and LOP deviations are too large to be consistent with sticky-price models in conjunction with data on price-setting behavior. Models of goods-market arbitrage and non-traded inputs, in contrast, restrict the unconditional volatility of PPP and LOP deviations. This is where the link lies. If the unconditional volatility restrictions are supported by the data — as our study suggests — then we are led to rethink our interpretation of the time-series evidence. Rogoff (1996), for instance, interprets the evidence as suggesting, "International goods markets, though becoming more integrated all the time, remain quite segmented, with large trading frictions across a broad range of goods." Our view is that this is too broad a brush. While it is certainly true for Big Macs, the set of goods for which it is suspect goes beyond gold bullion. Moreover, theory is informative for which goods are in the set and which are not. A promising avenue for future work involves further integration of arbitrage-based models — which impose absolute bounds on

[12]See, for example, Jeffrey A. Frankel and Andrew K. Rose (1996), Christian J. Murray and David H. Papell (2003), and Rogoff (1996).

LOP deviations — with models which describe behavior within the bounds, such as sticky-price models and models where most trade is at the level of intermediate inputs, not final products.

Acknowledgments

In addition to participants at numerous seminars and conferences, we thank Stephen Cosslett, Mick Devereux, Paul Evans, Burton Hollifield, John Rogers, Kjetil Storesletten, Stan Zin, and, in particular, Charles Engel for helpful comments. We gratefully acknowledge the financial support of the National Science Foundation (SES-0136979) and the Carnegie Bosch Institute.

Data Appendix

"Understanding European Real Exchange Rates"
by Mario J. Crucini, Christopher I. Telmer and Marios Zachariadis

This appendix provides further description of our data sources and manipulations and tabulates the supplemental data used in our paper.

National retail price data. The retail price data were compiled and published by Eurostat, the statistical agency of the European Community, in cooperation with the national statistical agencies of the countries that participated. While all of the price data we utilize is published we are unaware of available electronic copies. All prices refer to cash prices paid by final consumers, including taxes, both VAT and any others paid by the purchaser. Sales points are selected is such a way that the sample selected is representative of the distribution in the capital city. Prices are collected at different locations so that the average price is representative of the distribution within the city. These data were not available electronically so we had a private firm key-punch the commodity codes, commodity descriptions and prices into an electronic format.

Data Reconciliation. In order to explain the price dispersion across goods that exists in our data we constructed measures of tradeability and the costs of non-traded inputs into production The constructed variables for tradeability and non-traded inputs from input-output tables are available at different levels of detail. For this reason, and in order to make the most of the information available for each of these factors, we matched the retail price data with each of the variables using two-digit, three-digit, and four-digit classifications depending on the level of detail available for each of the variables rather than attempting to match all variables using the same level of detail. The input-output data are also available at a three-digit level of detail that extends to four-digits for some industry groups. In order to reconcile the data as accurately as possible, we used the ISIC codes and descriptions available in the User Guide of the OECD International Sectoral Database. A description of each of our variables is as follows.

- *Tradeability.* We obtained data on imports, exports, and gross output for the period 1973 to 1990 from the 1994 edition of the OECD STAN Database. We use thirty-two non-overlapping subdivisions of manufacturing for which sufficient data are available and to the extent that they are relevant to the commodities in our price dataset. We also constructed additional tradeability indices for agriculture (sector 1) and electricity, gas, and water (sector 4) using the 1994 edition of the OECD Sectoral Database, which provides value-added instead of gross output data. Unfortunately, we only have this data for six countries: Belgium, Denmark, France, Germany, Italy, and the United Kingdom. We assigned a zero trade share to the following industries: restaurants and hotels, transport, storage and communication, inland transport, maritime and air transport, communication, financing, insurance, real estate and business services, community, social and personal services. Otherwise, our measure of tradeability is calculated as:

$$\theta_k = \frac{\sum_{j=1}^{m_k} (X_{kj} + M_{kj})}{\sum_{j=1}^{m_k} Y_{kj}},$$

  where for each sector k we sum over all countries j which have data for that sector. X_{kj} (M_{kj}) stands for exports (imports) of sector k

from country j and Y_{kj} stands for the gross output of sector k by country j.

- *Input–Output Data.* We use the input-output matrix for the United Kingdom in 1988. These data were compiled by Keith Maskus and Allan Webster (1995). We thank Tom Prusa for suggesting this data source, which is available at the National Bureau of Economic Research home page Non-traded inputs are assumed to include: utilities, construction, distribution, hotels, catering, railways, road transport, sea transport, air transport, transport services, telecommunications, banking, finance, insurance, business services, education health and other services We compute the cost share of non-traded intermediate inputs computed as,

$$\Phi_k = \sum_{s=1}^{S} \phi_{ks},$$

where ϕ_{ks} is the share of non-traded intermediate input s in the total cost of the output of sector k

Nominal exchange rates. We obtained daily data on nominal exchange rates from the New York Federal Reserve Bank's web page The Eurostat survey provides a 2–3 month window during which the survey was conducted for each good (for each of our 4 cross-sections). Accordingly, the nominal exchange rate we use is an average of the daily values over the respective months for each good. Data and programs are available at http://bertha.tepper.cmu.edu/eurostat.

VAT data. We obtained country-specific data on VAT rates for 23 different categories of goods and services for each of the years 1975, 1980, 1985 and 1990. We then categorized each of our goods into one of these categories and then divided each individual price by it's associated country/year-specific VAT rate to arrive at before-VAT prices. All of our analysis in Tables 4–6 of our paper, and Fig. 3, use these before-VAT prices. The VAT rates across EU countries are taken primarily from the European Commission publication "VAT rates applied in the member states of the European Community" (2002) the OECD publication "Taxing Consumption" and the Ernst and Young publication "Vat and Sales Taxes Worldwide: A Guide to Practice and Procedures in 61 Countries" (1996). Secondary sources on VAT rates include the Tax Executives Institute publication "Value-Added Taxes: A Comparative Analysis" (1992) Alan Tait's "Value Added Tax: International Practice and Problems" (1988) and George Carlin's "Value- Added Tax: European Experience and Lessons for the United States" (1980). The data are available at http://bertha.tepper.cmu.edu/eurostat.

Real GDP Per-Capita was obtained from Penn World Tables 6.1 for each of the years corresponding to our cross-sections.

A statistical appendix and more extensive data appendix are available from the authors upon request.

Reference

Maskus, Keith, and Allan Webster, 1995, Factor specialization in U.S. and U.K. trade: Simple departures from the factor-content theory, *Swiss Journal of Economics and Statistics* 1 (131).

Table A1. Non-traded input cost shares.

Category	Input share	Category	Input share
Agriculture	0.144	Glass	0.195
Forestry and fishing	0.318	Clay refractories	0.201
Milk and milk products	0.080	Cement, concrete	0.259
Meat, fruit, veg, fish processing	0.096	Iron and steel; plant	0.111
Oils and fats, grain products	0.124	Non-ferrous metals	0.092
Bread, biscuits etc	0.104	Metal castings etc	0.119
Sugar, confectionery	0.139	Office machinery, computers	0.103
Foods, nes	0.174	Other machinery	0.116
Alcoholic drink	0.097	Telecomms equipment	0.120
Soft drink	0.160	Domestic electric appliances	0.135
Tobacco	0.046	Electronic consumer goods	0.113
Woven textiles	0.095	Electronic components	0.147
Hosiery, other knitted goods	0.097	Electric lighting equipment	0.106
Carpets etc	0.112	Shipbuilding and repairing	0.134
Clothing and furs	0.096	Motor vehicles and parts	0.090
Leather and leather goods	0.073	Other vehicles	0.110
Footwear	0.086	Instrument engineering	0.149
Wood furniture	0.107	Other manufacturing	0.122
Paper and board products	0.135	Utilities	0.157
Printing and publishing	0.211	Hotels, catering etc	0.144
Synthetic resins, man-made fibers	0.134	Railways	0.272
Paints, dyes etc	0.154	Road transport etc	0.151
Soap and toiletries	0.226	Air transport	0.253
Chemicals nes	0.133	Transport services	0.204
Mineral oil processing	0.054	Telecomms and postal	0.124
Rubber and plastic products	0.127	Business services etc	0.134
		Other services	0.304

Values are based on the author's calculations, deriving from the 1988 input-output matrix for the U.K., compiled by Maskus and Webster (1995) and available at http://www.nber.org. Further details are available in the Data Appendix.

Table A2. Trade shares.

Industry	Trade share			
	1975	1980	1985	1990
Agriculture, hunting, forestry and fishing	0.26	0.41	0.38	0.56
Food	0.27	0.26	0.29	0.31
Beverages	0.20	0.25	0.28	0.33
Tobacco	0.06	0.17	0.21	0.21
Textiles	0.44	0.53	0.64	0.70
Wearing apparel	0.48	0.47	0.58	0.71
Leather products	0.47	0.63	0.77	0.82
Footwear	0.42	0.58	0.73	0.77
Furniture and fixtures	0.17	0.23	0.29	0.32
Paper and paper products	0.40	0.45	0.54	0.61
Printing and publishing	0.15	0.15	0.16	0.15
Industrial chemicals	0.58	0.75	0.90	0.98
Other chemicals	0.29	0.44	0.54	0.57
Chemical products, n.e.c.	0.25	0.46	0.59	0.65
Misc. products of petroleum and coal	0.62	0.46	0.42	0.36
Rubber products	0.40	0.50	0.58	0.62
Plastic products, n.e.c.	0.21	0.27	0.30	0.28
Pottery, china etc.	0.23	0.28	0.26	0.25
Non-metal products, n.e.c.	0.19	0.19	0.21	0.22
Iron and steel	0.37	0.43	0.48	0.52
Non-ferrous metals	0.69	0.66	0.71	0.73
Fabricated metal products, except machinery and equipment	0.28	0.34	0.39	0.40
Office and computing machinery	1.08	1.24	1.35	1.40
Machinery and equipment, n.e.c.	0.56	0.56	0.60	0.62
Electrical machinery	0.38	0.44	0.52	0.61
Radio, television and communication equipment	0.50	0.49	0.62	0.79
Electrical apparatus, n.e.c.	0.39	0.47	0.49	0.54
Shipbuilding and repairing	0.53	0.40	0.42	0.44
Motor vehicles	0.51	0.58	0.66	0.72
Motorcycles and bicycles	0.55	0.50	0.62	1.00
Professional goods	1.00	1.13	1.52	1.49
Other manufacturing n.e.c.	0.94	1.20	1.39	1.47
Electricity, gas and steam and water	0.63	1.16	0.84	0.68

Source: OECD Sectoral Database and OECD STAN Database. The following industries (not shown) have been assigned a zero trade share: restaurants and hotels, transport, storage and communication, inland transport, maritime and air transport, communication, financing, insurance, real estate and business services, community, social and personal services.

References

Balassa, Bela. "The Purchasing-Power Parity Doctrine: A Reappraisal." *Journal of Political Economy*, 1964, *72*(6), pp. 584–96.

Baumol, William J. and Bowen, William G. *Performing arts: The economic dilemma.* New York: Twentieth Century Fund, 1966.

Crownover, Collin; Pippenger, John and Steiger-wald, Douglas G. "Testing for Absolute Purchasing Power Parity." *Journal of International Money and Finance*, 1996, *15*(5), pp. 783–96.

Crucini, Mario J. and Shintani, Mototsugu. "Persistence in Law-of-One-Price Deviations: Evidence from Micro-price Data." Vanderbilt University Working Paper No. 02-W22R, 2004.

Cumby, Robert E. "Forecasting Exchange Rates and Relative Prices with the Hamburger Standard: Is What You Want What You Get with McParity?" National Bureau of Economic Research, Inc., NBER Working Papers: No. 5675, 1996.

Dumas, Bernard. "Dynamic Equilibrium and the Real Exchange Rate in a Spatially Separated World." *Review of Financial Studies*, 1992, *5*(2), pp. 153–80.

Engel, Charles. "Real Exchange Rates and Relative Prices: An Empirical Investigation." *Journal of Monetary Economics*, 1993, *32*(1), pp. 35–50.

Engel, Charles and Rogers, John H. "How Wide Is the Border?" *American Economic Review*, 1996, *86*(5), pp. 1112–25.

Engel, Charles and Rogers, John H. "European Product Market Integration after the Euro." *Economic Policy*, 2004, *19*(39), pp. 347–75.

Ethier, Wilfred. "Internationally Decreasing Costs and World Trade." *Journal of International Economics*, 1979, *9*(1), pp. 1–24.

Eurostat. *Price structure of the community countries.* Luxembourg: Commission of European Communities, Issues from 1975, 1980, 1985, and 1990.

Evans, Carolyn L. "The Economic Significance of National Border Effects." *American Economic Review*, 2003, *93*(4), pp. 1291–312.

Flam, Harry. "Product Markets and 1992: Full Integration, Large Gains?" *Journal of Economic Perspectives*, 1992, *6*(4), pp. 7–30.

Frankel, Jeffrey A. and Rose, Andrew K. "A Panel Project on Purchasing Power Parity: Mean Reversion within and between Countries." *Journal of International Economics*, 1996, *40*(1–2), pp. 209–24.

Froot, Kenneth A.; Kim, Michael and Rogoff, Kenneth. "The Law-of-One-Price over 700 Years." National Bureau of Economic Research, Inc., NBER Working Papers: No. 1532, 1995.

Ghosh, Atish R. and Wolf, Holger C. "Pricing in International Markets: Lessons from the Economist." National Bureau of Economic Research, Inc., NBER Working Papers: No. 4806, 1994.

Giovannini, Alberto. "Exchange Rates and Traded Goods Prices." *Journal of International Economics*, 1988, *24*(1/2), pp. 45–68.

Haskel, Jonathan and Wolf, Holger. "The Law of One Price — A Case Study." *Scandinavian Journal of Economics*, 2001, *103*(4), pp. 545–58.

Isard, Peter. "How Far Can We Push the 'Law of One Price'?" *American Economic Review*, 1977, *67*(5), pp. 942–48.

Knetter, Michael M. "Price Discrimination by U.S. and German Exporters." *American Economic Review*, 1989, *79*(1), pp. 198–210.

Knetter, Michael M. "International Comparisons of Price-to-Market Behavior." *American Economic Review*, 1993, *83*(3), pp. 473–86.

Kravis, Irving B. and Lipsey, Robert E. "Toward an Explanation of National Price Levels." Princeton University, Princeton Studies in International Finance: No. 52, 1983.

Krugman, Paul R. "Pricing to Market When the Exchange Rate Changes," in Sven W. Arndt and J. David Richardson, eds., *Real-financial linkages among open economies*. Cambridge, MA: MIT Press, 1987, pp. 49–70.

Lutz, Matthias. "Pricing in Segmented Markets, Arbitrage Barriers, and the Law of One Price: Evidence from the European Car Market." *Review of International Economics*, 2004, *12*(3), pp. 456–75.

Murray, Christian J. and Papell, David H. "Do Panels Help Solve the Purchasing Power Parity Puzzle?" *Journal of Business and Economic Statistics*, 2005, *23*(4), pp. 410–415, DOI: 10.1198/073500105000000072.

Mussa, Michael. "Nominal Exchange Rate Regimes and the Behavior of Real Exchange Rates: Evidence and Implications." *Carnegie-Rochester Conference Series on Public Policy*, 1986, *25*, pp. 117–213.

Obstfeld, Maurice and Rogoff, Kenneth. "Exchange Rate Dynamics Redux." *Journal of Political Economy*, 1995, *103*(3), pp. 624–60.

Parsley, David C. and Wei, Shang-Jin. "Explaining the Border Effect: The Role of Exchange Rate Variability, Shipping Costs, and Geography." *Journal of International Economics*, 2001, *55*(1), pp. 87–105.

Parsley, David C. and Wei, Shang-Jin. "How Big and Heterogeneous Are the Effects of Currency Arrangements on Market Integration?" Vanderbilt University, Financial Markets Research Center Working Paper: No. 0013, 2003.

Richardson, J. David. "Some Empirical Evidence on Commodity Arbitrage and the Law of One Price." *Journal of International Economics*, 1978, *8*(2), pp. 341–51.

Rogers, John H. "Price Level Convergence, Relative Prices, and Inflation in Europe." Board of Governors of the Federal Reserve System (U.S.), International Finance Discussion Papers: No. 699, 2001.

Rogers, John H. and Jenkins, Michael. "Haircuts or Hysteresis? Sources of Movements in Real Exchange Rates." *Journal of International Economics*, 1995, *38*(3–4), pp. 339–60.

Rogoff, Kenneth. "The Purchasing Power Parity Puzzle." *Journal of Economic Literature*, 1996, *34*(2), pp. 647–68.

Samuelson, Paul A. "Theoretical Notes on Trade Problems." *Review of Economics and Statistics*, 1964, *46*(2), pp. 145–54.

Sanyal, Kalyan K. and Jones, Ronald W. "The Theory of Trade in Middle Products." *American Economic Review*, 1982, *72*(1), pp. 16–31.

Sercu, Piet; Uppal, Raman and Van Hulle, Cynthia. "The Exchange Rate in the Presence of Transaction Costs: Implications for Tests of Purchasing Power Parity." *Journal of Finance*, 1995, *50*(4), pp. 1309–19.

Stockman, Alan C. and Tesar, Linda L. "Tastes and Technology in a Two-Country Model of the Business Cycle: Explaining International Comovements." *American Economic Review*, 1995, *85*(1), pp. 168–85.

Chapter 3

Understanding Long-Run Price Dispersion*

Mario J. Crucini

Department of Economics, Vanderbilt University, Nashville, TN, USA
mario.j.crucini@vanderbilt.edu

and

Hakan Yilmazkuday

Department of Economics, Florida International University, Miami, FL, USA
hakan.yilmazkuday@fiu.edu

Abstract. A unique panel of retail prices spanning 123 cities in 79 countries from 1990 to 2005 is used to uncover the novel properties of long-run international price dispersion. At the PPP level, almost all of price dispersion is attributed to unskilled wage dispersion. At the level of individual goods and services, the average contribution of these wages is significantly reduced, reflecting that good-specific sources of price dispersion, such as trade costs and good-specific markups, tend to average out across goods. At the LOP level, borders and distance contribute about equally to price dispersion that is rising in the distribution share.

Keywords: Real exchange rates; Purchasing power parity; Law of one price; Dynamic panel

*This chapter originally appeared in *Journal of Monetary Economics*, 2014, **66**, 226–240.

1. Introduction

The Law-of-One-Price is the theoretical proposition that, absent official and natural barriers to trade, international prices are equated in common currency units, and a laborer's purchasing power (i.e., real wage) is determined only by their labor productivity. A stark empirical implication of this proposition is that the cross-country correlation between price levels and wage levels is zero. As is well known, this implication of goods market integration is grossly at odds with the data. The Penn Effect, in recognition of the ambitious work of Alan Heston, Irving Kravis and Robert Summers who developed the Penn World Tables, shows a strong positive correlation between international price levels and per capita income.

Figure 1 shows the microeconomic counterpart of this fact using the panel data of our study. *Microeconomic* in this context means the prices of individual goods and services across cities of the world, as opposed to aggregate price levels at the national level. Specifically, each point in the scatterplot is the price of an individual good

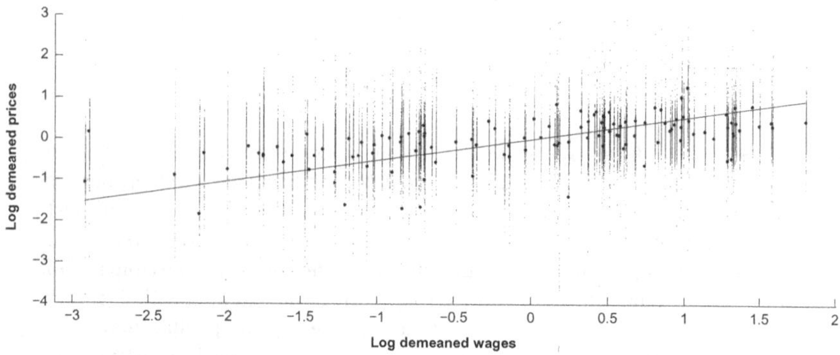

Fig. 1. Relative price levels and relative wages of domestic help.

Note: Each x-coordinate is a city wage relative to the world average. For the large dots, the y-coordinates are the price levels of each city relative to the world price level. The price levels are computed as consumption-expenditure-weighted average of the individual prices. The line through the scatterplot is an ordinary least squares estimate with slope 0.52 and a standard error of (0.05), using the price levels. For the small dots, the y-coordinates are prices of individual goods and services relative to the world average price of those items.

or service in a particular city plotted against the *hourly wage of domestic cleaning help* in that particular city. Prices and wages have been averaged over the period from 1990 to 2005 to eliminate transitory deviations associated with business cycles and exchange rate fluctuations.[1] As far as we know, this is the first study to use time-averaged data to study long-run deviations from the LOP and Purchasing Power Parity. The points labeled with an asterisk are price levels computed as expenditure-weighted averages of the individual prices.

In Fig. 1, the estimated line through the scatter of price levels has a slope of 0.52 and an R^2 value of 0.37.[2] In words: a doubling of wages is associated with a 52 percent higher price level. This finding is typically associated with the seminal works of Harrod (1933), Balassa (1964), and Samuelson (1964); however, the HBS theory assumes that LOP holds for traded goods but not for non-traded goods. According to this view, called the classical dichotomy, there should be a horizontal line traced out by traded goods for which the LOP holds and a line with a slope of unity for non-traded goods. The trivial example is the hourly wage of domestic help itself, which produces a slope of one by recognizing that the market price of this non-traded service is, in fact, the hourly wage for unskilled labor. Figure 1, obviously, is not much more sympathetic to the classical dichotomy than it is to complete market integration.

To help resolve this puzzle, this paper estimates distribution and trade cost wedges using a trade model augmented with a retail distribution sector (developed in Crucini and Yilmazkuday, 2009). We have two sets of results, one for relative price levels (PPP) and the other at the level of individual goods (LOP). Regarding PPP,

---

[1]Specifically, there are 300 goods and services (up to missing observations) for each city and there are 123 cities in total. The prices and wages used to construct these time-averages are from the Economist Intelligence Unit (EIU) World Cost of Living Survey which spans 79 countries.

[2]The estimation is by geometric mean regression to consider for possible measurement errors in both the price and the wage data. A common set of consumption expenditure weights are used for all cities. These consumption expenditure weights are taken from the PWT, averaged across all OECD nations.

the variance of price levels for international city pairs is found to be almost entirely explained by international wage differences, 92% by our estimate. Both the absolute amount of price dispersion and the relative importance of wage differences falls when the sample is restricted to cities in countries at similar stages of development while the role of retail productivity increases. The contribution of cross-city wage differences falls to 8% when the sample is restricted to city pairs within the same country. It is important to keep in mind that the amount of price level dispersion across cities that are located in the same country is a trivial 3–5%; as such, a modest amount of wage or retail productivity variance goes a long way in terms of accounting for the lion's share of the variance. The thrust of the PPP analysis is that when long run price level differences are consequential, the differences are attributable to the level of economic development, not traditional trade frictions.

The table turns dramatically in favor of borders and trade costs and away from wages and retail productivity, as explanatory factors, when the focus is LOP deviations. Pooling all international city pairs, the explanatory power of the HBS theory (wage dispersion) falls by a factor of three, to about 32%. Traditional theories of trade that emphasis distance and borders now account for the lion's share of price dispersion, about 41%. City effects account for almost none of the international LOP variation. Essentially, this is because international LOP deviations are both large and idiosyncratic to the good once we condition on the wage level. The remainder is a residual term, which may reflect good and location-specific markups as well as other variables omitted from the model.

2. The Model

The model consists of an arbitrary number of cities, each inhabited by two representative agents. One representative agent is a manufacturer who specializes in the production of a single good and exports this good to all other cities of the world. The second representative agent is a retailer who imports all of the manufactured goods and makes the goods available in retail outlets in her city of operation.

To import a good, the retailer must pay an iceberg shipping cost over the factory-gate price in the producer's location. The shipping cost is hypothesized to be increasing in the distance shipped and may take a discrete jump if a national border is crossed. The retailing activity is labor intensive with the retailers allocating their non-leisure time across all of the goods they sell. Some cities have more productive retailers than others which is captured by total-factor-productivity (TFP) at the retail level, specific to the city, common to all goods the retailer sells. Part of the TFP effect might be local public infrastructure and private capital, neither of which is modeled here.[3]

Turning to the details, the retailing technology for each good is Cobb–Douglas in retailer hours, N_{ij}, and the quantity of the imported manufactured good, G_{ij}, with TFP level, Z_j:

$$R_{ij} = Z_j N_{ij}^{\alpha_i} G_{ij}^{1-\alpha_i}. \tag{1}$$

While the production function is restricted to be common to all locations, it is very flexible across goods. It captures pure labor services (e.g., baby-sitting services) with α_i equal to one and internet purchases (e.g., Amazon.com book purchases), α_i equal to zero, and all points in between.

The retailer in city, j, minimizes cost of each good, i, by optimally choosing the two inputs needed to produce the good: (i) the amount of the traded input, G_{ij}, to import and (ii) the fraction of her time devoted to the good, N_{ij}:

$$\min_{N_{ij}, G_{ij}} (W_j N_{ij} + Q_{ij} G_{ij}) \tag{2}$$

Note that the W_j reflects the single opportunity cost of time relevant to the problem, that of the retailer. The two constraints on this minimization problem are the production function, (1) and that total

[3]In an earlier version of the paper (Crucini and Yilmazkuday, 2009), we included capital as a factor of production. The simpler formulation here focuses on aggregate retail efficiency, labor in the retail sector and trade costs. To the extent public and private infrastructure capital alter efficiency, these would be allocated to the TFP term.

hours available in the period are exhausted between leisure hours and total time allocated to all retail goods.

The resulting retail price is a Cobb–Douglas aggregate of the price (inclusive of trade cost) that the retailer paid to acquire the traded input, Q_{ij}, and the retailer's opportunity cost of time, W_j:

$$P_{ij} = \frac{W_j^{\alpha_i} Q_{ij}^{1-\alpha_i}}{Z_j}. \tag{3}$$

It is important to note that the weights on the two inputs are good specific. Not surprisingly, all retail prices decrease in proportion to total factor productivity in retailing, Z_j, and increase in proportion to retail input prices, W_j and Q_{ij} (with the factor of proportionality being their respective cost shares).

The factory-gate price of the traded input is determined as follows. A manufacturer in each city operates a simple linear technology, $Y_i = A_i N_i^m$, and maximizes profits from world-wide sales. She charges the same factory-gate price to all destination markets, $Q_{ii} = \tilde{W}_i / A_i$, where $\tilde{W}_i$ is the manufacturing wage in city i and A_i is productivity in manufacturing. The complete equilibrium solution to the model is presented in a separate technical appendix (see Crucini and Yilmazkuday, 2009).

For the purposes of studying relative prices, the only remaining piece of information needed is the relationship between the factory gate price and the destination price. We assume a proportional, good and location-specific shipping cost: $Q_{ij} = (1 + \tau_{ij}) Q_{ii}$.

The prediction of this model for the common-currency relative price of good i in city j relative to city k is

$$\frac{P_{ij}}{P_{ik}} = \frac{Z_k}{Z_j} \left(\frac{W_j}{W_k}\right)^{\alpha_i} \left(\frac{Q_{ij}}{Q_{ik}}\right)^{1-\alpha_i}. \tag{4}$$

Taking logs gives the object of interest

$$p_{ijk} = -z_{jk} + \alpha_i w_{jk} + (1 - \alpha_i) q_{ijk}$$

where $p_{ijk} = \log(P_{ij}/P_{ik})$, $z_{jk} = \log(Z_j/Z_k)$, $w_{jk} = \log(W_j/W_k)$, and $q_{ijk} = \log(Q_{ij}/Q_{ik})$.

3. The Estimation Approach

Taking the model to the data involves a number of empirical challenges. We have rich data with which to measure LOP deviations and reliable measures of wages across cities in our panel, but we lack both measures of retail productivity and micro-level data on traded input prices. This section describes the three-step approach taken to identify distribution shares, the α_i's for each good, city-level retail productivities, the z_j's, and trade costs between any city pair at the good level.

The first stage utilizes the available data on price and wages across cities to estimate a good-specific distribution share α_i, by regressing LOP deviations on the wage ratio

$$p_{ijk} = \alpha_i w_{jk} + \theta_{ijk}, \tag{5}$$

where, according to the model, the residual is $\theta_{ijk} = -z_{jk} + (1 - \alpha_i)q_{ijk}$. The slope parameter in the relationship between prices and relative wages in the HBS scatterplot of Fig. 1 is the empirical counterpart to α_i.

The parameter, α_i, is estimated by geometric mean regression (GMR). That is, we estimate the following two regressions:

$$p_{ijk} = \hat{\alpha}_i w_{jk} + \varepsilon_{ijk}$$

$$w_{jk} = \hat{\gamma}_i p_{ijk} + \epsilon_{ijk}.$$

The GMR estimate is the geometric average of the coefficient from the first regression and the inverse of the coefficient from the second regression, $\hat{\alpha}_i^G = \sqrt{\hat{\alpha}_i/\hat{\gamma}_i}$. As described in Kennedy (2003), this estimator is consistent when the two variables have comparable measurement error variances relative to the variance of the true underlying economic variables.

The second stage regression uses the residuals from the first stage regression

$$\hat{\theta}_{ijk} = p_{ijk} - \hat{\alpha}_i^G w_{jk}$$

and pools all goods and bilateral city pairs to estimate city fixed-effects $(-z_{jk})$

$$\hat{\theta}_{ijk} = -z_{jk} + \varphi_{ijk}$$

where $-z_{jk} \equiv -\mu_j + \mu_k$ is the retail productivity differential and the residual, $\varphi_{ijk} = (1 - \alpha_i)q_{ijk}$, represents the traded input cost ratio, which is assumed to be mean zero across goods, for each bilateral pair. Note that while the z's capture retail productivities under the assumption of perfect competition, they would also capture city-specific markups if retailers in each city have market power. Since we cannot separately identify retail productivity and retail markups, we will call z_j's (log) retail productivities simply to be consistent with our competitive equilibrium model of retailing and trade. Estimation at this stage is by OLS.

The third stage considers relative prices of traded inputs, q_{ijk}. To place some structure on these trade costs, consider the no-arbitrage condition for good i, across city pair j and k

$$-\delta_i d_{jk} - \rho_i B_{jk} \leq q_{ijk} \leq \delta_i d_{jk} + \rho_i B_{jk} \tag{6}$$

where $\delta_i d_{jk} + \rho_i B_{jk}$ is the trade cost between city j and city k for good i; $d_{jk} > 0$ is the log distance between cities j and k, $\delta_i > 0$ is the elasticity of trade costs with respect to distance for traded good i, B_{jk} is a border dummy taking a value of 1 if cities k and j are in different countries (and 0 otherwise), and $\rho_i > 0$ is the logarithm of the additional cost of crossing the border between city j and k (if one exists) with traded-input i. While the inclusion of distance is to capture geographical barriers to trade, the inclusion of a border dummy is to capture official barriers to international trade. As is evident from the specification above, the border effect estimated here differs across goods, but is common to all border crossings.

Equation (6) is a standard arbitrage condition showing that arbitrage is profitable in the sense of shipping goods from city k to city j only if the price in city j is high enough relative to the price in city k to cover the arbitrage costs in that direction: $q_{ijk} > \delta_i d_{jk} + \rho_i B_{jk}$. Conversely, goods should be shipped from city j to city k when the price in city j is sufficiently low: $-q_{ijk} > \delta_i d_{kj} + \rho_i B_{kj}$.

Since the traded input cost ratios, $(1-\alpha_i)q_{ijk}$, are estimated by the $\hat{\varphi}_{ijk}$'s, the sign of $\hat{\varphi}_{ijk}$ provides useful information on the profitable direction of arbitrage. Since trade costs measured by $\delta_i d_{jk} + \rho_i B_{jk}$ are positive, positive values of estimated φ_{ijk}'s will be associated with city j importing from city k, and negative values of φ_{ijk}'s will be associated with city j exporting to city k, according to our model. Thus, the direction-of-arbitrage indicator function $\mathbf{I}_{ijk}$ is set to a value of 1 or −1 according to:

$$\hat{\mathbf{I}}_{ijk} = \begin{cases} 1 & \text{if } \hat{\varphi}_{ijk} > 0\, j \text{ imports from } k \\ -1 & \text{if } \hat{\varphi}_{ijk} < 0\, k \text{ imports from } j \end{cases} \tag{7}$$

The importance of controlling for local distribution costs by using $\widehat{\varphi}_{ijk}$ rather than the real exchange rates themselves should be evident: if we did not do this, our indicator function would suggest that all goods are imported by rich nations from poor ones due to the lower price levels in poor countries at the retail level (recall Fig. 1). Clearly the first and second stages of the regression are crucial prior steps since they remove the local distribution cost component.

Consider, now, choosing the variables, κ_{ijk} and η_{ijk}, such that Eq. (6) holds with equality:

$$-\delta_i d_{jk} - \rho_i B_{jk} - \kappa_{ijk} = q_{ijk} = \delta_i d_{jk} + \rho_i B_{jk} + \eta_{ijk}.$$

Note that given the sign conventions for these plug-in values, they satisfy $\kappa_{ijk} \leq 0$ and $\eta_{ijk} \leq 0$. By using the estimated direction-of-arbitrage indicator $\widehat{\mathbf{I}}_{ijk}$, these two equalities can be combined in the following expression:

$$q_{ijk} = \widehat{\mathbf{I}}_{ijk}(\delta_i d_{jk} + \rho_i B_{jk}) + c_i + \varepsilon_{ijk} \tag{8}$$

where $\varepsilon_{ijk} = \hat{\iota}_{ikj}\eta_{ijk} + \hat{\iota}_{ijk}\kappa_{ijk} - c_i$. The presence of c_i is to ensure that $E_{jk}(\varepsilon_{ijk}) = 0$. The indicator $\hat{\iota}_{ikj}$ takes a value of 1 if the direction of trade is from city k to city j (and 0 otherwise), $\hat{\iota}_{ijk}$ takes a value of −1 if the direction of trade is from city j to city k (and 0 otherwise). The two indicators add up to the original one: $\widehat{\mathbf{I}}_{ijk} = \hat{\iota}_{ikj} + \hat{\iota}_{ijk}$. Using $\hat{\varphi}_{ijk} = (1-\hat{\alpha}_i)q_{ijk}$ (the fitted residuals from the second stage regression) and estimated $\widehat{\alpha}_i$'s from the first stage regression: $\hat{q}_{ijk} = \hat{\varphi}_{ijk}/(1-\hat{\alpha}_i)$. Thus, all the variables necessary to estimate Eq. (8) are available: the estimated relative input cost, $\widehat{q}_{ijk}$, the direction of trade indicator, $\widehat{\mathbf{I}}_{ijk}$, greater circle distance and border dummies (d_{jk} and B_{jk}).

Although we have confidence about what the good-specific intercept and residuals ($c_i + \varepsilon_{ijk}$) do not represent, namely relative distribution costs (wage and retail productivity components), border-related costs, or distance-related costs, there are a number of plausible alternative explanations for what they do represent. The sources of these deviations from LOP unexplained by the model include: measurement error in retail prices, deviations from LOP that are below the threshold arbitrage value, trade costs that do not depend on distance or borders (e.g., trade finance) and markups specific to goods rather than common to bilateral locations.

4. The Data

We use city-level data on retail prices, wages, and the greater-circle distance in our empirical work. The prices and wages are from the World Cost of Living Survey conducted by the Economist Intelligence Unit (EIU). The surveys took place in 123 cities, located in 79 countries. The vast majority of the cities in the survey are national capitals and since urban areas are typically densely populated with higher per capita income than rural areas, these cities account for a significant fraction of global consumption and production; they are also typically major ports and centralized trading locations (see Fig. 2). The larger number of cities than countries is due to the fact that the survey includes multiple cities in a few countries. Noteworthy are the 16 U.S. cities included in the survey; the next largest number of cities surveyed equals 5 in Australia, China and Germany. Our sample is annual from 1990 to 2005. Up to data availability for particular years and cities, the number of goods and services surveyed by EIU staff is 300. Each price observation is collected from the same retail outlet over time. Examples of goods found in the survey are as follows: *Butter* (*500 grams*), *Compact disc album*, *Light bulbs* (*two*, *60 watts*). Typical examples of services are as follows: *Dry*

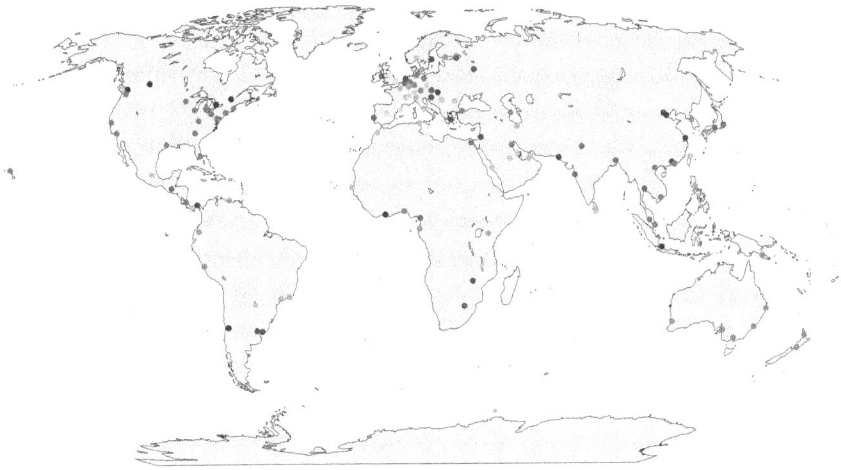

Fig. 2. Cities surveyed by the Economist Intelligence Unit.

Note: Each symbol marks the location of a city surveyed by the EIU. There are 123 in total. Most of the cities are national capitals located on the coast in the cases of nations not land-locked. Cases in which multiple cities are surveyed in the same country are marked with a common color. (For interpretation of the references to color in this figure legend, the reader is referred to the web version of this paper.)

cleaning, mans suit (standard high-street outlet), baby-sitters rate per hour (average), Hilton-type hotel, single room, one night including breakfast (average).

Let $P_{ij,t}$ be the price of good i, in city j and year t in U.S. dollars. The object of interest is the long-run bilateral price deviation across city pair j and k, computed as the time-averaged log-relative price

$$p_{ijk} \equiv T^{-1} \sum_t p_{ijk,t}$$

where $p_{ijk,t} \equiv \log(P_{ij,t}/P_{ik,t})$.

To gain an appreciation of the relative importance of long-run price dispersion compared to time series price variation, Fig. 3 presents kernel density estimates of relative prices. The solid lines are the distributions of the time-averaged prices, p_{ijk}, while the dashed lines are the distributions of the annual deviations of relative prices from these long-run levels, $p_{ijk,t} - p_{ijk}$. The two charts on the left are distributions for U.S. city pairs and the two charts on the right are

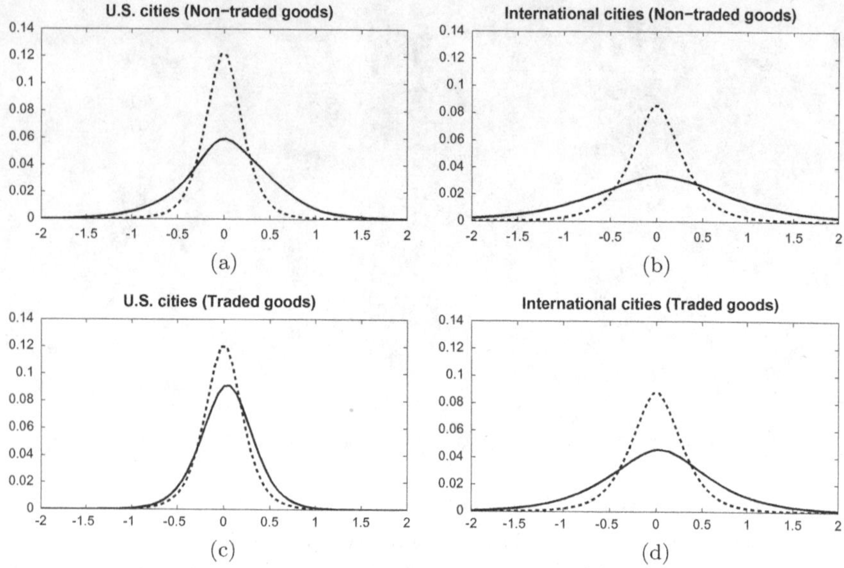

Fig. 3. Kernel density estimates of price distributions.

Note: The solid lines are kernel density estimates of the distribution of p_{ijk}, time averaged LOP deviations over the period 1990–2005. The dashed lines are kernel density estimates of the distribution of time series deviations from these long-run values. Each chart contains a different location and commodity grouping as indicated by the headers.

all international cross-border city pairs. The charts in the top row include only non-traded goods prices while the charts in the bottom row include only traded goods prices.

If the LOP held *always and everywhere*, all the distributions would be degenerate at zero. Such a situation would describe a world of frictionless trade in goods markets and instantaneous arbitrage. Given the continuous and often large movements of nominal exchange rates and what is known about the infrequency of local currency price changes, it is not surprising that the dashed lines reveal transitory deviations of relative prices from their long-run means. What is very surprising is the distribution of the long-run means themselves. In each case, with the possible exception of traded goods across U.S. cities, the dispersion of the long-run price distribution is greater than the variation of the time series deviations around these long-run

Table 1. Price distributions (summary statistics).

	Traded goods		Non-traded goods	
	U.S. no border	World border	U.S. no border	World border
		Standard deviation		
Long-run	0.294	0.681	0.543	1.069
Short-run	0.250	0.412	0.258	0.488
		Interquartile range		
Long-run	0.385	0.796	0.616	1.092
Short-run	0.295	0.417	0.295	0.430

Note: The long-run values have been calculated by the time-averaged prices, while the short-run values have been calculated as deviations from the long-run values.

means. Put differently, the time series movements seem less puzzling in light of the size of the long-run deviations. This motivates our focus on estimating the sources of long-run relative price deviations.

Table 1 presents summary statistics related to the data in Fig. 3. The least amount of price dispersion is found in U.S. traded goods, 0.29 and the greatest amount is found in the case of non-traded goods involving international border crossings, 1.07. Remarkably, non-traded goods in the U.S. actually have less price dispersion than do traded goods internationally, 0.54 compared to 0.68. Inter-quartile differences yield similar measures of price dispersion. As originally discovered by Crucini and Telmer (2012), time series variation is typically less than the long-run variance, with the possible exception of traded goods across U.S. cities, and even in this case, one of the two measures (inter-quartile difference) also gives a ranking consistent with the broader samples. Notice also that the distinction between traded and non-traded goods is obvious in the long-run measure. This contrasts with the existing international finance literature where the time series variance of non-traded and traded real exchange rates are found to be very comparable (Engel, 1999; Crucini and Landry, 2012).

The remaining data utilized are wages, measures of distribution costs and distance. Directly measuring trade costs is a significant challenge in the literature. Hummels (2001) provides the most comprehensive estimates of sectoral trade costs using import unit values, a more direct method than employed here. Unfortunately, these estimates are available for a very limited number of countries and are more aggregated than our retail price data. Instead, we follow the gravity literature in trade and use the greater circle distance between cities in the EIU sample to estimate trade costs in LOP deviations at the retail level. The implied trade costs are consistent with Hummels estimates.

The wage measure is *hourly rate for domestic cleaning help* (*average*) from the EIU survey. This wage measure is chosen for a number of reasons: (i) it is city-specific, consistent with our retail prices; (ii) it spans the entire 1990–2005 sample period; (iii) the number of missing observations is substantially lower than the alternative available wage series in the EIU survey (i.e., only 269 missing observations out of 7503 city pairs, less than 4% of the sample), and (iv) it has a high cross-sectional correlation with alternative source of wage data at the country level.

Sectoral U.S. NIPA data and U.S. input–output tables are used to cross-validate the distribution share measures estimated from our regression model. Our model recovers close to 300 good-specific distribution shares while the U.S. data provide 57 sectoral distribution shares and the input–output data span 33 sectors. The NIPA shares are computed as the value the producers receive relative to the value consumers pay for the output of a particular sector. For the typical traded good, the distribution margin computed using the consumer value less the producer value relative to the consumer value is about 50%. That is, the retail price is about twice the producer price. However, for services, the same NIPA data would produce an estimate of the distribution margin close to zero. Consider a visit to the doctor's office to receive an expensive vaccine injection by a nurse. Because of the arms length nature of the transaction, it appears as though what the consumer pays, the producer gets. Most existing studies record the distribution margin to be zero in these situations. However, the economic concept that the distribution margin is intended to capture in our model is the distinction between retail prices and traded inputs. The goal is to treat the labor services of the nurse at the doctor's office in a consistent manner with the labor services of the salesperson at Walmart. To our knowledge, this issue has not been dealt with in the existing literature because the focus has been mostly on traded goods.[4] Since the CPI consists of a large and growing fraction of services, measuring the distribution share for the service sector is an important facet of our work.

5. The Results

This section reports our findings, beginning with a careful review of the parameter estimates obtained by the three-stage regression approach using the full sample of international cities. Next, the implications of these estimates for geographic price dispersion at the good level (i.e., deviations from LOP) are reported using variance decompositions. Results that serve to contrast heterogeneity across goods and the role of national borders are highlighted. Finally, the LOP deviations are aggregated and a variance decomposition of PPP is conducted.

5.1. *Parameter estimates*

The distribution share of each good α_i is estimated by the first-stage regression using the GMR estimator described in the previous section. The mean $\hat{\alpha}_i$ estimate is 0.48, while the median adjusted R^2 of the first-stage regression is 0.34 (both taken across goods). Recall that using price levels computed from the same data and the same wage measure (Fig. 1), the slope coefficient was 0.52 and the R^2 was 0.37. As we shall see below, the higher slope coefficient in the aggregate for PPP is to be expected since, according to the model, it represents a consumption-expenditure-weighted average of the microeconomic distribution shares. Since non-traded goods tend to carry the largest consumption shares and involve more distribution

[4]See, for example, Burstein *et al.* (2003). Following a conversation between Crucini and Rebelo, the distribution margin in Burstein *et al.* (2005, 2007) makes an approximate correction for this effect.

costs (non-traded inputs), it is expected that the PPP slope exceeds the simple average LOP slope in the cross-section.

Given that a considerable number of variables implied by our theory that are omitted in the first stage regression, it is natural to ask how our distribution share estimates compare to distribution shares in the U.S. NIPA accounts and input–output tables. Since the latter are more aggregated than our estimates, we average our good-level estimates within each NIPA sector. Table 2 compares our microeconomic estimates to the more aggregated NIPA values at six points in the distribution. The median distribution share is estimated to be 0.45 compared to 0.41 using US NIPA data. The estimated values match remarkably closely throughout the distribution except at the very high-end of the distribution: at the third quartile the estimated distribution share is 0.55 compared to 0.75 in the US NIPA.

In summary, our estimates are broadly consistent with direct U.S. NIPA measures, but our estimates are preferred in the context of our study for three reasons. First, they are good specific allowing our subsequent analysis and variance decompositions to exploit the richness of our micro-price data. Second, the prices are consistent with the wage data since both are taken from the same EIU survey. By consistent, we mean not averaged across occupations and covering the same 123 cities as the price survey. Third, the U.S. distribution shares are not necessarily representative of those in other nations. Our estimates are literally global estimates.

Table 2. Distribution shares.

	Estimated from EIU micro-data	U.S. Sectoral NIPA data
Minimum	0.20	0.17
First quartile	0.36	0.36
Median	0.45	0.41
Mean	0.48	0.53
Third quartile	0.55	0.75
Maximum	1.00	1.00

Note: Since the distribution shares in the U.S. NIPA are more aggregated than the estimates of distribution shares in this paper, the good-level estimates have been averaged within each NIPA sector.

Table 3. Retail productivity trade costs and borders.

	Retail productivity (B_j)	Distance elasticity (δ_i)	Border effect (ρ_i)
Minimum	0.50	0.00	0.02
First quartile	0.75	0.04	0.21
Median	0.97	0.05	0.33
Mean	1.09	0.09	0.52
Third quartile	1.24	0.08	0.49
Maximum	3.32	2.15	5.30

Note: Each column independently depicts the summary statistics for the corresponding variable/parameter.

The second stage of the estimation process recovers the retail productivity of each city (Z_j) and yields a median adjusted R^2 of 0.40. Table 3 provides summary statistics for the Z_j's, which are all statistically significant at 5% level. The mean and median are not informative because they reflect an arbitrary choice of units in which to measure productivity. What is interesting are the large differences in productivity across cities, the third quartile city is 65% more productive than the first quartile city. In terms of the retail sector, the most productive city is 6.6 (3.32/0.50) times more productive than the least productive city.

To cross-validate our inference about retail productivity, the estimated Z_j's are compared to distribution sector productivities from the GGDC Productivity Level Database. This database covers only 18 of the 79 countries in the EIU sample. For countries in the EIU sample with more than one city in the price survey, we take the simple average of city-level retail productivities as our estimate of national retail productivity. The correlation between the two estimates of retail productivity across the 18 countries common to both samples is 0.48.

The effects of trade costs are estimated in the third-stage regression described earlier, which have a median adjusted R^2 of 0.61. The summary statistics for distance elasticities (δ_i's), which are all statistically significant at the 5% level, are reported in Table 3. The median distance elasticity is 0.05 which implies that price deviations increase by 40% per 1,000 miles of distance between the source and destination. Taking into account that traded inputs account for only a fraction of the retail price, the average effect of 1,000 miles of distance on retail prices is given by $\exp(\hat{\delta}_i(1-\hat{\alpha}_i)d_{jk})-1$. Evaluated at the median values of both the distance elasticities and distribution share parameters implies about a 21% increase in the retail price from source to destination from the trade cost channel.

The calculation above does not take into account the possible impact of market segmentation associated with national borders. The border effects are statistically significant at the 5% level. Borders are also economically significant. For the median good, the border adds 33% to the traded-input price (see Table 3). Taking into account the share of traded inputs in the production of the median retail good using, $\hat{\rho}_i(1-\hat{\alpha}_i)$, the average border wedge is 18%. Engel and Rogers (1996) have popularized the transformation of price deviations into distance equivalent measures. The border effect in distance equivalent units is computed as $\exp(\hat{\rho}_i/\hat{\delta}_i)$. The average border effect across goods, pooling all location pairs, is 735 miles. The median border width is 522 miles. As one might expect, the differences across goods are large. Moving from the first quartile of the distribution of the border effect to the third quartile, the border width increases from a mere 38 miles to an astounding 55,322 miles.[5] Interestingly, the first quartile contains the traded good, *banana*, while the third quartile contains the non-traded good, *a three course dinner for four people.* What this suggests to us it that extrapolating the distance metric becomes less useful as the item in question becomes inherently less traded in the sense of being produced mostly with local inputs. In such cases it is preferable to report price dispersion and attempt to account for that dispersion with something other than iceberg shipping costs.

The cumulative explanatory power of the three-stage estimation is a useful metric for summarizing the completeness of our model

[5]The baseline border width estimate of Engel and Rogers (1996) was 75,000 miles. It is not possible to make a direct comparison between our estimates and theirs for a number of reasons. First, they use the time series variance of changes in relative prices. Second, they use CPI data aggregated to roughly two-digit categories. Third, they focus on U.S.–Canada city pairs.

in accounting for price dispersion. The median R-bar squared value across goods is 0.72. In other words, the parsimonious set of controls account for the bulk of good-level heterogeneity in long-run price deviations. Having described the parameter estimates and their economic interpretations, it is now possible to decompose the variance of LOP and PPP deviations into the contributions of retail productivity, wages, distance and borders.

5.2. *Variance decompositions*

The goal is to explain the variance of relative prices across all unique city pairs, good-by-good[6]:

$$V_i = var_{jk}(p_{ijk})$$

and for price levels in the aggregate, $V = var_{jk}(p_{jk})$. We begin with the analytics of how international price dispersion in underlying factor inputs translates into variance in final goods prices at the microeconomics and macroeconomics levels.

Starting with microeconomic sources of price dispersion, the larger the V_i, the greater are the deviations from LOP over the geography of locations index by j and k. The natural economic benchmark for the lower bound is when the LOP holds across all bilateral pairs used in the calculation, in which case, $V_i = 0$. The model is designed to elucidate the sources of price dispersion emanating from plausible real frictions related to economic geography.

Recall that the log-relative price consists of three main components, two related to retailing (relative TFP in retailing and the relative wages of the retailers) and the relative cost of acquiring the traded input:

$$p_{ijk} = -z_{jk} + \alpha_i w_{jk} + (1 - \alpha_i) q_{ijk}.$$

---

[6]The variance metric is different from the one used by Crucini *et al.* (2005) to study price dispersion across European capital cities. They normalized prices to their cross-city means, $var_j(p_{ij} - \bar{p}_i)$, which does not allow for the role of bilateral distance in the trade cost component of our structural model.

Substituting our model of the traded input component into this equation gives the rather intimidating expression,

$$p_{ijk} = -z_{jk} + \alpha_i w_{jk} + (1-\alpha_i)[\hat{\mathbf{I}}_{ijk}(\delta_i d_{jk} + \rho_i B_{jk}) + c_i + \varepsilon_{ijk}]. \tag{9}$$

The variance decomposition will be computed using $var(p_{ijk}) = cov(p_{ijk}, p_{ijk})$ with the second p_{ijk} replaced by all of the terms on the right-hand-side of (9). The resulting variance decomposition is

$$1 = \underbrace{\beta_{iz} + \alpha_i \beta_{iw}}_{\text{Distribution costs}} + \underbrace{(1-\alpha_i)\delta_i \beta_{id} + (1-\alpha_i)\rho_i \beta_{iB}}_{\text{Trade costs}} + \underbrace{(1-\alpha_i)\beta_{ie}}_{\text{Unexplained}}.$$

The use of the notation β is natural here since the contribution of each component to the variance is effectively a regression coefficient. For example, $\beta_{iw} = cov_{jk}(w_{jk}, p_{ijk})/var_{jk}(p_{ijk})$ is the coefficient from a regression of relative wages on relative prices of good i across all city-pairs. Essentially this component tells us the role of international wage dispersion on retail price dispersion of good i, across locations. The fact that β_{iw} is pre-multiplied by the coefficient α_i means that a fixed amount of geographic wage dispersion has an effect on retail price dispersion that is increasing in the share of distribution in cost.

The contribution of traded inputs is more nuanced, involving a traditional trade cost component and a border effect. As one would expect, both terms are weighted by the cost share of traded inputs $(1-\alpha_i)$. The first component is a traditional shipping cost and involves the product of δ_i and β_{id}. Recall that δ_i is the good-specific elasticity of trade cost with respect to distance; ceteris paribus, a good that is more costly to transport will contribute more to the variance of retail prices. The more subtle part of the expression is the covariance between relative prices at the retail level and interaction of the direction of trade indicator and distance, the $\beta_{id} = cov(\hat{\mathbf{I}}_{ijk} d_{jk}, p_{ijk})/var_{jk}(p_{ijk})$ term. Due to the presence of the indicator function and how it was defined, this is the coefficient of a regression of the absolute value of the relative price of traded inputs on the retail price. Intuitively, we want to relate trade costs to distance in a symmetric fashion in the sense that the distance matters, not the direction of trade. The absolute value ensures that trade costs are non-negative in the estimation equation. Basically, if retail price deviations are increasing in the estimated trade cost, which themselves are rising in distance, then trade costs contribute positively to long-run price dispersion. The contribution is greater for locations separated by greater distances since $\delta_i > 0$. Holding distance fixed, goods that are more costly to ship, greater δ_i, will exhibit more long-run price dispersion. The border effect contributes only to the variance of cross-border city pairs and does so as a level effect, not as a function of distance. The level effect is good specific due to the presence of ρ_i.

Turning to relative price levels and PPP, consider the cost-of-living index for city j motivated by reference to a Cobb–Douglas aggregator function:

$$P_j = \prod_i (P_{ij})^{\omega_i}$$

where ω_i, is the consumption-expenditure-share of good i.

Using the equation for LOP (9) and the aggregator above, the log deviations from PPP may be written as

$$\begin{aligned} p_{jk} = z_k - z_j + \left(\sum_i \omega_i \alpha_i\right) w_{jk} + \sum_i \omega_i (1-\alpha_i) \hat{\mathbf{I}}_{ijk} \delta_i d_{jk} \\ + \sum_i \omega_i (1-\alpha_i) \hat{\mathbf{I}}_{ijk} \rho_i B_{jk} + \sum_i \omega_i (1-\alpha_i) c_i \\ + \sum_i \omega_i (1-\alpha_i) \varepsilon_{ijk} \end{aligned} \tag{10}$$

where $p_{jk} = \log(P_j/P_k)$ is the aggregate real exchange rate across city pair j and k.

The variance decomposition of real exchange rates (using Eq. (10)) is

$$1 = \underbrace{\beta_z + \omega\beta_w}_{\text{Distribution costs}} + \underbrace{\sum_i \omega_i (1-\alpha_i)[\delta_i \beta_{id} + \rho_i \beta_{iB}]}_{\text{Trade costs}} + \underbrace{\sum_i \omega_i (1-\alpha_i) \beta_\varepsilon}_{\text{Unexplained}}$$

where $\omega = \sum_i \omega_i \alpha_i$ and the β's are now covariances using the same right-hand-variables as before, but with the aggregate real exchange rate, p_{jk}, replacing the LOP deviations.

5.2.1. *Variance decomposition across goods*

Figures 4 and 5 present the variance decomposition in the cross-section of goods, sorted by the estimated distribution share, $\hat{\alpha}_i$. At the left-hand boundary are goods with 0.20 of their cost attributed to distribution inputs and the rest of the cost attributed to the traded good itself. Unleaded gasoline is an example of such a good. The

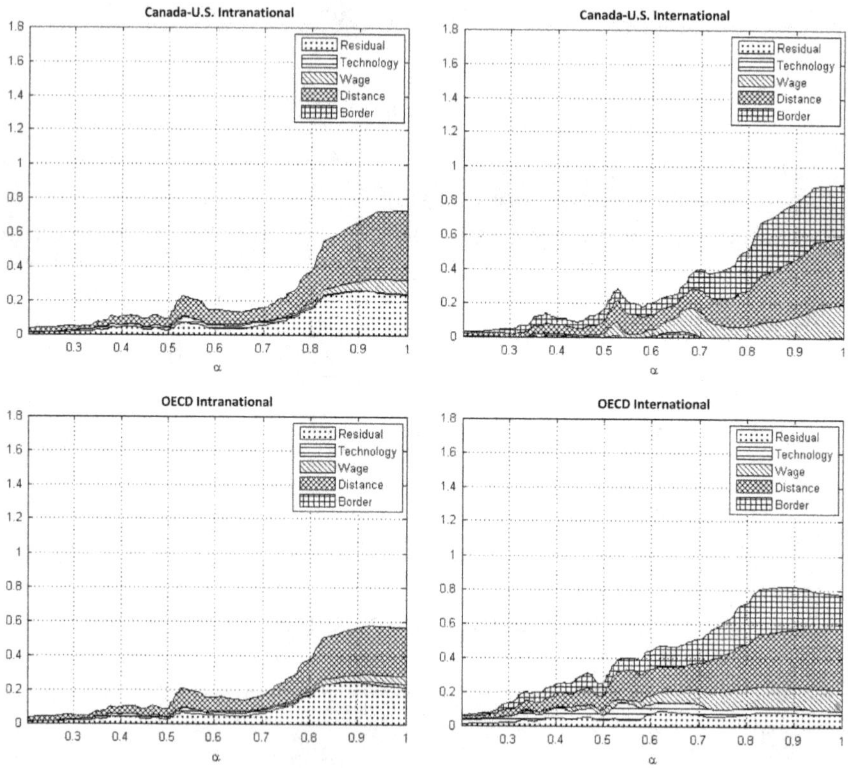

Fig. 4. Sources of price dispersion and the distribution share (a_i).

Note: The figures show the sources of price dispersion with respect to the distribution share (a_i).

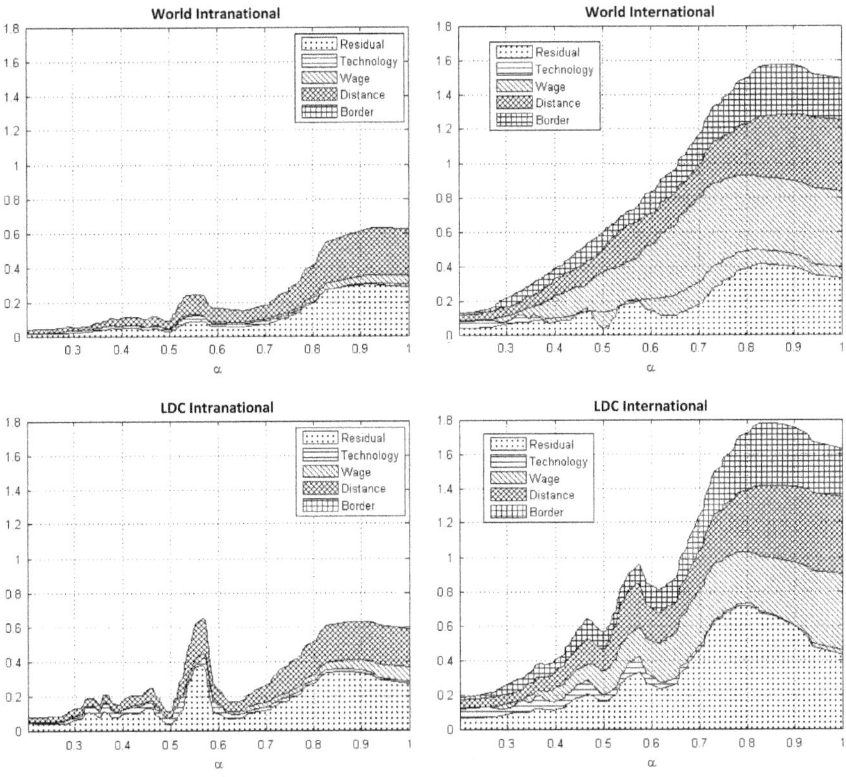

Fig. 5. Sources of price dispersion and the distribution share (a_i).

Note: The figures show the sources of price dispersion with respect to the distribution share (a_i).

right-hand boundary is a pure service, such as the hourly wage of baby-sitters. The variance of retail prices (V_i) is the upper contour. We clearly see a positive relationship between the distribution share and price dispersion. The increases are substantial. For example, goods involving the lowest distribution share practically satisfy the LOP in the case of Canada and the United States and among OECD cities, whereas the deviations for services approach 80%. The countries included in the sample matter for both the absolute level of price dispersion and the relative contributions of various components. Price dispersion is uniformly greater across LDC city pairs and World city pairs than across cities of the OECD or North America.

It is important to point out that the obvious contribution of non-traded inputs in these figures contrasts sharply with much of the existing international finance literature where skepticism regarding the value of the HBS theory originated. In that literature, the time series variance of the real exchange rates of two sub-indices of the CPI are typically used to elucidate the HBS theory (e.g., Engel, 1999). Recall, however, that in Table 1 the short-run variance (a measure of time series variance) failed to reveal a sharp difference in variability of real exchange rates across traded and non-traded goods. That classification, however, is based on applying the HBS theory to final goods, not intermediate inputs. Crucini and Landry (2012) show that the time series variance of LOP deviations is in fact rising in the distribution share. In other words, when the HBS theory is applied to intermediate inputs, it is successful in accounting for differences in both the long-run and the short-run property of price dispersion.

Turning to the details, intranational price dispersion, displayed in the left-hand charts, is largely accounted for by distance. International price dispersion is driven significantly by three components: wages, distance and borders. The relative importance of the three depends on the set of locations under examination and differs across goods. As expected, the wage component becomes more important as we move from, say unleaded gasoline to baby-sitting services (left-to-right along the x-axis). This is because the distribution share is much higher for the latter than the former item and wage differences play a crucial role in distribution costs.

The absolute amount of price dispersion also depends on the set of locations used in the analysis. Samples of cities which span nations at very different level of development will exhibit more price dispersion with a large role for distribution costs and wages. The reason for this is obvious, unskilled labor is relatively abundant and cheap in poorer countries than in richer ones and thus there is a large wedge driven between retail prices across those city pairs. As we move from the World or LDC geography of locations to the OECD or North America total price dispersion falls as wage dispersion also falls.

5.2.2. *Variance decomposition for the average good*

As the previous sub-section demonstrated, the underlying sources of deviations from the LOP depend on where in the distribution of goods one looks. This sub-section provides a summary of the decomposition for the good in the cross-section with the average amount of geographic price dispersion. In particular, Table 4 reports the averages across goods of total long-run price dispersion and the estimated contribution of each cost component to that average.

The averages reported in Table 4 are influenced by the fact that goods are not equally distributed over the distribution shares of 0.2–1.0 displayed in the figures. For example, the modal good is a food item with a distribution share of about 0.37 (whereas the median share is 0.45). The columns labelled NB report results that use only within country city pairs in the analysis whereas the columns labelled

Table 4. Accounting for long run deviations from LOP.

	World		LDC		OECD		CAN–US	
	NB	B	NB	B	NB	B	NB	B
Price dispersion	15.03	58.63	24.83	64.83	13.33	31.58	14.19	18.53
	Absolute contribution of							
Border effect	–	10.39	–	11.13	–	7.98	–	7.55
Distance	6.44	13.70	7.57	14.70	6.55	10.42	7.04	8.18
Distribution sector	2.56	18.74	5.21	18.08	1.96	8.53	2.25	3.40
Service wages	0.42	18.70	1.10	10.71	0.19	2.22	0.15	2.77
Retail productivity	2.14	0.04	4.10	7.37	1.76	6.31	2.10	0.63
Residual	5.93	15.54	11.93	20.67	4.74	4.49	4.82	−0.76
	Percentage contribution of							
Border	–	17.7	–	17.2	–	25.3	–	40.7
Distance	42.9	23.4	30.5	22.7	49.2	33.0	49.6	44.1
Distribution sector	17.0	32.0	20.9	27.9	14.7	27.0	15.9	18.4
Service wages	2.8	31.9	4.4	16.5	1.4	7.0	1.1	14.9
Retail productivity	14.2	0.1	16.5	11.4	13.2	20.0	14.8	3.4
Residual	39.4	26.5	48.0	31.9	35.5	14.2	33.9	−4.1
Average miles	856	4054	564	3944	896	3216	1083	1134

Notes: LDC stands for less developed countries, CAN–US stands for Canada–U.S., NB stands for no border, B stands for border. Average miles represent the average distance separating cities.

B report results that use only city pairs separated by a national border. The main column headings, LDC, OECD and CAN-US, describe the regions in which these cities are located while WORLD is the entire pooled sample of 123 cities. The upper panel of the table reports the absolute geographic variance coming from each economic channel while the lower panel reports the proportion of the total variance accounted for by each economic channel.

Table 4 shows the dominant factor accounting of geographic microeconomic price dispersion are trade costs. Recall that trade costs are the sum of traditional trade costs (distance) and a border effect. The border effect for the average good is between 7.55% and 10.39%. Distance contributes between 6.44% and 14.7%. The heterogeneity across location in the role of distance is intuitive: it reflects the differences in the average distance separating bilateral city pairs in the respective columns. Intranational city pairs are almost by definition, cities that are closer together with greater circle distances averaging 856 miles compared to 4054 for international pairs. The absolute contribution of distance is predicted to increase from 6.55 to 13.70 as a consequence. An interesting exception is North America where intranational city pairs are almost as far apart as international city pairs, 1083 versus 1134. Consequently, distance is estimated to account for a comparable amount of absolute price dispersion in the last two columns, 7.04 versus 8.18.

The role of distribution costs, which is the sum of service wages and retail productivity, depends on the city pairs included in the comparison. As one might expect, the role of distribution costs is significantly elevated when the comparisons involve cities in different countries. The reason for this is that the cost of moving from one city to another to arbitrage wage differences is much lower within countries than across them. This is why within-country wage dispersion is often ignored in macroeconomic models whereas across country wage dispersion constitutes a central question in the development literature. It is not necessary for us to determine the underlying sources of labor unit cost differences across cities to conduct our variance decompositions. For example, they could be driven mostly by prohibitive costs of cross-border arbitrage due to limits on legal immigration or institutions that limit technological progress in the service sector.

Consistent with this discussion, the absolute contribution of distribution costs ranges from 3.4% for cross-border cities pairs in North America (CAN-US) to 18.74% worldwide. Canada and the United States are obviously at similar stages of development and much more economically and financially integrated than most other country pairs. When comparisons involve city pairs within the same country, distribution costs are understandably very similar as evident in the dispersion measures that range from a low of 1.96% for within country cities pairs in the OECD sub-sample to a high of 5.21% in the LDC sub-sample. The greater role of retail productivity in the LDC sample may reflect great variance in retail infrastructure cost across cities within China and India compared to cities within countries like the United States, Canada, Germany and Australia, which account for a disproportionate number of intranational city pairs in the larger sample.

Turning to proportions of variance explained, in the lower panel of Table 4, for cross-border city pairs (B), the contribution shares of borders, distance and distribution are each substantial with the ranking dependent somewhat on the set of countries used in the analysis. Trade costs (sum of borders and distance) ranges in contribution from 40% to 60% of total LOP variation and always exceed that of distribution costs.[7] It is notable that the contribution of distribution costs is more stable across country groups than are the separate contributions of service wages and retail productivity.

It is important to note that despite shorter distance and thus lower trade costs between cities within countries (NB), trade costs actually account for a larger fraction of total price dispersion intranationally than internationally because the absolute variance is

[7]The absolute variance attributed to the width of the border is comparable across panels, but accounts for a larger share of price dispersion for Canada and the United States because the absolute amount of dispersion in prices is substantially lower between Canada and the United States than almost anywhere else, including the OECD sample, 18.53 versus 31.58.

smaller intranationally. Within countries, distance accounts for close to half of overall dispersion and this is robust across the panels.

To summarize, the model has provided a useful conceptual framework with which to conduct a variance decomposition of long-run LOP deviations into the role of distance, borders, wages, retail productivity and a residual. The relative importance of the factors depends on the good and set of locations in a fashion that makes intuitive sense. Distance and borders loom large in general and wages differences (consistent with HBS) seem particularly important once the analysis moves outside the OECD (i.e., once comparisons involve countries at very different income levels). We turn now to the aggregate implications of our model for PPP.

5.2.3. *Variance decomposition of price levels*

Macroeconomic analysis, of course, takes place at a much more aggregated level than these micro-price data. It is natural to ask how the sources of international price variation differ at the aggregate level from what was documented in the previous section.

The most obvious consequence of aggregation is that it eliminates spatial variation in relative prices specific to individual goods. The magnitude of the variance reduction, however, is larger than one might have expected. As is evident in Table 5, the dispersion in price levels across locations is on the order of one-fourth to one-fifth as large as the mean level of dispersion at the level of individual goods and services.[8]

Two obvious sources of variation that would average out across goods are measurement error and trade costs. Classical measurement error is, by definition, independently distributed across goods. The fact that the residual variance, particularly for the cross-border pairs where measurement error is likely to be greater, falls from 15% to 0.5% (WORLD) is consistent with this view. The absolute and proportional contribution of borders and trade costs are also

[8]The averaging-out property of LOP deviations was first documented by Crucini *et al.* (2005) in the context of mostly EU capital cities over the period from 1975 to 1990 at five-year intervals.

Table 5. Accounting for long-run deviations from PPP.

	World		LDC		OECD		CAN–US	
	NB	B	NB	B	NB	B	NB	B
Price dispersion	3.53	15.89	4.53	15.48	3.14	10.07	3.33	5.15
	Absolute contribution of							
Border effect	—	0.12	—	0.18	—	0.23	—	0.18
Distance	0.82	1.01	0.28	1.53	0.85	1.95	0.93	1.26
Distribution sector	2.10	14.12	2.80	12.50	1.74	7.47	1.89	3.43
Service wages	0.28	14.55	0.31	8.78	0.18	1.35	0.16	3.69
Retail productivity	1.82	−0.43	2.49	3.72	1.57	6.13	1.73	−0.25
Residual	0.62	0.67	1.44	1.25	0.55	0.36	0.51	0.22
	Percentage contribution of							
Border effect	—	0.8	—	1.2	—	2.3	—	3.5
Distance	23.2	6.4	6.2	9.9	27.1	19.4	27.9	24.4
Distribution sector	59.4	88.8	61.8	80.8	55.5	74.2	56.7	66.7
Service wages	7.9	91.5	6.8	56.7	5.7	13.4	4.8	71.5
Retail productivity	51.4	−2.7	55.0	24.0	50.0	60.9	52.0	−4.8
Residual	17.5	4.2	31.7	8.1	17.3	3.6	15.3	4.2

Note: LDC stands for less developed countries, CAN–US stands for Canada–U.S., NB stands for no border, B stands for border.

mitigated by aggregation. This is also quite intuitive. Countries long-run trade imbalances are modest. Consequently, the high relative price of goods that a nation imports is counter-balanced by the low relative price of goods that it exports. Provided trade costs are not too asymmetric across goods across ledgers of the trade balance, they will tend to average out in the cross-section. Table 5 indicates that the absolute variance contribution of trade costs falls from a range of 5–15% for individual relative prices (LOP) toward a range of 1–2% for relative price levels (PPP).

Contrast this with the economic role of the distribution margin. By definition, the relative costs of distribution is location specific, not good specific. Table 5 shows that at that aggregate level, relative wages account for virtually the entire variance (91.5%) when all cross-border city pairs are included in the calculation. Note that the coefficient on w_{jk} in Eq. (10) can be estimated from a regression of log relative price levels on log relative wages. Such a regression produces a coefficient of 0.55 on wages and an R^2 of 0.85. According to the microeconomic model of distribution, the same coefficient can be estimated from the micro-price data simply by calculating the consumption-expenditure-weighted average of distribution shares, $\sum_i \omega_i \alpha_i$. And what is this sum? Exactly 0.55!

This implies that an important facet of macroeconomic analysis is the interaction of tastes and technology in determining the local or non-traded factor content of consumption expenditure. That is, tastes enter into the determine of expenditure shares, ω_i, and the patterns of tastes across goods may amplify or mitigate the role of the distribution share in accounting for PPP deviations. In modern data the covariance of the expenditure share and the distribution share is positive in the cross-section. Goods with relatively high distribution shares tend to account for a larger share of consumption expenditure than those with below average distribution shares. Thus, the expenditure-weighted distribution share is higher than the average distribution share across goods (0.55 versus 0.48).

The results for *intranational* city pairs provide an interesting contrast. As one would expect, labor mobility tends to eliminate the role of wages in accounting for deviations from PPP. To a first approximation, the variance shifts from wages to retail productivity. This seems reasonable because retailing involves significant time-to-build and an immobile factor (land), which limits arbitrage across locations. An evolving literature asks how big-box retailers such as Walmart may alter the distribution margin across locations. It is also important not to overstate the implications of the PPP analysis across cities within countries. The absolute dispersion of prices is relatively minor and this limits our ability to identify the contributions of different components with the same degree of accuracy as in the international case.

6. Discussion

Our competitive model completely abstracts from markups. There are two places where it seems natural to allow for markups over marginal cost. The first is at the retail level, a markup of retail prices over the unit cost of retailing (including both distribution and traded input costs) that differs across city pairs. A city may have a relatively high price level than we predict based on relative wage costs and relative traded input costs (i.e., $p_{jk} - \hat{\alpha}w_{jk} - q_{jk} = -z_{jk} > 0$) either because it has a relatively inefficient retail sector ($z_{jk} < 0$, perhaps due to poor public infrastructure) or because retailers have market power and choose to set different markups over marginal cost across cities. In the latter case, the $z_{jk} < 0$ term could reflect a relatively high markup in city j compared to k, not relative inefficiency in retail in city j compared to k. Arguably, cities with inefficient infrastructure may also tend to be those with less competitive retailing. Consider a very efficient big-box retailer such as Walmart in a U.S. suburb compared to an open market in the center of Istanbul. One would expect the average markup over marginal cost to fall upon Walmart's entry into the Istanbul market in the same fashion that Walmart has lowered retail prices in the United States over time. While this is plausible, our data are simply not up to the task of exploring these alternative interpretations of the retail productivity term and these issues are thus left to future work.

The second place a markup would naturally appear is between the factory gate price and the price the retailer pays for the traded input, q_{ijk}. Thus some of the variation in traded prices we attribute to borders, distance and a residual term could be due to markups that exporters charge to the various destination markets. Where such a markup over cost on imported goods gets allocated in our variance decomposition depends crucially on its covariance with other location-specific variables used in our regression framework. If the markup is not correlated with wages, distance or borders, it will be relegated to the residual term.

More problematic is the idea that markups of retail prices over factory gate prices are positively correlated with wages in the destination market since this is inconsistent with the orthogonality assumption used to estimate the distribution share. The notion that markups are increasing in the wage levels in the destination market was first theoretically developed in Alessandria (2004) and empirical tested by Alessandria and Kaboski (2011). They estimated a robust positive correlation between good-level U.S. export unit values and aggregate wage levels in the destination market. They attribute this correlation to costly search by consumers in retail markets. The implication of this line of reasoning for our work is that our regression coefficient would overestimate the distribution cost share based on a standard omitted regressor bias argument.[9]

Identification of markups, of course, is a challenge confronting many sub-fields of macroeconomics. The model that we develop and estimate is based on the premise that markets are perfectly competitive. The NIPA is constructed along these same lines in the sense that payments to labor and capital exhaust value added, there is no separate line item for markups over unit cost. An important task going forward is to consider how bargaining power and imperfect competition leads shares of payments to factors of production that exceed their shares in the production function. All that may be claimed at this point is that both our estimating approach and variance accounting of LOP and PPP deviations are consistent with the NIPA constructs.

7. Conclusion

The growth of international trade and financial integration has moved the fields of international trade and international finance ever closer. This is a healthy development, bringing together the microeconomic details of trade theory such as patterns of specialization and the extensive margin of trade with the central facets of macroeconomic theory, dynamic equilibrium concepts and expectation formation. The fact that trade focuses on absolute deviations from the LOP while finance focuses on relative deviations from PPP has been an impediment to progress. Recent efforts to expand the availability of large-scale micro-price panels allows absolute deviations from PPP to be traced back to LOP deviations as was done in this paper.

The amount of price dispersion at the good level is 3–5 times larger than at the aggregate, PPP level. The main cause of this

[9]That is, if an omitted regressor (markup) is positively correlated with an included regressor (wages), the coefficient on the included regressor (the distribution margin) is biased upward.

averaging out of deviations specific to the good is attributed to trade costs and a residual term. The residual term may involve markups specific to the good and bilateral city pair as well as measurement error. What remains at the PPP level is largely a wage effect consistent with the HBS theory, though how dominant this factor is depends on the set of countries studied. Retail productivities and trade costs remain substantial at the PPP level for OECD countries, while they are dwarfed by wage effects when all international cities are pooled, consistent with the impression given by Fig. 1.

Effectively, this means that theories intended to match relative prices both within the OECD and between the OECD and the rest of the world will need to include both a rich trade structure drawn from trade theory and a role for the distribution margin and markups. The importance of markups relative to real costs of wholesale and distribution remains an open question.

Acknowledgments

We especially thank Mary Amiti, Eric Bond, Paolo Pesenti and Robert Vigfusson for valuable comments and criticisms as well as participants at numerous conferences and seminars.

We gratefully acknowledge the financial support of the National Science Foundation (SES-1030164).

References

Alessandria, George, 2004. International deviations from the law of one price: the role of search frictions and market share. *Int. Econ. Rev.* 45 (4), 1263–1291.

Alessandria, George, Kaboski, Joseph, 2011. Pricing-to-market and the failure of absolute PPP. *Am. Econ. J. Macroecon.* 3 (1), 91–127.

Balassa, Bela, 1964. The purchasing power parity doctrine: a reappraisal. *J. Polit. Econ.* 72, 584–596.

Burstein, Ariel, Neves, Joao, Rebelo, Sergio, 2003. Distribution costs and real exchange rate dynamics during exchange-rate based stabilizations. *J. Monet. Econ.* 50 (6), 1189–1214.

Burstein, Ariel, Eichenbaum, Martin, Rebelo, Sergio, 2005. Large devaluations and the real exchange rate. *J. Polit. Econ.* 113 (4), 742–784.

Burstein, Ariel, Eichenbaum, Martin, Rebelo, Sergio, 2007. Modeling exchange rate passthrough after large devaluations. *J. Monet. Econ.* 54 (2), 346–368.

Crucini, Mario J., Landry, Anthony, 2012. Accounting for real exchange rates using micro-data. Vanderbilt University, National Bureau of Economic Research, Working Paper No. 17812.

Crucini, Mario J., Telmer, Chris I., Zachariadis, Marios, 2005. Understanding European real exchange rates. *Am. Econ. Rev.* 95 (3), 724–738.

Crucini, Mario J., Telmer, Chris I., 2012. Microeconomic sources of real exchange rate variation. National Bureau of Economic Research, Working Paper No. 17978.

Crucini, Mario J., Yilmazkuday, Hakan, 2009. A model of international cities: implications for real exchange rates NBER Working Paper No. 14834.

Engel, Charles, 1999. Accounting for US real exchange rates. *J. Polit. Econ.* 107 (3), 507–538.

Engel, Charles, Rogers, John H., 1996. How wide is the border? *Am. Econ. Rev.* 86 (5), 1112–1125.

Harrod, Roy.F., 1933. *International Economics.* James Nisbet and Cambridge University Press, London.

Hummels, David, 2001. Toward a Geography of Trade Costs. Unpublished manuscript.

Kennedy, Peter, 2003. *A Guide to Econometrics.* MIT Press, Cambridge, MA.

Samuelson, Paul, 1964. Theoretical notes on trade problems. *Rev. Econ. Stat.* 46, 145–154.

Chapter 4

Persistence in Law of One Price Deviations: Evidence from Micro-Data*

Mario J. Crucini

Department of Economics, Vanderbilt University, Nashville, TN, USA
mario.j.crucini@vanderbilt.edu

and

Mototsugu Shintani

Department of Economics, Vanderbilt University, Nashville, TN, USA and Institute for Monetary and Economic Studies, Bank of Japan, Tokyo, Japan
mototsugu.shintani@vanderbilt.edu

Abstract. Using an extensive micro-price panel, we find a positive cross-sectional relationship between LOP persistence and the distribution margin, which we measure using sectoral U.S. data, as suggested by the classical dichotomy. The median level of persistence (across goods) is low, and there is no evidence of a border effect: the half-life of a deviation is about 19 months across OECD cities and just 1 month lower across cities in the U.S. Aggregating our micro-data using a variety of weighting methods shows PPP persistence to be in the range of 1–2 years, over the 1990–2005 period. These results challenge three widely held views: (i) the

*This chapter originally appeared in *Journal of Monetary Economics*, 2008, **55**(3), 629–644.

classical dichotomy is irrelevant; (ii) high persistence is a robust feature of aggregate real exchange rates; and (iii) border crossings necessarily generate greater real exchange rate persistence.

Keywords: Real exchange rates; Purchasing power parity; Law of one price; Dynamic panel

1. Introduction

Much of what is known about real exchange rates originates from studies that use aggregate price indices, such as the consumer price index. After decades of scrutiny, the consensus is that aggregate real exchange rates are stationary, but very persistent, with estimated half-lives in the range of 3–5 years. Three authoritative studies that span this range are: Choi *et al.* (2006) who focus on 21 OECD countries over the period 1973–1998 and arrive at a point estimate of 3.0 years; Frankel and Rose (1996) who utilize a panel of 150 countries over the period 1948–1992 and estimate the half-life to be about 4 years; and Murray and Papell (2005) who conduct bias-corrections using similar data and arrive at a point estimate of 4.6 years.

The conventional wisdom is that this level of persistence is due to the fact that many goods in the consumption basket are not traded, as emphasized by the two-sector open economy macroeconomic models developed by Salter (1959) and Swan (1960). As the reasoning goes, since the forces of arbitrage are weak or indirect among non-traded goods, volatile and persistent real exchange rates are less puzzling, if not entirely expected.

Actual evidence on the implications of the classical dichotomy for real exchange rate persistence, however, is both limited and decidedly mixed. Using CPI sub-indices partitioned into traded and non-traded components, Engel (1999) finds real exchange rate variability to be quite similar across the two. Betts and Kehoe (2006) find modest differences by focusing carefully on pairs of nations that engage extensively in trade with each other. An emerging literature looks directly at sub-indices of the CPI and producer price indices and finds lower half-lives for traded goods than non-traded goods. Unfortunately these estimates tend to be imprecise (Kim, 2004; Kim and Ogaki, 2004).

In response to these empirical findings, the pendulum has swung sharply in the direction of treating all goods alike. The *New Open Economy Macroeconomics* paradigm developed by Obstfeld and Rogoff (1995) and Svennsson and van Wijnbergen (1989) has all goods sharing a common markup and the same degree of nominal price stickiness in either the buyer's or the seller's currency. Chari *et al.* (2002) show that this approach fails to deliver the level of volatility and persistence observed in the aggregate real exchange rate even when a generous length of price non-adjustment with time-dependent pricing is assumed at the outset.

The goal of this paper is to use a novel data set on local currency prices of individual retail goods and services in major cities to shed new light on these two paradigms in open economy macroeconomics. Our data span all major categories of private consumption with the exception of medical services. Most countries of the world are represented and multiple cities are sampled in some countries, notably the United States. The sample is annual from 1990 to 2005. These international retail price surveys, conducted by the Economist Intelligence Unit (EIU), are the most comprehensive in existence in terms of coverage of goods, locations and time periods. Moreover, the intent of the survey is to develop cost of living comparisons, so the goods and services are reasonably comparable across cities as the law of one price (LOP) and purchasing power parity (PPP) propositions require.

We have three sets of results, the first relating to the persistence of LOP deviations for the median good in our cross-section, the second relating to differences in persistence across goods and the third relating to persistence in aggregate real exchange rates constructed from the micro-price data. For each retail item, we estimate a good-specific persistence parameter by pooling cities belonging to one of the following groups: OECD countries, non-OECD countries (referred to below as LDCs) and the United States.

The half-life of LOP deviations for the median good is 19 months for the OECD cities, 12 months for the LDC cities and 18 months for the U.S. cities. The similarity of the OECD and U.S. estimates indicates the absence of a border effect in persistence.

Following the logic of the classical dichotomy we partition items into two categories and find that non-traded goods have more persistence than traded goods in all three sets of locations. The median half-life for non-traded goods is 24 months in both the OECD and U.S. panels, 6 months higher than the median for traded goods. For LDC locations the difference in the medians across categories is just 2 months. As a check on the common practice of labelling consumption categories as traded and non-traded and estimating persistence across them, we also compute means under categorical classification (e.g., treat all food items as traded and all housing items as non-traded); this has no significant impact on the ability to distinguish the two classes of goods. We refer to this as *categorization bias* and conclude that it has a minor effect.

Despite this success for the classical dichotomy, there exists considerable overlap in the persistence distributions for traded and non-traded goods. Approximately 25% of traded goods have persistence levels above the median for the non-traded goods (the reverse is also true). We explore the ability of *compositional bias*, the notion that individual retail goods contain different proportions of non-traded and traded inputs, to account for this feature of the data. Extending the work of Crucini *et al.* (2005), we utilize highly disaggregated U.S. NIPA data on retail and manufacturing gross output along with input–output data to measure sectoral *distribution margins*. These margins encompass all real costs associated with the movement of goods and services from the producer to the consumer plus markups over marginal cost. Moving from a service which uses no measurable traded inputs in its production (e.g., baby-sitting services) to a good with the lowest distribution margin in our data (e.g., automobiles, 0.17), persistence drops from 27 to 14 months. Extrapolating outside the range of our data, to a purely traded good with no distribution margin, the half-life is predicted to drop an additional 1.5 months, to about 1 year.

The cross-border results on LOP persistence invite comparisons to international studies that focus on individual goods. Goldberg and Verboven (2005) estimate half-lives of relative price deviations for automobiles in the range of 16–19 months; they focus on Europe.

For OECD cities, we estimate the median half-life of LOP deviations for automobiles at 14 months. Cumby (1996) finds the half-life of international price deviations in Big Mac hamburgers to be about 12 months. The LOP for ground beef has a half-life of 12 months when we pool all international locations. What distinguishes our results from existing micro-studies is the breadth of the cross-section, leading to implications for aggregate real exchange rate persistence.

We emulate the aggregation methods used by national statistical agencies to the extent possible given data limitations. Since we do not have access to the micro-data that national statistical agencies use in construction of the CPI, our consistency checks are indirect. First, the EIU and the BLS surveys are compared in terms of the sampling intensities across major consumption categories. The two surveys match up closely with the exception of medical services, which are virtually non-existent in the EIU cross-section.[1] Both surveys include more individual items the higher the expenditure share of the category in question.

As a second check, the micro-data are aggregated using expenditure shares and persistence estimates of our constructed real exchange rates are compared to those obtained using official CPI data. For international locations, the two yield virtually identical persistence. Simply put, in terms of sample composition or in terms of implications for aggregate persistence, our micro-data tell basically the same story as the official data.

What is interesting is that the official CPI data indicate half-lives of 14 months for the OECD and 16 months for the LDC, well below the consensus range of half-lives of 36–60 months. Thus persistence of aggregate real exchange rates over the period 1990–2005 is lower than over the entire post-Bretton Woods period, which has been the focus of the existing literature. Our finding of the fast international price adjustment in recent years seems to be in line with the evidence

[1]Given that many countries deliver medicine and education almost exclusively through the public sector, price data for these sectors are often sparse and when they exist, they do not typically correspond to market determined prices.

of very frequent price changes in the United States reported in Bils and Klenow (2004) as well as in some other countries.[2]

The fact that the persistence of LOP deviations for the median good matches closely with aggregate real exchange rate persistence using official CPI data (which in turn match persistence in real exchange rates constructed from the micro-data) is a point of contrast with a recent finding by Imbs *et al.* (2005). They found aggregate real exchange rates across 10 European countries plus the United States exhibited much higher persistence than the median level of persistence across 19 sub-indices of the CPI index. Given that we fail to find aggregation bias in our international data, but do find it within the U.S., our results present a challenge to their claim that aggregation bias is a general answer to the PPP puzzle.

It is important to note that the lack of a border effect in persistence is entirely consistent with Engel and Rogers (1996) finding of a positive border effect in the time series variance of real exchange rates. Our results suggest that their border effect is primarily to be found in the innovation variance and not the transitional dynamics (i.e., persistence coefficients).

2. The Data

The source of our retail price data is the EIU's *Worldwide Cost of Living Survey.*[3] To our knowledge this is the most extensive ongoing survey of retail prices conducted by a single organization on a global scale. Given our focus, a significant advantage over other price surveys that have similar coverage of goods is the geographic breadth of locations and its annual frequency. Most existing micro-price surveys are so infrequent as to render them useless for addressing time series issues. In terms of locations, most aggregative studies

[2]For example, Ahlin and Shintani (2007) report that the price change frequencies were even higher during the high inflation period in Mexico.

[3]The target market for the data source is corporate human resource managers who use it to help determine compensation levels of their employees residing in different cities of the world. While the goods and services reflect this objective to some extent, the sample is extensive enough to overlap significantly with what appears in a typical urban consumption basket.

have focused on the U.S. real exchange rate vis-à-vis a few other large industrialized countries.

The survey includes 123 cities and spans 79 countries. The maximum number of goods and services priced in any given year is 301. When estimating international persistence, one city from each country is chosen. When estimating intranational persistence, U.S. cities are used due to the paucity of within country pairs elsewhere in the survey.[4] The available sample runs from 1990 to 2005.

The dynamic panel estimation pools data across locations and time, not goods. Since the raw data contain a number of missing observations, balanced panels are constructed by selecting goods and locations in the following way. First, if a country undergoes a currency reform, it is eliminated from the sample.[5] Second, for each good, cities that present less than a full complement of time series data are removed from the panel for that particular good. In selecting the city to use when more than one city is available in a country we pick the city that comes first alphabetically, among cities with available data for that good and country. Table 1 presents the 90 cities, located in 63 countries, that survive the selection criterion. The number of goods for which a particular city is used in the panel estimation is noted in parentheses next to the city name.

Supplemental data come from four additional sources. The first two provide consumption expenditure weights used to aggregate the micro-price data. National expenditure weights come from the International Comparison Project. For the 23 OECD countries, the 1990 expenditure weights which divide consumption into 78 expenditure categories are used. For 19 LDC countries, the 1996 weights which divide consumption into 26 expenditure categories are used. Bureau of Labor Statistics consumption expenditure shares are used for the intranational, U.S., analysis. These are *city-level* expenditure weights. For the 13 cities in the U.S. micro-sample, the

[4]The EIU surveys 16 U.S. cities, the next largest number of cities surveyed equals 5 in Australia, China and Germany.

[5]The excluded countries are: Argentina, Brazil, Ecuador, Mexico, Peru, Poland, Russia, and Uruguay.

Table 1. Locations.

Asia	Tripoli, Libya (51)	Stockholm, Sweden (252)[a]
Bahrain, Bahrain (230)[b]	Casa Blanca, Morocco (199)[b]	Geneva, Switzerland (262)[a]
Dhaka, Bangladesh (133)	Lagos, Nigeria (204)	Zurich, Switzerland (6)[a]
Beijing, China (144)	Dakar, Senegal (197)[b]	Istanbul, Turkey (253)[a]
Hong Kong, Hong Kong (242)[b]	Johannesburg, South Africa (253)	London, UK (261)[a]
New Delhi, India (57)	Tunis, Tunisia (186)[b]	Belgrade, Yugoslavia (105)
Mumbai, India (146)	Harare, Zimbabwe (200)	
Jakarta, Indonesia (183)[b]		*Oceania*
Tehran, Iran (181)	*Europe*	Adelaide, Australia (251)[a]
Tel Aviv, Israel (255)[b]	Vienna, Austria (263)[a]	Brisbane, Australia (12)[a]
Osaka Kobe, Japan (244)[a]	Brussels, Belgium (263)[a]	Melbourne, Australia (2)[a]
Tokyo, Japan (7)[a]	Prague, Czech (188)	Perth, Australia (2)[a]
Amman, Jordan (137)	Copenhagen, Denmark (264)[a]	Sydney, Australia (2)[a]
Seoul, Korea (167)	Helsinki, Finland (255)[a]	Auckland, NZ (257)[a]
Kuala Lumpur, Malaysia (244)	Lyon, France (261)[a]	Wellington, NZ (5)[a]
Karachi, Pakistan (192)[b]	Paris, France (7)[a]	*United States**
Manila, Philippines (211)[b]	Berlin, Germany (265)[a]	Atlanta (248)
Al Khobar, Saudi Arabia (203)	Dusseldorf, Germany (5)[a]	Boston (257)
Jeddah, Saudi Arabia (17)	Athens, Greece (247)[a]	Chicago (251)
Singapore, Singapore (256)[b]	Budapest, Hungary (255)[b]	Cleveland (249)
Colombo, Sri Lanka (212)[b]	Dublin, Ireland (248)[a]	Detroit (260)
Taipei, Taiwan (215)	Milan, Italy (263)[a]	Houston (250)
Bangkok, Thailand (257)[b]	Rome, Italy (5)[a]	Los Angeles (248)
Abu Dhabi, UAE (238)	Luxembourg, Luxembourg (260)[a]	Miami (253)
Dubai, UAE (11)	Amsterdam, Netherlands (260)[a]	New York (234)
Africa	Oslo, Norway (233)[a]	Pittsburgh (235)
Abidjan, Côte d'Ivoire (242)[b]	Lisbon, Portugal (267)[a]	San Francisco (230)
Cairo, Egypt (197)[b]	Bucharest, Romania (1)	Seattle (252)
Nairobi, Kenya (233)[b]	Barcelona, Spain (268)[a]	Washington DC (255)

Table 1. (*Continued*)

North America	Cleveland, USA (3)[a]	*South America*
Calgary, Canada (250)[a]	New York, USA (1)[a]	Santiago, Chile (257)[b]
Montreal, Canada (15)[a]		Bogota, Columbia (235)
Toronto, Canada (3)[a]	*Central America*	Asuncion, Paraguay (250)
Atlanta, USA (249)[a]	San Jose, Costa Rica (230)	Caracas, Venezuela (238)[b]
Boston, USA (11)[a]	Guatemala City, Guatemala (221)	
Chicago, USA (5)[a]	Panama City, Panama (242)[b]	

Notes: Number in parentheses are the number of goods in the analysis for which that city is used. Cities included in United States group (*) are used only for the intranational analysis.
[a]City belongs to OECD group.
[b]Selected LDCs for CPI construction.

1994 weights which divide consumption into 210 ELI (Entry Level Items) are used.[6]

In each case, the individual goods in the EIU micro-sample are placed into consumption categories at the level of aggregation of the available consumption expenditure weights. Under CPI weighting, each price gets a weight $\omega_{c,j}/N_c$, where $\omega_{c,j}$ is the expenditure weight for consumption category c in location j and N_c is the number of surveyed prices in that category.

The other two sources of data are the U.S. NIPA and the U.S. input–output tables. These sources are used to construct the distribution margin, intended to measure the difference between what final consumers pay and what producers receive. The NIPA data by personal consumption expenditure category record the expenditure of final consumers at final purchaser prices and at producer prices. The difference between these valuations is transportation cost plus wholesale and retail margins (inclusive of real costs of distribution,

[6]We thank Randy Verbrugge at the BLS for providing these data.

markups and taxes).[7] For service items, the NIPA record both the purchaser value and the producer value at purchaser prices. This occurs because transactions in these sectors take place at arms length between producers and final consumers. For example, viewed from these NIPA data, a doctor is the producer of both medical goods and medical services. To overcome this deficiency, input–output matrices are used to back-out the cost share of non-traded inputs for service items.

Table 2 reports summary information about our sample of goods and distribution margins. The table is arranged according to the broad classifications of goods in the U.S. CPI. There are seven major headings: food and beverages, housing, apparel and upkeep, transportation, medical care, entertainment and other goods and services. For each major heading the table reports the number of EIU goods, the survey sampling intensity (for both the EIU and BLS), the BLS consumption expenditure weights (these are the national expenditure weights used to construct the U.S. CPI) and the distribution share.

Many of the goods in the EIU sample are priced in two types of retail outlets. The column labelled "Prices EIU" counts both while the column sample proportions avoids double counting of goods (this is also true of BLS numbers to which they are being compared). Most categories of goods have similar sampling intensities across the EIU and BLS. Two exceptions are food and beverages and medical services. Food and beverages items make up about 40% of the EIU micro-sample, compared to about one quarter of the BLS sample. Thus, the EIU over-samples this category relative to the BLS. Medical services are under-represented in the EIU, possibly due to the fact that in many countries they are publicly provided. The remaining categories have similar sampling patterns across the two surveys.

[7]See also, Burstein *et al.* (2003) who use aggregative measures of distribution cost to account for aggregate real exchange rate movements in Argentina.

Table 2. Prices surveyed and distribution margins.

BLS category	Prices EIU	Sample proportion EIU	Sample proportion BLS	CPI Weight	Distribution share Mean	Distribution share Low	Distribution share High
Food and beverages	125	0.41	0.24	0.20	0.39	0.22	0.75
Housing	48	0.22	0.26	0.39	0.72	0.34	1.00
Apparel and upkeep	32	0.10	0.16	0.06	0.52	0.52	0.59
Transportation	20	0.13	0.11	0.19	0.55	0.17	0.94
Medical care	2	0.01	0.06	0.06	0.36	N.a.	N.a.
Entertainment	11	0.07	0.09	0.04	0.52	0.32	0.75
Other goods and services	17	0.06	0.07	0.07	0.46	0.37	0.85

Notes: Prices are the number of items priced in the EIU survey, including cases in which the same good is priced in two outlets. Sample proportions are the fractions of items by category, here we eliminate multiple outlets (i.e., a good price in two types of retail outlets is counted only once). Distribution share is computed as described in the text. Mean is weighted by number of items in the price survey assigned to a particular distribution share, low and high are ranges of sectoral distribution shares in the consumption category.

The more novel information in the table are the distribution shares. When the distribution share is 0 or 1, the good is traded or non-traded in the usual sense of the classical dichotomy. Numbers between these extremes reflect the role of distribution costs in influencing the difference between the producer price and the purchaser price. As is obvious from the table, goods tend to fall on a continuum rather than neatly into dichotomous bins. The housing category comes closest to reaching the upper bound of a non-traded good (0.72). Other categories have distribution margins in the neighborhood of 0.36–0.55, in a range of ambiguity relative to the classical dichotomy.

The broad averages also obscure variation at lower levels of aggregation. Food and beverages has a mean share of 0.39, but food away from home has a distribution share of 0.75 due to the importance of non-traded inputs and possibly higher markups, while fish has a distribution share of only 0.22. Housing contains both housekeeping supplies with a distribution share of 0.34 and housekeeping services with a share of 1.0. These measures point to the practical value of thinking of individual retail goods as composites of traded and local inputs with the relative importance of the inputs differing across goods. We will exploit this variation at the micro-level to gauge the role of *compositional bias* in LOP persistence.

3. Methodology

We take it as self-evident that the goal of applied real exchange rate research is to improve our understanding of LOP deviations at the level of individual goods and services analogous to how the literature on the frequency of micro-price adjustment fits into the closed economy macroeconomics literature. In this section we lay out a conceptual framework taking us from the aggregate real exchange rate all the way down to individual LOP deviations that are the focus of our study.

The standard empirical approach to the classical dichotomy is built upon Cobb–Douglas preferences over non-traded and traded consumption, giving rise to the ideal consumption deflator for location j:

$$P_{j,t} = W_{j,t}^{\gamma} T_{j,t}^{1-\gamma}, \tag{1}$$

where $W_{j,t}$ ($T_{j,t}$) is the domestic currency price index for non-traded (traded) goods. Taking logarithms of both sides and subtracting from the counterpart in location k (after conversion to location j's currency unit) defines the bilateral CPI real exchange rate in terms of the real exchange rates of non-traded and traded goods:

$$q_{jk,t} = \gamma w_{jk,t} + (1-\gamma) t_{jk,t}, \tag{2}$$

where $q_{jk,t} \equiv \log(S_{jk,t} P_{j,t}/P_{k,t})$, $S_{jk,t}$ is the nominal exchange rate for the bilateral pair j and k, and $w_{jk,t}$ and $t_{jk,t}$ are the real exchange rates for non-traded and traded goods across the same two locations. Throughout, lower case variables are logarithms of common currency *relative* prices.

There are two practical reasons why this common approach may be poorly suited to address the classical dichotomy. The first is that national statistical agencies do not create consumption categories with the intent of achieving a division of the commodity space into traded and non-traded goods. Suppose we choose the non-traded category to be household services and the traded category to be food. In the BLS classification, food includes both meals at home and food away from home. Household services include both the rental costs of dwellings and utilities. In other words, broad aggregates inevitably mix items at different ends of the tradeability continuum.

To be more concrete, let $\alpha > \frac{1}{2}$ be the expenditure share of rental of dwelling in household services (so the non-traded category is dominated by non-traded goods). Suppose, also for expositional convenience, that food is the mirror image of household services in the sense that α is the share of traded goods in the food category. The aggregate real exchange rate expressed in terms of these four real exchange rates (dropping the bilateral location subscript) is:

$$q_t = \gamma[\alpha r_t + (1-\alpha)u_t] + (1-\gamma)[(1-\alpha)a_t + \alpha f_t], \tag{3}$$

where r_t is the international relative price for rental of dwellings, u_t, a_t, f_t, are the relative prices of utilities, food away from home and food at home. Clearly the two components in square braces fail to capture the relative prices we hope to isolate from each other.

In theory, the classical dichotomy is recovered by appropriate aggregation of the sub-indices:

$$q_t = [\alpha\gamma r_t + (1-\gamma)(1-\alpha)a_t] + [\gamma(1-\alpha)u_t + (1-\gamma)\alpha f_t]. \tag{4}$$

In practice, the data required to achieve ideal aggregation are not publicly available. We refer to the practice of placing items into the wrong bins as *categorization bias.* We saw in Table 2, many examples of this bias at the top level of CPI aggregation.

The second challenge is that each, individual, retail good is a composite of traded inputs and non-traded inputs. This drives the classical dichotomy down to the micro-level and renders all final goods non-traded (Ethier, 1982; Sanyal and Jones, 1982). This concept has recently been applied with some success by Crucini *et al.* (2005) to explain geographic price dispersion across European cities. At the level of an individual good i, the LOP deviation becomes

$$q_{i,jk,t} = \alpha_i w_{jk,t} + (1 - \alpha_i) t_{i,jk,t}, \tag{5}$$

where $w_{jk,t}$ represents the relative cost of non-traded inputs faced by retailers in locations j and k, common to all goods. $t_{i,jk,t}$ is the relative price of the individual traded input across the same bilateral pair. The expectation is that the persistence and unconditional variability of $w_{jk,t}$ exceeds that of $t_{i,jk,t}$ due to the weaker forces of arbitrage at work on the non-traded component. This is what we refer to as *compositional bias*.[8]

This problem is potentially not solvable even with micro-data because it requires the researcher to observe input choices and input prices at the level of individual products and services. Our strategy is to use the distribution margin — the gap between retail and producer prices to proxy for α_i — thereby assigning distribution costs to the non-traded component, $w_{jk,t}$. By this logic, the higher the distribution share the more persistent we expect the deviation from the LOP for the retail item to be.

Before turning to the statistical model, it is useful to examine some features of the price distributions. Figure 1 presents kernel density estimates of $q_{i,jk,t}$ in 2005 separately for traded and non-traded goods (the classical dichotomy) for all available cross-border pairs (OECD and LDC cities) and for bilateral U.S. city pairs. We see a wide support for these price distributions, indicative of significant cross-sectional variation in deviations from the LOP. We also see that the least dispersed prices are the traded goods across U.S. cities and the most dispersed prices are non-traded goods across cities separated by a border. Somewhat surprising is the observation that traded goods across the international pairs have more price dispersion than do non-traded goods across U.S. cities. This suggests

[8]In an interesting recent paper, Parsley and Wei (2007) deconstruct the Big Mac using a subset of data from the EIU and find that non-traded inputs into Big Mac production have more persistence than traded inputs (ingredients).

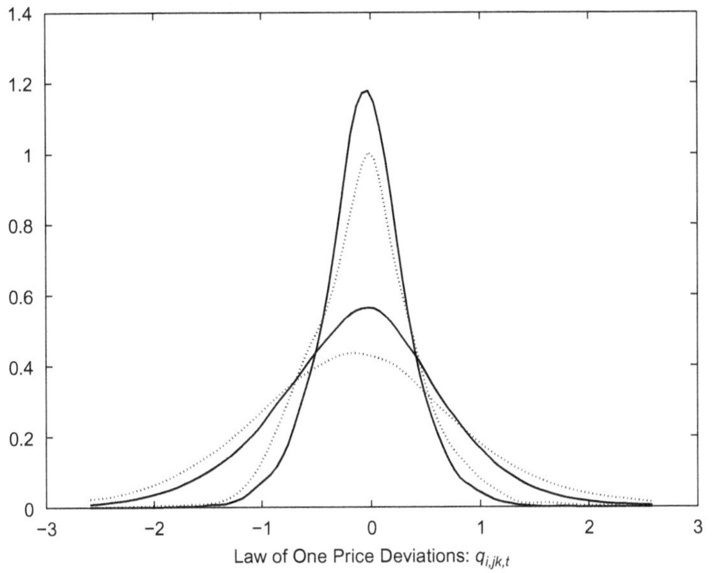

Fig. 1. Kernel density estimates of Law of One Price Deviations in 2005. Ordered from least dispersed to most dispersed: U.S. traded goods, U.S. non-traded goods, international traded goods and international traded goods.

an interaction between tradeability and location in shaping price dispersion.

What a price distribution at a point in time cannot tell us is how much of the observed price dispersion is due to long-run deviations from the LOP and how much is due to the lingering effects of past shocks.

To accomplish this we estimate persistence of LOP deviations specific to good i, pooling all cities indexed by j and k, belonging to a particular group of locations (OECD, LDC or U.S. cities). Following much of the existing PPP literature we estimate a first-order autoregressive model:

$$q_{i,jk,t} = \eta_{i,jk} + \rho_i q_{i,jk,t-1} + v_{i,jk,t}, \tag{6}$$

where $\eta_{i,jk}$ is the time-invariant individual city-pair-specific effect, assumed to have variance σ_η^2. Provided $|\rho_i| < 1, q_{i,jk} = \eta_{i,jk}/(1 - \rho_i)$ may be viewed as the steady-state level of $q_{i,jk,t}$ in the sense that it represents the limit of the sample mean of $q_{i,jk,t}$ conditional on $\eta_{i,jk}$.

We say that good i exhibits *absolute price convergence* if $\eta_{i,jk} = 0$ for all j, k. We use the term *conditional price convergence* to refer to a situation in which the deviations persist in the long-run, $\sigma_{\eta}^2 > 0$. We assume the $v_{i,jk,t}$ have mean zero conditional on $\eta_{i,jk}$ and lagged $q_{i,jk,t}$'s and variance σ_v^2.

Thus, the price distribution at a point in time is the convolution of long-run deviations, the current period shock and the transitory effects of shocks occurring in the past (assuming $\rho_i \neq 0$). Since we have absolute price data, the statistical model allows us to parse the variance into these three components. In contrast, most of the existing literature uses index numbers and is only able to parse the variance into the last two components since absolute price levels are necessary to quantify the role of $\eta_{i,jk}$ (this is why the constant term in the PPP literature is viewed as a nuisance parameter).

4. Results

4.1. *Testing for unit roots*

We conduct tests of the unit root null good-by-good, pooling all bilateral city pairs. Since we have far more bilateral pairs than time periods, we employ a unit root test for short panels developed by Harris and Tzavalis (1999). The test statistics are based on the least squares dummy variable (LSDV) estimator of ρ_i in (6) and converge to a standard normal distribution under the null hypothesis of a unit root, as the cross-sectional dimension N (i.e., number of city pairs) grows to infinity with fixed T (i.e., number of years).

Panel A of Table 3 summarizes the results. In the two international panels, we are able to reject the unit root null for virtually every good. Interestingly, for the OECD, the two goods for which we are unable to reject the unit root null are both labor services: the average cost of labor per hour and hourly wages paid to a babysitter. Evidence is only mildly weaker for U.S. cities, likely due to the availability of fewer bilateral locations to estimate the good-specific persistence level.

Table 3. Tests for unit roots and absolute price convergence.

Significance level	OECD	LDC	U.S.
	Panel A: Unit root rejection frequencies		
10%	0.97	0.99	0.88
5%	0.97	0.99	0.86
1%	0.97	0.99	0.83
	Panel B: Absolute convergence rejection frequencies		
10%	0.93	0.92	0.76
5%	0.90	0.87	0.73
1%	0.75	0.71	0.70
Number of goods	269	268	256
Number of city pairs	225	393	71

Notes: Panel A reports the proportion of goods for which the null hypothesis of unit root is rejected using the panel unit root test of Harris and Tzavalis (1999) using the LSDV estimator. Panel B reports the proportion of goods for which the null hypothesis of no individual effects is rejected using the test based on the distance between GMM objective functions evaluated at estimates under both conditional and absolute convergence.

In summary, overwhelming support is found for the hypothesis that when a disturbance alters the relative price of a good from its location-specific mean, the deviations are temporary, not permanent. This conclusion holds both within and across countries.

4.2. *Absolute versus conditional price convergence*

Having established that relative prices are indeed stationary, good-by-good, and with absolute price data in hand, we are now in a position to consider the alternatives of absolute and conditional price convergence. We employ Arellano and Bond's (1991) generalized method of moments (GMM) estimator.[9]

[9]To allow for conditional convergence, one may employ the LSDV estimator using the dummy variable to capture $\eta_{i,jk}$. The LSDV estimator, however, does not provide a consistent estimator when time dimension T is small and fixed. In contrast, our panel unit root test based on LSDV estimator works with fixed T since the test statistics are corrected for asymptotic bias.

The two-step GMM estimator of ρ_i is based upon the first difference transformation of (6)

$$q_{i,jk,t} - q_{i,jk,t-1} = \rho_i(q_{i,jk,t-1} - q_{i,jk,t-2}) + (v_{i,jk,t} - v_{i,jk,t-1}) \quad \text{for } t = 3, \ldots, T \qquad (7)$$

with instruments selected from the following orthogonality conditions:

$$E[q_{i,jk,s}(v_{i,jk,t} - v_{i,jk,t-1})] = 0 \quad \text{for} \quad s = 1, \ldots, t-2 \quad \text{and} \quad t = 3, \ldots, T. \qquad (8)$$

This choice of instruments, originally proposed by Holtz-Eakin *et al.* (1988) and Arellano and Bond (1991), is known to provide a consistent estimator for fixed T and large N under fairly general assumptions.[10]

The GMM estimator for the dynamic panel model based on the moment conditions (8) is valid under price convergence to any long-run level, whether it is characterized by absolute or conditional price convergence. However, in the case of absolute price convergence, the lack of individual effect, or $\eta_{i,jk} = 0$, in (6) provides $T-1$ additional valid moment conditions $E[q_{i,jkt}v_{i,jk,t-1}] = 0$ for $t = 2, \ldots, T$ (Holtz-Eakin, 1988). This introduces another GMM estimator that incorporates the new moment conditions in addition to those listed as Eq. (8) to estimate persistence under the null of absolute convergence. The distance between the GMM objective functions using these two alternative GMM estimates provides the inputs necessary to test the absolute price convergence hypothesis.[11]

The lower panel of Table 3 reports the results. We reject the absolute price convergence hypothesis in the international context for 75% of the goods at the 1% level of significance. The rejection frequencies are similar across groups of locations. Since physical commodities and services are not traded in a frictionless environment, rejection of

[10]We also follow Arellano and Bond (1991) for the choice of a weighting matrix in the first-step of the GMM estimation.

[11]The details of this test are provided in the Crucini and Shintani (2006).

absolute convergence is not too surprising. Based on these findings, the remainder of our analysis allows for long-run deviations from the LOP.

4.3. *Persistence of LOP deviations*

Three issues are of interest relating to the rate at which international relative prices move back to their steady-state levels following a "shock." The first is the level of persistence of the median good in each group of locations. The second is the issue of differences in persistence levels across goods in each group. The third is the relationship between LOP persistence and PPP persistence.

4.3.1. *The median good*

Table 4 presents summary statistics on LOP persistence. We see, first of all, that the persistence of the median good ranges from 0.51 to 0.65 across the three groups of locations. These values correspond to a half-life range of 12–19 months, well below the lower bound of the 36–60 month consensus range for PPP. Relative prices adjust quickest across the LDC cities, where the median half-life is 12 months. The latter finding is consistent with the view that greater volatility of nominal exchange rates and higher inflation rates give rise to faster price adjustment in LDC countries.[12] The finding that persistence is comparable across U.S. cities to what we see across OECD cities is striking as it suggests the absence of a border effect in persistence.

4.3.2. *Traded goods, non-traded goods and distribution margins*

Figure 2 presents kernel estimates of the distributions of ρ_i, organized by group of locations and according to the classical dichotomy of traded and non-traded goods. Each column is a group of locations within the OECD at the left and the U.S. cities at the right. The

[12]This faster adjustment in LDCs was found in the cross country study of PPP by Cheung and Lai (2000).

Table 4. Persistence of LOP deviations.

	OECD	LDC	U.S.
	Panel A: Half-life (months)		
All goods	19	12	18
Non-traded goods	24	14	24
Traded goods	18	12	17
	Panel B: Persistence estimates with standard errors in parentheses		
All goods	0.65 (0.006)	0.51 (0.006)	0.63(0.004)
Non-traded goods	0.71 (0.004)	0.56 (0.005)	0.71(0.004)
Traded goods	0.63 (0.006)	0.49 (0.006)	0.61(0.004)
	Panel C: Number of estimates (goods)		
All goods	269	268	256
Non-traded goods	59	58	53
Traded goods	210	210	203
	Panel D: Median number of city pairs		
All goods	231	435	78
Non-traded goods	231	465	78
Traded goods	231	406	78

Notes: All of the statistics are medians of the distribution (across goods) of the estimates with the exception of the number of goods, which refers to the number of estimated persistence parameters. The latter is also the number of goods over which the medians are computed. The rows "all goods" refer to median taken across all the data, while the rows "traded goods" and "non-traded goods" refer to medians taken only across goods of that type. Categorization of observations into traded and non-traded is available at: http://www.vanderbilt.edu/Econ/faculty/Crucini/home.html.

first row of figures shows the distribution of persistence estimates for all goods, the next two rows are those of the classical dichotomous categories referred to as traded and non-traded. Non-traded items include labor services, such as haircuts and the service flow from land and buildings, such as the rental price of a furnished apartment. The vertical line in each chart is the median of the distribution.

While the differences across groups of locations are noteworthy, the differences across individual goods are extraordinary. The first and third quartiles of parameter estimates for the OECD pairs are 0.55 and 0.73, respectively. Since our standard errors are typically below 0.02, one cannot ascribe much of this heterogeneity to sampling

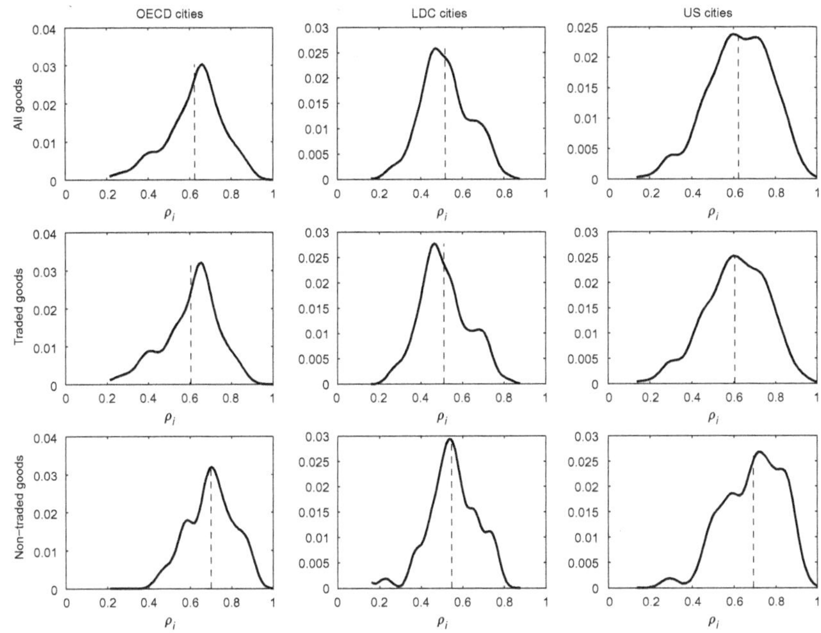

Fig. 2. Kernel estimates of the distribution of persistence estimates by good and location category.

error. In half-lives this persistence range translates to between 14 and 26 months.

Beginning our examination of cross-sectional differences in persistence, goods are placed into traded and non-traded categories. Table 4 reports the median persistence estimates in each of these groups. As expected, the persistence of non-traded retail goods is higher than traded retail goods for all three groups of locations. The median OECD half-life increases from 18 to 24 months as we move from traded goods to non-traded goods. Comparable results are found for the U.S. cities, with smaller differences arising in the LDC.

Turning to *categorization bias* we assign food, clothing and transportation to the tradeable category and housing, medical care and entertainment to the non-tradeable category (other goods and services are omitted, since the category is inherently ambiguous). Note that only 1 in 10 goods placed in the non-tradeable categories are in fact traded goods based on the dichotomous classification,

Table 5. Regression of persistence on the distribution share.

	OECD	LDC	U.S.	Pooled
Average persistence	0.624	0.518	0.622	0.494
a	0.513(0.050)	0.478(0.039)	0.527(0.068)	0.506(0.034)
b	0.220(0.085)	0.086(0.066)	0.209(0.115)	0.172(0.057)
R^2	0.20	0.06	0.11	0.09

Notes: $\widehat{\rho}_l = a + b\alpha_i +$ *residuals.* Numbers in parentheses are standard errors.

while 4 of 10 goods in the tradeable group are in fact non-traded. For the OECD cities, the median half-life of LOP deviations for goods belonging to the non-traded goods categories is 22 months, slightly lower than the 24 months found using the dichotomous rule good-by-good. For traded goods, the half-life is exact, to the month, to the median traded good reported earlier. *Categorization bias* appears to be a minor issue, at least when one uses persistence estimated from micro-price data.

To investigate *compositional bias* we regress the persistence estimates on the distribution share and a constant. Since our shares are more aggregated than our prices, we first average persistence across goods falling within the same distribution share bin. Table 5 reports our findings. The distribution share enters with the expected positive sign in all cases: LOP persistence rises as the distribution share rises. Moving from automobiles to baby-sitting services, which are associated with the extremes of our distribution shares, persistence rises from 13 to 21 months. Figure 3 shows the persistence estimates for all three groups of locations and the regression line for the pooled specification (which pools all three groups and estimates a single regression line).

We conclude from this analysis that *compositional bias*, associated with the fact that retail prices defray costs of both traded and non-traded inputs is helpful in understanding cross-sectional differences in LOP persistence.

4.3.3. *Persistence of PPP deviations*

Recall from Fig. 2, that very few of the persistence estimates reached levels consistent with the consensus range of 36–60 months

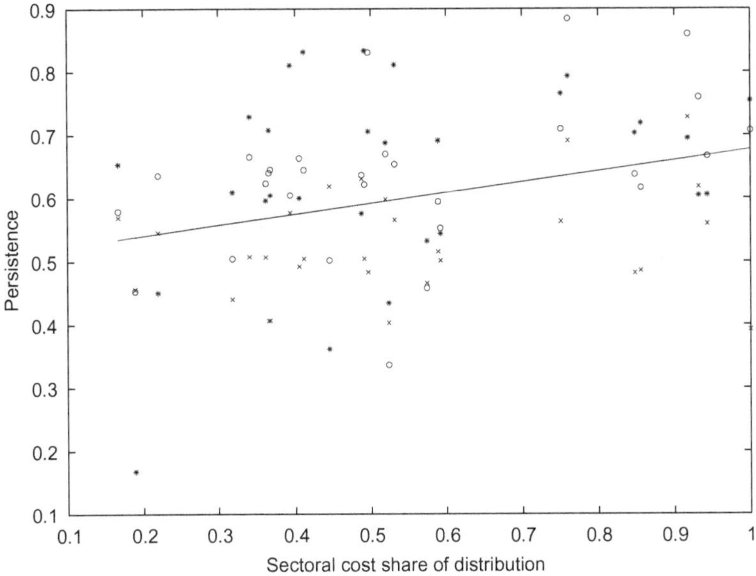

Fig. 3. Scatterplot of sectoral-mean persistence estimates against sectoral distribution shares. Circles indicate OECD persistence, x's indicate LDC persistence and '∗' indicate U.S. persistence. The solid line is the fitted regression line pooling all data.

found in the PPP literature. We explore three explanations for this disparity.

First, it could be a matter of weighting. Most items in the EIU and BLS micro-samples are traded goods with low persistence while expenditure in the CPI consists mostly of high persistence, non-tradeables. A second possibility is aggregation bias. Imbs *et al.* (2005) find higher persistence in the real exchange rates constructed from aggregate CPI data than in those constructed from disaggregated sub-indices that comprise the CPI. They studied 11 European countries plus the United States over the period 1981–1995. The third possibility is that real exchange rate persistence is lower during the 1990–2005 period compared to the entire post-Bretton Woods era.

All three possibilities are considered by aggregating the micro-data with weights used by national statistical agencies and by estimating the model with official CPI data, both at the national level and the U.S. city level.

Turning to the details, Table 6 shows the results of GMM estimation applied after the micro-data have been aggregated using the following weighting methods:

1. CPI weights: Weights are national weights for the international data and city-specific weights for the U.S. cities.
2. Common (good-specific) weights: Weights are category-specific, not location specific, thus yielding a common consumption basket for cities within each group, but differing across groups. Expenditure weights used are averages across locations within each group (i.e., all OECD cities are assigned a common expenditure weight equal to the average expenditure weight across the OECD countries; U.S. city weights are average weights across U.S. cities).
3. Equal weights: A consumption basket containing one of each item in the micro-panel.

Before turning to the results, it is important to highlight the fact that we use the same set of goods and services in each group for our aggregation results. In our good-by-good results our goal was to maximize the number of locations in a group to improve estimation precision. Here our goal is to isolate the impact of aggregation methods on aggregate persistence. Consequently we keep the set of goods and services the same in each group and change only the aggregation method. We report medians across goods in each group again, to reflect changes in the sample composition at the micro-level. The medians are almost identical in the OECD and U.S. sample, and increase by 2 months for the LDC countries compared to our earlier results.

The first row of entries in Table 6 are estimates using official CPI aggregates. Estimates in the first panel of Table 6 are based on our CPI indices constructed from the EIU micro-data. The half-lives of PPP deviations are 14 and 16 months for the LDC and OECD countries using the official indices compared to 16 months for both groups when we use our CPI indices. The BLS city-level price indices have a half-life of 56 months, almost twice what we find by aggregating the EIU for the same U.S. cities.

Table 6. Persistence of PPP deviations.

	Half-lives in months			Persistence estimates		
	OECD	LDC	U.S.	OECD	LDC	U.S.
Official CPI	14	16	56	0.55	0.59	0.86
		Panel A: All goods				
CPI weights	16	16	26	0.59	0.60	0.73
Common weights	20	15	32	0.65	0.57	0.77
Equal weights	17	13	26	0.61	0.54	0.72
Median good	18	16	18	0.63	0.59	0.63
		Panel B: Non-traded goods				
CPI weights	18	17	50	0.63	0.61	0.85
Common weights	22	15	39	0.68	0.57	0.81
Equal weights	23	12	52	0.70	0.51	0.85
Median good	21	17	30	0.68	0.61	0.76
		Panel C: Traded goods				
CPI weights	15	20	25	0.58	0.66	0.72
Common weights	18	17	23	0.63	0.61	0.70
Equal weights	17	14	18	0.60	0.56	0.63
Median good	18	16	17	0.62	0.59	0.61
		Panel D: Sample size				
	Number of goods			Number of city pairs		
All goods	173	64	190	231	136	77
Non-traded goods	34	20	30	253	136	78
Traded goods	139	44	160	231	136	78

Notes: Official CPIs are the aggregate consumer price indices constructed by the national statistical agencies (these are country level indices except for the U.S., which are urban indices for the cities matching our EIU data). The other entries are our PPP constructs as described in the text.

Table 6 also reports persistence of sub-indices. The middle panel is an index for non-traded goods and the third panel is an index of traded goods prices; these are counterparts to $w_{jk,t}$ and $t_{jk,t}$ discussed earlier. The first observation to make is that, with the exception of the U.S. cities, the method of weighting does not have a predictable (or large) effect on the estimated half-lives. We focus on CPI weights from here on.

Comparing the half-lives of PPP deviations under CPI weighting to the median LOP persistence estimate, we see that the median good provides a very reliable estimate of aggregate persistence for cross-border pairs. The OECD persistence level *decreases* from 18 to 16 months as we move from the median good to PPP, while the LDC half-lives are basically unchanged. U.S. half-lives increase from 18 months for the median good to 26 months for CPI weighting. As Table 6 shows, much of this increase appears specific to non-traded goods, where the median half-live is 30 months, compared to 50 months for the non-traded good sub-index we construct.

In summary, aggregation bias appears not to be a robust feature of the data. It arises in the European sample that Imbs *et al.* (2005) study and in our U.S. city level data, but not in our broader OECD and LDC samples.[13] The aggregation results also reinforce the view that the EIU micro-sample is representative of the broader consumption basket since these data tell basically the same story as official aggregate price indices.

4.4. *Robustness*

Employing an alternative estimator, the LSDV estimator, persistence rises for the median good, but with the exception of the LDC group these changes are small. The ranking of persistence across traded and non-traded goods is preserved across all panels of locations.

Since the LSDV estimator, with finite time series observations, is known to be biased downward even if N is large, the estimates are adjusted with the well-known formula for the dynamic panel derived by Nickell (1981). This adjustment fails to alter the estimates in a quantitatively significant fashion. Our favored estimator, GMM is not asymptotically biased as long as N tends to infinity, but it may suffer from bias when N is finite. As no closed form bias formula is available to make the adjustment to the GMM estimates, a Monte Carlo procedure was employed. Computing the bias adjustment over a grid of $\rho, \sigma_\eta^2/\sigma_v^2$ and N, the finite sample bias turns out to have a very minor impact on our GMM estimates.

[13] See Chen and Engel (2005) for more on the issue of aggregation bias in the PPP literature.

The fact that the micro-data are collected across quite distinct markets makes the possibility of measurement error a concern. The presence of measurement error in $q_{i,jk,t}$ produces a correlation between instruments dated $t - 2$ and the error in first differences, $v_{i,jk,t} - v_{i,jk,t-1}$, and thus the moment conditions (8) become invalid (see Holtz-Eakin *et al.*, 1988 for more on the reasoning). In the presence of measurement error, it is appropriate to use instruments dated $t - 3$ and earlier. This measurement-error-robust estimator based on a reduced number of moment conditions also produces evidence of rapid price convergence, very similar to the results we report in the text. Furthermore, Hausman tests cannot reject the null hypothesis of no measurement error except for some of the goods in the LDC panel.

We conclude from this battery of robustness checks that rapid price adjustment with half-lives in the range of 1–2 years is a robust finding, not distorted by the estimation technique, small sample bias or classical measurement error.

5. Conclusion

Persistence in LOP deviations vary significantly across goods and are positively related to the distribution share: goods involving larger increases in value added and markups in the move from the producer to the consumer have higher persistence. This reinvigorates the classical dichotomy approach at the level of inputs into the production of final goods and services.

Much faster international price convergence is found in this study compared to the existing PPP literature. This finding appears to reflect a dramatic downward shift in the half-lives of PPP deviations in the last 15 years of the post-Bretton Woods era. More work needs to be done to determine if persistence in international price deviations are stable over time.

It seems important to rethink priors about why persistence should be of a particular level at the outset. The perceived wisdom draws from the notion that deviations from the LOP should be small and highly transitory. Our evidence suggests this view holds to a closer approximation for traded inputs than final goods; haircuts differ from PCs. Since long-run, absolute, deviations for non-traded goods appear to be very large, there is a greater range of persistence and innovation variance parameters (e.g., nominal exchange rate movements) consistent with a no-arbitrage condition for haircuts than for PCs. Would this not also imply potential instability of persistence and time series variability for the relative price of non-traded goods across locations? We think so. Much remains to be done.

Acknowledgments

We are especially thankful for detailed and constructive comments provided by Charles Engel, Yanqin Fan, David Parsley, John Rogers, Andy Rose and Randy Verbrugge. We also thank numerous seminar and conference participants. The authors gratefully acknowledge the financial support of the National Science Foundation (SES-0136979, SES-0524868). We thank Inkoo Lee and Hakan Yilmazkuday for very able research assistance, financed by the grant. The views expressed in the paper are those of the authors and are not reflective of those of the Bank of Japan.

References

Ahlin, C., Shintani, M., 2007. Menu costs and Markov inflation: a theoretical revision with new evidence. *Journal of Monetary Economics* 54 (3), 753–784.

Arellano, M., Bond, S., 1991. Some tests of specification for panel data: Monte Carlo evidence and an application to employment equations. *Review of Economic Studies* 58 (2), 277–297.

Betts, C.M., Kehoe, T.J., 2006. U.S. real exchange rate fluctuations and relative price fluctuations. *Journal of Monetary Economics* 53 (7), 1297–1326.

Bils, M., Klenow, P.J., 2004. Some evidence on the importance of sticky prices. *Journal of Political Economy* 112 (5), 947–985.

Burstein, A.T., Neves, J.C., Rebelo, S., 2003. Distribution costs and real exchange rate dynamics during exchange-rate-based stabilizations. *Journal of Monetary Economics* 50 (6), 1189–1214.

Chari, V.V., Kehoe, P.J., McGrattan, E.R., 2002. Can sticky price models generate volatile and persistent real exchange rates? *Review of Economic Studies* 69 (3), 533–563.

Chen, S.S., Engel, C., 2005. Does "aggregation bias" explain the PPP puzzle? *Pacific Economic Review* 10 (1), 49–72.

Cheung, Y.W., Lai, K.S., 2000. On cross-country differences in the persistence of real exchange rates. *Journal of International Economics* 50 (2), 375–397.

Choi, C.Y., Mark, N.C., Sul, D., 2006. Unbiased estimation of the half-life to PPP convergence in panel data. *Journal of Money, Credit and Banking* 38 (4), 921–938.

Crucini, M.J., Shintani, M., 2006. Persistence in law-of-one-price deviations: evidence from micro-data. Working Papers 06-W16, Department of Economics, Vanderbilt University.

Crucini, M.J., Telmer, C.I., Zachariadis, M., 2005. Understanding European real exchange rates. *American Economic Review* 95 (3), 724–738.

Cumby, R.E., 1996. *Forecasting exchange rates and relative prices with the hamburger standard: is what you want what you get with McParity?* National Bureau of Economic Research, Working Paper No. 5675.

Engel, C., 1999. Accounting for U.S. real exchange rate changes. *Journal of Political Economy* 107 (3), 507–538.

Engel, C., Rogers, J.H., 1996. How wide is the border? *American Economic Review* 86 (5), 1112–1125.

Ethier, W.J., 1982. National and international returns to scale in the modern theory of international trade. *American Economic Review* 72 (3), 389–405.

Frankel, J.A., Rose, A.K., 1996. A panel project on purchasing power parity: mean reversion within and between countries. *Journal of International Economics* 40 (1–2), 209–224.

Goldberg, P.K., Verboven, F., 2005. Market integration and convergence to the Law of One Price: evidence from the European car market. *Journal of International Economics* 65 (1), 49–73.

Harris, R.D.F., Tzavalis, E., 1999. Inference for unit roots in dynamic panels where the time dimension is fixed. *Journal of Econometrics* 91 (2), 201–226.

Holtz-Eakin, D., 1988. Testing for individual effects in autoregressive models. *Journal of Econometrics* 39 (3), 297–307.

Holtz-Eakin, D., Newey, W., Rosen, H.S., 1988. Estimating vector autoregressions with panel data. *Econometrica* 56 (6), 1371–1395.

Imbs, J., Mumtaz, H., Ravn, M.O., Rey, H., 2005. PPP strikes back: aggregation and the real exchange rate. *Quarterly Journal of Economics* 120 (1), 1–43.

Kim, J., 2004. Half-lives of deviations from PPP: contrasting traded and non-traded components of consumption baskets. *Review of International Economics* 12 (1), 162–168.

Kim, J., Ogaki, M., 2004. Purchasing power parity for traded and non-traded goods: a structural error correction model approach. *Monetary and Economic Studies* 22 (1), 1–26.

Murray, C.J., Papell, D.H., 2005. Do panels help solve the purchasing power parity puzzle? *Journal of Business and Economic Statistics* 23 (4), 410–415.

Nickell, S., 1981. Biases in dynamic models with fixed effects. *Econometrica* 49 (6), 1417–1426.

Obstfeld, M., Rogoff, K., 1995. Exchange rate dynamics redux. *Journal of Political Economy* 103 (3), 624–660.

Parsley, D., Wei, S., 2007. A prism into the PPP puzzles: the micro-foundations of Big Mac real exchange rates. *The Economic Journal* 117 (523), 1336–1356.

Salter, W.E.G., 1959. Internal and external balance: the role of price and expenditure effects. *Economic Record* 35 (71), 226–238.

Sanyal, K.K., Jones, R.W., 1982. The theory of trade in middle products. *American Economic Review* 72 (1), 16–31.

Svennsson, L.E.O., van Wijnbergen, S., 1989. Excess capacity, monopolistic competition, and international transmission of monetary disturbances. *The Economic Journal* 99 (397), 785–805.

Swan, T.W., 1960. Economic control in a dependent economy. *Economic Record* 36 (73), 51–66.

Part II

Business Cycles, Risk Sharing and Asset Market Structure

Chapter 5

On International and National Dimensions of Risk Sharing*

Mario J. Crucini

Department of Finance, Wharton School, University of Pennsylvania, Philadelphia, PA, USA

Abstract. This paper contributes to the empirical literature that tests the implications of risk sharing across regions or countries. Rather than test the null of full insurance, the estimation method produces a parameter that measures the fraction of the annuity value of individual income that individuals of different regions (or nations) pool. Comparing the provinces of Canada, the states of the United States, and the G-7 countries, I find similar degrees of risk sharing within regions of Canada and the U.S. that exceed the risk sharing that occurs across countries. Specifically, more than two-thirds of the fitted annual variation in regional consumption is common to all regions compared to less than one-third in the case of G-7 countries.

1. Introduction

The empirical literature on consumption risk sharing has grown rapidly in recent years to encompass studies of individuals, regions, and nations. At the level of the individual, Mace (1991) used the U.S. Consumer Expenditure Survey, regressing individual consumption growth on average consumption growth and individual income growth and found that income growth is a significant regressor

*This chapter originally appeared in *The Review of Economics and Statistics*, 1999, **81**(1), 73–84.

for some, but not all, categories of consumption. Using the U.S. Panel Study of Income Dynamics, Cochrane (1991) found that the distribution of food consumption shifts across individuals who are unemployed for more than 100 days due to illness and involuntary job loss (but not for illness of less than 100 days) spells of unemployment following an involuntary job loss, loss of work due to strike, or an involuntary move.

International macroeconomists have tested the null hypothesis of full consumption risk sharing in panels of regional and national data. Using data for the U.S. and OECD countries, Atkeson and Bayoumi (1993) rejected the null of full insurance in both panels. Examining the G-7 countries, Obstfeld (1994a) found that international risk sharing is more complete following 1973 than before, yet Germany appears to have been very successful at international diversification of its consumption risks while Canada has not. Lewis (1996) found that consumption growth had a smaller common component in a group of countries that imposed capital controls compared to a group of countries that did not.

In testing the null of complete risk sharing, researchers have effectively computed the probability that average consumption growth explains all of the variance of fitted individual consumption growth. Taken together, these studies present substantial evidence against full insurance.

However, risk-sharing theory produces full consumption insurance only under stringent assumptions (that contracts can be written and enforced at zero cost, for example). More generally, the theory predicts that individuals will choose to pool risk to the extent that the costs and benefits are equated. Given that the costs and benefits of risk sharing may differ across individuals and indeed across different contingencies, individuals will choose different levels of risk sharing or choose different groups with whom they wish to pool risk. (These issues are discussed in a recent symposium. See the contributions by Townsend (1995), Morduch (1995), and Besley (1995) and, for a more rigorous treatment, references cited therein.)

Once we recognize that risk sharing may be imperfect, we would expect the results of tests of consumption risk sharing to depend on the groups included in the test and the extent to which shocks occurring over the period of observation are fully insured against, partially insured against, or not insured against. Tests of the null of complete insurance are not equipped to uncover these differences. One robust prediction of imperfect risk sharing is that, after controlling for common income shocks, consumption should move together more closely across individuals that engage in more risk sharing.

I formalize this idea by adapting a permanent income model to allow for varying degrees of income pooling. The consumption equation that emerges is consistent with risk-sharing behavior ranging from complete income pooling to portfolio autarky. The appropriate definition of permanent income in this setting is a weighted average of individual permanent income and permanent per capita income of each individual engaged in risk sharing. The weights on these two components of permanent income are determined by the fraction of an individual's income stream that is contributed to the risk-sharing pool. Using this model as an empirical tool, I can address two different questions. The first question is the same as has been asked in most of the existing literature: Do regions or countries engage in complete risk sharing? Employing panel data that includes the Canadian provinces, U.S. states, and G-7 countries that use this novel consumption specification, I am able to address a more general question: What is the extent of consumption risk sharing, and how does it differ across regions and countries?

Averaging across regions within each panel dataset set, I find that more than two-thirds of the variance of fitted consumption growth at the regional level (i.e., U.S. states and Canadian provinces) is attributable to average consumption growth compared to at most one-third for the G-7 countries. Regional income growth is also a key explanatory variable for regional consumption growth, but it is more important at the national level than at the state or provincial level.

The remainder of the paper is organized into five sections. Section 2 develops a simple model of incomplete risk sharing and an estimable equation to recover the risk-sharing parameter. Section 3 describes the data sources. Section 4 presents the estimation results and decomposes the variance of consumption growth into aggregate and regional components. Section 5 discusses econometric issues, and Section 6 concludes.

2. Incomplete Risk Sharing

Consider a population of J individuals that engage in risk sharing with member j selling fraction λ_j of her income stream in exchange for a claim to the pooled income streams of all J agents (each of whom contribute potentially different fractions of their own income). The total date t amount in the pool is $Y_{at} \equiv (1/\Lambda)\sum_{j=1}^{J}\lambda_j Y_{jt}$, where Y_{jt} is the income of individual j at time t and $\Lambda \equiv \sum_{j=1}^{J}\lambda_j$. The practical difficulty with this construct is that the pooled resource depends on the unknown fraction contributed by each individual. The problem is dealt with by maintaining the assumption that individuals in a particular risk-sharing group each contribute the same amount, but the parameters may differ across groups.[1] Regions within a country may pool a different fraction of their resources within national boundaries than countries pool as a group, for example. Imposing this restriction, the pooled resource is a simple average of the per capita income of each individual within the group and the flow of individual income after risk pooling is defined as $\bar{Y}_{jt} \equiv \lambda Y_{at} + (1-\lambda)Y_{jt}$, where $Y_{at} \equiv (1/J)\sum_{j=1}^{J} Y_{jt}$.

Suppose also that individuals smooth consumption by borrowing or lending at a fixed exogenous real interest rate. We arrive at the familiar decision rule for the change in consumption but with the relevant measure of income altered as a consequence of risk sharing:

$$\Delta C_{jt} = (1-\beta)\sum_{k=0}^{\infty}\beta^k[E_t\bar{Y}_{jt+k} - E_{t-1}\bar{Y}_{jt+k}]. \tag{1}$$

[1]See Sorensen and Yosha (1996) and Hess and Shin (1997) for evidence of risk-sharing patterns that differ across regions or industry groups within the United States.

Summing the decision rule over all individuals leads to the following expression for the average change in consumption:[2]

$$\Delta C_{at} \equiv \frac{1}{J}\sum_{j=1}^{J}\Delta C_{jt}$$

$$= (1-\beta)\sum_{k=0}^{\infty}\beta^{k}[E_tY_{at+k} - E_{t-1}Y_{at+k}]. \quad (2)$$

Substituting Eq. (2) into Eq. (1), the original decision rule becomes

$$\Delta C_{jt} = \lambda\Delta C_{at}$$

$$+(1-\lambda)(1-\beta)\sum_{k=0}^{\infty}\beta^{k}[E_tY_{jt+k} - E_{t-1}Y_{jt+k}]. \quad (3)$$

To avoid the verbose labels of average regional consumption and average regional income, I will use the term *aggregate consumption* and *aggregate income* to refer to averages across regions or countries in the exposition that follows. Equation (3) makes clear that the appropriate definition of permanent income is quite different in the presence of risk sharing than it is in its absence. Regional consumption growth responds with a unit coefficient to permanent income that is defined as the linear combination of the annuity value of innovations to aggregate per capita and regional per capita income, and not with a unit coefficient to each component separately.

To this point, we have been using the levels of consumption and income. In practice, aggregate economic variables appear to follow log-linear processes rather than linear processes. The equations estimated below will use first differences of the logarithm of consumption and income. The appendix presents the log-linear approximation in moving from levels to log levels. From this point on, all variables will be identified by lowercase letters to denote the logarithm of the level.

---

[2]Specifically, each term in the infinite sum can be rewritten as follows: $E_t\bar{Y}_{jt+k} - E_{t-1}\bar{Y}_{jt+k} = E_t[\lambda Y_{at+k} + (1-\lambda)Y_{jt+k}] - E_{t-1}[\lambda Y_{at+k} + (1-\lambda)Y_{jt+k}] = \lambda[E_tY_{at+k} - E_{t-1}Y_{at+k}] + (1-\lambda)[E_tY_{jt+k} - E_{t-1}Y_{jt+k}]$. Taking the average of these terms across j gives equation (2).

Now we consider the issue of forecasting regional income. In the context of a cross-sectional study of income and consumption, it seems natural to entertain the possibility that regional and aggregate income growth are interdependent. The type of interdependence relevant for evaluating unexpected changes in regional wealth is the impact of regional or aggregate "news" on the future path of regional income growth. To illustrate this point, consider the joint data-generating process for aggregate and regional income in Eq. (4):

$$\Delta z_{jt} = A_j \Delta z_{jt-1} + v_{jt} = \sum_{s=0}^{\infty} A_j^s v_{jt-s}, \tag{4}$$

where

$$\Delta z'_{jt} = [\Delta y_{at} \quad \Delta y_{jt}], \quad v'_{jt} = [v_{ajt} \quad v_{jt}],$$

$$A_j = \begin{pmatrix} A_j^{11} & A_j^{12} \\ A_j^{21} & A_j^{22} \end{pmatrix}.$$

Under these assumptions about the income processes, consumption growth will follow:

$$\begin{aligned} \Delta c_{jt} &= \lambda \Delta c_{at} + (1-\lambda)\Delta yp_{jt} \\ &= [\lambda B_j^{11} + (1-\lambda) B_j^{21}] v_{ajt} \\ &\quad + [\lambda B_j^{12} + (1-\lambda) B_j^{22}] v_{jt}. \end{aligned} \tag{5}$$

The coefficients on aggregate and regional news (i.e., the innovations from Eq. (4)) are multivariate versions of the Hansen-Sargent (1980) formula with B^{ij} defined as the ijth element of $(I - \beta A_j)^{-1}$ weighted by the risk-sharing parameters.

The response of consumption to an innovation in aggregate and regional income will depend on how the two income processes are dynamically related and on the extent of risk sharing. Regional consumption will respond to aggregate innovations directly to the extent that agents pool risk (the first of the four terms in Eq. (5)), and indirectly to the extent that innovations to aggregate income convey information about the future path of regional income growth (as indicated by the second of the four terms in Eq. (5)). So long as risk sharing is less than perfect ($\lambda < 1$), regional income innovations will matter for analogous reasons: directly as a source of income and indirectly as information about future aggregate income.

The model predicts that consumption growth will be positively correlated across regions for two reasons. First, regional permanent income may be positively correlated across regions. Consumption comovements on this account may have nothing to do with risk sharing. Second, to the extent that individuals share risk, their wealth levels are directly related, which introduces the second source of comovement.

Estimation proceeds in two stages. First, the income processes are estimated for each region in the dataset: the 10 Canadian provinces, the 48 contiguous U.S. states, and the G-7 countries. The first-stage estimates are used to construct a time series of innovations to permanent income for each region. The second-stage regressions use these time series as the second regressor in the regional consumption equations.

I consider three specifications for regional income growth:

$$\begin{pmatrix} \Delta y_{at} \\ \Delta y_{jt} \end{pmatrix} = \begin{pmatrix} A_j^{11} & A_j^{12} \\ A_j^{21} & A_j^{22} \end{pmatrix} \begin{pmatrix} \Delta y_{at-1} \\ \Delta y_{jt-1} \end{pmatrix} + \begin{pmatrix} v_{ajt} \\ v_{jt} \end{pmatrix} \tag{6a}$$

$$\Delta y_{jt} = \rho j \Delta y_{jt-1} + v_{jt} \tag{6b}$$

$$\Delta y_{jt} = v_{jt}. \tag{6c}$$

Estimates of the unexpected changes in regional permanent income ($\Delta\widehat{yp}_{jt}$) are computed from these models and are used in the second-stage regression:

$$\Delta c_{jt} = \lambda_j \Delta c_{at} + (1 - \lambda_j)\Delta\widehat{yp}_{jt} + \epsilon_{jt}. \tag{7}$$

The error entering the estimated relationship is interpreted as a measurement error in consumption growth or an individual taste shock that is uncorrelated with the innovation to permanent income as in Mace (1991). Each equation is estimated separately to avoid the problem of regressing regional consumption growth on its cross-sectional mean (which would return a unit coefficient on Δc_{at} by construction).

Recall that the theory allows individuals to contribute different fractions of their income, but we cannot define the aggregate as a function of these unknown parameters. Instead, we allow the risk-sharing parameters to vary across individuals but still maintain the aggregation assumption consistent with common λ's. We evaluate the implications of this maintained assumption using a Monte Carlo procedure in Section 5. All regressions are estimated by ordinary least squares.[3]

3. The Data

The Canadian data are from *Provincial Economic Accounts,* published by Statistics Canada. Provincial deflators for final demand are used to deflate both GDP and consumption. The Canadian provincial consumption data are conceptually closer to national income accounting measures than their U.S. counterparts.

The consumption data for U.S. states are from *Statistical Abstract of the United States: Retail Sales by Type of Store and State.* The consumption data are deflated by the national deflator for consumption of nondurable goods and services. The United States output data of state personal income are from *State Personal Income 1929–1987: Estimates and a Statement of Sources and Methods,* published by the U.S. Department of Commerce, Bureau of Economic Analysis. The income figures are deflated using the aggregate U.S. GNP deflator.

The international data are from the country pages of the World Tables published by the World Bank in the Fall 1990 update (World Bank, 1991). Output is nominal gross domestic product divided by

[3]The standard errors from OLS are correct in this application since only unanticipated regressors from the first-stage regression enter the second regression. See Pagan (1984), model 4, for a demonstration of this result.

the GDP deflator. Consumption is private consumption of goods and services, also deflated by the GDP deflator.

While a detailed description of the individual data series is provided in the appendix, a few comments about the regional data sources are in order. The state-level U.S. consumption series are based on retail purchases of food, general merchandise, furniture, household appliances, automotive products, drugs, and purchases made at eating and drinking establishments. While the Canadian consumption data also rely on retail trade surveys, these surveys are supplemented with data from other sources. Statistics Canada also includes a broader set of goods and services than is covered by the U.S. data. For example, energy consumption is either obtained directly or calculated with data on prices and consumption by province. Consumption also includes the rental value of the stock of housing, and expenditures on education, health, and financial services. Given the growth in the importance of services in aggregate consumption, the addition of these items is particularly important in recent years.

Comparable sample periods are used across the three panels to facilitate cross-sectional comparisons. The regressions are estimated for 1973 to 1991 for the Canadian provinces, 1972 to 1990 for the U.S. states, and 1970 to 1987 for the G-7 countries.

The sense that incomplete risk sharing might be helpful in understanding patterns of international and interregional income and consumption correlations is apparent in Figs. 1 and 2. These figures present smoothed histograms of cross-regional consumption and income growth correlations for each panel dataset.

Income growth correlations are comparable across the Canadian provinces and OECD countries with cross-regional correlations that average 0.38 and 0.32, respectively. However, cross-provincial consumption growth correlations tend to be *higher* than cross-provincial income growth correlations (0.56 versus 0.38), while international consumption growth correlations tend to be *lower* than international income growth correlations (0.14 versus 0.32). The average correlation of consumption growth rates across U.S. states is 0.40, which is also much higher than is observed across countries, but it

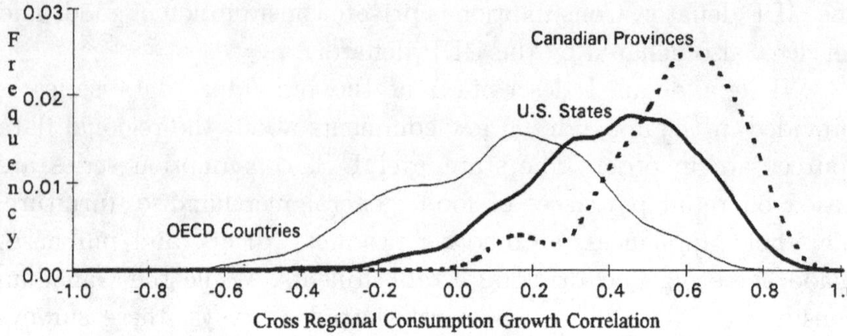

Fig. 1. Regional consumption correlations (Kernel estimates).

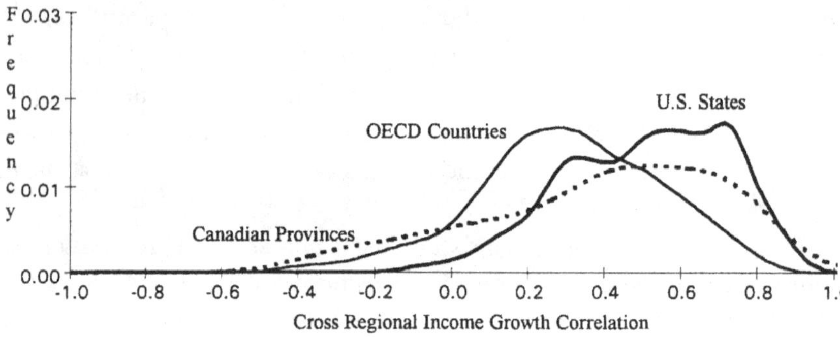

Fig. 2. Regional income correlations (Kernel estimates).

Note: The densities are constructed using a normal kernel with band width $1.06\sigma_x T^{2/10}$; where σ_x is the cross-sectional standard deviation of x, a pair-wise correlation of either consumption or income growth across two regions in a given panel.

is lower than the average cross-correlation of income growth across states (which equals 0.50). However, retail sales proxy for the U.S. state consumption data, which may downward bias the consumption correlations relative to the provincial and national data.

A simple interpretation of these correlation patterns is that, while risk sharing is less than perfect in all three panels, more risk sharing is taking place across regions within national boundaries than is taking place across countries. The remainder of the paper presents formal evidence on the validity of this interpretation of the data.

4. The Results

I begin by reporting the results of estimating the income processes. Table 1 reports the number of regions for which a one-sided hypothesis test reveals a positive or negative coefficient at the 10% level of significance, the weighting coefficients for innovations to regional and aggregate income denoted "multipliers" (the $\hat{B}^{ij}$, defined in the previous section), and the R-squared. These last two statistics are averaged across all regions within each panel.[4]

A greater number of statistically significant coefficients are found in estimating the regional income equations than in estimating the aggregate income equations. For Canada, only five of the provinces have coefficients in the aggregate income equation that are significantly different from zero (compared to nine in the case of the provincial income equations). The R-squared of the provincial income regressions are, on average, twice as large as those for the aggregate income equations (0.19 versus 0.08). Based on these results, it appears that aggregate income growth is approximately a random walk, while provincial income growth is predictable from the past growth rates of both provincial and aggregate income growth.

The same patterns are true for the U.S. states. Aggregate income growth helps predict future state income growth, but the reverse tends not to be the case. Of the 48 state-level regressions with aggregate U.S. income growth as the dependent variable, only 17 of the 96 coefficients are statistically significant (compared to 46 of 96 coefficients for the regressions with state income as the dependent variable). The G-7 results indicate that the annual growth rate of national income is well approximated by a random walk.

The last two columns of Table 1 report the results for the univariate, first-order, autoregressive model of regional income growth. Two, fifteen, and zero coefficients are significantly different from zero for the Canadian provinces, U.S. states, and G-7 countries respectively. The univariate model generally fits regional income growth less well

[4]Results for each region that correspond to the summary statistics in tables 1 through 4 are available from the author upon request.

Table 1. First-stage income regressions.

	Bivariate specification						Univariate specification	
	Aggregate income			Regional income				
Statistic	A^{11}	A^{12}	R^2	A^{22}	A^{21}	R^2	$\hat{\rho}_j$	R^2
Results for the Canadian Provinces								
Sign tests	[0, 2]	[2, 1]		[3, 2]	[0, 4]		[0, 2]	
Multipliers	0.85	0.19	0.08	1.21	–0.14	0.19	1.14	0.08
Results for the U.S. States								
Sign tests	[4, 3]	[7, 3]		[23, 5]	[6, 12]		[15, 0]	
Multipliers	0.99	0.21	0.10	1.54	–0.22	0.17	1.36	0.08
Results for the G-7 Countries								
Sign tests	[1, 0]	[0, 1]		[0, 1]	[1, 0]		[0, 0]	
Multipliers	1.05	0.03	0.15	0.97	0.09	0.14	1.09	0.02

Notes: The first row of entries for each panel (e.g., $[x, y]$) are the number of statistically significant positive (+) or negative (–) coefficients in each regional block, at the 10% level. The second row of entries report $\hat{B}_{ij}$, the ijth element of $(I - \beta A_j)^{-1}$, the weighting coefficients for innovations to income. The value of β used was 0.98. The sample periods are 1973 to 1991 for Canada, 1972 to 1990 for the U.S., and 1970 to 1987 for the G-7 nations. The parameter $\hat{\rho}_j$ refers to the coefficient on lagged income growth in the univariate specification.

than does the bivariate model, as is evident in the fewer statistically significant coefficients and lower R-squared in the univariate case.

The second row for each panel dataset reports the multipliers: the coefficients on aggregate and/or regional income innovations that are implied jointly by the estimated parameters and the permanent income hypothesis. To interpret the entries, consider the average of the estimated multipliers applicable to provincial income in the provincial income equation, which equals 1.21. This coefficient means that a unit innovation to current provincial income growth has approximately a 1.21% effect on permanent provincial income. Conditional on the aggregate income innovation not changing, provincial consumption growth would be predicted to be more variable than the innovations to provincial income growth.

The coefficients A_j^{21} give the impact of a unit innovation to aggregate income on regional permanent income. Since these parameters are typically less than unity, changes in aggregate income have a modest impact on regional permanent income. However, the impact of regional and aggregate innovations to income on the actual path of regional permanent income over time also depends on the relative volatility of the innovations.[5]

To summarize, regional income growth appears to be predictable based on its own history as well as the history of average income growth. However, the parameters that describe this process are imprecisely estimated. Since it is not clear which specification yields the best construct for changes in regional permanent income, in the results that follow I employ each of the three measures of the innovations to permanent income:

(i) one from the regional income equation in the bivariate system;
(ii) one from the univariate model of regional income growth; and
(iii) regional income growth itself, which amounts to assuming that income changes are permanent and unpredictable.

Table 2 presents the central findings. Each panel reports estimation results for one panel dataset, while each row within a panel refers to a different income specification. The table reports the estimated risk-sharing parameters and standard error of the estimates averaged across all regions within each regional block. The average R-squared of these regressions are reported in the third column. The last four columns consider alternative hypotheses about the magnitude of each individual regional estimate.

As the first column of the table indicates, the estimated provincial and state-level risk-sharing parameters are close to the complete risk-sharing benchmark of unity. Values tend toward 0.9 across these regions with negligible differences arising from the regional block

[5]As a way of summarizing the dynamic interaction of regional and aggregate income, I computed the correlation of the fitted values of aggregate and regional income growth. The correlation is computed from the estimated parameters of the A matrix and the innovation covariance matrix. The correlations range from an average of 0.70 for the Canadian provinces to just under 0.80 for the G-7 countries.

Table 2. Risk sharing parameter estimates.

Income process	Mean statistics $\hat{\lambda}$	$\text{se}(\hat{\lambda})$	R^2	Number of regions for which a 95% confidence interval encompasses a risk sharing parameter equal to: $\hat{\lambda}=1$	$1>\hat{\lambda}>0$	$\hat{\lambda}=0$	$\hat{\lambda}=1$ or 0
	Results for the Canadian Provinces						
Bivariate	0.90	(0.08)	0.74	6	4	0	0
Univariate	0.89	(0.08)	0.74	6	4	0	0
Random walk	0.88	(0.08)	0.75	6	4	0	0
	Results for the U.S. States						
Bivariate	0.94	(0.31)	0.51	31	3	2	9
Univariate	0.84	(0.34)	0.50	29	2	3	13
Random walk	0.88	(0.32)	0.50	33	3	2	10
	Results for the G-7 Countries						
Bivariate	0.60	(0.26)	0.45	2	2	2	1
Univariate	0.44	(0.19)	0.57	1	2	4	0
Random walk	0.37	(0.21)	0.57	1	2	4	0

Notes: The risk-sharing regressions are estimated by ordinary least squares. The regressors are the average consumption growth across regions within a regional block and the unexpected change in permanent income computed from the first-stage regressions reported in Table 1.

considered, and with modest differences arising from the specification of the income-generating process.

In contrast, the average estimated risk-sharing parameter is much lower — between 0.37 and 0.6 — for the G-7 countries. While the average parameter estimate for the G-7 countries is sensitive to the income specification, the average G-7 estimate is lower than the average regional estimate in every case. The largest average point estimate of 0.6 for the G-7 countries is only approximately two-thirds of the corresponding average across either the Canadian provinces or U.S. states.

The estimated equations account for a considerable fraction of the time-series variation in regional consumption growth. The R-squared ranges from 0.45 for the G-7 countries (for the bivariate income specification) to 0.75 for the Canadian provinces (for the unit root income specification). Despite the differences in the relative importance of aggregate consumption and regional permanent income in the regressions, the fit of the equations are comparable in terms of R-squared across the U.S. states and G-7 countries.

We fail to reject complete consumption insurance for 6 of the 10 provinces and 33 of the 48 states, but only 1 of the 7 countries. Consistent with the implications drawn from the average point estimates across regional blocks, risk sharing is less evident across countries than across regions within countries.

The value of nesting full insurance and portfolio autarky is apparent from the provincial results. The fifth column of the table reports the number of regions for which the 95% confidence interval for λ falls between 0 and 1. Four of the ten provinces satisfy this condition. These four provinces provide statistical evidence against either extreme hypothesis that risk sharing is complete or nonexistent. Few U.S. states satisfy this condition, even though many point estimates lie between 0 and 1 since the standard errors on the U.S. estimates are quite large (though still comparable to those for G-7 countries). In fact, for the random-walk specification the parameter estimates for ten U.S. states have confidence intervals that include both 0 and 1.

The results for the univariate specification present basically the same picture: no strong evidence against full insurance for most states, a slim majority of provinces, and only one country. The results using the bivariate income specification leave the basic conclusions unchanged for the provinces and states, but the results for the G-7 countries are mixed. Two countries are consistent with full insurance, two with no insurance, two fall in between these extremes, and one is consistent with either extreme.

The test of full insurance performed by Mace (1991) on individual U.S. consumption data is closest to the test $\lambda = 1$ using the specification in the last row of the middle panel of Table 2. There are two important differences. First, I have a modest cross-section (at most 48 regions versus thousands of individuals), but a considerably longer time series (20 years versus 4 years). Second, I do not impose $\lambda_j = \lambda$ across units within each panel. The results I obtain for

Table 3. Tests of overidentifying restrictions.

Income process	Number of regions	Number of rejections at P-values 0.10	0.05	0.01
		Results for the Canadian Provinces		
Bivariate	10	3	2	0
Univariate	10	1	1	0
Random walk	10	2	1	0
		Results for the U.S. States		
Bivariate	48	6	5	2
Univariate	48	6	4	1
Random walk	48	7	5	3
		Results for the G-7 Countries		
Bivariate	7	1	1	1
Univariate	7	1	1	1
Random walk	7	1	1	1

Notes: The table reports the results of likelihood ratio tests of the restriction that the coefficient on aggregate consumption and individual permanent income sum to unity. Each entry in the table gives the number of regions that reject that restriction at a significance level of 10%, 5%, or 1% using a chi-squared distribution with one degree of freedom. The first column gives the total number of regions in each regional block.

the U.S. are consistent with Mace's findings of substantial, but incomplete, insurance among individuals in the U.S.

Table 3 tests the overidentifying restriction that the coefficients on average consumption growth and the innovation to regional permanent income sum to unity. Very few regions reject this restriction, and there is virtually no difference across income specifications. At the 1% level, the restriction is not rejected in a single province and is rejected in only one country. At most, three state-level regressions are found to be inconsistent with this restriction at the 1% level. The results of this test suggest the value of defining permanent income such that it includes risk-sharing behavior, even when risk sharing is incomplete.

I draw four conclusions from the analysis to this point. First, the mean estimates across regions within the risk-sharing blocks indicate that risk sharing is more extensive across regions within countries (where the mean-risk sharing parameter tends to 0.9) than across countries (where the average of the risk-sharing parameters tends to about 0.5). Second, the sampling error of the U.S. estimates are such that the test of complete insurance lacks power against quite economically different alternatives. An additional implication of this fact is the lack of statistical evidence that the extent of risk sharing differs across the U.S. states and Canadian provinces, contrary to what one might infer from the raw consumption growth correlations displayed in Fig. 1. Third, the Canadian provincial estimates provide statistical evidence in favor of the incomplete risk-sharing specification rather than either extreme of full insurance or portfolio autarky. Fourth, the international data provide strong evidence against full insurance across countries and weak evidence against portfolio autarky.

To consider the economic significance of different degrees of risk pooling, I use the estimated equations to decompose the variance of fitted consumption growth into aggregate and regional components. The variance of fitted consumption growth of region j is

$$\begin{aligned}\mathrm{var}(\Delta\hat{c}_{jt}) = {} & \hat{\lambda}_j^2\mathrm{var}(\Delta c_{at}) + (1-\hat{\lambda}_j)^2\mathrm{var}(\Delta\widehat{yp}_{jt}) \\ & + 2\hat{\lambda}_j(1-\hat{\lambda}_j)\mathrm{cov}(\Delta c_{at}, \Delta\widehat{yp}_{jt}). \qquad (8)\end{aligned}$$

It is natural to think of this variance expression as arising from a portfolio decision to hold fraction $\hat{\lambda}_j$ of the market portfolio, which pays a stochastic dividend equal to the annuity value of changes in aggregate permanent income, and fraction $1-\hat{\lambda}_j$ of a "regional security" paying the annuity value of changes to regional permanent income. Under complete risk sharing, consumption variance is equal to the variance of the market dividend; under portfolio autarky, consumption variance is equal to the variance of the annuity value of innovations to regional permanent income.

The components of the variance of fitted regional consumption growth described in Eq. (8) are averaged across all regions within each panel and reported in Table 4. If risk sharing were complete, all of the variance would be accounted for by the aggregate component,

Table 4. Variance decomposition of consumption growth.

Income process	Aggregate component	Regional component	Covariance component
	Results for the Canadian Provinces		
Bivariate	0.72	0.06	0.21
Univariate	0.68	0.08	0.24
Random walk	0.68	0.09	0.23
	Results for the U.S. States		
Bivariate	0.92	0.13	−0.06
Univariate	0.78	0.14	0.08
Random walk	0.86	0.10	0.03
	Results for the G-7 Countries		
Bivariate	0.34	0.39	0.26
Univariate	0.16	0.58	0.26
Random walk	0.14	0.64	0.22

Notes: The first column gives the fraction of the variance of fitted regional consumption growth accounted for by the variance of changes in aggregate consumption growth; the second column gives the fraction accounted for by the variance of changes in regional permanent income; and the final column gives the fraction accounted for by the covariance between aggregate consumption growth and changes in regional permanent income. Equation (8) was used to construct the variance decomposition. The values in the table are averages across all regions within a particular panel.

and we would not reject the null hypothesis of complete risk sharing. We see a tendency for this in the Canadian provincial and U.S. state data. Between 78% and 92% of the variance in fitted state consumption growth is accounted for by the common component compared to lower, yet large, proportions of 68% and 72% for the provinces. The main difference between the two lies in the importance of the covariance term between regional income and aggregate consumption. For the provinces, this term accounts for approximately 20% of the variance in regional consumption compared to almost zero for the U.S. states. However, these differences are quite minor compared to what we observe in the international data, in which less than one-third of the variance of fitted national consumption growth is accounted for by the common component.

5. Econometric Issues

Before concluding, I consider two econometric issues. First, the use of the simple average change in consumption in the regional consumption equation was derived after imposing the assumption that each region contributed the same fraction of their income stream to the risk-sharing pool. The consumption specification that was estimated used this aggregation method to define the first regressor but allowed the risk-sharing parameters to vary across regions within each panel. I use Monte Carlo simulations to consider the implications of this procedure. Second, the theoretical model equates the change in aggregate consumption with the innovation to aggregate permanent income, yet the regression equation used the former construct as the first regressor in the consumption equation. I consider the implications of replacing aggregate consumption growth with changes in aggregate permanent income as the first regressor in the regional consumption equation.[6]

Since the aggregation bias will depend on the extent to which the true risk-sharing parameters differ across regions, it is useful to begin with some remarks on the cross-sectional patterns of these parameters found within each panel dataset. The estimates of the risk-sharing parameters for the Canadian provinces are quite close numerically — ranging from a low of 0.72 for British Columbia, to a high of 0.99 for Prince Edward Island and New Brunswick. In fact, these numbers understate the degree of homogeneity of the estimates, because British Columbia is the clear outlier with the remaining provinces having estimates between 0.83 and 0.99. (See the first column of Table 5.) The estimates are more diverse for the G-7 countries ranging from a low of approximately zero for the United Kingdom to a high of 0.86 for Germany. The dispersion of risk-sharing parameter estimates within each panel is also apparent in their cross-sectional standard deviation, which equals only 0.08 for the Canadian provinces compared to 0.28 for the G-7 countries and 0.35 for the U.S. states. In the Monte Carlo experiments that

[6] I thank John Campbell for suggesting I pursue this line of inquiry.

Table 5. Monte Carlo results: aggregation of consumption.

			Monte Carlo with measurement error in:			
	Empirical estimates		Consumption		Consumption and income	
Region	λ	se(λ)	λ	se(λ)	λ	se(λ)
	Results for the Canadian Provinces					
Newfoundland	0.87	(0.11)	0.87	(0.06)	0.86	(0.06)
P.E.I.	0.99	(0.08)	0.97	(0.04)	0.97	(0.04)
Nova Scotia	0.83	(0.05)	0.83	(0.04)	0.83	(0.04)
New Brunswick	0.99	(0.04)	0.98	(0.03)	0.97	(0.03)
Quebec	0.94	(0.18)	0.96	(0.08)	0.95	(0.07)
Ontario	0.86	(0.08)	0.86	(0.07)	0.87	(0.07)
Manitoba	0.84	(0.07)	0.86	(0.10)	0.88	(0.09)
Saskatchewan	0.84	(0.05)	0.85	(0.03)	0.85	(0.03)
Alberta	0.91	(0.05)	0.92	(0.02)	0.92	(0.02)
British Columbia	0.72	(0.10)	0.74	(0.07)	0.75	(0.07)
Average	0.88	(0.08)	0.88	(0.06)	0.89	(0.05)
	Results for the G-7 Countries					
Canada	0.38	(0.16)	0.35	(0.11)	0.45	(0.12)
France	0.12	(0.24)	0.18	(0.13)	0.36	(0.15)
Germany	0.86	(0.29)	0.67	(0.25)	0.87	(0.19)
Italy	0.29	(0.16)	0.29	(0.10)	0.42	(0.11)
Japan	0.38	(0.26)	0.41	(0.11)	0.53	(0.12)
U.K.	0.00	(0.25)	0.01	(0.11)	0.19	(0.14)
U.S.A.	0.57	(0.11)	0.50	(0.12)	0.60	(0.12)
Average	0.37	(0.21)	0.34	(0.13)	0.49	(0.13)

Note: Each Monte Carlo statistic is an average across 100 replications.

follow, I set the true risk-sharing parameters equal to the provincial estimates to explore aggregation bias in a case when is it negligible and use the G-7 estimates to explore aggregation bias in a case when it is significant.

The Monte Carlo procedure uses a random-walk specification of income and involves the following steps. First, I construct the quantity of pooled income using the estimated risk-sharing parameters from the baseline regression for the Canadian panel as the truth, for example, to get

$$\Delta y_t^* = (1/\hat{\Lambda}) \sum_{j=1}^{10} \hat{\lambda}_j \Delta y_{jt}, \tag{9}$$

where

y_{jt} = the logarithm of actual provincial income data for province j in year t,
$\hat{\Lambda} \equiv \sum_{j=1}^{10} \hat{\lambda}_j$,
$\hat{}$ = an estimated parameter,
$*$ = a constructed variable.

Under the random-walk assumption, province j's consumption growth is given by

$$\Delta\tilde{c}_{jt}^* = \widehat{\lambda}_j \Delta y_t^* + (1 - \widehat{\lambda}_j)\Delta y_{jt} + \epsilon_{jt}, \tag{10}$$

where ϵ_{jt} introduces consumption measurement error and in what follows a "$\sim$" denotes a variable measured with error. Following the practice of section 4, the first regressor is the simple average of consumption growth across the ten provinces given here as $\Delta\widetilde{c}_{at}^* = (1/10)\sum_{j=1}^{10} \Delta\widetilde{c}_{jt}^*$. The estimated equation for province j is

$$\Delta\widetilde{c}_{jt}^*(n) = \lambda_j(n)\Delta\widetilde{c}_{at}^*(n) + (1 - \lambda_j(n))\Delta\widetilde{y}_{jt} + \eta_{jt}(n), \tag{11}$$

where

$\lambda_j(n)$ = the estimated risk-sharing parameter,
$\Delta\widetilde{y}_{jt}$ = $\Delta y_{jt} + v_{jt}(n)$ is income growth plus measurement error,
$\eta_{jt}(n)$ = the regression residual, each indexed by the Monte Carlo run number n.

The process is repeated until 100 independent trials are completed for each of the ten provinces, and the entire procedure is replicated for each of the G-7 countries.

The measurement errors in consumption and income are drawn from a normal distribution with mean zero and standard deviation equal to 0.707, about one-fourth of the variance of consumption and income growth of a typical region. Experiments are run also with income measurement error set equal to zero. The statistics that follow are averages across the 100 Monte Carlo replications for each of the ten provinces and seven countries.

Table 5 reports the individual risk-sharing parameters for each province of Canada and each country of the G-7. The first two columns are the baseline estimates and standard errors from the random-walk specification, the averages of which were reported in Table 2. The remaining four columns are the Monte Carlo results for cases with consumption measurement error only and for cases with both consumption and income measurement error. All results use the simple average of consumption growth as the first regressor, which is inconsistent with the theory unless risk-sharing parameters are in fact the same in each region.

Before turning to the results of the Monte Carlo, it is useful to consider how employing the simple average versus a weighted average might be expected to affect the results. Recall that the true weight for a given region is λ_j/Λ compared to the weight used in estimation of $1/J$. Regions with above-average risk-sharing parameters receive too low a weight in the aggregate, and this is exacerbated if the average risk-sharing parameter in the panel is low. For example, Germany's income growth should receive a weight of 0.29 (i.e., $\widehat{\lambda}_{Ger}/\widehat{\Lambda}_{G-7} = 0.86/2.96 = 0.29$) based on the estimated risk-sharing parameters of Germany and the rest of the G-7 countries, but, in an equally weighted average, it gets a weight of only 0.14. We would expect the risk-sharing parameter for Germany to be biased downward on this account.

Beginning with the case that deals with only consumption measurement error, we see that the cross-provincial average risk-sharing parameter in the Monte Carlo is equal to its true value of 0.88. Absent the rounding of results, the bias is 0.75% of the true average. The minute extent of the bias is not surprising since the greatest difference between the true weight and the assumed weight is only about 0.02 for British Columbia, and the differences for the remaining provinces are typically less than 0.01.

Turning to the G-7 countries, the Monte Carlo estimates of nations having true risk-sharing parameters above the average, such as Germany at 0.86 and the United States at 0.57, are downward biased to 0.67 and 0.50 as expected, since their consumption growth rates are given a lower-than-appropriate weight in the construction of the aggregate consumption variable. Regions with risk-sharing parameters close to the panel mean (Canada, Japan, and Italy) are biased only a negligible amount, while France and the U.K. are based upward. The biases tend to average out in the cross-section so that the Monte Carlo estimate of the cross-sectional mean risk-sharing parameter is only slightly downward biased at 0.34 compared to the true value of 0.37.

Turning to the case with measurement error in regional income growth in addition to the measurement error in regional consumption growth, we expect the coefficient on income to be downward biased. In the context of a multiple regression, the other coefficient will also be biased even if the variable to which it is attached is not measured with error unless the regressors are orthogonal. Given that the true coefficient on the income variable and the correlation of the regressors are positive, the coefficient on aggregate consumption will be biased upward resulting in an overestimate of the extent of risk sharing.

For the Canadian provinces, the introduction of measurement error in regional income is of minor consequence, since the true coefficient on income is typically below 0.10 to begin with. The average of the risk-sharing parameters across provinces is biased upward by only 0.01 from 0.88 to 0.89. The results for the G-7 countries are affected in a more substantial way, with the average risk-sharing parameter recovered by the Monte Carlo at 0.49, compared to the true cross-sectional average of 0.37. The biases tend to be largest for the regions with true coefficients on income that are the largest. Compared to the results with only consumption measurement error, the risk-sharing parameter for Germany is biased upward from 0.67 to 0.87 (approximately 26%), while the estimate for the U.K. is biased upward from 0.01 to 0.19.

The Monte Carlo experiments demonstrate that the aggregation procedure alone does not induce quantitatively significant coefficient bias, so not knowing the risk-sharing parameters in advance is not necessary to recover them from the data. However, when income is measured with substantial error (recall the variance of the measurement error is 25% of income growth), the risk-sharing parameter is biased upward.

The variance decompositions (not reported) are consistent with the biases in the risk-sharing parameters found in Table 5. The Canadian provincial results are virtually unaffected, but the fraction of consumption variance attributed to the aggregate component is biased upward for the G-7 countries from a true crosscountry average of 0.14 to 0.27.

The possibility of income measurement error in the data suggest that the risk-sharing parameters and the variance decompositions overstate the risk sharing among G-7 countries, thus reinforcing the conclusion that risk sharing is more extensive across regions within countries than it is across nations.

Next, I turn to the issue of using aggregate consumption growth rather than the innovation to aggregate permanent income as the first regressor in the empirical specification. That is, the estimated equation in the Monte Carlo experiments for province j is

$$\Delta\widetilde{c}^*_{jt}(n) = \lambda_j(n)\Delta\widetilde{y}^*_{at}(n) + (1 - \lambda_j(n))\Delta\widetilde{y}_{jt} + \eta_{jt}(n), \qquad (12)$$

where

$$\begin{aligned}\Delta\widetilde{y}^*_{at}(n) &= (1/10)\textstyle\sum_{j=1}^{10}[\Delta y_{jt} + v_{jt}(n)],\\ y_{jt} &= \text{actual income growth in province j},\\ v_{jt}(n) &= \text{a measurement error added to this income}\\ &\quad\ \text{growth in Monte Carlo run } n.\end{aligned}$$

The remaining variables are as defined in the previous Monte Carlo experiment.

The only difference between this experiment and the previous one is that the construction of the first regressor is affected by measurement error in regional income rather than measurement error in regional consumption. The result is to induce some positive correlation into the two regressors due to a common measurement error in both. In practice, this effect is minor, because the measurement errors are independent across regions and this source of variance averages out in the process of aggregation.

As anticipated, the Monte Carlo results are basically unaffected by this change of variables. Table 6 reports these results along with actual estimates. Beginning with the Monte Carlo estimates in the last two columns of the table, the average risk-sharing parameter across countries is 0.47 for the G-7 countries compared to 0.49 in the Monte Carlo with mismeasured aggregate consumption as the first regressor. (The average across provinces is 0.89, the same (up to rounding error) as the previous Monte Carlo experiment.)

The conclusion to draw from this analysis is that, if income were truly a random walk and risk sharing was taking place among permanent income consumers, replacing aggregate consumption growth with aggregate income growth is of no consequence in recovering the true risk-sharing parameters.

The first two columns of Table 6 present the actual estimated risk-sharing parameters that obtain when aggregate income growth replaces aggregate consumption growth as the first regressor. The estimates are reasonably close to the true values in the case of the Canadian provinces, averaging 0.71 compared to a true average of 0.89, but the G-7 parameter estimates are severely biased downward to an average of 0.13 compared to a true average of 0.47. What are we to conclude from this last Monte Carlo experiment?

The interpretation that follows most directly from the available evidence is a logical extension of recent work by Cochrane (1994). Cochrane uses the bivariate relationship between consumption and income under the maintained assumption that the permanent income hypothesis is correct to decompose income into permanent and transitory components. Consumption, then, completely summarizes all consumer's information about long-run GNP. Here, aggregate consumption summarizes all the consumer's information about long-run movements in aggregate permanent income, which is relevant to individual consumption decisions to the extent that risk sharing is taking place. Under this interpretation, my results indicate that aggregate consumption growth is a better proxy for aggregate permanent income than the proxy constructed by averaging individual permanent income changes. This is particularly relevant for the country-level analysis.

Table 6. Monte Carlo results: aggregate permanent income.

Region	Empirical estimates		Monte Carlo estimates	
	λ	se(λ)	λ	se(λ)
Results for the Canadian Provinces				
Newfoundland	0.55	(0.21)	0.87	(0.06)
Prince Edward Island	1.15	(0.17)	0.98	(0.05)
Nova Scotia	0.60	(0.10)	0.82	(0.05)
New Brunswick	0.98	(0.14)	0.98	(0.04)
Quebec	0.16	(0.20)	0.96	(0.08)
Ontario	0.27	(0.22)	0.87	(0.07)
Manitoba	0.91	(0.30)	0.87	(0.10)
Saskatchewan	0.96	(0.09)	0.85	(0.03)
Alberta	0.97	(0.10)	0.92	(0.03)
British Columbia	0.53	(0.24)	0.75	(0.08)
Average	0.71	(0.18)	0.89	(0.06)
Results for the G-7 Countries				
Canada	0.27	(0.22)	0.44	(0.13)
France	−0.31	(0.20)	0.35	(0.16)
Germany	0.34	(0.61)	0.86	(0.22)
Italy	0.13	(0.21)	0.37	(0.12)
Japan	−0.04	(0.28)	0.50	(0.13)
United Kingdom	−0.07	(0.27)	0.15	(0.14)
United States	0.60	(0.19)	0.60	(0.14)
Average	0.13	(0.28)	0.47	(0.15)

Note: Each Monte Carlo statistic is an average across 100 replications.

6. Conclusions

Two main conclusions emerge from the results. First, there is evidently much more risk sharing across the Canadian provinces and the U.S. states than there is across the G-7 countries. Second, the absolute amount of risk sharing in terms of the variance of fitted changes in annual consumption is very large for the provinces and states. Each of these observations has important implications for research lying at the intersection of international finance and macroeconomics.

As is well known from the empirical work on international portfolio diversification, investors have financial portfolios that are severely home-biased. Tesar and Werner (1995) report that the proportion of foreign stocks in domestic equity portfolios of industrialized countries rarely exceeds 5%. The risk-sharing parameter estimates for the G-7 imply that individuals hold at least one-third of their wealth in an internationally diversified portfolio, though 5% is within a 95% confidence interval of the risk-sharing parameters for three of the G-7 countries.

The results found here support some recent attempts to measure the welfare gains of perfect international financial market integration. Obstfeld (1994b) presents numerical simulations that suggest further international financial market integration would result in both large welfare gains and greater comovement of international consumption growth. The benefits from complete international risk sharing among twenty OECD countries were calculated by van Wincoop (1994) to be between 1.8% and 5.6% of per capita consumption. These estimates suggest that the costs of international risk sharing are actually quite high if the costs and benefits are equated. The cross-sectional differences identified here may be consistent with small costs of risk sharing that are higher at the international level compared to the national level.

An alternative interpretation of the results is that aggregate consumption is a proxy for common movements in regional permanent income that are poorly estimated by the income regressions. Under this interpretation, the results over-estimate the risk sharing if these common movements are not the result of risk pooling behavior. Two possibilities seem plausible. Some of the variation in consumption undoubtedly reflects intertemporal substitution due to interest rate variation that the model assumed was absent. Not only would this induce common movements in consumption over time, it might also explain some of the differences across regions and nations, since evidence exists on the inequality of real interest rates across countries. (See, for example, Mark (1985).)

The second possibility is that aggregate consumption is a proxy for common movements in permanent income that is quantitatively more important at the regional level than at the national level. One example is Jaffe *et al.* (1993), who find evidence that knowledge spillovers (measured by citation patterns) are larger across regions within the U.S. than between the U.S. and foreign countries.

Fiscal policy may also contribute to the differences within and across countries. Bayoumi and Masson (1995) estimate that approximately thirty cents of the cyclical variation in state income is offset by fiscal variables in the U.S. compared to approximately seventeen cents for the Canadian provinces. Asdrubali *et al.* (1996) find a lower but still economically significant estimate of the impact of U.S. fiscal policy with approximately 13% of the smoothing of consumption across U.S. states accounted for by this channel. It could be that national governments provide more insurance against regional variation in income than private markets find efficient to provide nations against national variation in income, thus increasing regional consumption comovement relative to international consumption comovement.

Each of the explanations above presupposes some form of financial market incompleteness, yet only recently have the quantitative implications of incomplete markets been explored. Recent models (Baxter and Crucini (1995); Cole (1988); Conze *et al.* (1993); Kollmann (1996)) predict that regional consumption correlations are lower when asset markets are restricted and disturbances have persistent idiosyncratic components. However, these models abstract from both monetary and fiscal policy and typically compare only a limited menu of asset choices. Richer versions of these models will be useful in sorting out the plausibility of the various channels of consumption smoothing and risk sharing that are suggested by the existing empirical literature.

Acknowledgments

The current version was improved by incorporating the suggestions of Pok-sang Lam, Chris Telmer, Ken West, and two anonymous referees. An earlier version entitled "International Risk Sharing: A Simple Comparative Test," (Crucini, 1993) benefitted from the comments of Paul Evans, Nelson Mark, and workshop participants at the GSIA Carnegie-Mellon University, the Wharton School, the University of

Pennsylvania, Ohio State University, New York University, and the University of Rochester. I thank Wayne Strayer and Sejong Wang for their research assistance. Any errors that remain are the sole responsibility of the author.

Appendix

The data used in the paper are real per capita values of the sources described below.

A.1. Canadian Provincial Data

The Canadian data is from *Provincial Economic Accounts,* published by Statistics Canada from 1971 to 1991. The data are at the annual frequency. To my knowledge, these data represent that first attempt to provide a comprehensive set of macroeconomic accounts at a regional level of aggregation. Personal expenditure on consumer goods and services at 1986 prices is calculated at the same level of detail as the national estimates. Spending on goods by province relies, for the most part, on monthly and annual Retail Trade Surveys, the Census of Merchandising (1961, 1966, and 1971), the 1968 and 1974 Retail Commodity Surveys, and surveys of alcoholic beverages, motor vehicles, etc. Energy consumption is either obtained directly or calculated with data on prices and consumption by province.

Spending on services relies on more sources than spending on goods. The stock of housing is multiplied by average rent per dwelling to allocate gross rents. Expenditures on education, health, and financial services are obtained from administrative data and survey results from the Bank of Canada, Revenue Canada, the Public Accounts, and Statistics Canada. Commercial services are estimated for benchmark years and interpolated where suitable annual or subannual surveys are available.

Provincial GDP is an income-based measure, converted to constant prices; it includes

- wages, salaries, and supplementary labor income;
- corporation profits before taxes;

- interest and miscellaneous investment income;
- accrued net income of farm operators from farm production;
- net income of nonfarm unincorporated business, including rent;
- inventory valuation adjustment;
- indirect taxes less subsidies; and, finally,
- capital consumption allowances.

The supplementary income included in gross domestic product includes unemployment compensation and workers' compensation. Wages, salaries, and supplementary income are recorded from income tax forms ("T-4 Supplementary") by province of employment.

Corporation profits before taxes are allocated by one of three methods. The allocation is based appropriately on operating surplus for manufacturing, mining, and construction. Profits in utilities, transportation, communication, storage, and commercial services are distributed on the basis of taxable provincial income. Trade and finance allocations rely entirely on wages and salaries. Due to data limitations it is not possible in all cases to eliminate factor incomes from outside the province.

Interest and miscellaneous investment income is allocated by a number of methods. For example, interest income of persons for deposit, bond, and mortgage interest receipts is based on either tabulated data by Revenue Canada or surveys. Imputed interest of chartered banks, mortgage loan companies, and trust companies is based on deposit liabilities.

Accrued net income of farm operators from farm production is calculated annually from farm cash receipts, income in kind of farm producers, change in farm-held inventories and farm expenses.

The GDP numbers are converted to real terms using a final demand deflator as no separate implicit deflator is available for gross domestic product.

As stated in the reference volume accompanying the provincial data used in this study, Statistics Canada provides data quality ratings based on the following three criteria: "(i) the national estimates are deemed of good quality; (ii) the provincial estimation or allocation procedure presents no major conceptual problem; and (iii) the estimation or allocation method is appropriate (i.e., is consistent with national accounting practices and relies on directly relevant information) and uses information of good quality (i.e., which requires minimal adjustments for classification, coverage or valuation)."

A rating of 1 indicates that all of the three conditions are met; a rating of 2 is assigned when one condition is not met, while a rating of 3 indicates that two or more conditions are not met. Among the components of income-based GDP wages, salaries, and supplementary income, accrued net income of farm operators from farm production and indirect taxes less subsidies have a rating of 1; interest and miscellaneous investment income and capital consumption allowances have a rating of 2; and corporation profits before taxes, net income of nonfarm unincorporated business (including rent), and inventory valuation adjustment have a rating of 3. Among the components of consumption expenditure, personal expenditure on durable goods, semidurable goods, and nondurable goods have a rating of 1; personal expenditure on services has a rating of 2.

A.2. U.S. State Level Data

The U.S. data was generously provided by Paul Evans.

The consumption data is from the *Statistical Abstract of the United States,* Table No. 1317: Retail Sales by Type of Store and State. The value used is that for total sales, all stores.

The income data is from *State Personal Income: 1929–1987: Estimates and a Statement of Sources and Methods,* published by the U.S. Department of Commerce, Bureau of Economic Analysis. The more important administrative record data include the state unemployment insurance programs, the social insurance programs, the federal income tax program, the veterans benefit program, and the military payroll system, each from their respective government departments. The two important censuses are the censuses of agriculture and population. Income includes: wages, salaries, other labor income, proprietor's income, personal dividend income, personal interest income, rental income of persons; transfer payments, personal contributions for social insurance, and a residence adjustment.

Proprietor's income, personal dividend income, personal interest income, rental income of persons, and transfer payments are recorded on a place-of-residence basis, while the remaining components are recorded on a place-of-work basis. The residence adjustment is a method of converting the place-of-work components to place-of-residence components. The residence adjustment uses industry-level, journey-to-work data that records the number of wage and salary workers and their average earnings by county of work for each county of residence. The net flows relative to total regional income are used to estimate place-of-residence numbers from the place-of-work data.

A.3. International Data

The international data are from the country pages of the World Tables, published by the World Bank in the Fall 1990 update. The data are available on diskette with menu-driven software for selecting countries, sample periods, and series.

Private consumption is the market value of all goods and services purchased or received as income in kind by individuals and nonprofit institutions. It excludes purchases of dwellings, but includes imputed rent of owner-occupied dwellings. It includes any statistical discrepancy in the use of resources.

GDP is the sum of GDP at factor cost and indirect taxes less subsidies. The GDP deflator is the current price estimate of GDP divided by the constant price estimate.

A.4. Log-Linear Approximation

This section of the appendix provides details of the log-linear approximation involved in transforming the data from levels to log levels.

The linearization of the consumption function proceeds as in Campbell and Mankiw (1989). The additional part of the linearization particular to my model is the transformation of the level individual income, defined as the linear combination of the level of aggregate and individual per capita income into its logarithm.

The definition of income under the incomplete risk-sharing specification is

$$\bar{Y}_{it} \equiv \lambda Y_{at} + (1-\lambda)Y_{it}.$$

Taking the logarithm of $\bar{Y}_t^i$ with some simple manipulation leads to

$$\begin{aligned}\bar{y}_{it} \equiv \log \bar{Y}_{it} &= \log\left[\lambda Y_{at}\left(1+\frac{1-\lambda}{\lambda}\frac{Y_{it}}{Y_{at}}\right)\right]\\ &= \log\lambda + y_{at} + \log\left[1+\frac{1-\lambda}{\lambda}\exp\left(y_{it}-y_{at}\right)\right].\end{aligned}$$

The approximation is

$$\begin{aligned}\bar{y}_{it} &\approx \log\lambda + y_{at} + (\kappa{+}(1-\theta)(y_{it}-y_{at}))\\ &= \log\lambda + \kappa + \theta y_{at} + (1-\theta)y_{it}\end{aligned}$$

where

$$\begin{aligned}\theta &\equiv 1 - \frac{(1-\lambda)\exp\left(y_i-y_a\right)}{\lambda+(1-\lambda)\exp\left(y_i-y_a\right)}\\ \kappa &\equiv \log\left[1+\frac{1-\lambda}{\lambda}\exp(y_i-y_a)\right]\\ &\quad - \frac{(1-\lambda)\exp\left(y_i-y_a\right)}{\lambda+(1-\lambda)\exp\left(y_i-y_a\right)}(y_i-y_a).\end{aligned}$$

Taking the first difference operator through the approximation gives

$$\Delta\bar{y}_{jt} \approx \theta\Delta y_{at} + (1-\theta)\Delta y_{it}.$$

From the definition of θ, it goes to unity as λ goes to unity. Thus, the coefficient on the growth of aggregate income goes to unity as risk sharing increases as required.

References

Asdrubali, Pierfederico, Bent E. Sorensen, and Oved Yosha, "Channels of Interstate Risk Sharing: United States, 1963–1990," *Quarterly Journal of Economics* CXI 4 (1996), 955–1006.

Atkeson, Andrew, and Tamin Bayoumi, "Do Private Capital Markets Insure Regional Risks? Evidence from the United States and Europe," *Open Economics Review* 4 (1993), 303–324.

Bayoumi, Tamin, and Paul R. Masson, "Fiscal Flows in the United States and Canada: Lessons for Monetary Union in Europe," *European Economic Review* 19 (1995), 253–274.

Baxter, Marianne, and Mario J. Crucini, "Business Cycles and the Asset Market Structure of Foreign Trade." *International Economic Review* 36 (November 1995), 821–854.

Besley, Timothy, "Nonmarket Institutions for Credit Risk Sharing in Low Income Countries," *Journal of Economic Perspectives* 9 (Summer 1995), 115–127.

Campbell, John, and Gregory Mankiw. "Consumption, Income and Interest Rates: Reinterpreting the Time Series Evidence," in Olivier Blanchard and Stanley Fisher (eds.), *NBER Macroeconomics Annual* (Cambridge: MIT Press, 1989), 185–216.

Cochrane, John, "A Simple Test of Consumption Insurance," *Journal of Political Economy* 99 (October 1991), 957–976.

Cochrane, John, "Permanent and Transitory Components of GNP and Stock Prices," *Quarterly Journal of Economics* 109(1) (February 1994), 241–265.

Cole, Harold, "Financial Structure and International Trade," *International Economic Review* 29(2) (May 1988), 237–259.

Conze, A., J.M. Lasry, and J. Scheinkman, "Borrowing Constraints and International Comovements," In Robert Becker *et al.* (eds.), *General Equilibrium Growth and Trade: The Legacy of Lionel McKenzie* (Volume 2, Toronto: Academic Press, 1993), 460–489.

Crucini, Mario J., "International Risk Sharing: A Simple Comparative Test," unpublished manuscript (March 1993).

Hansen, Lars Peter, and Thomas J. Sargent, "Formulating and Estimating Dynamic Linear Rational Expectations Models," *Journal of Economic Dynamics and Control* 2 (February 1980), 7–46.

Hess, Gregory, and Kwanho Shin, "Risk Sharing by Households Within and Across Regions and Industries," Mimeo (February 1997).

Jaffe, Adam B., Manuel Trajtenberg, and Rebecca Henderson, "Geographic Localization of Knowledge Spillovers as Evidenced by Patent Citations," *Quarterly Journal of Economics* 108(3) (August 1993), 577–598.

Kollmann, Robert, "Incomplete Asset Markets and the Cross-Country Consumption Correlation Puzzle," *Journal of Economic Dynamics and Control* 20 (1996), 945–961.

Lewis, Karen, "What Can Explain the Apparent Lack of International Consumption Risk Sharing," *Journal of Political Economy* 104(2) (April 1996), 267–297.

Mace, Barbara, "Full Insurance in the Presence of Aggregate Uncertainty," *Journal of Political Economy* 99 (October 1991), 928–956.

Mark, Nelson, "Some Evidence on the International Inequality of Real Interest Rates," *Journal of International Money and Finance* 4(2) (June 1985), 189–208.

Morduch, Jonathan, "Income Smoothing and Consumption Smoothing," *Journal of Economic Perspectives* 9 (Summer 1995), 103–114.

Obstfeld, Maurice, "Are Industrial Country Consumption Risks Globally Diversified?" In Leonardo Leiderman and Assaf Razin, (eds.), *Capital Mobility: The Impact on Consumption, Investment, and Growth* (New York: Cambridge University Press, 1994a).

Obstfeld, Maurice, "Risk-Taking, Global Diversification, and Growth," *American Economic Review* 84(5) (December 1994b), 1310–1329.

Pagan, Adrian, "Econometric Issues in the Analysis of Regressions with Generated Regressors," *International Economic Review* 25 (February 1984), 221–247.

Sorensen, Bent E., and Oved Yosha, "Income and Consumption Smoothing Among U.S. States: Regions or Clubs?" Mimeo (June 1996).

Statistics Canada, Provincial Economic Accounts, Annual Estimates 1961 to Date, Ministry of Supply and Services Canada (1991).

Tesar, Linda, and Ingrid Werner, "Home Bias and High Turnover," *Journal of International Money and Finance* 14(4) (August 1995), 467–492.

Townsend, Robert M., "Consumption Insurance: An Evaluation of Risk-Bearing Systems in Low-Income Countries," *Journal of Economic Perspectives* 9 (Summer 1995), 83–102.

United States Department of Commerce, Bureau of Economic Analysis. State Personal Income: 1929–1987: A Statement of Sources and Methods.

United States Department of Commerce, Bureau of the Census. Statistical Abstract of the United States. (Washington D.C.: U.S. Government Printing Office.)

van Wincoop, Eric, "Welfare Gains from International Risk Sharing," *Journal of Monetary Economics* 34(2) (October 1994), 175–200.

World Bank, World Tables, Washington, D.C. (1991).

Chapter 6

Business Cycles and the Asset Structure of Foreign Trade*

Marianne Baxter

Department of Economics, University of Virginia, Charlottesville, VA, USA and National Bureau of Economic Research, Cambridge, MA, USA

and

Mario J. Crucini

Department of Economics, Ohio State University, Columbus, OH, USA

Abstract. International financial markets are widely believed to be important for the international transmission of business cycles, since they determine the extent to which individuals can smooth consumption in the presence of country-specific shocks to income. Using a two-country equilibrium model with restricted asset trade, we find that the absence of complete financial integration may not be important if shocks to national economies have low persistence or are transmitted rapidly across countries. However, if shocks are highly persistent or are not transmitted internationally, the extent of financial integration is central to the international transmission of business cycles.

*This chapter originally appeared in *International Economic Review*, 1995, **36**(4), 821–854.

1. Introduction

Economists have long understood that financial markets play a central role in the international propagation and transmission of business cycles. Morgenstern's (1959) book is a classic reference on this subject, but discussions of the link between financial markets and business cycles can be found in the earlier writings of Mitchell (1927) who attributed the positive and increasing correlation of international business cycles to the growth of international financial markets. The extent of international financial integration *should* be important for international business cycles, since an important function of financial markets is to permit individuals to smooth consumption in response to fluctuations in income. Thus the extent to which a country can trade on world financial markets will determine the extent to which its citizens can insure themselves against nation-specific components of business-cycle risk. The goal of the present paper is to provide a detailed analysis of the channels through which international financial linkages affect international business cycles.

Our framework is a two-country, single-good, general equilibrium model related to those used in the "open economy real business cycle" literature. This literature highlights the transmission of international business cycles in an equilibrium setting through the influences of interest rates and asset prices.[1] However, this literature is often criticized for its treatment of international financial market linkages. That is, this literature assumes that individuals have access to complete international contingent-claims markets which permit them to pool all risks. A second strand of literature studies business cycles in small open economies. These studies typically restrict access to international risk sharing in ways that seem, empirically, to be more reasonable than the assumption of complete markets.[2] But these analyses are necessarily silent on the factors affecting world interest rates and asset prices.

---

[1]See, for example, the surveys by Backus, Kehoe, and Kydland (1995) and Baxter (1995).

[2]See, for example, the contributions of Cardia (1991), Correia, Neves, and Rebelo (1995), and Mendoza (1991).

This paper develops a two-country, general equilibrium model in which individuals have incomplete access to international risk sharing. Using this model as our laboratory, we evaluate the importance of financial market linkages for international business cycles, by comparing its predictions to the complete markets model. Our main findings are as follows. First, we find that restricting asset trade to noncontingent bonds alone does not importantly alter the predictions of the standard, complete markets model. If the international productivity process is trend stationary with substantial international "spillovers" of productivity shocks, the two models are essentially indistinguishable. If, however, productivity in each country follows a random walk without spillovers but with correlated innovations, restricting asset trade alters the predictions of the model along several important dimensions. In particular, under this parameterization, the complete markets model predicts low cross-country output correlations and near-perfect consumption correlations; the bond economy conversely predicts high output correlations and low consumption correlations. This finding is important, since the complete markets model has been heavily criticized for its counterfactual prediction of near-perfect international consumption correlations for a wide range of parameterizations. With random walk shocks, restricting asset markets brings the consumption correlation down substantially.

Second, we find that the major differences in the macroeconomic response to shocks under the alternative asset structures are due almost entirely to differential wealth effects. In particular, we find strong differences across asset structures when productivity follows a random walk. In this case, under complete markets, individuals receiving a favorable productivity shock experience a negative wealth effect. This is because the optimal insurance character of equilibrium requires them to increase labor supply while transferring a large proportion of the additional output to residents of the other country. In the bond economy, however, individuals own all the risky claims to their country's output. Thus individuals receiving a favorable productivity shock experience a positive wealth effect which induces them to increase consumption by more than in the complete markets economy and, more importantly, causes them to decrease labor input.

Although our primary goal was to understand the relationship between financial integration and business cycles, this analysis also contributes to the growing literature that uses quantitative theory to understand international business cycles. Specifically, we show that the model with restricted asset market linkages provides an explanation for the empirical observation that international consumption correlations are lower than international output correlations. Further, we find that the model with restricted asset markets can generate correlations between productivity and labor input that are much closer to those observed in the data, compared with those generated by a standard closed-economy model driven by technology shocks alone. That is, restricted asset trade is another possible resolution of the so-called "Dunlop-Tarshis" observation, which is the low correlation of productivity and labor input observed in the data.[3]

Although the dominant source of differences across asset structures was found to lie in wealth effects, consumption and leisure are strongly affected in both asset structures by interest rate effects and wage effects. Thus the general equilibrium structure, in which interest rates and asset prices are determined endogenously, is important for understanding the way in which economies respond to exogenous shocks. This consideration is important even if the economy in question is "small" in the sense of producing a small share of world output.

Our work is related to that of Cole (1988), who studied the implications of financial structure for business cycles in a two-period model with production. More recently, the relationship between asset markets and real activity has been studied by Conze, Lasry, and Sheinkman (1990), and Kollman (1993). They find, as we do, that restrictions on asset markets lead to lower international correlations of consumption. Constantinides and Duffie (1991) find that, when idiosyncratic shocks are purely permanent, there is no bond trade

[3]See Christiano and Eichenbaum (1992) for more discussion, and a different proposed resolution of the puzzle based on government spending shocks combined with important measurement error in labor input.

in equilibrium. However, in our model permanent shocks affect the marginal productivity of capital, so trade in bonds occurs even with unit-root shocks. Telmer (1993) studies an endowment economy with asset trade restricted to bonds only, and finds that this restriction has little effect on asset prices when idiosyncratic shocks are stationary. Heaton and Lucas (1995) use an endowment economy with restricted asset trade to study the effects of market incompleteness on asset returns.

The paper is structured as follows. Section 2 describes the model economy and discusses aspects of the solution procedure that differ from prior, complete markets analyses. Section 3 begins with a review of previous work on estimating the stochastic process for productivity, and presents some new results. Taken together, these results suggest that productivity shocks are highly persistent, are correlated across countries, and may contain unit roots. Therefore, we compare the predictions of the complete markets model to the predictions of the model with restricted asset markets under two alternative parameterizations of the productivity process: (i) a trend-stationary process with innovations that are correlated across countries and with international transmission of shocks, and (ii) a difference-stationary process without transmission but with correlated innovations. We find that the empirical implications of the models are very sensitive to the specification of the stochastic process for productivity. If productivity follows a trend-stationary process with highly persistent shocks and international transmission, the business cycle implications of the incomplete markets economy are very similar to those of the complete markets economy. However, if productivity follows a random walk without transmission, the implications of the alternative models are quite different. Section 4 explores the economic forces behind the differential response under alternative asset structures by studying the dynamic response to a productivity shock originating in one country. Using King's (1990) method for decomposing consumption and labor responses into wealth and substitution effects, we find that differences across asset structures — when they exist — can be traced primarily to differential wealth effects. Section 5 briefly summarizes the paper's main results and discusses avenues for future research.

2. The Model

The basic structure of this model, in terms of preferences and technology, is identical to the structure in Baxter and Crucini (1993). The main difference arising from restrictions on asset trade appears in the flow constraints (budget, constraints), which differ across the two models. Foreign country variables are denoted by stars, and all variables are in national per capita terms.

Preferences. Individuals consume two goods: a produced consumption good, C, and leisure, L. They maximize expected lifetime utility, given by

$$E_0 \sum_{t=0}^{\infty} \beta^t \frac{1}{1-\sigma}[C_t^{\theta} L_t^{1-\sigma}]^{1-\sigma}, \quad \text{home country;} \tag{1}$$

$$E_0 \sum_{t=0}^{\infty} \beta^t \frac{1}{1-\sigma}[(C_t^*)(L_t^*)^{1-\theta}]^{1-\sigma}, \quad \text{foreign country.} \tag{2}$$

In each country, individuals are subject to the constraint that hours worked in the marketplace plus hours of leisure cannot exceed the time endowment, normalized to one unit:

$$\begin{aligned} 1 - L_t - N_t &\geq 0, \quad \text{home country;} \\ 1 - L_t^* - N_t^* &\geq 0, \quad \text{foreign country.} \end{aligned} \tag{3}$$

Technology. Production functions exhibit constant returns to scale, and production of the single final good requires the input of both labor and capital. Capital used in production in a specific country is not necessarily owned by residents of that country; thus, K_t represents capital in place in the home country, not necessarily capital owned by residents of the home country. Labor is internationally immobile. Letting N_t denote labor employed in the home country, these production functions are given by

$$Y_t = A_t K_t^{1-\alpha}(X_t N_t)^{\alpha}, \quad \text{home country;} \tag{4}$$

$$Y_t^* = A_t^*(K_t^*)^{1-\alpha^*}(X_t^* N_t^*)^{\alpha^*}, \quad \text{foreign country.} \tag{5}$$

In these production functions, the variables X_t and X_t^* represent the level of purely labor-augmenting technical change in the home and foreign countries, respectively, and each grows at a common, constant gross rate: $\gamma = X_{t+1}/X_t = X^*_{t+1}/X^*_t$. The variables A_t and A^*_t represent the stochastic component of the productivity variable, and are assumed to follow a vector Markov process.

New capital goods are internationally mobile, and all investment is subject to costs of adjustment governed by the function $\phi(I/K)$, with $\phi > 0, \phi' > 0, \phi'' < 0$, as in Hayashi (1982). Capital accumulates over time according to

$$K_{t+1} = (1-\delta)K_t + \phi(I_t/K_t)K_t, \quad \text{home country;} \tag{6}$$

$$K^*_{t+1} = (1-\delta)K^*_t + \phi(I^*_t/K^*_t)K^*_t, \quad \text{foreign country.} \tag{7}$$

Capital adjustment costs have been incorporated to slow the response of investment to location-specific shocks. Because there is a single good produced in two different countries, capital owners have a strong incentive to locate new investment in the more-productive location (so long as productivity shocks are persistent). Without some friction in the capital adjustment process, the model would display excessive volatility of investment.

2.1. *Complete markets*

The first model that we shall study is also, in many ways, the simplest. There are two countries in the world, and individuals in the two countries are free to trade any state-contingent asset they wish. Thus, in equilibrium, individuals will bear no idiosyncratic risk. Since the consumption/investment good is internationally mobile, there is a single world resource constraint for this good. Letting π denote the fraction of the world population residing in the home country, the world resource constraint is

$$\pi[Y_t - C_t - I_t] + (1-\pi)[Y^*_t - C^*_t - I^*_t] \geq 0. \tag{8}$$

The equilibrium of this economy consists of a set of functions describing the behavior of endogenous variables such as consumption, saving, investment, and so forth, as functions of the exogenous shocks to the model (i.e., the productivity shocks). Before solving our model, we transform it to remove deterministic trend components; this is accomplished by dividing all home country variables by X_t and all foreign country variables by X_t^*. Lowercase letters are used below to denote transformed variables. Note that labor and leisure cannot have deterministic trends; otherwise, the time constraints would eventually be violated. These variables continue to be represented by uppercase letters. Finally, the common rate of time preference for all individuals in the transformed world economy is $\tilde{\beta} \equiv \beta\gamma^{\theta(1-\sigma)}$. The Appendix discusses the details of the approach that we use to solve for this model's competitive equilibrium.

2.2. *General equilibrium in a two-country world with restricted asset markets*

The model differs from the general equilibrium economy described in Section 2.1 above in that agents are restricted to trade only goods and noncontingent real debt. For simplicity, but without loss of generality, the single debt instrument is a one-period discount bond. We let r_t denote the world rate of return on risk-free securities, and let $P_t^B \equiv (1 + r_t)^{-1}$ denote the price per unit of one-period discount bonds purchased in period t. B_{t+1} denotes the quantity of bonds purchased in period t (maturing in $t + 1$). Following our earlier convention of letting lowercase letters refer to the transformed economy, we let $b_t \equiv B_t/X_t$ denote the value of bonds in the transformed economy. Then the flow budget constraint for the home country in period t is

$$\gamma P_t^B b_{t+1} + c_t + i_t \leq y_t + b_t, \tag{9}$$

and for the foreign country is

$$\gamma P_t^B b_{t+1}^* + c_t^* + i_t^* \leq y_t^* + b_t^*. \tag{10}$$

The boundary conditions for the incomplete-markets economy are

$$\lim_{t\to\infty} \tilde{\beta}^t p_t b_{t+1} = 0, \tag{11}$$

$$\lim_{t\to\infty} \tilde{\beta}^t p_t^* b_{t+1}^* = 0, \tag{12}$$

where p_t, p_t^* are the multipliers associated with the constraints (9) and (10).

As before, let π be the fraction of world population residing in the home country. Then, since bonds are in zero net supply at the world level, bond market clearing requires that

$$\pi b_t + (1 - \pi) b_t^* = 0. \tag{13}$$

By permitting asset accumulation, we have introduced a new parameter: the steady state level of assets relative to output. In closed economies and in multicountry models with fully pooled equilibria, each country's holdings of assets which are in zero net supply must be constant along any equilibrium path. In general, however, whenever there are multiple countries and incomplete risk pooling, the steady state level of asset holdings will not be invariant to shocks to the world economy. We set $\theta_b = b/y = 0$ so that per capita wealth is equal across countries in the deterministic steady state.

The Appendix describes in detail how we solve for competitive equilibrium in this model. The key insight is that the shifting wealth distribution associated with market incompleteness can be appropriately accounted for by adding one country's current bond holdings to the model's state vector. That is, the distribution of bond holdings across countries in the world is a sufficient statistic for the history of the economy in terms of determining current decisions by individuals. Thus models with market incompleteness can be analyzed using the methods developed for complete markets models with J countries, with the modification that the state space must be expanded. In this case, the state space must include the bond holdings of $J - 1$ of the countries.

3. Implications for Business Cycles

In this section we examine the implications for the character of international business cycles of restricting the portfolio of internationally tradable assets. We begin by reviewing the international stylized facts, and then discuss the calibration of our model. We turn next to the measurement and estimation of the productivity process. Whether asset markets are important depends importantly on the properties of the stochastic process for productivity. For this reason, this section also presents some new empirical evidence on international productivity.

3.1. *Open economy business cycles*

Table 1 presents summary business cycle statistics for eight OECD countries. To render the data stationary, all variables have been filtered with the Hodrick and Prescott (1980) filter. The central stylized facts of business cycles are similar across countries: (i) there is a tendency for consumption to be less volatile than output while investment is more volatile; (ii) output movements are highly persistent; and (iii) consumption and investment are both strongly procyclical. The lower panel of Table 1 shows that both outputs and consumptions have a tendency to covary positively across countries, but international consumption correlations tend to be lower than international output correlations. Finally, labor market data for the United States shows that (i) labor input is less volatile than output, as is average labor productivity; (ii) labor input is highly correlated with output, as is the average product of labor, and (iii) average labor productivity and the level of labor input are roughly uncorrelated. Labor market statistics for other countries are omitted since accurate measures of total labor input are not readily available.

3.2. *Calibration and model solution*

In our model, the world comprises two equally-sized countries with identical preferences and technology. The parameters of preferences and technology are the same as in Baxter and Crucini (1993). The coefficient of relative risk aversion is set at σ =2, which is in the range of many empirical estimates. Labor's share is $\alpha = 0.58$; as noted in King, Plosser, and Rebelo (1988a) this is the average postwar value of labor's share in GNP, excluding proprietor's income. The discount factor, β, is set so that the steady state annual real interest rate is 6.5 percent; the average quarterly gross growth rate of the economy is $\gamma = 1.004$, and the quarterly depreciation rate is $\delta = 0.025$. These parameter values were set so that the model's steady state matches the average postwar behavior of the U.S. economy. The business-cycle behavior of the model is insensitive to modest perturbations in these parameters; for a sensitivity analysis of the complete markets model, see Baxter and Crucini (1993).

Table 1. Business cycle statistics for 8 OECD countries.

	Relative volatility			Contemporaneous correlation		
Country	σ_c/σ_y	σ_i/σ_y	σ_{nx}/y	ρ_y	$\rho(c, y)$	$\rho(i, y)$
Australia	0.69	2.17	1.46	0.67	0.62	0.55
Canada	0.88	2.83	0.83	0.79	0.72	0.62
France	0.89	1.92	0.81	0.79	0.58	0.45
Germany	0.70	3.40	0.88	0.71	0.64	0.80
Italy	0.82	2.49	1.76	0.78	0.70	0.80
Japan	1.12	2.31	0.93	0.74	0.47	0.60
Switzerland	0.77	2.88	1.50	0.70	0.74	0.73
United States	0.67	3.00	0.41	0.84	0.88	0.90

	Correlation with same U.S. variable		Additional labor market statistics for the U.S.	
Country	Output	Consumption		
Australia	0.24	0.11	σ_N/σ_y:	0.84
Canada	0.77	0.65	$\sigma_{\text{prod}}/\sigma_y$:	0.57
France	0.50	0.28	$\rho(N, y)$:	0.83
Germany	0.44	0.45	$\rho(\text{prod}, y)$:	0.54
Italy	0.47	0.23	$\rho(\text{prod}, N)$:	–0.04
Japan	0.42	0.41		
Switzerland	0.28	0.22		
United States	1.00	1.00		

Note: With the exception of the U.S. labor market statistics, all statistics are taken from Baxter and Crucini (1993). The data is from the International Financial Statistics, and is quarterly postwar data, with coverage varying by country. This is the same database used by Backus, Kehoe, and Kydland (1992) who graciously provided us with their data.

Statistics for U.S. labor markets were taken from Baxter and King (1991); the original data source was Citibase. The data is quarterly data from 1955:1–1990:3. In this table, "N" denotes labor input (hours worked), and "prod" denotes productivity computed as output per man-hour.

All data has been detrended using the Hodrick-Prescott (1980) filter.

The adjustment cost function is specified as follows. Since we are interested in the near steady state dynamics of the model economy, we do not need to specify a particular functional form for adjustment costs. Rather, we need only specify the near steady state behavior of the adjustment cost function. That is, we must specify the level, slope, and curvature of this function at the steady state point. Thus we set ϕ' so that the steady state value of Tobin's "q" is one — that is, the model with adjustment costs has the same deterministic steady state as the model without adjustment costs. Further, the elasticity of the investment-capital ratio with respect to Tobin's "q" is $\eta = -(\phi'/\phi'') \div (i/k) = 15$. Alterations in this elasticity primarily affect the volatility of investment, thus we have set this parameter so that the model generates realistic investment volatility.

It is well known that the system of equations that implicitly defines the equilibrium of the one-sector closed-economy model does not have an analytic solution, except in a small number of special cases. A variety of numerical methods have recently been developed for obtaining approximate solutions to a particular nonlinear equilibrium problem: see the summary paper by Taylor and Uhlig (1990) and the papers cited therein. One method which has been shown to work well for the closed-economy neoclassical model is log-linear approximation of the equilibrium decision rules that solve the Euler equations; see, for example, Dotsey and Mao (1992). The point around which the approximation is taken is the model's initial deterministic steady state. The resulting linear system is solved by application of standard linear systems theory, as described in King, Plosser, and Rebelo (1987).

3.3. *Measuring productivity*

Following the work of Solow (1957), it has become commonplace to measure disembodied productivity (A_t and A_t^*, in our notation) as a residual from a Cobb-Douglas production function. In the notation of our model, the "Solow residuals" would be measured as

$$\log(A_t) \equiv \log(y_t) - (1-\alpha)\log(k_t) - \alpha\log(N_t)$$
$$\log(A_t^*) \equiv \log(y_t^*) - (1-\alpha^*)\log(k_t^*) - \alpha^*\log(N_t^*).$$

Measurement of the Solow residual therefore requires measures of output, capital input, labor input, and factor shares. For the United States, measures of all these variables are available, although there naturally is substantial disagreement concerning the accuracy of these measures. For other countries, in many cases, the necessary data are not readily available. Backus, Kehoe, and Kydland (1992) used output data and employment data to construct estimates of Solow residuals for the United States, Canada, and an aggregate of six European countries. These measures omit the term involving capital input. Further, the mismeasurement of labor input by using employment in place of total hours worked is a potentially serious problem: Burdett and Wright (1989) show that for many European countries, more of the variance in total labor input is explained by hours variation than by employment variation. Despite the measurement problems, the Backus *et al.* (1992), estimates provide a valuable starting point, and we begin by briefly reviewing their findings.

Backus, Kehoe, and Kydland (1992) modeled the productivity shock process as the following vector-autoregressive process:

$$\begin{bmatrix} \log A_t \\ \log A_t^* \end{bmatrix} = \begin{bmatrix} \rho & \nu \\ \nu^* & \rho^* \end{bmatrix} \begin{bmatrix} \log A_{t-1} \\ \log A_{t-1}^* \end{bmatrix} + \begin{bmatrix} \epsilon_t \\ \epsilon_t^* \end{bmatrix} \tag{14}$$

where $E(\epsilon) = E(\epsilon^*) = 0$ and $E(\epsilon^2) = \sigma_\epsilon^2$, $E((\epsilon^*)^2) = \sigma_{\epsilon^*}^2$, and $E(\epsilon_t, \epsilon_t^*) = \psi$ for all t. Backus, Kehoe, and Kydland (1992) estimated Eq. (14) for (i) the United States versus Canada, and (ii) the United States versus an aggregate of six European countries. Their estimates are given below; standard errors are in parentheses.

$$\begin{matrix} \text{U.S.:} \\ \text{Canada:} \end{matrix} \begin{bmatrix} \log A_t \\ \log A_t^* \end{bmatrix} = \begin{bmatrix} 0.796 & 0.131 \\ (0.079) & (0.052) \\ 0.000 & 0.989 \\ (0.093) & (0.060) \end{bmatrix} \begin{bmatrix} \log A_{t-1} \\ \log A_{t-1}^* \end{bmatrix} + \begin{bmatrix} \epsilon_t \\ \epsilon_t^* \end{bmatrix};$$

$$\rho(\epsilon_t, \epsilon_t^*) = 0.434$$

$$\begin{array}{l} \text{U.S.:} \\ \text{Europe:} \end{array} \begin{bmatrix} \log A_t \\ \log A_t^* \end{bmatrix} = \begin{bmatrix} 0.904 & 0.052 \\ (0.074) & (0.041) \\ 0.149 & 0.908 \\ (0.064) & (0.036) \end{bmatrix} \begin{bmatrix} \log A_{t-1} \\ \log A_{t-1}^* \end{bmatrix} + \begin{bmatrix} \epsilon_t \\ \epsilon_t^* \end{bmatrix};$$

$$\rho(\epsilon_t, \epsilon_t^*) = 0.258.$$

We see from these estimates that shocks to productivity are highly persistent, and that there is some evidence of transmission of shocks from one country to another ($\nu, \nu^* > 0$). Further, the innovations to productivity are positively correlated across countries.[4]

Because the Backus *et al.* (1992) estimates indicate that shocks to the productivity process are highly persistent and that the transmission or "spillover" parameters are positive but carry large standard errors, we investigated the hypothesis that the Solow residuals follow a random walk without spillovers, but with possibly correlated innovations.[5] Panel A of Table 2 reports the results of the $J(p, q)$ test for a unit root and zero transmission in each of the three Solow residual series generated by Backus, Kehoe, and Kydland (1992) (Canada, Europe, and the United States). In each case, we fail to reject the null hypothesis at conventional significance levels.

A natural next question is whether there is a cointegrating relationship between the Solow residual time series. Panel B of Table 2 reports the results of tests for cointegration: there is evidence of cointegration between the United States and Canada, but the evidence for cointegration is weaker for the United States and Europe. Based on these results, we estimated a vector error correction model for the United States and Canada, and a standard VAR in first differences for the United States and Europe; the results are in Table 2, Panel C. There appears to be no significant international transmission of shocks, with the possible exception of transmission

[4]See also a recent contribution by Reynolds (1993). Her findings show that, in many cases, the spillover parameters are not significantly different from zero.
[5]All test statistics used in this analysis are discussed in Park (1990).

Table 2. Statistical properties of international Solow residuals.

Panel A: Park and Choi $J(p, q)$ test for unit root

The null hypothesis is a unit root: the hypothesis is rejected if the test statistic is smaller than the critical value.

Measure of solow residual (time period)		Test statistic			
		$J(1, 2)$	$J(1, 3)$	$J(1,4)$	$J(1, 5)$
United States	(1965:3–1988:3)	0.124	0.645	0.699	0.745
Canada	(1965:3–1988:3)	0.343	1.346	1.948	3.461
United States	(1970:2–1986:4)	0.010	0.255	0.275	0.309
Europe	(1970:2–1986:4)	0.740	0.946	0.967	1.179
critical values:		1% 8.6e-5	0.011	0.055	0.123
		5% 0.002	0.055	0.160	0.295
		10% 0.009	0.120	0.290	0.452

Panel B: Tests for cointegration

We used Park's canonical cointegrating regression to estimate α_1 such that log $\log A_t - \alpha \log A_t^* = \epsilon_t$, a stationary random variable. Next, we used Park's $H(p, q)$ test for stochastic cointegration; p-values are given in the table below. In each case, the United States is the unstarred variable (i.e., α is the coefficient on Canada and Europe).

			p-values			
	$\hat{\alpha}$	$se(\hat{\alpha})$	$H(1, 2)$	$H(1, 3)$	$H(1, 4)$	$H(1, 5)$
United States–Canada	0.580	0.061	0.313	0.523	0.707	0.462
United States–Europe	0.603	0.041	0.046	0.039	0.082	0.145

Panel C: Estimates of stochastic processes for Solow residuals

Δ denotes the first difference of the log of a variable, i.e., $\Delta A_t \equiv \log A_t - \log A_{t-1}$; as before the United States is the unstarred country. Standard errors are in parentheses.

United States–Canada:

$$\Delta A_t = \underset{(0.001)}{0.003} + \underset{(0.117)}{0.113}\, \Delta A_{t-1} + \underset{(0.101)}{0.048}\, \Delta A_{t-1}^* - \underset{(0.052)}{0.074}(A_{t-1} - A_{t-1}^*) + u_t$$

$$\Delta A_t^* = \underset{(0.001)}{0.005} + \underset{(0.131)}{0.283}\, \Delta A_{t-1} + \underset{(0.112)}{0.035}\, \Delta A_{t-1}^* - \underset{(0.058)}{0.021}\,(A_{t-1} - A_{t-1}^*) + u_t^*$$

$$\hat{\sigma}_u^2 = 8.38e^{-3}; \quad \hat{\sigma}_{u^*}^2 = 9.34e^{-3}; \quad \hat{\rho}(u, u^*) = 0.392.$$

(*Continued*)

Table 2. (*Continued*)

United States–Europe:
(error-correction term omitted due to lack of cointegration)

$$\Delta A_t = \underset{(0.001)}{0.002} + \underset{(0.126)}{0.003}\ \Delta A_{t-1} + \underset{(0.134)}{0.193}\ \Delta A^*_{t-1} + u_t$$

$$\Delta A^*_t = \underset{(0.001)}{0.005} + \underset{(0.110)}{0.196}\ \Delta A_{t-1} - \underset{(0.117)}{0.076}\ \Delta A^*_{t-1} + u^*_t$$

$$\hat{\sigma}^2_u = 9.07e^{-3};\quad \hat{\sigma}^2_{u*} = 7.95e^{-3};\quad \hat{\rho}(u, u^*) = 0.228.$$

Note: All the tests reported in this table are discussed in Park (1990).

between the United States and Canada. Based on these estimates, we cannot reject the hypothesis that productivity in each country follows a random walk with drift, without transmission, but with innovations that are positively correlated across countries. In the remainder of the paper, we therefore examine the business cycle implications of alternative asset structures under two assumptions concerning the stochastic process for productivity: (i) Backus *et al.* (1992) "symmetrized parameterization," which is characterized by trend-stationary shocks with correlated innovations and substantial international transmission ("spillovers"); and (ii) a random walk process for productivity without spillovers, but with correlated innovations.

3.4. *Trend stationary productivity with spillovers*

We begin by comparing the cyclic behavior of the complete markets economy to that of the bond economy when the stochastic process for productivity is given by the Backus *et al.* (1992) "symmetrized parameterization" of the relationship between United States and European productivity under which $\rho = \rho^* = 0.906, \upsilon = \upsilon^* = 0.088$, and $\psi = 0.258$. Under this parameterization, innovations to productivity are positively correlated across countries ($\psi > 0$) and shocks that originate in one country "spill over" to the other country at the rate of 8.8 percent per quarter ($\nu = 0.088$). We set the innovation variances equal to one.[6]

[6]Since our log-linear solution algorithm generates decision rules that display certainty equivalence, only the scale of volatility changes as we change the

Table 3. Trend stationary shocks.

(1) Results for complete markets economy
(2) Results for economy trading noncontingent bonds and goods only

	Standard deviation		Relative standard deviation		Persistence		Correlation w/y, lag 0			Other correlations	
	(1)	(2)	(1)	(2)	(1)	(2)	(1)	(2)		(1)	(2)
Output	2.01	1.99	1.00	1.00	0.75	0.76	1.00	1.00	y, y^*	0.04	0.06
Consumption	0.97	0.98	0.48	0.49	0.81	0.81	0.82	0.84	c, c^*	0.95	0.92
Investment	3.72	3.55	1.85	1.79	0.73	0.74	0.98	0.97	i, i^*	0.02	0.12
Labor	1.07	1.02	0.53	0.51	0.73	0.72	0.91	0.91	N, N^*	−0.70	−0.67
Wage	1.13	1.14	0.56	0.57	0.80	0.80	0.92	0.93	w, w^*	0.75	0.72
Net exports	0.57	0.59	0.29	0.30	0.80	0.80	0.65	0.65	s, i	0.95	0.94
Bonds	0.00	3.22	0.00	1.62	0.00	0.98	0.00	0.23	w, N	0.66	0.69

Table 3 compares the response of the complete markets economy to the economy which is restricted to financial trade in bonds alone when both economies are driven by the trend-stationary productivity shock with spillovers. The statistics reported in this table are the model's population moments for Hodrick-Prescott (1980) filtered time series.[7] Surprisingly, the differences between the business cycle implications of these two (apparently) very dissimilar models are really quite minor. Compared with the complete markets economy, the bond economy displays similar volatility of output, consumption, investment, labor input, the wage rate, and the net export ratio.[8] In the bond economy, however, bond holdings as a

innovation variances. Relative volatilities, such as the standard deviation of consumption divided by the standard deviation of output, are invariant in this setup to the size of the shock variance.

[7]The population moments for the filtered time series are computed using the rational polynomial version of the Hodrick-Prescott filter applicable to an infinite sample of data, as discussed in King and Rebelo (1993). Even though the incomplete markets model implies that there is a unit root component to each country's real quantity variables, the HP filter contains four differences in the numerator of the rational polynomial, so that population moments for the filtered series are well-defined. For comparison, we also computed these statistics using long simulations of the model — the approach yielded very similar results.

[8]In our model, the wage rate equals the average product of labor.

fraction of output are about three times as volatile as output. Bond holdings have zero variance in the complete markets economy; a well-known characteristic of fully-pooled equilibria is that asset holdings need not fluctuate. In terms of persistence, the two models are essentially indistinguishable except, once again, for the behavior of bond holdings.

Turning to the contemporaneous correlation of macroeconomic aggregates with output, we see that the bond economy generally predicts higher correlations of most variables with same-country output, although the numerical differences are very small. The bond economy predicts higher international correlations of output, investment, and labor input, and smaller international correlations between consumption and wage rates. The within-country correlation between saving and investment is slightly lower in the bond economy compared with the complete markets economy. This might seem surprising, since one's intuition is that closing asset markets, thus forcing individuals to bear more country-specific risk, would act to increase within-country saving-investment correlations. However, this "basic saving measure" (defined as output minus consumption) need not be a good measure of true saving in an open economy, as discussed by Obstfeld (1986) and Stockman and Svensson (1987).

Finally, the asset structure is of minor importance for the predicted correlation between the wage rate and the level of labor input. The complete markets economy predicts a correlation of 0.66, which is about the same as the predictions of the closed-economy real business cycle model calibrated to U.S. data (e.g., the model in Baxter and King (1991) predicts a correlation of 0.65). Restricting asset trade to bonds alone has the effect of slightly increasing the predicted correlation, to a level of 0.69. In the U.S. data, this correlation is –0.04.

How do these models do overall in terms of generating empirically accurate predictions? As discussed by Backus, Kehoe, and Kydland (1992) and Baxter and Crucini (1993), the complete markets economy does reasonably well in matching the within-country stylized facts concerning volatility and persistence of macro aggregates. Much more problematic are the complete markets model's implications for cross-country correlations of output, consumption, investment, and labor input. Specifically, this model has difficulty generating positive output comovement (and correspondingly positive comovement of investments and labor inputs across countries). Further, the model predicts a level of cross-country consumption correlation that is much too high relative to the data.

Because individuals are subject to idiosyncratic (nation-specific) risk in the bond economy, in equilibrium this economy will display nation-specific fluctuations in consumption. Thus we expect that the international correlation between consumptions should be lower in the bond economy, and it is — but not much lower. The complete markets economy predicts an international consumption correlation of 0.95, while the bond economy predicts a correlation of 0.92. (Table 1 shows that the empirical correlations range from 0.11 to 0.65.)

Similarly, we expect the absence of insurance against labor income risk in the bond economy to alter the response of labor input to productivity shocks. In the complete markets economy, the response to a positive productivity shock in one country generates an increase in labor input in the productive country, and a tendency for a decline in labor input in the relatively unproductive country. Because of the optimal insurance character of the complete markets equilibrium, workers in the productive country agree to "share" some of the additional output generated by the increase in productivity and labor input, in exchange for similar "sharing" when the other country receives a positive productivity shock. In the bond economy, individuals can only smooth consumption across time (by buying or selling bonds); they cannot smooth consumption across different "states of nature" because of the absence of contingent securities. This reduces the tendency for labor input to decline in the temporarily unproductive location (we will discuss the details of these mechanisms further in Section 4). But again, while we see this effect in somewhat higher international correlations between output, investment, and labor input, the effect is not strong enough to make the bond economy a good description of the international data along these dimensions.

In summary, with trend-stationary shocks and substantial spillovers, we find that restricting international trade in financial assets to noncontingent bonds alone has very minor effects on the model's predictions for the business cycle behavior of the key macroeconomic aggregates. In particular, restricting asset markets helps only slightly in remedying the chief empirical failings of the one-sector international equilibrium business cycle model, which are (i) high international consumption correlations; (ii) negative international correlations of output, labor input, and investment; and (iii) a strong, positive correlation between labor input and real wages.

3.5. *Random-walk productivity without spillovers*

As shown in Section 3.3, we cannot reject the statistical hypothesis that the logs of total factor productivity follow random walk processes without spillovers but with correlated innovations. This section therefore examines the implications of this process for the behavior of the complete markets economy and the bond economy. Table 4 presents the two models' predictions for the central business cycle statistics, under the assumption that $\rho = \rho^* = 1,\ \nu = \nu^* = 0$ (as in Table 3, these are Hodrick-Prescott filtered population moments). All other parameters, including the contemporaneous correlation of the shocks and the innovation variances, are the same as in Table 3.

Table 4. Unit root in productivity.

(1) Results for complete markets economy
(2) Results for economy trading noncontingent bonds and goods only

	Standard deviation		Relative standard deviation		Persistence		Correlation w/y, lag 0			Other correlations	
	(1)	(2)	(1)	(2)	(1)	(2)	(1)	(2)		(1)	(2)
Output	2.58	1.59	1.00	1.00	0.87	0.82	1.00	1.00	y, y^*	−0.41	0.54
Consumption	1.03	1.67	0.40	1.05	0.82	0.80	0.72	0.85	c, c^*	0.89	−0.28
Investment	11.84	4.74	4.60	2.98	0.77	0.78	0.71	0.74	i, i^*	−0.92	−0.50
Labor	1.58	0.71	0.61	0.45	0.89	0.78	0.93	0.19	N, N^*	−0.91	−0.56
Wage	1.25	1.62	0.48	1.02	0.83	0.80	0.89	0.90	w, w^*	0.50	−0.11
Net exports	2.39	1.61	0.93	1.01	0.81	0.77	−0.18	−0.28	s, i	0.74	0.04
Bonds	0.00	8.18	0.00	5.13	0.00	0.98	0.00	0.35	w, N	0.66	−0.25

It is immediately evident from Table 4 that there are important differences between the complete markets economy and the bond economy. In contrast to the results for the trend stationary with spillovers parameterization, reported in Table 3, market structure matters a great deal when shocks are permanent and there is no transmission. First, the volatility of output, investment, and labor input are substantially higher in the complete markets economy, compared with the bond economy; in fact investment and labor input are about twice as volatile in the complete markets economy. Recall that one effect of the complete risk-pooling in the complete markets economy is a strong increase in labor input in response to positive productivity shocks. Because of the complementarity of labor input and capital input, the stronger labor response in the complete markets setting is accompanied by a stronger investment response and, consequently, a stronger output response.

The most striking differences between the models appear when we look at the international correlations of output and consumption. As noted above, a well-known failing of the complete markets model is its robust prediction of too high an international consumption correlation, combined with a too-low prediction for the international correlation of outputs. In Section 3.2, we saw that the bond economy shares this flaw when shocks to total factor productivity are trend stationary and subject to spillovers. When the shocks are purely permanent, as in Table 4, the complete markets economy continues to exhibit this counterfactual pair of predictions; in fact, the predictions for output correlations are even worse (i.e., even more strongly negative). But when the bond economy is subject to purely permanent shocks, this model predicts a substantial, *positive* international output correlation (0.54) and a *negative* consumption correlation (−0.28)! (While this configuration of correlations is unusual in the data, Baxter and Crucini 1993 did find this pattern of positive output correlations and negative consumption correlations for four country pairs.)

With random walk productivity, the two asset structures also differ importantly in their implications for the cyclic behavior of labor input. The bond economy predicts a weak (0.19) contemporaneous correlation of labor with output compared to the prediction of 0.93 for the complete markets economy. However, despite the fact that asset market restrictions have increased output correlations to an empirically reasonable level, the bond economy continues to underpredict international co-movement of labor input and investment. With the random walk specification, both asset structures predict a negative correlation between the net export ratio and output, which is characteristic of most OECD countries. Under this parameterization, the complete markets model continues to predict high saving-investment correlations but the bond economy does not. In fact, the predicted correlation of 0.04 in the bond economy is much lower than saving-investment correlations typically found in the data for this measure of saving. (As noted earlier, however, this "basic saving" measure may not be an accurate measure of true saving in the economy.) Finally, the complete markets model predicts a substantial positive correlation between productivity and labor input, while the bond economy generates a strongly negative correlation. In the data, these variables are roughly uncorrelated.

Figure 1 shows how cross-country consumption and output-consumption correlations, as well as within-country productivity-labor correlations, depend on the persistence of the shock and market structure. The top panel has results for the complete markets economy; the bottom panel has results for the bond economy. With complete markets, increasing persistence of the shock process leads to lower cross-country output correlations. The productivity-labor correlation also decreases with increased persistence, but never approaches the approximately zero correlation observed in the data. Changing persistence has a negligible (positive) effect on cross-country consumption correlations.

In the incomplete markets economy, by contrast, consumption correlations decrease dramatically as persistence rises, as does the correlation between productivity and labor input. At the same time, cross-country output correlations rise with increased persistence. The economic mechanisms behind these effects are explored in the next section.

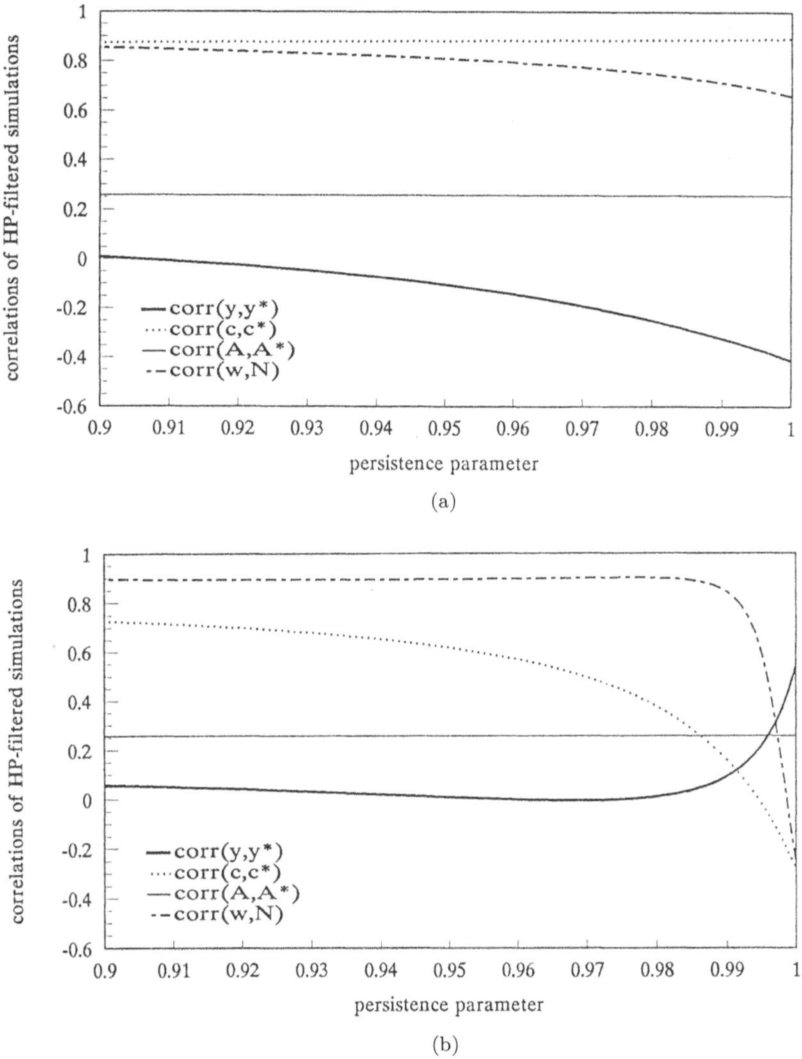

Fig. 1. (a) Complete markets model without spillovers. (b) Incomplete markets model without spillovers.

4. Dynamic Response to a Productivity Shock

The preceding section explored the implications for the summary statistics of business cycles of alternative assumptions concerning (i) the stochastic process for productivity shocks and (ii) market structure. The chief findings of that section were that restricting financial trade to noncontingent bonds alone had minor effects on the business cycle statistics when productivity was assumed to follow a trend stationary process exhibiting high persistence with substantial international transmission of shocks. However, when productivity contained a unit root, the restrictions on asset trade had important effects.

In order to explore the economic mechanisms behind these differential responses, this section studies the impulse responses of the alternative models when driven by the trend-stationary process of Section 3.4 versus random walk shocks, as in Section 3.5. Throughout, we study the response of the world economy to a 1 percent increase in total factor productivity which originates in the home country: $\hat{A}_t = 0.01$.

4.1. *Random Walk Productivity*

In many ways the responses to purely permanent shocks are easier to understand, so we start with this case. Figure 2 plots the responses of aggregate quantity variables in the two countries, and Fig. 3 plots the responses of real wages, real interest rates, and bond holdings.

Figure 2 shows that, under both asset structures, home country output, consumption, and investment increase in response to the shock, while foreign country investment falls. However, labor market behavior across countries is sensitive to the asset structure, as is the cross-country behavior of consumption and output. First, under complete markets, labor input increases in the home country and falls in the foreign country; the reverse is true in the bond economy. Second, under complete markets, consumptions move together across countries while outputs move in opposite directions. In the bond economy, by contrast, consumptions move in opposite directions while output rises in both countries (at least for the first few periods).

Figure 3 shows that the real interest rate implications of the shock are virtually identical under the two asset structures; and that the positive productivity shock causes the home country wage rate to rise under both structures, reflecting the positive effect of the shock on labor productivity. However, the foreign country wage rate rises

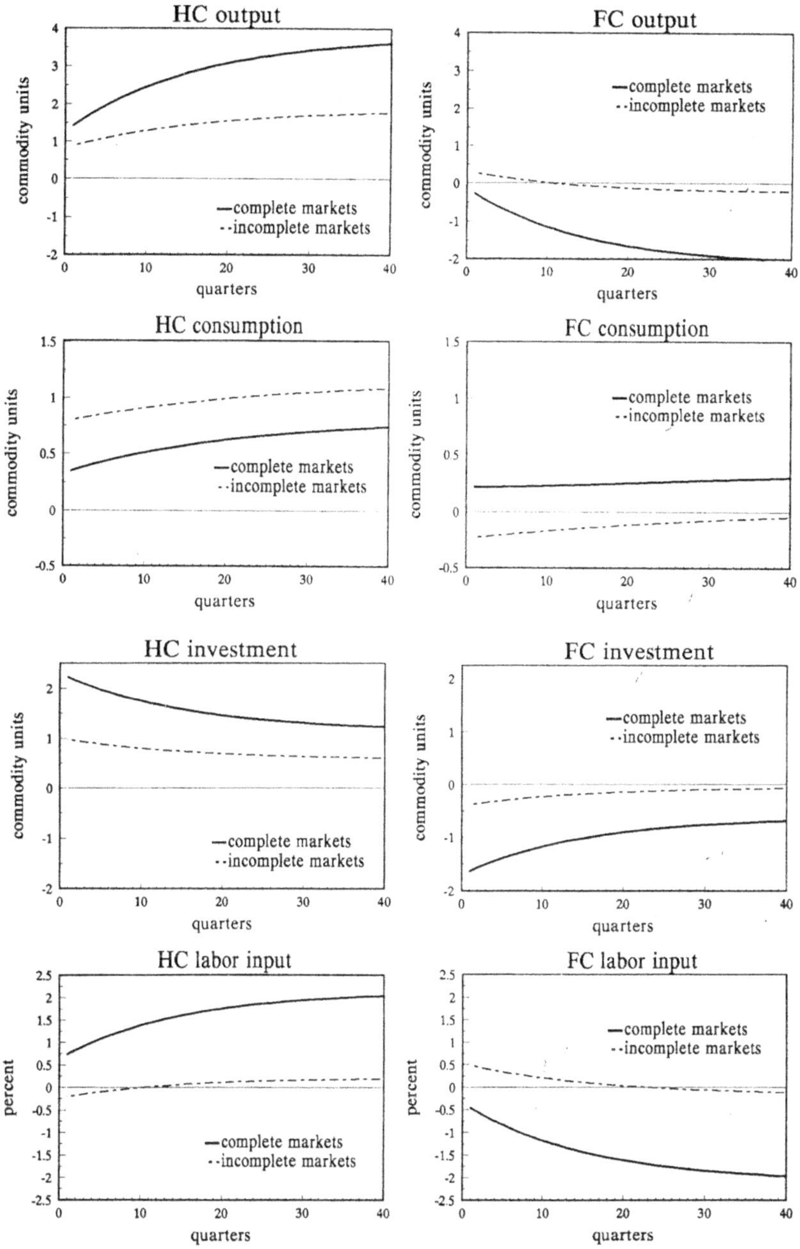

Fig. 2. Random walk productivity without spillovers: Quantity responses to positive productivity shock in home country.

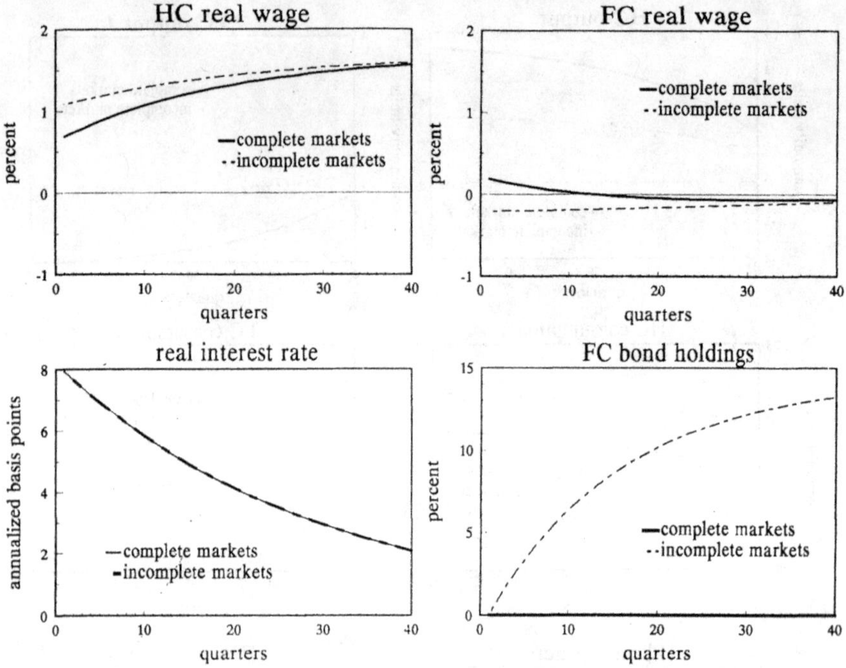

Fig. 3. Random walk productivity without spillovers: Price and interest rate responses to positive productivity shock in home country.

on impact in the complete markets economy but falls in the bond economy, mirroring the labor responses. Finally, with asset trade restricted to bonds alone, the foreign country accumulates bonds in response to the productivity shock in the home country, (there is no change in asset holdings in the complete markets economy). We have already seen that, in the bond economy, the foreign country responds by decreasing consumption and increasing labor input; thus they must be accumulating bonds over time. When adjustment to the shock is complete, the foreign country will work less and consume less than in the pre-shock steady state; however, a higher share of this consumption will be financed by the interest generated by the increased shock of debt accumulated over the transition path.

Figures 2 and 3 illustrate that the within-country and cross-country responses of consumption and labor are sensitive to the asset structure. In order to gain additional insight into the reasons why consumption and labor responses differ across asset structures, we employ King's (1990) "Hicksian" method for decomposing the consumption and labor supply responses into (i) a wealth effect, (ii) a real interest rate effect, and (iii) a wage effect. The wealth effect is computed as follows. First, compute the discounted present value of the change in utility caused by the altered time path of consumption and leisure (in response to the shock). Next, compute the constant consumption and leisure profiles that yield the same change in utility, using initial steady state wages and interest rates. The real interest rate effect is that part of the response due to alterations in the interest rate alone, holding fixed wealth and wage rates at their initial steady state levels; the wage effect is computed in a similar fashion. These effects are plotted in Fig. 4a.

Beginning with the wealth effect on home country consumption, we find that the positive productivity shock has a positive wealth effect in the bond economy, but has a negative wealth effect under complete markets. The positive wealth shock in the bond economy is easy to understand — the positive productivity shock means that more output can be obtained using the same level of inputs. In the bond economy, these inputs are completely domestically owned. Because individuals value both consumption and leisure, the natural response to a positive wealth shock (holding fixed all prices) is to consume more and work less; we see that the wealth effect on labor input is in fact negative in the bond economy (Fig. 4b).

Why is the home country wealth effect on consumption negative under complete markets? Recall that, under complete markets, the response to a location-specific positive productivity shock is for individuals living in the productive location to increase labor supply, taking advantage of the increase in productivity, while transferring some of the proceeds of the increased labor input to individuals living in less productive locations. Although home country consumption rises in response to the shock, home country leisure falls so much that home country discounted utility actually falls in response to the shock. Thus, the home country suffers a negative wealth effect.

In addition to the wealth effect, the productivity shock also induces substitution effects associated with (i) alterations in the time

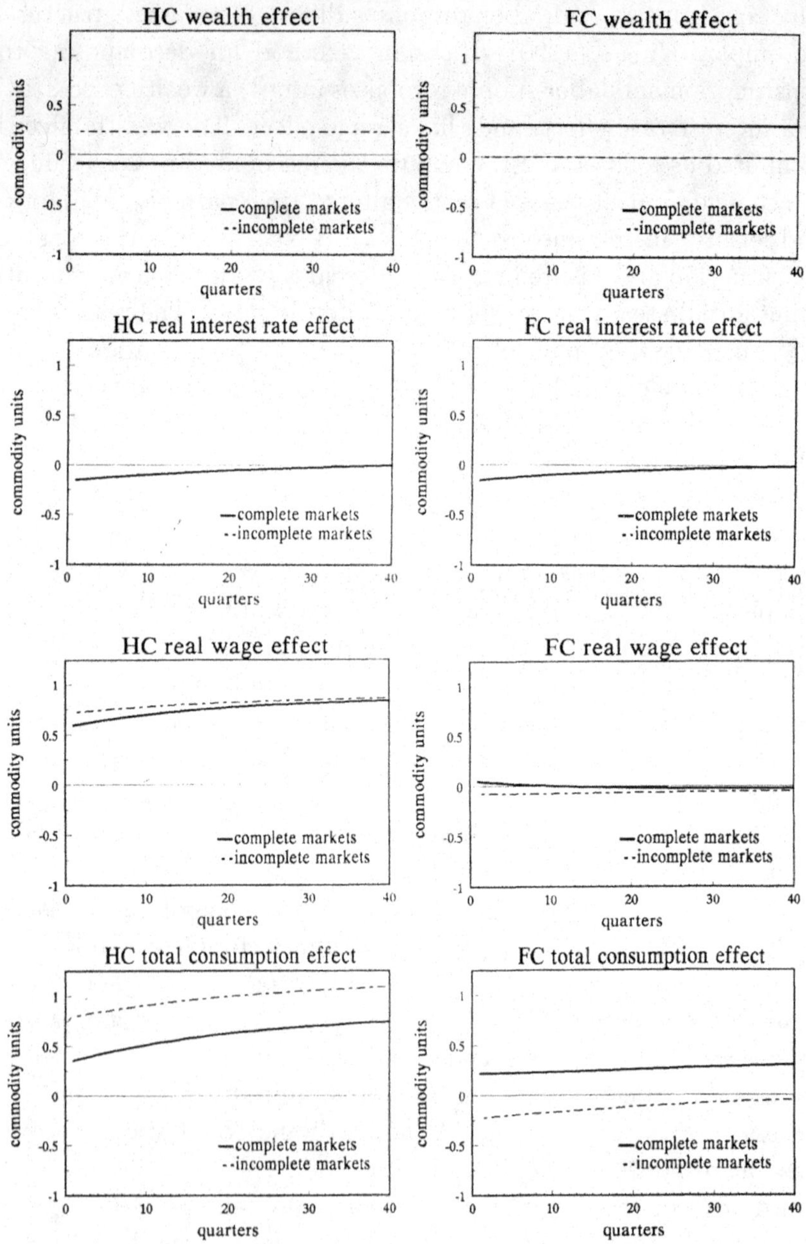

Fig. 4a. Random walk productivity without spillovers: Hicksian decomposition of consumption response.

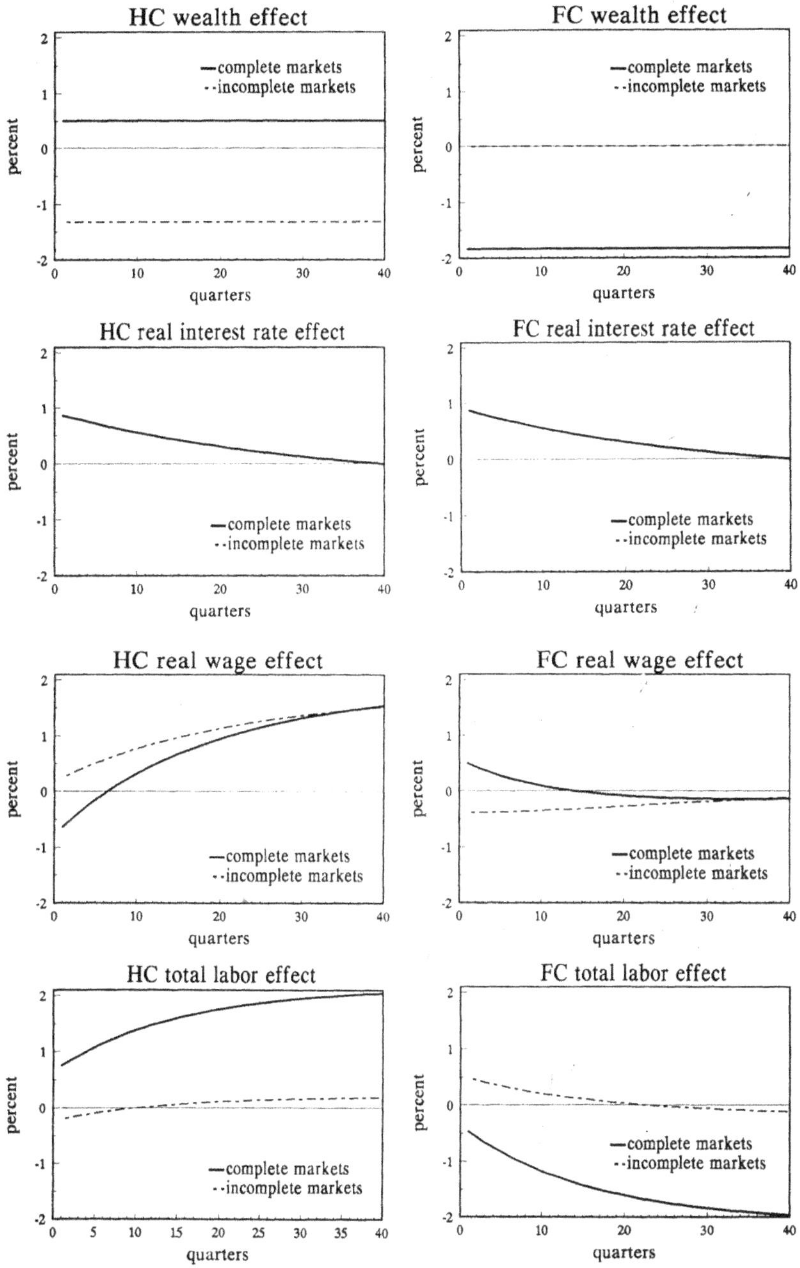

Fig. 4b. Random walk productivity without spillovers: Hicksian decomposition of labor response.

profile of real interest rates (the intertemporal price of consumption), and (ii) alterations in the time profile for the real wage rate. Since the real interest rate response is virtually identical under the two asset structures (see Fig. 3), the substitution effect stemming from this channel is also virtually the same across the two cases. The substitution effect on home consumption arising from the increase in the wage profile is positive and similar in both cases, reflecting the fact that wages rise in response to the shock under both asset structures. Thus in the home country, the differential consumption response under the alternative asset structures is almost entirely due to differences in the size of the wealth effect.

Similar arguments explain the responses of home country labor supply (Fig. 4b). Under complete markets, the wealth effect on labor is positive; i.e., the negative wealth effect induces an increase in labor input. With financial trade restricted to bonds alone, the productivity shock implies a positive wealth shock, thus labor input falls. As with home country consumption, the discount rate effects are nearly identical across the two market structures: the increase in current real interest rates (an increase in the price of current leisure, relative to future leisure) leads to an increase in labor supply from this channel. The wage effect on labor input is positive in the bond economy, but negative in the complete markets economy. As with the consumption response, the biggest difference between the labor response across asset structures lies in the wealth effects. Because the wealth effects are of different sign under the alternative market structures, we find that labor input rises on impact in the complete markets setting, but falls on impact in the bond economy.

In the foreign country it is also the case that the dominant differences across the asset structures lie in the wealth effects. In the bond economy, foreign country residents do not own productive factors located in the home country. Because there is no international transmission of the productivity shock, there is a zero wealth effect of the shock on foreign consumption and labor supply. Under complete markets, however, there is a positive wealth effect on consumption and a negative wealth effect on labor supply. With optimal labor insurance, the efficient arrangement calls for the less-productive country to "take a paid vacation," working less and consuming more. Under complete markets, the strength of the wealth effect in depressing labor input is sufficient to counteract positive substitution effects from the increase in the real interest rate and the increase in the real wage rate. Thus, on impact, foreign labor input rises in response to the shock in the bond economy, but falls in the complete markets economy.

Finally, in this case the incomplete markets model generates the interesting prediction that cross-country output correlations exceed the cross-country correlation of productivity. The Hicksian decompositions help us understand this result, as follows. If we write out the production functions as

$$\log y_t = \log A_t + (1 - \alpha) \log k_t + \alpha \log N_t \tag{15}$$

$$\log y_t^* = \log A_t^* + (1 - \alpha) \log k_t^* + \alpha \log N_t^*, \tag{16}$$

then the correlation between y_t and y_t^* depends on the cross-correlations of all the variables in (15) and (16). In particular, negative cross-country correlations of labor input and capital would tend to make outputs less correlated than the Solow residuals. In the bond economy with random walk productivity, however, the output correlations exceed the productivity correlations because there is a positive correlation between the home country productivity shock and foreign labor input. When there is a positive domestic productivity shock, foreign labor input rises due to the interest rate effect (the wealth effect is zero, and the wage effect is slightly negative); these effects can be seen in Figs. 2 and 4. The negative comovement between labor inputs arises because the increase in domestic productivity causes an initial decline in domestic labor input: here, the wealth effect temporarily outweighs the combined influences of the wage and interest rate effects.

4.2. *Trend-stationary shocks with spillovers*

Figures 5 to 7 plot the dynamic response to an innovation in home country productivity when productivity follows the trend-stationary process with spillovers specified in Section 3. We have already seen,

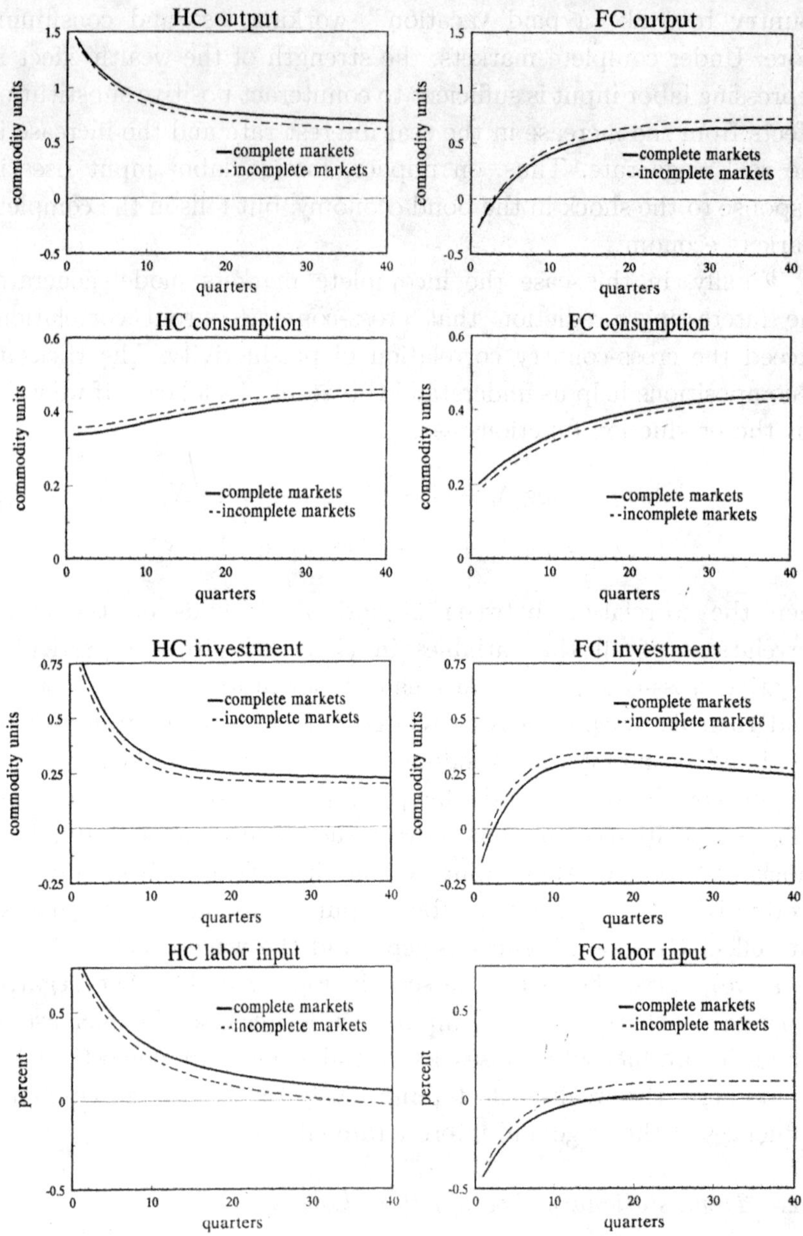

Fig. 5. Trend-stationary productivity with spillovers: Quantity responses to positive productivity shock in home country.

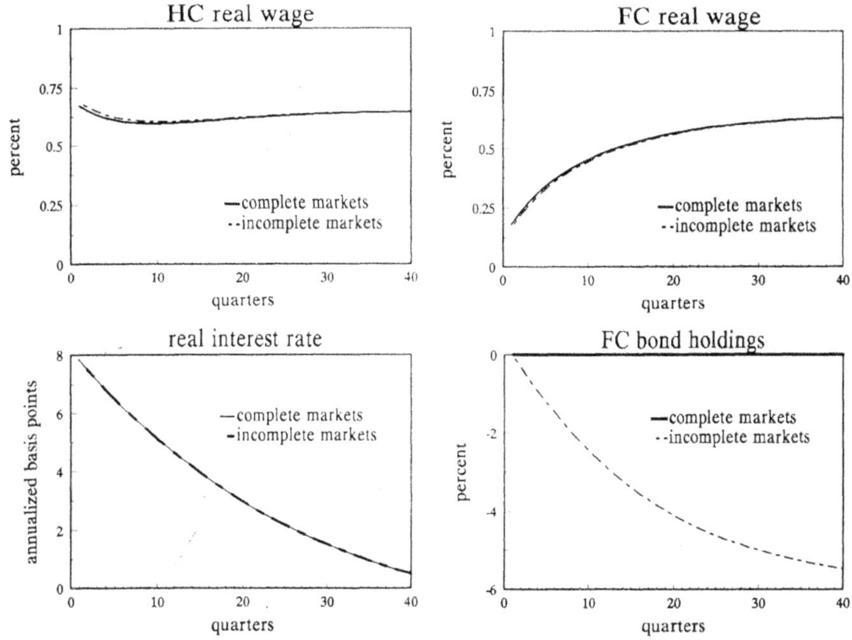

Fig. 6. Trend-stationary productivity with spillovers: Price and interest rate responses to positive productivity shock in home country.

in Table 3, that the summary statistics of business cycles are largely invariant to the asset structure under this parameterization of the productivity process. The dynamic responses detailed in Figs. 5 to 7 give a similar impression: the responses of the quantity variables (Fig. 5) and prices and interest rates (Fig. 6) show very similar responses under the alternative asset structures. The only significant difference is that, in the bond economy, assets are decumulated in the foreign country in response to the home country productivity shock, whereas there is no change in asset holdings in the complete markets economy.

The Hicksian decompositions of the consumption and labor responses plotted in Fig. 7 confirm the general impression that, with the trend-stationary process, there is little practical difference between the two asset structures. Recall that, with random walk productivity shocks, the primary difference across asset structures was due to differential wealth effects. In Fig. 7, we see that the wealth effects on the two countries of the productivity shock are first of all small, and second, are virtually indistinguishable across the two asset structures. The wealth effect of a temporary shock will always be smaller than the wealth effect of a permanent shock of the same size, so that this in itself is not surprising. The fact that the wealth effects are almost identical across asset structures is more surprising, and this is largely due to the fact that the productivity shock is transmitted across countries over time via the "spillover" parameter, v. In fact, 8.8 percent of the shock is transmitted each quarter, and apparently this is rapid enough so that the wealth effects of the shock are nearly identical across countries even when asset trade is restricted to bonds alone (the wealth effect is identical across countries under complete markets). As before, the real interest rate effects are virtually identical across countries and across asset structures.

Figure 7a is useful in understanding the forces behind negative international comovement of labor input under this parameterization. Although the wealth effects and real interest rate effects of the shocks are approximately the same across countries, the wage effects are quite different. The wage effect on home country labor is positive, reflecting the higher productivity due to the shock itself, combined with a rapid run-up in investment (see Fig. 5). In the foreign country, there is no immediate effect on productivity, although individuals in that country realize that productivity will increase in the future due to the "spillovers." That is, labor productivity in the foreign country is low, on impact, compared with its expected future value. Intertemporal substitution considerations mean that foreign country residents are induced to increase current leisure with the expectation of lower future leisure when the spillover effect brings increased productivity to the foreign country.

Once we understand the importance of the international transmission of the shock (the "spillover") for the wealth effects on labor and consumption, it is easy to understand why foreign country residents decumulate bonds in response to the shock. As noted above, these permanent-income consumers know that the favorable shock

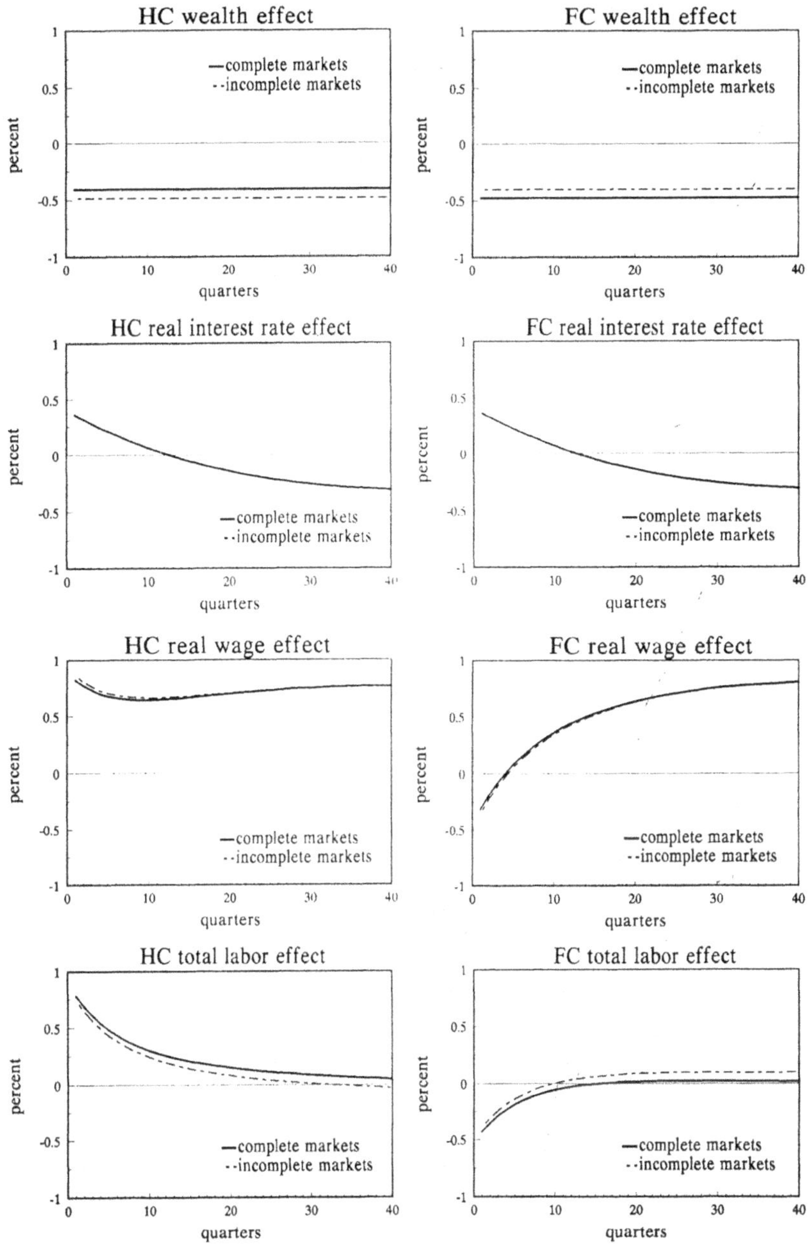

Fig. 7a. Trend-stationary productivity with spillovers: Hicksian decomposition of labor response.

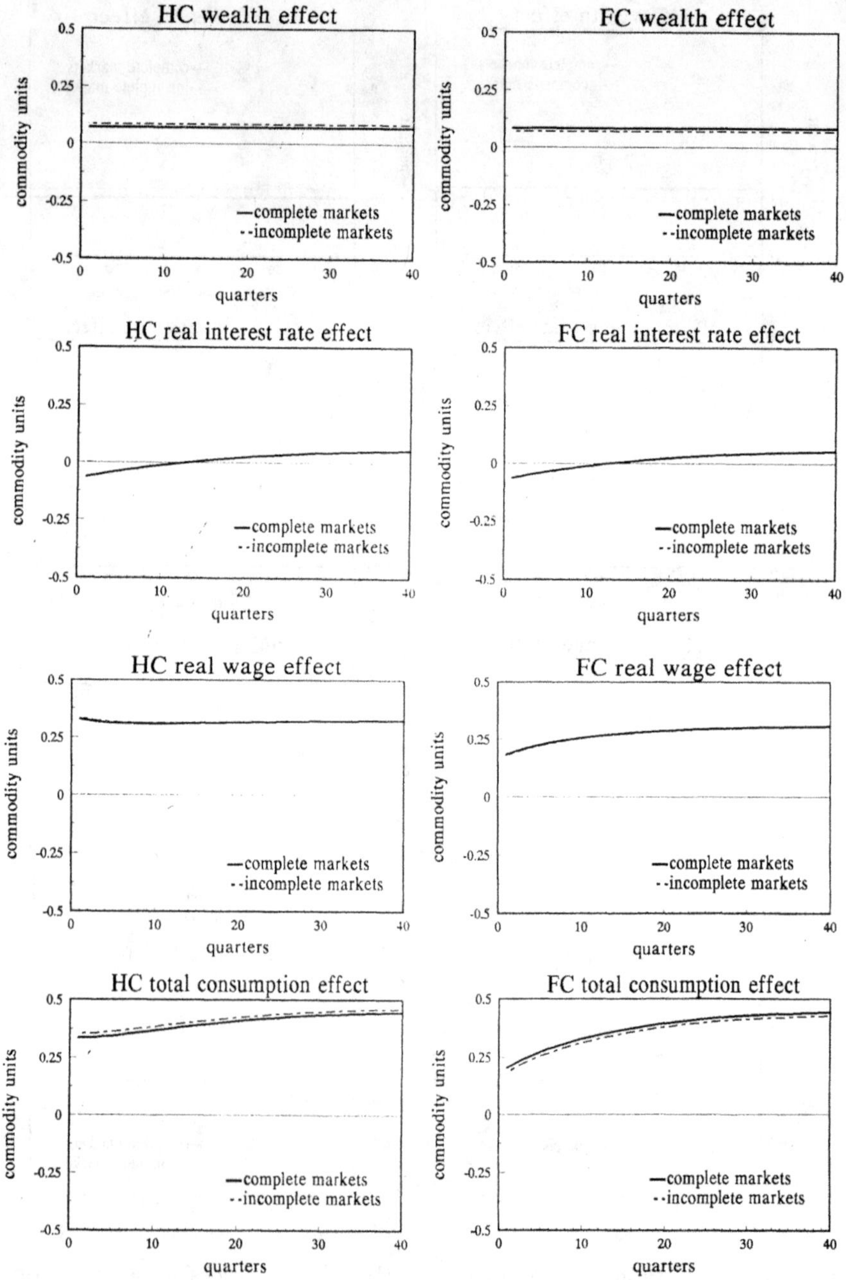

Fig. 7b. Trend-stationary productivity with spillovers: Hicksian decomposition of consumption response.

will be coming to their country in a few quarters — rapidly enough that the positive wealth effect is nearly as large as in the originating economy. But on impact, productivity in the foreign country is low relative to its expected future level. Thus individuals respond on impact to the positive wealth shock by decreasing current labor supply and increasing current consumption, financing part of current consumption from the proceeds of bond sales.

In summary, we find that with trend-stationary shocks and spillovers, the absence of risk-sharing arrangements stemming from asset market restrictions is, not important for the character of international business cycles. With this parameterization of the productivity shock process, nearly all of the fluctuations in productivity are common across countries, i.e., there is little scope for risk sharing in the first place, although there is a role for intertemporal trade since productivity arrives in the nonoriginating country with a lag. Because a real discount bond is the ideal instrument for undertaking intertemporal trade, the restriction of asset markets to bonds alone has little effect on equilibrium outcomes.

5. Conclusions

This paper has explored the importance of financial market linkages for the character of international business cycles. We have found that restrictions on asset trade may be important for business cycles, but that this result is sensitive to the stochastic process for productivity. In particular, restrictions on asset trade are more important (i) the more persistent is the shock, and (ii) the smaller are international spillovers of productivity shocks. When there are important differences across asset structures, these can be traced to important differences in wealth effects.

This paper also contributes to the technical literature on solving dynamic models by providing an example of how Euler equation methods can be extended in a straightforward fashion to the study of suboptimal dynamic economies. In particular, this paper illustrates how one can compute equilibrium in models in which departures from optimality arise due to constraints on individuals' opportunities for risk pooling, without suffering a significant increase in conceptual or computational complexity. Because the equilibrium behavior of dynamic models can always be characterized as the solution to a system of Euler equations (augmented by market clearing conditions and equilibrium "consistency conditions"), the same approach can be used to study other models in which departures from optimality arise for a number of possible reasons, such as monopolistic behavior, market incompleteness, or imperfect information.

Appendix

This appendix discusses the procedures that we use to solve the models described in this paper. We begin by discussing the complete-markets model, and then turn to models with restrictions on asset trade. Throughout, the notation is the same as described in Section 2.

A.1. *Complete markets*

Competitive equilibrium in the complete markets economy is also Pareto optimal, thus this equilibrium can be found by carrying out a standard Lagrangian problem, as specified below:

$$\begin{aligned}\max \mathscr{L} = E_0 \sum_{t=0}^{\infty} \tilde{\beta}^t \{ &[\pi u(c_t, L_t) + (1-\pi) u(c_t^*, L_t^*)] \\ &+ \pi w_t (1 - L_t - N_t) + (1-\pi) w_t^* (1 - L_t^* - N_t^*) \\ &+ \pi \lambda_t [(1-\delta) k_t - (\gamma k_{t+1} - \phi(i_t/k_t) k_t)] \\ &+ (1-\pi) \lambda_t^* \left[(1-\delta) k_t^* - \left(\gamma k_{t+1}^* - \phi(i_t^*/k_t^*) k_t^*\right)\right] \\ &+ p_t[\pi(A_t F(k_t, N_t) - c_t - i_t) \\ &+ (1-\pi)(A_t^* F(k_t^*, N_t^*) - c_t^* - i_t^*)]\}.\end{aligned}$$

The multipliers on the constraints in the Lagrangian have the following natural interpretations as (utility-denominated) shadow prices:

w_t, w_t^*: wage rate
λ_t, λ_t^*: price of existing capital
p_t: price of the final good (price of new capital).

The competitive equilibrium for this economy is found by solving the system of first-order necessary conditions plus "consistency conditions" arising from this Lagrangian problem. The competitive equilibrium for this particular economy is Pareto optimal, but this approach works more generally for nonoptimal competitive equilibria; see Baxter (1991).

Letting D denote the total derivative of a function of a single variable, and letting D_j denote the partial derivative of a function with respect to its jth argument, the first-order necessary conditions for this Lagrangian problem are

$$c_t : D_1u(c_t, L_t) - p_t = 0 \tag{17}$$

$$L_t : D_2u(c_t, L_t) - w_t = 0 \tag{18}$$

$$N_t : p_t A_t D_2 F(k_t, N_t) - w_t = 0 \tag{19}$$

$$i_t : \lambda_t D\phi(i_t/k_t) - p_t = 0 \tag{20}$$

$$k_{t+1} : E_t\mu(i_{t+1}/k_{t+1})\tilde{\beta}\lambda_{t+1} + \tilde{\beta}E_t p_{t+1}A_{t+1}D_1F(k_{t+1}, N_{t+1}) \\ -\gamma\lambda_t = 0 \tag{21}$$

$$w_t : 1 - L_t - N_t = 0 \tag{22}$$

$$\lambda_t : k_{t+1} = (1-\delta)k_t + \phi(i_t/k_t)k_t \tag{23}$$

$$p_t : \pi[y_t - c_t - i_t] + (1-\pi)[y_t^* - c_t^* - i_t^*] = 0, \tag{24}$$

for all $t \geq 0$, where $\mu(z) \equiv [\phi(z) - zD\phi(z) + (1-\delta)]$. There are foreign-country analogues to Eqs. (17) to (23), and a transversality condition for capital in each country.

We solve the model by taking a log-linear approximation to the model's initial deterministic steady state. The resulting linear system is solved by application of standard linear systems theory, as described in King, Plosser, and Rebelo (1987). The planner weights are implicit in the steady state shares of world output consumed by residents of each country; we set these shares as part of the calibration exercise. As shown by Rebelo (1987) and discussed in detail in King, Plosser, and Rebelo (1988b) it is not necessary to solve for the planner weights when solving the model by log-linear approximation, since the weights are absent from the linearized Euler equations.

A.2. *A partial equilibrium model of a small open economy*

This subsection describes a model of an open economy that is assumed to be too small to affect the world interest rate. This is a partial equilibrium model because the representative consumer in the small open economy optimizes in the face of an exogenous process for the world interest rate. Solving the small open economy model is a useful first step toward constructing a general equilibrium model with restricted asset trade. The flow budget constraint, or asset accumulation equation, for the small open economy is

$$\gamma P_t^B b_{t+1} + c_t + i_t \leq y_t + b_t. \tag{25}$$

To solve the small open economy model, we specify the following Lagrangian problem and then solve the resulting system of first-order conditions:

$$\begin{aligned}\max \mathscr{L} = E_0 \sum_{t=0}^{\infty} \tilde{\beta}^t \{ & u(c_t, L_t) \\ & + w_t(1 - L_t - N_t) \\ & + \lambda_t[(1-\delta)k_t - (\gamma k_{t+1} - \phi(i_t/k_t)k_t)] \\ & + p_t(y_t + b_t) - \gamma P_t^B b_{t+1} - c_t - i_t)\}.\end{aligned}$$

The first-order necessary conditions obtained by maximizing the Lagrangian with respect to $c_t, L_t, N_t, i_t, k_{t+1}, w_t$, and λ_t, are exactly the same as the corresponding efficiency conditions for the complete-markets economy described above, together with the transversality conditions for debt holdings (Equations (11) and (12)). There are two first-order conditions that are different: these are the efficiency conditions for b_{t+1} and for p_t (i.e., the flow budget constraint) which follow.

$$(b_{t+1}) : \tilde{\beta} E_t p_{t+1} - \gamma p_t P_t^B = 0 \tag{26}$$

$$(p_t) : b_t + A_t F(k_t, N_t) - c_t - i_t - P_t^B \gamma b_{t+1} = 0. \tag{27}$$

The steady state real interest rate is determined by Eq. (26): $\gamma P^B = \tilde{\beta}$.[9] The remaining first-order conditions determine the evolution of all endogenous variables as functions of the controlled states (b_t, k_t), the corresponding costates (p_t, λ_t), and the exogenous variables (A_t, P_t^B). As before, the model can be linearized and solved using the procedure outlined in King, Plosser, and Rebelo (1987).

A.3. *General equilibrium with restricted asset markets*

Next, we consider a two-country world in which each country can trade a noncontingent real bond with residents of the other country. That is, the representative individual in each country faces the same problem as the individual described above in the small open economy. The only difference is that, in general equilibrium, the interest rate process is not exogenous. Rather, the interest rate adjusts to clear the bond market. In particular, bond-market clearing requires that

$$\pi b_t + (1-\pi) b_t^* = 0, \tag{28}$$

since bonds are in zero net supply in the world economy.

Combining Eq. (28) with aggregate financial asset accumulation equation

$$\begin{aligned} \pi P_t^B b_{t+1} + (1-\pi) P_t^B b_t^* \geq \pi[b_t + y_t - c_t - i_t] \\ +(1-\pi)[b_t^* + y_t^* - c_t^* - i_t^*] \end{aligned} \tag{29}$$

implies goods-market clearing (due to Walras' Law)

$$\pi(A_t F(k_t, N_t) - i_t - c_t) + (1-\pi)(A_t^* F(k_t^*, N_t^*) - c_t^* - i_t^*) \geq 0. \tag{30}$$

The first-order necessary conditions for the representative individuals' problem are given by Eqs. (17) to (23) (with foreign-country

[9]Recall that we assumed that $\tilde{\beta}$ is the same for all countries in the world, so that (26) holds for each country, and $R\tilde{\beta} = \gamma$ is also a world general equilibrium condition. This requirement also guarantees that no country grows arbitrarily wealthy over time in the deterministic version of the model.

analogues), together with the following:

$$(b_{t+1}) : \tilde{\beta} E_t p_{t+1} - \gamma p_t P_t^B = 0 \tag{31}$$

$$(b_{t+1}^*) : \tilde{\beta} E_t p_{t+1}^* - \gamma p_t^* P_t^B = 0 \tag{32}$$

$$p_t : b_t + A_t F(k_t, N_t) - c_t - i_t - P_t^B \gamma b_{t+1} = 0, \tag{33}$$

$$p_t^* : b_t^* + A_t^* F(k_t^*, N_t^*) - c_t^* - i_t^* - P_t^B \gamma b_{t+1}^* = 0. \tag{34}$$

In world general equilibrium, the interest rate process implicit in P_t^B is endogenously determined: from (31) and (32), we have $P_t^B = \tilde{\beta} E_t(p_{t+1}/\gamma p_t) = \tilde{\beta} E_t(p_{t+1}^*/\gamma p_t^*)$.

The key issue is how to compute the world general equilibrium. The procedure we use is as follows. First, we drop one of the asset accumulation equations (i.e., one of Eqs. (33) and (34)) since Eq. (28) implies that, in a two-country world, only one of the asset stocks is independent. We let this be the foreign country's asset stock. Second, we treat the home country's shadow price (p) as an additional control variable. This augmented system determines the world control vector as a function of the world controlled state vector $[k_t, k_t^*, b_t^*]$; the world costate vector $[\lambda_t, \lambda_t^*, p_t^*]$; and the exogenous variables $[A_t, A_t^*]$. Third, we impose the equilibrium condition that $P_t^B = \tilde{\beta} E_t(p_{t+1}/\gamma p_t)$. That is, we replace P_t^B with the expression $\tilde{\beta} E_t(p_{t+1}/p_t)$ in the accumulation equation.

This three-step procedure yields a dynamic system that can be linearized and solved in the standard manner. Note that the new state variable — the foreign country's bond holdings — is a sufficient statistic for the current distribution of wealth. Further, the solution satisfies the transversality conditions (11) and (12).

Acknowledgments

We have received valuable comments on this paper from two anonymous referees, as well as workshop participants at the International Monetary Fund, the 1992 NBER Summer Institute, Ohio

State University, Simon Fraser University, University of British Columbia, University of Virginia, and University of Washington. We are responsible for any remaining errors. Dave Backus generously provided us with the Solow residual time series used in Section 3; Masao Ogaki provided us with his computer programs for unit root and cointegration tests, and aided us in their implementation. Neither of these individuals retains any culpability for the uses to which we put their material. The first draft of this paper was completed while Baxter was a visitor at the Institute for Empirical Macroeconomics; she is grateful for the support of the IEM and the National Science Foundation.

References

Backus, D., P. Kehoe, and F. Kydland, "International Real Business Cycles," *Journal of Political Economy* 100 (1992), 745–775.

Backus, D., P. Kehoe, and F. Kydland, "International Business Cycles: Theory and Evidence," in T. Cooley, ed., *Frontiers of Business Cycle Research* (Princeton: Princeton University Press, 1995), 331–356.

Baxter, M., "Approximating Suboptimal Dynamic Equilibria: An Euler Equation Approach," *Journal of Monetary Economics* 27 (1991), 173–200.

Baxter, M., "International Trade and Business Cycles," in G. Grossman and K. Rogoff, eds., *Handbook of International Economics* 3 (Amsterdam: North-Holland, 1995).

Baxter, M., and M. Crucini, "Explaining Saving-Investment Correlations," *American Economic Review* 83 (1993), 416–436.

Baxter, M., and R. King, "Productive Externalities and Cyclical Volatility," Institute for Empirical Macroeconomics Discussion Paper No. 53, Federal Reserve Bank of Minneapolis, November 1991 (forthcoming *European Economic Review*).

Burdett, K. and R. Wright, "Unemployment Insurance and Short-Time Compensation: The Effects on Layoffs, Hours Per Worker, and Wages," *Journal of Political Economy* 97 (1989), 1479–1496.

Cardia, E., "The Dynamics of a Small Open Economy in Response to Monetary, Fiscal, and Productivity Shocks," *Journal of Monetary Economics* 28 (1991), 411–434.

Christiano, L. and M. Eichenbaum, "Current Real-Business-Cycle Theories and Aggregate Labor Market Fluctuations," *American Economic Review* 82 (1992), 430–450.

Cole, H., "Financial Structure and International Trade," *International Economic Review* 29 (1988), 237–259.

Constantinides, G. and D. Duffie, "Asset Pricing with Heterogeneous Consumers," Mimeo, Stanford University, 1991.

Conze, A., J. M. Lasry, and J. Scheinkman, "Borrowing Constraints and International Comovements," Mimeo, University of Chicago, 1990.

Correia, I., J. Neves, and S. Rebelo, "Business Cycles in a Small Open Economy," *European Economic Review* (forthcoming 1995).

Dotsey, M. and C. S. Mao, "How Well Do Approximation Methods Work?" *Journal of Monetary Economics* 29 (1992), 25–58.

Hayashi, F., "Tobin's Marginal q and Average q: A Neoclassical Interpretation," *Econometrica* 50 (1982), 213–224.

Heaton, J. and D. Lucas, "The Importance of Investor Heterogeneity and Financial Market Imperfections for the Behavior of Asset Prices," *Carnegie Rochester Conference Series on Public Policy* 42 (forthcoming 1995).

Hodrick, R. and E. Prescott, "Post-War U.S. Business Cycles: An Empirical Investigation," Mimeo, Carnegie Mellon University, 1980.

King, R., "Value and Capital in the Equilibrium Business Cycle Program," in L. McKenzie and S. Zamagni, eds., *Value and Capital: Fifty Years Later* (London: MacMillan, 1990).

King, R., C. Plosser, and S. Rebelo, "Technical Appendix to 'Production, Growth, and Business Cycles'," Mimeo, University of Rochester, 1987.

King, R., C. Plosser, and S. Rebelo, "Production, Growth, and Business Cycles I: The Basic Neoclassical Model," *Journal of Monetary Economics* 21 (1988a), 195–232.

King, R., C. Plosser, and S. Rebelo, "Production, Growth, and Business Cycles II: New Directions," *Journal of Monetary Economics* 21 (1988b), 309–342.

Kollman, R., "Incomplete Asset Markets and International Real Business Cycles," Mimeo, University of Montreal, 1993.

Mendoza, E., "Real Business Cycles in a Small Open Economy," *American Economic Review* 81 (1991), 797–818.

Mitchell, W., *Business Cycles: The Problem and Its Setting* (New York: National Bureau of Economic Research, 1927).

Morgenstern, O., *International Financial Transactions and Business Cycles* (Princeton: Princeton University Press, 1959).

Obstfeld, M., "Capital Mobility in the World Economy: Theory and Measurement," *Camegie-Rochester Conference Series on Public Policy* 24 (1986), 55–104.

Park, J. Y., "Testing for Unit Roots and Cointegration by Variable Addition," *Advances in Econometrics* 8 (1990), 107–133.

Rebelo, S., "Tractable Heterogeneity and Near-Steady-State Dynamics," Mimeo, Northwestern University, 1987.

Reynolds, P., "International Comovements in Production and Consumption: Theory and Evidence," Mimeo, University of Southern California, 1992.

Reynolds, P., "International Comovements in Aggregate Productivity: An Empirical Analysis," Mimeo, University of Southern California, 1993.

Solow, R., "Technical Progress and the Aggregate Production Function," *Review of Economic Studies* 39 (1957), 312–320.

Stockman, A. and L. Svensson, "Capital Flows, Investment, and Exchange Rates," *Journal of Monetary Economics* 19 (1987), 171–202.

Taylor, J. and H. Uhlig, "Solving Nonlinear Stochastic Growth Models: A Comparison of Alternative Solution Methods," *Journal of Business and Economic Statistics* 8 (1990), 1–18.

Telmer, C. I., "Asset-Pricing Puzzles and Incomplete Markets," *Journal of Finance* 48 (1993), 1803–1832.

Chapter 7

Trends and Cycles in Small Open Economies: Making the Case for a General Equilibrium Approach*

Kan Chen

BBVA Research,
Houston, TX, USA

and

Mario J. Crucini

Department of Economics, Vanderbilt University,
Nashville, TN, USA
and National Bureau of Economic Research,
Cambridge, MA, USA
mario.j.crucini@vanderbilt.edu

Abstract. Economic research into the causes of business cycles in small open economies is almost always undertaken using a partial equilibrium model. This approach is characterized by two key assumptions. The first is that the world interest rate is unaffected by economic developments in the small open economy, an exogeneity assumption. The second assumption is that this exogenous interest rate combined with domestic productivity is sufficient to describe equilibrium choices. We demonstrate the failure of the second assumption by contrasting general and partial equilibrium approaches to the study of a cross-section of small open economies. In doing so, we provide a method for modeling

*This chapter originally appeared in *Journal of Economic Dynamics and Control*, 2016, **72**, 159–168.

small open economies in general equilibrium that is no more technically demanding than the small open economy approach while preserving much of the value of the general equilibrium approach.

Keywords: Small open economy; Business cycle; Productivity

1. Introduction

The veracity of business cycles differs dramatically across countries. Figure 1 presents a comprehensive view: it displays the standard deviation of annual output and consumption growth rates computed over the period 1971–2011 for 66 countries (countries are ranked from the most to least volatile).[1] The standard deviation of output growth ranges from an astounding 24.3% in Iraq (not shown) to a mere 1.58% in Australia; the median country is Luxembourg (3.53%). An important goal of quantitative business cycle theory is to explain these differences.

In this respect, the work-horse small open economy model has considerable appeal because it is possible to treat the world interest

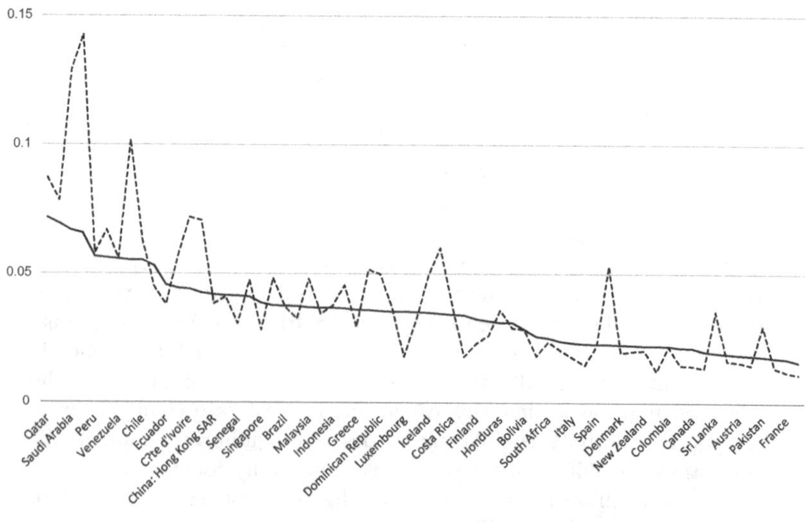

Fig. 1. International business cycles.

[1]The PWT 8.1 starts from 1951 and ends in 2011. The starting year of 1971 allows for a comprehensive and balanced cross-country panel.

rate as given (i.e., determined in the rest-of-the-world), an exogeneity assumption and conduct a partial equilibrium analysis. Aguiar and Gopinath (2007) is a recent leading example of this approach. They argue persuasively that much of the cross-country heterogeneity in the veracity of business cycles is accounted for by differences in the relative importance of permanent and transitory shocks to total factor productivity. The logic is simple. A permanent shock leads to larger jump in consumption than a persistent, but transitory, shock because it entails a larger wealth effect. Output, to a reasonable first-approximation, follows the path of productivity and therefore inherits the volatility and persistence properties of the shock itself. Altering the relative importance of the two shocks therefore allows one to match the standard deviation of output and consumption patterns displayed in Fig. 1. Applying this method to 13 emerging and 13 developed economies, Aguiar and Gopinath find that the permanent component accounts for 84% of productivity growth for emerging markets compared to 61% for developed countries.[2]

The use of a partial equilibrium model comes at a cost however, as it fails to capture any meaningful economic interactions across nations. The most obvious is the international correlation of business cycles. To fill this gap, we revisit the study of AG, using the two-country general equilibrium model developed by Baxter and Crucini (1995). The BC model is a natural choice because it shares virtually all features of preferences, technology and the asset market structure of AG, while closing the model by imposing world market clearing in the goods market and the market for one-period non-contingent bonds.

In our simulations, the 'home' country is parameterized to mimic the business cycle of an aggregate of (listed in descending economic size) the United States, Japan, the United Kingdom, Germany, Italy, France, Canada and Australia (hereafter the G-8). This massive economic block effectively determines the world interest rate (marginal product of capital). The 'foreign' country is one of the 58 economies in our panel dataset. Individual countries are rotated

[2]Note that they do not report a variance decomposition of output growth in their paper, though productivity and output tend to move closely in neoclassical models of the business cycle.

through in separate model simulations to produce the entire cross-section of business cycle implications that are consistent with the domestic and foreign business cycle facts.

Total factor productivity in the G-8 is the sum of a pure random walk component and a transitory but persistent component. Matching the standard deviation of: (i) consumption growth, (ii) income growth and (iii) the consumption — GDP ratio for the G-8 block yields an estimated standard deviation of 0.9% (1.2%) for the innovation to the permanent (transitory) component. The persistence of the transitory component is 0.9. The implication of these estimates is that the transitory component contributes 58% to the standard deviation of TFP growth, compared to 42% for the stationary component. These estimates are broadly consistent with the less structural approach of Crucini and Shintani (2015) they estimate a bivariate error-correction model of output and consumption growth for each country of the G-8 and find comparable contributions of stochastic trend and cycle shocks to output growth.

For each country outside of the G-8, we match the standard deviation of output growth, the standard deviation of consumption and the correlation of output and consumption growth of each country with the output and consumption growth of the G-8 block. To accomplish this — in addition to an idiosyncratic permanent and transitory shock to productivity in each country — we allow for a spillover from the G-8 permanent and transitory shock. The productivity spillovers from the G-8 is the point of departure from the partial equilibrium approach and allows us to match international business cycle comovement of consumption and output.[3]

On average (across countries), the permanent shocks account for 45% of output growth in developing countries compared to 51% in developed countries. These results contrast sharply with AG who attribute 84% of productivity growth to permanent shocks for emerging markets compared to 61% for developed countries. While there are a number of differences in terms of the sample

[3]Consistent with the partial equilibrium approach, there are no productivity spillovers from the small countries to the large countries: a block-exogeneity assumption.

of countries and sample period, the main driver of the difference is our general equilibrium approach and the additional empirical discipline of matching international business cycle comovement. We demonstrate this in two ways.

First, we use a small open economy model to match national business cycle moments (excluding international comovement) in our cross-section and find the permanent shocks must account for twice as much of output growth for developing countries compared to developed countries, which is even more skewed in the direction of AG's earlier findings. This demonstrates that our results using the same modeling approach as AG also imply a dominant role for permanent shocks in developing countries. The even larger roll of the permanent shock may be a consequence of the Great Recession.

Second, shocks to the exogenous interest rate play a non-trivial role, accounting for about 25% of output growth variation in the average country (both developing and developed). Since the real interest rate is stationary in the model, it is impossible to determine the role of permanent and transitory shocks in accounting for real interest rate fluctuations without a general equilibrium model. To demonstrate the identification issue, when we incorporate the international spillovers of productivity estimated from the general equilibrium model, the real interest rate plays almost no role in the small open economy version despite the fact that the small open economy with spillovers of productivity produces virtually the same variance decomposition as the general equilibrium model with spillovers.

The lessons here are stark. The logical contradiction of the small open economy approach is that any comovement of business cycles through productivity transmission (or endogenous propagation) must be attributed to domestic productivity or the 'world' interest rate. And yet, the world interest rate is not determined by the business cycle of the small open economy leading to a fundamental issue of identification and mis-specification of the variance decomposition.

2. The One-Sector Stochastic Growth Model

Our use of the basic one-sector, two-country stochastic growth model is motivated by two objectives. The first is to stay as close as possible to the model specification utilized by AG. The second is to ensure that the general equilibrium and partial equilibrium versions of the model are structurally compatible. Three sources of novelty are introduced into these otherwise standard models. First, careful attention is given to international productivity spillovers from the large G-8 block to each individual nation. Second, the cross-section of countries is comprehensive. Third, general equilibrium and partial equilibrium models are explicitly compared. The general equilibrium model is the one-sector, two country, DSGE model developed by Baxter and Crucini (1995). The partial equilibrium version of this model omits the world goods market clearing condition and adds a stochastic process to capture the evolution of the world interest rate.[4] This section begins by quickly reviewing common features of these two versions of the one-sector model and concludes with a discussion of the differences.

2.1. *Preferences and technology*

Individuals in each country have Cobb-Douglas preferences over consumption and leisure

$$U(C_{jt}, L_{jt}) = \beta^t \frac{1}{1-\sigma} \left[C_{jt}^{\theta} L_{jt}^{1-\theta} \right]^{1-\sigma}, \tag{1}$$

where parameter $\theta \in (0,1)$, and the inter-temporal elasticity of substitution is $1/\sigma$.

The final good is produced using capital and labor. The production function is Cobb-Douglas and each country experiences stochastic fluctuations in the level of factor productivity, A_{jt},

$$Y_{jt} = A_{jt} K_{jt}^{1-\alpha} N_{jt}^{\alpha}. \tag{2}$$

The stochastic processes for productivity will involve both permanent and transitory components each potentially with a common G-8 (world) component and an idiosyncratic or nation-specific component. These stochastic processes are described in more detail below.

[4] AG incorporate a domestic interest rate response to home debt relative to productivity, but this plays a minor quantitative role in their exercise.

The capital stock in each country, depreciates at the rate δ and is costly to adjust:

$$K_{jt+1} = (1-\delta)K_{jt} + \phi(I_{jt}/K_{jt})K_{jt}, \tag{3}$$

where $\phi(\cdot)$ is the adjustment cost function. As in Baxter and Crucini (1995), adjustment costs have the following properties: (i) at the steady-state, $\phi(I/K) = I/K$ and $\phi'(I/K) = 1$ so that in the deterministic solution to the model the steady state with and without adjustment costs are the same and (ii) $\phi' > 0$, $\phi'' < 0$.

2.2. *Closing the model*

Following Baxter and Crucini (1995), the two country general equilibrium model is closed by imposing one intertemporal budget constraint and world goods market clearing. The intertemporal budget constraint is

$$P_t^B B_{jt+1} - B_{jt} = Y_{jt} - C_{jt} - I_{jt} \tag{4}$$

where B_{jt+1} denotes the quantity of bonds purchased in period t by country j. P_t^B is the price of a bond purchased in period t and maturing in period $t+1$. The bond is not state-contingent, it pays one physical unit of consumption in all states of the world. Implicitly this defines, r_t, the real rate of return for the bond (i.e., $P_t^B \equiv (1+r_t)^{-1} < 1$). The price of this bond is endogenous in the two-country equilibrium model, determined by the market-clearing condition in the world bond market.

The world goods market clearing condition is:

$$\pi_0(Y_{0t} - C_{0t} - I_{0t}) + \pi_j(Y_{jt} - C_{jt} - I_{jt}) = 0, \tag{5}$$

where π_j denotes the fraction of world GDP produced by country j. These weights are necessary to define market clearing because the quantities in the constraint are in domestic per capita terms.

The small open economy is closed with an inter-temporal budget constraint identical to (4). However, the discount rate follows an exogenous stochastic process describe below. In addition, the following boundary condition is imposed:

$$\lim_{t\to\infty} \beta^t p_{jt} B_{jt+1} = 0,$$

where p_{jt} is the multiplier on the inter-temporal budget constraint of the representative agent in country j.

Parameterization of tastes and technology are set to values commonly used in the literature. The value of β is set to be 0.954, so that the annual real interest rate is 6.5%. The parameter of relative risk aversion σ is 2 and labor's share α in the production function is 0.58. In the Cobb-Douglas preference function, $\theta = 0.233$. The depreciation rate of capital, δ, is assigned a value of 0.10. The elasticity of the investment-capital ratio with respect to Tobin's Q is $\eta = -(\phi'/\phi'') \div (i/k) = 15$.

2.3. *Exogenous shocks*

Moving from theory to quantitative implications requires estimation of the stochastic process for productivity in each country. Partial equilibrium models require specification of stochastic processes for home country productivity and the domestic interest rate. General equilibrium models require the estimation of stochastic processes for both home and foreign productivity since the interest rate is endogenous. Our specification and estimation method for each of these stochastic processes is discussed in turn below.

2.3.1. *Total factor productivity*

Beginning with the G-8 aggregate, indexed by 0, the logarithm of productivity is the sum of a non-stationary and a stationary component, $\ln A_{0t} = \ln A_{0t}^P + \ln A_{0t}^T$. The non-stationary component follows a pure random walk,

$$\ln A_{0t}^P = \ln A_{0t-1}^P + \ln \varepsilon_{0t}^P, \tag{6}$$

and the stationary component follows an AR(1) process:

$$\ln A_{0t}^T = \rho_0 \ln A_{0t-1}^T + \ln \varepsilon_{0t}^T. \tag{7}$$

The innovations are drawn from independent normal distributions with different standard deviations: $\varepsilon_{0t}^{T} \sim N(0, \sigma_0^T)$, $\varepsilon_{0t}^{P} \sim N(0, \sigma_0^P)$.

As the G-8 is by far the largest region and we assume that productivity spillovers are from the G-8 to each nation of the G-60 and not the reverse. Simulations of the closed economy version of the benchmark model are used to estimate the parameters of the productivity components of the G-8 (effectively this involves setting $\pi = 1$ in the general equilibrium model described earlier). Inputs into the estimation are G-8 aggregates, constructed as country-size-weighted averages of output growth, consumption growth and the logarithm of the consumption-output ratio.

Productivity parameters are chosen to match the observed sample variances of these three key macroeconomic variables. The outcome of the moment-matching exercise is reported in Table 1. The average difference (across countries) between the moments from the data and from the model simulation, reported in the upper panel of the table, is less than 10% in all cases. The estimated persistence of the stationary component of productivity is 0.90, which, when converted to a quarterly estimate matches closely with the existing closed economy real business cycle literature that focuses exclusively

Table 1. Estimates of G-8 productivity processes.

	Data	Model
Standard deviation of:		
GDP growth	1.78	1.80
Consumption growth	1.14	1.14
Consumption-GDP ratio	1.22	1.20
G-8 productivity parameters		
Std. dev. of permanent innovation	0.9	
Persistence	0.90	
Std. dev. of transitory innovation	1.2	

Notes: The upper panel reports the moments of G-8 data in the first column that are matched with the model simulations reported in the second column. The closed economy version of the model is simulated 2700 times with the range of parameters as follows: $\widehat{\rho}_0 \in [0.40, 0.95]$, $\widehat{\sigma}_0^T \in [0.006, 0.02]$ and $\widehat{\sigma}_0^P \in [0.006, 0.02]$. The parameters that best fit the model to the data are reported in the lower panel.

on persistent, but transitory shocks and output fluctuations at business cycle frequencies. It is interesting that the innovations to the permanent and transitory components are of the same order of magnitude, with standard deviations of 0.9 and 1.2, respectively. When combined with the estimated persistence of the stationary component, the implication is that the unconditional variance of the transitory shock adds about 16% *more* to the variance of productivity growth than the permanent shock.

The specification of total factor productivity of the small open economies (nations outside of the G-8 block) is more novel. We have a no-spillover case and a spillover case. In the no-spillover case, the structure is analogous to the G-8 specification:

$$\ln A_{jt} = \ln A_{jt}^P + \ln A_{jt}^T.$$

The permanent component of TFP in country j is,

$$\ln A_{jt}^P = \ln A_{jt-1}^P + \ln \varepsilon_{jt}^P, \tag{8}$$

and the stationary component is an AR(1) process:

$$\ln A_{jt}^T = \rho_j \ln A_{jt+1}^T + \ln \varepsilon_{jt}^T. \tag{9}$$

As was the case of innovations to the components of TFP of the G-8, ε_{jt}^P, ε_{jt}^T, are *i.i.d.* draws from normal distributions both with mean zero, but different standard deviations. For expositional convenience, the distributions are expressed as: $\varepsilon_{jt}^T \sim N(0, \nu_j^T \sigma_0^T)$, $\varepsilon_{jt}^P \sim N(0, \nu_j^P \sigma_0^P)$. Thus, v_j^P and v_j^T, are the standard deviations of the innovations to the permanent and temporary components of productivity in country j *relative* to their counterparts in the G-8, estimated earlier. For purposes of parsimony and tractability, the persistence of the transitory component of TFP in all countries is set equal to its G-8 counterpart: $\rho_j = \widehat{\rho}_0 = 0.90\ \forall j$.[5]

[5]While this choice of persistence for the stationary component is based on maintaining some aspects of tractability and symmetry across countries, it turns out that this is equivalent to a quarterly persistence of 0.96 and thus consistent with the findings of Aguiar and Gopinath (2007). They estimated persistence of their transitory component of productivity at the quarterly frequency of 0.97 for

The second specification of total factor productivity is the correctly specified one in the sense that it is estimated by simulating the two country general equilibrium model. Specifically, with the G-8 productivity processes estimated from the closed economy general equilibrium model, the stochastic process for TFP in the small open economy in the two-country general equilibrium model is specified as: $\ln A_{jt} = \ln A^P_{jt} + \ln A^T_{jt} + \omega^P_j \ln A^P_{0t} + \omega^T_j \ln A^T_{0t}$. The parameters ω^P_j and ω^T_j are factor loadings capturing non-stationary and stationary productivity spillovers from the G-8 to country j. These spillovers are necessary to match international business cycle comovement patterns across the G-8 and individual small open economies in our panel data.

Thus, the correct structural model is taken to be the two-country general equilibrium model with a block-recursive bivariate model for TFP of country j and the G-8 ($j = 0$):

$$\begin{bmatrix} \ln A_{jt} \\ \ln A_{0t} \end{bmatrix} = \begin{bmatrix} 1 & 1 & \omega^P_j & \omega^T_j \\ 0 & 0 & 1 & 1 \end{bmatrix} \begin{bmatrix} \ln A^P_{jt} \\ \ln A^T_{jt} \\ \ln A^P_{0t} \\ \ln A^T_{0t} \end{bmatrix}.$$

As a matter of accounting, the true productivity process of the small open economy is the sum of four terms, the first two terms are permanent and temporary components coming from domestic productivity and the second two terms are permanent and temporary productivity spillovers from the G-8.

Naturally, the response of an open economy to a permanent or temporary productivity shock will depend on whether the shock is of home or foreign origin. As we shall see, the spillovers are necessary to match the international correlation of business cycles, which are absent from the set of moments available using the partial equilibrium approach. This is what distinguishes general equilibrium

Canada and 0.95 for Mexico, respectively. Moreover, they find that this value is close to what the persistence of transitory component of productivity equals for a number of other developed countries.

analysis from partial equilibrium analysis of international business cycles.

To estimate the nation-specific factor loadings on G-8 productivity components, ω_j^P and ω_j^T, and the *relative* standard deviations of nation-specific productivity innovations, v_j^T and v_j^P, the general equilibrium open economy model is used. Specifically, in each simulation, the G-8 takes the role of the home economy and nation j (a nation outside the G-8) takes the role of the foreign economy in the model. The relative size of the small country is set to the fraction of world GDP that country produces, on average, over the sample period of observation. The model is simulated for a range of values for the innovation variance of the permanent and transitory shock to the small country relative to the G-8 value (keeping the G-8 processes as previously estimated) to match: (i) the variance of GDP growth of country j; (ii) the variance of consumption growth of country j; (iii) the correlation of GDP growth between the G-8 and country j and (iv) the correlation of consumption growth between the G-8 and country j.

The heterogeneity of business cycles across developing and developed countries is stark (see Table 2). The standard deviation of output growth is almost twice as high in developing countries

Table 2. Estimates of G-60 productivity processes.

	Developing		Developed	
	Data	Model	Data	Model
Std. dev. of GDP	4.93	5.51	2.60	2.87
Std. dev. of consumption	5.93	5.61	2.12	2.46
Corr. with G-8 GDP	0.09	0.09	0.62	0.61
Corr. with G-8 consumption	−0.08	−0.06	0.47	0.37
Innovation standard deviations relative to G-8 counterparts				
$\nu_j^P \in [0.1, 15]$		3.13		0.61
$\nu_j^T \in [0.1, 15]$		1.98		0.78
Factor loadings on G-8 spillovers				
$\omega_j^P \in [-15, 15]$		−0.53		1.83
$\omega_j^T \in [-15, 15]$		0.40		0.67

compared to developed countries, 4.93 versus 2.60. Notice also that the standard deviation of consumption is higher than that of output in developing countries (5.93 versus 4.93) while it is lower in developed countries (2.12 versus 2.60). Recall that the permanent income reasoning of AG plays a key role in their attributing a dominant role for permanent shocks in developing countries to match this ranking. The additional moments to be matched in the general equilibrium model are the international comovement of consumption growth and output growth. These correlations are also quite distinct across the two groups with strong positive comovement of income growth (0.62) between the median developed economy and the G-8 and positive, but lower consumption growth correlations (0.47). In contrast, the median developing country has a near zero correlation with the G-8 business cycle by either measure (output or consumption growth).[6]

The stochastic processes for productivity, by allowing for both idiosyncratic and common components to permanent and transitory movements in national productivity is able to capture both the standard deviation patterns of income and consumption growth in each nation as well as the correlation of business cycles between each nation and the G-8 block. It is not surprising, for example, that the standard deviation of productivity innovations are estimated to be much higher in developing countries. Less obvious and more interesting is a comparison of the two components that determine country-specific component of national productivity: the innovations to the permanent component to productivity has a standard deviation three times that of the G-8 (3.13) and the stationary component has a standard deviation of twice that of the G-8 (1.98). In contrast, the country specific components of national productivity are relatively

[6]Backus *et al.* (1992) coined the phrase 'international comovement puzzle' in recognition that models featuring complete financial markets predict consumption growth correlations to be near unity, bounding the output correlation from above. Their work focused on developed nations within the G-8 block. The puzzle is preserved in the developed nations sample and the puzzle worsens dramatically when the sample is extended to developing countries.

smooth for the developed countries: the permanent component has a standard deviation of innovations 0.61 times that of the G-8 and the stationary component is 0.78 times that of the G-8.

Turning to the factor loadings linking national productivity to the G-8 productivity levels, the spillover from G-8 productivity shocks to productivity level in the developed world is positive for both permanent and transitory shocks, but the permanent shock has a factor loading of 1.83, almost three times that of the transitory component (0.67). The factor loadings for developing countries are both smaller and the loading on the permanent G-8 shock is actually negative. This pattern of spillovers are required to match the low correlation of output growth (0.09) and negative correlation of consumption growth (−0.08) between the G-8 and developing countries. This is where the general equilibrium incomplete markets model is particularly useful. Essentially, what matters for consumption comovement is the correlation of wealth in each country with that of the G-8 block. The negative factor loading on the permanent G-8 shock for developing countries shifts output and particularly consumption comovement towards zero for that group of nations.

2.3.2. *Interest rate shocks*

In the SOE model, domestic productivity shocks play a central role as they should, just as is the case in the general equilibrium model. However, unlike the general equilibrium model, foreign productivity shocks are not explicitly included in the set of exogenous shocks faced by small open economies and interest rate shocks are intended to summarize the relevant international business cycle spillovers. As there has not been any systematic research into the ability of interest rate disturbances to capture the response of a small open economy to anything other than an unexpected change in the interest rate itself, it seems essential to elucidate the issue.

To explore the implications of exogenously specified interest rates we assume as Mendoza (1991) did that the discount rate follows an AR(1) process:

$$\ln P_{jt}^{B} = \gamma_j \ln P_{jt}^{B} + \ln \varepsilon_{jt}^{B}, \tag{10}$$

Table 3. Bond price shock parameters.

	Developing		Developed	
Spillovers	Yes	No	Yes	No
Persistence	0.30	0.54	0.24	0.69
Innovation standard deviations	0.003	0.006	0.004	0.005

where $0 < \gamma_j < 1$ denotes the persistence of the logarithm of the bond price, and ε_{jt}^{B} is an *iid* draw from a normal distribution with zero mean and standard deviation σ_j^B.[7]

From a general equilibrium perspective, the bond price is redundant as it is determined almost entirely by G-8 productivity when the model is closed. When added as a separate forcing process in the small open economy model along with the productivity processes, some of the variance of output and consumption that should be attributable to domestic or foreign productivity is incorrectly attributed to the real interest rate. Turning to the results, Table 3 reports the persistence and innovation variance of the bond price for the two groups of countries for two parameterizations. The column labeled 'Yes' is the case in which G-8 productivity spillovers are included and the case labeled 'No' are the case in which these spillovers are absent. The contrast of these cases is intended to explore the consequences of ignoring international business cycle comovement in the moment matching exercise.

Beginning with the no-spillover case, which is most relevant to partial equilibrium calibration, the persistence averages 0.54

[7]Recent extensions of this basic approach allow for a differential to arise between the domestic interest rate and the world interest rate and for that differential to be a function of domestic productivity, as Uribe and Yue (2006). The latter formulation is intended to allow for the possibility that changes in domestic productivity change the probability of default and this feeds back into banks willingness to lend. While this is an important extension of the basic framework, this formulation, once again, abstracts from the differential response of a country to a home and global productivity change.

for developing countries and 0.69 for developed countries while the standard deviation averages about 5.5 basis points. Including spillovers from the G-8 significantly reduces the role of interest rate shocks by: reducing the persistence needed for both groups of countries and, particularly for the developing countries while cutting the innovation variance in half. The diminished role of the interest rate shocks when spillovers are included goes in the right direction in terms of general equilibrium reasoning, but a more direct evaluation is to examine the output variance decomposition across the model variants, to which we now turn.

3. Variance Decomposition

With the calibration of the DGSE and SOE models complete, we are in a position to compute variance decompositions of output growth into the underlying exogenous sources of variation under the null and alternative model. Recall, the null model is the two-country general equilibrium model with international productivity spillovers.

Table 4 reports the results using the small open economy model without spillovers as this corresponds most closely to the analysis of AG. Beginning with the pooled results for all countries the permanent and transitory shocks account for virtually identical

Table 4. Output variance decompositions, small open economy model.

	Variance decomposition					
Source of shock type of shock	Home permanent	Home transitory	World interest rate	Total	Number of countries	Std. dev. of output
All countries	36.93	36.97	26.10	100	58	4.3
Developing	43.13	30.51	26.37	100	40	4.9
Developed	23.15	51.34	25.51	100	18	2.8
AG sample	25.70	46.72	27.58	100	20	3.1
Developing	29.97	43.03	27.00	100	9	4.0
Developed	21.81	50.07	18.12	100	11	2.3

Notes: Productivity spillovers are abstracted from this specification because they would not be identified using the small open economy model.

fractions of output growth fluctuations, 37% (74% combined). The world interest rate accounts for the remaining 26%. However, these averages obscure heterogeneity in the cross-section. Dividing the sample into developing and developed countries the asymmetry point out by AG shows up vividly: the permanent shock accounting for about 43% of the variance in developing countries compared to 23% in the case of developed economies. The interest rate plays a relative minor role in both cases, but is more important for the developed economies than the developing economies.

This no-spillover benchmark is even more stark in amplifying the role of permanent shocks in developing countries than the original AG result. The result is sensitive to the sample of countries. Using 20 countries that are common across our study and theirs, the permanent shock accounts for 30% for developing countries and 22% in developed countries. The sensitivity to countries included in the analysis reflects substantial differences in business cycle variability within each group, an issue we address below.

Turning to Table 5, the result when the simulation model is correctly specified as a two country general equilibrium model with productivity spillovers, the asymmetry in the contribution of permanent and transitory shocks across the country groups is now the *reverse* of what AG found. That is, the permanent shocks now play a relatively more important role in the case of the developed countries, 51% versus 45% for developing countries. Notably this tendency is even more pronounced in the narrower sample used by AG (51% versus 35%). The right-most panel uses the partial equilibrium model with spillovers to show that when the productivity processes of correctly specified, the partial equilibrium approach gives quantitatively similar results. However, this should not be construed as indicating the potential for the partial equilibrium model to correctly identify the relevant business cycle shocks. Recall, the spillover case was based upon the general equilibrium simulations that also matched international business cycle comovement.

Further problems of identification are evident in the lower panel of Table 5, which breaks the permanent and transitory components into the contributions of home productivity and G8 spillovers.

Table 5. Output variance decompositions, model comparisons.

Model	DSGE				SOE				
Source of shock type of shock	Home + G8 permanent		Home + G8 transitory		Home + G8 permanent		Home + G8 transitory		Interest rate
All countries	46.9		53.1		41.3		53.2		5.4
Developing	45.2		54.8		42.8		54.4		2.7
Developed	50.8		49.2		38.0		50.5		11.5
Aguiar and Gopinath	43.3		56.7		32.6		57.0		10.4
Developing	34.9		65.1		30.2		64.0		5.8
Developed	51.0		49.0		34.8		50.8		14.4
Source of Shock Type of Shock	Home P	G8 P	Home T	G8 T	Home P	G8 P	Home T	G8 T	Interest rate
All countries	23.6	23.4	38.5	14.6	22.5	18.8	37.9	15.3	5.4
Developing	30.6	14.6	44.2	10.6	29.5	13.4	43.6	10.8	2.7
Developed	8.1	42.7	25.8	23.4	7.1	30.9	25.3	25.2	11.5

In particular, the small open economy model does not reproduce the correct decomposition of the permanent and temporary components into home and foreign (spillovers). For example, in the case of developed countries, the correct decomposition of the permanent shocks is to assign 42.7% of the variation to a spillover from the G-8. The small open economy model assigns 30.9% to this spillover. The reason the prediction is so far off is that the small open economy predicts that agents will respond in the same fashion to shocks of domestic or foreign origin provided they have the same stochastic properties (i.e., permanent or transitory) whereas this is obviously not the case in a general equilibrium context where the source of the shock is of paramount importance in determining the quantitative response and often the sign of the response.

The results are even more apparent at the country level since the specification errors tend to be highly skewed. Figure 2 depicts the fraction of output growth variance attributable to the permanent shocks (home and G-8 spillover) predicted by the general equilibrium and partial equilibrium models. Since the interest rate is endogenous

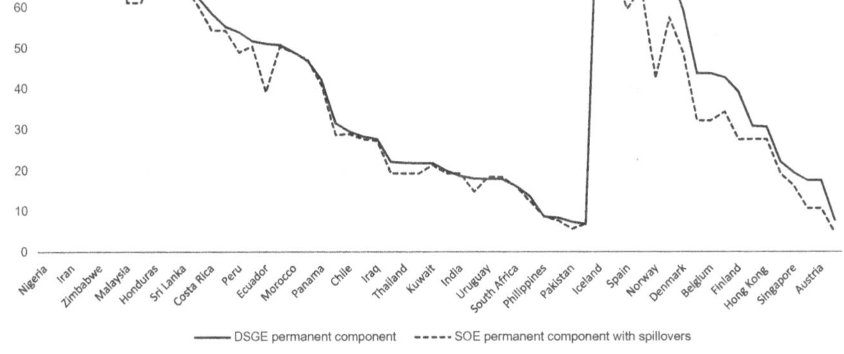

Fig. 2. Proportion of output growth variance accounted for by permanent shocks: comparison of DSGE model and SOE with productivity spillovers.

in the general equilibrium model, the fraction of variance attributed to productivity is typically an upper envelope of that predicted by the small open economy. The reader is reminded that in this exercise the spillovers estimated using the general equilibrium model are included in the partial equilibrium simulations in this comparison to give the partial equilibrium model the best chance of matching the general equilibrium null model. Since the spillovers are not identified in the partial equilibrium model these comparisons should be viewed as lower bounds on the errors: only if the productivity processes could be directly observed would this small open economy specification be feasible to simulate and compare to the small open economy results in Fig. 2.

Figure 3 presents a more pragmatic comparison. It contrasts the small open economy approach under the correct specification with productivity spillovers from G-8 and the more common practice (as in AG) where the small open economy model is simulated with only domestic permanent and transitory shocks. Note that the small

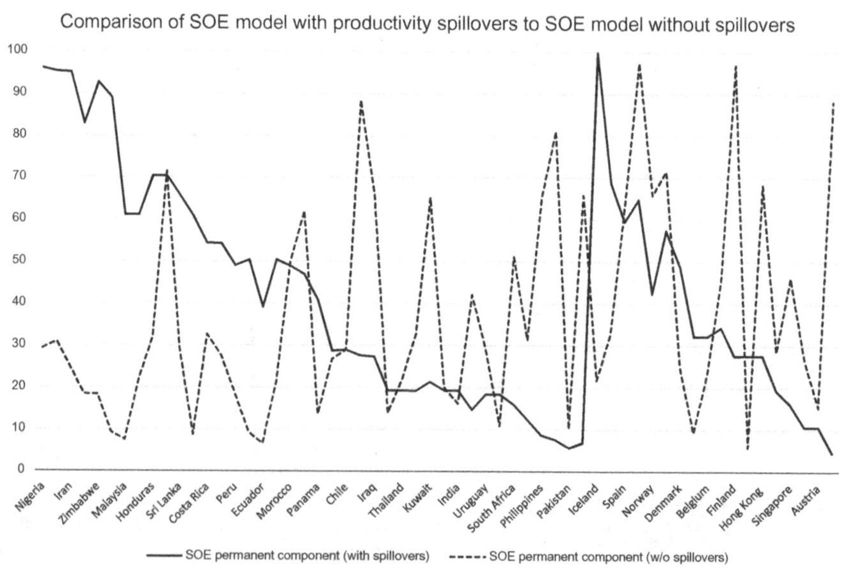

Fig. 3. Proportion of output growth variance accounted by permanent shocks: comparison of SOE model with productivity spillovers to SOE model without spillovers.

open economy approach gets the correct variance decomposition on average (across countries) even when spillovers are ignored. However, the errors of variance accounting country-by-country are obviously very substantial and not randomly distributed in the cross-section. The role of permanent shocks is underestimated when spillovers are ignored for developed economies, but overestimated when spillovers are ignored in the case of developing countries.

4. Concluding Remarks

In this paper we have compared the performance of a standard SOE model with an analytically comparable two-country DSGE model. We conducted variance decomposition for 58 small economies using both models. We find that the main limitation of the SOE model is that it cannot capture the role of TFP spillovers from the G-8 since it ignores international business cycle correlation in the moment-matching exercise. This result is robust in the entire cross-section of nations, but is more quantitatively important for small developed countries, who share more of a stochastic trend in productivity with the G-8 than do developing countries.

The exercise shows that it is simply not true that the small open economy framework is justifiable on the grounds that small economies do not affect the world interest rate. The practical difficulty with the small open economy approach is that it greatly limits the ability of researchers to capture the differential national responses of internationally integrated economies to common and idiosyncratic shocks, be they permanent or transitory in nature. What matters is not just how persistence the shocks are, but also how idiosyncratic they are.

Our paper has provided a methodology that allows researchers to study economic interactions of a large number of heterogeneous and small open economies in general equilibrium without exploding the dimensionality of the state space. Essentially it boils down to modeling a large aggregate economic region in general equilibrium with a small open economy. One limitation of way this approach is developed here is that it abstracts from the possibility that shocks outside of the G-8 are large enough to alter the world interest rate. With the emergence of the BRICs, for example, it seems important to extend the approach to allow for more than one block of nations to alter the equilibrium dynamics of the smaller economies that comprise the rest of the world. We leave this extension to future work.

References

Aguiar, M., Gopinath, G., 2007. Emerging market business cycles: the cycle is the trend. *J. Political Econ.* 115, 69–102.

Backus, D.K., Kehoe, P.J., Kydland, F.E., 1992. International real business cycles. *J. Political Econ.* 100, 745–775.

Baxter, M., Crucini, M.J., 1995. Business cycles and the asset structure of foreign trade. *Int. Econ. Rev.* 36, 821–854.

Crucini, M.J., Shintani, M., 2015. Measuring international business cycles by saving for a rainy day. *Can. J. Econ./Rev. Can. D.'économique* 48, 1266–1290.

Mendoza, E.G., 1991. Real business cycles in a small open economy. *Am. Econ. Rev.* 81 (September), 797–818.

Uribe, M., Yue, V.Z., 2006. Country spreads and emerging countries: Who drives whom? *J. Int. Econ.* 69, 6–36.

Chapter 8

International Risk Sharing and Commodity Prices*

Martin Berka

Victoria University of Wellington,
Wellington, New Zealand

Mario J. Crucini

Department of Economics, Vanderbilt University,
Nashville, TN, USA
mario.j.crucini@vanderbilt.edu

and

Chih-Wei Wang

Pacific Lutheran University,
Tacoma, WA, USA

Abstract. Cole and Obstfeld (1991) exposited a classic result where equilibrium movements in the terms of trade could make ex ante risk-sharing arrangements unnecessary: a unity elasticity of substitution across goods and production specialization. This paper extends their model to N countries and M commodities ($N > M$). Here the terms of trade provides insurance against commodity-specific shocks, not country-specific shocks. Using commodity-level production data at the national level and world commodity prices, we document significant terms of trade variability and positive responses of nation-specific production to terms of trade improvements. The endogenous terms of trade insurance mechanism highlighted in CO is virtually non-existent.

*This chapter originally appeared in *Canadian Journal of Economics*, 2012, **45**(2), 427–447.

1. Introduction

Financial markets provide a mechanism through which individuals and firms are able to transform the cash flows from their economic activities across time and states of nature. The consumption risk-sharing literature attempts to provide an overall assessment of the outcomes of these financial market linkages by examining how closely consumption allocations conform to the idealized world in which complete contingent claims shield individuals entirely from idiosyncratic variation in their income. The empirical literature on this topic is broad, ranging from microeconomic approaches that study individual income and consumption dynamics using, for example, the U.S. Consumption Expenditure Survey (CEX) to macroeconomic approaches, using income and product accounts at the national or regional level. Examples of the microeconomic approach are Cochrane (1991) and Mace (1991), while examples of the macroeconomic approach are Canova and Ravn (1996) and Lewis (1996).[1]

At the national level, the empirical risk-sharing literature has been mostly focused on the large industrialized countries, in part owing to the dominant fraction of world output that they produce, but also because of the relatively short time spans of reliable developing country data available at the time the literature emerged in the early 1990s. This omission has a number of implications. First, the omission is significant in the sense that the welfare implications of risk sharing for a majority of the world's population has not been examined. This omission would also be important for studies of industrialized countries in the sense that, while individual developing nations contribute very little to global capital flows, in the aggregate the flow of capital between developing and developed countries is actually quite large and growing rapidly. Second, given the more volatile and idiosyncratic nature of the business cycles in developing countries, these nations evidently have much more to gain from risk sharing with each other and through integration with industrialized countries than industrialized nations gain from pooling risks among

[1]See Hess and van Wincoop (2000) for insightful comparisons of approaches at the regional and national levels.

themselves. Thus, the welfare implications of risk sharing may be understated when the focus is placed on the most economically stable nations who share a large common factor in their business cycle variation.

To gain an appreciation for the heterogeneity in business cycle experiences around the world, consider Fig. 1. It plots the standard deviation of the growth rates of consumption and GDP for 161 countries using the Penn World Tables (PWT) over the sample period 1971 to 2005.[2] The standard deviation of GDP growth ranges from an astounding 27.5% in Lebanon to a mere 1.88% in the Netherlands; the median country is Samoa (5.16%). The United States, the most scrutinized country in the business cycle literature, is hardly representative: it ranks 149th. OECD nations occupy 16 of the 20 least volatile positions in the ranking. The often cited business cycle fact that the ratio of the standard deviation of consumption growth relative to output growth is much less than 1 in the United States is a feat achieved by only 11 of the 161 nations in the PWT (the line at the bottom of the figure presents this ratio by country along with the U.S. benchmark value of 0.69). The median volatility ratio is 1.18. Note, also, that nations with more GDP volatility tend to have more consumption volatility: the correlation of output and consumption volatility across nations is 0.76.

The benchmark international risk-sharing model in which nations pool output endowments in a mutual fund and each nation is allocated consumption in proportion to total world output predicts that consumption volatility will be equalized across countries and, furthermore, it will be equal to the variance of world GDP. In the data, however, the median consumption standard deviation is 6.63, four times the standard deviation of world GDP growth of 1.69.[3] The standard deviation of world consumption growth is even lower than that of world GDP growth (1.12), suggesting that extending the endowment version of the risk-sharing model to allow for

[2]Using the Hodrick-Prescott filter gives qualitatively similar results.

[3]World GDP and consumption growth are computed as a country-size weighted averages of national GDP and consumption growth, respectively. The country size weights used are the averages over the sample period.

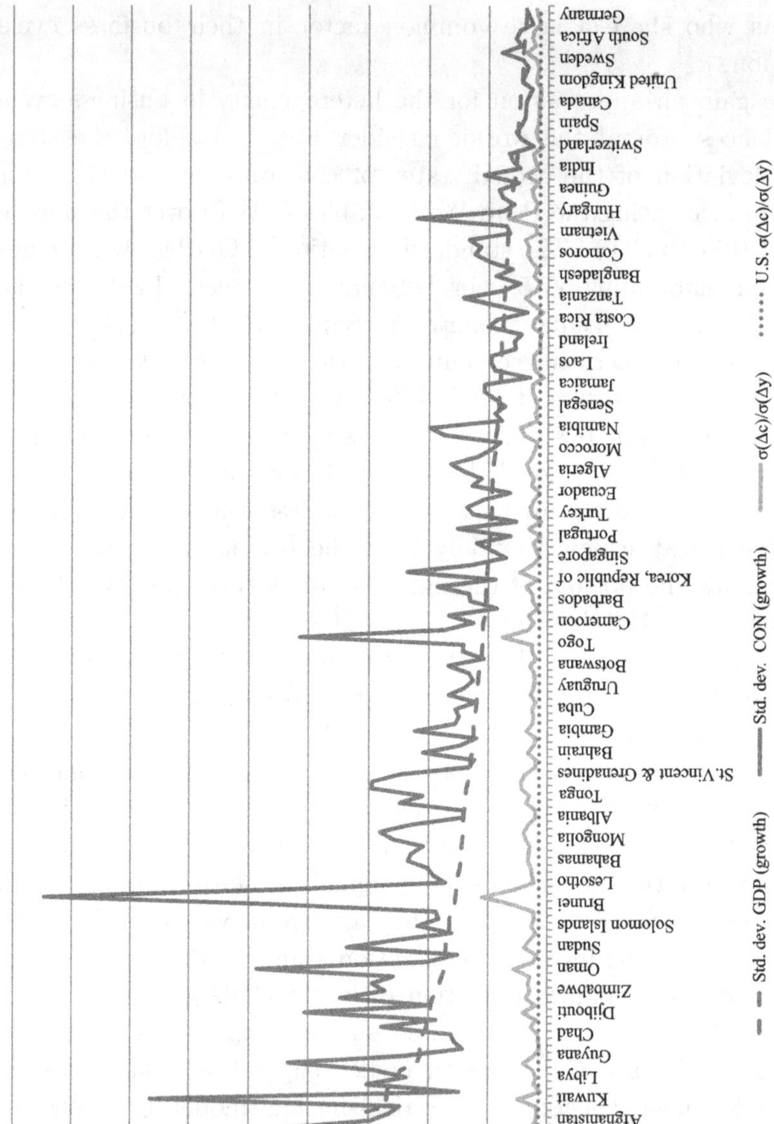

Fig. 1. International business cycles standard deviation of output and consumption growth.

intertemporal substitution would allow consumption variability fall below output variability by a significant margin. Interestingly, the world consumption volatility ratio is 0.66, only slightly lower than the U.S. level. Taken at face value, these facts suggest considerable GDP risk at the national level and limited amounts of risk sharing. Below, we provide reduced-form estimates that one-third of national GDP variability is pooled among nations.

With a shift in focus to the full sample of nations of the world, it is productive to move from a one-sector macroeconomic model emphasizing the gains from intertemporal trade to a trade model emphasizing variation in the terms of trade. The classic general equilibrium trade model of risk sharing is Cole and Obstfeld (1991). In their two-country model, each nation receives a stochastic endowment of a perishable commodity. When the elasticity of substitution across goods is unity, the equilibrium terms of trade and relative endowments move in equal and opposite directions. Consequently, the same consumption allocations arise under financial autarky as under complete risk sharing: asset markets are redundant.

We extend the Cole and Obstfeld model in a number of directions to more accurately assess the terms of trade channel. Two crucial theoretical extensions are (i) to allow multiple producers of each primary commodity and (ii) to allow for incomplete specialization. By allowing for multiple producers of each primary commodity, we show that the terms of trade insurance mechanism of the original paper remains in effect for the group of nations (or individuals) that specialize in the production of a primary commodity but provides absolutely no insurance against idiosyncratic variation in production levels across members of the group producing the same commodity. Allowing for incomplete commodity specialization reduces supply-side risk to the extent shocks are good or sector specific, but tends to amplify the impact of nation-specific disturbances because the terms of trade effect is muted. Since our focus is on countries most vulnerable to terms of trade risk, we assume the numeraire good (a composite manufactured good) is produced by one 'country' and consider this to be an aggregate of the G-7 nations. The diversification of production across most of the goods in the consumption basket greatly reduces the output and consumption variance of the G-7 group.

Much of the novelty of the analysis lies in the empirical work, which exploits a panel of physical production data of individual primary commodities at both the national and the world level. To incorporate the broadest possible picture of the role of commodity prices in the business cycle variation of nations we use a cross-section of 66 countries. The number of countries is substantially lower than the 161 nations available in the PWT, which is a limitation forced by the available panel of commodity production and export data. We find a very substantial idiosyncratic component to annual production changes, which based on the theory cannot be insured by movements in the terms of trade. In fact, the results are even more stark, since by measuring production variation it is possible to examine the covariance of production changes in each country with the relative price of the primary commodities that it exports. This covariance is large and positive in most cases, which effectively means that supply changes actually reinforce the effect of relative prices on export earnings, which is the opposite of the Cole and Obstfeld mechanism. Put differently, the primary commodity supply shocks that the Cole and Obstfeld theory focused upon appear to be the exception rather than the rule.

To make this a bit more concrete, consider the international coffee market. When the demand for coffee on the global market increases, owing to a world cyclical expansion, what do we expect will happen in individual countries that depend on coffee for a large fraction of their income and export earnings? If income elasticities of demand are unitary and the world production possibility frontier is shifting out in a neutral fashion (neutral in the sense of all dimensions of the commodity space), all commodity supplies and demands will increase in the same proportion and relative prices and relative demands will remain unchanged. More of everything is produced and consumed at exactly the same relative prices as before the expansion took place. A more realistic expectation is that asymmetric movements in prices and quantities will occur, at least in the short run. In other words, we would expect changes in the terms of trade. This is an empirical question informed in part by the fact that the typical primary commodity relative price is procyclical, extremely volatile, and persistent. Thus, in a typical global expansion, the income of the coffee producer is likely to rise, owing to a terms of trade improvement, which may be reinforced by a positive supply response. This is not meant to completely downplay the role of commodity supply shocks. Exogenous crop failures do have significant implications for nations that concentrate their production in a few primary commodities. It is also true that the concentration of production is sufficiently high that a shock in one or a few locations could move the world price significantly in the manner described by the Cole and Obtsfeld model. Brazil, for example, produces about one-third of the world coffee supply and it and Colombia and Vietnam account for more than 50% — again, an empirical question that our panel data is well suited to address.

We find that the negative correlation between a relative commodity price and its production level needed to provide the endogenous terms of trade risk sharing in the Cole and Obstfeld model is largely inoperative in the real world. While there are periods in which a commodity relative price increases as the relative quantity of its global production falls, these periods and commodities are the exceptions to the rule. Most of the time the correlation is either ambiguous or positive. Drilling down to the level of a nation makes matters worse, since a positive correlation is prevalent, consistent with a positive supply response to a terms of trade improvement. In other words, the quantity movements reinforce the relative price movements on export earnings rather than working to mitigate the effect as would be true in the Cole and Obstfeld model. Finally, the terms of trade are where most of the variance lies in the change in export earnings. This suggests either an inelastic supply curve for the primary commodity due to capacity constraints in the short run or possibly wealth effects working to offset the substitution effects that would typically lead to an expansion of commodity supply.

Overall, we find that the model predicts high consumption variance in nations that have more volatile terms of trade, and it accounts for about 15% of the cross-sectional variation in consumption volatility in the data. However, the marginal impact of variation in export revenue is too great; as we move from a country with a 10% predicted standard deviation of consumption growth to twice that level, the increase in the standard deviation of consumption growth in the actual data is only about 1.4%, not 10%. As the model assumes complete specialization in primary commodities and abstracts from non-traded goods, it is not surprising that it predicts excess consumption sensitivity to the terms of trade. The main point, however, is that the terms of trade is not providing the insurance channel attributed to it by the Cole and Obstfeld benchmark model. In fact, the data seem to point to an important role for changes in world commodity demand that, first of all, move relative prices and relative quantities in the same direction and, second of all, move relative prices by far more than relative quantities, at least in the short run. The relatively high variance of price compared with quantity seems inconsistent also with the unitary elasticity of substitution in demand. More plausibly, the elasticity of both demand and supply of primary commodities relative to manufactured goods is quite below unity. Finally, national production changes tend to be dominated by nation-specific variation, adding an important idiosyncratic component to national consumption even for producers of the same commodities.

2. The Data

The macroeconomic data on Gross Domestic Product and private consumption for 161 countries is from version 6.3 of the Penn World Tables (PWT). These data are annual and the sample period is 1970 to 2005. The commodity price and physical quantity of production data are from the *Commodity Research Bureau Yearbook*, 2009. The prices are annual averages of U.S. dollar spot market prices. The quantity data are production data by country and total world production. The difference between the world production estimate and the sum of national production levels is a residual referred to as 'other' in what follows. Subject to availability, the commodity price and production data start in 1970 and end in 2005. The commodity export data by country are collected from the United

Nations Commodity Trade Statistics (UN Comtrade) Database. The sample periods are 1962–2002 for the SITC classification and 1988–2009 for the HS classification.[4]

2.1. *Macroeconomic fluctuations*

When output is modelled as a stochastic and perishable endowment, full risk pooling is achieved by having each nation hold shares in a global mutual fund paying dividends equal to world GDP. A natural starting point for a discussion of international risk sharing, therefore, is a variance decomposition of world output.

World GDP growth is defined as a country-size weighted average of national GDP growth rates:

$$\Delta y_t = \sum_i \pi_i \Delta y_{it}, \tag{1}$$

where y_{it} is the logarithm of real GDP (Layspeyres) for country i, and π_i is the fraction of world GDP produced by country i, on average, over the period 1971 to 2005. Figure 2 presents the entire distribution of country sizes, with the largest countries at the bottom of the figure and successively smaller countries added until the total of 100%, is achieved. The extreme skewness of the world country-size distribution is readily evident: of the 161 countries in the full sample, 147 of them contribute significantly less than 1% of world GDP.

Owing to the large number of countries, it is economical to use a non-standard variance decomposition:

$$var(\Delta y_t) = \sum_i \pi_i cov(\Delta y_t, \Delta y_{it}). \tag{2}$$

Dividing both sides by the variance of world output growth leads to the variance decomposition:

$$1 = \sum_i \pi_i \beta_i, \tag{3}$$

[4]See the Data Appendix for more details about data sources and index construction.

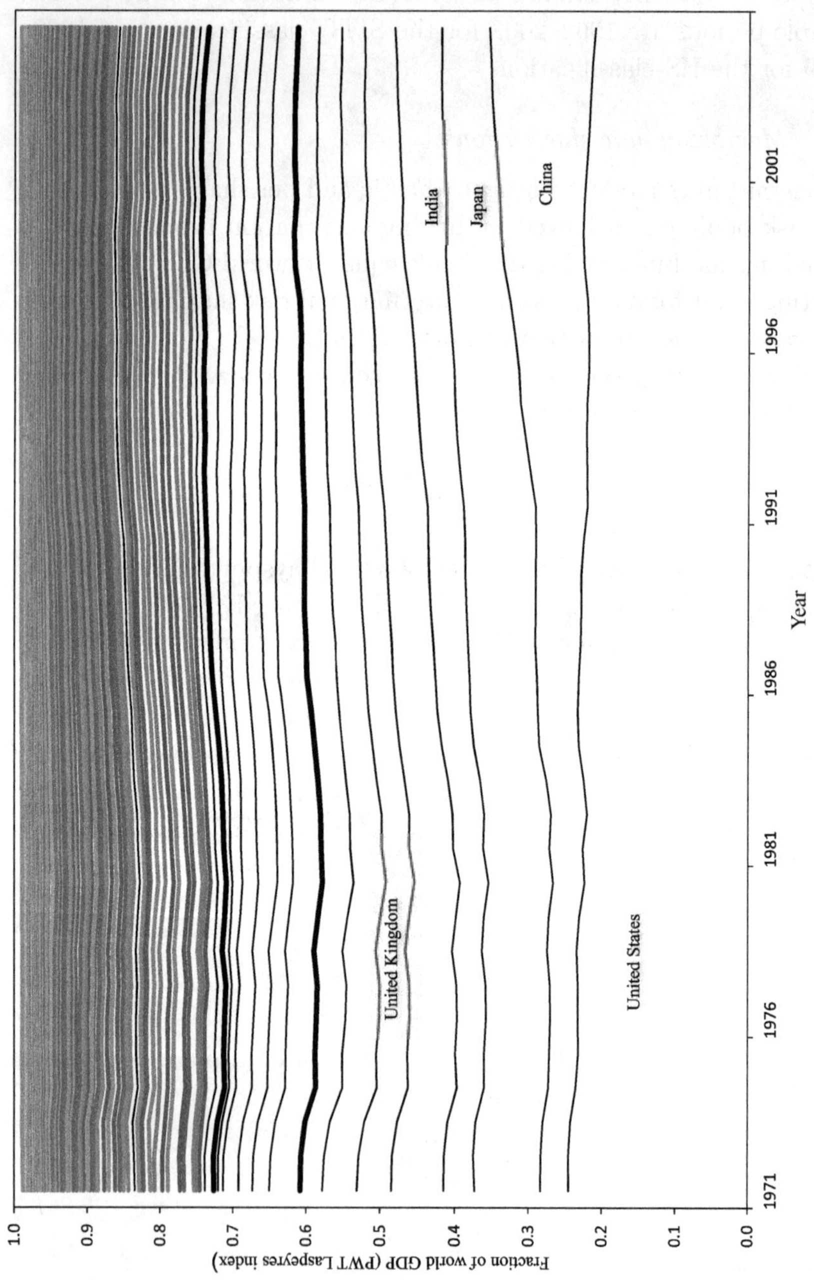

Fig. 2. The evolution of relative country size.

where $\beta_i \equiv cov(\Delta y_t,\ \Delta y_{it})/var(\Delta y_t)$. By construction, the country-size weighted average β is 1.

The U.S. ranks first in this variance decomposition, which is not very surprising. What is surprising is that the U.S. accounts for 35% of the variance despite producing only 23% of world output (the U.S. share of world GDP in the PWT data). The difference reflects the fact that the beta of the U.S. is 1.52. Put differently, while the U.S. may have one of the most stable growth rates in the world, it is more volatile than world GDP and has a high correlation with world GDP, thus giving it a beta far in excess of 1.

About 15% of the world's nations, 23 to be exact, have negative betas, indicating that the variance of world GDP falls as a consequence of their inclusion in the portfolio. Among this group, China and Indonesia are notable because of their economic size. At the other extreme are countries where βs far exceed unity; oil exporters tend to fall into this category. Saudi Arabia, for example, contributes one-fifth as much to world GDP variance as the U.S., despite being about 30 times smaller economically.

The fact that the income betas are very different from unity suggests considerable scope for international risk sharing. For evidence on the extent to which risk sharing occurs, the consumption side of the ledger is relevant. The analogous variance decomposition of world consumption is $1 = \Sigma_i \pi_i \alpha_i$, where $\alpha_i \equiv cov(\Delta c_t,\ \Delta c_{it})/var(\Delta c_t)$.

As is well known, complete risk sharing in the one-sector endowment economy implies the equality of marginal utility across nations. Moreover, under the assumption that consumption is separable from other arguments of the utility function and takes the form, $(1-\sigma)^{-1}c^{1-\sigma}$, complete international risk sharing implies $\Delta c_t = \Delta c_{it}$. In terms of the world consumption growth variance decomposition this means the distribution of the αs is degenerate: $\alpha_i = 1$.[5]

[5]The reader will recognize that the international business cycle literature has shown how difficult it is to reduce the consumption correlation below unity under risk pooling even when assumptions such as separable utility are relaxed and preference shocks are introduced.

Figure 3 presents a scatterplot of the consumption αs against the income βs. The figure also contains three lines. The horizontal line is the relationship between the two parameters under the null hypothesis of complete risk sharing. The 45-degree line is consistent with national GDP and consumption moving with each other, which is inconsistent with risk sharing. The third line is a least-squares estimate of the relationship between the αs and the βs in the data. The slope of the line is 0.7, suggesting that 70% of GDP risk is not pooled among nations. In sum, the macroeconomic time series are consistent with a considerable amount of idiosyncratic variation in national GDP available to be pooled, yet the majority of the consumption risks remain specific to the nation.

2.2. *Commodity market fluctuations*

Developing countries would seem to be the ideal setting in which to investigate the Cole and Obstfeld proposition that the positive wealth

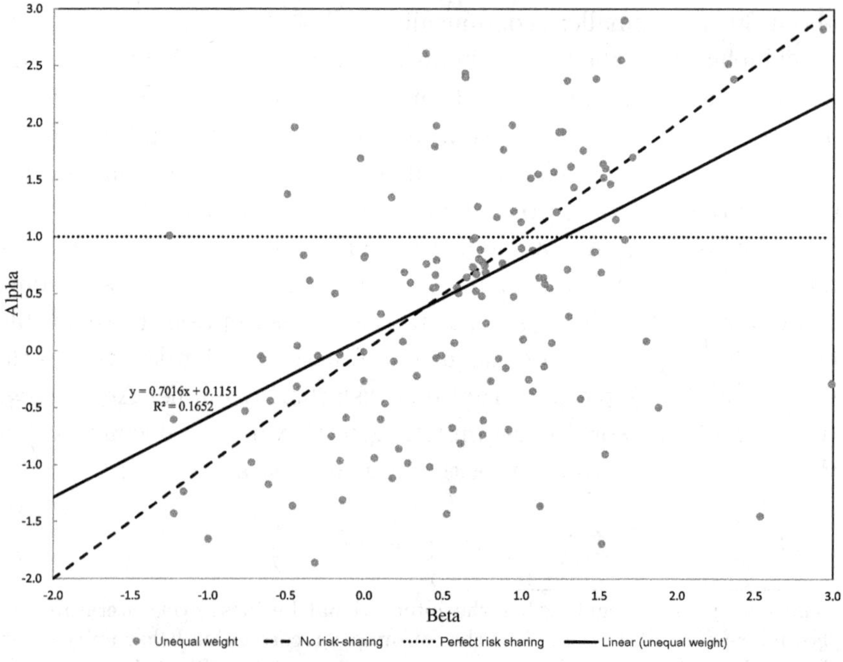

Fig. 3. Risk-sharing regression.

effects of an increase in the physical output of a commodity are completely offset by a deterioration in the terms of trade. Developing nations are typically highly specialized in exports. Moreover, the physical quantity of primary commodity production is arguably more susceptible to exogenous sources of variation than is true of manufactured goods and services produced in industrialized nations.

The properties of commodity price fluctuations have been thoroughly documented in the existing literature. The typical primary commodity price fluctuates by an order of magnitude larger than other goods or services in the CPI basket. Economists continue to debate whether they are random walks or are cointegrated with the price level.[6] Less is known about the evolution of the quantity of world production and we know of no study that investigates nation-specific variation in production levels. This section intends to fill these gaps in the literature before turning to their risk-sharing implications.

2.2.1. *World commodity price and quantity indices*

The panel data consist of spot U.S. dollar prices and physical production of 33 primary commodities. The price data are U.S. dollar spot prices from centralized exchanges. The production data are physical production by major producers and world production levels.

The analysis begins at the level of world commodity price and quantity indices, each constructed using sample average production value weights, denoted θ_j:

$$\theta_j \equiv T^{-1} \sum_t \frac{P_{jt} Y_{jt}}{\sum_j P_{jt} Y_{jt}}, \tag{4}$$

where P_{jt} is the international price of commodity j in year t and Y_{jt} is world physical production of commodity j in the same year. The

[6]See Wang (2011) for evidence on persistence of commodity prices relative to the CPI and the role of permanent and transitory shocks in the evolution of nominal commodity prices.

commodity price and quantity indices are defined as

$$\tilde{z}_{ct} \equiv \sum_j \theta_j z_{jt}, \; z = p, \, y, \tag{5}$$

where lower case variables are logarithms of their upper case counterparts (thus, the indices should be viewed as geometric averages of the micro-data with production shares as the weights).

The commodity price index is trending over time, owing to inflation (in U.S. dollar terms), while the commodity quantity index is trending because of the interactions of economic growth and technological innovation. The presumption is that economic growth increases the demand of primary commodities, while technological innovation allows producers to economize on these inputs or develop substitutes for them over time. For this reason, we normalized by the U.S. CPI for the price index (p_t) and we normalized by world real GDP (y_t) for the quantity index. We refer to these as the relative price and relative quantity indices in what follows and denote them by $p_{ct} = \tilde{p}_{ct} - p_t$ and $y_{ct} = \tilde{y}_{ct} - y_t$, respectively.

Figure 4 plots the levels of the relative commodity price and quantity indices from 1970 to 2005. For the Cole and Obtsfeld risk-sharing channel to be operating across the industrialized and developing world these two indices would need to be equal in slope and opposite in sign. In fact, they are very unequal in slope (notice different vertical scales) and equal in sign. Primary commodities are becoming relatively inexpensive and relatively scarce at the same time. The property of a secular decline in the relative price of primary commodities is called the Prebisch-Singer hypothesis and has been the subject of intense empirical study for some time. Note that the implication of these two series for the world share of expenditure on primary goods is astounding: the relative price decline is on the order of 100%, while the quantity decline is about 20%; thus, the 2005 share of world expenditure on primary commodities is about one-half what it was in 1970.

Figure 5 presents the same variables in growth rates to focus on the higher-frequency movements in consumption and income that

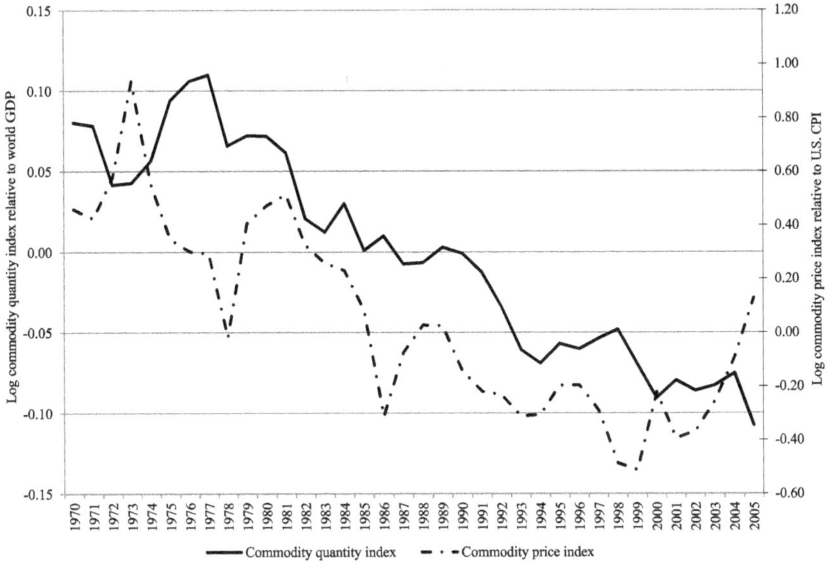

Fig. 4. Commodity quantity and price trends.

often are the focus of the risk-sharing and business cycle literature. The correlation of the two variables is now ambiguous (–0.08) and the relative volatility of prices is greatly amplified, to a factor of about 10. There are periods in which the correlation of relative prices and quantities is strongly negative, suggestive of a dominance of 'supply shocks.' Taking five-year moving averages of the correlations centered on the early 1970s and the late 1980s and 1990s, we see that the correlation averages –0.6. While interesting, the standard error is very large and these periods are not typical of the last quarter-century of evidence.

2.2.2. *Deconstruction of world commodity price and quantity indices*

It is tempting to relate the annual changes in relative commodity prices to the patterns of business cycle heterogeneity documented in Fig. 1. As we move up along the business cycle volatility profile of nations in Fig. 1, the commodity concentration of output and particularly exports is rising, suggesting an important role for

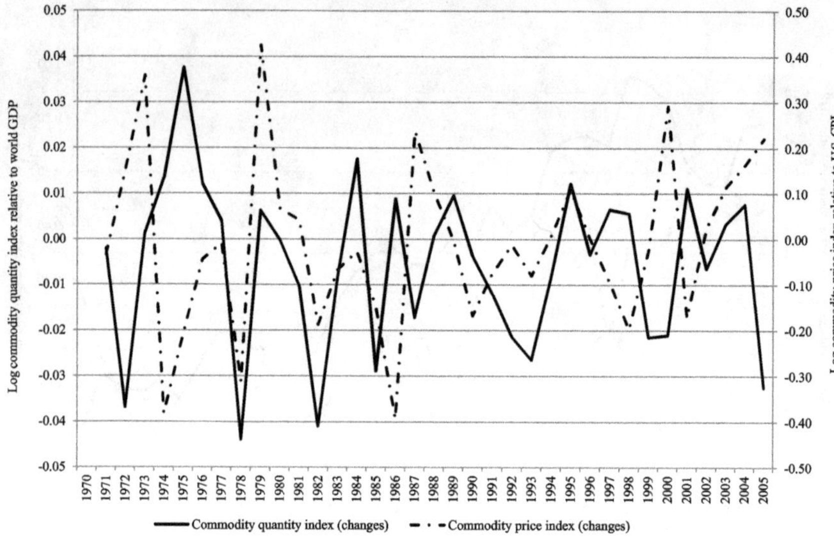

Fig. 5. Commodity price and production changes.

commodity prices in elevating the volatility of GDP and consumption in small, developing nations, compared with large industrialized ones.

Since primary exports of developing countries tend to be highly concentrated in a single or small number of items, it is instructive to begin this investigation by decomposing the variance of the world commodity relative price and quantity indices into the contributions of individual commodities using the same variance decomposition method employed earlier. The variance decomposition of the commodity price index is thus $1 = \Sigma_j \theta_j \gamma_{jc}$, where θ_j is once again the production value weight of commodity j and $\gamma_{jc} = cov(\Delta p_{jt}, \Delta p_{ct})/var(\Delta p_{ct})$ is the contribution of commodity j's relative price to the variance of the world relative price index before production share-weighting. Here we define $\Delta p_{jt} = \Delta \tilde{p}_{jt} - \Delta p_t$ as the change in the logarithm of the U.S. dollar price of commodity j, $\Delta \tilde{p}_{jt}$ relative to U.S. CPI inflation (to be consistent with our definition of Δp_{ct}). The analogous variance decomposition of the quantity index is $1 = \Sigma_j \theta_j \beta_{jc}$ where $\beta_{jc} = cov(\Delta y_{jt},\ \Delta y_{ct})/var(\Delta y_{ct})$.

Table 1 presents the variance decomposition of the commodity relative price index on both an equal and production-value-weighted basis. When commodities are weighted equally in the price index, commodities such as oranges and corn oil contribute far more than the average good and petroleum contributes far less. When world production value weights are used, the picture changes because petroleum has a production value share of 36% compared with 3.3% under equal weighting. On a production value-weighted basis, oil now accounts for about 68% of the variance of the commodity price index changes: twice its production share. Only eight other commodities account for 1% or more of the commodity price variance: corn oil, eggs, iron, milk, rice, soybeans, sugar, and wheat.

Table 2 presents the variance decomposition of the commodity relative quantity index on both an equal and production-value-weighted basis. Some parallels and some differences emerge in a comparison of price and quantity indices. Petroleum stands out much less starkly in the value-weighted commodity quantity index, accounting about one-third of the variation, which happens to match its value share. The other difference between the price and quantity data is that, unlike commodity prices, the production levels tend to move more independently of one another. There are some commodity production changes that have a negative covariance with the aggregate quantity index, such as iron, oranges, petroleum, tallow, and zinc. This means there is more averaging out of quantity changes across commodities than is true of price changes, which cautions against casual interpretations of relative price and quantity variation in terms of structural elasticities of supply and demand. The averaging out of quantity changes, though, is evidence of a significant role for commodity-specific supply changes that are not as evident in the relative price series. We turn, next, to nation-specific patterns of specialization and production changes.

2.2.3. *National and world commodity supplies*

Bidarkota and Crucini (2000) investigated the consumption risks faced by primary commodity-exporting developing countries under the assumption that the quantity of production was constant, since

Table 1. Variance decomposition of commodity price index (levels).

	Equally weighted		Production share weighted	
	Weight	Var share	Weight	Var share
Aluminum	3.3	0.7	1.1	0.2
Apples	3.3	5.2	0.9	0.2
Butter	3.3	1.9	1.7	0.5
Cocoa	3.3	2.7	0.4	0.1
Coffee	3.3	2.1	0.3	0.0
Copper	3.3	1.3	1.4	0.3
Corn	3.3	3.7	2.1	0.8
Corn oil	3.3	6.1	4.3	4.2
Cotton	3.3	2.2	2.1	0.3
Eggs	3.3	3.3	3.0	1.5
Hides	3.3	3.1	0.9	0.1
Iron	3.3	2.8	6.8	5.8
Lead	3.3	2.4	0.4	0.1
Milk	3.3	0.4	10.7	2.6
Nickel	—	—	—	—
Oranges	3.3	12.6	0.1	0.0
Palm oil	—	—	—	—
Peanuts	3.3	0.9	0.6	0.1
Pepper	3.3	3.2	1.2	0.3
Petroleum	3.3	1.1	36.4	68.5
Potatoes	3.3	5.9	—	—
Rice	3.3	1.1	8.5	3.5
Rubber	3.3	3.1	0.5	0.2
Rye	—	—	—	—
Soy Meal	3.3	4.8	0.3	0.1
Soy oil	3.3	6.7	0.8	0.6
Soybeans	3.3	5.1	2.3	1.1
Sugar	3.3	4.1	4.6	4.7
Tallow	3.3	6.3	0.2	0.2
Tin	3.3	1.4	0.2	0.1
Wheat	3.3	3.1	6.3	3.9
Wool	3.3	1.7	1.3	0.2
Zinc	3.3	1.2	0.7	0.2
Totals	100.0	100.0	100.0	100.0

Table 2. Variance decomposition of commodity quantity index.

	Equally weighted		Production share weighted	
Commodity	Weight	Var share	Weight	Var share
Aluminum	3.4	1.8	1.0	0.5
Apples	3.4	4.2	0.9	−0.7
Butter	3.4	3.0	1.8	3.6
Cocoa	3.4	10.7	0.4	0.4
Coffee	3.4	11.3	1.5	−0.3
Copper	3.4	2.8	1.9	1.6
Corn oil	3.4	10.5	4.4	12.3
Cotton	3.4	8.5	2.2	4.5
Eggs	3.4	0.4	3.1	−2.1
Hides	3.4	0.3	1.0	0.1
Iron	3.4	−0.6	7.1	4.4
Lead	3.4	1.2	0.4	−0.1
Milk	3.4	4.5	11.1	19.8
Nickel	3.4	3.5	0.6	0.4
Oranges	3.4	−3.7	0.1	−0.1
Palm oil	3.4	2.7	0.5	−1.0
Peanuts	3.4	9.2	1.3	0.6
Pepper	—	—	—	—
Petroleum	3.4	−1.2	34.2	34.2
Potatoes1	—	—	—	—
Rice	3.4	2.2	8.9	3.8
Rubber	3.4	0.6	0.5	0.1
Rye	3.4	10.8	0.3	0.8
Soy meal	—	—	—	—
Soy oil	3.4	2.8	0.7	−0.7
Soybeans	3.4	5.7	2.3	2.3
Sugar	3.4	2.3	4.8	4.8
Tallow	3.4	−2.0	0.2	−0.1
Tin	3.4	5.1	0.2	0.3
Wheat	3.4	2.8	6.5	9.3
Wool	3.4	1.5	1.4	0.9
Zinc	3.4	−0.7	0.7	0.2
Totals	100.0	100.0	100.0	100.0

they lacked production data by country. This section explores the cross-sectional and time series properties of commodity production by major world producers.

For each of our 33 primary commodities we have annual production data for major producers and total world production. The distinction between world and nation-specific variation is important for our analysis. Changes in the world supply of commodities are arguably related to changes in world demand and the equilibrium supply responses those changes evoke. Changes in commodity supply at the level of a country relative to the world are arguably related to exogenous supply shocks specific to that country.

Figure 6 plots the world market shares of coffee production for 12 major producers. Brazil and Columbia are the two dominant producers, accounting for a fairly stable 50% share of world production. By the end of the sample Vietnam has risen from being a marginal producer to contributing a share comparable to that of Columbia. There is considerable annual variation in Brazil's share of world production.

Figure 7 focuses on petroleum production. In this category the production levels are somewhat more concentrated across the 10 major producers displayed than was true of coffee. The U.S. and Russia exhibit secular declines in their share of world production from 35% to about 20%, most of which is picked up by the 'other' category. The breakup of the Soviet Union is the main reason for the dramatic decline in the share accounted for by Russia, evident in the early 1990s. Also evident are the higher frequency movements in the production shares of Saudi Arabia and Iran. Between 1975 and 1981, the Iranian share of world production falls precipitously. Some of the early decline is taken up by increases in Saudi Arabia; later some new entrants (those at the top of the chart) account for some of the change in composition.

3. The Model

The starting point of discussion is the seminal paper by Cole and Obstfeld (1991), who developed a sharp theoretical benchmark for

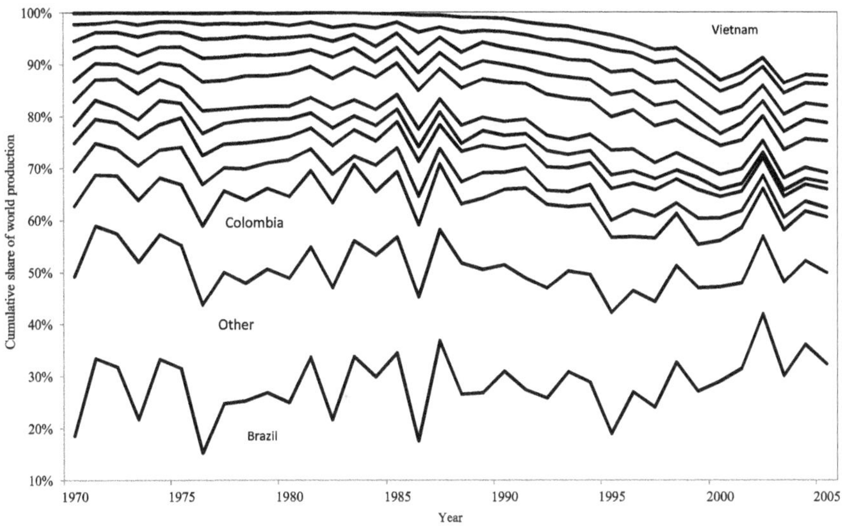

Fig. 6. Coffee world production shares, by country.

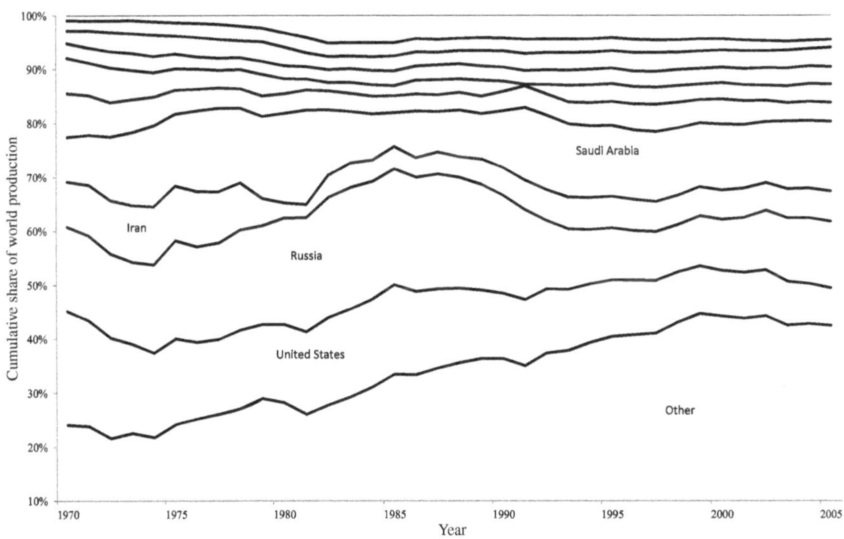

Fig. 7. Petroleum world production shares, by country.

commodity risk sharing. Specifically, in an endowment economy setting with complete specialization and Cobb-Douglas preferences, they demonstrated that in a two-country world, the movement of a nation's terms of trade was sufficient to make financial markets redundant.

The economic mechanism works as follows. The first country specializes in X and the second in Y. In a frictionless world, with Cobb-Douglas preferences, the relative price of the two goods is, $P^* \equiv P_Y/P_X = (1-\theta)X/\theta Y$, where X and Y are the realizations of the endowments of the two goods, and θ is the Cobb-Douglas weight on good X. Thus, any variation in relative supply is offset one-for-one with a relative price change. When countries are in financial autarky and trade only one physical object for another, the allocations in a competitive equilibrium are the same as the allocations when countries pool risks to their individual endowments. Effectively, equilibrium terms of trade adjustments provide insurance against supply shocks.

Consider the more general case: a world populated by a large developed bloc, the OECD, and a smaller bloc of developing countries each of whom is specialized in the production of a single primary commodity. Note that, while each country may be specialized, there may be more than one specialist in each good.

The maximization problem of country i, specializing in production of commodity j is

$$\max U(C_{it}) = \prod_{k}^{N} C_{ikt}^{\theta_k}$$

$$\text{subject to: } \sum_{k} P_{kt}C_{ikt} \leq P_{jt}Y_{jt}. \tag{6}$$

$P_{jt}Y_{jt}$ is the value the single exported commodity fetches on world markets, but it could, in general, be thought of as the market value of the entire export basket of country i with appropriate definitions of the aggregates. The demand for good k, by country i, is

$$C_{ikt} = \theta_k \frac{P_{jt}}{P_{kt}} Y_{jt}. \tag{7}$$

Taking a geometric weighted average across commodities gives

$$\prod_k^N C_{ikt}^{\theta_k} = \prod_k^N \left(\theta_k \frac{P_{jt}}{P_{kt}} Y_{jt}\right)^{\theta_k}$$

$$P_t C_{it} = \Theta P_{jt} Y_{jt}. \tag{8}$$

The last line indicates that an appropriately defined aggregate real consumption index, C_{it}, and consumer price index, P_t, when multiplied, equal nominal income accruing to country i from selling commodity j, up to a scalar normalization. Specifically,

$$P_t = \prod_k^N P_{kt}^{\theta_k} \text{ and } C_{it} = \prod_k^N C_{ikt}^{\theta_k} \text{ and } \Theta \equiv \prod_k^N \theta_k^{\theta_k}.$$

3.1. *Model implications*

Since aggregate consumption, so defined, maps into welfare and wealth, what we would like to know is how consumption changes with relative prices and endowments. Taking the first-difference of the logarithm of the last equation and denoting logarithms of upper case variables as lower case variables, we have

$$\Delta c_{it} = (\Delta \tilde{p}_{jt} - \Delta p_t) + \Delta y_{jt}. \tag{9}$$

In words: changes in aggregate consumption of country i, consist of a terms of trade effect, $\Delta \tilde{p}_{jt} - \Delta p_t$, and an endowment effect. The terms of trade effect is the change in the value of the endowment relative to the change in the value of value of the consumption basket, at the initial endowment level. The endowment effect is the change in physical quantity produced, which at fixed prices leads to a proportional change in aggregation consumption. Thus, the volatility of consumption depends on the variance of the terms of trade and production as well as the covariance between the two. The covariance term is the key element of the Cole and Obtsfeld asset market redundancy result.

To see this, consider a pair of countries each specializing in a particular good and note how relative prices and quantities behave in equilibrium. Note that price level inflation is $\Delta p_t = \theta_1 \Delta \tilde{p}_{1t} + \theta_2 \Delta \tilde{p}_{2t}$;

then the consumption growth rates of country 1 and 2 (from (9)) are given by

$$\Delta c_{1t} = \Delta\tilde{p}_{1t} - [\theta_1\Delta\tilde{p}_{1t} + \theta_2\Delta\tilde{p}_{2t}] + \Delta y_{1t}$$
$$\Delta c_{2t} = \Delta\tilde{p}_{2t} - [\theta_1\Delta\tilde{p}_{1t} + \theta_2\Delta\tilde{p}_{2t}] + \Delta y_{2t}, \tag{10}$$

and the consumption growth differential is

$$\Delta c_{1t} - \Delta c_{2t} = (\Delta\tilde{p}_{1t} - \Delta\tilde{p}_{2t}) + (\Delta y_{1t} - \Delta y_{2t}) = 0. \tag{11}$$

The last equality holds by virtue of the fact that relative prices and relative quantities move in proportion and in opposite directions: the 'market value' changes cancel. Thus, consumption moves one-for-one across countries, as implied by risk sharing despite the fact that no risks are pooled ex ante: the terms of trade does all the work.

The subtlety in applying this result in practice is that it actually is referring to good-specific risk, not country-specific risk. In the model with complete specialization in production the two are the same, but in practice they are not. Recall Figs. 6 and 7 which show the national levels of coffee and petroleum production across producers of the world. To see what happens when countries remain specialized but there are multiple producers of the two goods (less goods than countries),[7] let the output of country i of commodity j, y_{ijt}, consist of both a commodity-specific shock, y_{jt}, and an idiosyncratic shock specific to both the commodity and the country, ϵ_{ijt}:

$$y_{ijt} = y_{jt} + \epsilon_{ijt}, \tag{12}$$

where $E_i(y_{ijt}) = y_{jt}$ is the commodity-specific component, while ϵ_{ijt} captures i.i.d. deviations from this level across countries that produce good j.

[7]It may seem odd to have the number of countries exceed the number of goods rather than the reverse, but this is more a consequence of the arbitrariness of using countries as the unit of account than the thrust of our argument. The important point is that we break the singularity of country and sector shocks.

Aggregate consumption in country i, still has the terms of trade component, but now the quantity must be indexed by the good and country to reflect the nation-specific component of the endowment:

$$c_{it} = \tilde{p}_{jt} - p_t + y_{ijt}. \tag{13}$$

Consider, now, two randomly selected countries, a and b, that produce goods, 1 and 2, respectively, subject to idiosyncratic as well as nation-specific risks; the previous result, (11), becomes (after trivial substitutions)

$$\Delta c_{at} - \Delta c_{bt} = (\Delta\tilde{p}_{1t} - \Delta\tilde{p}_{2t}) + \Delta y_{a1t} - \Delta y_{b2t}. \tag{14}$$

Substituting the country-specific realizations with their assumed stochastic processes gives us

$$\Delta c_{at} - \Delta c_{bt} = (\Delta\tilde{p}_{1t} - \Delta\tilde{p}_{2t}) + (\Delta y_{1t} + \Delta\epsilon_{a1t} - \Delta y_{2t} - \Delta\epsilon_{b2t}), \tag{15}$$

and using the relationship between relative prices and quantities in the Cobb-Douglas formulation, gives

$$\Delta c_{at} - \Delta c_{bt} = \Delta\epsilon_{a1t} - \Delta\epsilon_{b2t}. \tag{16}$$

Remarkably, each country bears all of its idiosyncratic risks!

What has happened to the risk-sharing facet of movements in the terms of trade? Essentially, the relative price movements of one commodity to another still provide insurance, but the group that is insured is the industry that produces that good. This is easily demonstrated by averaging the consumption allocations across individuals in the same country who specialize in different sectors:

$$E_i(\Delta c_{i1t}) - E_i(\Delta c_{i2t}) = E_i(\Delta\epsilon_{i1t} - \Delta\epsilon_{i2t}) = 0. \tag{17}$$

In words: equilibrium terms of trade adjustments insure the producers who happen to have a change in production exactly equal to the world sectoral change. Thus, in the absence of ex ante risk sharing all *idiosyncratic* output deviations are completely borne by the individual countries. Note, also, that if all sector risks are idiosyncratic to the nation, the terms of trade will be constant and all risks will be borne by the individual producers.

The extent to which national production levels move with the world aggregate and in response to the terms of trade is an empirical question, which our data allow us to investigate in detail in the next section.

4. Consumption Risk Sharing and the Terms of Trade

This section applies the logic of the Cole-Obtsfeld model, extended to the case of non-specialization, to conduct a variance decomposition. The variance decomposition is that of national consumption growth relative to world consumption growth with the variance allocated to terms of trade variation, world production variation, and nation-specific production variation.

The starting point is the construction of the commodity terms of trade from world commodity relative prices and the national commodity export data. Toward this end, each country's terms of trade is constructed as an export-share-weighted index of changes in primary commodity relative prices, $\Delta p_{it} = \Delta \tilde{p}_{it} - \Delta p_t$:

$$\Delta p_{it} = \sum_j \omega_{ij} \Delta p_{jt}. \tag{18}$$

Recall that p_{jt} is, as before, the U.S. dollar price of commodity j in world markets relative to the U.S. CPI. Thus, when Δp_{jt} is positive, commodity j's inflation exceeds that of the U.S. consumption basket (which is treated as the import deflator), indicating a relative price increase and a terms of trade improvement for exporters of commodity j. The ω_{ij} are country and commodity-specific export weights computed from our panel:

$$\omega_{ij} \equiv T^{-1} \sum_t \frac{P_{jt} Y_{ijt}}{\sum_j P_{jt} Y_{ijt}}. \tag{19}$$

Note that the use of common, as opposed to country-specific, commodity prices on the right-hand-side of the index construction assumes that the Law-of-One-Price holds internationally for these goods and for the basket of imports.

We return, now, to the logic of the CO model. Recall that the generic equation for consumption growth for country i producing commodity j is $\Delta c_{it} = (\Delta\tilde{p}_{jt} - \Delta p_t) + \Delta y_{jt}$. The case of non-specialization involves replacing the j subscripts with i subscripts indicating the terms of trade and production value of country i, given its pattern of specialization:

$$\Delta c_{it} = (\Delta\tilde{p}_{it} - \Delta p_t) + \Delta y_{it}. \tag{20}$$

Aggregating across all countries gives the deviation of consumption growth of country i relative to world consumption growth, which represents the deviation from complete risk sharing:

$$(\Delta c_{it} - \Delta c_t) = (\Delta\tilde{p}_{it} - \Delta p_t) + (\Delta y_{it} - \Delta y_t). \tag{21}$$

The goal is to decompose these deviations from complete risk sharing, $\Delta c_{it} - \Delta c_t$, into microeconomic sources of risk based on the available data. The variance of the change in consumption of country i relative to the world (the G-7 supplier of manufactured goods) is

$$var(\Delta c_{it} - \Delta c_t) = var[(\Delta\tilde{p}_{it} - \Delta p_t) + (\Delta y_{it} - \Delta y_t)]. \tag{22}$$

This should be viewed as the amount of commodity revenue risk to be shared after taking into account non-diversifiable movements in world consumption or income and allowing for endogenous covariances among variables to offset some of the underlying risks. One such endogenous covariance is the negative covariance of the terms of trade with aggregate world output of a commodity highlighted in the CO model.

To ensure a full variance decomposition, other sources of consumption variation are ignored and the focus is on decomposing the right-hand side, which is, given our data, nominal commodity export earnings relative to nominal world GDP. Drilling down to the commodity level on the right-hand side, we have

$$\Delta x_{it} = \Delta c_{it} - \Delta c_t = (\Delta\tilde{p}_{it} - \Delta p_t) + (\Delta y_{it} - \Delta y_t)$$
$$= \underbrace{\sum_j \omega_{ij}(\Delta\tilde{p}_{jt} - \Delta p_t)}_{=\text{terms of trade}} + \underbrace{\sum_j \omega_{ij}(\Delta y_{jt} - \Delta y_t)}_{+\text{world production}}$$
$$+ \underbrace{\sum_j \omega_{ij}(\Delta y_{ijt} - \Delta y_{jt})}_{+\text{nation-specific production}} \tag{23}$$

and the resulting variance decomposition, in terms of the β-method is

$$1 = \sum \omega_{ij}(\beta_{pj} + \beta_{yj} + \beta_{yij}).$$

- $\beta_{pj} = cov(\Delta\tilde{p}_{jt} - \Delta p_t, \Delta x_{it})/var(\Delta x_{it})$ captures the pure terms of trade effect, the change in value of the exported commodity holding physical production fixed at steady-state shares (ω_{ij}).
- $\beta_{yj} = cov(\Delta y_{jt} - \Delta y_t, \Delta x_{it})/var(\Delta x_{it})$ captures the common world changes in the production of commodity j, relative to world GDP.
- $\beta_{yij} = cov(\Delta y_{ijt} - \Delta y_{jt}, \Delta x_{it})/var(\Delta x_{it})$ captures the contribution of nation-specific changes in the production of commodity j, that is, relative to world commodity production of that commodity.

Table 3 reports the results of this variance decomposition, focusing on the top exported commodity of each country in our panel. We focus on the top commodity since this commodity accounts for three-fourths of the variation, in our primary export variable for the median country and virtually all of the variation for half of the countries.

Variation in the terms of trade is by far the dominant contributor to export earnings, accounting for about 82% of the variance for the median country. The terms of trade of the top exported commodity alone accounts for about two-thirds of this variation. The next most important contributor to export earnings variability is the nation-specific component of the quantity of primary commodities produced, at 15% for the median country. Again, the top export accounts for

Table 3. Variance decomposition of export earnings.

Country	Std. Dev. of primary exports	First-ranked commodity	Terms of trade	Nation-specific production	World production	Total contribution to variance	Other commodities
Argentina	19.9	corn	12.8	30.7	−2.4	41.1	58.9
Australia	18.6	wheat	16.8	31.7	0.3	48.8	51.2
Bangladesh	34.8	rice	95.4	5.9	−1.3	100.0	—
Belgium-Luxembourg	21.3	zinc	51.5	17.2	4.8	73.5	26.5
Bolivia	29.8	tin	58.9	26.7	11.0	96.7	3.3
Brazil	24.5	coffee	37.8	16.1	5.4	59.3	40.7
Burkina Faso	23.7	cotton	42.1	61.0	−3.1	100.0	—
Cameroon	35.0	cocoa	85.4	12.7	1.9	100.0	—
Canada	13.6	petroleum	22.4	1.3	2.3	26.0	74.0
Chile	36.2	copper	95.9	3.2	0.9	100.0	—
China	17.2	iron	49.6	3.1	5.2	58.0	42.0
Colombia	49.4	coffee	94.3	−2.6	8.0	99.7	0.3
Costa Rica	52.1	coffee	88.9	7.9	3.2	100.0	—
Cote d'Ivoire	36.0	cocoa	42.8	8.0	5.5	56.3	43.7
Cuba	33.4	sugar	56.6	42.3	1.2	100.0	—
Dominican Republic	34.5	cocoa	62.7	38.9	−1.6	100.0	—
Ecuador	50.9	cocoa	42.7	51.8	5.5	100.0	—
Egypt	25.4	cotton	51.7	42.9	5.2	99.9	0.1
El Salvador	65.1	coffee	71.3	23.4	5.3	100.0	—
Ethiopia	51.5	coffee	93.2	0.4	6.4	100.0	—

(Continued)

Table 3. (*Continued*)

Country	Std. Dev. of primary exports	First-ranked commodity	Terms of trade	Nation-specific production	World production	Total contribution to variance	Other commodities
EU-27	18.6	sugar	50.3	5.0	−0.4	54.9	45.1
France, Monaco	24.3	iron	81.9	1.4	5.9	89.2	10.8
Germany	24.4	iron	76.0	2.1	5.6	83.8	16.2
Ghana	32.3	cocoa	79.1	15.9	5.0	100.0	—
Greece	23.8	cotton	39.7	24.0	7.4	71.1	28.9
Guatemala	52.5	coffee	92.9	0.7	6.4	100.0	—
India	20.8	cotton	28.7	−0.7	7.7	35.7	64.3
Indonesia	21.9	petroleum	56.8	2.3	1.2	60.3	39.7
Iran	30.4	petroleum	73.5	26.9	−0.4	100.0	—
Italy	24.5	iron	96.2	−3.5	5.0	97.7	2.3
Japan	28.2	iron	91.1	3.1	5.3	99.5	0.5
Kazakhstan	27.3	zinc	36.9	60.6	2.5	100.0	—
Korea, Republic	32.0	iron	64.7	32.7	2.5	99.9	0.1
Kuwait	51.7	petroleum	23.2	76.8	0.1	100.0	—
Malaysia	24.5	rubber	67.6	13.6	4.0	85.2	14.8
Mexico	22.9	petroleum	55.2	12.2	−0.2	67.2	32.8
Morocco	47.9	oranges	90.1	6.4	3.5	100.0	—
Myanmar (Burma)	34.3	rice	96.9	4.7	−1.6	100.0	—

Table 3. (*Continued*)

Country	Std. Dev. of primary exports	First-ranked commodity	Terms of trade	Nation-specific production	World production	Total contribution to variance	Other commodities
Netherlands	23.6	tallow	89.6	11.4	−1.0	100.0	—
New Caledonia	25.6	iron	99.7	0.0	0.0	99.7	0.3
New Zealand	18.6	milk	51.9	7.2	−3.8	55.3	44.7
Nigeria	25.5	cocoa	35.6	19.0	4.4	58.9	41.1
Norway	35.5	aluminum	92.7	2.6	4.7	100.0	—
Pakistan	27.0	rice	59.6	7.2	−1.5	65.2	34.8
Paraguay	31.7	soybeans	46.0	66.1	−12.1	100.0	—
Peru	37.1	copper	85.7	13.2	0.3	99.2	0.8
Philippines	33.4	rice	99.3	2.4	−1.8	100.0	—
Poland	36.7	copper	92.3	7.9	−0.1	100.0	—
Portugal	79.7	tin	−0.8	101.2	−0.3	100.0	—
Romania	31.4	wool	92.5	7.6	−0.1	100.0	—
Russian Federation	19.9	petroleum	75.5	10.5	0.7	86.7	13.3
Saudi Arabia	30.9	petroleum	76.8	22.1	1.0	100.0	—
Senegal	44.6	peanuts	10.0	82.7	7.4	100.0	—
South Africa	28.0	oranges	83.2	1.9	2.3	87.4	12.6
Spain	27.8	oranges	91.4	−10.5	4.8	85.7	14.3

(*Continued*)

Table 3. (*Continued*)

Country	Std. Dev. of primary exports	First-ranked commodity	Terms of trade	Nation-specific production	World production	Total contribution to variance	Other commodities
Sri Lanka	27.5	rubber	85.5	8.8	5.7	100.0	—
Switzerland	19.0	iron	41.7	0.0	0.0	41.7	58.3
Thailand	20.7	rice	45.9	4.4	−1.0	49.3	50.7
Turkey	22.7	cotton	65.9	15.6	9.4	90.9	9.1
Uganda	53.3	coffee	86.8	6.8	6.4	100.0	—
Ukraine	23.8	sugar	75.1	23.2	−2.3	96.0	4.0
United Kingdom	30.3	iron	60.2	24.7	3.7	88.7	11.3
Uruguay	28.9	wool	92.9	6.1	1.0	100.0	—
USA and Puerto Rico	16.0	iron	18.3	5.4	2.8	26.5	73.5
Venezuela	26.5	petroleum	86.3	5.6	−0.1	91.8	8.2
Vietnam	30.2	coffee	39.5	12.3	0.4	52.1	47.9

the bulk of this variation. World supply variation is trivial, having a median absolute value contribution of about 3.5%.

Approximately one in three countries have a negative contribution to world production, which is consistent with the terms of trade channel of Cole and Obstfeld, but the magnitude of this variation is so modest that it contributes very little to the overall variance. Nation-specific production changes are overwhelmingly positive contributors to variability. This means countries tend to increase their production when their terms of trade improves, suggestive of an endogenous supply response and thus reinforcing the effect of terms of trade variation.

Figure 8 plots the decomposition of the predicted variance of $\Delta c_{it} - \Delta c_t$ into the contribution of the terms of trade, national production, and world production for each country in the cross-section. While it is obvious that the terms of trade dominates the variance decomposition in most countries, there is a substantial minority of cases in which changes in domestic production relative to world production is the dominant factor. For twenty nations, variation in the physical production of the top export commodity, accounts for more than 20% of the total predicted variation.

Figure 9 plots the actual standard deviation of consumption growth against the predicted variance of consumption growth, excluding outliers.[8] A linear regression produces a slope coefficient of 0.14 and an R^2 of 16%. That the two are strongly positively correlated despite the fact that many sources of consumption variation are ignored is evidence of the importance of these commodity terms of trade changes and supply responses. There are many reasons that the coefficient is less than unity: most countries in the sample produce some manufactured goods as well as non-traded goods, for example.

[8]The figure and regression lines do not include extreme outliers of the distribution, countries with terms of trade standard deviations in excess of 40% (Portugal, El Salvador, Uganda, Guatemala, Costa Rica, Kuwait, Ethiopia, Ecuador, Colombia, Morocco, Senegal), and countries with consumption growth standard deviations exceeding 10% (Saudi Arabia, Nigeria).

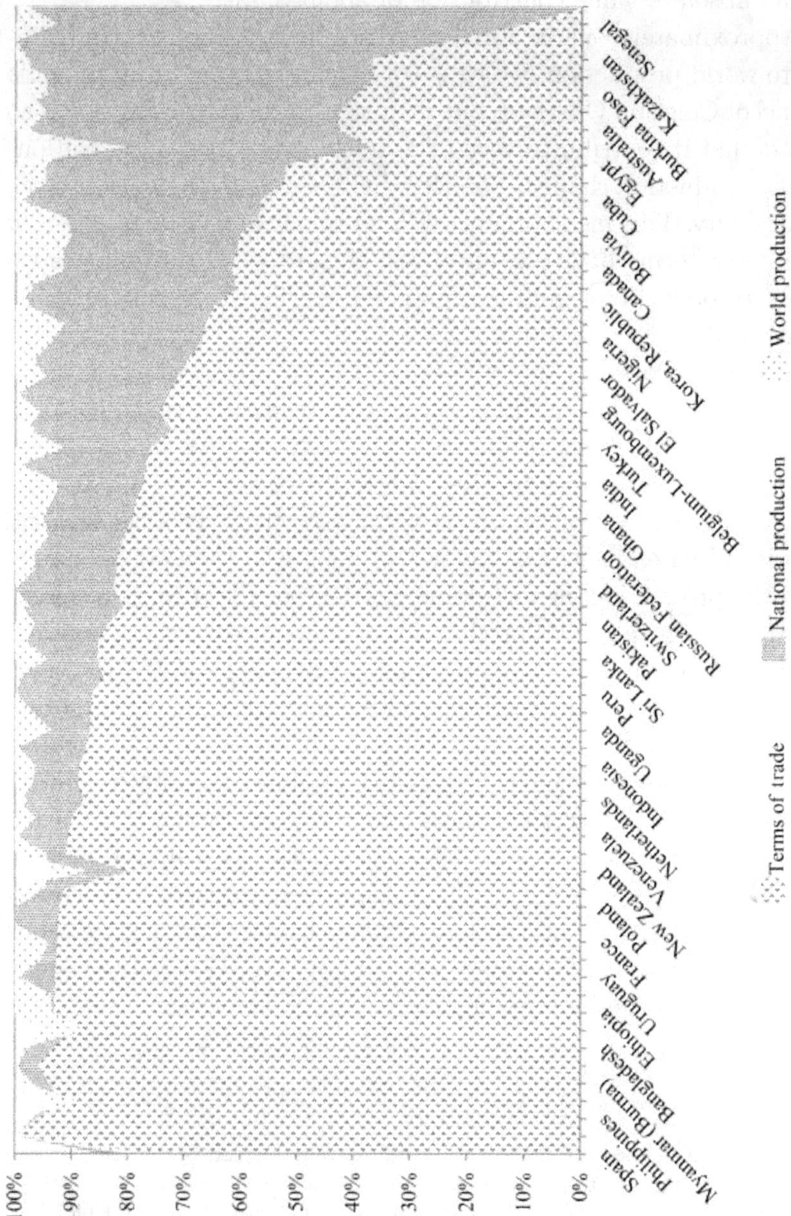

Fig. 8. Sources of deviations from risk sharing.

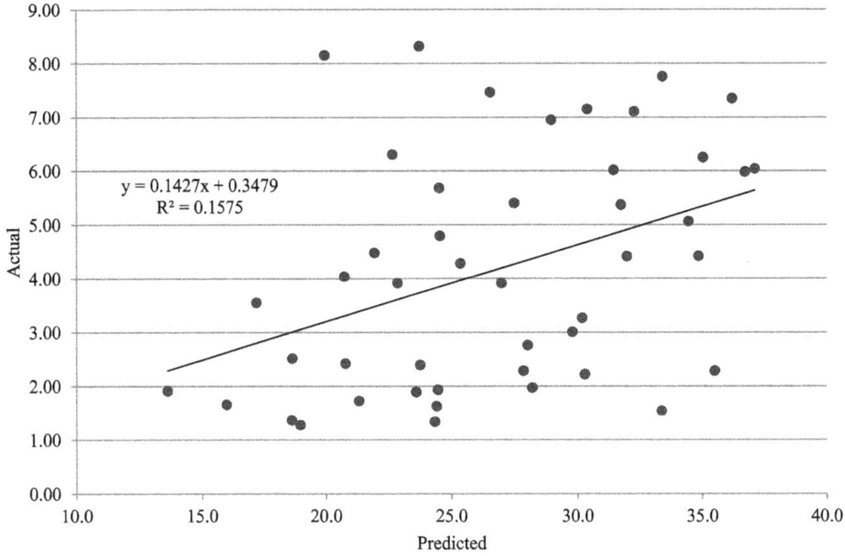

Fig. 9. Actual and predicted consumption growth.

5. Conclusion

The heterogeneity of business cycles across countries outside the large industrialized ones is vast. The hypothesis put forward here is that a substantial fraction of this heterogeneity reflects a concentration of exports in a single or small number of primary commodities. We estimate this fraction to be about 16%.

Specialization in primary commodities poses risks that are significant because of the highly volatile and unpredictable nature of world commodity prices. These risks may be further amplified when production is also somewhat beyond the control of individuals and firms, owing to weather and national policy instability or when the short-term elasticity of supply is very low.

The implications of these trade patterns for the long run was emphasized by Prebisch (1950) and Singer (1950), who documented a secular decline in relative commodity prices and later in the immiserizing growth theory of Bhagwati (1958). Business cycle implications of the terms of trade have been studied by Kose (2002), Kouparitsas (1997a), and Mendoza (1995). These studies have focused on the aggregate terms of trade and also abstracted from idiosyncratic movements in production in the cross-section of countries specializing in the same commodity.

The focus here has been to emphasize the heterogeneity across countries and the role of individual primary commodities in shaping the heterogeneity through idiosyncratic production shifts across countries by commodity. We find evidence that national production responses almost always magnify, rather than dampen, the impact of commodity price movements on a nation's export earnings. In other words, while there may be a risk-sharing effect in terms of negative comovements of commodity relative supplies and commodity relative prices at the world level, this effect is swamped by a positive covariance of national production and the relative price of the export commodity, which amplifies export earnings variation. It could be that the elastic supply responses of developing countries are themselves enhanced by underlying risk-sharing arrangements in accord with the theoretical work of Baxter and Crucini (1995). Further study is needed to investigate this possibility.

Our analysis is subject to a number of important caveats. In particular, the import side of the trade balance has been broad-brushed. We assumed all countries import a common consumption basket in exchange for a small number of exported primary commodities. It will be interesting to measure the import side of the trade balance more carefully and incorporate imports of primary commodities as inputs into domestic production. The analysis above has also abstracted from dynamic considerations, including permanent income theory, capital accumulation, credit market frictions, and interest rate movements. Each of these facets are extensions in progress. Much remains to be done.

Acknowledgments

Crucini gratefully acknowledges the financial support of National Science Foundation (SES-1030164). Crucini is also affiliated with the NBER. We thank Nicolas Coeurdacier for very helpful comments.

Data Appendix

"INTERNATIONAL RISK-SHARING AND COMMODITY PRICES"

Martin Berka, Mario J. Crucini and Chih-Wei Wang

Country Code: Three-letter Codes and Country Names

AFG Afghanistan
AGO Angola
ALB Albania
ARE United Arab Emirates
ARG Argentina
ATG Antigua and Barbuda
AUS Australia
AUT Austria
BDI Burundi
BEL Belgium
BEN Benin
BFA Burkina Faso
BGD Bangladesh
BGR Bulgaria
BHR Bahrain
BHS Bahamas
BLZ Belize
BMU Bermuda
BOL Bolivia
BRA Brazil
BRB Barbados
BRN Brunei
BTN Bhutan
BWA Botswana
CAF Central African Republic
CAN Canada
CHE Switzerland
CHL Chile
CHN China
CIV Côte d'Ivoire
GIN Guinea
GMB Gambia
GNB Guinea-Bissau
GNQ Equatorial Guinea
GRC Greece
GRD Grenada
GTM Guatemala
GUY Guyana
HKG Hong Kong
HND Honduras
HTI Haiti
HUN Hungary
IDN Indonesia
IND India
IRL Ireland
IRN Iran
IRQ Iraq
ISL Iceland
ISR Israel
ITA Italy
JAM Jamaica
JOR Jordan
JPN Japan
KEN Kenya
KHM Cambodia
KIR Kiribati
KNA St. Kitts & Nevis
KOR Korea, Republic of
KWT Kuwait
LAO Laos
NIC Nicaragua
NLD Netherlands
NOR Norway
NPL Nepal
NZL New Zealand
OMN Oman
PAK Pakistan
PAN Panama
PER Peru
PHL Philippines
PLW Palau
PNG Papua New Guinea
POL Poland
PRI Puerto Rico
PRT Portugal
PRY Paraguay
ROM Romania
RWA Rwanda
SAU Saudi Arabia
SDN Sudan
SEN Senegal
SGP Singapore
SLB Solomon Islands
SLE Sierra Leone
SLV El Salvador
SOM Somalia
STP Sao Tome and Principe
SUR Suriname
SWE Sweden
SWZ Swaziland

CMR Cameroon
COG Congo, Republic of
COL Colombia
COM Comoros
CPV Cape Verde
CRI Costa Rica
CUB Cuba

CYP Cyprus
DJI Djibouti
DMA Dominica
DNK Denmark
DOM Dominican Republic
DZA Algeria
ECU Ecuador
EGY Egypt

ESP Spain
ETH Ethiopia
FIN Finland
FJI Fiji
FRA France
GAB Gabon

GBR United Kingdom
GER Germany
GHA Ghana

LBN Lebanon
LBR Liberia
LBY Libya
LCA St. Lucia
LKA Sri Lanka
LSO Lesotho
LUX Luxembourg

MAC Macao
MAR Morocco
MDG Madagascar
MDV Maldives
MEX Mexico
MHL Marshall Islands
MLI Mali
MLT Malta

MNG Mongolia
MOZ Mozambique
MRT Mauritania
MUS Mauritius
MWI Malawi
MYS Malaysia

NAM Namibia
NER Niger
NGA Nigeria

SYC Seychelles
SYR Syria
TCD Chad
TGO Togo
THA Thailand
TON Tonga
TTO Trinidad & Tobago
TUN Tunisia
TUR Turkey
TWN Taiwan
TZA Tanzania
UGA Uganda

URY Uruguay
USA United States
VCT St. Vincent & Grenadines
VEN Venezuela
VNM Vietnam
VUT Vanuatu
WSM Samoa
ZAF South Africa
ZAR Congo, Dem. Rep.
ZMB Zambia
ZWE Zimbabwe

Original Data: Description

1. Macroeconomic Data

Code	Description.
O.RYccc	Real GDP for country ccc (country code).
O.RCccc	Real private consumption for country ccc (country code).
O.USCPI	U.S. Consumer Price Index, all urban consumers (CPI-U), 1982 – 84 = 100.

2. Commodity Price and Production Data

Code	Description, Units.
O.pcom1	Aluminum price, United States, in cents per pound.
O.pcom2	Apples price, United States, in cents per pound.
O.pcom3	Butter price, United States, in cents per pound.

O.pcom4	Cocoa price, United States, in dollars per metric ton.
O.pcom5	Coconut oil price, United States, in cents per pound.
O.pcom6	Coffee price, United States, in cents per pound.
O.pcom7	Copper price, United States, in cents per pound.
O.pcom8	Corn price, United States, in cents per bushel.
O.pcom9	Cotton price, United States, in cents per pound.
O.pcom10	Eggs price, United States, in cents per dozen.
O.pcom11	Hides price, United States, in cents per pound.
O.pcom12	Iron price, United States, in dollars per metric ton.
O.pcom13	lead price, United States, in cents per pound.
O.pcom14	Milk price, United States, in cents per pound.
O.pcom15	Nickel price, United States, in cents per pound.
O.pcom16	Oranges price, United States, in dollars per box.
O.pcom17	Palm oil price, United States, in cents per pound.
O.pcom18	Peanuts price, United States, in cents per pound.
O.pcom19	Petroleum price, United States, in dollars per barrel.
O.pcom20	Rice price, United States, in dollars per 100 pounds.
O.pcom21	Rubber price, United States, in cents per pound.
O.pcom22	Rye price, United States, in cents per bushel.
O.pcom23	Soybean meal price, United States, in dollars per short ton.
O.pcom24	Soybean oil price, United States, in cents per pound.
O.pcom25	Soybeans price, United States, in cents per bushel.
O.pcom26	Sugar price, United States, in cents per pound.
O.pcom27	Tallow price, United States, in cents per pound.
O.pcom28	Tin price, United States, in cents per pound.
O.pcom29	Wheat price, United States, in cents per bushel.
O.pcom30	Wool price, United States, in cents per pound.
O.pcom31	Zinc price, United States, in cents per pound.
O.qcom1	Aluminum world production, 1000 metric tons.
O.qcom2	Apples world production, 1000 metric tons.
O.qcom3	Butter world production, 1000 metric tons.
O.qcom4	Cocoa world production, 1000 metric tons.
O.qcom5	Coconut oil world production, 1000 metric tons.
O.qcom6	Coffee world production, Thousands of 60 Kilogram Bags.
O.qcom7	Copper world production, 1000 metric tons.
O.qcom8	Corn world production, 1000 metric tons.
O.qcom9	Cotton world production, Thousands of 480-Pound Bales.
O.qcom10	Eggs world production, Millions of Eggs.
O.qcom11	Hides world production, 1000 metric tons.
O.qcom12	Iron world production, 1000 metric tons.
O.qcom13	lead world production, 1000 metric tons.
O.qcom14	Milk world production, 1000 metric tons.
O.qcom15	Nickel world production, metric tons.
O.qcom16	Oranges world production, 1000 metric tons.

O.qcom17	Palm oil world production, 1000 metric tons.
O.qcom18	Peanuts world production, 1000 metric tons.
O.qcom19	Petroleum world production, 1000 Barrels Per Day.
O.qcom20	Rice world production, 1000 metric tons.
O.qcom21	Rubber world production, 1000 metric tons.
O.qcom22	Rye world production, 1000 metric tons.
O.qcom23	Soybean meal world production, 1000 metric tons.
O.qcom24	Soybean oil world production, 1000 metric tons.
O.qcom25	Soybeans world production, 1000 metric tons.
O.qcom26	Sugar world production, 1000 metric tons.
O.qcom27	Tallow world production, 1000 metric tons.
O.qcom28	Tin world production, metric tons.
O.qcom29	Wheat world production, 1000 metric tons.
O.qcom30	Wool world production, metric tons.
O.qcom31	Zinc world production, metric tons.

3. Commodity Export Data

Code	Description, Classification.
O.extotSITC	Total exports by country, SITC classification.
O.exSITCcom1	Aluminum exports by country, SITC classification.
O.exSITCcom2	Apples exports by country, SITC classification.
O.exSITCcom3	Butter exports by country, SITC classification.
O.exSITCcom4	Cocoa exports by country, SITC classification.
O.exSITCcom5	Coffee exports by country, SITC classification.
O.exSITCcom6	Copper exports by country, SITC classification.
O.exSITCcom7	Corn exports by country, SITC classification.
O.exSITCcom8	Corn oil exports by country, SITC classification.
O.exSITCcom9	Cotton exports by country, SITC classification.
O.exSITCcom10	Eggs exports by country, SITC classification.
O.exSITCcom11	Hides exports by country, SITC classification.
O.exSITCcom12	Iron exports by country, SITC classification.
O.exSITCcom13	Lead exports by country, SITC classification.
O.exSITCcom14	Milk exports by country, SITC classification.
O.exSITCcom15	Oranges exports by country, SITC classification.
O.exSITCcom16	Peanuts exports by country, SITC classification.
O.exSITCcom17	Pepper exports by country, SITC classification.
O.exSITCcom18	Petroleum exports by country, SITC classification.
O.exSITCcom19	Potatoes exports by country, SITC classification.
O.exSITCcom20	Rice exports by country, SITC classification.
O.exSITCcom21	Rubber exports by country, SITC classification.
O.exSITCcom22	Soybean Meal exports by country, SITC classification.
O.exSITCcom23	Soybean oil exports by country, SITC classification.
O.exSITCcom24	Soybeans exports by country, SITC classification.
O.exSITCcom25	Sugar exports by country, SITC classification.
O.exSITCcom26	Tallow exports by country, SITC classification.

O.exSITCcom27	Tin exports by country, SITC classification.
O.exSITCcom28	Wheat exports by country, SITC classification.
O.exSITCcom29	Wool exports by country, SITC classification.
O.exSITCcom30	Zinc exports by country, SITC classification.
O.extotHS	Total exports by country, HS classification.
O.exHScom1	Aluminum exports by country, HS classification.
O.exHScom2	Apples exports by country, HS classification.
O.exHScom3	Butter exports by country, HS classification.
O.exHScom4	Cocoa exports by country, HS classification.
O.exHScom5	Coffee exports by country, HS classification.
O.exHScom6	Copper exports by country, HS classification.
O.exHScom7	Corn exports by country, HS classification.
O.exHScom8	Corn oil exports by country, HS classification.
O.exHScom9	Cotton exports by country, HS classification.
O.exHScom10	Eggs exports by country, HS classification.
O.exHScom11	Hides exports by country, HS classification.
O.exHScom12	Iron exports by country, HS classification.
O.exHScom13	Lead exports by country, HS classification.
O.exHScom14	Milk exports by country, HS classification.
O.exHScom15	Oranges exports by country, HS classification.
O.exHScom16	Peanuts exports by country, HS classification.
O.exHScom17	Pepper exports by country, HS classification.
O.exHScom18	Petroleum exports by country, HS classification.
O.exHScom19	Potatoes exports by country, HS classification.
O.exHScom20	Rice exports by country, HS classification.
O.exHScom21	Rubber exports by country, HS classification.
O.exHScom22	Soybean Meal exports by country, HS classification.
O.exHScom23	Soybean oil exports by country, HS classification.
O.exHScom24	Soybeans exports by country, HS classification.
O.exHScom25	Sugar exports by country, HS classification.
O.exHScom26	Tallow exports by country, HS classification.
O.exHScom27	Tin exports by country, HS classification.
O.exHScom28	Wheat exports by country, HS classification.
O.exHScom29	Wool exports by country, HS classification.
O.exHScom30	Zinc exports by country, HS classification.

Original Data: Source

Macroeconomic data

O.RYccc	Penn World Table Version 6.3.
O.RCccc	Penn World Table Version 6.3.
O.USCPI	The Bureau of Labor Statistics.

Commodity price and production data (O.pcom1 – O.pcom31, O.qcom1 – O.qcom31) are collected from the CRB Commodity

Yearbook 2009. Mass Conversion Factors: 1 metric ton = 2204.62262 pounds, 1 kilogram = 2.20462262 pounds, 1 metric ton = 39.368 bushels (56 pound bushel).

Commodity export data (O.extotSITC, O.exSITCcom1 – O.exSITCcom30, O.extotHS, O.exHScom1 – O.exHScom30) are collected from United Nations Commodity Trade Statistics (UN Comtrade) Database, for selected countries. Sample period: 1962-2002 (SITC classification), 1988–2009 (HS classification). Selected countries: Argentina, Australia, Bangladesh, Belgium-Luxembourg, Bolivia, Brazil, Burkina Faso, Cameroon, Canada, Chile, China, Colombia, Congo, Costa Rica, Côte d'Ivoire (Ivory Coast), Cuba, Ecuador, Egypt, El Salvador, Ethiopia, EU-27, France, Germany, Ghana, Greece, Guatemala, India, Indonesia, Iran, Italy, Japan, Kazakhstan, Korea, Republic, Kuwait, Malaysia, Mexico, Morocco, Myanmar (Burma), Netherlands, New Caledonia, New Zealand, Nigeria, Norway, Pakistan, Paraguay, Peru, Philippines, Poland, Portugal, Romania, Russian Federation, Saudi Arabia, Senegal, South Africa, Spain, Sri Lanka, Switzerland, Liechtenstein, Thailand, Turkey, Uganda, Ukraine, United Kingdom, United States, Uruguay, Uzbekistan, Venezuela, Vietnam, Zimbabwe.

Constructed series: Description

C.DYccc	Real GDP growth rate for country ccc (country code).
C.DCccc	Real private consumption growth rate for country ccc (country code).
C.1	Commodity price index
C.2	Commodity quantity index
C.3	Commodity export shares, by country

Construction of Series

C.DYccc The first difference of the logarithm of the real GDP for country ccc (O.RYccc).

C.DCccc The first difference of the logarithm of the real private consumption for country ccc (O.RCccc).

C.1 A production-value-weighted average of commodity prices (O.pcom1 – O.pcom31). Weights are the sample average production value shares, computed as individual commodity production values divided by the total world commodity production values.

C.2 A production-value-weighted average of commodity quantities (O.qcom1 – O.qcom31). Constructed in the analogous fashion to C.1, using sample average production value weights.

C.3 Commodity export shares are computed as the value of individual commodity exports (O.exSITCcom1 – O.exSITCcom30, O.exHScom1 – O.exHScom30) divided by the value of total exports (O.extotSITC, O.extotHS) for each country.

References

Baxter, Marianne, and Mario J. Crucini (1995) 'Business cycles and the asset structure of foreign trade,' *International Economic Review* 36, 821–54.

Bhagwati, Jagedish (1958) 'Immiserizing growth: a geometrical note,' *Review of Economic Studies* 25, 201–5.

Bidarkota, Prasad, and Mario J. Crucini (2000) 'Commodity prices and the terms of trade,' *Review of International Economics* 8, 647–66.

Canova, Fabio, and Morten Ravn (1996) 'International consumption risk sharing,' *International Economic Review* 37, 573–601.

Cochrane, John (1991) 'A simple test of full consumption insurance,' *Journal of Political Economy* 99, 957–76.

Cole, Harold, and Maurice Obtsfeld (1991) 'Commodity trade and international risk sharing: how much do financial markets matter?' *Journal of Monetary Economics* 28, 3–24.

Hess, Gregory, and Eric van Wincoop, eds (2000) *Intranational Economics* (Cambridge: Cambridge University Press).

Kose, Ayhan M. (2002) 'Explaining business cycles in small open economies: "How much do world prices matter?"' *Journal of International Economics* 56, 299–327.

Kouparitsas, Michael A. (1997a) 'A dynamic macroeconomic analysis of NAFTA,' *Economic Perspectives,* Federal Reserve Bank of Chicago, January, 14–35.

Lewis, Karen K. (1996) 'What can explain the apparent lack of international consumption risk sharing?' *Journal of Political Economy* 104, 267–97.

Mace, Barbara (1991) 'Full insurance in the presence of aggregate uncertainty,' *Journal of Political Economy* 99, 928–56.

Mendoza, Enrique (1995) 'The terms of trade, the real exchange rate, and economic fluctuations,' *International Economic Review* 36, 101–37.

Prebisch, Raoul (1950) *The Economic Development of Latin America and Its Principal Problems* (New York: United Nations).

Singer, Hans W. (1950) 'The distribution of gains between investing and borrowing countries,' *American Economic Review* 40, 473–85.

Wang, Chih-Wei (2010) 'Trend-cycle decompositions of commodity prices,' Mimeo, Pacific Lutheran University.

Part III

Models of International Prices

Chapter 9

Oil Prices and the Terms of Trade*

David K. Backus

Stern School of Business, New York University,
New York, NY 10012, USA
and National Bureau of Economic Research,
Cambridge, MA 02138, USA

and

Mario J. Crucini

Department of Economics, Ohio State University,
Columbus, OH 43210, USA

Abstract. The combination of substantial terms of trade variability and unstable correlation patterns of trade prices with output and trade volumes has led some to suggest a break in the link between trade volumes and prices. We find that oil accounts for much of the variation in the terms of trade over the last twenty five years and its quantitative role varies significantly over time. And since our dynamic general equilibrium model predicts that the economy responds differently to oil supply shocks than to other shocks, changes in their relative importance helps to account for the unstable correlations in the data.

Keywords: Oil; Productivity; Terms of trade; Real exchange rates; International transmission of business cycles

*This chapter originally appeared in *Journal of International Economics*, 2000, **50**(1), 185–213.

1. Introduction

Relative price movements remain the central issue in international macroeconomics, with their source a continuing object of speculation and debate. We study one such price, the terms of trade, which we define as the ratio of the import deflator to the export deflator in national income and product accounts. In four countries for which quarterly data are available for four decades, we find that the terms of trade has been highly variable relative both to real output and to the predictions of existing dynamic general equilibrium models of trade (Backus *et al.*, 1994, for example, or Stockman and Tesar, 1995). This variability, moreover, has been substantially greater over the last twenty years than the first twenty. We also find that the correlation of terms of trade movements with real output and trade volumes varies widely over time and across countries.

We show that a large part of the variability of the terms of trade is associated with extreme movements in oil prices. Accordingly, we study the terms of trade and its correlation with other variables in a setting in which events affecting the production of oil interact with the production and sale of other goods. The structure blends the Backus *et al.* (1994) model of two large industrial countries with the Crucini and Kahn (1996) treatment of international trade in intermediate inputs into production. In our theoretical economy, two industrialized countries produce imperfectly substitutable goods using capital, labor, and oil. These two goods are then aggregated into final consumption and investment goods. A third country produces oil but consumes final goods.

This structure mimics in a simple way the interaction between large industrialized countries and largely non-industrial oil producers. The result allows us to study the responses of trade flows and real output to changes in oil production and industrial productivity. As one might expect, the volatility and comovements of the terms of trade depend on the nature and source of disturbances. We consider three different disturbances: a domestic productivity shock, a foreign productivity shock, and an oil supply shock. As in earlier work, productivity shocks alone produce little in the way of terms of trade volatility. The reason, ironically, is that the model generates insufficient variability in export and import quantities. Since quantities and prices are linked (the relative price equals the marginal rate of substitution), lack of variability in the quantities is inherited by the prices unless we adopt unrealistically low substitution elasticities.

Two features of the model help us to account for terms of trade variability. First, the supply of oil becomes partly exogenous, leading to dramatic price changes. We think this fits our experience in the 1970s quite well. Second, the technology exhibits little opportunity to substitute oil for capital and/or labor. As a result, relatively small variations in the quantity of oil are associated with substantial variation in its relative price.

The same mechanism helps to account for the unstable correlation between the terms of trade and output. In the model, fluctuations in the terms of trade and output generated by productivity shocks are positively correlated, while those generated by oil shocks are negatively correlated. A domestic productivity disturbance leads to an increase in domestic output and a fall in the relative price of the domestic good — an increase in the terms of trade. Oil supply disruptions, on the other hand, lead to output reductions in countries that use imported oil as an input into production and therefore an inverse relation between the terms of trade and output. Unstable correlations are the result, in this setting, of changes over time in the composition of shocks hitting the economy. We elaborate on these and other features of the model in the remainder of the paper.

2. International Business Cycles

We start by reviewing properties of business cycles in eight developed countries between 1955 and 1990, with an emphasis on prices and quantities of traded goods. We then turn to the price of oil. Quarterly national income and product account data are from the Organisation for Economic Cooperation and Development's (OECD's) Quarterly National Accounts. Other sources are described in Appendix A. Unless otherwise noted, statistics are computed after application of the Hodrick and Prescott (1997) filter. Three variables are transformed in a way that merit special mention. We measure net exports as the ratio of net exports to output, both measured in nominal terms. We measure the terms of trade as the ratio of implicit deflators for imports and exports. Finally, we compute a trade ratio of export to import quantities.

2.1. *Business cycles across countries*

We begin with a review of some of the features of international business cycles that have been highlighted in the existing literature. Table 1 reports standard deviations, correlations with output, and international correlations of various macroeconomic aggregates.

We see that trade variables are uniformly more volatile than aggregate output and are often more volatile than investment. The standard deviation of output ranges from 0.89 in France to 2.17 in Germany while the standard deviation of investment ranges from 2.64 to 5.63 in the same two countries. Trade variables are substantially more volatile than output, with the standard deviation of the trade ratio ranging from a low of 3.66 in France to a high of 9.94 in Australia. The terms of trade is also quite volatile, with the standard

Table 1. Business cycle statistics for eight OECD countries.

	Standard deviation					Cross–correlation of					
Country	y	c	i	x/m	p	(y,nx)	(y,p)	(p,nx)	(y,y^{us})	(c,c^{us})	(i,i^{us})
Australia	1.54	1.08	3.79	9.94	5.21	−0.19	−0.30	−0.07	0.32	−0.10	0.19
Canada	1.53	1.36	4.54	4.60	2.44	−0.43	−0.11	0.06	0.70	0.53	0.11
France	0.89	0.88	2.64	3.66	3.50	−0.30	−0.14	−0.51	0.43	0.40	0.25
Germany	2.17	2.30	5.63	3.90	2.61	−0.05	−0.09	−0.00	0.37	0.23	0.34
Italy	1.69	1.32	3.28	4.89	3.50	−0.68	0.38	−0.66	0.40	0.03	0.31
Japan	1.60	1.35	3.94	7.29	5.68	−0.23	−0.09	−0.50	0.21	0.28	0.21
United Kingdom	1.49	1.61	3.62	3.94	2.64	−0.25	0.22	−0.54	0.46	0.35	0.31
United States	1.70	1.22	5.29	6.73	2.90	−0.30	−0.08	0.28	1.00	1.00	1.00

Notes: Statistics are based on Hodrick-Prescott-filtered data. Variables are y, real gross national production; c, real consumption; i, real investment; x, real exports; m, real imports; p, ratio of import price index to export price index; nx nominal exports less nominal imports divided by nominal gross national product. Except for the net export ratio all variables are transformed to logarithms before filtering. The sample periods are: Australia, 1960:1 to 1990:3; France, 1970:1 to 1990:3; Germany, 1968:1 to 1990:3; Italy, 1970:1 to 1990:2; Japan, 1955:2 to 1990:3; United Kingdom, the United States and Canada, 1955:1 to 1990:3.
Source: OECD, *Quarterly National Accounts*.

deviation ranging between 2.44 for Canada and 5.68 for Japan. Note that the terms of trade is uniformly less volatile than the trade ratio, though some of the differences are small.

The next three columns of Table 1 report correlations between key international variables. The correlation of net exports and output is robustly negative, ranging from –0.05 for Germany to –0.68 for Italy. However, the correlations of the terms of trade with output and net exports vary widely across countries. The terms of trade is approximately acyclical, in the sense that its correlation with output is small on average, but it ranges between 0.38 for Italy and –0.30 for Australia. The correlation of the terms of trade and net exports ranges from –0.66 for Italy to 0.28 for the US.

The final three columns report the correlations of each country's output, consumption, and investment with the same US variable. We see that all of these macroeconomic aggregates tend to be positively correlated, with output more strongly correlated across countries than consumption or investment.

2.2. *Business cycles across periods*

The dramatic oil price increases of the early 1970's and 1980's and subsequent collapse are salient features of international price behavior in the postwar economy. Given the net trade exposure of industrialized countries in energy and oil, it would be surprising if some dimension of international business cycles were not affected by the rapid emergence of these shocks. We search for evidence of this by examining business cycles across different time periods.

In Table 2 we divide the sample into three periods. We refer to the middle period, 1973:1 to 1986:4, as the OPEC regime, when the most dramatic shifts in oil prices occurred. Many of the statistics change significantly as we move from the early postwar period to the OPEC years, but not all the changes are in the same direction. Beginning with output, volatility rose in France, the United Kingdom, and the United States, but fell in Germany and Japan. Consumption volatility rose in Italy, Japan, the United Kingdom, and the United States, but fell in Australia and Germany. Investment volatility rose in Australia, France, Italy, and the United States, but fell in Germany and Japan.

Table 2. Business cycle statistics by subperiod.

Country	Standard deviation					Cross-correlations					
	y	c	i	x/m	p	(y,nx)	(y,p)	(p,nx)	(y,y^{us})	(c,c^{us})	(i,i^{us})
Panel A: Pre-OPEC period											
Australia	1.60	1.25	2.94	11.33	4.99	−0.38	−0.30	−0.05	−0.13	0.05	0.25
Canada	1.49	1.37	4.51	4.60	1.56	−0.60	−0.24	0.16	0.57	0.64	0.28
France	0.59	0.72	1.60	2.03	2.57	0.30	−0.47	−0.79	0.20	0.37	0.85
Germany	3.72	4.29	9.21	4.81	1.97	0.11	−0.10	0.52	−0.15	−0.13	−0.08
Italy	1.31	0.61	1.44	4.17	3.91	−0.72	0.77	−0.57	−0.64	−0.16	−0.63
Japan	1.85	1.26	4.49	7.97	3.29	−0.24	0.06	−0.63	−0.17	0.06	−0.21
United Kingdom	1.27	1.23	3.18	4.06	2.32	−0.31	0.47	−0.39	0.18	0.29	0.08
United States	1.34	0.90	3.67	6.13	1.39	−0.12	0.44	0.27	1.00	1.00	1.00
Panel B: OPEC period											
Australia	1.61	0.93∨	4.19∧	8.55∨	5.19	0.04∧	−0.30	−0.25	0.56∧	−0.18	0.18
Canada	1.69	1.44	4.72	5.02	3.39∧	−0.25∧	−0.02	−0.01	0.80∧	0.47	−0.02∨
France	1.00∧	1.01	2.99∧	4.09∧	3.97	−0.37∨	−0.20	−0.53	0.44	0.42	0.19∨
Germany	1.64∨	1.41∨	4.39∨	3.73	2.80∧	−0.19	−0.23	−0.14∨	0.80∧	0.61	0.63∧
Italy	1.92	1.55∧	3.83∧	5.44	3.54	−0.67	0.31∨	−0.69	0.46∧	0.01∧	0.35∧
Japan	1.42∨	1.59∧	3.63∨	7.26	7.88∧	−0.20	−0.28∨	−0.50	0.62∧	0.43	0.58∧
United Kingdom	1.80∧	2.05∧	3.89	3.66	3.12∧	−0.15	0.00∨	−0.69	0.59∧	0.35∧	0.45∧
United States	2.21∧	1.63∧	7.36∧	8.03∧	4.28∧	−0.42	−0.24∨	0.37	1.00	1.00	1.00

Table 2. (*Continued*)

	Standard deviation					Cross-correlations					
Country	y	c	i	x/m	p	(y,nx)	(y,p)	(p,nx)	(y,y^{us})	(c,c^{us})	(i,i^{us})
					Panel C: Post-OPEC period						
Australia	1.09	0.97	4.92	9.52	5.71	−0.44	−0.36	0.53	0.84	0.74	0.86
Canada	1.01	0.96	4.00	2.66	1.41	−0.51	−0.59	0.18	0.93	0.79	0.84
France	0.60	0.33	1.49	2.79	2.05	0.50	0.89	0.50	0.22	−0.04	0.60
Germany	0.93	0.86	3.20	2.34	2.50	0.08	0.78	−0.16	−0.32	0.02	0.06
Italy	0.55	0.37	1.14	2.59	2.43	−0.70	0.47	−0.46	0.75	0.57	0.53
Japan	0.82	0.63	1.72	2.64	4.86	−0.49	0.58	−0.81	0.02	−0.20	0.23
United Kingdom	1.15	1.36	4.59	4.65	1.79	−0.63	0.51	0.09	0.57	−0.41	0.52
United States	0.91	0.83	1.60	3.36	1.63	0.02	0.50	−0.67	1.00	1.00	1.00

Notes: Each of the three panels are sample statistics computed over different periods. The first sample begins with the first available observation and ends at 1972:4, the second sample is from 1973:1 to 1986:4 and the last sample is from 1987:1 to the last available observation. In the second panel, $\wedge$ and $\vee$ indicates a statistically significant increase and decrease in the moment, respectively. The variances are tested for shifts at the 5% level using critical values $F(n-1,\ m-1)$ where n is the number of observations in the OPEC regime (56) and m is the number of observations available before 1973:1 which varies by country (n and m are reverse to test for statistically significant declines in the variances). The correlations are indicated as significantly changed across periods if the 80% confidence intervals for the two periods do not overlap. The intervals are constructed as $[1+\rho-(1-\rho)e^{x}]/[1+\rho+(1-\rho)e^{x}] \geq \rho \leq [1+\rho-(1-\rho)e^{-x}]/[1+\rho+1(1-\rho)e^{-x}]$ where $x = 2c/\sqrt{n-3}$, c is the critical value (here 1.282), and n is the number of observations (see Hogg and Tanis (1983), p. 451). See the notes to Table 1 for variable definitions and exact sample periods.

The trade variables display a more consistent pattern across the two samples. The standard deviation of the trade ratio is about the same in both periods. The terms of trade, however, exhibits much more volatility during the OPEC period, increasing substantially in five of the eight countries and rising in absolute terms in every country. The correlation of output and net exports remains robustly negative, though it declines in France while rising in Australia and Canada. The correlation of the terms of trade and net exports is not significantly different in the OPEC period. The correlation of the terms of trade and output falls significantly in four countries.

Cross-country correlations indicate greater conformity of business cycles with the United States during the OPEC period than before. This is particularly evident in output correlations, which rise for all countries but France.

The focus of the remainder of the paper will be to explain three observations about the OPEC period: (i) greater volatility of the terms of trade without an associated increase in the volatility of the trade ratio; (ii) smaller correlations of the terms of trade with output (particularly among oil importers); and (iii) increased cross-country correlations of output. Increased variability of the terms of trade can be traced directly to the price of oil, which we examine next.

2.3. *Oil prices*

The basic facts relating to the oil price shocks of the 1970's are familiar to most of us: the nominal price of a barrel of crude oil jumped by over 300 percent from \$2.7 in 1973 to \$11.2 in 1974, rose another 200 percent to 34.4 in 1981 before falling to about half this price by the late 1980's. Given the importance of oil as an internationally traded commodity and the volatility of its price, oil shocks could potentially explain virtually all of the terms of trade variation from the early 1970's to mid-1980's. We explore that possibility in this section.

Our monthly nominal oil price index is a simple average of US dollar prices in three major markets: Brent, Dubai, and West Texas. The series is converted to a quarterly frequency by averaging. The

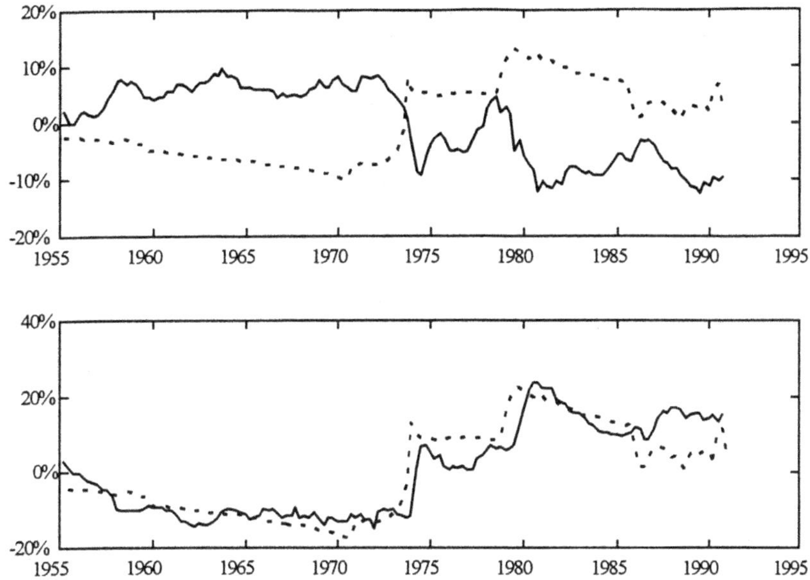

Fig. 1. The figure presents the terms of trade expressed as the ratio of the implicit deflator for imports to exports (solid lines) for Canada (upper panel) and the United States (lower panel). The dashed line is the international price of crude petroleum expressed in constant U.S. dollars (see Appendix A for the details of its construction) and normalized such that the sample standard deviation matches the standard deviation of the terms of trade with which it is plotted.

resulting price index is then divided by the quarterly U.S. GDP deflator to arrive at a constant dollar measure of oil prices.

Figure 1 plots the oil price index against the terms of trade for Canada and the United States with the oil price series normalized so that its standard deviation matches that of the terms of trade for the country against which it is plotted. Two observations can be made directly from the figure. First, the terms of trade is remarkably volatile, shifting on many occasions by 20% or more in a few years. The most dramatic shifts in the terms of trade are synchronous with changes in the relative price of oil. The second obvious feature of the series is the negative correlation between the two relative prices in Canada and the positive correlation in the United States. These patterns almost certainly reflect the fact that the United States is a net importer of oil while Canada is a net exporter.

Table 3. Oil prices and the terms of trade.

	Net fuel trade share (annual data)			Terms of trade			
				Correlation with oil price		Standard deviation	
Country	1970	1975	1987	Level	HP-cycle	Overall	Ex. Energy
Australia	−0.5	3.0	13.3	0.17	−0.60	8.10	8.22
Canada	1.2	2.8	5.5	−0.47	−0.47	6.51	6.05
France	−10.4	−20.6	−9.2	0.49	−0.05	6.08	3.60
Germany	−5.0	−12.5	−6.9	0.45	0.09	7.36	4.95
Italy	−10.1	−22.6	−11.6	0.60	0.25	8.02	5.03
Japan	−20.2	−44.8	−20.4	0.50	0.14	12.76	6.28
United Kingdom	−8.6	−15.9	3.1	−0.25	0.36	7.63	5.23
United States	−3.3	−21.4	−11.5	0.63	0.16	5.99	3.25

Notes: The correlation of the terms of trade and relative price of oil is computed using quarterly data over the OPEC period, 1973:1 to 1986:4. The net fuel trade shares are annual, computed as the ratio of the nominal trade balance in fuel divided by the average level of nominal imports plus exports for the year indicated above each column and expressed as a percentage. The last two columns report the annual standard deviation of the terms of trade in raw terms (ratio of import to export price index) and our estimate adjusted to exclude the impact of relative fuel prices as described in Appendix B. Both series are filtered using the Hodrick-Prescott (1997) filter with smoothing parameter equal to 100.

Table 3 reports the net trade share for all fuels for each country in the sample at three points in time: 1970, 1975, and 1987. The share is computed as the ratio of the nominal trade balance in fuels divided by the nominal average level of exports plus imports in a given year, expressed as a percentage. We see that countries with little or no domestic oil production have large negative trade balances in fuel. The most obvious example is Japan, which in 1970 had a net fuel share of trade of −20.2%.

The first oil price shock altered net fuel trade shares in a predictable way. Between 1970 and 1975, the deficits in fuel trade almost exactly double in France, Germany, Italy, and Japan (all countries that have substantial net import shares of fuel during the entire sample period). The United States' net export share of fuel changes even more, moving from −3.3% to −21.4%. By 1987, the deficits had largely reversed themselves. Some of the reversal was due to the collapse of the relative price of oil in the mid-1980's, but some was also likely due to energy conservation. Other major alterations to fuel trade balances were the increased positive position of fuel in the trade balances of Australia and Canada (moving from approximate balance to 13.3% and from 1.2% to 5.5%, respectively) and the emergence of the United Kingdom as a net exporter of fuel (attributable to the rapid growth of North Sea oil production).

The next two columns of Table 3 report the correlation of each country's terms of trade and the relative price of crude oil in the world market (in terms of US goods) computed using both log-levels of variables and their HP-cyclical components. We find a negative correlation between the terms of trade and oil for the only country that is consistently a net exporter of oil — Canada. The correlation is robustly positive for the countries that were consistently net importers of oil with the exception of France and Germany where the correlation of the cyclical components are close to zero. The correlation for the United Kingdom changes from −0.25 to 0.36 as we move from log-levels to cyclical fluctuations.

The correlations are suggestive of an important role for oil's relative price in the cyclical and secular evolution of the terms of trade. How important? We answer this question by comparing the volatility of the overall terms of trade to an estimate of the non-fuel terms of trade. Our estimate of the non-fuel terms of trade is the overall terms of trade multiplied by the net export share of fuels. The estimate will be crude unless the ratio of the quantity of fuel to non-fuel trade is constant (see the discussion in Appendix B). The standard deviation of the annual terms of trade and our non-fuel terms of trade estimates are shown in the final two columns of Table 3.

As one might anticipate, the smallest adjustment in the volatility of the terms of trade occurs for countries with small or ambiguous trade exposure: rising slightly in Australia from 8.10 to 8.22 percent per year; falling somewhat in Canada from 6.51 to 6.05; and falling in the United Kingdom from 7.63 to 5.23. More dramatic changes are found for the large net importers, where the non-fuel terms of trade is typically one-fourth as volatile as the overall terms of trade. After adjusting for the impact of oil, the volatility of the terms of trade of the smaller countries is comparable or greater than that for the larger countries.

3. The Model

We extend the two-good, two-country, stochastic growth model of Backus *et al.* (1994) to incorporate a third country that sells oil. Each of the three countries specializes in the production of a single good. The first two goods satisfy the consumption and investment needs of all three countries. We denote them as good a and good b and interpret them as manufactures. The third good is oil (o), which is used to produce manufactures. We use the same indexes to refer to countries as we use for goods.

3.1. *The economic environment*

Consumers in each country maximize the expected value of lifetime utility, given by:

$$E_0 \sum_{t=0}^{\infty} \beta^t U(c_t^j,\, L_t^j),\ \beta < 1\ j = a, b, o. \tag{1}$$

where consumption, c, is a CES aggregate of the home good, a, and the foreign good, b, and L is leisure.

The production of each manufactured good makes use of labor N, physical capital k, and oil o, as inputs. Output in country j is y^j and is affected by a stochastic productivity variable denoted z^j that is described in detail below.

$$y_t^j = z_t^j F(k_t^j,\, N_t^j,\, o_t^j),\ j = a, b. \tag{2}$$

The key point of our departure from existing models of the macroeconomic impact of oil shocks is that we endogenize the price of oil. We accomplish this by having the world supply of oil, y^o, at any point in time equal the sum of two parts:

$$y_t^o = z_t^o + F(N_t^o) \tag{3}$$

an exogenous component z^o which in practice we treat as OPEC oil supply and an endogenous component, $F(N^o) = N^\alpha$, which we treat as the supply originating from non-OPEC oil producers.

The technology differs in two respects from that of Backus *et al.* (1994). One is that final consumption and investment goods are separate composites of a and b. The aggregator for investment is

$$i_t^j = i(a_{it}^j, b_{it}^j), \ j = a, b. \tag{4}$$

where $i(a,b) = [\psi a^{1-\mu} + (1-\psi)b^{1-\mu}]^{1/(1-\mu)}$ and the subscript i identifies the use of a and b in the investment process. The other is that physical capital formation is subject to adjustment costs, as in Baxter and Crucini (1995):

$$k_{t+1}^j = (1-\delta)k_t^j + \phi(i_t^j/k_t^j)k_t^j, \ j = a, \ b. \tag{5}$$

with $\phi > 0, \phi' > 0, \phi'' < 0$. The resource constraints for the three goods are

$$y_t^a = \sum_{j=a,b,o} a_{ct}^j + \sum_{j=a,b} a_{it}^j \tag{6}$$

$$y_t^b = \sum_{j=a,b,o} b_{ct}^j + \sum_{j=a,b} b_{it}^j \tag{7}$$

$$y_t^o = o_t^a + o_t^b \tag{8}$$

where a_{ct}^j refers to the amount of good a used in country j for consumption purposes. Note that physical investment does not take place in the oil producing country and we abstract from the use of oil by oil producing countries. Similarly, time allocations satisfy

$$1 - L_t^j - N_t^j = 0, \ j = a, b, o; \tag{9}$$

the unit endowment is divided between work and leisure.

We solve the model by exploiting the equivalence between competitive equilibria and Pareto optima. An optimum is the solution to the maximization of:

$$\sum_{t=0}^{\infty} \beta^t \{\omega^a U(c_t^a, L_t^a) + \omega^b U(c_t^b, L_t^b) + \omega^o U(c_t^o, L_t^o)\} \quad (10)$$

subject to the constraints implied by Eqs. (5)–(9). We approximate the first-order necessary conditions of the planning problem in a neighborhood of the steady state. We specify log-linear stochastic processes for the shocks and calibrate the functional forms of preferences and technology. The resulting linear dynamic rational expectations model is then solved using standard techniques (King *et al.* (1988), for example).

3.2. *Calibration*

We explore the impact in the model of changes in the supply of oil. The specifics depend, to some extent, on the choice of parameters. We stay as close as possible to the values used by Backus *et al.* (1994), but consider alternatives when they seem interesting. The complete set of parameter values is summarized in Table 4. A brief sketch of the logic behind these choices follows.

The functional form of preferences for the industrial countries is exactly as in BKK:

$$U(c, L) = [c^\theta L^{1-\theta}]^{1-\gamma}/(1-\gamma)$$

where $0 < \theta < 1$, $\gamma > -1$. Consumption is a CES function of the home and foreign manufactured good: $c = [\psi a^{1-\mu} + (1-\psi)b^{1-\mu}]^{1/(1-\mu)}$. The elasticity of substitution between the two goods is $1/\mu$.

With these preferences, the curvature properties of the utility function are completely determined by three parameters: the intertemporal substitution parameter (γ), the fraction of time spent in the workplace (governed by θ), and the willingness of individuals to substitute between domestic and foreign goods. We set the first two of these parameters, as well as the discount factor, the share

Table 4. Benchmark parameter values.

			Parameter value	
	Description	Symbol	Quarterly model	Annual model
Preferences	Discount factor	β	0.99	0.96
	Intertemporal substitution	$1/\gamma$	0.5	0.5
	Atemporal substitution	$1/\mu$	1.5	1.5
	Fraction of time spent working	$\bar{N}$	0.3	0.3
Technology	Labor's share	α	0.64	0.64
	Depreciation rate of capital	δ	0.025	0.10
	Cost of adjustment parameter	η	1000	1000
Trade	Industrial country shares	s_x	0.15	0.15
Oil sector	Energy cost-to-value added	ξ	0.10	0.10
	Elasticity of substitution k, o	$1/\nu$	0.09	0.09
	OPEC's share of oil output	ϕ^o	(0.3, 0.5)	0.5
	Labor parameter	α	0.64	0.64
Productivity shocks	Persistence		0.906	0.83
	Spillover		0.088	0.16
	Innovation variance		0.00825	NA
OPEC oil supply	Persistence		0.97	0.88
	Innovation variance		(0.0099, 0.0114)	NA

Note: The standard deviations of innovations to OPEC oil supply differ across regimes as shown within the parentheses with the first entry referring to the non-OPEC regimes and the second entry referring to the OPEC regime.

of value added going to capital, and the depreciation rate, equal to values suggested by Kydland and Prescott (1982). The elasticity of substitution between domestic and foreign goods (σ) is set at 1.5 for both the consumption and investment aggregator. Costs of adjustment in capital accumulation are essentially set to zero by calibrating $\eta = -(D\phi(i/k)/D^2\phi(i/k))/(i/k)$, the elasticity of the investment–capital ratio with respect to Tobin's "q", to equal to 1000.

The two industrial countries are of equal size, but each consumes a disproportionate amount of its own good. Given that we abstract from non-traded goods, this last feature is needed to ensure that trade shares are not unrealistically high. For simplicity we assume that the oil producer likes a and b equally well so that $a^o = b^o$. The only remaining pieces of information we need to arrive at the steady-state values of quantity ratios are a trade share for the industrialized countries; the ratio of oil use to value added; and the fractions of imports for consumption and investment purposes. We set the first two parameters at 15% and 10% to approximate the share of trade in industrialized countries and the cost share of energy for the United States, respectively. We assume a common home bias for both consumption and investment goods so that the ratio of imports of consumption goods to investment goods equals the ratio of total expenditure on consumption goods to investment goods.

Turning to the oil market we consider features of both the supply and demand.

The sensitivity of the demand for oil to changes in industrial country output depend, in part, on how oil enters the production function — one of the most studied and least resolved issues in empirical macroeconomics. Part of the difficulty stems from the different roles played by oil in industrialized countries. Nordhaus (1980) notes that many components of the physical capital stock are engineered in ways that makes substitution possible only when the existing capital is scrapped. A good example is the transportation sector, in which energy use depends largely on the fuel efficiency of the outstanding stock of automobiles. The energy consumption of this sector responded gradually to increases in oil prices during the 1970s, as old vehicles were gradually replaced with more fuel efficient models. Electricity generation is another sector in which infrastructure requirements can make energy substitution costly. Conservation would reduce the end-use demand, but the relationship between physical inputs of oil and other factors of production would be closer to Leontief than Cobb-Douglas. Berndt and Wood (1979) evaluate the conflicting evidence on capital and energy substitutability, in which estimates of complementarity and substitutability have been found. In Jorgensen (1986, p. 9) the conclusion is made that energy and capital are on the borderline between substitution and complementarity.

We follow Kim and Loungani (1992), in nesting capital and oil as a CES function within a Cobb-Douglas production function: $y = zN^{\alpha}[\eta k^{1-v} + (1-\eta)o^{1-v}]^{(1-\alpha)/(1-v)}$ with $0 < \alpha < 1, v > 0, \eta > 0$ and the elasticity of substitution between capital and oil equal to $1/v$.

We explore the sensitivity of our results to alternative parameterizations of capital-energy substitutability but our baseline choice of the parameter v is 11, which translates into an elasticity of substitutability of 0.09, compared to the value 0.7 used by Kim and Loungani (1992). The lower elasticity seems more plausible for an investigation focusing on business cycles, while an elasticity approaching one might be more appropriate for analysis of the secular changes in energy use (Atkeson and Kehoe, 1994, for example). We will see, in any case, that a high elasticity of substitution produces strongly counterfactual implications for the time series of prices and quantities in the world oil market. Basically, if other inputs into production are highly substitutable for oil (in a technological sense) it will be next to impossible to match the observed changes in the quantity of oil production that we observe in the data.

Oil supply behavior introduces some new issues. Much of the literature on the supply-side of the oil market bases supply or pricing decisions on optimal behavior given a particular market structure. See, for example, the excellent survey by Cremer and Salehi-Isfahani (1991). We assume that OPEC supply decisions are taken as exogenous by agents in the two industrialized countries and the non-OPEC oil producer. To see how this assumption allows us to map existing data on OPEC and non-OPEC oil supply into our model consider the linearized version of our "supply" function:

$$\hat{y}_t^o = \phi^o \hat{z}_t^o + (1 - \phi^o)\alpha \hat{N}_t^o \tag{11}$$

where ϕ^o is OPEC's market share which we treat as constant in the deterministic steady state. We associate $\hat{z}_t^o$ with OPEC oil production

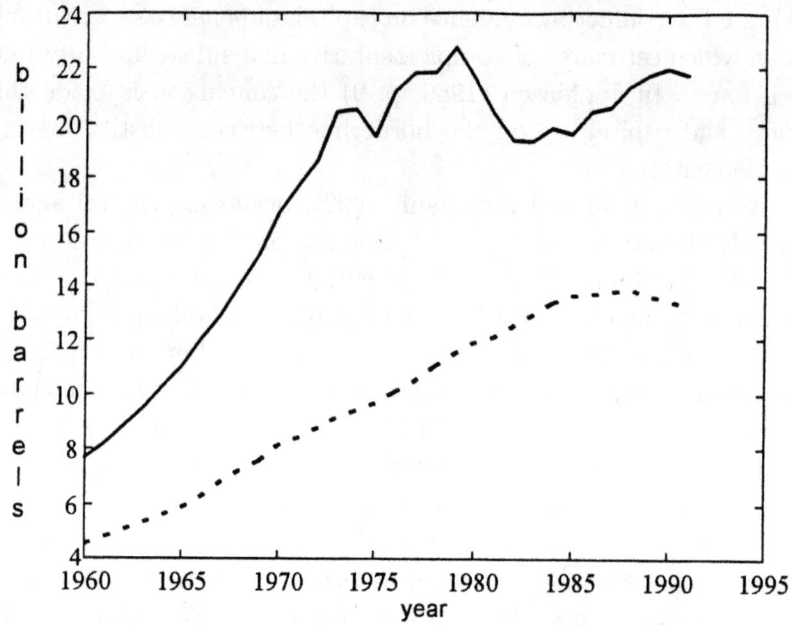

Fig. 2. The figure presents the annual production volume of crude petroleum for all major producers (solid line) and for non-OPEC countries (dashed line).

data, and allow $(1-\phi^o)\alpha\hat{N}_t^o$ to be determined by the endogenous choice of effort by non-OPEC producers. Our formulation makes clear what an oil shocks is: a change in the supply of oil by OPEC, holding fixed the remaining exogenous variables (in our model home and foreign productivity). Note that there is no guarantee that we will match — or even come close to — either the total amount of oil produced in the world economy or its world relative price without putting some restrictions on the endogenous part of oil supply.

The empirical counterparts to the two components of world oil supply are displayed in Fig. 2. Non-OPEC supply is measured from the axis to the dashed line while OPEC supply is the distance from the dashed to the solid line which is total world production measured in billions of barrels per year. We see that non-OPEC oil supply is quite smooth suggesting that supply is not highly responsive to either changes in OPEC production or the dramatic changes in the relative price of oil. For this reason, we adopt a preference specification for the non-OPEC oil producers consistent with an inelastic labor supply response to changes in real wages:

$$U(c, L) = c^{1-\gamma}/(1-\gamma) + \theta_L v(L). \tag{12}$$

We use the same intertemporal elasticity of substitution in consumption, $1/\gamma$, as for the industrialized countries, but set the elasticity $\xi_{LL} = LD^2v(L)/Dv(L)$ equal to -10 which when combined with the fraction of time spent devoted to market activity matches the upper bound on the labor supply elasticity of prime age males found in Pencavel (1986).

That leaves us with the shocks. Our world economy is driven by three disturbances: home productivity shocks, foreign productivity shocks, and oil supply shocks. Much of our analysis utilizes the quarterly OECD data, but since our oil production data is annual we use simulations from an annual version of the model to evaluate our characterization of the world oil market. Complete parameterization of the model requires that we also specify forcing processes consistent with the assumed length of a decision period. Thus we present evidence on both the quarterly and annual properties of the shocks.

The processes for technology shocks are based on observed properties of Solow residuals. In the quarterly model, we use the same symmetric bivariate first-order autoregressive process as Backus *et al.* (1994):

$$\begin{pmatrix} z_t^a \\ z_t^b \end{pmatrix} = \begin{pmatrix} 0.906 & 0.088 \\ 0.088 & 0.906 \end{pmatrix} \begin{pmatrix} z_{t-1}^a \\ z_{t-1}^b \end{pmatrix} + \begin{pmatrix} \epsilon_t^a \\ \epsilon_t^b \end{pmatrix}, \tag{13}$$

where z_t^a and z_t^b are Solow residuals computed for the United States and Europe, respectively. The standard deviations of both innovations are 0.008325 and the correlation between them is 0.258. With annual data (computed by taken averages of quarterly productivity levels), we estimate a similar system for the period 1972 to 1989:

$$\begin{pmatrix} z_t^a \\ z_t^b \end{pmatrix} = \begin{pmatrix} 0.858 & 0.092 \\ 0.281 & 0.804 \end{pmatrix} \begin{pmatrix} z_{t-1}^a \\ z_{t-1}^b \end{pmatrix} + \begin{pmatrix} \epsilon_t^a \\ \epsilon_t^b \end{pmatrix}. \tag{14}$$

The standard deviations of the innovations are 0.0161 and 0.0190, respectively, and the correlation between them is 0.67. Following the approach taken for the quarterly model, we use a symmetric matrix A with the same eigenvalues as the matrix estimated in Eq. (14) to get:

$$A = \begin{pmatrix} 0.83 & 0.16 \\ 0.16 & 0.83 \end{pmatrix}. \tag{15}$$

In both cases, productivity shocks are persistent and exhibit two sources of positive correlation across countries: the correlation between the innovations and the positive off-diagonal elements of A.

In the absence of quarterly oil production data, we interpolate the annual OPEC production data (using a quadratic interpolation of the annual data from 1961 to 1991) and estimate a first-order autoregressive model for z_t^o:

$$z_t^o = 0.977 z_{t-1}^o + \epsilon_t^o \tag{16}$$

With $\sigma_{\epsilon^o} = 0.0099$. Estimating the same process over the OPEC period (1973:1 to 1986:4) we get almost the same coefficient, 0.971 but the standard deviation of the innovations rises to 0.0114.

Using the original annual series of OPEC production data from 1961 to 1991 we get:

$$z_t^o = 0.882 z_{t-1}^o + \epsilon_t^o, \tag{17}$$

with an innovation standard deviation of 0.0828. Note that the innovations of OPEC oil supply have a standard deviation five times larger than the annual productivity measures. We set OPEC's market share, ϕ^o, at 0.3, which is a lower bound on OPEC's share of world oil production.

3.3. *Impulse response analysis*

We use impulse response functions to illustrate the economic mechanisms that might give rise to the unstable correlations of

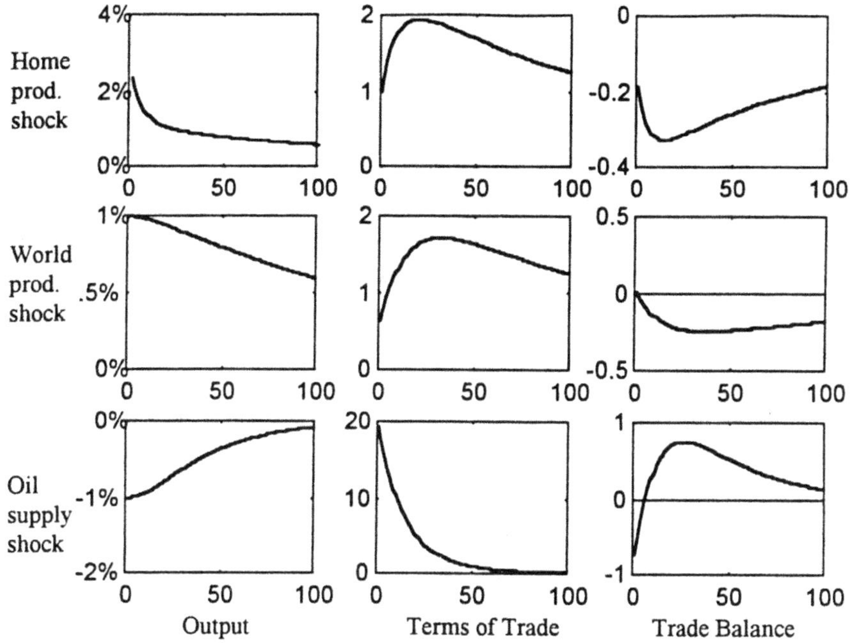

Fig. 3. The figure presents the impulse responses of the home country to a 1% increase in home productivity (upper panel), a 1% increase in both home and foreign productivity (middle panel), and an oil supply reduction of sufficient size to lower world output by 1% (lower panel).

trade prices and quantities documented in Section 2. To emphasize the roles played by different shocks, we trace out the dynamic responses of output, the terms of trade, and the trade balance to three different shocks: a positive innovation to home productivity; a positive innovation to world productivity; and a negative oil supply shock. The first two disturbances are set such that world output rises by 1 percent on impact while the third is set so that world output falls by 1 percent on impact. The magnitudes of the innovations needed to achieve this are: a 1.85% increase in home productivity, a 0.93% increase in productivity in both industrial countries, and a 22.1% decline in OPEC oil supply. Figure 3 presents the time paths of output, the terms of trade, and net exports in the home country (each in a separate column) in response to the three types of disturbances (each in a separate row).

Beginning with a home productivity shock, we see that output rises in the home country, as does its terms of trade, and the trade balance moves into deficit. The increase in output is due to the productivity led boom in which both effort and physical investment move above their steady state levels for an extended period of time. The terms of trade rises for two reasons. First, the home country is more productive and therefore produces more of its good. Because the country is also large it drives down the world relative price of its export (causing a deterioration of its terms of trade). Reinforcing this effect is the fact that an increase in world output drives up the relative price of oil which is an import of the home country (recall that the terms of trade is the import price index divided by the export price index). The response of the trade balance is familiar from the existing international real business cycle research where a persistent productivity led boom cases consumption and investment to rise by a sufficient amount to result in a trade deficit. Evidence on this channel may be found in empirical work by Glick and Rogoff (1995) and Sachs (1981).

The second panel shows the response of the home country to an equal increase in productivity in both industrialized countries. Again output rises but the terms of trade response is muted and the trade balance moves into deficit. The terms of trade effect is muted because the relative price of the two manufactured goods does not change when productivity increases simultaneously in the two industrialized countries. Without oil as an imported input into production and given the symmetry of the two industrial countries, common disturbances across countries would not alter the terms of trade. However, the relative price of oil rises due to increased oil demand and the terms of trade rises on this account. The trade deficit is a consequence of consumption smoothing by the oil producer and the impact of an investment boom in both industrialized countries.

The last panel shows the response of the home country to a reduction in OPEC oil supply of the magnitude needed to reduce world output by 1%. Note that despite the inelastic labor supply of non-OPEC oil producers, the OPEC supply shock must be very large to induce a worldwide recession; OPEC supply must fall by 22.1%

to reduce world output by 1%. The decline needed would be even higher with a production function that allowed more substitutability between capital and oil or a more elastic labor supply on the part of non-OPEC suppliers. We see the terms of trade increases very dramatically, rising by 20% on impact (though it decays rapidly). The trade balance moves into deficit initially before turning into a surplus after about one year.

We can see from these experiments that the volatility of the terms of trade and its correlation with output depend crucially on the source of the disturbance. When productivity shocks are the dominant source of economic fluctuations we expect to see a positive correlation of the terms of trade and output for oil importers while the opposite correlation should prevail when oil shocks are dominant. Accompanying the shift to a greater role for oil shocks should be a dramatic increase in the variance of the terms of trade.

4. Oil and Business Cycles

We assess the role of oil in international business cycles in two ways. First, we consider how a change in the variability of oil shocks relative to productivity shocks alters the character of business cycles. Second, we use time series simulations to compare the actual time paths of economic variables to predictions of the model conditioned on the measured sequence of shocks over the period from 1971 to 1989.

4.1. *Business cycle regimes*

We use the term regime to refer to a shift in the time series properties of oil supply which we characterize as involving a change in OPEC's share of world oil production and a coincident change in the volatility of OPEC's oil supply. We refer to the OPEC regime as a time period during which OPEC's market share is 50% and the standard deviation of the innovations to OPEC oil supply is 0.0114; both having risen from benchmark values of 0.30 and 0.0099, respectively. Recall that these last two statistics are from our analysis of the time series properties of OPEC oil supply. The OPEC market shares are based on the data used in Fig. 2, which shows a sharp rise in the world share of oil production accounted for by OPEC between

Table 5. OPEC and the international business cycle.

	Country averages		Model predictions	
Country	1955:3 1972:4	1973:1 1987:1	Pre-OPEC	OPEC
	Standard deviations:			
Output	1.65	1.66	1.60	1.60
Consumption	1.45	1.45	1.07	1.09
Investment	3.88	4.37	4.61	4.75
Trade ratio	5.64	5.72	1.05	1.14
Terms of trade	2.75	4.27	1.71	3.00
	Cross-correlations:			
Output and net exports	−0.25	−0.28	−0.55	−0.48
Output and terms of trade	0.08	−0.12	0.49	0.22
Terms of trade and net exports	−0.18	−0.31	−0.60	−0.59
	Correlations with U.S.:			
Counterpart				
Output	−0.02	0.61	0.09	0.09
Consumption	0.15	0.30	0.79	0.80
Investment	0.07	0.34	−0.68	−0.59

Notes: The country averages are simple averages of the statistics in the first and second panels of Table 2. The model predictions are population moments for HP filtered results.

1960 and 1970. Pre-OPEC and post-OPEC regimes mark a return to "normalcy" in the sense that the market share and volatility of oil supply return to baseline parameter settings.

The first two columns of Table 5 report the cross-country averages of the individual country statistics that were reported in Table 2. We summarize the salient features of pre-OPEC and OPEC regimes as follows. The volatility of consumption and income are virtually unchanged across the two periods while investment volatility rises modestly. The volatility of the terms of trade rises sharply from 2.75 to 4.27, accompanied by almost no change in the volatility of the trade ratio. The correlation of the terms of trade and output falls from 0.08 to −0.12. The international comovement of output rises from −0.02 to 0.61 while investment comovement increases from 0.07 to 0.32.

Beginning with the pre-OPEC period, we see that the model does a reasonably good job in capturing volatility with the notable exception of the trade variables. Output is more volatile than consumption but less so than investment, both of which we see in international data. The presence of oil combined with exogenous fluctuations in its supply increases the standard deviation of the terms of trade from 0.48 in BKK to 1.71. This prediction as well as the volatility of the trade ratio (at 1.05) remain an order of magnitude below the standard deviations of their empirical counterparts in the pre-OPEC period of 5.64 and 2.75, respectively.

The model correctly predicts the sign of the correlation between output and net exports, output and the terms of trade, and the terms of trade and net exports. Again, the magnitudes are quite far off from their empirical counterparts: net exports are too sharply counter-cyclical, −0.55 in the model compared to −0.25 in the data; the terms of trade are too sharply pro-cyclical, 0.49 in the model compared to 0.08 in the data; and the correlation of the terms of trade and net exports is too low, −0.60 in the model compared to −0.18 in the data. The comovement of international output is about right, −0.02 in the data and 0.09 in the model. As with virtually all dynamic equilibrium models that feature complete markets and physical capital as the mobile factor, the international correlation of consumption is too high and the international correlation of investment is too low (negative in fact).

More interesting to us is that the model predicts a number of significant changes in the character of the international business cycles across the two regimes. The presence of large oil shocks increases the volatility of the terms of trade, investment, and the trade ratio while reducing the correlation of output and the terms of trade. Each of these could be anticipated from the impulse response analysis. They also mimic some of what we see in the data, although the magnitudes differ. The predicted increase in investment volatility is too small, rising from 4.61 to 4.75, while rising from 3.88 to 4.37 in the data. The predicted increase in the volatility of the trade ratio is a bit too large, rising from 1.05 to 1.14, while rising very modestly from 5.64 to 5.72 in the data. The predicted decline in the correlation of the terms of trade and output is dramatic in both the model, falling from 0.49 to 0.22, and in the data where it falls from 0.08 to −0.12. The international comovement of output, consumption and investment is virtually unchanged in the model (except for a modest increase in the case of investment) compared to quite dramatic increases in the data. However, the comovement of international business cycles continues into the post-OPEC period so it is unclear what to make of this shift in terms of oil's role.

4.2. *Sensitivity analysis*

We have used our model to suggest how output, the terms of trade, and the trade balance would evolve in response to different shocks over the post World War II period. While the model predicted an increase in the volatility of the terms of trade and a reduction in the comovement of output and the terms of trade during the OPEC period, it was less successful in matching the actual magnitudes of business cycle statistics. The question is whether the discrepancies that remain are sensitive to changes in the model's parameter values or theoretical structure.

Table 6 presents a detailed sensitivity analysis. The first two rows of the table present the cross-country averages of business cycle moments for all countries and countries that are consistently net importers (France, Italy, Germany, Japan, and the United States).

We begin our sensitivity analysis by stepping back and considering the moment predictions of the model in the presence and absence of each type of disturbance. Consider first a case in which variation in productivity is the only source of business cycle fluctuations. We see in Table 6 that this parameterization of the model is basically identical to the baseline version we used to describe the pre-OPEC period except that the correlation of output and the terms of trade is higher. The standard deviation of output is 1.59, only slightly lower than in the presence of oil supply shocks. While oil shocks alone can produce substantial variation in output (0.38), they are incapable of replicating the volatility of output that we see in the data, which averages about 1.58 across industrialized countries.

Table 6. Sensitivity analysis.

	Standard deviation					Domestic comovement			International comovement		
	y	c	i	x/m	p	(y, nx)	(y, p)	(p, nx)	(y, y^{us})	(c, c^{us})	(i, i^{us})
International data:											
All countries	1.58	1.39	4.09	5.62	3.56	−0.30	−0.03	−0.24	0.42	0.25	0.25
Oil importers	1.61	1.42	4.16	5.29	3.64	−0.31	0.00	−0.28	0.35	0.23	0.28
Model predictions:											
Pre-OPEC	1.60	1.07	4.61	1.05	1.71	−0.55	0.49	−0.60	0.09	0.79	−0.68
No oil shocks	1.59	1.08	4.55	1.04	1.20	−0.58	0.76	−0.69	0.08	0.79	−0.73
No productivity shocks	0.38	0.39	3.45	1.19	6.90	0.56	−0.94	−0.79	0.98	1.00	1.00
High trade share	1.52	1.02	7.25	2.31	1.17	−0.33	0.74	−0.39	0.20	0.97	−0.87
Low substitution across goods	1.53	1.10	4.37	1.22	1.74	−0.52	0.58	−0.62	0.18	0.70	−0.65
Inelastic oil demand	1.55	1.14	4.43	1.05	2.68	−0.25	0.33	−0.91	0.05	0.81	−0.77
Elastic oil supply	1.62	1.03	4.76	0.89	0.99	−0.62	0.73	−0.72	0.12	0.77	−0.58
Low energy cost share	1.58	1.10	4.39	1.16	1.47	−0.39	0.77	−0.55	0.09	0.73	−0.73

Note: The parameters that change across cases are: Pre-OPEC benchmark (see Table 4); No oil shocks, $\sigma^2_{\epsilon^o} = 0.8325 \times 10^{-6}$; No productivity shocks, $\sigma^2_{\epsilon^j} = 0.8325 \times 10^{-6}$, $j = a, b$; High trade share, $s_x = 0.5$; Low substitution across goods, $1/\gamma = 0.1$; Inelastic oil demand, $v = 100$. Elastic oil supply, uses the same preference specification for the oil producer as for the industrial countries which gives rise to a more elastic labor supply curve. Low energy cost share uses an energy cost share of 0.05.

Examination of the other moments makes clear how dramatically the international business cycle is altered as we move from a productivity driven business cycle to a cycle driven only by oil shocks: the volatility of the terms of trade rises from 1.20 to 6.90; the correlation of the terms of trade and output falls from 0.76 to −0.94; the international correlation of output goes from 0.08 to almost unity; and the international correlation of investment goes from −0.73 to 1.00.

The next two experiments consider a larger trade share and a lower substitutability of goods a and b. Increasing the trade ratio makes the aggregator functions for consumption and investment more symmetric across countries. Our intuition is that this will make the model look more like the one sector model in terms of international comovement of consumption and investment thereby increasing consumption correlations while reducing investment correlations across countries. In fact the international correlation of consumption rises from 0.79 in the baseline to 0.97 while the international correlation of investment falls from −0.68 to −0.87.

Altering the substitutability of the two goods would be expected to increase price variability relative to quantity variability based on the relationship between relative prices and quantities in general equilibrium. However, the presence of oil complicates the relationship, since both the terms of trade and quantity ratio are now functions of all three goods. Making goods a and b less substitutable increases the variability of oil demand since output of the two industrialized countries will be more highly correlated in this case (output correlations increase from 0.09 to 0.18). As a result, the ratio of price variability to quantity variability actually falls modestly as we lower the substitution elasticity.

The next two experiments illustrate the effect on the economy of alterations in parameters that govern key features of the oil market, a less elastic demand for oil (approximately a Leontief relationship between oil and capital) and a more elastic oil supply, which we accomplish by using the same preferences for the oil producer that we use for the other two countries which gives rise to a more elastic labor supply.

Our intuition was that the first of these would give rise to changes in business cycles similar to an increase in oil supply shocks. We find that this is the case. The volatility of the terms of trade increases from 1.71 in the pre-OPEC benchmark to 2.68 while the correlation of output and the terms of trade falls from 0.49 to 0.33, and the correlation of the terms of trade and the trade balance falls from −0.60 to −0.91.

In contrast to this case, the more elastic oil supply case mimics quite closely the case without oil supply shocks. The reason for this should be obvious. If oil supply responds endogenously to offset OPEC quantity changes the total world oil supply will reflect mainly fluctuations in demand for oil driven by productivity changes. As such we would expect the relative price of oil to be less volatile and the terms of trade and output to be positively correlated as in the productivity model. In fact the terms of trade volatility drops from the pre-OPEC benchmark of 1.71 to 0.99 while the correlation of the terms of trade and output increases from 0.49 to 0.73. Lowering the energy cost share has qualitatively similar effects.

4.3. *Simulations*

We conclude our empirical analysis of the model by considering it's ability to match the actual time path of economic variables over the period in which oil supply disturbances were most dramatic. We focus our attention on four aggregates: U.S. GDP, European GDP, the relative price of crude oil, and the world production of oil.

The procedure we use to generate the simulations is as follows. We calibrate an annual version of the baseline model including the forcing processes of U.S. and European productivity and OPEC oil production data as described in the calibration section. We transform the linearized model into first-difference form and compute changes in the endogenous variables as functions of the actual sequences of changes in the three forcing processes.[1] The sequences of growth

---

[1]One limitation of our analysis is that we do not adjust the computation of the Solow residual to account for the mismeasurement induced by variation in oil use. The presumption that oil and capital are not highly substitutable in the short-run

rates that result are accumulated and then filtered using the Hodrick-Prescott filter with a smoothing parameter of 100.

Figure 4 presents simulation results along with their empirical counterparts. Each column displays the time path of a different economic variable: oil prices, world oil production, U.S. output, and European output. The first row of the figure presents simulations using all three shocks while the second row presents simulations with only productivity shocks.

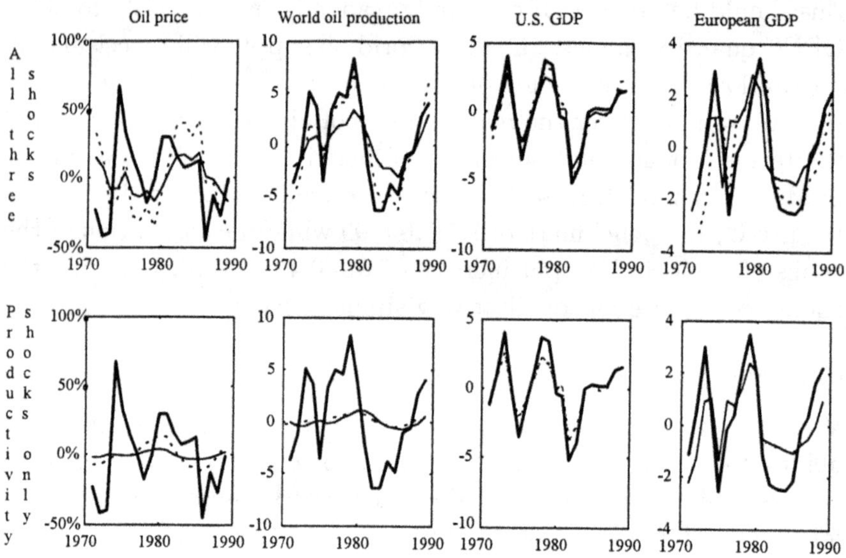

Fig. 4. Simulation results from the model using actual productivity changes in the U.S. and Europe and oil supply shocks (OPEC production changes) as inputs. The upper panel presents the results with all three shocks simultaneously while the lower panel shows the model predictions when only productivity disturbances (for the U.S. and Europe) are used in the simulation. All variables are percentage deviations from HP trends. The thick solid lines are actual sample paths. Simulations are performed over the period 1971–1989 using the baseline calibration with inelastic labor supply (dashed line) and elastic labor supply (thin solid line).

---

would tend to limit the quantitative impact of such adjustments. We currently do not have energy use available on an international basis so we leave this as a topic for future research.

Beginning with the productivity driven model, in the lower panel of the figure, we see very modest oil price fluctuations and almost no variation in oil production. This is largely independent of the elasticity of oil supply — we get some additional oil price volatility when the preferences of the oil producer are such that labor supply is inelastic, but not much.

Turning to the upper panel which shows the simulations using all three shocks we see that adding oil supply disturbances increases both the oil price and oil production variation dramatically. We also see that the inelastic supply case (our benchmark parameterization) does a better job of matching the magnitude of fluctuations in these markets than does a more elastic supply specification.

More difficult to see in Fig. 4 is much of a quantitative role for oil shocks in explaining the actual path of U.S. and European output beyond what is accounted for by the productivity shocks. Table 7 makes the differences across the simulations transparent by comparing the standard deviations of the sample paths and their RMSE relative to the actual data.

We see that the baseline parameterization that incorporates both shocks does are very good job of matching the standard deviations of the four series over the period 1970 to 1989. The standard deviation of world oil output is predicted to be 4.12 compared to 4.43 in the data while the comparable statistics for the relative price of oil are 27.49 and 28.99. The standard deviations of the simulated output cycles of the U.S. and Europe are also very close to their empirical counterparts. Turning to the RMSE statistics which also take into account the ability of the simulated paths to actually track the data we see similar degrees of success with one notable exception. As is apparent in Fig. 4, the model misses the timing of the oil price changes and underpredicts the magnitude of the first oil price shock in 1973.

The model is much less successful when only one type of disturbance is used to generate the simulations. Continuing with the baseline simulation, we see that the productivity model does a reasonable job of matching output variability but a very poor job of matching the volatility of either the relative price or quantity of

Table 7. Simulation results.

Variable	Data	Baseline parameterization: Both shocks	Baseline parameterization: Productivity shocks	Baseline parameterization: Oil shocks	Elastic oil supply: Both shocks	Elastic oil supply: Productivity shocks	Elastic oil supply: Oil shocks
Panel A: Standard deviations							
World oil output	4.43	4.12	0.45	4.12	1.92	0.55	1.91
World oil price	28.99	27.49	7.76	28.98	11.95	2.39	12.93
U.S. GDP	2.42	2.21	1.61	1.01	1.81	1.62	0.47
European GDP	1.95	1.98	1.26	0.86	1.49	1.24	0.37
Panel B: Root mean squared errors							
World oil output		1.62	4.35	1.62	2.91	4.37	2.93
World oil price		37.53	26.63	38.25	30.92	28.52	30.88
U.S. GDP		0.77	0.90	2.07	0.74	0.89	2.26
European GDP		1.13	1.25	1.41	1.12	1.23	1.78

Notes: The data and simulations are annual from 1970 to 1989. The GDP data are from the World Bank, *STARS database* with European GDP being an aggregate of each EC member's GDP. Trends are removed from the data and simulations using the Hodrick and Prescott (1997) filter with smoothing parameter set equal to 100. Simulations are produced for a case in which U.S. and European productivity and OPEC oil supply shocks are included, labelled *Both shocks*; a case in which only U.S. and European productivity shocks are included, labelled *Productivity shocks*; and a case in which only OPEC oil supply shocks are included, labelled *Oil shocks.* The parameterization *Elastic Oil Supply* uses the same preference specification for the oil producer as for the industrial countries which gives rise to a more elastic labor supply curve.

oil that we observe over the sample period of study. In particular, the productivity driven model can only account for about 1% of the observed relative price variation in oil. The case with only oil shocks has the opposite problem with only modest output variation and almost exactly the right amount of oil price and quantity variation. We see also from Table 7 that moving to a more elastic supply of oil reduces the explanatory power of the model in all dimensions, but particularly in terms of matching the behavior of the oil market.

We conclude this section with a brief discussion of the contribution of oil shocks and productivity shocks to the overall U.S. business cycle. Finn (1995) estimates energy price shocks contribute between 7.47 and 18.75 percent to U.S. output volatility compared estimates of between 2.6% and 12% produced by Kim and Loungani (1992).[2]

Recall that theirs are partial equilibrium models so that the persistence and volatility of energy prices are calibrated to match the actual data. In our model the price of oil is endogenously determined, given the path of productivity and oil supply (both exogenous and endogenous parts). The parameterization that uses an inelastic labor supply for the endogenous part of oil supply matches the volatility of the relative price of oil almost exactly and is therefore the natural one to compare to the variance decompositions performed by Finn and Kim and Loungani. Using this parameterization we estimate that OPEC oil supply changes account for about 17.4% of U.S. output variation, a figure at the high end of existing estimates.

Our novel contribution to the literature that aims to evaluate the relative important of oil price movements for U.S. business fluctuations is in providing evidence that their contribution is more likely to be at the high end of estimates coming out of existing calibration exercises. We arrive at this conclusion based on the observation that such estimates are more plausible because they obtain in parameterizations that produce both the right amount of price and quantity volatility in the world market for crude petroleum.

5. Conclusions

Recently a number of authors have examined the role of trade in intermediate inputs for the character of international business cycles. Most of these studies have focused on the role of intermediate inputs in producing more comovement in international output than found in one sector models (see for example, Ambler *et al.* (1995) or Costello and Praschnik (1993)). Exceptions are Kouparitsas (1995), who demonstrates that the pattern of North–South specialization gives rise to volatile terms of trade across developing and developed

---

[2]Both of these studies assume perfect competition, for a quantitative analysis of oil price shocks on the U.S. economy under imperfect competition see Rotemberg and Woodford (1996).

economies, and Boileau (1997), who shows that trade in equipment can add volatility to the terms of trade of industrialized countries.[3]

We found that the Hamilton (1983) view of the U.S. business cycle has important implications for international business cycles too. We documented how changes in the terms of trade in major industrialized countries during the period 1972 to 1987 were driven primarily by the dramatic changes in the relative price of a single commodity — oil. Using a suitably adapted dynamic equilibrium model of international business cycles, we found that unstable relationships between relative prices and quantities are to be expected when oil price shocks play vastly different roles across time periods. Once we control for the sources of shocks driving the terms of trade the comovement and volatility of the terms of trade, output, and the trade balance become less puzzling.

Given the timing of the oil price shocks, the increased volatility in the terms of trade since Bretton Woods seems largely due to the increased volatility in the relative price of oil rather than the increased volatility of nominal or real exchange rates. A direction that we plan to pursue in future research is to relate the properties of the terms of trade to similar properties of real exchange rates documented by Mussa (1986) and others. Although the two relative prices are conceptually and operationally different, preliminary analysis shows that they are positively correlated in the data. The question then is whether the striking change in the variability of real exchange rates between the pre-1972 Bretton Woods fixed exchange rate regime and the more recent floating exchange rate period is related to the similar change in the behavior of oil prices. Perhaps further work will tell us more.

[3]In a separate paper Kouparitsas (1997) demonstrates how variation in the price of primary commodities (fuel and non-fuel primary commodity price indices) relative to manufactures account for most of terms of trade variation in developing countries and much of it in industrialized countries. Bidarkota and Crucini (1997) show that changes in developing country's terms of trade are typically dominated by fluctuations in the world price of a single primary commodity.

Acknowledgments

We are indebted to two anonymous referees for helpful comments on an earlier version of the paper. Betty Dow at the World Bank provided generous help with oil data.

Appendix A.

A.1. *Data sources*

Quarterly macroeconomic aggregates. The quarterly macroeconomic aggregates: gross domestic product, consumption, investment, exports, imports, civilian employment are the same series used in Backus *et al.* (1995). The countries are Australia, Canada, France, Germany, Italy, Japan, the UK, the US, and Europe (an aggregate constructed by the OECD). The sample periods for the quarterly data are given in note to Table 1.

Annual macroeconomic aggregates and fuel shares of trade. The annual macroeconomic data (US GDP and Economic Community GDP) are taken from the World Bank's *World Tables: Fall 1990 Update,* which is available in machine-readable form as the *STARS database.* Annual fuel imports and exports are taken from the same source. Imports are measured on a customs basis and include freight, while exports are free on board.

Oil production data. From 1970 to 1989, the annual world production data are from Knight-Rider Commodity Research Bureau's *Commodity YearBook,* various issues. The data are found in the table entitled: "World Production of Crude Petroleum, by Specified Countries." From 1973 to 1989, the OPEC crude oil production data are from and the Energy Information Administration's *Monthly Energy Review, December 1995.* The data are found in Table 1b, "World Crude Oil Production." Data for 1970–1972 are from the same CRB Table as the world totals, but among OPEC members include only: Libya, Iran, Iraq, Kuwait, Indonesia, Saudi Arabia, and Venezuela (the Monthly Energy Review also included Gabon, Qatar, United Arab Emirate which together accounted for about 10% of OPEC production in 1973). The CRB totals are scaled up by factor 1.1 to make the series comparable across periods.

Oil price data. The annual data are nominal price data from the World Bank's *Commodity Trade and Price Trends.* The index is constructed using quantity weights for a larger number of markets than is the monthly index described below. The sample runs from 1955 to 1990. The monthly nominal oil price data were provided by Betty Dow of the World Bank. The index is a simple average of the U.S. dollar prices for crude in three major international markets: Brent, Dubai, and West Texas. The sample is monthly from 1950 to 1995. The series is converted to quarterly taking the average of the monthly index within the quarter. Both price series are converted to real terms using the quarterly U.S. CPI-U inflation index.

Appendix B.

B.1. *Estimates of the non-fuel terms of trade*

The estimates of the non-fuel terms of trade are constructed from the overall terms of trade and the shares of non-fuel exports and imports as follows. Let P_t^m be the price index for imports in the current period, consisting of both fuel and non-fuel commodities with prices and quantities: $P_t^{mf}, P_t^{mnf}, Q_t^{mf}$, and Q_t^{mnf}, respectively. We can write the current price of imports relative to a base period as:

$$
\begin{aligned}
\frac{P_t^m}{P_0^m} &= \frac{P_t^{mf} Q_t^{mf} + P_t^{mnf} Q_t^{mnf}}{P_0^{mf} Q_t^{mf} + P_0^{mnf} Q_t^{mnf}} \\
&= \frac{P_t^{mnf}}{P_0^{mnf}} \frac{1}{S_t^{mnf}} \frac{P_0^{mnf} Q_t^{mnf}}{P_0^{mf} Q_t^{mf} + P_0^{mnf} Q_t^{mnf}} \\
&= \frac{P_t^{mnf}}{P_0^{mnf}} \frac{1}{S_t^{mnf}} \cdot Q_t^m
\end{aligned}
$$

where S_t^{mnf} is the share of non-fuel imports relative to total imports (in current value terms) and Q_t^m is the ratio of the quantity of non-fuel imports to the quantity of total trade (both evaluated at base period prices). Repeating this process for the export price index and taking the ratio of the import price index to the export price index to the right-hand-side we have:

$$\frac{P_t^{mnf}}{P_t^{xnf}} = \frac{P_t^m}{P_t^x}\frac{S_t^{mnf}}{S_t^{xnf}}\frac{Q^m}{Q^x}$$

Given the data at hand, we must ignore the time variation in the physical quantity of fuel to non-fuel trade in our estimate setting $Q_t^i = Q^i$, $i = m, x$.

References

Ambler, S., Cardia, E., Zimmermann, C., 1995. Intermediate Goods and the International Business Cycle, Mimeo, Centre de Recherche sur l'Emploi et les Fluctuations Economiques, Universite du Quebec.

Atkeson, A., Kehoe, P.J., 1994. Putty-clay capital and energy. Federal Reserve Bank of Minneapolis Staff Report.

Backus, D.K., Kehoe, P.J., Kydland, F.E., 1994. Dynamics of the trade balance and the terms of trade: the J-curve? *American Economic Review* 84, 84–103.

Backus, D., Kehoe, P., Kydland, F., 1995. International business cycles: theory and evidence. In: Cooley, T.F. (Ed.), *Frontiers of Business Cycle Research.* Princeton University Press, Princeton.

Bidarkota, P., Crucini, M.J., 1997. Commodity Prices and the Terms of Trade, Ohio State University Working Paper 98–01, December.

Baxter, M., Crucini, M.J., 1995. Business cycles and the asset market structure of foreign trade. *International Economic Review* 36, 821–854.

Berndt, E.R., Wood, D.O., 1979. Engineering and econometric interpretations of energy-capital complementarity. *American Economic Review* 69(3), 342–354.

Boileau, M., 1997. Trade in Capital Goods and the Volatility of Net Exports and the Terms of Trade, Mimeo, University of Toronto.

Costello, D.M., Praschnik, J., 1993. Intermediate Goods and the Transmission of International Business Cycles, Mimeo, University of Western Ontario.

Cremer, J., Salehi-Isfahani, D., 1991. *Models of the Oil Market.* Harwood Academic Publishers, New York.

Crucini, M.J., Kahn, J., 1996. Tariffs and aggregate economic activity: lessons from the Great Depression. *Journal of Monetary Economics* 38, 427–468.

Finn, M., 1995. Variance properties of Solow's productivity residuals and their cyclical implications. *Journal of Economic Dynamics and Control* 19, 1249–1281.

Glick, R., Rogoff, K., 1995. Global versus country-specific productivity shocks and the current account. *Journal of Monetary Economics* 35, 159–192.

Hamilton, J., 1983. Oil and the macroeconomy since World War II. *Journal of Political Economy* 91, 228–248.

Hodrick, R., Prescott, E., Post-war, U.S., 1997. business cycles: an empirical investigation. *Journal of Money, Credit, and Banking* 29, 1–16.

Hogg, R.V., Tanis, E.A., 1983. *Probability and Statistical Inference.* Macmillan Publishing, New York.

Jorgensen, D.W., 1986. The great transition: energy and economic change. *The Energy Journal* 7(3), 1–13.

Kim, I., Loungani, P., 1992. The role of energy in real business cycle models. *Journal of Monetary Economics* 29, 173–189.

King, R.G., Plosser, C.I., Rebelo, S.T., 1988. Production, growth, and business cycles: I. The basic neoclassical model. *Journal of Monetary Economics* 21, 195–232.

Kouparitsas, M., 1997. North–South terms of trade: an empirical investigation, Federal Reserve Bank of Chicago, Working Paper No. 97–5, September.

Kouparitsas, M., 1995. North–South asset markets and business cycle transmission, Mimeo.

Kydland, F., Prescott, E., 1982. Time to build and aggregate fluctuations. *Econometrica* 50, 1345–1370.

Mussa, M., 1986. Nominal exchange rate regimes and the behavior of real exchange rates: evidence and implications. Carnegie-Rochester Conference Series on Public Policy 25, 117–214.

Nordhaus, W.D., 1980. Oil and economic performance in industrialized countries. Brookings Papers on Economic Activity 2, 341–399.

Pencavel, J., 1986. Labor supply of men: a survey. In: Ashenfelter, O., Layard, R. (Eds.), *Handbook of Labor Economics.* North-Holland, Amsterdam.

Rotemberg, J.J., Woodford, M., 1996. Imperfect competition and the effects of energy price increases on economic activity. *Journal of Money, Credit, and Banking* 28, 549–577.

Sachs, J., 1981. The current account and macroeconomic adjustment in the 1970's. Brookings Papers on Economic Activity 12, 201–268.

Stockman, A.C., Tesar, L.L., 1995. Tastes and technology in a two-country model of the business cycle: explaining international comovements. *American Economic Review* 85, 168–185.

Chapter 10

Distribution Capital and the Short- and Long-Run Import Demand Elasticity*

Mario J. Crucini

Department of Economics, Vanderbilt University, Nashville, TN, USA
mario.j.crucini@vanderbilt.edu

and

J. Scott Davis

Research Department, Federal Reserve Bank of Dallas, Dallas, TX, USA
scott.davis@dal.frb.org

Abstract. The elasticity of substitution between home and foreign goods is one of the most important parameters in international economics. The international macro literature, which is primarily concerned with short-run business cycle fluctuations, assigns a low value to this parameter. The international trade literature, which is more concerned with long-run changes in trade flows following a change in relative prices, assigns a high value to this parameter. This paper constructs a model where this discrepancy between the short- and long-run elasticities is due to frictions in distribution. Goods need to be combined with a local non-traded input, distribution capital, which is good specific. Home and foreign goods may be close substitutes, but if distribution capital is slow to adjust then agents cannot shift their consumption in the short run

*This chapter originally appeared in *Journal of International Economics*, 2016, **100**, 203–219.

following a change in relative prices, and home and foreign goods appear as poor substitutes in the short run. In the long run this distribution capital can be reallocated, and agents can shift their purchases following a change in relative prices. Thus the observed substitutability gets larger as time passes.

Keywords: Distribution services; Import demand elasticity

1. Introduction

The elasticity of substitution between home and foreign goods, also called the Armington elasticity, is arguably the key parameter in dynamic equilibrium models of international trade. The Armington elasticity ties the time series variation in exports and imports to movements in the terms of trade via a static first-order condition present in many work-horse models. Trade models demonstrate the importance of this parameter in determining the impact of trade policy on trade flows and welfare. Macro models rely on this parameter to determine the business cycle effects of certain macro shocks and the general business cycle properties of international macro models.

The problem, as highlighted in Ruhl (2005) and Arkolakis *et al.* (2012) , is that the trade literature and the international macro literature do not agree on the value of this parameter. Macro models, which are concerned with short-run fluctuations, generally ascribe a low value to this parameter. Backus *et al.* (1994) assign a value of 1.5 to the Armington elasticity and discuss how the model fails to replicate the negative co-movement between the terms of trade and net exports when the elasticity is too high (above 3). In the calibration of their model, Kose and Yi (2006) use this same value. Stockman and Tesar (1995) use a Cobb-Douglas (unitary elasticity) to aggregate home and foreign goods. Heathcote and Perri (2002) estimate the Armington elasticity to be 0.9, using an equation that links changes in the real exchange rate to changes in net exports and relative production. Corsetti *et al.* (2008b) use a value close to this, 0.85. They arrive at this value by calibrating their model to match certain features of the data, most notably, second moments of the real exchange rate and the terms of trade. Enders *et al.* (2011) construct a model to specifically explain the path of the real exchange rate and the terms of trade following either a productivity or government spending shock. They find that the model calibrated with a high elasticity of substitution yields counterfactual results as to the response of the real exchange rate following a shock. Similarly, in estimations using data on relative prices and import shares, Blonigen *et al.* (1999) use quarterly data and find an average elasticity of about 0.81.

On the trade side, in their survey of the literature on trade costs, Anderson and van Wincoop (2004) report that the import demand elasticity is generally found to lie between 5 and 10. Hillberry *et al.* (2001) find long run estimates of the elasticity between 4 and 8. Hertel *et al.* (2007) backs the elasticity parameter out of an estimated gravity model after estimating the elasticity of trade costs with respect to distance and finds the elasticity is about 5. In a similar fashion, Obstfeld and Rogoff (2000) find that when the elasticity of substitution is equal to 6, the observed home bias in trade can be reconciled with estimated international trade costs. Head and Reis (2001), Clausing (2001), and Romalis (2007) each estimate the elasticity using U.S.–Canadian trade data from before and after the passage of the Canada–U.S. Free Trade Agreement and find the elasticity is between 6 and 11. Eaton and Kortum (2002) estimate a parameter that can be thought of as an import demand elasticity and find a value of 8.

Hooper *et al.* (1998) and Gallaway *et al.* (2003) use a regression framework that allows them to distinguish between short- and long-run elasticities. They find that import demand elasticities are typically much larger in the long run than they are in the short run. The mechanism most often associated with these conflicting short-run and long-run responses is the notion that changes in relative prices at the wholesale level do not pass through into final consumer prices. Campa and Goldberg (2005) and many other papers document the low pass through of exchange rate changes into import prices.

This paper presents a novel mechanism to explain why exports and imports may be slow to respond to a change in relative prices, and thus why the observed import demand elasticity may be low in the short run but high in the long run. In the model, traded goods need to be combined with local distribution services before they are consumed. However, these services are allocated separately to the distribution of home and foreign goods. Specifically, labor employed in distribution is assumed to be costless to reallocate across sectors within the period, whereas distribution capital is predetermined and costly to reallocate across sectors.[1] While the home and foreign goods may be viewed as highly substitutable by consumers (parameterized by a high Armington elasticity) distribution capacity creates a short-run bottleneck, the result of which is to make trade quantities appear unresponsive to trade prices in the short-run as seen in the data. In practical terms, distribution capital could be anything from port capacity, which can impose a capacity constraint on the quantity of imported goods until port capacity is expanded, to good-specific retail outlets, like a BMW dealership or a Louis-Vuitton store, which would limit retail sales of imported varieties of a good (cars or handbags) until more retail space can be built. Intuitively, the short-run decline of import prices brought on by a foreign productivity improvement is partially canceled out by the increase in the marginal cost of distribution of imports, mitigating the demand for imports in the current period. As time passes, distribution capital is reallocated across sectors and the response of trade to the changing wholesale price is greater, consistent with a higher elasticity of substitution.

So in this paper we make two contributions. First, we empirically show that there is a role for a local-non-traded input in the production of retail goods. To show this our empirical strategy is to make use of a panel of micro-price data. What we observe is the fact that when the time-series variation in micro-prices is divided into a good-specific component and a location-specific component; the local component of the price displays a lot of volatility and persistence and is only imperfectly correlated across sectors. This is consistent with the notion that the pass-through of wholesale price changes

[1]In the U.S. input-output tables, labor's share of value added in the retail and wholesale trade and transportation sectors is about 58%.

(or cost shocks from the perspective of retailers) is both incomplete and heterogeneous across locations. The fact that retail prices do not move one-to-one with import prices is the familiar question that is the focus of the well-developed international exchange-rate passthrough literature. The asymmetries across sectors are novel here and points to frictions that impede the reallocation of distribution services across goods in the same location. While this mechanism is likely to be ubiquitous, it is quite compelling in terms of home versus foreign (imported) goods.

In our second contribution, we take what we learn about the retail goods production technology and incorporate this into the workhorse international real business cycle model in Backus *et al.* (1994). We build on Corsetti *et al.* (2008b) who develop a two-country general equilibrium business cycle model with a distribution sector. They show that this modification, along with incomplete markets leads to significant improvements in the ability of real business cycle models to account for a number of existing international finance puzzles. In their formulation, as well as in Burstein *et al.* (2003) it is assumed that the sale of a physical unit of the final good in the home market requires a fixed quantity of non-traded inputs. This assumption makes the traded price index a time invariant linear combination of the wholesale price index of tradables and the price index of non-tradables.[2]

We build upon these models that incorporate a distribution sector by specifying that capital used in distribution is a specific factor which is costly to adjust across the distribution of home and foreign goods, and thus our model can help account for the cross-sector heterogeneity in the location-specific component of prices

[2]It is also important to point out similarities and differences between our model and the models of Corsetti and Dedola (2005) and Corsetti *et al.* (2008a). These models rely on market power at the level of the traded good firm, and thus the presence of a distribution sector can endogenously lead to firm pricing-to-market behavior and violations of the law of one price. We intentionally abstract from firm market power in this paper and instead focus on goods produced is highly competitive markets, so here distribution affects the final consumer price of a good, not the wholesale producer price.

that we observe in the micro-price data.[3] When the parameters of this equilibrium model are calibrated to match the volatility and co-movement of the traded and non-traded components of the micro-price data, the model predicts that the empirical elasticity of substitution between home and foreign goods is low in the short run but gets larger as time passes and these short-run frictions in the distribution sector dissipate. Moreover, because capital adjustment is endogenous, the time horizon along which the short-run and long-run elasticities are reconciled is also endogenous. Thus our contribution lies both in a substantive extension of the Corsetti *et al.* (2008b) model and in the unique microeconomic data that is used to calibrate and estimate the facets of the distribution sector that our model highlights.

A number of important contributions also attempt to reconcile the short-run and long-run elasticity of substitution across the trade and macroeconomic literature. Attention was first drawn to this issue by Ruhl (2005) who contrasts the response of trade flows to temporary productivity shocks and permanent tariff changes along with associated shift in adjustment from the intensive to the extensive margin. Ramanarayanan (2013) emphasizes the role of investment irreversibility in production and importation of intermediate inputs in generating a slow buildup in the response of quantities to permanent trade liberalization. These papers emphasize different channels and manufacturing decisions while abstracting from the distribution sector, which is our focus. Close in spirit to our model is Drozd and Nosal (2012b) who construct a search model where sales require some marketing capital. This marketing capital is sluggish, and thus quantities demanded will adjust slowly in the short run following a change in international relative prices.[4]

[3]Thus by explicitly modeling the distribution sector and short-run supply constraints in the distribution sector, this paper provides a basis for the reduced-form import adjustment cost function in Erceg *et al.* (2005) or the convex costs to adjusting the stocks of domestic and imported durable goods in Engel and Wang (2011).

[4]Similarly, demand persistence is introduced in a reduced form way into a Ricardian model of trade by Arkolakis *et al.* (2012) with consumers switching

In all of these models, short-run frictions (be they stickiness in buyer–supplier relationships or sluggishness in market share and marketing capital) are a form of short-run trade friction that prevent the quantity demanded of imports from adjusting fully in the short term following a change in international relative prices. To this list of short-run frictions this paper adds a durable and specific factor in the production of retail goods, distribution capital. The size of this short-run friction in distribution is then calibrated using micro-price data to show how this friction in distribution is indeed a type of short-run trade friction that can help to reconcile observations of a low short-run import demand elasticity with observations of a high long-run import demand elasticity.

The rest of this paper is organized as follows. The decomposition of final goods prices in our micro-price data into traded and non-traded components is presented in Section 2. From these microprices we can learn more about the retail goods production technology and the specific factors that are involved in the distribution of wholesale goods. The equilibrium international real business cycle model is presented in Section 3. In the version of the model without local non-traded inputs, the model collapses to the benchmark IRBC model in Backus *et al.* (1994). Using the information gained from the decomposition of the micro-price data, the benchmark calibration of the model is presented in Section 4. The results from the different versions of the model are presented in Section 5. First we solve analytically for the observed import demand elasticity following a change in the relative price of imports. We then compare the different versions of the model, the version with a high elasticity of substitution as measured in the international trade literature, the version with the low elasticity as measured in the international macro literature, and the version with the high elasticity of substitution but a local non-traded component that is inelastically supplied in the short run. The version of the model with the high Armington elasticity of substitution combined with distribution-specific capital

---

to the lowest price source with some probability or staying with the existing source otherwise.

is able to reconcile the seemingly contradictory calibrations of trade and business cycles models. Finally, Section 6 concludes.

2. The Distribution Sector

Much of what is known about the size of the distribution sector comes from the US National Income and Product Accounts (NIPA). Specifically, sectoral data showing the amount paid by consumers relative to the value received by manufacturers for goods sold. The difference between these two monetary values as a ratio of consumer expenditure is referred to as the distribution margin. In an accounting sense, this margin includes shipping costs associated with the movement of goods from the factory gate to the final consumer, value added in the distribution sector, and markups at each point in the vertically integrated market chain. The aggregate US distribution margin is approximately 50% (Crucini and Yilmazkuday, 2014) with only a fraction of this wedge attributable to traditional trade costs.

Whereas the steady-state properties of the distribution wedge have recently been established, little is known about their business cycle properties. This section is intended to fill this void. To accomplish this, we use a panel dataset of retail prices for over 300 goods in 123 cities where the price of each good in each city is observed annually from 1990–2005. The dataset covers over 300 items representative of what consumers regularly purchase. We exclude pure labor services (e.g., domestic cleaning help) and aggregate the items into six sectors: food, clothing, property and rents, transportation, utilities and other consumer goods. The full list of goods in the dataset and how they are grouped into six categories is presented in the appendix. Because our model abstracts from nominal rigidities and nominal exchange rate fluctuations, we restrict our empirical work to 13 U.S. cities, the list of these 13 cities is also presented in the appendix.

In this decomposition of the micro-price data, we allow there to be three components of the final good price: a good-specific component, μ_{it}, a location-specific component, μ_{jt}, and a location and good specific component, μ_{ijt}. In the data set we observe $\tilde{p}_{ijt}$, the retail price of the good from sector i in city j at time t. Crucini and Yilmazkuday (2014) estimate the distribution margin for each good in the EIU dataset and the sectoral distribution shares used here, s_i, are averages of their good-level estimates within each of our six sectors.[5] Given these prices and the distribution margins the following regression is estimated:

$$\tilde{p}_{ijt} = (1 - s_i)\mu_{it} + s_i\mu_{jt} + s_i\mu_{ijt} \tag{1}$$

and further, we can calculate the total distribution cost, $\hat{c}_{ijt} = \frac{\tilde{p}_{ijt}-(1-s_i)\mu_{it}}{s_i}$.

We begin with a variance decomposition of the retail price into the contributions of the wholesale price, wage margin and rental margin (and the sum of the latter two, the distribution margin). The variance decomposition uses the covariances between the retail price and the estimated fixed effects components to avoid arbitrary assignment of covariances among the components.[6] Table 1 reports the variance decomposition of the prices in each sector into that caused by time-series fluctuations in the sector-specific price component ($(1-s_i)\mu_{it}$), the location-specific price component ($s_i\mu_{jt}$), and the sector and location specific component ($s_i\mu_{ijt}$). The table

Table 1. Variance decompositions of the final goods prices in six sectors.

		Total variance	Good-specific	City-specific	Idiosyncratic
Sector	$1 - s_i$	$\tilde{p}_{ijt}$	$(1 - s_i)\mu_{it}$	$s_i\mu_{jt}$	$s_i\mu_{ijt}$
Food	0.62	0.10	1.28	−0.16	−0.12
Other	0.49	0.09	0.54	−0.09	0.56
Transportation	0.48	0.09	0.16	0.18	0.65
Clothing	0.48	0.15	0.26	0.15	0.59
Utilities	0.19	0.27	0.10	0.28	0.61
Property	0.07	0.31	—	−0.08	1.08
Average	0.39	0.17	0.39	0.05	0.56

[5]The distribution margins, s_i, are good specific, but common across all locations and constant time.

[6]The variance decomposition method follows Crucini and Landry (2012).

also reports the number of micro-prices used in the aggregation to the consumption category level and the simple average share of traded goods in value (s_i is the distribution share). The categories are ordered from those with the lowest distribution share (food at 0.38) to the highest (property at 0.93).

The most obvious feature of the decomposition is that most of the business cycle movements in retail prices are accounted for by the idiosyncratic component, which in the model is the sector and location-specific distribution cost. The next most dominant contribution is the good-specific component. The city-specific component common to all goods is not inconsequential, but is relatively minor quantitatively. Next we will turn to see how the workhorse international real business cycle model can be modified to reflect the fact that in the micro-price data, such a large component of the fluctuations in the price of a good seems to be driven by this location-specific component (distribution) and a large share of this distribution component of the price seems to be sector-specific (distribution capital).

3. The Model

There are two countries, home and foreign. Foreign variables are written with an asterisk (*) and home variables are not. In the following description of the model, foreign equations are omitted for brevity.

3.1. *Firms*

For the purposes of exposition, it is useful to think of each country as comprised of two sectors. Firms in one sector produce wholesale goods using capital and labor. Firms in the second sector distribute either home produced goods or imported goods to final consumers. These firms combine wholesale goods with distribution services.

Distribution services are produced using labor and distribution capital:

$$d_{Z,t} = A_t \left[(1 - \hat{\alpha}_d)^{\frac{1}{\eta}} (N_{dZ,t})^{\frac{\eta-1}{\eta}} + (\hat{\alpha}_d)^{\frac{1}{\eta}} (K_{dZ,t})^{\frac{\eta-1}{\eta}} \right]^{\frac{\eta}{\eta-1}}, \quad Z = D, M \tag{2}$$

where N_d and K_d are the labor and capital employed in the distribution sector, and A_t is a country specific total factor productivity parameter. Notice that this production function is the same for domestic goods, denoted with subscripts D, and imported goods, denoted with subscripts M.[7] The input demand functions for capital and labor in distribution sector Z are given by: $K_{dZ,t} = (\hat{\alpha}_d)\left(\frac{r_{Z,t}}{c_{Z,t}}\right)^{-\eta}\frac{d_{Z,t}}{A_t^{1-\eta}}$, $N_{dZ,t} = (1-\hat{\alpha}_d)\left(\frac{w_t}{c_{Z,t}}\right)^{-\eta}\frac{d_{Z,t}}{A_t^{1-\eta}}$, $Z = D, M$.

Firms in the distribution sector combine wholesale goods $(y_{Z,t})$ and distribution services $(d_{Z,t})$ to produce the retail quantity of the good, $\tilde{y}_{Z,t}$ according to a CES production function:

$$\tilde{y}_{Z,t} = \left[(Y_{Z,t})^{\frac{\gamma-1}{\gamma}} + \kappa^{\frac{1}{\gamma}}(d_{Z,t})^{\frac{\gamma-1}{\gamma}}\right]^{\frac{\gamma}{\gamma-1}}, \quad Z = D, M \tag{3}$$

where κ is the weight on distribution services, and γ is the elasticity of substitution between wholesale goods and distribution services. In the absence of distribution costs ($\kappa = 0$), $\tilde{y}_{D,t} = y_{D,t}$ and $\tilde{y}_{M,t} = y_{M,t}$, and the model collapses to Backus *et al.* (1994).

The resource constraint for the home produced good is:

$$y_{D,t} + y^*_{M,t} = A_t N_t^{1-\alpha} K_t^{\alpha} \tag{4}$$

where $y_{D,t}$ and $y^*_{M,t}$, are domestic uses of the home good and exports, respectively. N_t and K_t are labor and capital employed in the production of home country goods. From this production function, the demand for labor and capital are given by $N_t = (1-\alpha)\frac{MC_t}{w_t}(y_{D,t} + y^*_{M,t})$ and $K_t = \alpha\frac{MC_t}{r_t}(y_{D,t} + y^*_{M,t})$ where w_t is the home real wage rate (in terms of the home consumption good), r_t is the rental rate of physical capital employed in the production of home goods, and $MC_t = \frac{1}{A_t}\left(\frac{w_t}{1-\alpha}\right)^{1-\alpha}\left(\frac{r_t}{\alpha}\right)^{\alpha}$.

[7] $\hat{\alpha}_d$ is the weight on capital in the production function, if the elasticity of substitution, $\eta = 1$, $\hat{\alpha}_d$ would also be the share of distribution costs devoted to capital. When $\eta \neq 1$, the capital share is instead a function of the steady state wage and rental rate, $\alpha_d = \frac{\hat{\alpha}_d(r)^{1-\eta}}{\hat{\alpha}_d(r)^{1-\eta}+(1-\hat{\alpha}_d)(w)^{1-\eta}}$. In Section 4 where we calibrate this parameter, to gain intuition we will calibrate capital's share of distribution costs, α_d but for a given steady state wage and rental rate, there is a one-to-one relationship between the capital share, α_d, and the parameter $\hat{\alpha}_d$.

3.2. *Aggregate demand*

Following Backus *et al.* (1994), home and imported goods are combined in an Armington (1969) aggregator function with an elasticity of substitution ρ to provide households with consumption, C_t, investment in capital used in production of the home good, I_t, and investment in distribution capital, $I_{d,t}$:

$$C_t + I_t + I_{d,t} = y_t = \left[(\omega)^{\frac{1}{\rho}} (\tilde{y}_{D,t})^{\frac{\rho-1}{\rho}} + (1-\omega)^{\frac{1}{\rho}} (\tilde{y}_{M,t})^{\frac{\rho-1}{\rho}} \right]^{\frac{\rho}{\rho-1}}. \quad (5)$$

The demand for domestically produced or imported final goods as a function of aggregate expenditure is:

$$\begin{aligned} \tilde{y}_{D,t} &= \omega (\tilde{p}_{D,t})^{-\rho} y_t \\ \tilde{y}_{M,t} &= (1-\omega)\,(\tilde{p}_{M,t})^{-\rho} y_t \end{aligned} \quad (6)$$

where $\tilde{p}_{D,t}$ ($\tilde{p}_{M,t}$) is the retail price of domestic (imported) goods relative to the price of the home consumption good.

3.3. *Prices*

This section presents a number of useful analytical expressions linking firm marginal costs and market prices to price indices.

Substituting the demand functions in Eq. (6) into the aggregator function in Eq. (5) yields:

$$\left[\omega (\tilde{p}_{D,t})^{1-\rho} + (1-\omega)\,(\tilde{p}_{M,t})^{1-\rho} \right]^{\frac{1}{1-\rho}} = 1.$$

From the production function in Eq. (3), the retail prices of domestic and imported goods relative to the home aggregate price deflator are:

$$\begin{aligned} \tilde{p}_{D,t} &= \left[(p_{D,t})^{1-\gamma} + \kappa (c_{D,t})^{1-\gamma} \right]^{\frac{1}{1-\gamma}} \\ \tilde{p}_{M,t} &= \left[(p_{M,t})^{1-\gamma} + \kappa (c_{M,t})^{1-\gamma} \right]^{\frac{1}{1-\gamma}} \end{aligned} \quad (7)$$

where $p_{D,t}(p_{M,t})$ is the wholesale price of the domestic (imported) good, and $c_{D,t}(c_{M,t})$ is the cost of domestic (import) distribution services. The parameter κ and the steady state prices of the final good and of distribution services are used to compute the steady state distribution margin, $s = \kappa\left(\frac{c_D}{p_D}\right)^{1-\gamma} = \kappa\left(\frac{c_M}{p_M}\right)^{1-\gamma}$.

Wholesale goods are produced by firms engaged in perfect competition, and thus the price of a home produced good is equal to its marginal cost of production, MC_t, and the price of a foreign produced good is equal to its marginal cost of production, MC_t^*. The relative price of the domestic good in the home market is thus $p_{D,t} = MC_t$ while the relative price in the home market of the imported good is $p_{M,t} = \frac{MC_t^*}{Q_t}$, where Q_t is the real exchange rate defined as the foreign price level divided by the home price level.

From the production functions for domestic and imported distribution services, the marginal costs of distribution are given by:

$$
\begin{aligned}
c_{D,t} &= \frac{1}{A_t}\left[(1-\tilde{\alpha}_d)(w_t)^{1-\eta} + \tilde{\alpha}_d(r_{D,t})^{1-\eta}\right]^{\frac{1}{1-\eta}} \\
c_{M,t} &= \frac{1}{A_t}\left[(1-\tilde{\alpha}_d)(w_t)^{1-\eta} + \tilde{\alpha}_d(r_{M,t})^{1-\eta}\right]^{\frac{1}{1-\eta}}
\end{aligned} \tag{8}
$$

where $r_{D,t}$ is the rental rate of capital used for domestic distribution services, $r_{M,t}$ is the rental rate for capital used in import distribution.

3.4. *Capital stocks*

There are three separate types of capital in each country, capital used in production, K_t, and capital used in distribution of either domestic or imported goods, $K_{dD,t}$ and $K_{dM,t}$. Capital employed in the production of goods evolves according to the usual capital accumulation equation:

$$K_{t+1} = (1-\delta)K_t + I_t. \tag{9}$$

Distribution capital is earmarked for domestic or imported distribution services. We will consider two cases for how this capital is allocated. In the first case we assume that there is one stock of capital dedicated to distribution. This stock of distribution capital, $K_{d,t}$, evolves according to the following capital accumulation equation:

$$K_{d,t+1} = (1-\delta)K_{d,t} + \phi\left(\frac{I_{d,t}}{K_{d,t}}\right)K_{d,t} \tag{10}$$

where this distribution capital can be allocated to domestic goods distribution or imported goods distribution, $K_{d,t} = K_{dD,t} + K_{dM,t}$. The adjustment cost for distribution capital is described by the concave function $\phi(\cdot)(\phi' > 0$ and $\phi'' < 0)$.

In the second case, the two markets for distribution capital are segmented in the sense that capital cannot be reallocated between the distribution of domestic goods and the distribution of imports. The two types of distribution capital each evolve according to their own capital accumulation equation:

$$K_{dZ,t+1} = (1-\delta)K_{dZ,t} + \phi\left(\frac{I_{dZ,t}}{K_{dZ,t}}\right)K_{dZ,t}, \quad Z = D,\, M. \tag{11}$$

The total investment in distribution capital, $I_{d,t}$, is allocated to investment in domestic or imported goods distribution, $I_{d,t} = I_{dD,t} + I_{dM,t}$.

The difference between these two cases highlights the key mechanism in this paper. In the first case, where there is only one stock of distribution capital, capital can be reallocated between domestic goods distribution and imported goods distribution within the period, and thus the rental rates of these two types of capital must be equal in equilibrium $r_{D,t} = r_{M,t}$. This ensures that in equilibrium the cost of domestic goods distribution is the same as the cost of imported goods distribution, $c_{D,t} = c_{M,t}$.

This first case, where the costs of distribution are equal across goods, is very similar to the distribution sector in Corsetti *et al.* (2008b). In the second case, where the markets for the two types of distribution capital are segmented, this equality in distribution costs holds in a long-run steady state, but need not hold in the short run. Specifically, this market segmentation forms a friction in the market for distribution services, and it leads to the result that highly substitutable home and foreign goods may appear as poor substitutes in the short run. If there is a sudden shift in international relative prices that makes foreign goods cheaper at the wholesale level, the quantity demanded of imports will increase. However, if distribution capital cannot be reallocated away from domestic goods distribution to imported goods distribution, this increased quantity demanded for imports will strain the existing stock of imported goods distribution capital, leading to a bottleneck in the distribution of imported goods. The cost of imported goods distribution, $c_{M,t}$, will increase, and this will partially reverse the initial fall in the price of foreign goods at the wholesale level.

3.5. *Households*

The one representative household per country derives utility from consumption and leisure. The household in the home country maximizes expected lifetime utility given by:

$$E_0 \sum_{t=0}^{\infty} \beta_t \frac{1}{1-\sigma} \left[(1-h_t)^{\theta} (C_t)^{1-\theta} \right]^{1-\sigma} \tag{12}$$

where σ is the coefficient of relative risk aversion and $h_t = N_t + N_{dD,t} + N_{dM,t}$

International asset markets are complete and thus, households share one worldwide budget constraint:

$$\begin{aligned} C_t + I_t + I_{d,t} + Q_t \left(C_t^* + I_t^* + I_{d,t}^* \right) \\ = w_t h_t + r_t K_t + r_{D,t} K_{dD,t} + r_{M,t} K_{dM,t} \\ + Q_t \left(w_t^* h_t^* + r_t^* K_t^* + r_{D,t}^* K_{dD,t}^* + r_{M,t}^* K_{dM,t}^* \right). \end{aligned} \tag{13}$$

3.6. *Productivity*

In this real business cycle model, fluctuations in total factor productivity drive business cycle fluctuations. The A_t and A_t^* variables in Eq. (4) are exogenous country-specific shocks. Using data on gross value added, total employment, and gross fixed capital formation from the OECD's STAN database, we estimate two series of total factor productivity for the United States and the combination of Germany, France, Italy, the Netherlands, Belgium, Austria, and Finland from 1977–2007. The data is available at annual frequency, we first estimate a VAR(1) with the two series using the annual data, and then we impose symmetry and convert this annual process to a quarterly process. The resulting quarterly shock process for the model is:

$$\begin{bmatrix} A_{t+1} \\ A^*_{t+1} \end{bmatrix} = \begin{bmatrix} 0.83 & 0 \\ 0 & .083 \end{bmatrix} \begin{bmatrix} A_t \\ A^*_t \end{bmatrix} + \begin{bmatrix} \varepsilon_t \\ \varepsilon^*_t \end{bmatrix} \tag{14}$$

where $\mathrm{var}(\varepsilon_t) = \mathrm{var}(\varepsilon^*_t) = 0.12$ and $\mathrm{corr}(\varepsilon_t, \varepsilon^*_t) = 0.31$.

This shock process assumes that TFP is the same across both the production sector and the distribution sector within a country, as in the production functions in Eqs. (4) and (2). Alternatively we can assume that there is a separate TFP process for the distribution sector, and thus the A_t in Eq. (2) is replaced with A^d_t. There are now four TFP processes to estimate, so with the STAN data, instead of considering total value added, total employment, and total capital formation in order to find aggregate TFP, we can consider these same series separated into industry and service sectors. Thus using both industrial and service sector TFP for both the U.S. and Europe, we can estimate a VAR(1) with the four TFP variables, A_t, A^*_t, A^d_t, and A^{d*}_t. Again, this data is available at an annual frequency, so after estimating the annual process, imposing symmetry across countries, and converting to a quarterly process, the resulting shock process for the model is:

$$\mathbf{A}_{t+1} = \rho \mathbf{A}_t + \varepsilon_t$$

where $\mathbf{A}_t = \left[A_t \; A^*_t \; A^d_t \; A^{d*}_t \right]'$ and $E(\varepsilon_t \varepsilon'_t) = \mathbf{\Omega}$, where

$$\rho = \begin{bmatrix} 0.78 & 0.06 & 0.07 & -0.19 \\ 0.06 & 0.78 & -0.19 & 0.07 \\ 0.00 & 0.02 & 0.84 & -0.07 \\ 0.02 & 0.00 & -0.07 & 0.84 \end{bmatrix}$$

and

$$\mathbf{\Omega} = \mathbf{10}^{-1} \times \begin{bmatrix} 6.92 & 0.63 & 0.32 & 0.77 \\ 0.63 & 6.92 & 0.77 & 0.32 \\ 0.32 & 0.33 & 0.97 & 0.47 \\ 0.33 & 0.32 & 0.47 & 0.97 \end{bmatrix}.$$

4. Model Parameters

A full list of the model's parameters and their values is found in Table 2. The first six parameters: θ, the exponent on leisure in the Cobb-Douglas utility function, σ, the coefficient of relative risk aversion, α, the capital share, β, the discount factor, ω, the weight on domestic goods in the Armington aggregator function, and δ, the capital depreciation rate, are all taken from Backus *et al.* (1994) and found throughout the international real business cycle literature.

4.1. *Distribution sector parameters*

The last four parameters in Table 2, γ, α_d, η, and χ are the key parameters in distribution.[8] To identify these parameters, second moments of the good-specific, location-specific, and good and location-specific components of the final goods estimated in the second section are used in a moment matching exercise.

Table 2. Parameter values.

Symbol	Value	Description
θ	0.66	Weight on leisure in the household's utility function
σ	2	Coefficient of relative risk aversion
α	0.36	Capital share in the production of traded goods
β	0.99	Discount factor
ω	0.85	Exogenous preference for home goods
δ	0.025	Capital depreciation rate
γ	.0001	Elasticity of substitution between wholesale goods and distribution services
α_d	0.58	Capital share in distribution costs
η	0.32	Elasticity of substitution between capital and labor in distribution
χ	0.125	Capital adjustment cost parameter for capital used in distribution

[8] χ describes the capital adjustment cost for capital used in distribution. Specifically $\chi = \frac{\phi''\left(\frac{I_{dD,t}}{K_{dD,t}}\right)}{\phi'\left(\frac{I_{dD,t}}{K_{dD,t}}\right)} \frac{I_{dD,t}}{K_{dD,t}} = \frac{\phi''\left(\frac{I_{dM,t}}{K_{dM,t}}\right)}{\phi'\left(\frac{I_{dM,t}}{K_{dM,t}}\right)} \frac{I_{dM,t}}{K_{dM,t}}$.

Table 3. Volatility, persistence, and co-movement of the traded and non-traded price components in the micro-price data.

St. Dev.	μ_{jt}	0.12
St. Dev. relative	μ_{it}	0.69
to μ_{jt}	c_{ijt}	0.65
Autocorrelation	μ_{jt}	0.66
	μ_{it}	0.45
	c_{ijt}	0.45
Correlation	μ_{it}, μ_{jt}	−0.27
	c_{ijt}, μ_{jt}	0.34
	μ_{it}, c_{ijt}	−0.44

First calculate the variance, persistence, and the co-movement of each one of the components of the retail price which were identified in the second section. These statistics are presented in Table 3.[9] From the micro-price data we estimate six series of the sector-specific price component (μ_{it}), thirteen series of the location-specific price component (μ_{jt}) and 78 series of the sector and location specific component ($\hat{c}_{ijt}$). A simple average of the individual moments from each one of these series is reported in Table 3.

Within the model we linearize our retail price index (7) and the marginal cost of distribution (8), then fluctuations in the price of the final good, $\tilde{p}_{ijt}$, may be expressed as a combination of the fluctuations in the wholesale price, $\tilde{p}_{it}$, the wage rate (non-sector specific input into distribution in location j), $\hat{w}_{jt}$, and the rental rate for sector-specific distribution capital in the same location, $\hat{r}_{ijt}$:

$$\tilde{p}_{ijt} = (1 - s_i)\tilde{p}_{it} + s_i(1 - \alpha_d)\hat{w}_{jt} + s_i\alpha_d\hat{r}_{ijt}.$$

[9]Since the price data, $\tilde{p}_{ijt}$, is nominal, the first step is to remove the nominal trend. This can be done in a number of different ways, like removing the U.S. CPI, or using a time dummy. There are also non-stationary shifts in relative prices that may complicate any attempt to measure short-run fluctuations of micro-price data. We test the robustness of our estimates of the moments of μ_{it}, μ_{jt} and $\hat{c}_{ijt}$ to different detrending methods. The details and the results from those robustness tests are presented in the appendix.

The model described in the previous section is solved with a linear approximation and simulated in order to produce moments and impulse responses of key variables. A moment matching exercise is employed to find the combination of γ, α_d, η and χ that minimizes the squared distance between the moments presented in Table 3 and the corresponding moments from simulations of the model. This requires simulating the model over a four-dimensional grid. The combination of the four parameters that minimize the square deviation from the estimated moments are listed in the bottom four rows of Table 2. The EIU data is available at a yearly frequency, so the moments are calculated from yearly data. The model is a quarterly model, but when considering the second moments of the price components $\hat{w}_t$, $\hat{p}_{it}$, and $\hat{c}_{it}$ for this moment matching exercise, we will use the simulated prices at a yearly frequency.

The optimal combination of γ, α_d, η and χ is chosen by varying all four parameters simultaneously, but to gain some intuition about the separate role of each of these four parameters related to the distribution sector, in Table 4 we vary one of these four parameters, while holding the other three constant.

The effect of varying the elasticity of substitution between tangible goods and distribution services, γ, is shown in columns 2–6 from the top half of Table 4. The simulated method of moments exercise finds that the optimal value of $\gamma \approx 0$, implying that tangible goods and distribution services are perfect compliments. The table reports the effect of increasing γ while holding all other parameters constant. As γ increases, there is very little change in either the volatility or the persistence of the wage rate, $\hat{w}_t$. However, the relative volatility of both the wholesale price and distribution cost fall as γ increases. In the data, both wholesale prices, $\hat{p}_i$, and distribution costs, $\hat{c}_i$, are about two-thirds as volatile as the wage rate. When wholesale goods and distribution services are perfect compliments, the model is able to replicate these relative volatilities. As γ increases and the two become more substitutable, these relative volatilities fall, when $\gamma = 0.8$, the price of wholesale goods and the cost of distribution are both about a third as volatile as the wage

Table 4. Calibrating the value of the parameters used in distribution.

			γ					α_d				
		Data	0.00	0.2	0.40	0.60	0.80	1.00	0.79	0.58	0.37	0.16
St. Dev.	$\hat{w}_t$	0.12	0.56	0.57	0.58	0.59	0.59	0.59	0.56	0.56	0.58	0.62
St. Dev. relative	$\hat{p}_{it}$	0.69	0.68	0.56	0.49	0.43	0.39	1.05	0.88	0.68	0.50	0.39
to $\hat{w}_t$	$\hat{c}_{it}$	0.65	0.63	0.51	0.43	0.37	0.33	1.04	0.85	0.63	0.42	0.27
Autocorrelation	$\hat{w}_t$	0.66	0.85	0.83	0.82	0.82	0.81	0.97	0.92	0.85	0.78	0.70
	$\hat{p}_{it}$	0.45	0.48	0.52	0.55	0.58	0.60	0.45	0.45	0.48	0.59	0.86
	$\hat{c}_{it}$	0.45	0.46	0.50	0.54	0.57	0.59	0.45	0.44	0.46	0.54	0.84
Correlation	$\hat{p}_{it}, \hat{w}_t$	−0.27	−0.33	−0.35	−0.35	−0.35	−0.34	0.18	−0.07	−0.33	−0.62	−0.67
	$\hat{c}_{it}, \hat{w}_t$	0.34	0.30	0.30	0.30	0.29	0.28	−0.19	0.04	0.30	0.60	0.72
	$\hat{p}_{it}, \hat{c}_{it}$	−0.44	−0.99	−0.98	−0.98	−0.98	−0.97	−0.99	−0.99	−0.99	−0.97	−0.94
			η					χ				
		Data	0.16	0.24	0.32	0.40	0.48	0.00	0.06	0.125	0.19	0.25
St. Dev.	$\hat{w}_t$	0.12	0.55	0.55	0.56	0.57	0.57	0.61	0.58	0.56	0.55	0.54
St. Dev. relative	$\hat{p}_{it}$	0.69	0.81	0.74	0.68	0.64	0.60	0.43	0.61	0.68	0.73	0.77
to $\hat{w}_t$	$\hat{c}_{it}$	0.65	0.77	0.70	0.63	0.58	0.54	0.37	0.56	0.63	0.68	0.72
Autocorrelation	$\hat{w}_t$	0.66	0.89	0.87	0.85	0.83	0.82	0.85	0.86	0.85	0.84	0.83
	$\hat{p}_{it}$	0.45	0.42	0.45	0.48	0.50	0.53	0.27	0.40	0.48	0.52	0.55
	$\hat{c}_{it}$	0.45	0.40	0.43	0.46	0.48	0.51	0.19	0.37	0.46	0.51	0.54
Correlation	$\hat{p}_{it}, \hat{w}_t$	−0.27	−0.26	−0.30	−0.33	−0.36	−0.38	0.06	−0.23	−0.33	−0.40	−0.44
	$\hat{c}_{it}, \hat{w}_t$	0.34	0.23	0.27	0.30	0.32	0.34	−0.14	0.18	0.30	0.37	0.42
	$\hat{p}_{it}, \hat{c}_{it}$	−0.44	−0.99	−0.99	−0.99	−0.99	−0.98	−0.92	−0.98	−0.99	−0.99	−0.99

rate. Hence, γ must be small, implying that wholesale goods and distribution services are compliments, to replicate the volatility of price components that we see in the data. Our estimates of a perfect complementarity between wholesale goods and distribution services largely validates the calibration by Burstein *et al.* (2003, 2007), and Corsetti *et al.* (2008b).

In columns 7–11 of the top half of the table we vary α_d, the capital share in the production of distribution services from 0.16 to 1. Again we see that varying α_d has little effect on the volatility of the wage rate. Allowing the capital share to decrease reduces the relative volatilities of the wholesale price and the distribution costs. The major effect of decreasing α_d is in the co-movement between the wage rate and wholesale prices or between the wage rate and distribution costs. In the data, the correlation between the wage rate and the cost of distribution is about 0.34. When α_d is high, and thus there is very little labor used in distribution, the model predicts that the comovement between the two should be negative. As α_d decreases and thus there is more labor used in distribution, the correlation between the two will increase. However, as α_d gets too small, the correlation between the two gets too large, so to replicate the positive but modest correlation between the wage rate and the cost of distribution, α_d should be about 0.58.

Similarly, in the data, the correlation between the wage rate and wholesale priccs is about -0.27. In the model, when α_d is large, the two are positively correlated, but as α_d decreases, this correlation falls, but again, to replicate the negative, but modest, correlation, α_d should be about 0.58.

In columns 2–6 of the bottom half of the table we vary η, the elasticity of substitution between capital and labor in the production of distribution services. Again we see that allowing η to vary has little effect on the volatility or the persistence of the wage rate. However, as η increases capital and labor in distribution become more substitutable, and the relative volatilities of both the distribution cost and the wholesale price falls. When η is small, and capital and labor in distribution are nearly perfect compliments, both distribution costs and the wholesale prices should be about as volatile as the wage rate. When η is higher and capital and labor are closer substitutes, these two prices are about half as volatile as the wage rate, in order to match the relative volatilities that we observe in the data, η should be about 0.32.

Finally, columns 7–11 in the bottom half of the table present the results from simulations of the model where χ, the distribution capital adjustment cost parameter varies. Again, allowing χ to vary has little effect on the volatility or the persistence of the wage rate. Note that in contrast to the other three cases in Table 4, only when we vary χ do we see any significant effect on persistence. In the data, both the distribution cost and the wholesale price have a first-order autocorrelation coefficient of about 0.45. When $\chi = 0$, implying that there are no costs to adjusting the stocks of distribution capital, the persistence of these two variables is counterfactually low. Similarly, when χ is low, the relative volatilities of the two prices is too low, the correlation between the wage rate and the cost of distribution is too low, and the correlation between the wage rate and wholesale prices is too high. In order to replicate the moments we observe in the data, the model needs a modest investment adjustment cost parameter of 0.125.

The four distribution parameters are calibrated to ensure that simulations of the model produce the moments of the price components, $\hat{w}_t$, $\hat{p}_{it}$, and $\hat{c}_{it}$, presented in Table 3. These model simulations are carried out under the estimated productivity shock process described in Section 3. If instead of using the estimated shock process we were to assume a more persistent shock process then the optimal calibrated parameters would change.

The results from this exercise are presented in the online appendix. As the assumed shock persistence increases the calibrated value of the capital adjustment cost parameter, χ_d, increases. The reason for this is simple. This is because as the shock persistence rises, so do the gains from expanding distribution capacity and thus distributors are more willing to pay the adjustment cost. In order to enable simulations of the model to match certain properties of the micro-price data, namely the volatility of the distribution margin, the capital adjustment cost parameter must increase as assumed shock persistence increases. As is shown in the online appendix, when the model is re-simulated with the more persistent shock process and the new optimal value of the capital adjustment cost parameter, the key results do not change.

Of course, in this calibration exercise, the selected parameter values depend on the particular model and shock process. The microprice data includes prices for hundreds of goods over 13 locations. Each of these good-location observations is potentially subject to its own idiosyncratic fluctuations, arising from everything from demand or taste shocks to measurement error. This data is then used to calibrate a model with two locations and two shocks that conforms to the standard workhorse international real business cycle model. We do acknowledge that the mapping between observed micro-prices and a stylized model of the business cycle is imperfect. Combining these hundreds of goods into six broad sectors eliminates a lot of this idiosyncratic variation.

Since direct observations of the distribution margin are for the most part unavailable, one needs to rely on an indirect empirical strategy. Our empirical justification for distribution capital is based on the observation that the law-of-one-price does not hold at the retail level: there is both a good and a location specific component to prices of traded goods, and the local component displays a lot of volatility and persistence while being imperfectly correlated across sectors. The only way to justify these facts in a model with perfect competition and the free movement of goods is to introduce a location and sector specific component to the retail goods production technology.

Relaxing the assumption of perfect competition and the free movement of goods segments markets there are mechanisms (including markup variation across markets) through which idiosyncratic demand or taste shocks could explain the same observations. In defense of our assumption, the goods in this micro-price dataset are disproportionately grocery items and the locations are exclusively U.S. cities. Thus, our sample is drawn from a sub-set of the consumption basket that is more likely to be characterized by our maintained assumption of perfect competition and the free movement of goods. There are, of course, many other items in the consumption basket that fail to satisfy these stylized assumptions, such as medical services, non-generic drugs and other trade-marked goods. Models featuring marketing capital, imperfect competition and search, such as in Drozd and Nosal (2012) offer insights into sources of price dispersion in these sectors of the economy, which would be further amplified for cross-border city pairs as emphasized in the voluminous pricing-to-market literature.

Under these assumptions, our results confirm the findings and assumptions in other papers that highlight the role of distribution, like the complementarity between wholesale goods and distribution services in Burstein *et al.* (2003, 2007), and Corsetti *et al.* (2008b). In addition to this, however, our model provides a potential explanation for the elasticity puzzle at the intersection of the international trade and international macro literatures. The fact that the workhorse international real business cycle model, when calibrated to reflect that the law-of-one-price does not hold at the retail level, can explain this puzzle is evidence in favor of the fact that there is a location and sector specific component to distribution capital.

5. Results

5.1. *Distribution costs and the observed elasticity of substitution*

The elasticity of substitution between home and foreign goods is defined as the percentage change in relative quantities divided by the percentage change in relative prices:

$$\varepsilon_t = \frac{d\ln\left(\frac{y_{M,t}}{y_{D,t}}\right)}{d\ln\left(\frac{p_{D,t}}{p_{M,t}}\right)}. \tag{15}$$

To find this elasticity in terms of the model's structural parameters, consider the demand functions in Eq. (6) and find an expression for

$\ln\left(\frac{\tilde{y}_{M,t}}{\tilde{y}_{D,t}}\right)$[10]:

$$\ln\left(\frac{\tilde{y}_{M,t}}{\tilde{y}_{D,t}}\right) = \ln\left(\frac{1-\omega}{\omega}\right) - \rho \ln\left(\frac{\tilde{p}_{M,t}}{\tilde{p}_{D,t}}\right).$$

If $\tilde{p}_{D,t} = p_{D,t}$ and $\tilde{p}_{M,t} = p_{M,t}$, then the elasticity, ε_t equals the structural parameter ρ. If however, the price of imports relative to domestic goods at the wholesale level varies over time relative to that at the retail level, then the elasticity ε_t becomes a function of other parameters in the model, and in general is time varying.

To see this, expand the elasticity expression in Eq. (15):

$$\varepsilon_t = \frac{d\ln\left(\frac{\tilde{y}_{M,t}}{\tilde{y}_{D,t}}\right)}{d\ln\left(\frac{\tilde{p}_{D,t}}{\tilde{p}_{M,t}}\right)} \frac{d\ln\left(\frac{\tilde{p}_{D,t}}{\tilde{p}_{M,t}}\right)}{d\ln\left(\frac{p_{D,t}}{p_{M,t}}\right)} = \rho \frac{d\ln\left(\frac{\tilde{p}_{D,t}}{\tilde{p}_{M,t}}\right)}{d\ln\left(\frac{p_{D,t}}{p_{M,t}}\right)}.$$

Thus the change in relative quantities following a change in wholesale prices is the Armington elasticity of substitution between home and foreign goods, ρ, multiplied by the elasticity of relative prices at the consumer level with respect to changes in relative prices at the wholesale level. Given the expressions for the final consumer prices in Eq. (7), this elasticity can be written as:

$$\frac{d\ln\left(\frac{\tilde{p}_{D,t}}{\tilde{p}_{M,t}}\right)}{d\ln\left(\frac{p_{D,t}}{p_{M,t}}\right)} \approx \frac{(1-s)\, d\ln\left(\frac{p_{D,t}}{p_{M,t}}\right) + s d\ln\left(\frac{c_{D,t}}{c_{M,t}}\right)}{d\ln\left(\frac{p_{D,t}}{p_{M,t}}\right)}$$

Thus the observed elasticity of substitution between domestic and imported goods following a change in wholesale prices is:

$$\varepsilon_t = \rho\left((1-s) + s\frac{d\ln\left(\frac{c_{D,t}}{c_{M,t}}\right)}{d\ln\left(\frac{p_{D,t}}{p_{M,t}}\right)}\right).$$

[10]The model is calibrated such that γ, the elasticity of substitution between intermediate goods and distribution services is equal to zero. As such, the ratio of imported to domestic goods inclusive of distribution inputs moves in exact proportion to actual trade flows of physical goods: $d\ln\left(\frac{\tilde{y}_{M,t}}{\tilde{y}_{D,t}}\right) = d\ln\left(\frac{y_{M,t}}{y_{D,t}}\right)$. If instead $\gamma > 0$, then the expression linking wholesale quantities and retail quantities will be more complicated, but the intuition is the same.

There are two inputs into the production of distribution services, non-sector specific labor and sector specific capital. From Eq. (8), fluctuations in the ratio of the two distribution margins, $d\ln\left(\frac{c_{D,t}}{c_{M,t}}\right)$, can be written as:

$$d\ln\left(\frac{c_{D,t}}{c_{M,t}}\right) = (1-\alpha_d)\,d\ln\left(\frac{w_t}{w_t}\right) + \alpha_d d\ln\left(\frac{r_{D,t}}{r_{M,t}}\right) = \alpha_d d\ln\left(\frac{r_{D,t}}{r_{M,t}}\right).$$

Thus the observed elasticity of substitution, ε_t, is:

$$\varepsilon_t = \rho\left((1-s) + s\alpha_d \frac{d\ln\left(\frac{r_{D,t}}{r_{M,t}}\right)}{d\ln\left(\frac{p_{D,t}}{p_{M,t}}\right)}\right). \tag{16}$$

This expression for the observed elasticity of substitution, ε_t, highlights the difference between the two cases regarding the market for distribution capital described by the capital accumulation equations in Eqs. (10) and (11). In the case with integrated markets for domestic goods and import distribution capital, capital can be reallocated between the two within the period, and the equality $r_{D,t} = r_{M,t}$ will always hold in equilibrium. Thus the expression for the observed elasticity of substitution becomes $\varepsilon_t = (1-s)\rho$ as in Corsetti *et al.* (2008b).

In the second case there are segmented markets for domestic good and import distribution capital. Following the shift in the quantity demanded of imported and domestic wholesale goods, the demand for imported goods distribution services will increase and the demand for domestic goods distribution services will fall. Labor used in the production of distribution services can be reallocated within the period, but distribution capital cannot be reallocated. Thus following a change in relative wholesale prices that leads to an increased demand for imports and a decreased demand for domestic goods, there is an excess demand for imported goods distribution capital and an excess supply of domestic goods distribution capital. This implies that the equilibrium cost of domestic goods distribution capital should fall and the cost of imported goods distribution capital should rise. Thus the following inequality holds in the short run:[11]

$$\frac{d\ln\left(\frac{r_{D,t}}{r_{M,t}}\right)}{d\ln\left(\frac{p_{D,t}}{p_{M,t}}\right)} < 0.$$

Given this excess demand in one market and the excess supply in another, agents will change their future investment plans. Investment in imported goods distribution capital will increase and investment in domestic good distribution capital will decrease.

If there are no adjustment costs in the capital accumulation equations in Eq. (11) then plans for investment in new domestic or import distribution capital are changed and the capital stocks reach their new efficient level in the next period. If there are capital adjustment costs then the adjustment may be slower and it may take multiple periods to clear out any excess demand or supply in the market for distribution services and reach a point where $r_{D,t} = r_{M,t}$.

Given this change in the relative distribution costs, in the short run $\varepsilon_t < (1 - s)\rho$, and as time passes and capital is reallocated, ε_t approaches $(1 - s)\rho$.

The path of the observed elasticity of substitution following a productivity shock is presented in Fig. 1. The figure presents the path of the observed elasticity of substitution, as measured by Eq. (15) for 40 quarters following a shock in four different cases. The solid line in the figure refers to the case where the Armington elasticity of substitution between home and foreign goods is equal to 4 and there is no distribution sector. The dashed line in the figure refers to the case the Armington elasticity is equal to 0.9 and there is no distribution sector. The dotted line refers to the case where the Armington elasticity is equal to 8 but distribution costs make up approximately 50% of the final cost of a good, and the markets for the two types of distribution capital are integrated. The line with stars refers to the case where the Armington elasticity is equal to 8

[11]Empirically, Goldberg and Campa (2010) find that following a 1% exchange rate depreciation that results in a 1% increase in the price of foreign currency denominated imports at the dock, the distribution cost of imports falls by 0.47%.

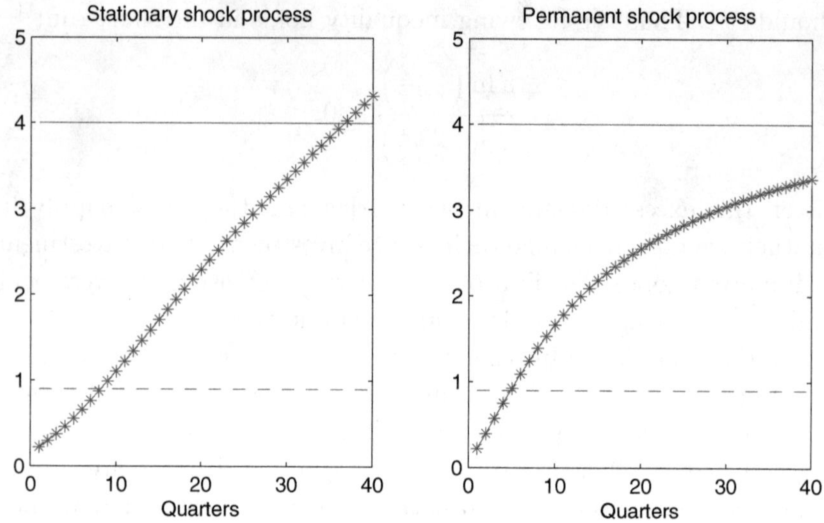

Fig. 1. Observed elasticity of substitution following a TFP shock. The solid line and the dashed line represent the model with no distribution and where the Armington elasticity is equal to 4 and 0.9, respectively. The dotted line and the line with stars represent the model where the structural elasticity is equal to 8 and there is distribution. In the dotted line distribution capital can be reallocated across sectors within the period. In the line with stars frictions prevent the reallocation of distribution inputs in the short run.

but distribution costs make up approximately 50% of the final cost of a good, and the markets for the two types of distribution capital are segmented. The figure on the left presents the observed elasticity of substitution in a model with a stationary shock process, the figure on the right presents the observed elasticity under a near-unit-root shock process.

In the two cases where there is no distribution sector the observed elasticity of substitution is simply equal to the Armington elasticity. When there is a distribution sector but the markets for distribution capital are integrated the observed elasticity is simply a constant and proportional to the Armington elasticity, $\varepsilon_t = (1 - s)\rho$. Thus given the parameter values, the dotted line lies on top of the solid line.

When the markets for the two types of distribution capital are segmented, the observed elasticity is initially close to zero since distribution capital is a state variable and cannot be instantaneously reallocated from the domestic goods sector to the imported goods sector (the reason it isn't exactly zero is that some labor can be shifted into distribution in the high demand sector, but since the elasticity of substitution between capital and labor in the distribution sector is low, the benefits of this labor reallocation are small). Agents cannot reallocate existing capital but can change investment plans subject to investment adjustment costs, so over time capital in one sector is allowed to depreciate without replacement while the stock of distribution capital increases in the other. Over time, as the stocks of distribution capital change, the observed substitutability between home and foreign goods increases.

Since the arguments in the numerator and denominator for the observed elasticity of substitution in Eq. (15) are deviations from the steady state, after a while this expression for the observed elasticity of substitution becomes nonsensical as variables return to their steady-state values in a model with stationary shocks. So while the observed elasticity definitely starts at a low value and increases with time, the elasticity is less precisely measured as the time from the initial shock increases. This is not so when shocks are nearly permanent. Here variables do not return to their steady state values, so the expression for the observed elasticity of substitution remains accurate. The figure shows that in a model with a near unit-root shock process, the observed elasticity of substitution in the model with frictions that prevent the reallocation of distribution capital begins at a low value and over time approaches its horizontal asymptote, $(1 - s)\rho$.

5.2. *Impulse responses*

The responses of home and foreign GDP and its components to a positive home TFP shock are presented in Figs. 2 and 3. Figure 2 presents the responses of home and foreign GDP and investment under the four cases mentioned earlier, where the Armington elasticity, ρ, is equal to 4 and the distribution margin is equal to 0, where the Armington elasticity is equal to 0.9 and the distribution margin is equal to 0, where the Armington elasticity is equal to 8, the distribution margin is set to 50% and there are no frictions in the

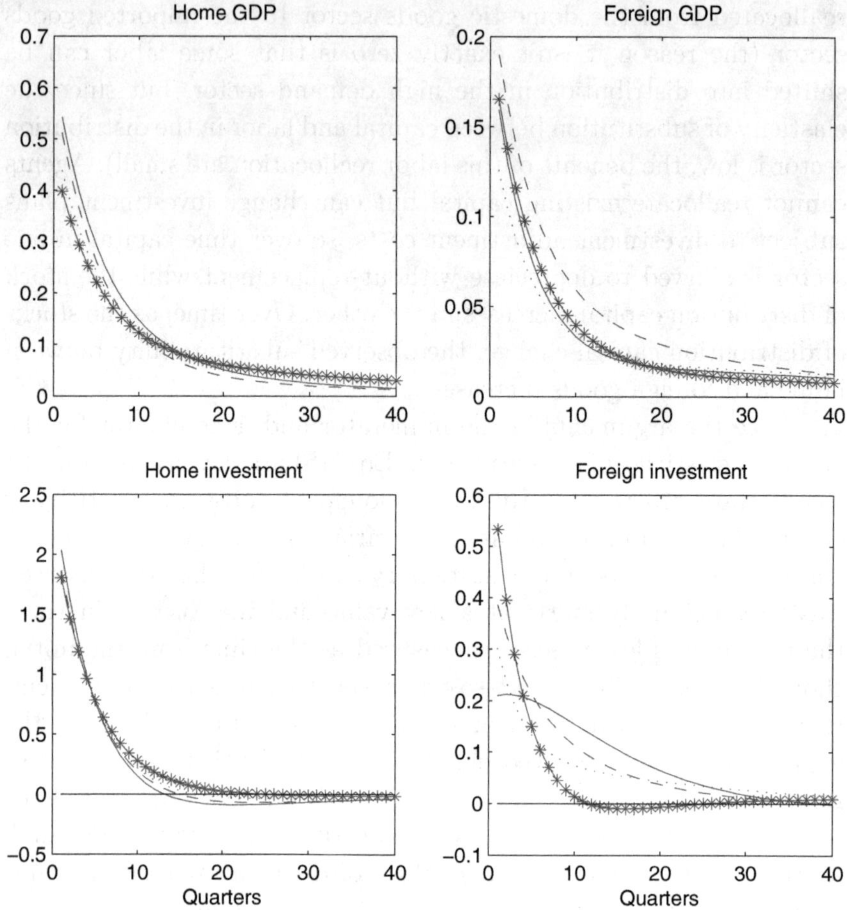

Fig. 2. The responses of home and foreign GDP and investment to a positive home TFP shock. The solid line and the dashed line represent the model with no distribution and where the Armington elasticity is equal to 4 and 0.9, respectively. The dotted line and the line with stars represent the model where the structural elasticity is equal to 8 and there is distribution. In the dotted line distribution capital can be reallocated across sectors within the period. In the line with stars frictions prevent the reallocation of distribution inputs in the short run.

market for distribution capital, and where the Armington elasticity is equal to 8, the distribution margin is set to 50% and there are frictions in the market for distribution capital. Figure 3 does the same for consumption and net exports.

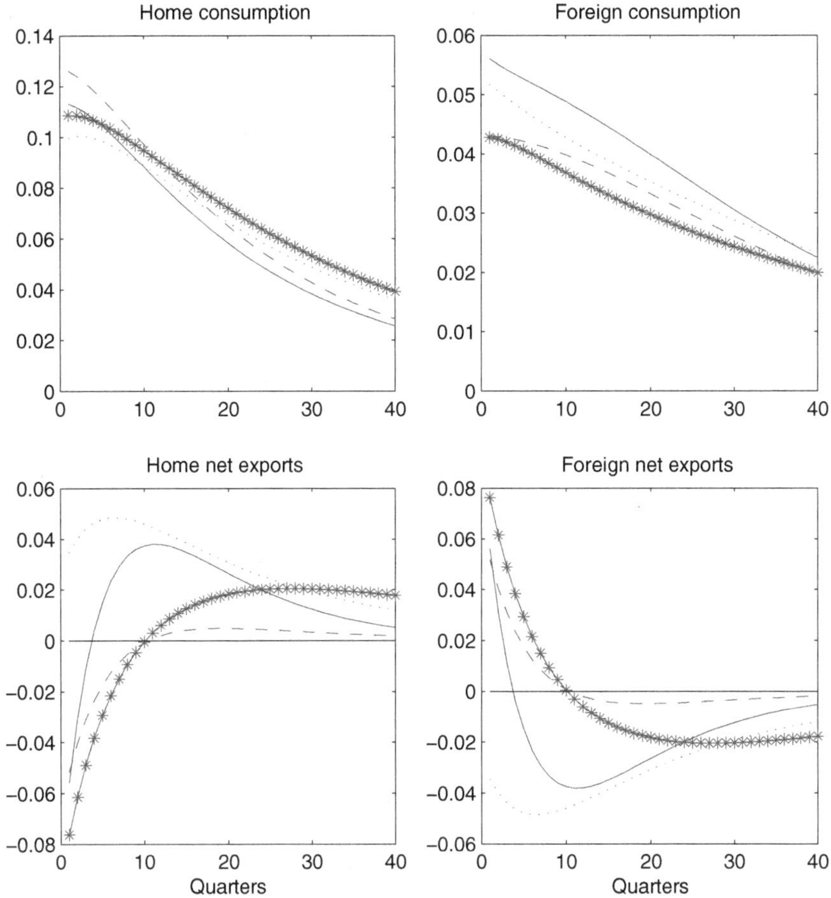

Fig. 3. The responses of home and foreign consumption and net exports to a positive home TFP shock. The solid line and the dashed line represent the model with no distribution and where the Armington elasticity is equal to 4 and 0.9, respectively. The dotted line and the line with stars represent the model where the structural elasticity is equal to 8 and there is distribution. In the dotted line distribution capital can be reallocated across sectors within the period. In the line with stars frictions prevent the reallocation of distribution inputs in the short run.

For the case where the elasticity is equal to 4 but there is no distribution sector, the figures show the familiar result for an international real business cycle model with complete international asset markets and a high degree of substitutability between home and foreign goods. Following a productivity shock in the home country, there is a sharp increase in home investment demand. The foreign country does not have the same increase in investment demand and any increase in foreign investment is tempered in order to ship goods to fuel the productivity induced investment boom in the home country. Thus in the immediate aftermath of the shock, before the benefits of the shock in terms of increased home production are felt, the home country runs a current account deficit and the foreign country runs a current account surplus.

Within a few quarters there is a reversal in the current account as the higher production leads to increased saving in the home country, some of this increased savings is shipped abroad in the form of high home current account surpluses. Thus after the first few quarters, the home country runs a large and persistent current account surplus and the foreign country runs a large and persistent deficit.

The current account dynamics change in significant ways when home and foreign goods are less substitutable. When the elasticity of substitution is equal to 0.9, the foreign goods can't as easily be used to fuel a home country investment boom, so there is more of an increase in foreign investment in the aftermath of the shock. Furthermore, once the increased home productivity leads to an increase in home production and home saving, foreign agents can't as easily consume the benefits of the productivity fueled boom in the home country and thus do not run large current account deficits when substitutability is low.

The responses from the model with a distribution sector but no frictions in distribution are very similar to the responses when the Armington elasticity is equal to 4. In both cases, home and foreign goods are highly substitutable, and the output from one country can easily be consumed in the other country, leading to a large a persistent current account surplus in the country that experiences the positive productivity shock.

The responses from the model with a distribution sector and frictions in distribution are very similar to the responses when the Armington elasticity is equal to 0.9. The observed long-run elasticity of substitution between home and foreign goods may be equal to 4, but in the short run, home and foreign goods are poor substitutes.

The figure shows that there is more of an increase in foreign investment in the immediate aftermath of the shock as foreign goods are not as easily diverted for use in the home country investment boom. Furthermore, without adequate distribution channels, foreign agents cannot as easily substitute the excess production from the home country for their own goods, so foreign agents import less and run a smaller trade deficit.

Following a shock to productivity in one country, prices and quantities need to adjust to restore equilibrium. Figures 2 and 3 show that when there is low substitutability between home and foreign goods, there is not much response to net exports following a shock, so it must be that most of the burden of adjustment falls on international relative prices.[12]

Figure 4 shows the responses of the home country terms of trade and the real exchange rate following a positive home TFP shock. When the technological elasticity of substitution is equal to 4 and there is no distribution sector there is little movement in either the terms of trade or net exports following a shock. This is also true when there is a distribution sector, but there are no frictions in distribution. When the elasticity of substitution is equal to 0.9, there is much more movement in both the terms of trade and the real exchange rate. Similarly when the Armington elasticity of substitution is equal to 8 but there are frictions in distribution there is significant movement in both the terms of trade and the real exchange rate following the shock. Thus when there are distribution costs and a distribution sector that is slow to adjust, the economy with a high elasticity of substitution acts a lot like the economy with a low elasticity of substitution, following a shock, quantity variables like exports and imports cannot adjust quickly to restore equilibrium, so the burden of adjustment falls on prices like the terms of trade and the real exchange rate.

[12]A similar argument (but one that relied on incomplete pass-through to explain the low substitutability) is given in Devereux and Engel (2002) to explain the high volatility of exchange rates that we observe in the data.

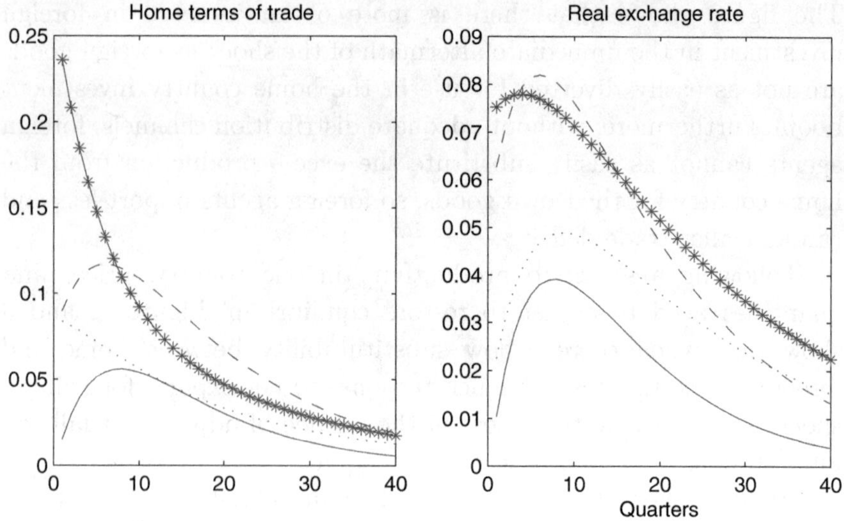

Fig. 4. The response of the home country terms of trade and the real exchange rate to a positive home TFP shock. The solid line and the dashed line represent the model with no distribution and where the Armington elasticity is equal to 4 and 0.9, respectively. The dotted line and the line with stars represent the model where the structural elasticity is equal to 8 and there is distribution. In the dotted line distribution capital can be reallocated across sectors within the period. In the line with stars frictions prevent the reallocation of distribution inputs in the short run.

5.3. *Volatility and co-movement of certain macro variables*

The standard deviation and co-movement of GDP, the components of GDP, and international prices like the terms of trade and the real exchange rate are listed in Table 5. The first column of the table lists these moments calculated from U.S. data. The data is quarterly from 1984 to 2007. The rest of the table presents these moments as calculated from simulations of the model.

The simulations of the model are conducted under the four alternative parameterizations that were used in the impulse response analysis. The table shows that when the Armington elasticity is equal to 4 and there is no distribution sector, simulations of the model yield too little volatility in both consumption and international prices like the terms of trade or the real exchange rate, a low crosscountry

Table 5. Volatility and co-movement of GDP and its components in the data and from simulations of the model under different elasticities of substitution and distribution costs.

			Distribution	No	No	Yes	Yes
			Elasticity	4	0.9	8	8
		Data	Frictions	N/A	N/A	No	Yes
St. Dev.	GDP	0.92		0.75	0.70	0.60	0.55
	NX	0.28		0.19	0.14	0.05	0.08
Volatility	C	0.89		0.23	0.27	0.26	0.30
relative	I	3.14		3.84	3.67	4.68	4.49
to GDP	N	0.85		0.55	0.53	0.40	0.30
	Ex	3.86		1.16	1.02	0.82	1.04
	Im	3.37		1.13	1.13	0.71	1.30
	Tot	2.14		0.16	0.40	0.35	1.02
	Q	4.14		0.11	0.28	0.16	0.37
Co-movement	C	0.84		0.91	0.92	0.89	0.92
with	I	0.91		0.96	0.98	0.98	0.98
GDP	NX	−0.41		−0.42	−0.53	0.48	−0.49
	N	0.81		0.99	0.99	0.97	0.98
	Ex	0.54		0.26	0.41	0.86	0.09
	Im	0.82		0.87	0.99	0.25	0.83
	Tot	0.29		0.27	0.41	0.59	0.50
	Q	−0.02		0.27	0.41	0.37	0.45
Cross-country	GDP	0.52		0.26	0.42	0.25	0.50
co-movement	C	0.76		0.61	0.36	0.64	0.46
	I	0.67		−0.12	0.09	−0.04	0.25
	N	0.47		0.17	0.44	−0.17	0.77
	Ex	0.63		−0.07	0.36	−0.19	−0.39
Correlation	Tot,NX	−0.13		0.34	−0.65	0.93	−0.97
	Q,NX	−0.05		0.34	−0.65	0.96	−0.81

Notes: (i) The statistics taken from the data are from quarterly U.S. data from 1984–2007. The cross-country statistics are between the U.S. and the Euro Area. (ii) All variables, both from the data and those from model simulations, are logged (except NX) and HP filtered with a smoothing parameter of 1600.

co-movement in production variables like output, investment and employment, and a high cross-country co-movement in consumption.

These features of the model were shown earlier in the impulse response analysis. Following a positive shock in one country, the country that experienced the positive shock can easily export their surplus production to the less productive country. This leads to too much consumption smoothing, and since quantities adjust so easily in order to clear markets internationally, there is not much movement in either the terms of trade or the real exchange rate. The high substitutability of home and foreign goods means that agents are willing to change the composition of their consumption basket and take advantage of productivity differentials across countries to maximize total consumption, and this results in a low cross-country correlation in production and a high cross-country correlation in consumption.

When the elasticity of substitution between home and foreign goods is 0.9, the low substitutability between home and foreign goods means that the country that experiences a positive shock cannot as easily export their surplus production to the foreign country. This implies that net exports are less volatile and consumption is more volatile. Lower substitutability means that production responsibilities cannot as easily be "shared" between countries, so cross-country output co-movement is higher and cross-country consumption co-movement is lower.

Given that home and foreign goods are not as easily substitutable, international prices like the real exchange rate and the terms of trade must move more to restore equilibrium following a shock. The relative volatilities of the terms-of-trade and the real exchange are much higher in the model with the low elasticity than in the model with the high elasticity. It should be noted that the relative volatilities are still far smaller than we observe in the data. This is a common feature of the international real business cycle model. Heathcote and Perri (2002) and Corsetti *et al.* (2008b) show that this problem of counterfactually small relative volatilities of the terms-of-trade and the real exchange rate is a feature of the international real business cycle model with complete markets. Chari *et al.* (2002) show that one needs to include sticky prices, preferences that are separable in consumption and leisure, and monetary shocks in order to replicate the relative volatilities of these two prices in a model.

In the version of the model where the Armington elasticity of substitution between home and foreign goods is equal to 8, there is a distribution sector, and there exists one integrated market for both domestic and import distribution capital, the volatility and co-movement from simulations of the model are very close to the moments predicted from the model with the high Armington elasticity. There is a distribution sector in this version of the model, but since distribution capital can be reallocated within the period, there are no frictions to limit the substitutability of home and foreign goods in the short run.

In the version of the model where the Armington elasticity of substitution between home and foreign goods is equal to 8, there is a distribution sector, and there are frictions in distribution due to the segmented markets for domestic and import distribution capital, the volatility and co-movement from simulations of the model are very close to the moments from the model with the low Armington elasticity. Even though the Armington elasticity is high, since distribution channels cannot be adjusted quickly following a shock, at short horizons home and foreign goods are much less substitutable. As a result, net exports are not very volatile, and the model can replicate the high volatility of the real exchange rate and the terms of trade even when the observed long-run elasticity of substitution between home and foreign goods is equal to 4 ($\varepsilon = \rho(1 - s)$). Since home and foreign goods are poor substitutes in the short run, there is less consumption smoothing, lower cross-country consumption correlation, and higher cross-country correlation in output, investment and employment.

As shown by Kehoe and Ruhl (2008), a discrepancy can arise between the definition of real *GDP* in the model and that in the data due to the fact that when calculating real *GDP* in the model, the quantity of imports is multiplied by the terms-of-trade. Kehoe and Ruhl (2008) show how large movements in the terms of trade can thus lead to a change in real *GDP* even though there was no actual change in real activity. Thus when exports and imports are measured with current prices, there is the possibility that changes in the moments of *GDP* and net exports are not due to an actual change in quantities but are simply due to movements in the terms of trade. Measuring exports and imports with constant prices removes this possibility. The results from these simulations are presented in the online appendix. There is no change in this paper's main results.

5.3.1. *The S-curve*

As discussed in Backus *et al.* (1994), the contemporaneous correlation between international relative prices like the terms of trade or the real exchange rate and net exports is low and maybe even negative, and the last two rows of Table 5 show that the correlation between the terms of trade and net exports or between the real exchange rate and net exports is negative in the United States. Furthermore, the table shows that simulations of the model where the Armington elasticity is equal to 4 yields a high contemporaneous correlation between relative prices and net exports. In the model, when there is a depreciation in the real exchange rate or the terms of trade that makes home goods relatively less expensive than goods produced abroad, there is an instantaneous improvement in the trade balance.

The table shows that when home and foreign goods are less substitutable, the contemporaneous correlation between relative prices and net exports falls. The model with a low substitutability between home and foreign goods predicts that the contemporaneous correlation between the terms of trade and net exports is about -0.36.

The version of the model with a distribution sector but no frictions in distribution also leads to a very high correlation between these international relative prices and net exports, reflecting the high elasticity of substitution between home and foreign goods. On the other hand, the model with frictions in distribution can replicate negative correlation between the real exchange rate and net exports. In this model, even though the Armington elasticity is high, frictions in the distribution sector ensure that home and foreign goods are poor substitutes in the short run.

Backus *et al.* (1994) go on to describe the S-curve. The fact that the correlation between the terms of trade at time t and net exports at time $t + n$ looks like a horizontal letter S as n goes from some negative integer to some positive integer. Most importantly, the S-curve shows the fact that the contemporaneous correlation between net exports and international relative prices is negative, but the correlation between relative prices today and net exports at time $t + n$ is positive for some positive n, implying that the immediate impact of an exchange rate depreciation may be a fall in the trade balance, but a depreciation eventually leads to an increase in net exports.

This S-like relationship between relative prices like the real exchange rate or the terms of trade and lags or leads of net exports is presented in Fig. 5. The figure shows the correlation between relative prices at time t and net exports at time $t+n$ as observed in the data for the United States and the Euro Area, and as predicted by the four versions of the model.

As observed from the S-curves in the data, the correlation between relative prices at time t and net exports at time $t + n$ is increasing as n increases. Thus there is a negative contemporaneous correlation between either the terms of trade or the real exchange rate and the current value of net exports, but this correlation increases for future values of net exports. When the Armington elasticity is equal to 4 and there is no distribution sector, or when there is a distribution sector but no frictions in distribution, the model cannot replicate this finding. Counterfactually the model finds that the correlation between relative prices at time t and net exports at time $t + n$ falls as n increases.

However, when the short-run substitutability of home and foreign goods is low, either because the Armington elasticity is low or because frictions in the distribution sector hamper substitutability in the short run, the model can replicate the fact that the correlation between relative prices at time t and net exports at time $t+n$ starts at an initially low level and increases as n increases.

5.3.2. *Permanent shocks*

The results presented in Table 5 are found from simulations of the model under the calibrated shock process in Eq. (14). The results under this stationary shock process show that the fact that distribution capital used to distribute domestic goods cannot be reallocated to the distribution of imported goods creates a friction

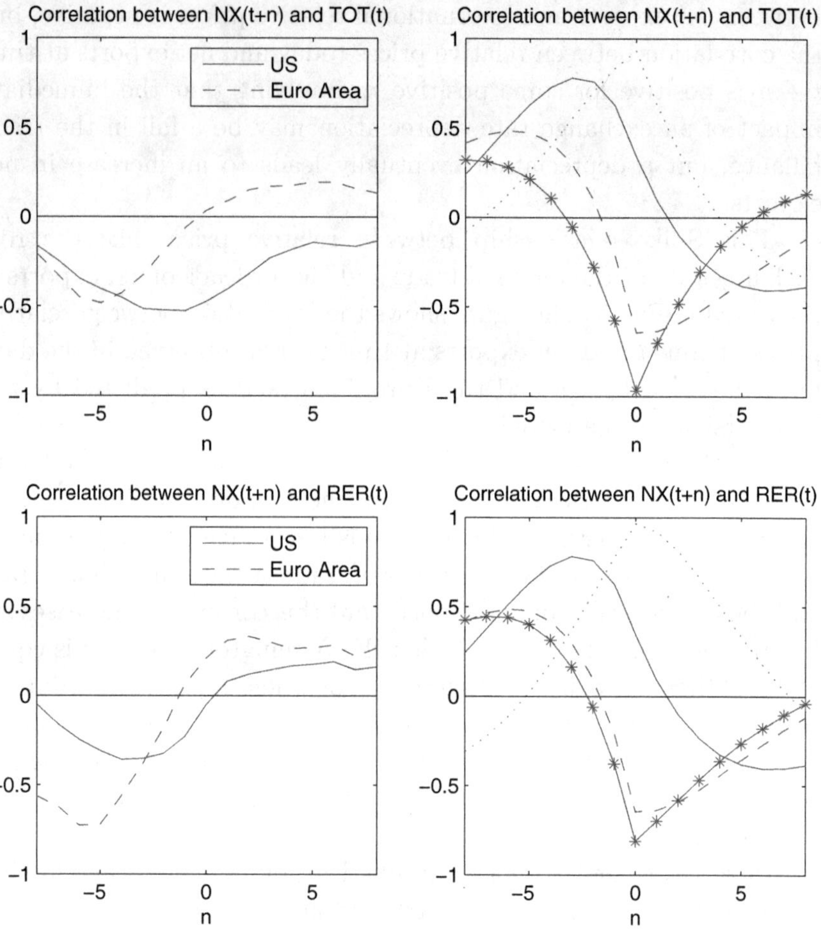

Fig. 5. The correlation between relative prices and lagged values of net exports. The solid line and the dashed line represent the model with no distribution and where the Armington elasticity is equal to 4 and 0.9, respectively. The dotted line and the line with stars represent the model where the structural elasticity is equal to 8 and there is distribution. In the dotted line distribution capital can be reallocated across sectors within the period. In the line with stars frictions prevent the reallocation of distribution inputs in the short run.

whereby highly substitutable home and foreign goods are actually poor substitutes in the short run.

Rabanal *et al.* (2011) show that the shock process driving shocks in the U.S. and the rest of the world is well captured by a vector error correction model, implying that shocks driving U.S. and rest of the world business cycles may have a unit-root component. We re-run this exercise using a near unit-root shock process. Specifically we calibrate the model such that the transition matrix in Eq. (14) is a 2×2 diagonal matrix with diagonal elements 0.999.

The simulated moments from this calibration of the model are presented in Table 6. The table shows that just as before, the model with a distribution sector where frictions prevent the reallocation of

Table 6. Volatility and co-movement of GDP from simulations of the model under different elasticities of substitution and distribution costs and a near permanent shock process.

		Distribution	No	No	Yes	Yes
		Elasticity	4	0.9	8	8
		Frictions	N/A	N/A	No	Yes
St. Dev.	GDP		0.69	0.55	0.58	0.52
	NX		0.22	0.04	0.06	0.10
Volatility	C		0.49	0.67	0.64	0.75
relative	I		3.66	2.11	3.47	2.82
to GDP	N		0.45	0.23	0.33	0.16
	Ex		1.31	0.91	1.07	1.28
	Im		1.25	1.09	0.89	1.70
	Tot		0.22	1.08	0.41	1.22
	Q		0.15	0.76	0.26	0.67
Co-movement	C		0.84	1.00	0.88	0.98
with	I		0.89	0.99	0.89	0.91
GDP	NX		−0.44	−0.45	0.57	−0.38
	N		0.91	0.98	0.79	0.72
	Ex		0.04	0.94	0.91	0.29
	Im		0.79	0.99	0.24	0.77
	Tot		0.28	0.45	0.64	0.51
	Q		0.28	0.45	0.55	0.54
Cross-country	GDP		−0.01	0.58	0.12	0.41
co-movement	C		0.88	0.59	0.88	0.74
	I		−0.72	0.35	−0.69	−0.41
	N		−0.74	0.55	−0.94	−0.64
	Ex		−0.42	0.93	−0.15	−0.25
Correlation	Tot,NX		0.48	−0.93	0.96	−0.89
	Q,NX		0.48	−0.93	1.00	−0.76

Notes: All variables are logged (except NX) and HP filtered with a smoothing parameter of 1600.

distribution capital from domestic goods distribution to imported goods distribution can be calibrated with the high elasticity of substitution from the trade literature but match the short-run business cycle moments from the international macro literature. This international real business cycle model with flexible prices and complete financial markets still cannot replicate the high volatility of these international relative prices that we observe in the data, but the model with distribution capital and frictions that slow the cross-sector reallocation of this capital leads to a significant increase in the volatility of these relative prices, bringing them more in line with the data than a model without distribution capital.

Figure 6 plots the volatility of the terms of trade as the Armington elasticity increases from 0.4 to 10 (Rabanal *et al.*, (2011) use 0.62, we use 8). We do this for 3 models, the model with no distribution sector, the model with a distribution sector but no frictions to prevent the reallocation of distribution capital in the short run and our benchmark model with a distribution sector, but with frictions preventing the reallocation of distribution capital in the short run. The figure plots the volatility of the terms of trade as a function of the Armington elasticity in each of the three models under the assumption of a near-unit-root shock process and our baseline shock persistence (autoregressive parameters of 0.999 and 0.83). Consistent with the findings of Rabanal *et al.* (2011), the volatility of the terms of trade increases rapidly as the shocks approach a unit root, but only when the Armington elasticity is very low. In particular, shock persistence has little effect on terms-of-trade volatility when the Armington elasticity is the high value measured by the trade literature.

5.3.3. *No capital adjustment costs*

In the version of the model where frictions prevent the reallocation of distribution capital from the domestic goods sector to the imported goods sector, when agents want to reallocate the stocks of distribution capital they must increase investment in one sector and decrease investment in the other sector. The capital accumulation equations in Eq. (11) assume that there is a cost to adjusting the stock of

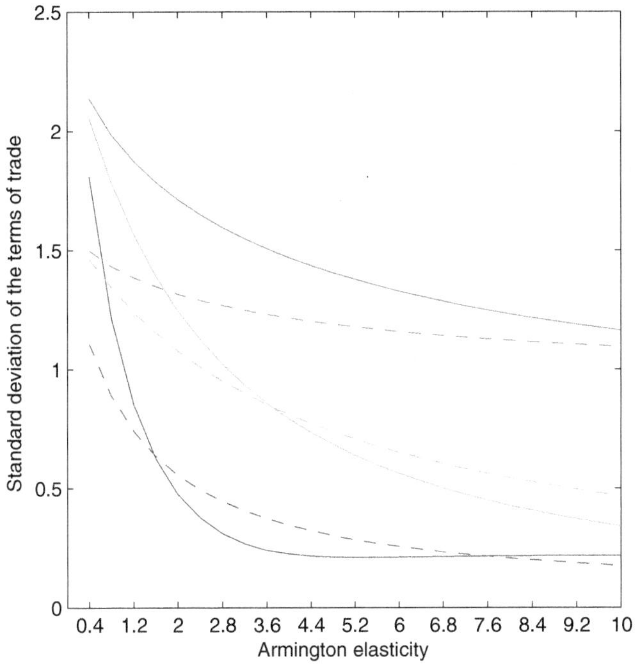

Fig. 6. The standard deviation of the terms-of-trade as a function of the Armington elasticity in each of the three models. The pair of lines at the bottom represent the model with no distribution sector. The pair of lines in the middle represent the model where this is a distribution sector, but where distribution capital can be reallocated across sectors within the period. The pair of lines at the top represent the model where there is a distribution sector, but capital cannot be reallocated across sectors within the period. In each case, the solid line represents the model under near-unit-root shocks and the dashed line represents a stationary shock process.

distribution capital, so reallocation takes multiple periods. In this way, the observed substitutability between home and foreign goods is low in the short run and with time approaches its long-run level.

If instead we assume no costs to capital adjustment, then capital used in distribution is still predetermined, but through investment complete reallocation can be achieved by the next period. In this case, the observed substitutability between home and foreign goods may be low in the period when the shock occurs, but reaches its steady-state level within one period. The volatility and co-movement of *GDP* and its components under this assumption are presented in Table 7. The results in this table show that when there are no costs to adjusting the stocks of distribution capital, the results from the model where frictions prevent the reallocation of distribution capital from domestic goods distribution to imported goods distribution look

Table 7. Volatility and co-movement of GDP and its components from simulations of the model. Simulated assuming there are no costs to adjusting the stock of distribution capital.

		Distribution	Yes	Yes
		Elasticity	8	8
		Frictions	No	Yes
St. Dev.	GDP		0.62	0.61
	NX		0.04	0.08
Volatility Relative to GDP	C		0.24	0.25
	I		6.01	6.07
	N		0.45	0.43
	Ex		0.82	1.17
	Im		0.74	1.11
	Tot		0.28	0.59
	Q		0.17	0.18
Co-movement with GDP	C		0.85	0.85
	I		0.35	0.40
	NX		0.31	−0.11
	N		0.99	0.98
	Ex		0.82	0.41
	Im		0.58	0.62
	Tot		0.56	0.41
	Q		0.31	0.34
Cross-country co-movement	GDP		0.29	0.36
	C		0.59	0.60
	I		0.27	0.31
	N		0.10	0.25
	Ex		0.35	−0.31
Correlation	Tot,NX		0.79	−0.69
	Q,NX		0.85	0.44

Notes: All variables are logged (except NX) and HP filtered with a smoothing parameter of 1600.

very similar to the results from the model where there is just one stock of distribution capital that can be reallocated across different goods. Specifically, the model predicts low volatilities of international relative prices, it results in a much higher co-movement between net exports and *GDP*, it predicts lower cross-country business cycle co-movement, and it cannot replicate the negative co-movement between international relative prices and net exports. Thus the key feature of the model with distribution capital that allows it to replicate the short-run business cycle moments while still calibrated to match the high Armington elasticity from the trade literature is the slow readjustment of stocks of domestic goods and imported goods distribution capital.

5.3.4. *Separate shocks in the production and distribution sectors*

The results presented so far have assumed that both the production and distribution sectors within a country are affected by the same country-specific TFP shock. This was done to ensure that the results from the model without the distribution sector could be easily compared with the results from the model with a distribution sector. However, as mentioned in Section 3, it may be more realistic to assume that within each country there are two shocks, a production sector shock, A_t, that affects the manufacturing sector, and a service sector shock, A_t^d, that affects the distribution sector. We use data from the OECD's STAN database to calculate country and sector specific TFP processes for both the manufacturing sector and the service sector, and the results from the estimation of this VAR(1) process with these four shocks was presented in Section 3.

The results from simulations of this model are presented in Table 8. Now the comparison between the model with no distribution sector and the model with a distribution sector is not as easy. Since the shocks to the production sector are more volatile than shocks to the services sector, it is not as clear-cut to compare a model where all of the economy is engaged in manufacturing to one where half is manufacturing and half is distribution.

Table 8. Volatility and co-movement of GDP and its components in the data and from simulations of the model under different elasticities of substitution and distribution costs. Simulated assuming separate shocks for the production and distribution sectors.

	Distribution	No	No	Yes	Yes
	Elasticity	4	0.9	8	8
	Frictions	N/A	N/A	No	Yes
St. Dev.	GDP	0.75	0.70	0.70	0.55
	NX	0.19	0.14	0.44	0.14
Volatility relative to GDP	C	0.23	0.27	0.21	0.28
	I	3.84	3.67	4.61	5.41
	N	0.55	0.53	0.57	0.77
	Ex	1.16	1.02	4.38	2.30
	Im	1.13	1.13	4.49	2.49
	Tot	0.16	0.40	1.44	4.58
	Q	0.11	0.28	0.17	0.34
Co-movement with GDP	C	0.91	0.92	0.79	0.88
	I	0.96	0.98	0.51	0.65
	NX	−0.42	−0.53	0.57	−0.09
	N	0.99	0.99	0.53	0.15
	Ex	0.26	0.41	0.53	−0.11
	Im	0.87	0.99	−0.56	0.03
	Tot	0.27	0.41	0.60	0.02
	Q	0.27	0.41	−0.25	0.26
Cross-country co-movement	GDP	0.26	0.42	0.12	0.78
	C	0.61	0.36	0.74	0.57
	I	−0.12	0.09	0.60	0.85
	N	0.17	0.44	0.10	−0.03
	Ex	−0.07	0.36	−0.82	0.02
Correlation	Tot,NX	0.34	−0.65	1.00	−0.96
	Q,NX	0.34	−0.65	−0.67	−0.77

Notes: All variables are logged (except NX) and HP filtered with a smoothing parameter of 1600.

That said, in the model with both sector- and country-specific shocks, most of the same features of the model with only country-specific shocks continue to hold. Namely the fact that in the model with a high elasticity of substitution, consumption volatility will be counterfactually low, the volatility of the terms of trade and the real exchange rate will be too low, cross-country GDP co-movement will be too low, and cross-country consumption correlation will be too high. These key failings of the model were brought on by the fact that home and foreign goods were too highly substitutable, and thus home and foreign agents could too easily smooth consumption following a county-specific shock. The model with both sector-and country-specific TFP shocks can still lead to key improvements in the ability of the model to match the data since frictions in the distribution sector still hamper the substitutability of home and foreign goods in the short run.

6. Conclusion

In the international macro literature a low elasticity of substitution between home and foreign goods is needed to explain short business cycle fluctuations, particularly movements in international relative prices such as the terms of trade and the real exchange rate. At the same time the international trade literature estimates a high value for this elasticity using data on the longer term change in trade patterns following a change in relative prices.

This paper presents a model that helps to reconcile these two apparently contradictory results. The true elasticity of substitution between home and foreign goods is high, like in the trade literature. However, in the short run there are frictions in distribution that makes home and foreign goods appear much less substitutable in the short run. The model is parameterized to produce this high long-term elasticity, but simulations of the model show that in the short run it behaves like an international macro model parameterized with a low elasticity of substitution. Specifically, the model is able to replicate the short-run volatility of the real exchange rate and the terms of trade. The model can also replicate the negative co-movement between relative prices and both GDP and net exports while still maintaining the high long-run substitutability that would satisfy the international trade literature.

In this model, frictions in the distribution of imported goods produce this time-varying elasticity. These distribution frictions can be thought of as one possible explanation for the larger phenomenon of the low pass through of changes in international relative prices into the relative prices of home and foreign goods at the consumer level. This is closely related, but not identical to the practice of firm pricing-to-market. As reviewed by Drozd and Nosal (2012a), distribution is one of a handful of explanations in the international macroeconomics literature for this pricing-to-market behavior. Pricing-to-market requires market power at the level of the wholesale good firm, and thus they can set a different price for the home and foreign markets. In this paper we have intentionally abstracted from firm market power and pricing-to-market.

By studying the behavior of consumer prices at the level of the individual good across locations, the empirical results in this paper suggest that there is a significant local non-traded component in the retail goods production technology and that there are significant frictions that make this local non-traded component sector specific in the short run. The empirical results in this paper are based on prices for goods in highly competitive markets, where prices are close to marginal costs. This allows us to highlight the retail goods production technology. An interesting direction for further research would be to then combine these insights with the literature that relies on firm market power and pricing-to-market to form a more complete picture of why changes in international relative prices may not fully pass through into the relative prices of home and foreign goods at the consumer level.

Acknowledgment

This paper was begun while Davis was a visiting researcher at the Bank of Estonia and while Crucini was a visiting Senior Fellow at the Globalization and Monetary Policy Institute, Federal Reserve Bank of Dallas. We would like to thank participants at the 2011 Midwest Macro Meetings, the 2012 meetings of the System Committee for International Economic Analysis at the Federal Reserve Bank of San Francisco, the 2013 North American Meetings of the Econometric Society, the 2013 Shanghai Macro Workshop, the 2013 meeting of the

Society for Economic Dynamics, the 2014 International Economics and Finance Society meetings in Beijing, the ICP working group, and seminar participants at UC-Davis, Dexel, and Auburn University. In addition we thank George Alessandria, Aurelijus Dabusinskas, Mick Devereux, Robert Feenstra, Jonathan Heathcote, Andre Kurmann, Finn Kydland, Sylvain Leduc, Andrea Raffo, Costas Syropoulos, Jian Wang, Lenno Uuskula and Mark Wynne for their many helpful comments and suggestions. The views in this paper are those of the authors and do not necessarily reflect the views of the Federal Reserve Bank of Dallas, the Federal Reserve System. Mario Crucini acknowledges the generous financial support of the National Science Foundation (SES #1030164).

Appendix A. Supplementary Material

Supplementary data to this article can be found online at http://dx.doi.org/10.1016/j.jinteco.2016.03.010.

References

Anderson, J.E., van Wincoop, E., 2004. Trade costs. *J. Econ. Lit.* 42 (3), 691–751.

Arkolakis, C. Samuel Kortum and Jonathan Eaton, 2011. Staggered Adjustment and Trade Dynamics, 2011 Meeting Papers 1322, Society for Economic Dynamics.

Armington, P., 1969. A Theory of Demand for Products Distinguished by Place of Production. *IMF Staff. Pap.* 16, 159–178.

Backus, D.K., Kehoe, P.J., Kydland, F.E., 1994. Dynamics of the trade balance and the terms of trade: The j-curve? *Am. Econ. Rev.* 84, 84–103.

Blonigen, B.A., Liebman, B.H., Wilson, W.W., 1999. Explaining Armington: What determines substitutability between home and foreign goods? *Can. J. Econ.* 32 (1), 1–21.

Burstein, A., Eichenbaum, M., Rebelo, S., 2007. Modeling exchange rate passthrough after large devaluations. *J. Monet. Econ.* 54 (2), 346–368.

Burstein, A., Neves, J.C., Rebelo, S., 2003. Distribution costs and real exchange rate dynamics during exchange-rate-based stabilizations. *J. Monet. Econ.* 50, 1189–1214.

Campa, J.M., Goldberg, L.S., 2005. Exchange rate pass through into import prices. *Rev. Econ. Stat.* 87 (4), 679–690.

Chari, V., Kehoe, P.J., McGrattan, E.R., 2002. Can sticky price models generate volatile and persistent real exchange rates. *Rev. Econ. Stud.* 69 (3), 533–563.

Clausing, K.A., 2001. Trade creation and trade diversion in the Canada–United States free trade agreement. *Can. J. Econ.* 34 (3), 677–696.

Corsetti, G., Dedola, L., 2005. A macroeconomic model of international price discrimination. *J. lnt. Econ.* 67, 129–155.

Corsetti, G., Dedola, L., Leduc, S., 2008. High exchange-rate volatility and low pass-through. *J. Monet. Econ.* 55 (6), 1113–1128.

Corsetti, G., Dedola, L., Leduc, S., 2008. International risk sharing and the transmission of productivity shocks. *Rev. Econ. Stud.* 75 (6), 443–473.

Crucini, M.J., Yilmazkuday, H., 2014. Understanding long-run price dispersion. *J. Monet. Econ.* 66, 226–240.

Crucini, M.J., Landry, A., 2012. Accounting for real exchange rates using micro-data. NBER Working Paper No. 17812.

Devereux, M.B., Engel, C., 2002. Exchange rate pass-through, exchange rate volatility, and exchange rate disconnect. *J. Monet. Econ.* 49, 913–940.

Drozd, L.A., Nosal,J.B., 2012. Pricing to Market in Business Cycle Models. Mimeo.

Drozd, L.A., Nosal, J.B., 2012. Understanding international prices: Customers as capital. *Am. Econ. Rev.* 102, 364–395.

Eaton, J., Kortum, S., 2002. Technology, geography, and trade. *Econometrica* 70, 1741–1779.

Enders, Z., Müller, G.J., Scholl, A., 2011. How do fiscal and technology shocks affect real exchange rates? New evidence for the United States. *J. lnt. Econ.* 83, 53–69.

Engel, C., Wang, J., 2011. International trade in durable goods: Understanding volatility, cyclicality, and elasticities. *J. lnt. Econ.* 83, 37–52.

Erceg, C.J., Guerrieri, L., Gust, C., 2005. SIGMA: A new open economy model for policy analysis. *Int. J. Cent. Bank.* 2 (1), 1–50.

Gallaway, M.P., McDaniel, C.A., Rivera, S.A., 2003. Short-run and long-run industry-level estimates of U.S. Armington elasticities. *N. Am. J. Econ. Financ.* 14, 49–68.

Goldberg, L.S., Campa, J.M., 2010. The sensitivity of the CPI to exchange rates: Distribution margins, imported inputs, and trade exposure. *Rev. Econ. Stat.* 92 (2), 392–407.

Head, K., Reis, J., 2001. Increasing returns versus national product differentiation as an explanation for the pattern of U.S.–Canada trade. *Am. Econ. Rev.* 91 (4), 858–876.

Heathcote, J., Perri, F., 2002. Financial autarky and international business cycles. *J. Monet. Econ.* 49, 601–627.

Hillberry, R., Anderson, M., Balistreri, E., Fox, A., 2001. The determinates of Armington taste parameters in CGE models, or why you love canadian vegetable oil. U.S. International Trade Commisson, Office of Economics Working Paper.

Hooper, P., Johnson, K., Marquez, J., 1998. Trade elasticities for the G-7 countries. Board of Governors International Finance Discussion Paper 609.

Hertel, Thomas, David Hummels, Maros Ivanic and Roman Keeney, 2007. How confident can we be of CGE-based assessments of Free Trade Agreements? *Econ. Model.* 24 (2007) 611–635.

Kehoe, T.J., Ruhl, K.J., 2008. Are shocks to the terms of trade shocks to productivity. *Rev. Econ. Dyn.* 11 (4), 804–819.

Kose, M.A., Yi, K.M., 2006. Can the standard international business cycle model explain the relation between trade and comovement? *J. lnt. Econ.* 68, 267–295.

Obstfeld, M., Rogoff, K., 2000. The six major puzzles in international economics: Is there a common cause? *NBER Macroecon. Annu.* 15, 339–390.

Rabanal, P., Rubia-Ramrez, J.F., Tuesta, V., 2011. Cointegrated TFP processes and international business cycles. *J. Monet. Econ.* 58, 156–171.

Ramanarayanan, Ananth, 2017. Imported Inputs, Irreversibility, and International Trade Dynamics, *J. Int. Econ.*, 104, 1–18.

Romalis, J., 2007. NAFTA's and CUSFTA's effect on international trade. *Rev. Econ. Stat.* 89 (3), 416–435.

Ruhl, K.J., February 2005. Solving the Elasticity Puzzle in lnternational Economics. Mimeo, University of Texas — Austin.

Stockman, A.C., Tesar, L.L., 1995. Tastes and technology in a two-country model of the business cycle: Explaining international comovement. *Am. Econ. Rev.* 85 (1), 168–185.

Chapter 11

Do Sticky Prices Increase Real Exchange Rate Volatility at the Sector Level?*

Mario J. Crucini

Department of Economics, Vanderbilt University, Nashville, TN, USA and National Bureau of Economic Research, Cambridge, MA, USA
mario.j.crucini@vanderbilt.edu

Mototsugu Shintani

Department of Economics, Vanderbilt University, Nashville, TN, USA
mototsugu.shintani@vanderbilt.edu

and

Takayuki Tsuruga

Graduate School of Economics, Kyoto University, Kyoto, Japan
tsuruga@econ.kyoto-u.ac.jp

Abstract. We introduce the real exchange rate volatility curve as a useful device to understand the relationship between price stickiness and the fluctuations in Law of One Price deviations. In the presence of both nominal and real shocks, the theory predicts that the real

*This chapter originally appeared in *European Economic Review*, 2013, **62**, 58–72.

exchange rate volatility curve is a U-shaped function of the degree of price stickiness. Using sector-level US-European real exchange rate data and frequency of price changes, we estimate the volatility curve and find the predominance of real effects over nominal effects. Good-by-good variance decompositions show that the relative contribution of nominal shocks is smaller at the sector level than what previous studies have found at the aggregate level, consistent with significant averaging out of good-specific real microeconomic shocks.

Keywords: Real exchange rates; Law of one price; Sticky prices; Nonparametric test for monotonicity

1. Introduction

Among international macroeconomists, it is widely believed that the variability of real exchange rates is increasing in the degree of price rigidity. A reasoning is found in a prominent textbook by Dornbusch *et al.* (2004):

> "Exchange rate overshooting results from the rapid response of exchange rates to monetary policy and the sluggish adjustment of prices. A monetary expansion will lead to an immediate depreciation but only a gradual increase in prices. Exchange rate overshooting implies that real exchange rates are highly volatile (p. 534)."

The basic idea is as follows. The nominal exchange rate is an asset price (since currencies are actively traded in the foreign exchange market) and thus it adjusts instantaneously in response to nominal shocks. However, if prices of many goods and services adjust sluggishly, the real exchange rate will be highly volatile because it comoves with the nominal exchange rate. The expectation, then, is a *positive* correlation between the volatility of real exchange rates and the degree of price stickiness if *nominal* shocks dominate the landscape, as they do in much theorizing on the topic. Quantitative investigations of this prediction have been undertaken, by Chari *et al.* (2002) who focus on the aggregate real exchange rates and by Kehoe and Midrigan (2007) who focus on Law of One Price (LOP) deviations.

An early advocate for the role of real shocks in the equilibrium determination of real exchange rates is Stockman (1980). Stockman casts his model in a flexible price setting, so that nominal shocks make no contribution to real exchange rate volatility. Crucini *et al.*

(2010), on the other hand, neutralize the effect of nominal shocks by focusing on intranational trade and investigate the role of real shocks on good-level real exchange rate volatility across cities in the presence of price rigidity. Unlike models emphasizing the role of the nominal shocks, their model predicts a *negative* correlation between price stickiness and real exchange rate variability because only *real* shocks affect real exchange rates across locations within a country.

The current paper puts these two views of real exchange rate determination on the same playing field by combining the model of Kehoe and Midrigan (2007) which emphasizes nominal shocks with the model of Crucini *et al.* (2010) which emphasizes real shocks. These models rely on the time dependent pricing assumption, but allow the frequencies of price changes to vary across goods, as measured in the micro-data. Under the synthesized framework, we theoretically explore the cross-sectional relationship between price stickiness and real exchange rate volatility at the level of individual goods. We refer to this relationship as the real exchange rate volatility curve: the functional relationship between the forecast error variance of the real exchange rate and the infrequency of price changes at the level of a good. When real shocks are absent, the volatility curve is upward-sloping: an increasing function of the price stickiness parameter and the good with the stickiest price should exhibit the greatest amount of real exchange rate variability. When nominal shocks are turned off, the volatility curve is downward-sloping: a decreasing function of the price stickiness parameter and the good with the stickiest price has the least amount of real exchange rate variability. When both real and nominal shocks are present, the real exchange rate volatility curve becomes U-shaped.

We estimate the volatility curve using sector-level real exchanges of Austria, Belgium, France, and Spain vis-à-vis the US, constructed by Kehoe and Midrigan (2007). We find that the estimated U-shaped curve is monotonically decreasing over the majority of the range of price stickiness. Our main findings regarding the shape of the curve are confirmed by both parametric and nonparametric estimation methods. The negative correlation together with the theoretical prediction of our model suggests the predominance of real shocks over nominal shocks in explaining the volatility of real exchange rates at the sector level.

At the aggregate level, the relative contribution of real and nominal shocks to real exchange rate variability has been typically evaluated in terms of forecast error variance decompositions (e.g., Clarida and Galí, 1994; Eichenbaum and Evans, 1995; Rogers, 1999).[1] Following this literature, we further conduct variance decompositions of real exchange rates at the sector level, and evaluate the relative contribution of nominal and real shocks. For the majority of goods, the contribution of nominal shocks is smaller than that of real shocks, and real shocks rise in dominance as the forecast horizon lengthens. To reconcile our microeconomic evidence with the macroeconomic evidence, it seems necessary to allow for large idiosyncratic real shocks at the sector level such that these microeconomic sources of variation average out in the move to the CPI-based real exchange rate (Broda and Weinstein, 2008; Bergin *et al.*, in press; Crucini and Telmer, 2012).

2. The Model

The theory combines the key features of Kehoe and Midrigan (2007) and Crucini *et al.* (2010). Both of these models assume heterogeneous price stickiness across goods, but the former relies on nominal exchange rate variations whereas the latter focuses on the labor productivity variations along with trade costs in explaining the volatility of good-level real exchange rates.

In what follows, we present a sketch of our model to discuss its main implications for good-level real exchange rate volatility.[2] The (log) real exchange rate for a bilateral pair of countries is defined as

$$q_{it} = s_t + p_{it}^* - p_{it}. \tag{1}$$

where p_{it} (p_{it}^*) denotes the (log) price index for good i in the home (foreign) country and s_t is the (log) nominal exchange rate, at period t.

[1] Some exceptions, such as Steinsson (2008), focus on the shape of impulse response function to evaluate the relative importance of nominal and real shocks.

[2] The full model is presented in Appendix A.

To introduce the real exchange rate volatility curve, some simplifying assumptions are made on the sources of real exchange rate variation. The first assumptions concern nominal shocks and exchange rates and we take these assumptions from Kehoe and Midrigan (2007). Let M_t and P_t be the money demand and aggregate price level, respectively. The nominal shocks in the model are the home and foreign money growth rate, $\mu_t = \ln(M_t/M_{t-1})$ and $\mu_1^* = \ln(M_t^*/M_{t-1}^*)$, which are independent and identically distributed (i.i.d.). We also assume that the period utility function is given by $\ln C_t - \chi L_t$, where C_t and L_t denote aggregate consumption and hours worked, respectively. The assumption on household preference, combined with a local-currency cash-in-advance constraint, $M_t = P_t C_t$, leads to the equality of the money growth differential and the nominal exchange rate growth (i.e., $\mu_t - \mu_t^* = \Delta s_t$). Conveniently, the i.i.d. process of the money growth rates gives rise to a nominal exchange rate s_t that follows a random walk, a characteristic similar to the data.[3]

The second assumptions concern real shocks and trade costs. Monopolistically competitive firms set prices of their goods, which are produced using a technology that is linear in labor and subject to productivity shocks: $Y_{it}(v) = A_{it}L_{it}(v)$, where $Y_{it}(v)$ is output and $L_{it}(v)$ is labor demand, for firms producing brand v of good i, and A_{it} is the labor productivity which varies by good i but is common across brands. Productivity shocks in logs in two countries ($a_{it} = \ln A_{it}$ and $a_{it}^* = \ln A_{it}^*$) are given by

$$a_{it} = z_t + \eta_t + \varepsilon_{it}, \quad a_{it}^* = z_t + \eta_t^* + \varepsilon_{it}^*. \tag{2}$$

Due to our microeconomic focus, the productivity shock for each good consists of three components: a possibly nonstationary global trend component (z_t), an i.i.d. nation-specific component (η_t and η_t^*) and an i.i.d. good-specific component (ε_{it} and ε_{it}^*).[4] Finally, firms in

[3]With the cost of losing computational simplicity of the real exchange rate volatility curve, we can also replace i.i.d. money growth with serially correlated money growth.

[4]Here we impose an i.i.d. assumption on nation- and good-specific components for ease of exposition. As in the case of nominal shocks, however, we can easily

each country are required to pay an iceberg transportation cost τ to send a good across the border. This transportation cost leads to home bias in consumption because the home variety of each good is cheaper than the imported variety of the same good. We denote the elasticity of substitution among differentiated products by θ and the discount factor by β; these parameters are assumed to satisfy $\theta > 1$ and $0 < \beta < 1$. Finally, firms reset their prices under Calvo-type pricing with the good-specific degree of price stickiness given by the probability of no price change λ_i.

The focal equation of the model is the first-order difference equation that nests equations by Kehoe and Midrigan (2007) and Crucini *et al.* (2010):

$$q_{it} = \lambda_i q_{it-1} + \lambda_i(\mu_t - \mu_t^*) + (1-\lambda_i)(1-\lambda_i\beta)\psi(a_{it} - a_{it}^*), \quad (3)$$

where $\psi = (1-(1+\tau)^{(1-\theta)})/(1+(1+\tau)^{(1-\theta)})$. The parameter ψ appears because a productivity shock to good i in one country asymmetrically transmits to the price indexes of the same good in two countries due to the home bias. The derivation of (3) is provided in Appendix A.

2.1. *The real exchange rate volatility curve*

Equation (3) together with i.i.d. assumptions of money growth differential $\mu_t - \mu_t^*$ (the nominal shock) and cross-country productivity differential $a_{it} - a_{it}^*$ (the real shocks) implies the k-period-ahead forecast error variance of the sector-level real exchange rate

$$\begin{aligned} Var_{t-k}(q_{it}) = \Lambda_{ik}[\lambda_i^2\, Var(\mu_t - \mu_t^*) &+ (1-\lambda_i)^2(1-\lambda_i\beta)^2\psi^2 \\ &\times Var(a_{it} - a_{it}^*)], \end{aligned} \quad (4)$$

where $\Lambda_{ik} = \sum_{j=1}^{k} \lambda_i^{2(j-1)}$. Equation (4) attributes the forecast error variance of the good-level real exchange rate to the variance of the

relax this assumption and introduce persistence without changing the qualitative implication of real exchange rate volatility curve. For the same reason, we further assume that variance of good-specific component is common across i. In the empirical part of the paper, the possibility of heterogenous variances of real shocks across goods is considered.

nominal shocks and the variance of the real shocks. Recall that price stickiness parameter λ_i is assumed to be common across countries but differs across goods. Viewed as a function of λ_i, this equation is called *the real exchange rate volatility curve.*

Note that the coefficient on the nominal shock $\lambda_i^2\Lambda_{tk}$ is increasing in λ_i, while the coefficient on the real shock $(1-\lambda_i)^2(1-\lambda_i\beta)^2\psi^2\Lambda_{ik}$ is decreasing in λ_i. Therefore, for any forecast horizon k, an increase in λ_i increases the contribution of the nominal effect (measured by $\Lambda_{ik}\lambda_i^2 Var(\mu_t-\mu_t^*)$) and decreases the contribution of the real effect (measured by $\Lambda_{ik}(1-\lambda_i)^2(1-\lambda_i\beta)^2\psi^2 Var(a_{it}-a_{it}^*)$) to the total forecast error variance of the good-level real exchange rate. These two opposing forces give rise to a real exchange rate volatility curve that is U-shaped over the support $\lambda_i \in [0,1]$.[5]

To gain some intuition behind the mechanism, recall that q_{it} is defined as $s_t+p_{it}^*-p_{it}$. To see the impact of nominal shocks, consider a positive money growth rate shock in the home country. The model predicts an immediate depreciation of the nominal exchange rate, that is, an increase in s_t. The responses of p_{it}, however, depend on the good-specific frequencies of price adjustment. For goods with prices that change every period, an increase in p_{it} completely offsets an increase in s_t keeping q_{it} unchanged. At the other end of the continuum, goods with prices that are extremely sticky will have q_{it} that basically follows the path of s_t with negligible pass-through of the nominal shock to p_{it}. The nominal effect on real exchange rate variability is amplified by sluggish adjustment of prices. Simply put: conditional on nominal shocks, the correlation between real exchange rate volatility and the degree of price stickiness is positive.

Turning to real shocks, consider a positive shock in home productivity in good i. In our model, this productivity shock has no equilibrium consequences for s_t. What it does is reduce both p_{it} and p_{it}^*, because firms in the home country sell their goods in both countries. However, due to home bias generated by trade costs, p_{it} will decrease more than p_{it}^*. This increases $p_{it}^*-p_{it}$ which results in an

[5]It can be easily shown that the real exchange rate volatility curve for $k=1$ is convex on $\lambda_i \in [0,1]$ as long as the variances of the two shocks are strictly positive.

increase in $q_{it} = s_t + p_{it}^* - p_{it}$. Because this channel requires prices to actually change and thereby induce asymmetric price changes across countries, it is more quantitatively important when prices are flexible. Conversely, the real effect is mitigated by sticky prices. Simply put: conditional on real shocks, the correlation between real exchange rate volatility and the degree of price stickiness is negative.

We note that household preferences and firm technology are key assumptions, producing a U-shaped real exchange rate volatility curve. The semi-log period utility along with the cash-in-advance constraint ensures that no real shocks affect the nominal exchange rate, generating the equivalence of $Var(\Delta s_t)$ to $Var(\mu_t - \mu_t^*)$. The assumption of the firms' linear technology in addition to the semi-log period utility and the cash-in-advance constraint allows us to derive the simple reduced form solution for the real exchange rates by making firms' optimal local-currency pricing depend solely on money supply and productivity and shutting down the quantity effect of the demand for goods on firms' pricing. As long as these assumptions are maintained, the U-shape is robust to the introduction of other real shocks such as preference and markup shocks (see Appendix B).

2.2. *Numerical examples*

Let us provide numerical examples to evaluate how different intensities of real and nominal shocks alter the shape of the real exchange rate volatility curve. We focus on the one-period-ahead forecast error variance by setting $k = 1$ in Eq. (4):

$$\begin{aligned} Var_{t-1}(q_{it}) = \lambda_i^2\, Var(\mu_t - \mu_t^*) + (1-\lambda_i)^2(1-\lambda_i\beta)^2\psi^2 \\ \times Var(a_{it} - a_{it}^*). \end{aligned} \tag{5}$$

The structural parameters are calibrated as follows: (i) the data are monthly, so the discount factor is set to $\beta = 0.96^{1/12}$; (ii) trade costs, broadly defined at the retail level, are in the neighborhood of $\tau = 0.5$; and (iii) the elasticity of substitution is set at $\theta = 10$.[6] Figure 1 shows

[6]Here we follow Carvalho and Nechio (2011) in setting the substitution across varieties within the same sector as $\theta = 10$. However, the shape of the curve is qualitatively insensitive to the values of θ and τ.

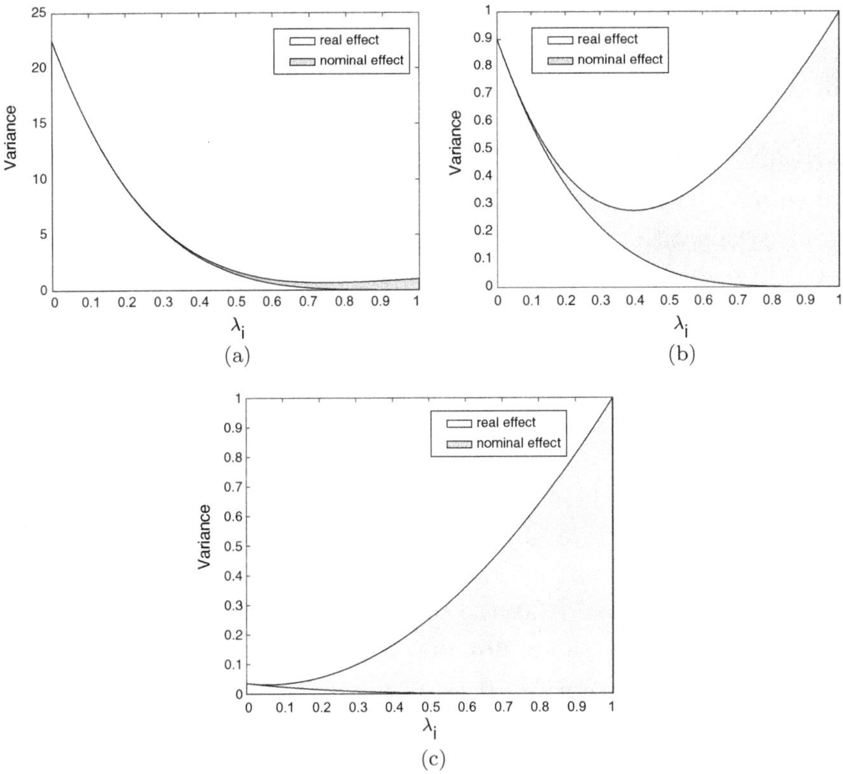

Fig. 1. Simulated real exchange rate volatility curves.

Notes: Each panel of the figure shows contributions of the nominal and real shocks on the sector-level real exchange rate volatility over the range of the degree of price stickiness. The volatility is measured by the one-period-ahead forecast error variance. For each good, the variances due to real and nominal shocks are indicated by the height of the white and grey areas. The combined height of the two areas corresponds to the total variance. Panels (a), (b) and (c) show the cases of $Std(a_{it} - a^*_{it})/Std(\mu_t - \mu^*_t) = 5, 1$, and $1/5$, respectively. The standard deviation of the nominal shocks is set to one.

the shape of the curve under three distinct stochastic environments: (a) $Std(a_{it}-a^*_{it})/Std(\mu_t-\mu^*_t) = 5$; (b) $Std(a_{it}-a^*_{it})/Std(\mu_t-\mu^*_t) = 1$; and (c) $Std(a_{it}-a^*_{it})/Std(\mu_t-\mu^*_t) = 1/5$.[7] The height of the volatility

[7]For all three cases, $Std(\mu_t - \mu^*_t)$ is normalized to 1%.

curve in each panel is the model's prediction for the total forecast error variance of the real exchange rate for a particular good indexed by λ_i. The white and shaded segments of a vertical line drawn at each λ_i give the contributions of real and nominal shocks, respectively. For example, real exchange rate fluctuations of goods with fully flexible price (e.g., crude petroleum) would be driven solely by real shocks while goods with completely rigid prices (e.g., postage stamps) would be driven solely by nominal shocks.

Each panel of the figure clearly suggests that the shape of the curve depends crucially on the relative magnitude of the two shocks. The U-shaped curves are minimized at $\lambda_i = 0.75$ in panel (a), 0.40 in panel (b), and 0.06 in panel (c). While shock structures in terms of variance ratios are symmetric between panels (a) and (c), the shapes of their volatility curves are asymmetric because of asymmetric roles played by nominal and real shock volatility.[8] This feature also explains that the curve in panel (b) is minimized at $\lambda_i = 0.40$ rather than 0.50, the midpoint of the unit interval.

When the real shock dominates, the model predicts that the volatility curve is downward-sloping almost its entire range as in panel (a). The middle panel (b), with equal variances of real and nominal shocks, displays an obvious U-shape. When the nominal shock dominates, the curve is upward-sloping over almost its entire range as in panel (c). In practice the sign of the correlation of price stickiness and real exchange rate volatility will depend on the distribution of goods in the sample as well as the relative importance of real and nominal shocks. In addition, since the real exchange rate volatility curve is U-shaped in general, introducing a nonlinear functional form in the regression, rather than relying a simple linear regression, is essential for detecting the underlying structure.

[8]Since β and ψ are close to unity in our setting, the curve can be approximated by $\lambda_1^2\, Var(\mu_t - \mu_t^*) + (1-\lambda_i)^4\, Var(a_{it} - a_{it}^*)$. This shows that the relative role of nominal and real shock volatilities is asymmetric since the weight on the former approaches 0 at a slower rate as $\lambda_i \to 0$, compared to the coefficient on the latter which approaches 0 at a faster rate as $\lambda_i \to 1$.

When the degree of price stickiness is uniformly distributed across goods, shaded and white areas in Fig. 1 can be interpreted as the cross-sectional average of the variance decomposition for each individual good. In panel (a), the shaded area (nominal effects) accounts for only 7% and the white area (real effects) contributes the remaining 93%. In contrast, the nominal effects account for 65% in panel (b) and 98% in panel (c). While the average variance decomposition is a convenient measure under the uniform distribution assumption, it should be noted that variance decompositions can still greatly vary across the individual goods. For example, consider two goods, one with $\lambda_1 = 0.25$ and the other with $\lambda_2 = 0.56$ in panel (b). These two real exchange rates turn out to have the same total forecast error variance. However, the relative contribution of nominal shocks is only 18% for the first good but 90% for the second good.

3. Empirical Analysis

3.1. *Data*

The empirical analysis focuses on (i) examining the relationship between the total variance of real exchange rates and the degree of price stickiness based on the theoretical volatility curve; and (ii) parsing this variance into the real and nominal effects at the disaggregated level. The data are from Kehoe and Midrigan (2007) and consist of 66 sectoral real exchange rates for four European countries (Austria, Belgium, France, and Spain) relative to the US from January 1996 to May 2006. The series are constructed by matching monthly, highly disaggregated price data from Eurostat and the Bureau of Labor Statistics and converting to a common-currency using spot nominal exchange rates obtained from the FRED database. The goal is to understand the time series properties of the real exchange rate for sector i for country j, vis-à-vis the US, $q_{ijt} = s_{jt} + p^*_{it} - p_{ijt}$, for $i = 1, \dots, N_j$ and $j = 1, \dots, 4$, where N_j is the number of sectors available both in country j and the US, p_{ijt} is the price for sector i in country j expressed in local currency, p^*_{it} is the US price for sector i in US dollar, S_{jt} is the domestic currency value of the US dollar. The Euro was officially introduced part-way through our sample. It should be noted that even before the introduction of the Euro, the volatility of the nominal exchange rate against the US dollar was quite similar across these European countries.[9] Thus, we expect that the role of the nominal shock may be similar across the four bilateral pairs, while that of the shock to productivity differentials is not known. In the analysis, we use a pooled regression of the four country-pairs as a benchmark but also run country-by-country regressions to allow for the different roles of the real shocks.

The country-specific frequencies of price changes for the US are from Bils and Klenow (2004) and those for each of the European countries are taken from the individual country studies by: Baumgartner *et al.* (2005) for Austria; Aucremanne and Dhyne (2004) for Belgium; Baudry *et al.* (2007) for France; Alvarez and Hernando (2006) for Spain. Since the degree of price stickiness of the same good is assumed to be common between paired countries and constant across time, Kehoe and Midrigan (2007) take the cross-country average monthly infrequencies of price changes within each sector. Thus, observed infrequency of price changes, λ_{ij}, represents the average value between country j and the US.[10]

For the purpose of our analysis, we compute the k-period-ahead forecast error variance, $Var_{t-k}(q_{ijt})$, from the sample variance of the quasi-difference $q_{ijt} - \lambda_{ij}^k q_{ijt-k}$, using the observed infrequency of price changes, λ_{ij}. When either λ_{ij} or q_{ijt} is missing or when the sample variance can be computed from only a short time sample, we exclude the sector from the sample. As a result, the number of sectors (N_j) is 57 for Austria, 46 for Belgium, 48 for France, and 31 for Spain. In the pooled case, the number of cross-sectional observations is 182. Figure 2 plots the density estimate of λ_{ij} when all the observations are pooled. It suggests that many observations are clustered around

[9] The standard deviations of the nominal exchange rate growth of the US dollar against the Austrian Schilling, Belgian Franc, French Franc, and Spanish Peseta were 2.36, 2.37, 2.35, and 2.36%, respectively.

[10] The details of the data construction are found in the appendix of Kehoe and Midrigan (2007).

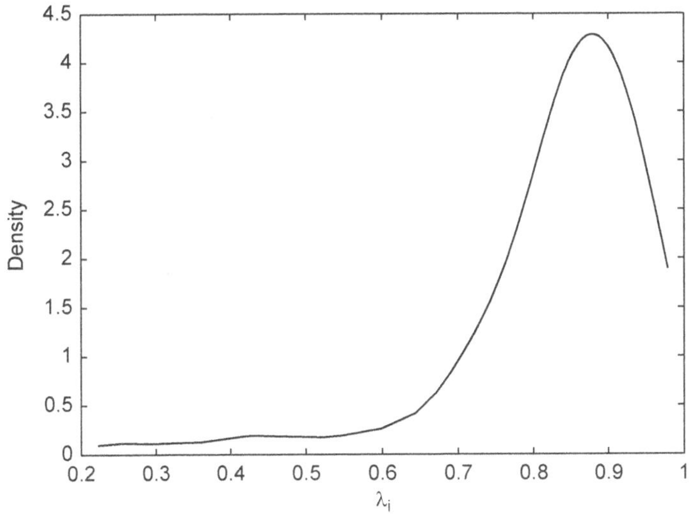

Fig. 2. Empirical distribution of price stickiness. Notes: The kernel density estimate of pooled λ_i's using standard Gaussian kernel combined with Silverman's rule of thumb for the bandwidth.

high values of λ_i. The empirical range of λ_{ij} in our dataset is given by $[\{\lambda_{\min}, \lambda_{\max}] = [0.223, 0.979]$. In what follows, country subscript j is dropped for notational simplicity.

3.2. *Estimation of the real exchange rate volatility curve*

Let V_i be the one-period-ahead forecast error variance of the real exchange rate. As a preliminary analysis, we first follow Kehoe and Midrigan (2007) and run a simple linear regression of V_i on λ_i pooling the data from all the countries. The estimated coefficient on λ_i is significantly negative with the adjusted R^2 of 70%.[11] Therefore, linear regression suggests that the real exchange rate volatility curve is downward-sloping, which is consistent with the finding of Kehoe and Midrigan (2007) who use the squared residuals from the first-order autoregression instead of our theoretical one-period-ahead forecast error variance based on observed λ_i.

[11]To be specific, the estimated linear model is given by $V_i = 0.013 - 0.014\lambda_i$.

Recall, however, that the theory predicts a nonlinear relationship, rather than the linear relationship, between the frequency of price adjustment and real exchange rate variability. For this reason, we employ Ramsey's (1969) regression specification error test to see whether the null hypothesis of linearity can be rejected. The resulting t-statistic is 5.36, which rejects the null hypothesis at the 1% significance level.[12] In what follows, we conduct two alternative nonlinear regression analyses, one using a parametric approach and the other using a nonparametric approach.

3.2.1. *Parametric approach*

Our regression analysis based on a parametric approach relies on the structural form of (5) which suggests both a quadratic term and a quartic term to be included as regressors:

$$V_i = b_1\lambda_i^2 + b_2(1-\lambda_i)^2(1-\lambda_i\beta)^2 + u_i, \tag{6}$$

where u_i is a regression error term. According to (5), regression coefficient b_1 should capture the nominal effects, due to $Var(\mu_t - \mu_t^*)$. The second regressor $(1-\lambda_i)^2(1-\lambda_i\beta)^2$ is constructed by setting $\beta = 0.96^{1/12}$. The regression coefficient, b_2, captures the real effects $\psi^2\ Var(a_{it} - a_{it}^*)$, with the restriction that the variance of productivity differentials is common across i. If the restriction is not satisfied, it captures the cross-sectional average of variance of real shocks.

Table 1 presents the estimation results of the quartic regression model (6).[13] In all cases, the estimated coefficients, b_1 and b_2, are significantly positive, which is consistent with the theory. The quartic

---

[12] We also tested the linearity for each country. The null hypothesis is rejected at 1% significance level for the Austrian and French cases. Weaker evidence of nonlinearity is obtained for Belgian and Spanish cases possibly because the power of the test is lower in smaller samples.

[13] In the pooled case, we run the regression with and without the cross product of country dummy variables and each regressor. In the table, we only report the result with country dummies D_{ji} for $j = 1, \ldots, 4$, which takes value 1 if the data are from country j. For example, reported b_1 is from $b_1\lambda_1^2 + \sum_{j=1}^4 b_{1j}D_{ji}\lambda_i^2$ with a restriction $\sum_{j=1}^4 b_{1j} = 0$. When country dummies are excluded, estimates of b_1 and b_2 are 0.0016 and 0.0456, respectively.

Table 1. Structural regressions.

	λ_i^2	$(1-\lambda_i)^2(1-\lambda_i\beta)^2$	Adj. R^2_{uc}	$\underline{\lambda}$
Pooled	0.0016	0.0718	0.789	0.793
	(0.0001)	(0.0076)		(0.008)
Austria	0.0012	0.0475	0.895	0.784
	(0.0001)	(0.0066)		(0.011)
Belgium	0.0021	0.0419	0.623	0.735
	(0.0004)	(0.0056)		(0.017)
France	0.0015	0.0411	0.905	0.763
	(0.0001)	(0.0040)		(0.009)
Spain	0.0017	0.1567	0.716	0.836
	(0.0002)	(0.0292)		(0.011)

Notes: The heteroskedasticity-consistent standard errors are in parentheses. The "Adj. R^2_{uc}" denotes the adjusted uncentered R^2. $\underline{\lambda}$ is the estimate of λ which minimizes the total variance.

regression is comparable to the linear regression in terms of the goodness of fit. The relative role of nominal and real shocks, as implied by the estimates b_1 and b_2, indicates a much larger role for real shocks.[14] Because the home bias term satisfies $0 \leq \psi^2 \leq 1, b_2$ can be considered as a lower bound on $Var(a_{it} - a^*_{it})$. The same argument establishes that $\sqrt{b_2/b_1}$ can be used as a lower bound for $Std(a_{it} - a^*_{it})/Std(\mu_t - \mu^*_t)$.

The lower bounds are inferred to be: 6.63, 6.17, 4.42, 5.30 and 9.64, for the pooled case and the Austrian, Belgian, French and Spanish nation-specific cases, respectively. Thus, the quartic regression result is very comparable to the numerical example of case (a) where $Std(a_{it} - a^*_{it})/Std(u_t - \mu^*_t) = 5$.

[14]We also conduct the robustness analysis, using the first-order autocorrelation (ρ_i) of the sector-level real exchange rates, rather than λ_1. In particular, we obtain the sample variance of $q_{it} - \rho_i q_{it-1}$ and run the quartic regression (6) by replacing λ_1 with ρ_i. Even when we use ρ_1 for the quartic regressions, the estimated coefficients are both significantly positive in the pooled regression and country-by-country regressions except for Spain and again suggest a large role for real shocks as in the case of λ_i.

Figure 3 further elucidates the shape of the volatility curve, showing the fitted curve and its derivative with respect to λ_i of the pooled quartic regression. The figure also includes the 95% confidence intervals computed using heteroskedasticity-robust standard errors. The fitted curve shown in the upper panel resembles panel (a) of Fig. 1 in terms of the shape of the curve, suggesting the importance of real effects. The fitted curve in the lower panel shows the monotonically increasing first derivative.

As reported in the last two columns of Table 1, estimates of b_1 and b_2 can be also used to locate the degree of price stickiness which minimizes the forecast error variance. For the pooled case, the variance of the real exchange rate is minimized at $\underline{\lambda} = 0.79$ which is somewhat close to the value of 0.75 from our numerical example with dominant real shocks. This frequency of price changes implies that the duration between price changes is 4.8 months.

3.2.2. *Nonparametric approach*

We now turn to the regression analysis based on a nonparametric approach. Note that the quartic regression (6) imposes a strict theoretical shape restriction on the real exchange rate volatility curve. To allow for a more general functional form of the real exchange rate volatility curve, we may consider the following nonparametric regression model:

$$V_i = m(\lambda_i) + u_i,$$

where m is an unknown conditional mean function. We are interested in the shape of $m(x)$ and its first derivative $m'(x)$. Here, we estimate the former using the local linear estimator and the latter using the local quadratic estimator. The pth order local polynomial estimator at a point $\lambda_i = x$ can be obtained by minimizing the weighted least squares criterion $\sum_{i=1}^{N}\{V_i - \sum_{k=0}^{p} \beta_k(\lambda_i - x)^k\}^2 K((\lambda_i - x)/h)$, where h is the bandwidth and K is a kernel function such that $\int K(u)du = 1$.[15] The solution is given by

[15] We employ the standard Gaussian kernel function for K. For the bandwidth h, we use the rule of thumb bandwidth selector designed for the local polynomial regression proposed by Fan and Gijbels (1996, p. 111).

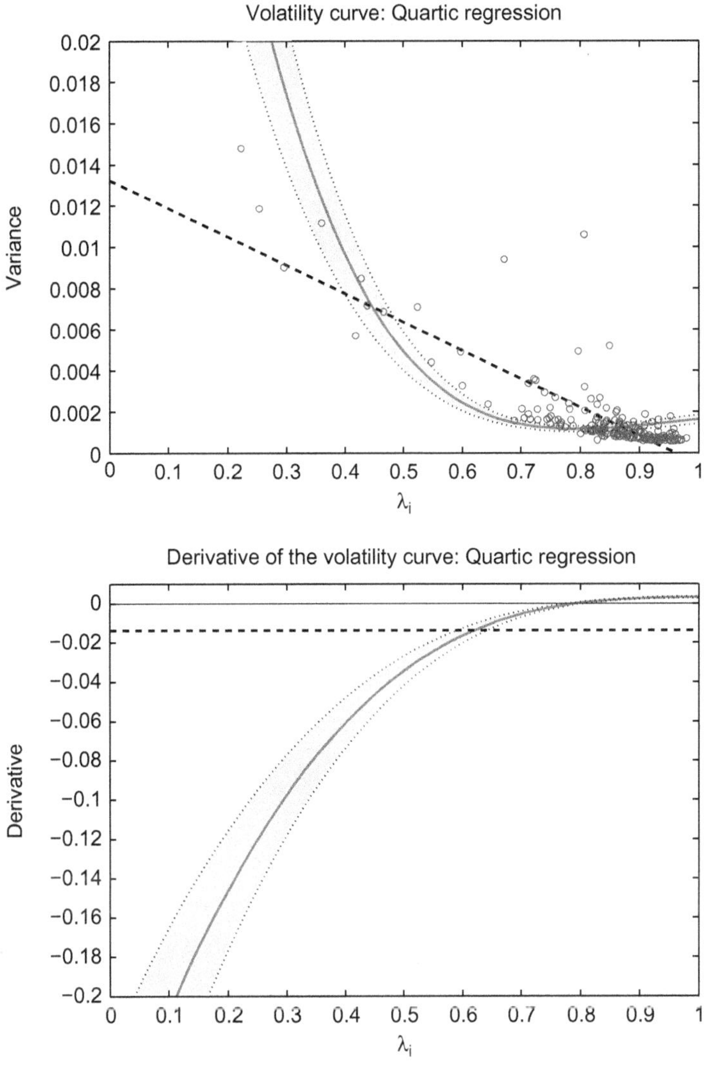

Fig. 3. Estimated real exchange rate volatility curves: parametric regression.

Notes: The upper panel shows the scatter plot of the one-period-ahead forecast error variance of the sector-level real exchange rates against the degree of price stickiness. The solid line in the upper panel shows the fitted curve based on the quartic regression with the 95% confidence interval bands. The lower panel represents the estimated derivative of the volatility curve with the 95% confidence interval bands. The dashed lines in both panels show the linear regression counterparts.

$\widehat{\beta} = (\widehat{\beta}_0, \ldots \widehat{\beta}_p)' = (X'WX)^{-1}X'WY$ where

$$X = \begin{bmatrix} 1 & (\lambda_1 - x) & \cdots & (\lambda_1 - x)^p \\ \vdots & \vdots & & \vdots \\ 1 & (\lambda_N - x) & \cdots & (\lambda_N - x)^p \end{bmatrix},$$

$Y = (V_1, \ldots, V_N)'$ and $W = \mathrm{diag}\{K\{(\lambda_1 - x)/h\}, \ldots, K\{(\lambda_N - x)/h\}\}$. Our local linear estimator of the function $m(x)$ is given by $\widehat{m}(x) = \widehat{\beta}_0$ when $p = 1$ while our local quadratic estimator of the first derivative is given by $\widehat{m}'(x) = \widehat{\beta}_1$ when $p = 2$. The (point-wise) confidence interval of $\widehat{\beta}_k$ is constructed from the heteroskedasticity-robust standard error defined as a square root of the (k, k) element of $s^2(x)(X'WX)^{-1}X'W^2X(X'WX)^{-1}$ where

$$s^2(x) = \frac{1}{\mathrm{tr}\{W - WX(X'WX)^{-1}X'W\}} \times \sum_{i=1}^{N} \left\{ V_i - \sum_{k=0}^{p} \widehat{\beta}_k (\lambda_i - x)^k \right\}^2 K\left(\frac{\lambda_i - x_i}{h}\right).$$

The upper panel of Fig. 4 shows the estimated curve using the local linear regression estimator with pooled data. The shape of the fitted curve shown as the solid line is very different from the linear regression fit shown as the dashed line. This suggests the plausibility of a nonlinear structure in the real exchange volatility curve. The lower panel of the figure shows the estimated first derivative of real exchange rate volatility curve based on the local polynomial regression, along with the confidence interval. The first derivative tends to be increasing in λ_i, which is consistent with the theoretical prediction. The slope of the curve is negative over the majority of the empirical range of λ_i with the exception of values close to one. The confidence intervals for the derivative include the positive region when λ_i is above 0.9, which could represent the dominating nominal effect.

Turning to a comparison between the quartic regression (6) and the nonparametric regression, both similarities and differences are evident. Both estimates imply convexity in the real exchange rate

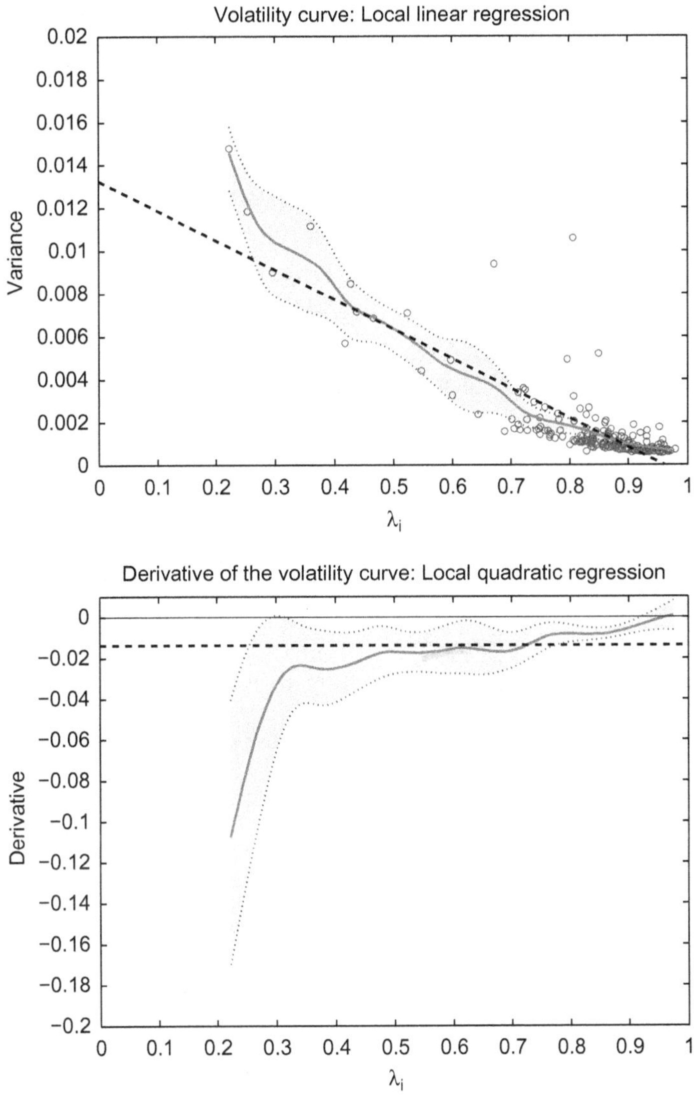

Fig. 4. Estimated real exchange rate volatility curves: nonparametric regression.

Notes: The upper panel shows the scatter plot of the one-period-ahead forecast error variance of the sector-level real exchange rates against the degree of price stickiness. The solid line in the upper panel shows the fitted curve based on the nonparametric regression with the 95% confidence interval bands. The lower panel represents the estimated derivative of the volatility curve with the 95% confidence interval bands. The dashed lines in both panels show the linear regression counterparts.

volatility curve. The most notable difference between the parametric and nonparametric estimates is the location of the bottom of the curve. The value of λ_i which minimizes the forecast error variance in the nonparametric regression is close to unity, much larger than the value predicted by the quartic regression.

To formally investigate the shape of the estimated curve, a nonparametric test of monotonicity developed by Ghosal *et al.* (2000) is employed. The testing procedure concerns the null hypothesis that the m function is an increasing function over a certain interval $[a, b]$, or $H_0 : m'(x) \geq 0$ for all $x \in [a, b]$. In the present context, the shape of the curve is examined over the observed range of the data, $[a, b] = [\lambda_{\min}, \lambda_{\max}]$. Their test statistic for $H_0 : m'(x) \geq 0$ is defined as the supremum of a U-statistic over $x \in [a, b]$.[16] The test for the decreasing function, or $H_0 : m'(x) \leq 0$, can be similarly constructed by replacing λ_i by $1-\lambda_i$. We also utilize the parametrically estimated value of $\underline{\lambda}$ and apply the test for $H_0 : m'(x) \leq 0$ using the range below $\underline{\lambda}$ and for $H_0 : m'(x) \geq 0$ using the range above $\underline{\lambda}$. Table 2 shows that the hypothesis of an increasing function in λ_i over $[a, b] = [\lambda_{\min}, \lambda_{\max}]$ is rejected, and that of decreasing function is not, based on a

---

[16]Formally, the test statistic is defined as $\sup_{x\in[a,b]}\sqrt{N}U(x)/\widehat{\sigma}(x)$ with

$$U(x) = \frac{2}{N(N-1)h^2} \times \sum_{1\leq i<j\leq N} \operatorname{sign}(V_i - V_j)\operatorname{sign}(\lambda_i - \lambda_j)K\left(\frac{\lambda_i - x}{h}\right)K\left(\frac{\lambda_j - x}{h}\right) \text{ and}$$

$$\widehat{\sigma}^2(x) = \frac{4}{3N(N-1)(N-2)h^4} \times \sum_{1\leq i<j\leq N, i\neq j\neq k} \operatorname{sign}(\lambda_i - \lambda_j)\operatorname{sign}(\lambda_i - \lambda_k)K^2\left(\frac{\lambda_i - x}{h}\right) \times K\left(\frac{\lambda_j - x}{h}\right)K\left(\frac{\lambda_k - x}{h}\right)$$

where sign(x) denotes the sign function which takes 1 if $x > 0, -1$ if $x < 0$ if and 0 otherwise. We follow the example of Ghosal *et al.* (2000) and use the quadratic kernel $K(x) = 0.75(1 - x^2)$ for $-1 < x < 1$ combined with $h = 0.5\,N^{-1/5}$.

Table 2. Tests of monotonicity.

H_0 and range	$m'(x) \leq 0$ $[\lambda_{\min}, \lambda_{\max}]$	$m'(x) \geq 0$ $[\lambda_{\min}, \lambda_{\max}]$	$m'(x) \leq 0$ $[\lambda_{\min}, \underline{\lambda}]$	$m'(x) \geq 0$ $[\underline{\lambda}, \lambda_{\max}]$
Pooled	−1.831	10.329	−1.822	10.329
	(1.000)	(0.001)	(1.000)	(0.182)
Austria	−1.546	4.927	−1.546	4.783
	(1.000)	(0.026)	(1.000)	(0.587)
Belgium	−0.647	4.608	−0.643	4.535
	(1.000)	(0.051)	(1.000)	(0.708)
France	−1.212	6.369	−1.212	6.243
	(1.000)	(0.004)	(1.000)	(0.578)
Spain	−1.281	5.098	−1.281	3.906
	(1.000)	(0.067)	(1.000)	(0.767)

Notes: Numbers in parentheses are P-values computed using the procedure explained in Ghosal *et al.* (2000).

conventional significance level. At the same time, both hypotheses of decreasing function over $[a, b] = [\lambda_{min}, \underline{\lambda}]$ and of increasing function over $[a, b] = [\underline{\lambda}, \lambda_{\max}]$ fail to be rejected. Therefore, the evidence from the nonparametric test on real exchange rate volatility curve does not contradict the U-shape prediction of the theory.

3.3. *Variance decomposition*

Let us now turn to the relative importance of the real and nominal effects at the sector level by directly using Eq. (4) at various horizons. Because the nominal shock, $\mu_t - \mu_t^* = \Delta s_t$, is observable according to the theory, the variance due to nominal effect can be estimated by $\lambda_i^2 \Lambda_{ik} \widehat{Var}(\Delta s_t)$, where $\widehat{Var}(\Delta s_t)$ is the sample variance of Δs_t. The relative contribution of nominal shocks to the k-period-ahead forecast error variance of the real exchange rate of sector i can be estimated by

$$FEV_i(k) = \frac{\lambda_i^2 \Lambda_{ik} \widehat{Var}(\Delta s_t)}{\widehat{Var}_{t-k}(q_{it})},$$

where $\widehat{Var}_{t-k}(q_{it})$ is the sample variance of the quasi-difference $q_{it} - \lambda_i^k q_{i,t-k}$. For the limiting case of $k \to \infty$, we utilize the sample variance of q_{it} and $[\lambda_i^2/(1-\lambda_i^2)]\widehat{Var}(\Delta s_t)$ to measure the relative contribution of the nominal shocks to the unconditional variance. For the purpose of evaluating the relative role of shocks, this approach has an advantage over the direct estimation of the volatility curve in the sense that it allows for heterogeneous variance of real shocks across sectors. Furthermore, as shown in Appendix B, this approach is robust in the presence of other types of real shocks, such as preference shocks and markup shocks.

Table 3 reports the summary statistics for the contributions of the nominal shocks to the forecast error variance of sectoral real exchange rates at monthly horizons of $k = 1, 3, 6, 12$ and ∞. Note that, unlike the variance decomposition of aggregate real exchange rates often reported in the literature, the decomposition is calculated for each sector i. The first row of the table shows the average contribution of nominal shocks, with the average taken across all sectors and all four bilateral pairs. The numbers in parentheses in the second row are the standard deviations of these contributions across goods. The remaining rows report corresponding results for each pair of countries.

Table 3. Percentage of forecast error variance accounted for by nominal shocks.

k	1	3	6	12	∞
Pooled	40.6	23.6	18.7	14.2	11.4
	(24.1)	(16.5)	(15.7)	(13.5)	(11.8)
Austria	48.6	30.5	25.7	20.3	17.1
	(24.4)	(16.9)	(17.1)	(15.7)	(16.3)
Belgium	34.9	19.9	15.3	11.4	8.9
	(23.0)	(14.9)	(13.6)	(11.2)	(8.2)
France	40.2	21.8	16.2	11.7	9.2
	(22.7)	(15.2)	(13.5)	(10.2)	(7.6)
Spain	35.2	18.9	14.6	11.1	7.9
	(24.5)	(16.4)	(15.6)	(13.3)	(8.0)

Notes: Numbers are in %. Each column corresponds to the cross-sectional average of the k-period-ahead forecast error variance of sector-level real exchange rates accounted for by nominal shocks. Numbers in parentheses are standard deviations.

For the one-period-ahead forecast error decomposition, nominal shocks account for about 40% of real exchange rate variation and range from a high of 49% for Austria to a low of 35% for Spain. The large standard deviations in the table imply that the contributions of nominal shocks differ considerably across goods. This cross-sectional dispersion is similar across countries. At the monthly horizon it seems sensible to conclude that the contribution of real shocks is at least as large as that of nominal shocks for many goods.

The role of nominal shocks becomes smaller as the horizon lengthens. At a horizon of 6 months, the relative contribution is about one half of the 1-month horizon. The long-run contribution of nominal shocks, evaluated at $k = \infty$, is lower than 10% for all countries except for Austria, thus leaving 90% to be explained by real shocks.

Let us now compare the variance decompositions of sector-level real exchange rates with previous studies involving the aggregate real exchange rate. Using a structural VAR model, Clarida and Galí (1994, Table 3) find that the relative contribution of nominal shocks to one-period-ahead forecast error variance of quarterly real exchange rate is 47% for Germany and 36% for Japan. In contrast, our three-month (the counterpart to one quarter) ahead variance decomposition indicates nominal shocks account for between 19 and 31%, depending on the country (see Table 3). Using over 100 years of annual UK-US real exchange rate data, Rogers (1999) finds that the contribution of nominal shocks to the one-year-ahead forecast error variance ranges from 19% to 60%, with a median value of 41%. Our 12-month ahead forecast error variance decomposition estimates indicate nominal shocks only account for about 14%. The benchmark estimates of Eichenbaum and Evans (1995, Table 1a) show a nominal shock contribution at horizons of 31- to 36-months averaging 38% for France, while our estimates imply long-run contributions between 9 and 12% for France. Thus, largely independent of the horizon or countries examined, nominal shocks play a more important role in accounting for aggregate real exchange rate fluctuations than for sector-level real exchange rate fluctuations.

What accounts for this difference in the micro and macro evidence? Our suspicion is that the real shocks tend to average out across sectors. Recall productivity shocks in (2) are expected to embody idiosyncratic sector-specific shocks ε_{it} and ε^*_{it}, at least in part. In our model, the aggregation of goods prices eliminates this idiosyncratic component but has no effect on the nominal shocks, μ_t and μ^*_t, which are common across sectors. In particular, (3) implies that idiosyncratic components of q_{it} is $\sum_{j=0}^{\infty} \lambda_i^j (1-\lambda_i)(1-\lambda_i\beta)\psi(\varepsilon_{it-j} - \varepsilon^*_{it-j})$ which is likely to be averaged out when the number of sectors increases. It is therefore not surprising that nominal and real shocks are more on par as contributors to real exchange rate variation at disaggregated level.

To see whether this averaging-out effect is present in our data, we can decompose the total variance of one-period ahead forecast error series, $e_{it} = q_{it} - \lambda_i q_{it-1}$, into the between-group variance and the within-group variance using the basic identity from the analysis of variance

$$\frac{1}{NT}\sum_{i=1}^{N}\sum_{t=1}^{T}(e_{it}-\bar{e})^2 = \frac{1}{T}\sum_{t=1}^{T}(e_t-\bar{e})^2 + \frac{1}{T}\sum_{t=1}^{T}\left[\frac{1}{N}\sum_{i=1}^{N}(e_{it}-e_t)^2\right], \tag{7}$$

where $\bar{e} = (NT)^{-1}\sum_{i=1}^{N}\sum_{t=1}^{T} e_{it}$ and $e_t = N^{-1}\sum_{i=1}^{N} e_{it}$. Substitution of (3) into (7) implies that the between-group variance (the first term) captures the contribution of common shocks $\lambda_i \Delta s_t + (1-\lambda_i)(1-\lambda_i\beta)\psi(\eta_t - \eta^*_t)$ and the within-group variance (the second term) captures the contribution of idiosyncratic shocks $(1-\lambda_i)(1-\lambda_i\beta)\psi(\varepsilon_{it} - \varepsilon^*_{it})$. Using the analysis of variance, we find that the ratio of within-group variance to total variance is 0.50, 0.57, 0.54, 0.40 and 0.34, for the pooled case and the Austrian, Belgian, French and Spanish nation-specific cases, respectively. Thus, the contribution of idiosyncratic shocks in the total variance seems to be large, which helps to reconcile the differences between the micro and macro findings.

Our findings appear consistent with recent micro studies including Crucini and Telmer (2012) who show that only a small fraction of

LOP changes are common to all goods, Broda and Weinstein (2008) who find that enormous volatility in the barcode prices is eliminated at the aggregate price level, and Bergin *et al.* (in press) who claim that idiosyncratic industry price shocks account for about 80% of variation in LOP deviations. Thus, explaining the LOP volatility only by nominal exchange rates would leave most of the variation unaccounted for. The decomposition performed here fills this gap with common and sector-specific real shocks.

4. Conclusion

We use a Calvo-type pricing model with real and nominal shocks to develop the concept of a real exchange rate volatility curve. The volatility curve has a U-shape as a function of the degree of price stickiness, implying an ambiguous correlation between the forecast error variance of real exchange rates and the degree of price stickiness. Using US-European real exchange rate data, the correlation was found to be negative over most of the range of observed degree of price stickiness. The downward-sloping profile suggested that for this micro-sample of goods and countries, real shocks account for most of the volatility of sectoral real exchange rates, though nominal shocks are important as well. The good with minimal real exchange rate volatility was estimated to have a duration between the price changes of about 4.8 months based on the benchmark quartic regression, and longer based on a nonparametric regression. However, to validate the generality of the theory, it is important to explore other samples of goods, cross-sections of countries and historical periods.

Our results also point to the value of examining cross-sectional differences in real exchange rate variability in order to flesh out the rich quantitative predictions of models of micro-price adjustment currently under development. Differences across goods help us to disentangle heterogeneous responses to common shocks due to differences in economic propagation mechanisms such as costs of price adjustment and trade costs from heterogeneity in the underlying shocks themselves. Averaging across goods, as is inevitable in the move to an aggregate real exchange rate, is not innocuous in terms of the weight given to real and nominal shocks. The same averaging may also lead to an under-appreciation of the sources of the risks that individuals and firms face. We hope to explore these possibilities in future work. Much remains to be done.

Acknowledgments

We thank Yasushi Iwamoto, Oleksiy Kryvtsov and seminar and conference participants at the Bank of Canada, the Board of Governors of the Federal Reserve System, Clemson University, the European Commission, the Federal Reserve Bank of Atlanta, the Federal Reserve Bank of Dallas, Hitotsubashi University, Kobe University, Kyoto University, Nagoya University, Osaka University, Otaru University of Commerce, Econometrics Society World Congress 2010, and Society for Economic Dynamics Annual Meeting 2011 for their helpful discussion and comments. We are grateful to John Taylor for his encouragement at the early stage of the project. We also thank Virgiliu Midrigan for providing the data and Subhashis Ghosal for providing the programing code. Crucini and Shintani gratefully acknowledge the financial support of NSF (SES-1030164). Tsuruga gratefully acknowledges the financial support of Grants-in-Aid for Scientific Research (24243044).

Appendix A. The Model

This appendix derives the real exchange rate volatility curve used in our numerical and empirical analysis. The model is based on a symmetric two-country model with heterogeneous price stickiness. Due to the symmetry of the model, we mostly focus on the equations of the home country.

Households. Households choose consumption and labor supply over an infinite horizon subject to a cash-in-advance (CIA) constraint. Let $C_{it}(v), C_{it}$, and C_t denote the consumption of brand v of good i, the consumption of good i aggregated across brands, and aggregate consumption, respectively. Each country has a continuum of goods $i \in [0, 1]$, each of which consists of a continuum of brand $v \in [0, 1]$. Brands of good i in the home country are indexed by

$v \in [0, 1/2]$ while those in the foreign country are indexed by $v \in (1/2, 1]$. We define C_{it} and C_t as $C_{it} = [\int_0^1 C_{it}(v)^{(\theta-1)/\theta} dv]^{\theta/(\theta-1)}$ and $C_t = [\int_0^1 C_{it}^{(\theta-1)/\theta} di]^{\theta/(\theta-1)}$, respectively. The home consumer maximizes

$$E_0 \sum_{t=0}^{\infty} \beta^t [U(C_t) - \chi V(L_t)], \tag{A.1}$$

where β is the household's discount factor and $E_0(\cdot)$ is the expectations operator. The functions are: $U(C_t) = C_t^{1-\sigma}/(1-\sigma)$ and $V(L_t) = L_t^{1-\phi}/(1-\phi)$, where $\sigma \geq 0$ and $\phi \geq 0$.

The households are faced with intertemporal budget and CIA constraints:

$$M_t + E_t(\gamma_{t,t+1} D_{t+1}) = R_{t-1} W_{t-1} L_{t-1} + D_t + (M_{t-1} - P_{t-1} C_{t-1}) + T_t + \Pi_t \tag{A.2}$$

$$M_t \geq P_t C_t, \tag{A.3}$$

where M_t, D_{t+1}, and $\gamma_{t,t+1}$ denote cash holding, state-contingent bond holding denominated in the home currency, and the nominal stochastic discount factor, respectively. Thus, $M_t + E_t(\gamma_{t,t+1} D_{t+1})$ on the left-hand side represents the nominal total value of wealth brought into the beginning of the period $t + 1$. On the right-hand side, the household receives labor income $(W_{t-1} L_{t-1})$ at the end of period $t - 1$ and earns nominal interest R_{t-1} per unit of labor income within period t in terms of the home currency. The household also carries the nominal bonds in amount of D_t and the cash remaining after consumption in amount of $M_{t-1} - P_{t-1} C_{t-1}$, where P_t is the aggregate price index given by $P_t = [\int P_{it}^{1-\theta} di]^{1/(1-\theta)}$ and P_{it} is the price index for good i given by $P_{it} = [\int P_{it}(v)^{1-\theta} dv]^{1-\theta}$. Finally, the household receives nominal transfers from the government, T_t and the nominal profits from firms, Π_t.

The foreign consumer has the same preference and the same constraints except that we express the intertemporal budget constraint in the foreign currency with the nominal exchange rate S_t. In particular, the budget constraint for the foreign consumer is given by

$$M_t^* + E_t\left(\frac{\gamma_{t,t+1}D_{t+1}^*}{S_t}\right) = \frac{S_{t-1}R_{t-1}}{S_t}W_{t-1}^*L_{t-1}^* + D_t^* + (M_{t-1}^* - P_{t-1}^*C_{t-1}^*) + T_t^* + \Pi_t^*. \quad (A.4)$$

The first-order conditions are standard

$$\frac{W_t}{P_t} = \chi\frac{V_L(L_t)}{U_C(C_t)}, \quad (A.5)$$

$$\gamma_{t,t-1} = \beta\left[\frac{U_C(C_{t+1})}{U_C(C_t)}\frac{P_t}{P_{t+1}}\right] = \beta\left[\frac{U_C(C_{t+1}^*)}{U_C(C_t^*)}\frac{S_tP_t^*}{S_{t+1}P_{t+1}^*}\right], \quad (A.6)$$

$$M_t = P_tC_t, \quad (A.7)$$

where $U_C(C_t) = C_t^{-\sigma}$ is the marginal utility of consumption and $V_L(L_t) = L_t^{-\phi}$ is the marginal disutility of labor.

Assumption 1. $\sigma = 1$ and $\phi = 0$.

Imposing Assumption 1 and combining the first-order conditions (A.5) and (A.7) yields

$$\frac{W_t}{P_t} = \chi\frac{M}{P_t}. \quad (A.8)$$

Using (A.6), the aggregate real exchange rate, Q_t, is proportional to the marginal utility ratio:

$$Q_t = \frac{S_tP_t^*}{P_t} = \kappa\frac{U_C(C_t^*)}{U_C(C_t)}, \quad (A.9)$$

where $\kappa = Q_0U_C(C_0)/U_C(C_0^*)$. In what follows, we assume that $\kappa = 1$. Furthermore, using (A.7) and (A.9) gives an expression for the nominal exchange rate:

$$S_t = \frac{M_t}{M_t^*}. \quad (A.10)$$

Firms. Firms in the home country sell their goods to home and foreign consumers.

Assumption 2. Firm's technology is linear in labor: $Y_{it}(v) = A_{it}L_{it}(v)$, where $Y_{it}(v)$ is output and $L_{it}(v)$ is labor demand, for firms producing brand v of good i, and A_{it} is the labor productivity which varies by good i but is common across brands.

Recall that the firm must pay trade cost, τ, to send one unit of goods into another country. Then, the resource constraint for the home market is

$$C_{it}(v) + (1+\tau)C^*_{it}(v) = A_{it}L_{it}(v) \quad \text{for} \quad v \in [0, 1/2], \quad \text{(A.11)}$$

and the resource constraint for the foreign market is

$$(1+\tau)C_{it}(v) + C^*_{it}(v) = A^*_{it}L^*_{it}(v) \quad \text{for} \quad v \in (1/2, 1]. \quad \text{(A.12)}$$

Prices are set in the buyers' currency (local currency pricing). We introduce the Calvo-type nominal price rigidities for firm's pricing. Every month, a fraction λ_i of firms are not allowed to change prices; the remaining fraction of firms reset prices. We allow for heterogeneity of this Calvo parameter across goods whereas we assume that it is common across countries. The optimal price for firms in the home country to sell good i in the home country, $P_{H,it}$, solves

$$\operatorname*{Max}_{P_{H,it}} E_t \sum_{h=0}^{\infty} \lambda_i^h \gamma_{t,t+h} \left[P_{H,it} - \frac{W_{t+h}}{A_{it+h}} \right] \left(\frac{P_{H,it}}{P_{it+h}} \right)^{-\theta} C_{it+h},$$

where W_t/A_{it} is the nominal marginal cost of production. Note that all firms face the common nominal marginal cost, implying that the optimal price is independent of v. The optimal price for firms in the foreign country to sell good i in the home country, $P_{F,it}$, solves

$$\operatorname*{Max}_{P_{F,it}} E_t \sum_{h=0}^{\infty} \lambda_i^h \gamma_{t,t+h} \left[P_{F,it} - (1+\tau)\frac{S_{t+h}W^*_{t+h}}{A^*_{it+h}} \right] \left(\frac{P_{F,it}}{P_{it+h}} \right)^{-\theta} C_{it+h}.$$

Shocks and model identities. We follow Kehoe and Midrigan (2007) and assume that the money growth rates μ_t and μ^*_t are i.i.d., such that the model predicts random walk behavior of the nominal exchange rate, consistent with the data. As stated in the main text, real shock is defined by (2).

Total transfers from the governments satisfy $T_t = M_t - M_{t-1} - (R_{t-1} - 1)W_{t-1}L_{t-1}$ and $T_t^* = M_t^* - M_{t-1}^* - (R_{t-1}S_{t-1}/S_t - 1)W_{t-1}^*L_{t-1}^*$. Hence, the total transfers in each country equal domestic money injections and interest payment of the government to correct distortion in the intra-temporal first-order condition for the households. The profits of firms accrue exclusively to consumers in the same country: $\Pi_t = \int_{i=0}^{1}\int_{v=0}^{1/2}\Pi_{it}(v)\,dv\,di$ and $\Pi_t^* = \int_{i=0}^{1}\int_{v=1/2}^{1}\Pi_{it}^*(v)\,dv\,di$. The labor market clearing conditions are $L_t = \int_{i=0}^{1}\int_{v=0}^{1/2}L_{it}(v)\,dv\,di$ and $L_t^* = \int_{i=0}^{1}\int_{v=1/2}^{1}L_{it}^*(v)\,dv\,di$. The state-contingent bond market clearing condition is $D_t + D_t^* = 0$. Finally, good market clearing conditions are given by (A.11) and (A.12).

Equilibrium dynamics. To derive the real exchange rate volatility curve, we approximate the first-order conditions and resource constraints by the log deviation from the steady state and derive the reduced form solution for the real exchange rates. In what follows, unless otherwise indicated, the log deviation of a generic variable X_t from the steady state is expressed as $x_t = \ln(X_t/X)$, where X is the steady state value of X_t. Also, we normalize all nominal prices by dividing by the nominal money stock in the place of consumption and by multiplying the labor productivity in the place of production to ensure the stationarity. For example, the normalized price of the nominal home price index for good i is given by $\overline{P}_{it} = P_{it}A_{it}/M_t$. Likewise, the normalized optimal reset prices for the home market are $\overline{P}_{H,it} = P_{H,it}A_{it}/M_t$ and $\overline{P}_{F,it} = P_{F,it}A_{it}^*/M_t$.

The log-linearized first-order conditions are

$$\overline{p}_{H,it} = \sum_{h=1}^{\infty}(\lambda_i\beta)^h E_t\Big[\mu_{t+h} - g_{t+h}^{A_i}\Big] = \lambda_i\beta\,(\eta_t + \varepsilon_{it}), \quad \text{(A.13)}$$

$$\overline{p}_{F,it} = \sum_{h=1}^{\infty}(\lambda_i\beta)^h E_t\Big[u_{t+h} - g_{t+h}^{A_i^*}\Big] = \lambda_i\beta\,(\eta_t^* + \varepsilon_{it}^*), \quad \text{(A.14)}$$

where $g_{t+1}^{A_i} = a_{it+1} - a_{it}$. Equations (A.13) and (A.14) indicate that the optimal reset prices are determined only by exogenous shocks.

The second equality in each equation arises from our assumptions about the stochastic processes of the shocks.

We next turn to the price index for good i. Due to Calvo pricing, $P_{it}^{1-\theta} = \lambda_i P_{it-1}^{1-\theta} + (1-\lambda_i)\left(P_{it}^{opt}\right)^{1-\theta}$, where P_{it}^{opt} denotes the composite of domestic and foreign reset prices in the home country, defined as $P_{it}^{opt} = \left[(1/2)P_{H,it}^{1-\theta} + (1/2)P_{F,it}^{1-\theta}\right]^{1/(1-\theta)}$. Log-linearizing the above indexes yields

$$\overline{p}_{it} = \lambda_i \overline{p}_{it-1} - \lambda_i \mu_t + \lambda_i g_t^{A_i} + (1-\lambda_i)\,\overline{p}_{it}^{opt}, \tag{A.15}$$

$$\overline{p}_{it}^{opt} = \omega \overline{p}_{H,it} + (1-\omega)\left(\overline{p}_{F,it} + \eta_t + \varepsilon_{it} - \eta_t^* - \varepsilon_{it}^*\right), \tag{A.16}$$

where ω is the expenditure share of the household in the home country given by $1/[1+(1+\tau)^{1-\theta}]$.

Let the sectoral real exchange rate be $Q_{it} = S_t P_{it}^*/P_{it}$. Note that the log real exchange rate at the sector level can be expressed by $q_{it} = \overline{p}_{it}^* - \overline{p}_{it} + a_{it} - a_{it}^*$. Then, (A.13)–(A.15) yields

$$q_{it} = \lambda_i q_{it-1} + \lambda_i(\mu_t - \mu_t^*) + (1-\lambda_i)(1-\lambda_i\beta)\psi(a_{it} - a_{it}^*), \tag{A.17}$$

where $\psi = 2\omega - 1 = \left(1-(1+\tau)^{(1-\theta)}\right)/\left(1+(1+\tau)^{(1-\theta)}\right)$. To derive (A.17), we used the fact that $\eta_t + \varepsilon_{it} - \eta_t^* - \varepsilon_{it}^*$ can be replaced with $a_{it} - a_{it}^*$ because a common stochastic trend z_t cancels out of the productivity differential.

Equation (A.17) describes equilibrium dynamics of real exchange rates at the sector level. The real exchange rate follows the AR(1) process and it immediately follows that the k-period-ahead forecast error variance is given by (4).

Appendix B. Extended Model with Preference and Markup Shocks

We present the robustness of the U-shape in the real exchange rate volatility curve by introducing two additional real shocks into the model: a preference shock in marginal labor disutility χ and a markup shock arising from variations in θ. We replace χ and θ by χ_t and θ_t, respectively. These shocks are country-specific so we use χ_t^* and θ_t^*

for the foreign country counterparts while the steady state values are common across countries. We assume that these shocks follow i.i.d. processes.

Given the above assumptions, the normalized log optimal prices can be written as

$$\overline{p}_{H,it} = (1-\lambda_i\beta)\left[\hat{\chi}_t - \frac{\hat{\theta}_t}{\theta-1}\right] + \lambda_i\beta(\eta_t + \varepsilon_{it}), \tag{B.1}$$

$$\overline{p}_{F,it} = (1-\lambda_i\beta)\left[\hat{\chi}_t^* - \frac{\hat{\theta}_t}{\theta-1}\right] + \lambda_i\beta(\eta_t^* + \varepsilon_{it}^*), \tag{B.2}$$

where $\hat{\theta}_t = \ln(\theta_t/\theta), \hat{\chi}_t = \ln(\chi_t/\chi)$, and $\hat{\chi}_t^* = \ln(\chi_t^*/\chi)$. Note that $\overline{p}_{F,it}$ has $\hat{\chi}_t^*$ rather than $\hat{\chi}_t$ because the labor in the foreign country is used for the production of the imported goods. In contrast, $\overline{p}_{F,it}$ remains affected by $\hat{\theta}_t$, because the markup is determined by the elasticity of substitution at the place of consumption.

Turning to the log-linearized price indexes, (A.15) continues to hold but (A.16) must be replaced by

$$\overline{p}_{it}^{opt} = \omega\overline{p}_{H,it} + (1-\omega)\left(\overline{p}_{F,it} + \eta_t + \varepsilon_{it} - \eta_t^* - \varepsilon_{it}^*\right) - \Psi\hat{\theta}_t, \tag{B.3}$$

where the coefficient Ψ is defined as

$$\begin{aligned}\Psi &= \frac{\theta}{\theta-1}\left\{\ln\overline{P}_{ii}^{opt} - \left[\omega\ln\overline{P}_{Hi} + (1-\omega)\ln\overline{P}_{Fi}\right]\right\}\\ &= \frac{\theta}{(\theta-1)^2}[(1-\omega)\ln(1-\omega) + \omega\ln\omega + \ln(2)] > 0.\end{aligned}$$

The second equality obtained from the definitions of ω and Ψ can be shown to be positive for any $\tau > 0$ and $\theta > 1$.[17] Combining (A.15)

---

[17]The detail of the derivation is available upon request.

and (B.1)–(B.3), we have the equation for q_{it}:

$$\begin{aligned} q_{it} &= \lambda_i q_{it-1} + \lambda_i(\mu_t - \mu_t^*) + (1-\lambda_i)(1-\lambda_i\beta)\psi(a_{it} - a_{it}^*) \\ &\quad - (1-\lambda_i)(1-\lambda_i\beta)\psi(\hat{\chi}_t - \hat{\chi}_t^*) \\ &\quad + (1-\lambda_i)\left(\frac{1-\lambda_i\beta}{\theta-1} + \Psi\right)(\hat{\theta}_t - \hat{\theta}_t^*). \end{aligned} \tag{B.4}$$

Consequently, the extended version of the real exchange rate volatility curve is

$$\begin{aligned} Var_{t-k}\left(q_{it}\right) = \left(\sum_{j=1}^{k} \lambda_i^{2(j-1)}\right) \Bigg[& \lambda_i^2\, Var\left(\mu_t - \mu_t^*\right) \\ & + (1-\lambda_i)^2(1-\lambda_i\beta)^2\psi^2[\,Var(a_{it} - a_{it}^*) \\ & + Var(\hat{\chi}_t - \hat{\chi}_t^*)] \\ & + (1-\lambda_i)^2\left(\frac{1-\lambda_i\beta}{\theta-1} + \Psi\right)^2 Var(\hat{\theta}_t - \hat{\theta}_t^*)\Bigg]. \end{aligned} \tag{B.5}$$

In (B.5), all the coefficients on the variance of real shocks are decreasing in λ_i. By contrast, the coefficient on the variance of nominal shock is increasing in λ_i. Therefore, for any forecast horizon, an increase in λ_i decreases the contribution of real shocks and increases the contribution of nominal shock.

References

Alvarez, L.J., Hernando, I., 2006. Price setting behaviour in Spain: stylised facts using consumer price micro data. *Economic Modelling* 24 (4), 699–716.

Aucremanne, L., Dhyne, E., 2004. How frequently do prices change? Evidence based on the micro data underlying the Belgian CPI. National Bank of Belgium Working Paper, No. 44.

Baudry, L., Le Bihan, H., Sevestre, P., Tarrieu, S., 2007. What do thirteen million price records have to say about consumer price rigidity? *Oxford Bulletin of Economics and Statistics* 69 (2), 139–183.

Baumgartner, J., Glatzer, E., Rumler, F., Stiglbauer, A., 2005. How frequently do consumer prices change in Austria? ECB Working Paper Series, No. 523.

Bergin, P.R., Glick, R., Wu, J.-L. The micro-macro disconnect of purchasing power parity. *Review of Economics and Statistics*, http://dx.doi.org/10.1162/REST_a_00335, in press.

Bils, M., Klenow, P.J., 2004. Some evidence on the importance of sticky prices. *Journal of Political Economy* 112 (5), 947–985.

Broda, C., Weinstein, D.E., 2008. Understanding international price differences using barcode data. NBER Working Paper, No. 14017.

Carvalho, C., Nechio, F., 2011. Aggregation and the PPP puzzle in a sticky price model. *American Economic Review* 101 (6), 2391–2424.

Chari, V.V., Kehoe, P.J., McGrattan, E.R., 2002. Can sticky price models generate volatile and persistent real exchange rates? *Review of Economics Studies* 69 (3), 533–563.

Clarida, R., Galí, J., 1994. Sources of real exchange-rate fluctuations: how important are nominal shocks?. *Carnegie-Rochester Conference Series on Public Policy* 41 (1), 1–56.

Crucini, M.J., Shintani, M., Tsuruga, T., 2010. The law of one price without the border: the role of distance versus sticky prices. *Economic Journal* 120 (544), 462–480.

Crucini, M.J., Telmer, C., 2012. Microeconomic sources of real exchange rate variability. NBER Working Paper, No. 17978.

Dornbusch, R., Fischer, S., Startz, R., 2004. *Macroeconomics.* McGraw-Hill, New York.

Eichenbaum, M., Evans, C., 1995. Some empirical evidence on the effects of monetary policy shocks on exchange rates. *Quarterly Journal of Economics* 110 (4), 975–1010.

Fan, J., Gijbels, I., 1996. *Local Polynomial Modelling and Its Applications.* Chapman & Hall, London.

Ghosal, S., Sen, A., van der Vaart, A.W., 2000. Testing monotonicity of regression. *The Annals of Statistics* 28 (4), 1054–1082.

Kehoe, P.J., Midrigan, V., 2007. Sticky prices and sectoral real exchange rates. Federal Reserve Bank of Minneapolis Working Paper, No. 656.

Ramsey, J.B., 1969. Tests for specification errors in classical linear least-squares regression analysis. *Journal of the Royal Statistical Society B* 31 (2), 350–371.

Rogers, J.H., 1999. Monetary shocks and real exchange rates. *Journal of International Economics* 49 (2), 269–288.

Steinsson, J., 2008. The dynamic behavior of the real exchange rate in sticky price models. *American Economic Review* 98 (1), 519–533.

Stockman, A.C., 1980. A theory of exchange rate determination. *Journal of Political Economy* 88 (4), 673–698.

Chapter 12

Noisy Information, Distance and Law of One Price Dynamics Across US Cities*

Mario J. Crucini

Department of Economics, Vanderbilt University,
Nashville, TN, USA
and National Bureau of Economic Research, Cambridge, MA, USA
and Centre for Applied Macroeconomic Analysis, Canberra, Australia
mario.crucini@vanderbilt.edu

Mototsugu Shintani

Department of Economics, Vanderbilt University,
Nashville, TN 37235-1819, USA
and RCAST, The University of Tokyo, Japan

and

Takayuki Tsuruga

Graduate School of Economics, Kyoto University,
Kyoto, Japan
and Centre for Applied Macroeconomic Analysis, Canberra, Australia

Abstract. US micro price data at the city level suggests that both the volatility and the persistence of law of one price deviations are rising in the distance between US cities. A standard two-city equilibrium model with trade costs can predict the relationship between volatility and

*This chapter originally appeared in *Journal of Monetary Economics*, 2015, **74**, 52–66.

distance but not between persistence and distance. We show that if there is imperfect information about the state of nominal aggregate demand, with noisy signals that are asymmetric across cities, then distance and persistence will be positively correlated. Our main results are shown to be robust to the introduction of sticky prices and multiple cities.

Keywords: Real exchange rates; Law of one price; Relative prices; Trade costs

1. Introduction

Trade costs still matter even among highly integrated economies. The empirical trade literature has shown a negative relationship between bilateral trade flows and distance to be robust across time and countries (see Disdier and Head, 2008). More recently, Anderson and van Wincoop (2004) survey the empirical literature on the law of one price (LOP) and emphasize the observed positive correlation between LOP deviations and distance. These correlations are across countries, and are consistent with a broad range of static trade theories in which distance proxies for trade costs.[1] The international macroeconomics literature has emphasized the time series properties of LOP deviations, specifically, their volatility and persistence. Most notably, Engel and Rogers (1996) and Parsley and Wei (2001) find a positive correlation between the time-series volatility of LOP deviations and distance. This correlation can be explained by using a variety of dynamic stochastic general equilibrium models of trade. For example, Crucini *et al.* (2010a, hereafter CST) develop a simple sticky price model where intranational LOP deviations are driven by time-varying productivity to account for the positive correlation between the time-series volatility and trade costs. In contrast to the volatility-distance correlation, less is known about the persistence-distance correlation.

The objective of this paper is to understand both empirically and theoretically whether LOP persistence is rising in the distance separating retail markets. Using micro data on price differences

[1]For example, these can be obtained either by a variant of a static Ricardian model of Eaton and Kortum (2002) or by the static trade model of Helpman *et al.* (2008) which emphasizes the self-selection of firms into export markets. See also Kano *et al.* (2013).

across US cities, both persistence and volatility are found to be positively correlated with the distance between cities. Whereas CST can produce a positive volatility-distance correlation, it fails to predict a positive persistence-distance correlation. To overcome this difficulty, the dynamic model of CST is extended with imperfect common knowledge as developed by Woodford (2003) and Angeletos and La'O (2009), among others.

In the macroeconomics literature, it has been widely argued that heterogeneous expectations help to generate more plausible predictions about the inflation-output trade-off than homogeneous expectations. Mankiw and Reis (2002) and Woodford (2003) extend the homogenous expectations models of Lucas (1972) and Phelps (1970) by introducing (i) heterogenous expectations with strategic complementarities in firm's decision making under monopolistic competition and (ii) nominal aggregate demand shocks which cannot be common knowledge even in the long-run. Subsequent work by Angeletos and La'O (2009) simplifies the second assumption to the case where shocks will be publicly known after one period and suggest that the introduction of sticky prices into the flexible price model of imperfect common knowledge can improve predictions on inflation and output dynamics.

Following this line of research, we introduce information frictions to explain the persistence and volatility of intra-national LOP deviations. Specifically, we modify the dynamic model of intra-national LOP deviations used in CST by introducing the assumption of heterogeneous expectations about the state of nominal demand across cities in the economy. Analytical results show that when information precision is heterogenous across cities, our two-city model produces a positive correlation between persistence and distance while preserving the prediction of the positive volatility-distance correlation produced by standard perfect information models. Our results are robust to extensions that include sticky prices or more than two cities.

The paper is organized as follows. Empirical findings from the US price data are explained in Section 2. Section 3 introduces the theoretical model and explores its implications for LOP dynamics. Section 4 reports on robustness analysis. Section 5 concludes.

2. Regressions

Using the US data, this section provides evidence on the persistence-distance correlation.

2.1. *Data*

The data are individual prices from the *American Chamber of Commerce Researchers Association* (ACCRA) *Cost of Living Index* produced by the Council of Community and Economic Research. The original ACCRA *Cost of Living Index* includes 75 goods and services across 632 cities. However, when a balanced panel from 1990:Q1 to 2007:Q4 is constructed, the number of items and cities are reduced to 48 and 52, respectively.[2]

In measuring the LOP deviations, we follow Crucini and Shintani (2008) and consider all possible city pairs for each good or service. Let $q_{j,k,t}(i)$ be the LOP deviation measured as the difference between the logarithm of the price of good i in city j and that of the same good in city k:

$$q_{j,k,t}(i) = \ln P_{j,t}(i) - \ln P_{k,t}(i),$$

for $i = 1, 2, \ldots, 48$ and for all $j, k = 1, 2, \ldots, 52$ with $j \neq k$. Because the number of cities is 52, the total number of city pairs is 1326 in our data set. For each of the 63, 648 (48×1326) series of relative prices, we compute persistence measures along with volatility measures, which are summarized in Table 1. Our persistence measures of $q_{j,k,t}(i)$ are: (i) the first-order autocorrelation, (ii) the sum of autoregressive coefficients (SAR), and (iii) the largest autoregressive (AR) root. The latter two persistence measures are computed by estimating univariate AR(p) models of $q_{j,k,t}(i)$ for each good and city pair separately (running 63,648 autoregressions in total).[3] The first three

[2]We closely follow Yazgan and Yilmazkuday (2011) in the construction of panel data. See their paper for the detailed explanation on the selection of items and cities.

[3]We compute the first-order autocorrelation simply by estimating a coefficient in an AR(1) model. For the SAR and the largest AR root, we select lag lengths of AR models based on the Bayesian Information Criterion (BIC).

Table 1. Summary statistics.

	Persistence measure			Volatility measure	
City pairs	ρ_q	SAR	Largest AR root	sd_q	$mapd_q$
All	0.520	0.534	0.542	0.136	0.158
	(0.151)	(0.149)	(0.147)	(0.038)	(0.045)
(Obs. = 63,648)	[0.238]	[0.244]	[0.246]	[0.057]	[0.089]
Less than 100 miles	0.482	0.493	0.503	0.127	0.127
	(0.174)	(0.173)	(0.166)	(0.040)	(0.046)
(Obs. = 624)	[0.250]	[0.254]	[0.250]	[0.056]	[0.076]
More than 2000 miles	0.563	0.578	0.585	0.150	0.243
	(0.145)	(0.147)	(0.147)	(0.045)	(0.108)
(Obs. = 3648)	[0.222]	[0.229]	[0.233]	[0.061]	[0.149]

Notes: Reported numbers are the averages of the estimated persistence and volatility measures over goods and services where the total number of observations is denoted by "Obs." The LOP deviations, $q_{j,k,t}(i)$, are calculated as the logarithm of the relative price of a good or service in a city to the same good or service in a different city. The sample period is over 1990:Q1–2007:Q4. Persistence measures are the first-order autocorrelations (ρ_q), the sum of autoregressive coefficients (SAR), and the largest autoregressive root (Largest AR root). The AR order is selected based on the BIC. Volatility measures are the standard deviation (sd_q) and mean absolute price difference ($mapd_q$). The numbers in parentheses are the between-group standard deviations across 48 items. The numbers in brackets are the total standard deviations. The upper panel shows statistics for all observations. The middle and lower panels show statistics among city pairs with distance being less than 100 miles and with distance being more than 2000 miles, respectively.

rows in the left panel of the table report the summary statistics for the persistence measures of $q_{j,k,t}(i)$ together with the standard deviations between 48 goods and across the entire sample. The full sample averages are 0.52 for the first-order autocorrelation, 0.53 for the SAR, and 0.54 for the largest AR root. These estimates are consistent with other studies that find persistence is low when micro-price data is used in place of CPI data. We also report the volatility measures used by Parsley and Wei (1996) in their study of the ACCRA *Cost of Living Index* over the period 1975:Q1–1992:Q4. The volatility measures, tabulated in the right panel, are the standard deviation (sd_q) and the mean absolute price difference ($mapd_q$), where the latter measure is defined as the time-series average of

$|q_{j,k,t}(i)|$. Pooling all goods and bilateral pairs, sd_q is 0.136 and $mapd_q$ is 0.158. Both of these are close to their counterparts in Parsley and Wei (1996), suggesting some robustness of these measures over time.

Table 1 also reports persistence and volatility measures of LOP deviations for city pairs whose locations are very close or are very far apart. The fourth to sixth rows of the table report the persistence and volatility for 13 city pairs in which the distance between cities is less than 100 miles. Both persistence and volatility take values below the averages of all city pairs. In contrast, when we pick 76 city pairs in which the distance between cities is more than 2000 miles, the averages of the persistence and volatility are above the averages of all city pairs. The contrast of these nearby and distant city pairings suggests that the persistence and volatility of LOP deviations are positively correlated to the distance separating the cities. In the next sub-section, we formally examine this relationship by regression analysis.

2.2. *Regression results*

The existing literature has assigned an important role for trade costs in the determination of LOP volatility. Specifically, Engel and Rogers (1996) and Parsley and Wei (1996, 2001), among many others, have found that the LOP volatility is positively associated with the distance separating city pairs, a proxy for the trade cost. The well-known volatility-distance correlation is also confirmed in our dataset. When we pool all goods and run the volatility-distance regression using two volatility measures reported in Table 1 with good-specific dummies, the coefficients on the logarithm of distance are found to be positive and significant. The magnitudes of estimated coefficients are broadly in line with Parsley and Wei (1996).[4]

Our main focus is the persistence-distance relationship, rather than the volatility-distance relationship. Thus, we use regression with

---

[4]In particular, the coefficient estimates are 0.008 with the standard errors (clustered by city pairs) of 0.0004 when the dependent variable is sd_q and 0.03 with the standard errors of 0.002 when the dependent variable is $mapd_q$.

its regressand replaced by persistence.

$$\rho_{q_{j,k}}(i) = a(i) + b \ln dist_{j,k} + u_{j,k}(i),$$

where $\rho_{q_{j,k}}(i)$ is the first-order autocorrelation of LOP deviations of good i between cities j and k, ln $dist_{j,k}$ is the logarithm of the great-circle distance between cities j and k, $a(i)$ is the good-specific fixed effect, and $u_{j,k}(i)$ is the regression error. For robustness, we also use SAR and the largest AR root as the regressand.

Table 2 reports the persistence-distance regression results for a variety of specifications. Specification (1) is the benchmark specification based on the above equation. The results show significantly positive correlations between all persistence measures and distance, based on standard errors clustered by city pairs reported below the estimates.[5] Suppose the distance between the cities increases from 100 miles to 2000 miles. Using the specification with the first-order autocorrelation as the regressand, the coefficient estimate of 0.02 implies that the LOP persistence is increased by 0.06 $(= 0.02 \times \ln(2000/100))$. The increment in persistence is essentially the same when we use the SAR or the largest AR root.

Specification (2) in Table 2 replaces the good-specific effects with the distribution cost shares used in Crucini and Shintani (2008) who find that goods with higher distribution cost shares exhibit higher LOP persistence.[6] The distribution share is the wedge between what final consumers pay and what producers receive. These distribution costs include retail costs, markups and taxes. The distribution share can be used as an alternative measure of nontradability and, in fact, is included in the trade cost measures reported in Anderson and van Wincoop (2004). Our distribution shares are constructed based on sectoral US data aggregated to the national level. Therefore, our distribution shares vary across items but not across city pairs. Since

[5]We also confirmed that the coefficients on distance were statistically significant based on standard errors clustered by goods.

[6]We compare the items from EIU's *Worldwide Cost of Living Survey* used in Crucini and Shintani (2008) with those from ACCRA dataset and construct the distribution share variable for our regression analysis.

Table 2. Persistence-distance regressions.

Dependent variables	ρ_q				SAR				Largest AR root			
Regressors	(1)	(2)	(3)	(4)	(1)	(2)	(3)	(4)	(1)	(2)	(3)	(4)
$\ln dist_{j,k}$	0.020	0.020	0.019	0.019	0.023	0.023	0.022	0.022	0.026	0.026	0.025	0.025
	(0.002)	(0.002)	(0.002)	(0.002)	(0.002)	(0.002)	(0.002)	(0.005)	(0.002)	(0.002)	(0.002)	(0.002)
$distribution\ share_i$		0.342		0.280		0.322		0.259		0.261		0.202
		(0.004)		(0.005)		(0.004)		(0.005)		(0.005)		(0.005)
λ_i			0.209	0.129			0.214	0.140			0.213	0.156
			(0.004)	(0.004)			(0.004)	(0.004)			(0.004)	(0.004)
Good dummies	Yes	No	No	No	Yes	No	No	No	Yes	No	No	No
Obs.	63,648	63,648	58,344	58,344	63,648	63,648	58,344	58,344	63,648	63,648	58,344	58,344
Adj. R^2	0.40	0.12	0.05	0.11	0.37	0.10	0.05	0.10	0.37	0.10	0.05	0.10

Notes: The regression models are estimated using data for 48 items and 1326 city-pairs. Standard errors clustered by city-pairs are given in parentheses below the coefficients. The regression coefficients are reported for distance ($\ln dist_{j,k}$), the distribution shares ($distribution\ share_i$) and the degree of price stickiness (λ_i). See the footnote of Table 1 for the detail of dependent variables. The number of observations (Obs.) in regressions are 63,648 for all items, and 58,344 if λ_i is used as a regressor, because no data of the degree of price stickiness is available for four items related to shelters (i.e., monthly rent for apartment, total home purchase price, mortgage rate, and monthly payment for house). The "Adj. R_2" in the last row denotes the adjusted R-squared.

the distance and distribution share are orthogonal to each other by construction, the coefficient on distance is essentially unaltered from specification (1). Consistent with the previous finding, the estimated coefficients on the distribution share are all positive and significant. The estimates indicate that the goods and services with higher distribution shares have a significantly slower speed of adjustment. The estimated coefficients range between 0.26 and 0.34, depending on what regressand is used. This additional regression confirms a positive relationship between trade cost and persistence when trade costs are proxied either by the distance which captures city-pair variation or by the distribution share which captures good-specific variation.

In specifications (3) and (4), we perform the robustness analysis by including the degree of price stickiness in the regressions. These specifications are in the spirit of earlier studies emphasizing the effect of price stickiness on persistence of good-level real exchange rates or LOP deviations (e.g., Kehoe and Midrigan, 2007; Crucini *et al.*, 2010b; Carvalho and Nechio, 2011). These studies show theoretically (and confirm empirically) that LOP persistence is rising in the degree of price stickiness. Here, we measure the good-level degree of price stickiness λ_i as the probability of no price change at a quarterly frequency measured by $(1-f_i)^3$, where f_i is the monthly frequency of price changes reported by Nakamura and Steinsson (2008). Again, in both specifications, the coefficient on distance is essentially unaltered from specification (1). The coefficients on the distribution share in specification (4) decrease somewhat, but remain positive and statistically significant. We also note that the coefficient on λ_i is positive which is consistent with theoretical predictions.

Our findings on the relationship between persistence and distance are broadly consistent with the few existing previous works. For example, Parsley and Wei (1996) report positive coefficients on the interaction terms of lagged relative prices and distance in augmented Dickey–Fuller regressions of relative prices between pairs of US cities. Their results imply that the convergence rate, measured by the SAR, is slower between cities that are further apart. Obstfeld and Taylor (1997) use disaggregated CPI data from 32 countries and US and

Canadian cities and estimate a threshold autoregressive model with the price difference following a random walk within the band of arbitrage but converging to the level of trade cost from outside the band. They regress the estimated threshold on distance and find a weak positive relationship between persistence and distance because observed persistence typically becomes higher when the band of inaction widens. Cecchetti *et al.* (2002) examine the persistence of deviations from purchasing power parity (rather than LOP) using aggregate price indexes of 19 US cities from 1918 to 1995, and find that both the SAR and half-lives are positively correlated with distance. Choi and Matsubara (2007) investigate sector-level price differences among Japanese cities from 1970 to 2002. They find that, for 22 out of 36 items, the estimated half-lives are positively correlated with distance. Although estimation results from previous works described above may not be directly comparable to ours due to the difference in data and methods, the positive relationship between persistence and distance has been gaining empirical support in the literature.

3. Model

In this section, we develop a model with imperfect information and investigate whether it can explain the observed positive correlation between persistence and distance, as well as the observed positive correlation between volatility and distance.

3.1. *A noisy information model*

We employ a flexible price version of CST that adds noisy information about aggregate nominal expenditure to explain the positive persistence–distance correlation. The economy consists of two cities 1 and 2 within the same country. The economy is populated by a single representative household and a continuum of firms. Trade is over a continuum of goods, which involves the iceberg transportation cost of τ per unit to carry goods between the two cities. Under monopolistic competition, firms set prices to satisfy demand for a particular good in a particular city (i.e., pricing to market). The representative household chooses consumption and labor supply over an infinite horizon subject to a cash-in-advance (CIA) constraint. The unit of time is one quarter.

We consider three levels of constant-elasticity-of-substitution (CES) aggregation. The lowest level of aggregation is across brands v. Here, brands produced in city 1 are indexed $v \in [0,1]$ while those produced in city 2 are indexed $v \in (1,2]$. The CES index for the consumption of a particular good $i \in [0,1]$ sold in a particular city $j(=1,2)$ is given by $C_{j,t}(i) = [(1/2)^{1/\xi} \int_0^2 C_{j,t}(i,v)^{(\xi-1)/\xi} dv]^{\xi/(\xi-1)}$, where ξ is the elasticity of substitution across varieties satisfying $\xi > 1$ and $C_{j,t}(i,v)$ denotes consumption for brand v of good i consumed in city j. Aggregating across the two cities gives national consumption of good i, $C_t(i) = [(1/2)^{1/\xi} \sum_{j=1}^{2} C_{j,t}(i)^{(\xi-1)/\xi}]^{\xi/(\xi-1)}$. Aggregating further across goods i gives aggregate national consumption, $C_t = [\int_0^1 C_t(i)^{(\xi-1)/\xi} di]^{\xi/(\xi-1)}$. The correspondent CES price indices for good i in city j, good i nationally, and aggregate national consumption are given by $P_{j,t}(i) = [(1/2) \int_0^2 P_{j,t}(i,v)^{1-\xi} dv]^{1/(1-\xi)}$, $P_t(i) = [(1/2) \sum_{j=1}^{2} P_{j,t}(i)^{1-\xi}]^{1/(1-\xi)}$, and $P_t = [\int_0^1 P_t(i)^{1-\xi} di]^{1/(1-\xi)}$, respectively.[7]

Households in this economy trade complete state-contingent financial claims and choose consumption (C_t) and labor supply (L_t) over an infinite horizon subject to budget and CIA constraints. The household instantaneous utility is given by $\ln C_t - \chi L_t$, resulting in the intra-temporal first-order condition between consumption and labor: $W_t/\mathrm{P}_t = \chi C_t$, where W_t is the nominal wage rate. The CIA constraint is $\Theta_t = P_t C_t$ and thus the nominal wage rate is proportional to the nominal money demand (or equivalently aggregate nominal expenditure): $W_t = \chi \Theta_t$. In this paper, we assume that the logarithm of aggregate nominal expenditure ($\theta_t = \ln \Theta_t$)

[7]One can also consider an alternative sequence of aggregations which interchanges the aggregation across cities j and the aggregation across goods i. While this allows for the general price indexes at the city level, such a change in the sequence of aggregation does not affect results in this paper.

follows a random walk process:

$$\theta_t = \theta_{t-1} + \varepsilon_t^\theta, \varepsilon_t^\theta \sim \text{iid}\, N(0, \sigma_\theta^2). \tag{1}$$

The firms' technology is

$$Y_t(i, v) = Z_t(i, v)[\Gamma_t^d(i, v)]^\alpha [L_t^d(i, v)]^{1-\alpha}, \tag{2}$$

where $Y_t(i, v), Z_t(i, v), \Gamma_t^d(i, v)$, and $L_t^d(i, v)$ denote output, exogenous productivity, the inputs of composite intermediate goods, and labor, respectively. Here $\alpha \in [0, 1)$ is the share of intermediate goods and represents the degree of strategic complementarities (see Huang *et al.*, 2004).

Note that the intermediate goods purchased by each firm are composites of all goods. Therefore, the market clearing condition for intermediate goods is given by $\int_0^1 \int_0^2 \Gamma_t^d(i, v)\, dv\, di = \Gamma_t$ where Γ_t is aggregate intermediate goods defined similarly to C_t with the brand-level intermediate goods sold in city j, denoted as $\Gamma_{j,t}(i, v)$. since firms must pay the iceberg transportation cost ($\tau > 0$) to carry their goods between cities, the market clearing conditions for each brand of each good satisfy

$$Y_t(i, v) = C_{1,t}(i, v) + \Gamma_{1,t}(i, v) + (1 + \tau)[C_{2,t}(i, v) + \Gamma_{2,t}(i, v)] \quad \text{for } v \in [0, 1], \tag{3}$$

$$Y_t(i, v) = (1 + \tau)[C_{1,t}(i, v) + \Gamma_{1,t}(i, v)] + C_{2,t}(i, tv) + \Gamma_{2,t}(i, v) \quad \text{for } v \in (1, 2]. \tag{4}$$

The market clearing condition for labor is given by $\int_0^1 \int_0^2 L_t^d(i, v)\, dv\, di = L_t$.

We assume that productivity ($z_t(i, v) = \ln Z_t(i, v)$) is common across brands, but specific to the good and the place of production:

$$z_t(i, v) = \begin{cases} z_{1,t}(i) & \text{for } v \in [0, 1] \\ z_{2,t}(i) & \text{for } v \in (1, 2], \end{cases} \tag{5}$$

where $z_{\ell,t}(i)$ follows a stationary ARMA process:

$$A_\ell^i(L) z_{\ell,t}(i) = B_\ell^i(L) \varepsilon_{\ell,t}^z(i), \quad \varepsilon_{\ell,t}^z(i) \sim \text{iid} N(0, \sigma_z^2(\ell)) \tag{6}$$

where $A_\ell^i(L)$ and $B_\ell^i(L)$ are lag polynomials for AR and MA components which differ across goods and the place of production. We further assume that $\sigma_z^2(\ell)$ is location specific such that the productivity innovations for good i are independently drawn from a distribution with a location-specific variance. Using these assumptions, we allow for the possibility that persistence and volatility of $z_{\ell,t}(i)$ are both good- and location-specific. Throughout this paper, we measure the persistence of $z_{\ell,t}(i)$ by the first-order autocorrelation $\rho_{z,\ell}(i)$ and assume that $0 < \rho_{z,\ell}(i) < 1$ for $i \in [0,1]$ and $\ell = 1, 2$.

Following Angeletos and La'O (2009), we assume that each period is divided in two stages. In stage 1, prices are set under imperfect information. In stage 2, the information on θ_t is revealed, and consumption and employment choices are made taking the prices determined in stage 1 as given. Building on the framework of Angeletos and La'O (2009), we introduce retail managers who decide prices for each firm. Managers set prices for the firm's brands in the city in which they live. The retail managers are assumed to be fully informed about the productivity of their own firm, but imperfectly informed about the current state of nominal aggregate demand.

In stage 1, retail managers receive idiosyncratic noisy signals $x_{j,t}(i, v)$ of θ_t:

$$x_{j,t}(i, v) = \theta_t + \varepsilon_{j,t}^x(i, v), \quad \text{where } \varepsilon_{j,t}^x(i, v) \sim \text{iid}N(0, \sigma_x^2(j)). \qquad (7)$$

We allow retail managers' signals and variability of noise $\varepsilon_{j,t}^x(i, v)$ to differ across cities j. Recall that $\sigma_z^2(\ell)$ is location specific. We also assume that $\sigma_x^2(j)$ is location specific such that $\varepsilon_{j,t}^x(i, v)$ is independently drawn from a distribution with a location-specific variance. This reflects the assumption that retail managers are isolated in city j in terms of their information and receive idiosyncratic signals of nominal aggregate demand with different levels of precision.

Following Angeletos and La'O (2009), in stage 2, aggregate nominal expenditure becomes common knowledge (see also, Fukunaga, 2007). We later discuss the possibility of replacing this assumption with an alternative of persistent informational deficiencies. Let $\mathbb{I}_{j,t}(i, v)$ and $\mathbb{I}'_{j,t}(i, v)$ be the information sets in period t, for the retail managers in city j at stages 1 and 2, respectively. Within period t, the retail managers' information set evolves as follows:

$$\mathbb{I}_{j,t}(i,v) = \mathbb{I}'_{j,t-1}(i,v) \cup [x_{j,t}(i,v), z_t(i,v)] \quad \text{and}$$
$$\mathbb{I}'_{j,t}(i,v) = \mathbb{I}_{j,t}(i,v) \cup \{\theta_t\}. \tag{8}$$

Note that the information is purely idiosyncratic: the information set differs across j, i, and v.

The log-linearization of the optimal individual prices, with suppressed constant terms, yields

$$p_{j,t}(i,v) = (1-\alpha)\mathbb{E}_{j,t}(\theta_t|i,v) + \alpha\mathbb{E}_{j,t}(p_t|i,v) - z_t(i,v), \tag{9}$$

where $p_{j,t}(i,v) = \ln P_{j,t}(i,v), p_t = \ln P_t$, and $\mathbb{E}_{j,t}(\cdot|i,v)$ denotes the expectation operator conditional on $\mathbb{I}_{j,t}(i,v)$.[8] Note that θ_t appears in (9) because the nominal wage rate in our model is proportional to the aggregate nominal expenditure.

The price index for good i sold in city 1 can be approximated by

$$p_{1,t}(i) = s\int_0^1 p_{1,t}(i,v)\,dv + (1-s)\int_1^2 p_{1,t}(i,v)dv, \tag{10}$$

where s is the steady state expenditure share on home-produced goods, or the "home bias" parameter satisfying $s > 1/2$. This home bias parameter s is given by

$$s = \frac{1}{1+(1+\tau)^{1-\xi}}.$$

Importantly, s is an increasing function of τ. The home bias makes the home city price index more sensitive to the price of home-produced goods than that of goods produced in the other city. Since a larger home bias is caused by more costly transportation of goods, s is increasing in τ. The price in city 2, $p_{2,t}(i)$, is similarly derived.

[8]See Appendix A.1 for the derivation of (9). In general, the optimal prices differ across the locations of sales because of the presence of the trade cost. However, since we suppressed the constant term which depends on the trade cost, (9) can be used for both cases of $j = k$ and $j \neq k$.

Finally, we address how expectations about nominal aggregate demand are formed. We use a standard signal extraction problem:

$$\mathbb{E}_{j,t}(\theta_t|i,v) = \kappa_j x_{j,t}(i,v) + (1-\kappa_j)\theta_{t-1} \quad \text{for } j = 1, 2. \tag{11}$$

where k_j is the steady-state Kalman gain defined as $\sigma_\theta^2/[\sigma_\theta^2 + \sigma_x^2(j)]$.

3.2. *Characterizing the equilibrium*

The model is solved by the method of undetermined coefficients. The resulting equilibrium prices are characterized by the following proposition:

Proposition 1. *Under the preference assumption* ($\ln C - \chi L$), *the CIA constraint, the stochastic processes of aggregate nominal expenditure* (1) *and productivity* (6), *and the imperfect information specified as* (7) *and* (8), *the aggregate price index is given by*

$$p_t = \omega\theta_t + (1-\omega)\theta_{t-1}, \tag{12}$$

where $\omega = (1-\alpha)\overline{\kappa}/(1-\alpha\overline{\kappa})$ *and* $\overline{\kappa} = (\kappa_1+\kappa_2)/2$. *The price indexes for good i sold in city* 1 *and* 2 *can be expressed as*

$$p_{1,t}(i) = (1-\alpha+\alpha\omega)\kappa_1\varepsilon_t^\theta + \theta_{t-1} - sz_{1,t}(i) - (1-s)z_{2,t}(i), \tag{13}$$

$$p_{2,t}(i) = (1-\alpha+\alpha\omega)\kappa_2\varepsilon_t^\theta + \theta_{t-1} - sz_{2,t}(i) - (1-s)z_{1,t}(i), \tag{14}$$

respectively. Also, the relative price $q_t(i) \equiv p_{2,t}(i) - p_{1,t}(i)$ *equals*

$$q_t(i) = \phi\varepsilon_t^\theta + (2s-1)z_t(i), \tag{15}$$

where $\phi = (1-\alpha)\kappa/(1-\alpha\overline{\kappa})$, $\kappa = \kappa_2 - \kappa_1$, *and* $z_t(i) = z_{1,t}(i) - z_{2,t}(i)$.

The proof is provided in Appendix A.2. Here $\bar{\kappa}$ may be interpreted as the level of information precision in the macroeconomy and κ is a measure of the spatial dispersion of information precision between the two cities. For ease of exposition, κ is referred to as the information difference, which is one of the key parameters of the model. Without loss of generality, let $\kappa_1 \le \kappa_2$ so that $\kappa \ge 0$. Finally, $z_t(i)$ represents the productivity difference between two cities.

Equations (13) and (14) indicate that $p_{j,t}(i)$ is affected by ε_t^θ, $z_{1,t}(i)$, and $z_{2,t}(i)$. Here, the response of $p_{j,t}(i)$ to ε_t^θ varies across cities, depending on the precision of signals that managers receive in each city. If managers in city j have less precise signals (larger $\sigma_x^2(j)$), individual prices in city j respond less to signals (smaller κ_j) and thus $p_{j,t}(i)$ is less sensitive to shocks to aggregate nominal expenditure. Also, $p_{j,t}(i)$ responds to productivity shocks in the home city more strongly than in the other city, due to the home bias in expenditure shares arising from trade costs (i.e., $s > 1/2$).

Difference in price responses between (13) and (14) generates the LOP deviations in (15). It should be noted that $q_t(i)$ now only depends on ε_t^θ and $z_t(i)$. First, the aggregate nominal demand shock ε_t^θ matters for $q_t(i)$. To see this, suppose productivity is equal across cities so that $z_t(i) = 0$. The difference in price responses to ε_t^θ gives rise to an LOP deviation that lasts for one period because ε_t^θ is assumed to be fully revealed to all managers in the next period.[9] The coefficient ϕ on ε_t^θ is increasing in the information differences. Second, the productivity difference between two cities $z_t(i)$ also drives LOP deviations.[10] To understand how $z_t(i)$ affects LOP deviations, suppose that $\varepsilon_t^\theta = 0$ and that productivity in city 1 increases by one percent. The difference in price responses to $z_{1,t}(i)$ leads to an LOP deviation because the productivity improvement in city 1 decreases the price of index in city 1 by larger amount than the price index in city 2. In this case, LOP deviations persist, depending on the persistence of the productivity difference. The coefficient $(2s - 1 > 0)$ on $z_t(i)$ is increasing in the size of the trade cost.

[9]A more general treatment would allow for the presence of persistent informational deficiencies. As in the case of Mankiw and Reis (2002) and Woodford (2003), the nominal shocks will have a longer effect.

[10]Note that $q_t(i)$ in (15) can always be approximated by the AR(p) process with a large p. This justifies the use of the AR(p) model in computing the persistence measures in Section 2. For example, when $z_{1,t}(i)$ and $z_{2,t}(i)$ follow an AR(1) process with common persistence parameter $\rho_z(i), q_t(i)$ can be expressed as an ARMA(1, 1) process, which has an AR(∞) representation.

The original CST model that assumes perfect information predicts the volatility–distance correlation, but not the persistence–distance correlation. Under flexible prices, LOP deviations in the CST model are given by $q_t(i) = (2s - 1)z_t(i)$, which can be obtained from Eq. (7) of CST (p. 427) combined with $\lambda_i = 0$. This matches with (15) in Proposition 1 under perfect information (i.e., $\kappa_1 = \kappa_2 = 1$), because $\phi = 0$ when $\kappa = 1 - 1 = 0$. In this case, the productivity difference alone drives the inter-city LOP deviations. From this equation, volatility increases with trade cost (or distance) because a rise in τ increases $2s-1$ and thus amplifies the fluctuation of $z_t(i)$ via $2s - 1$. In contrast, the persistence of LOP deviations is invariant to the trade cost τ, and simply equals $Z_t(i)\rho_z(i)$ due to the one-to-one relationship between $q_t(i)$ and $z_t(i)$.[11] In the next subsection, we show that the noisy information model explains both the volatility–distance and the persistence–distance correlations.

3.3. *Comparative statics*

We now discuss comparative statics of volatility and persistence of LOP deviations with respect to the trade cost, which is often proxied by distance. As emphasized in Kehoe and Midrigan (2007) and CST, both the strategic complementary parameter α and the productivity persistence parameter $\rho_{z,\ell}(i)$ play an important role in explaining the persistence and volatility of LOP deviations. With respect to the persistence, our model adds a third key parameter, κ, which captures the information differences between retail managers. As we will show below, the presence of asymmetric noisy information structure ($\kappa \neq 0$) allows us to account for the persistence–distance correlation.

Before proceeding, note that, given the independence of $z_{1,t}(i)$ and $z_{2,t}(i)$, the variance of $z_t(i)$ is simply the sum of variances of the location-specific productivity (i.e., $\text{var}[z_t(i)] = \text{var}[z_{1,t}(i)] + [z_{2,t}(i)]$). Consequently, the first-order autocorrelation of $z_t(i)$ can be expressed

[11]It is straightforward to show that the LOP persistence remains invariant to the trade cost, even when sticky prices are introduced into the model.

as a weighted average of the first-order autocorrelations of $z_{1,t}(i)$ and $z_{2,t}(i)$:

$$\rho_z(i) = \frac{\text{var}[z_{1,t}(i)]}{\text{var}\,[z_t(i)]}\rho_{z,1}(i) + \frac{\text{var}[z_{2,t}(i)]}{\text{var}\,[z_t(i)]}\rho_{z,2}(i). \tag{16}$$

Using (15), the standard deviation of the LOP deviation is $sd_q(i) = \sqrt{\text{var}[q_t(i)]}$ where

$$\text{var}[q_t(i)] = \phi^2\sigma_\theta^2 + (2s-1)^2\text{var}[z_t(i)]. \tag{17}$$

Thus, the variance of LOP deviation is rising in the information differences, because ϕ is increasing in κ.

Now, the first-order autocorrelation of $q_t(i)$ is given by

$$\rho_q(i) = \frac{(2s-1)^2\text{var}\,[z_t(i)]}{\phi^2\sigma_\theta^2 + (2s-1)^2\text{var}\,[z_t(i)]}\rho_q(i). \tag{18}$$

Notice that the persistence of LOP deviation is bounded from above by $\rho_z(i)$ and is falling in the extent of the information differences across retail managers.[12] We summarize the main results of our paper in the following proposition.

Proposition 2. *Under the maintained assumptions in Proposition 1, LOP deviations have the following properties:*

(i) *volatility measured by $sd_q(i)$ is increasing in the trade cost τ, $\partial sd_q(i)/\partial\tau > 0$;*
(ii) *persistence measured by $\rho_q(i)$ is independent of the trade cost τ when information about nominal aggregate demand θ_t is perfect (i.e., $\sigma_x(1) \to 0$ and $\sigma_x(2) \to 0$) or when information on θ_t is imperfect and information difference between managers in different cities is absent (i.e., $\kappa = 0$), $\partial\rho_q(i)/\partial\tau = 0$;*
(iii) *persistence measured by $\rho_q(i)$ is increasing in the trade cost τ when information about θ_t is imperfect and information difference between managers in different cities is present (i.e., $\kappa \neq 0$), $\partial\rho_q(i)/\partial\tau > 0$.*

[12] Appendix A.3 provides the derivations of (16)–(18).

The proposition implies that, when trade costs rise with the distance separating locations, the model with perfect information can account for the positive volatility–distance correlation discovered by the literature, but fails to predict the positive persistence–distance correlation. In contrast, the presence of an information difference across managers in different cities can account for both observations.[13]

To see the intuition for part (i) of Proposition 2, again suppose that there is a one percent increase in the location-specific productivity of city 1. If the trade cost is absent, the steady state expenditure share s equals 1/2, which implies that price indexes in both cities fall by the same amount and the relative price, $q_t(i) = p_{2,t}(i) - p_{1,t}(i)$, remains unchanged. In contrast, the presence of the trade cost causes home bias and the price index in city 1 falls more than that in city 2. Higher trade costs amplify this expenditure asymmetry which causes higher volatility of relative prices.

Let us now turn to part (ii) of Proposition 2. With perfect information, the effect of a change in θ_t on the price indexes in two cities cancels out because managers increase prices by the same amount in two cities. The same intuition applies to the case of the imperfect information without information difference. Because the same information precision of uninformed managers implies price increases by the same amount, in response to an increase in θ_t, the effect on the price indexes cancels out. In either of these cases, the relative prices are solely determined by the productivity differences and the persistence of $q_t(i)$ corresponds to the persistence of $z_t(i)$ which is independent of the trade cost.

The result of part (iii) of Proposition 2 can be explained as follows. When imperfect information is present with asymmetric information precision across managers in different cities, LOP

[13]As pointed out by an anonymous referee, Proposition 2 holds even if the assumption of heterogeneous information across retail managers given by (7) is replaced by the assumption of homogeneous information given by $x_{j,t}(i,v) = x_{j,t} = \theta_t + \sigma_x^2(j)\varepsilon_t^x$, where $\varepsilon_t^x \sim N(0,1)$. However, in such a case, dynamics of $q_t(i)$ will become more complicated and cannot be described simply by (15).

deviations with imperfect information consist of two components: the i.i.d. process $\phi\varepsilon_t^\theta$ and the persistent process of $(2s-1)z_t(i)$. Consequently, the persistence of LOP deviations is determined by the weighted average of the persistence of the two components. Thus, the persistence of $q_t(i)$ is bounded between zero and $\rho_z(i)$ and, in fact, the coefficient on $\rho_z(i)$ in (18) is the weight for the productivity difference. In the trivial case in which the home bias is zero ($s \to 1/2$), the LOP deviations are determined solely by i.i.d. innovations to aggregate nominal expenditure. As trade costs become larger, home bias increases ($s > 1/2$) and the contribution of the productivity difference to persistence rises. Therefore, when the trade cost is high, LOP deviations become more persistent. Indeed, the persistence of LOP rises from zero toward $\rho_z(i)$ as the trade cost increases.

Two additional remarks are useful at this point. First, it is of interest to see if the results in Proposition 2 continue to hold when Angeletos and La'O (2009) assumption of short-lived informational deficiencies is replaced by more persistent informational deficiencies, as in Mankiw and Reis (2002) and Woodford (2003). As long as informational deficiencies are less persistent than the productivity difference, our results remain valid. If $\bar{\kappa}$ is relatively large or α is relatively small, this condition is likely to be met under typical speed of informational deficiency adjustment considered in the modern imperfect information literature. Second, $z_t(i)$ disappears from (15) if the productivity $z_{\ell,t}(i)$ is common across two cities. Even when $z_t(i)$ is absent, if the model has city-specific preference shocks biased toward home goods and if the preference shocks in the two cities are persistent, the same qualitative results as in Proposition 2 can be obtained.[14] In this sense, our results do not critically depend on the assumption of the location-specific productivity.

3.4. *Numerical examples*

So far, persistence of $q_t(i)$ was demonstrated to be positively associated with trade costs in the noisy information model. At the same

[14]Details of this result is provided in Appendix A.4.

time, (18) shows that three key parameters $(\kappa, \alpha, \rho_z(i))$ determine the level of LOP persistence that arises in equilibrium. Here, we provide some assessment of the empirical relevance of the theory. We first ask how $\rho_q(i)$ changes over a plausible range of trade cost in the model. In particular, we show how $\rho_q(i)$ changes as a function of τ for various settings of κ, α, and $\rho_z(i)$, keeping the other parameters $\overline{\kappa}, \xi$, and $\text{var}[z_t(i)]/\sigma_\theta^2$ constant. We then evaluate the model based on its ability to replicate the estimated coefficient on distance in our persistence–distance regressions.

Beginning with the parameters whose values are kept constant throughout our analysis, the average of the Kalman gains across managers is set to $\overline{\kappa} = 0.5$, the benchmark value employed by Angeletos and La'O (2009) in their simulations. Conveniently, this makes κ lie on the unit interval [0,1]. The one extreme is $\kappa = 0$, where the noise-to-signal ratio is common across managers: $\sigma_x^2(1)/\sigma_\theta^2 = \sigma_x^2(2)/\sigma_\theta^2 = 1$. The other extreme is $\kappa = 1.00$, where one manager has no information about the shocks to θ_t while the other receives a perfect signal: $\sigma_x^2(1)/\sigma_\theta^2 = \infty$ and $\sigma_x^2(2)/\sigma_\theta^2 = 0$. The elasticity of substitution across goods is set to $\xi = 4$, a value taken from Broda and Weinstein (2006). Note that (18) implies that the persistence depends on the variance ratio, $\text{var}[z_t(i)]/\sigma_\theta^2$. We follow Crucini *et al.* (2013) and set $\sqrt{\text{var}[z_t(i)]/\sigma_\theta^2} = 5$.[15]

Grossman (1998) and Hummels (2001), among others, specify the relationship between trade costs and distance as a power function

$$\tau = c \times dist^{\delta}, \tag{19}$$

where *dist* is the distance between two locations, δ is the elasticity of τ with respect to distance and c is a constant. Following Anderson and van Wincoop (2004), we set $\delta = 0.30$, a consensus value in the empirical trade literature. If we assume that the average distance from the data in our regression analysis corresponds to the typical

[15]One of benchmark values of the standard deviation ratio of real shock to nominal shock was 5 in their analysis of international LOP. They claim that the value of 5 matches well with their data, compared to alternative values of 1 and 1/5.

trade cost value $\overline{\tau} = 0.20$ taken from the value used in CST, our sample implies the range of trade cost, $\tau \in [0.07, 0.30]$.[16]

Turning to the key parameters, κ, α, and $\rho_z(i)$ a wide range of values is considered. The information difference ranges upward from a base of no difference, $\kappa = 0, 0.20, 0.50$, and 0.80. Strategic complementarities include the values: $\alpha = 0, 0.45$, and 0.90. As shown in (18), the model suggests that $\rho_z(i)$ is the upper bound for $\rho_q(i)$. The lower panel of Table 1 shows that the LOP persistence for city pairs which are the farthest apart is 0.56 with a between-good standard deviation of 0.15. The persistence of productivity differences encompasses this level of LOP persistence: $\rho_z(i) = 0.30, 0.60$, and 0.90.

Figure 1 shows the relationship between $\rho_q(i)$ and $\ln\,\tau$, as well as the relationship between $sd_q(i)$ and $\ln\,\tau$, and their sensitivity to κ, when the other two key parameters are set at $\alpha = 0$ and $\rho_z(i) = 0.60$. The patterns confirm the properties proven in Proposition 2. The right panel of the figure shows that, regardless of values of information difference, the volatility of LOP deviations depends positively on $\ln\,\tau$.[17] In contrast, the curves for persistence in the left panel are upward-sloping only when κ is non-zero. If $\kappa = 0$, the persistence curve is flat, independent of $\ln\,\tau$ and equal to $\rho_z(i)(= 0.60)$. An increase in κ can be interpreted as a larger information difference between cities, and thus ϕ, ceteris paribus, increases. The increase in ϕ leads to a decline in the persistence of the LOP deviation because a larger information difference increases the importance of the i.i.d. nominal demand shock relative to the persistent productivity difference in the determination of the LOP deviations.

[16] Based on the US data, Anderson and van Wincoop (2004) estimate that total international frictions average 74 percent. These frictions are further divided into those arising from transportation costs amounting to a wedge of 21 percent and a border-related wedge of 44 percent ($1.74 = 1.21 \times 1.44$). Due to the absence of the international border in our model, our choice of $\overline{\tau} = 0.20$ seems reasonable for an average across bilateral city pairs.

[17] The volatility curve is drawn by fixing σ_θ^2 at 0.01 along with the assumption of $\sqrt{\text{var}[z_t(i)]/\sigma_\theta^2} = 5$.

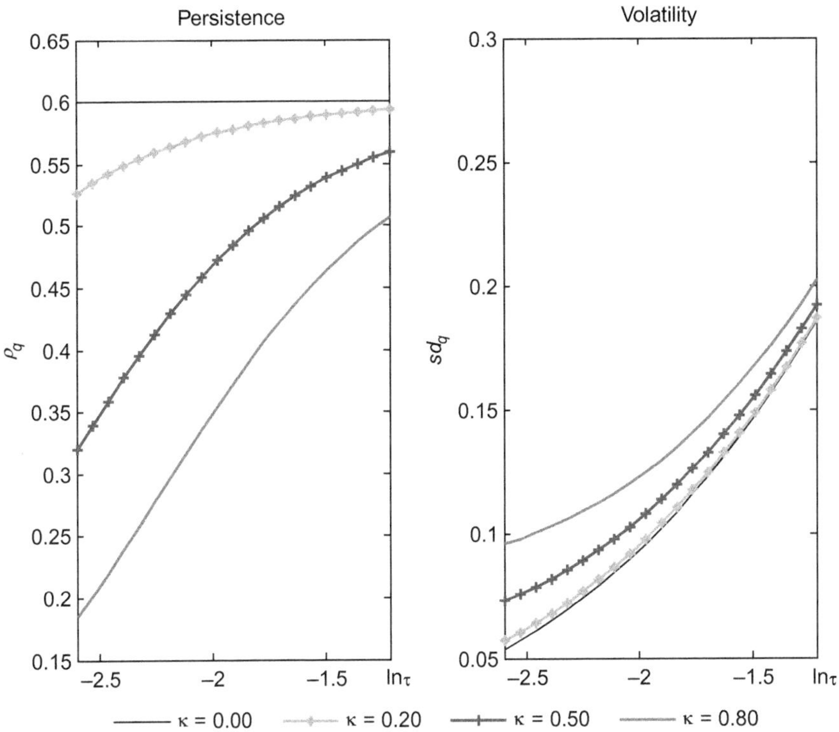

Fig. 1. Effect of information differences κ on persistence and volatility of LOP deviations.

Notes: Each line in the figure represents the first-order autocorrelation (the left panel) and the standard deviation (the right panel) of $q_t(i)$ against $\ln \tau$ for different values of κ. For parameterization we use $\alpha = 0, \rho_z(i) = 0.6, \overline{\kappa} = 0.5, \xi = 4,$ $\sqrt{\text{var}\{z_t(i)\}/\sigma_\theta^2} = 5, \overline{\tau} = 0.2,$ and $\delta = 0.3$.

Figure 2 shows persistence and volatility and their sensitivity to α, when the other two key parameters are fixed at $\kappa = 0.50$ and $\rho_z(i) = 0.60$. In Woodford's (2003) model of monetary non-neutrality where prices fluctuate according to shocks to aggregate nominal expenditure, he has emphasized that strategic complementarities can generate substantial persistence in output dynamics. We show that strategic complementarities also affect both the persistence and volatility of relative prices across locations. Stronger strategic complementarities raise the persistence because price indexes are

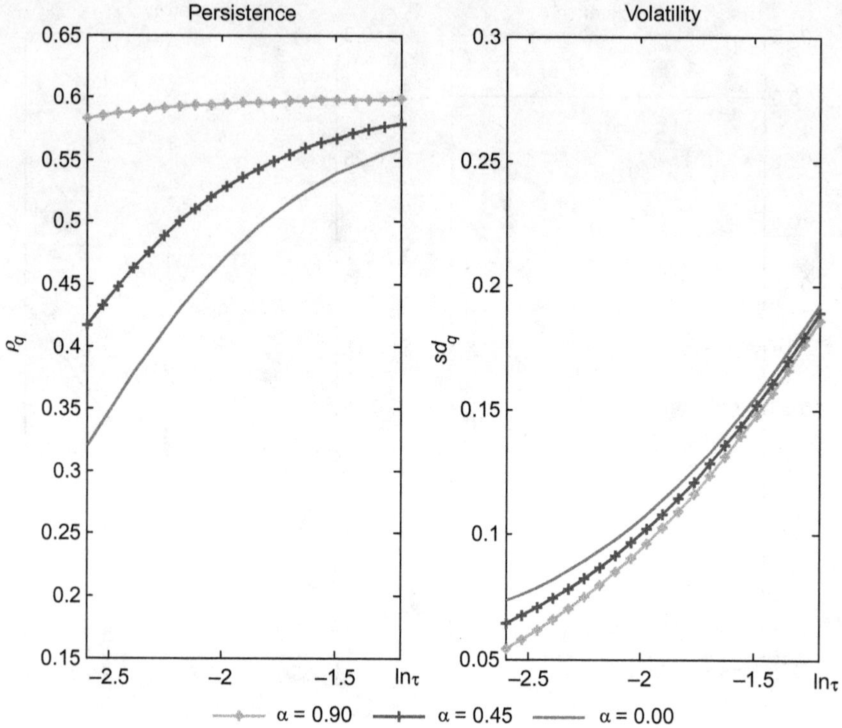

Fig. 2. Effect of strategic complementarities α on persistence and volatility of LOP deviations.

Notes: Each line in the figure represents the first-order autocorrelation (the left panel) and the standard deviation (the right panel) of $q_t(i)$ against $\ln \tau$ for different values of α. For parameterization except for α, we use $\kappa = 0.5, \rho_z(i) = 0.6$, $\overline{\kappa} = 0.5, \xi = 4, \sqrt{\text{var}\{z_t(i)\}/\sigma_\theta^2} = 5, \overline{\tau} = 0.2$, and $\delta = 0.3$.

more persistent, through smaller ϕ. However, smaller ϕ also dampens the volatility, since the effect of ε_t^θ on $q_t(i)$ is weakened.

Finally, Fig. 3 shows persistence and volatility and their sensitivity to $\rho_z(i)$, when the other two key parameters are set at $\alpha = 0$ and $\kappa = 0.50$. Not surprisingly, the left panel of the figure shows the higher $\rho_z(i)$ corresponds to the higher $\rho_q(i)$ since the latter is proportional to the former (see (18)). In contrast, the volatility of LOP deviations is the same for all $\rho_z(i)$ simply because $\text{var}[z_t(i)]$ and σ_θ^2 in (17) remain unchanged by changing $\rho_z(i)$.

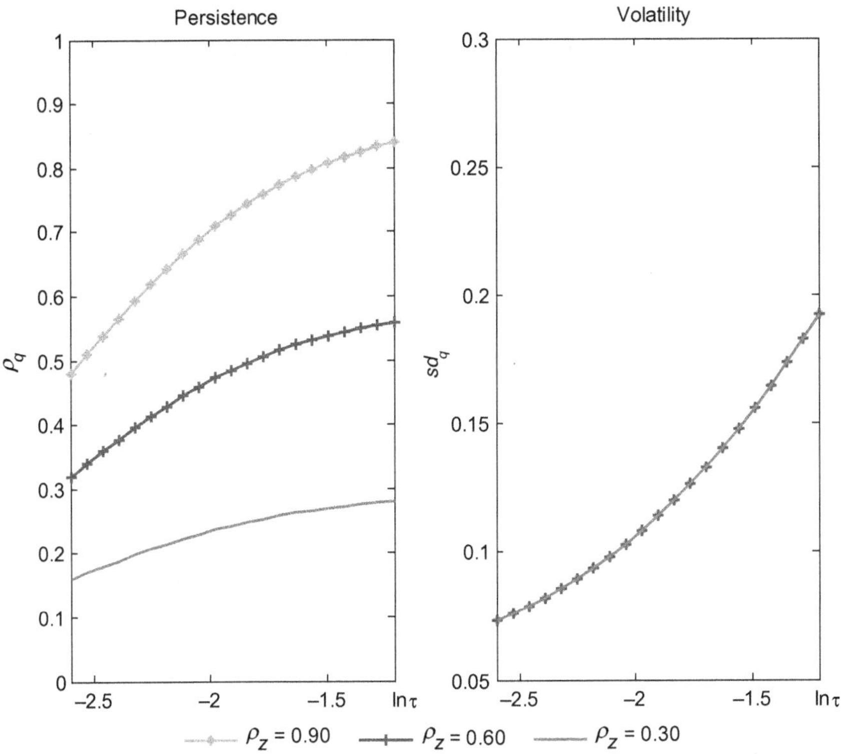

Fig. 3. Effect of the productivity persistence $\rho_z(i)$ on persistence and volatility of LOP deviations.

Notes: Each line in the figure represents the first-order autocorrelation (the left panel) and the standard deviation (the right panel) of $q_t(i)$ against $\ln\,\tau$ for different values of $\rho_z(i)$. For parameterization except for $\rho_z(i)$, we use $\kappa = 0.5, \alpha = 0, \overline{\kappa} = 0.5, \xi = 4, \sqrt{\text{var}\left\{z_t(i)\right\}/\sigma_\theta^2} = 5, \overline{\tau} = 0.2$, and $\delta = 0.3$.

While these figures are helpful in understanding the mechanism, we further investigate whether our model can reproduce the estimated coefficient on distance in our regression analysis. To answer this question, we calibrate the regression coefficient from the model based on the following procedure.

Note that our analysis in Section 2 employs a linear regression of LOP persistence on distance, whereas the first-order autocorrelation in (18) is non-linear in trade cost. We first linearly approximate (18) around $\ln\,\overline{\tau}$, and then use (19) to transform the coefficient on trade cost to that on distance. This predicted coefficient on distance corresponds to the slope of persistence curve in Figs. 1–3 evaluated at ln 0.20 (≈ -1.61) multiplied by $\delta = 0.30$. While the slope depends on all the key parameters, κ, α, and $\rho_z(i)$, we pay special attention to κ because the presence of information difference is the essential feature in producing the persistence–distance correlation in the noisy information model.

Panel A of Table 3 reports the coefficients on distance for various κ, using the baseline model for the purpose of matching the

Table 3. Calibrated regression slope in persistence-distance regressions.

	κ					κ Consistent with data	
Model specifications	0.20	0.40	0.50	0.60	0.80	LB	UB
A: The flexible price model							
$\alpha = 0.90, \rho_z(i) = 0.60$	0.000	0.001	0.001	0.002	0.004	—	—
$\alpha = 0.45, \rho_z(i) = 0.60$	0.003	0.013	0.019	0.026	0.041	0.449	0.570
$\alpha = 0.00, \rho_z(i) = 0.60$	0.007	0.024	0.034	0.044	0.061	0.319	0.405
$\alpha = 0.00, \rho_z(i) = 0.30$	0.003	0.012	0.017	0.022	0.030	0.483	0.648
$\alpha = 0.00, \rho_z(i) = 0.90$	0.010	0.036	0.051	0.066	0.091	0.255	0.320
B: The sticky price model ($\alpha = 0.00, \rho_z(i) = 0.60$)							
$\lambda_i = 0.35$	0.005	0.017	0.024	0.031	0.043	0.392	0.506
$\lambda_i = 0.65$	0.004	0.012	0.017	0.021	0.028	0.479	0.669
$\lambda_i = 0.95$	0.004	0.005	0.004	0.004	0.003	—	—
C: The three-city, flexible price model ($\alpha = 0.00, \rho_z(i) = 0.60$)							
$(\tau_{1,2}, \tau_{1,3}, \tau_{2,3}) = (0.2, 0.2, 0.2)$	0.016	0.047	0.060	0.068	0.074	0.197	0.251
$(\tau_{1,2}, \tau_{1,3}, \tau_{2,3}) = (0.2, 0.3, 0.1)$	0.012	0.037	0.047	0.055	0.063	0.234	0.300
D: The three-city, sticky price model ($\alpha = 0.00, \rho_z(i) = 0.60, \lambda_i = 0.65$)							
$(\tau_{1,2}, \tau_{1,3}, \tau_{2,3}) = (0.2, 0.2, 0.2)$	0.009	0.023	0.027	0.030	0.030	0.298	0.425
$(\tau_{1,2}, \tau_{1,3}, \tau_{2,3}) = (0.2, 0.3, 0.1)$	0.006	0.018	0.022	0.025	0.026	0.365	0.570

Notes: Each number in the table represents the coefficients on the logarithm of distance in persistence-distance regressions predicted by the noisy information models. The coefficients are obtained from the linear approximation of the theoretical first-order autocorrelation of $q_t(i)$ or $q_{2,1,t}(i) = p_{2,t}(i) - p_{1,t}(i)$ around $\overline{\tau} = 0.2$, along with the parameter values described in the main text. Lower bound (LB) and upper bound (UB) of κ that are consistent with the 95 percent confidence interval of regression slope in Table 1 are also shown. Panel A shows the baseline two-city flexible price model. Panel B shows the two-city model with price stickiness. Panels C and D are the three-city models with and without sticky prices, respectively. In the first rows of Panels C and D, all trade costs are assumed to be the same across all three city pairs. The second rows of Panels C and D show the case when trade costs between cities 1 and 2 differ from trade costs between other city pairs.

estimated coefficient of 0.02 in Table 2. Note that the standard errors reported in Table 2 imply that the 95 percent confidence interval of the estimated coefficient is given by [0.016, 0.024]. This provides lower and upper bounds for κ, which are reported in the last two columns of the table. The first three rows in the panel show the predicted coefficients for different levels of strategic complementarity, $\alpha = 0.90$, 0.45, and 0, with $\rho_z(i)$ fixed at 0.60. When strategic complementarities are strong, such as $\alpha = 0.90$, increasing the informational asymmetry has little effect on the slope coefficient, resulting in the failure of the model to replicate the persistence–distance relationship in the data. However, for smaller values of α, the model performs well over a reasonable range of κ. For example, the predicted range of κ is [0.45, 0.57] when $\alpha = 0.45$, while the predicted range is [0.32, 0.41] when $\alpha = 0$. Thus, the information difference required for replicating the estimated coefficient becomes smaller, as the degree of strategic complementarities becomes lower.

Next two rows show the effects of changing $\rho_z(i)$, while keeping $\alpha = 0$. When $\rho_z(i) = 0.30$, the required level of κ increases compared to the benchmark case of $\rho_z(i) = 0.60$. In contrast, when $\rho_z(i) = 0.90$, the required level of κ decreases. This simply reflects the fact that the change of $\rho_z(i)$ has a proportional effect on the slope of $\rho_q(i)$ and the predicted coefficient. At the same time, the range of κ that is consistent with the data becomes wider as $\rho_z(i)$ becomes smaller.

4. Discussion

In this section, we discuss the robustness of our results to the case of sticky prices or multiple cities.

4.1. *The role of price stickiness*

The baseline model assumes that prices of all goods are completely flexible. Empirical studies on micro price data, however, have discovered substantial heterogeneity in the degree of price stickiness across goods. In Section 2, we found that, even after controlling for the distribution share, LOP persistence was higher for goods whose prices changed less frequently. To take this feature into account, we follow Kehoe and Midrigan (2007) and CST in assuming that the degree of price stickiness differs across goods but is common across locations. Each period, retail managers can reset their price with a constant probability $1-\lambda_i$. To simplify the argument, let us assume $\alpha = 0$ and that $z_{1,t}(i)$ and $z_{2,t}(i)$ follow a common AR(1) process (i.e., $\rho_{z,1}(i) = \rho_{z,2}(i) = \rho_z(i)$ and $\sigma_z(1) = \sigma_z(2)$).

The LOP deviation from the noisy information model with sticky prices follows the first-order difference equation:

$$q_t(i) = \lambda_i q_{t-1}(i) + (1-\lambda_i)\left[\kappa\varepsilon_t^\theta + \frac{1-\lambda_i\beta}{1-\lambda_i\beta\rho_z(i)}(2s-1)z_t(i)\right], \quad (20)$$

where β is the discount factor satisfying $\beta \in (0,1)$.[18]

This can be compared to our flexible price model by setting $\lambda_i = 0$, to arrive at $q_t(i) = \kappa\varepsilon_t^\theta + (2s-1)z_t(i)$. The only difference between this equation and (15) is the absence of strategic complementarity ($\alpha = 0$), in which case $\phi = \kappa$. As λ_i increases, prices respond less to signals about nominal aggregate demand (i.e., demand channel) or to productivity (i.e., productivity channel). Thus, the persistence is rising and the volatility is falling in λ_i.

Proposition 2 continues to hold for (20) because the coefficient on $z_t(i)$ is still increasing in τ, due to the presence of $(2s-1)$ as in (15). Price stickiness mitigates the productivity channel even further than the demand channel through the coefficient $(1-\lambda_i\beta)/[1-\lambda_i\beta\rho_z(i)]$ (<1). While the quantitative implications become slightly different because of this coefficient, the higher trade cost still gives rise to more persistent $q_t(i)$ through larger home bias.

We investigate whether the model with sticky prices can quantitatively account for the regression results. The simple average of the degree of price stickiness across goods used in our regression analysis is 0.65. This value implies that prices remain fixed for 8.6 months on average, consistent with the findings of Nakamura and Steinsson (2008) who estimate the median duration of regular prices is 8–11 months. To account for substantial heterogeneity in the degree of price stickiness across goods, the cases of $\lambda_i = 0.35$ and 0.95 are

[18] Derivation of this equation is provided in Appendix A.5.

contrasted. Panel B of Table 3 reports the predicted regression slope from the model with sticky prices when $\alpha = 0$ and $\rho_z(i) = 0.60$. Other parameter values are same as the case of the baseline flexible price model. The results show that the model can replicate the estimated coefficient when λ_i is either 0.35 and 0.65. The range of κ consistent with the data becomes wider with sticky prices compared to the baseline flexible price model. However, when λ_i becomes as large as 0.95, the model fails to replicate the observed regression slope.

4.2. *Multi-city model*

The baseline framework is a two-city model, whereas the data span numerous cities. This section considers an N city extension of the model. Beginning with the price index in a representative city (e.g., city 1), we have

$$P_{1,t}(i) = \left[\frac{1}{N}\int_0^N P_{1,t}(i,v)^{1-\xi}dv\right]^{1/(1-\xi)}. \tag{21}$$

We derive the explicit solution for LOP deviations in the multi-city model where the trade cost can differ across city pairs.[19] In this multi-city model, we redefine the LOP deviations between cities 1 and 2 as $q_{2,1,t}(i) = \ln[P_{2,t}(i)/P_{1,t}(i)]$. We also denote $\tau_{\ell,j}$ by the iceberg transportation cost to carry goods from city ℓ to j, where $\tau_{\ell,j}$ satisfies the assumptions that $\tau_{\ell j} = \tau_{j,t}$ and $\tau_{j,j} = 0$. Under flexible prices, $q_{2,1,t}(i)$ is given by

$$q_{2,1,t}(i) = \phi_{2,1}\varepsilon_t^{\theta} + \sum_{\ell=1}^{N}(s_{\ell,1} - s_{\ell,2})z_{\ell,t}(i), \tag{22}$$

where

$$s_{\ell,j} = \frac{(1+\tau_{\ell,j})^{1-\xi}}{\sum_{m=1}^{N}(1+\tau_{m,j})^{1-\xi}} \quad \text{for } j = 1,2 \text{ and } \ell = 1,2,\ldots,N, \tag{23}$$

and $\phi_{2,1} = (1-\alpha)\kappa_{2,1}/(1-\alpha\overline{\kappa}), \overline{\kappa} = N^{-1}\sum_{j=1}^{N}\kappa_j$ and $\kappa_{2,1} = \kappa_2 - \kappa_1$. We note that $\overline{\kappa}$ is the average of information precision across

---

[19]Details of this derivation is provided in Appendix A.6.

all N types of managers while $\kappa_{2,1}$ remains the spatial dispersion of information precision between two cities under examination. The parameter $S_{\ell,j}$ is the steady-state expenditure share of consumption in city j on goods produced in city ℓ.

When $\ell = j$, this parameter can be understood as the home bias parameter as in the two-city model. Also, when $N = 2, s_{\ell,1} - s_{\ell,2}$, reduces to $2s-1$ for $\ell = 1$ and $1-2s$ for $\ell = 2$. Hence, (22) generalizes (15) in the two-city model.

Compared to the two-city model, the LOP deviations still include both temporary and persistent components and the coefficient on ε_t^θ remains effectively unchanged. However, there is no longer the productivity difference in (22). Instead, the productivity for each city contributes to dynamics of LOP deviations even when the relative price between cities 1 and 2 is considered. This is because the prices in cities 1 and 2 include prices of brands produced in all cities in the economy, as indicated in (21).

Let us assume that all $z_{\ell,t}(i)$ have a common variance and first-order autocorrelation (i.e., $\rho_{z,1}(i) = \rho_{z,2}(i) = \cdots = \rho_{z,N}(i)$ and $\text{var}[z_{1,t}(i)] = \text{var}\,[z_{2,t}(i)] = \cdots = \text{var}\,[z_{N,t}(i)]$). Then, the first-order autocorrelation of $q_{2,1,t}(i)$ is given by

$$\rho_{q,2,1}(i) = \frac{\psi^2 \text{var}\,[z_{1,t}(i)]}{\phi_{2,1}^2\sigma_\theta^2 + \psi^2 \text{var}\,[z_{1,t}(i)]}\rho_{z,1}(i), \tag{24}$$

where $\psi^2 = \sum_{t=1}^{N}(s_{\ell,1} - s_{\ell,2})^2$. The underlying structure of the LOP persistence shown in (24) is similar to that under the two-city model. As long as ψ is increasing in $\tau_{1,2}$, the model can still explain a positive persistence–distance correlation.

Unfortunately, we cannot determine the sign of the derivative of ψ with respect to $\tau_{1,2}$ in general. Hence, the need for simulations. As in the previous exercise, we linearly approximate (24) around $\ln \overline{\tau}$ and use (19) for $\tau_{1,2}$ in evaluating the model. For comparison purpose, we report the case of $N = 3, \alpha = 0$ and $\rho_{z,1}(i) = \rho_{z,2}(i) = \rho_{z,3}(i) = 0.60$ to see the marginal changes in results.[20]

[20]For the variance ratio of real and nominal shocks, we set $\sqrt{3 \times \text{var}\,[z_{1,t}(i)]/\sigma_\theta^2} = 5$.

Panel C of Table 3 shows the coefficients on distance for the three-city model for various values of κ (more precisely $\kappa_{1,2}$). In both rows of the panel, the partial derivative of $\rho_{q,2,1}(i)$ with respect to the log distance is computed numerically. The first row of the panel assumes that the trade cost is the same across all three city pairs. Under this assumption, κ required for replicating the estimated coefficient on distance is smaller than in the two-city model, while the range of κ that is consistent with the data is narrower. The second row of the panel allows for different trade costs between cities 1 and 3 and between cities 2 and 3. Here, while $\tau_{1,2}$ remains unchanged at 0.20, $\tau_{1,3}$ and $\tau_{2,3}$ are set to 0.30 and 0.10, respectively, to keep the average trade cost unchanged at $\overline{\tau} = 0.20$.[21] Under this parameterization, the required level of κ becomes slightly higher than the case of symmetric trade costs and the range of κ is wider, but neither change is very substantial. Hence, our calibration results suggest that, within a reasonable range of parameter values, the three-city model continues to imply a positive persistence–distance correlation and can still explain the observed regression coefficient. Similar results can be obtained even if we combine the multi-city model with sticky prices, as shown in Panel D of Table 3 with the choice of $\lambda_i = 0.65$. To sum up, the main predictions of the noisy information model are robust.

5. Conclusion

This paper studies micro price data across US cities to provide empirical evidence that persistence of intra-national LOP deviations is positively correlated with the distance between cities. To explain the empirical findings, we develop a model of time-varying productivity combined with imperfect information about nominal aggregate demand. Assuming that distance proxies trade cost between two cities, we found that the perfect information model can account for the observed positive volatility–distance correlation pointed out by

[21] Note that these additional parameter values fall within the range of $\tau \in [0.07, 0.30]$ in the data.

the literature but fails to predict the observed positive persistence–distance correlation. In contrast, the noisy information model can account for both observations if there is an information difference across managers in different cities. The key mechanism is that shocks arising from imperfect information are temporary while shocks from productivity are long-lived. When trade costs are low, the effect of the temporary nominal shock is strong relative to the effect of persistent real shocks on the persistence of LOP deviations. When the trade costs are high, the former is weak relative to the latter and the persistence of LOP deviations approaches the persistence of technology shocks. Under the perfect information, this change in relative contribution between nominal and real shocks does not arise because nominal shocks do not contribute to persistence in LOP deviations.

Our findings suggest the importance of imperfect information for better understanding persistent and volatile LOP deviations, while not ruling out other plausible mechanisms. For example, productivity spill-overs across manufacturers may be negatively correlated with distance. This could produce a positive persistence–distance correlation in LOP deviations. However, careful investigation of this requires highly disaggregated data on productivity.

Acknowledgments

We thank Jeff Campbell, Virgiliu Midrigan, Ricardo Reis, two anonymous referees, and seminar participants at Kyoto University, the University of Tokyo, Otaru University of Commerce for helpful comments and discussions. Crucini and Shintani gratefully acknowledge the financial support of National Science Foundation (SES-1030164). Shintani and Tsuruga gratefully acknowledge the financial support of Grant-in-aid for Scientific Research.

Appendix A. Supplementary Material

Supplementary material associated with this article can be found in the online version at http://dx.doi.org/10.1016/j.jmoneco.2015.06.003.

References

Anderson, J.E., van Wincoop, E., 2004. Trade costs. *J. Econ. Lit.* 42 (3), 691–751.

Angeletos, G.-M., La'O, J., 2009. Incomplete information, higher-order beliefs and price inertia. *J. Monet. Econ.* 56, 19–37.

Broda, C., Weinstein, D.E., 2006. Globalization and the gains from variety. *Q. J. Econ.* 121 (2), 541–585.

Cecchetti, S.G., Mark, N.C., Sonora, R.J., 2002. Price index convergence among United States cities. *Int. Econ. Rev.* 43 (4), 1081–1099.

Carvalho, C., Nechio, F., 2011. Aggregation and the PPP puzzle in a sticky-price model. *Am. Econ. Rev.* 101 (6), 2391–2424.

Choi, C.-Y., Matsubara, K., 2007. Heterogeneity in the persistence of relative prices: what do the Japanese cities tell us? *J. Jpn. Int. Econ.* 21 (2), 260–286.

Crucini, M.J., Shintani, M., 2008. Persistence in law of one price deviations: evidence from micro-data. *J. Monet. Econ.* 55 (3), 629–644.

Crucini, M.J., Shintani, M., Tsuruga, T., 2010a. The law of one price without the border: the role of distance versus sticky prices. *Econ. J.* 120, 462–480.

Crucini, M.J., Shintani, M., Tsuruga, T., 2010b. Accounting for persistence and volatility of good-level real exchange rates: the role of sticky information. *J. Int. Econ.* 81 (1), 48–60.

Crucini, M.J., Shintani, M., Tsuruga, T., 2013. Do sticky prices increase the real exchange rate volatility at the sector level? *Eur. Econ. Rev.* 62, 58–72.

Disdier, A.-C., Head, K., 2008. The puzzling persistence of the distance effect on bilateral trade. *Rev. Econ. Stat.* 90 (1), 37–48.

Eaton, J., Kortum, S., 2002. Technology, geography, and trade. *Econometrica* 70 (5), 1741–1779.

Engel, C., Rogers, J.H., 1996. How wide is the border? *Am. Econ. Rev.* 86 (5), 1112–1125.

Fukunaga, I., 2007. Imperfect common knowledge, staggered price setting, and the effects of monetary policy. *J. Money Credit Bank.* 39 (7), 1711–1739.

Grossman, G.M., 1998. Comment on Deardorff. In: Frankel, J.A. (Ed.), *The Regionalization of the World Economy*, University of Chicago Press, Chicago, pp. 29–31.

Helpman, E., Melitz, M., Rubinstein, Y., 2008. Estimating trade flows: trading partners and trading volumes. *Q. J. Econ.* 123 (2), 441–487.

Huang, K.X.D., Liu, Z., Phaneuf, L., 2004. Why does the cyclical behavior of real wages change over time? *Am. Econ. Rev.* 94 (4), 836–856.

Hummels, D., 2001. Toward a geography of trade costs. Unpublished manuscript.

Kano, K., Kano, T., Takechi, K., 2013. Exaggerated death of distance: revisiting distance effects on regional price dispersions. *J. Int. Econ.* 90 (2), 403–413.

Kehoe, P.J., Midrigan, V., 2007. Sticky prices and sectoral real exchange rates. Federal Reserve Bank of Minneapolis Working Paper No. 656.

Lucas, R.E., 1972. Expectations and the neutrality of money. *J. Econ. Theory* 4 (2), 103–124.

Mankiw, N.G., Reis, R., 2002. Sticky information versus sticky prices: a proposal to replace the New Keynesian Phillips curve. *Q. J. Econ.* 117 (4), 1295–1328.

Nakamura, E., Steinsson, J., 2008. Five facts about prices: a reevaluation of menu cost models. *Q. J. Econ.* 123 (4), 1415–1464.

Obstfeld, M., Taylor, A.M., 1997. Nonlinear aspects of goods-market arbitrage and adjustment: Heckscher's commodity points revisited. *J. Jpn. Int. Econ.* 11 (4), 441–479.

Parsley, D.C., Wei, S.-J., 1996. Convergence to the law of one price without trade barriers or currency fluctuations. *Q. J. Econ.* 111 (4), 1211–1236.

Parsley, D.C., Wei, S.-J., 2001. Explaining the border effect: the role of exchange rate variability, shipping costs, and geography. *J. Int. Econ.* 55 (1), 87–105.

Phelps, E.S., 1970. Introduction: the new microeconomics in employment and inflation theory. In: *Microeconomic Foundations of Employment and Inflation Theory.* Norton, New York, pp. 1–23.

Woodford, M., 2003. Imperfect common knowledge and the effects of monetary policy. In: Aghion, P., Frydman, R., Stiglitz, J., Woodford, M. (Eds.), *Knowledge, Information, and Expectations in Modern Macroeconomics: In Honor of Edmund S. Phelps*, Princeton University Press, Princeton, pp. 25–58.

Yazgan, M.E., Yilmazkuday, H., 2011. Price-level convergence: new evidence from U.S. cities. *Econ. Lett.* 110 (2), 76–78.

Part IV

Commercial Policy

Chapter 13

Sources of Variation in Real Tariff Rates: The United States, 1900–1940*

Mario J. Crucini

Department of Economics, The Ohio State University, Columbus, OH, USA

During the 1930's, commercial policy and international trade underwent rapid and dramatic change. Tariff levels in the United States reached heights described by Gottfried Haberler (1976) as "skyscraper duties," foreign countries retaliated (see e.g., Joseph M. Jones, 1934), and the volume of international trade fell precipitously.[1] The connection between these events and the internationalization of the U.S. depression remains the subject of considerable debate.

While trade theorists point to this episode as a classic example of beggar-thy-neighbor commercial policy, macroeconomists disagree about the role of the tariff war in the propagation of the world depression. Opinions range from Rudiger Dornbusch and Stanley Fischer's (1986) denial that the Hawley-Smoot Tariff Act was a

*This chapter originally appeared in *The American Economic Review*, 1994, **84**(3), 732–743.

[1]Total imports of 75 countries fell from $3 billion (in old U.S. gold dollars) to $1 billion between January 1929 and 1933, while nominal income in major industrial countries fell by less than 50 percent over the same period (Charles P. Kindleberger, 1973, p. 172).

"macroeconomic phenomenon," to Alan Meltzer's (1976) claim that Hawley-Smoot was a key contributor to the propagation of the Great Depression.

An essential part of interwar tariff history has been ignored in this debate. During the period from 1900 to 1940, many customs duties were specific, calling for a fixed nominal levy per physical unit imported. Under a specific duty, a decline in the nominal price of the import good causes an increase in the tariff as a percentage of the price of the good.[2] As is well known, the nominal price level changed dramatically during these years, a period which includes the inflation of World War I and the deflation of the 1930's.

This study carefully measures the impact of legislation and the price level on ad valorem equivalent tariff rates using time-series data on individual imported commodities. The tariff history that emerges from this study is remarkably different from that which has previously been told. I find that monetary policy, through its influence on nominal prices and therefore on the real value of specific duties, had larger effects on ad valorem equivalent tariff rates than did legislative amendments. This adds an intriguing dimension to the Friedman-Schwartz thesis that the depression was a monetary phenomenon, suggesting a novel deflationary channel by which the depression was internationalized.

1. Data

The data are compiled from the annual serial *The Foreign Trade and Navigation of the United States* (U.S. Department of Commerce, 1903–1940) and include the following: the physical quantity imported, the nominal value of imports, the ad valorem equivalent rate of duty, and the legislated rate of duty. Value of imports is measured as the foreign value or export value, whichever is higher, converted to U.S. dollars at the prevailing exchange rate.[3]

[2]This problem is mentioned by Dornbusch and Fischer (1986 p. 469) and Barry Eichengreen (1989 p. 15).

[3]Foreign value is defined as "... the market value or price at which the merchandise, at the time of exportation to the U.S. is offered for sale in the

In 1929, approximately 4,600 dutiable imports entered the United States. I used two selection criteria to reduce the panel data set to a manageable size. I required that the value of imports in 1929 exceed one million dollars and that the categorical definition of each commodity be maintained over the entire sample period.

The first constraint produced a sample of more than 70 commodities. The second criterion was satisfied for only 29 of these because legislative changes frequently involved alterations in tariff categories. Overall, the selection process resulted in surprisingly few commodities subject to pure ad valorem duties. To make the data set more representative of the aggregate data, cigarette papers, diamonds, and soap were added. These commodities were the largest imports, in terms of value in 1929, subject to pure ad valorem duties while also satisfying the second criterion. The final data set consists of 32 individual imported commodities, and the sample period runs from 1903 to 1940.[4]

Table 1 reveals the basic difficulty in representing thousands of dutiable imports with a modest-sized cross section. While the sample includes commodities from nine of the 14 tariff schedules and covers more than 20 percent of the value of dutiable imports in five cases, four categories are not represented at all. However, the excluded schedules, taken together, account for less than 15 percent of total U.S. dutiable imports. In terms of tariff levels, the ad valorem equivalent tariff rates are typically underestimated by the panel data set, with the exception of sugars and agricultural products.

---

principal markets of the country from which exported, including the costs of containers or coverings and all expenses incident to placing the merchandise in condition ready for shipment to the U.S. as defined in section 402 of the tariff Acts of 1922 and 1930" (quoted from the preface of *Foreign Trade and Navigation of the United States* [U.S. Department of Commerce, 1903–1940]).

[4]The peculiar starting date was determined by library resources that had some gaps in the set of *Foreign Trade and Navigation of the United States* volumes. It is feasible, using a complete Congressional set of these volumes, to extend the sample period both forward and backward in time.

Table 1. Comparison of aggregate U.S. data and panel data set in 1929.

Tariff schedule	Share of dutiable imports			Ad valorem equivalent tariff		
	Aggregate U.S. data	Panel data set	Percentage covered	Aggregate U.S. data	Panel data set	Percentage difference
Sugar, molasses, and manufactures thereof	10.7	9.4	87.6	84.0	93.7	−11.5
Tobacco and manufactures thereof	4.1	4.0	96.7	65.1	64.8	0.4
Manufactures of cotton	2.9	0.1	3.2	36.5	29.4	19.3
Sundries	16.5	4.1	24.5	37.6	26.1	30.5
Agricultural products and provisions	20.4	5.0	24.5	22.9	25.8	−12.4
Earths, earthenware, glassware	3.8	0.2	4.9	48.9	23.2	52.6
Metals and manufactures thereof	10.6	0.1	1.0	35.5	18.7	47.2
Chemicals, oils, and paints	7.6	0.4	5.9	30.7	18.3	40.6
Flax, hemp, jute, and manufactures thereof	8.9	5.3	59.5	19.0	8.3	56.2
Wood and manufactures thereof	1.2	0.0	0.0	24.7	NA	NA
Paper and books	1.7	0.0	0.0	25.3	NA	NA
Wool and manufactures thereof	8.3	0.0	0.0	50.8	NA	NA
Manufactures of silk and rayon	3.2	0.0	0.0	58.0	NA	NA
Spirits, wines, and other beverages	0.1	0.0	0.0	34.6	NA	NA
All schedules:	100.0	28.6	28.6	40.1	49.7	−23.8

Note: NA indicates that the information is not available; no commodity in this group is included in the data set.
Source: *Statistical Abstract of the United States* (U.S. Department of Commerce, 1932).

2. Sources of Variation in Real Tariff Rates

Early tariff history is complicated by the use of three types of duties: specific, ad valorem, or the two in combination. A specific duty taxes the physical quantity imported at a nominal rate, in contrast to the more familiar ad valorem duty which is levied as a percentage of the value imported. The price faced by domestic consumers will differ from the world price by the amount of the ad valorem equivalent tariff rate.

To define this ad valorem equivalent rate, let P_{jt} denote the nominal price of commodity j, in domestic currency, in period t, and let Q_{jt} denote the physical quantity imported. Let τ_{js} denote the ad valorem rate of duty, and let ω_{js} denote the specific duty, on commodity j, as legislated in period s, which might be some periods earlier. The ad valorem equivalent rate of duty is constructed by dividing customs duties collected, C_{jt}, by the value of imports. For a commodity subject to a combined duty the ad valorem equivalent rate is

$$\tau_{jt}^{*} = \frac{C_{jt}}{P_{jt}Q_{jt}} = \tau_{js} + \frac{\omega_{js}}{P_{jt}}. \tag{1}$$

The ad valorem equivalent rate, denoted τ_{jt}^{*}, is the sum of the ad valorem duty and the specific duty converted to an equivalent rate at the current price of the good.

The existing tariff literature focuses on the infrequent alterations in legislated duties, ignoring the continuous changes that arise as fluctuations in the nominal import price alter the real value of the specific duty. This section studies the impact of nominal prices on ad valorem equivalent tariff rates, adding an important chapter to U.S. tariff history.[5]

---

[5]Many of the contemporary tariff studies discuss specific duties across distant years without conversion to an ad valorem equivalent rate. See, for examples, the classic (and voluminous) work by Frank Taussig (1931) and the comparative analyses of adjacent pieces of tariff legislation by Taussig (1922) and Abraham Berglund (1923, 1930).

Toward this end, let P_t denote the import price index in period t. Equation (2) below uses this and earlier definitions to decompose movements in an ad valorem equivalent tariff rate into three components: (i) a component due to legislation (T^L_{js}); (ii) a component arising from movements in the import price index (T^P_{jt}); and (iii) a component attributable to movements in the relative price of the imported commodity (T^{RP}_{jt}):

$$\begin{aligned}\tau^*_{jt} &= \left[\tau_{js} + \frac{\omega_{js}}{P_{js-1}}\right] + \left[\frac{\omega_{js}}{P_{js-1}}\left(\frac{P_s}{P_t} - 1\right)\right] \\ &\quad + \left[\frac{\omega_{js}}{P_{js} - 1}\left(\frac{P_{js-1}}{P_{jt}} - \frac{P_s}{P_t}\right)\right] \\ &\equiv T^L_{js} + T^P_{jt} + T^{RP}_{jt}. \end{aligned} \tag{2}$$

Lagged prices were used in the above decomposition because tariff revisions often took a year or more from initial discussion to final implementation.

For a pure ad valorem duty, only the term τ_{js} is nonzero. In such a case, ad valorem equivalent rates and ad valorem duties coincide; the tariff rate jumps discretely at legislative dates and remains constant at all other dates. Ad valorem equivalent tariff rates will fluctuate continuously when specific duties are present, reflecting the interaction of all three components in Eq. (2).

2.1. *A tale of two histories*

In this subsection, I present two alternative histories implied by the tariff decomposition: a history focusing on legislative amendments, following the practice of previous research, and a second history incorporating the fact that many legislated duties were nominally denominated.

Ordered from top to bottom, Fig. 1 presents decompositions of ad valorem equivalent tariff rates for bristles, china clay, ostrich feathers, and flaxseed. The left-hand panel presents the ad valorem equivalent rate (solid line) and legislative component (dashed line), while the right-hand panel gives the price-level component (solid line) and relative-price component (dashed line).

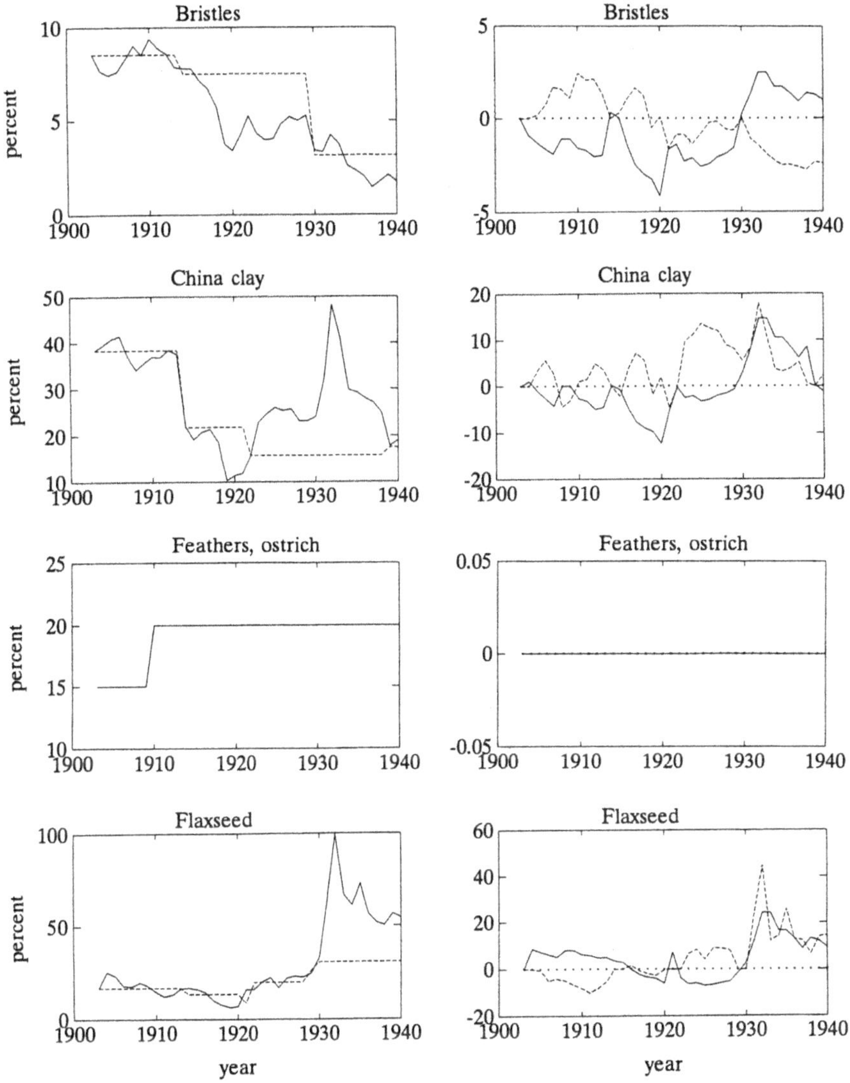

Fig. 1. Ad Valorem tariff rate decompositions.

Notes: The left-hand panels show the ad valorem equivalent tariff rate (solid line) and the legislative component (dashed line); the right-hand panels show the price-level component (solid line) and the relative-price component (dashed line).

The legislated duties declined in real terms, in two steps, for both bristles and china clay. As a rule of thumb, the ad valorem equivalent tariff rate on china clay is 3–4 times that on bristles. This rule of thumb fails miserably in the early 1930's. In 1932 the ad valorem equivalent tariff rate on china clay is ten times that on bristles. Sharp relative price movements account for the observed changes in relative protection across the two imports. The increasing relative price of bristles (relative to the import price index) decreases the real tariff rate on bristles, while the declining relative price of china clay increases the real tariff rate on china clay. The legislative history indicates modest changes in relative protection across the two commodities, which is obviously wrong for the 1930's.

The figures for ostrich feathers and flaxseed provide a perfect contrast between ad valorem and specific duties. Ostrich feathers were subject to a pure ad valorem tariff over the entire sample, increasing from 15 percent to 20 percent in 1910.

In contrast, flaxseed was subject to a nominal specific rate per bushel throughout the period. The specific duty changed from 25 cents in 1903 to 20 cents in 1914, to 30 cents in 1921, to 40 cents in 1922, to 56 cents in 1929, and finally to 65 cents in 1930. It is interesting to note that, despite the substantial (50-percent) nominal increase in the specific duty from 1914 to 1921, the ad valorem equivalent tariff rate actually declined.

Frequent legislative changes in the specific duty keep the legislative and ad valorem equivalent paths close until the early 1930's. By 1932, however, the ad valorem equivalent rate is three times the rate legislated in 1930. The modest changes in tariff rates indicated by the legislative history are dwarfed by the influences of nominal and relative prices in the 1930's.

The tariff histories of bristles, china clay, ostrich feathers, and flaxseed, are typical of other commodities in the data set. The view that legislative amendments are the only source of tariff variation leads one to underestimate the volatility of the ad valorem equivalent rates on individual commodities and masks the movements in relative tariff rates as measured by their ad valorem equivalents.

2.2. *Extremes of protection*

The time-series decompositions presented in the previous subsection uncovered large discrepancies between ad valorem equivalent tariff rates and initial legislated rates. This subsection examines the contribution of legislation and price changes to the variation in ad valorem equivalent tariff rates in two ways. First, I compare *levels* of protection at dates of legislative amendment to the maximum and minimum levels achieved from 1914 to 1933. Second, I look at *changes* in ad valorem equivalent tariff rates and compare legislative influences to price-induced changes.

The Underwood Act of 1914 reduced tariff rates, on average. The first question I consider is whether World War I inflation reduced ad valorem equivalent tariff rates significantly beyond the levels achieved by the Underwood Act. The Hawley-Smoot Tariff Act of 1930 is considered the high-water mark in the tariff history of the United States. The second question addressed is whether the deflation of the early 1930's added much to the increases attributable to Hawley-Smoot.

Table 2 examines the extremes of protection for each commodity in the panel data set. The first two columns report the year and the level of the lowest tariff rate between 1914 and 1928. The last two columns report the year and the level of the highest tariff rate between 1929 and 1933. The two middle columns report the tariff levels in 1914 and 1930, the years in which the Underwood Tariff Act and the Hawley-Smoot Tariff Act were passed into law.

Table 2 clearly shows that the extremes of protection followed the inflation of World War I and the deflation of the interwar period. In 17 of 32 cases, the lowest tariff rates were achieved between 1919 and 1927, rather than at the time the Underwood Act was passed into law. The highest tariff levels occurred, almost exclusively (23 of 32 cases), in 1932 or 1933. Only a single tariff rate reached its peak in 1931, and none did so in 1930. On average, Hawley-Smoot increased ad valorem equivalent tariff rates by a factor of 2 over the levels legislated in 1914, though 10 ad valorem equivalent rates actually declined. Comparing the minimum and maximum levels achieved from 1914 to 1933,

Table 2. Extremes of protection.

Commodity	1914–1928				1929–1933	
	Minimum				Maximum	
	Year	Tariff	Underwood	Hawley-Smoot	Tariff	Year
Almonds	1920	10.4	14.4	51.9	90.0	1932
Brazil and cream	1920	7.5	17.1	10.7	39.9	1933
Bristle	1920	3.4	7.8	3.4	5.3	1929
Burlap	1915	0.0	3.8	11.0	20.2	1932
Castor beans	1919	4.9	14.0	16.3	29.9	1933
China clay	1919	10.3	22.0	24.0	48.3	1932
Cigar and cheroots	1927	59.7	80.7	62.8	76.3	1931
Cigar filler, Cuban, stemmed	1922	40.6	92.1	62.4	87.0	1933
Cigar filler, unstemmed	1921	26.3	47.8	38.3	61.8	1933
Cigar filler, Cuban, unstemmed	1921	30.0	58.9	46.4	56.3	1933
Cigar leaf	1924	83.7	137.4	126.8	184.2	1932
Cigarette paper	1915	50.0	52.6	60.0	60.0	1929
Coconuts	1914	0.0	0.0	24.8	34.9	1933
Dates	1920	15.7	51.7	24.5	35.2	1933
Diamonds	1914	15.4	15.4	20.0	20.0	1929
Egg yolk, dried	1914	10.0	10.0	46.9	292.2	1933
Egg yolk, other	1914	10.0	10.0	35.3	136.4	1933
Feathers, for beds	1914	20.0	20.0	20.0	20.0	1929
Feathers, ostrich	1914	20.0	20.0	20.0	20.0	1929
Flaxseed	1919	6.3	16.7	33.2	99.5	1932
Matches in boxes	1918	4.9	17.6	30.3	76.3	1933
Mercury	1915	10.0	11.0	19.5	68.9	1932
Quebracho	1915	0.0	2.1	15.0	15.0	1929
Soap, Castille	1915	10.0	11.5	15.0	15.0	1929
Sugar, Cuban, 95°	1920	8.3	57.4	127.3	217.0	1932
Sugar, Cuban, 96°	1920	8.8	60.9	127.6	223.2	1932
Sugar, Cuban, 97°	1920	8.3	67.1	96.7	220.4	1933
Sugar, Cuban, 100°	1914	0.0	0.0	92.8	140.8	1932
Toilet water	1915	30.0	37.6	30.0	30.0	1929
Tracing cloth	1927	29.3	33.6	29.7	32.7	1932
Vanilla beans	1914	4.6	4.6	20.2	50.2	1933
Walnuts, shelled	1919	7.8	18.4	51.2	101.6	1933

Note: The reference years for the Underwood and Hawley-Smoot tariffs are 1914 and 1930, respectively.

tariffs, on average, increased by a factor of 8. Thus the estimated swing in tariff levels during the interwar period is mismeasured by a factor of 4 when the influence of the price level is ignored.

Table 3 decomposes the sample path of ad valorem equivalent tariff rates into legislative changes and intervening effects of price-level movements. The legislative changes include the Underwood Act

Table 3. Sources of variation in ad valorem equivalent tariff rates.

	Legislative changes				Price–induced changes			
Commodity	1914	1922	1930	Totals	1915–1920	1923–1929	1931–1933	Totals
Almonds	−10.7	12.0	12.2	13.5	−4.0	−22.5	32.3	5.8
Brazil and cream	17.1	14.4	−0.4	31.2	−9.6	−5.5	29.2	14.1
Bristle	−0.1	1.9	−1.8	−0.1	−4.4	1.0	0.3	−3.1
Burlap	−17.5	2.7	2.7	−12.1	−3.8	−0.6	5.4	1.0
Castor beans	−8.4	5.7	2.2	−0.5	−7.6	−0.5	13.6	5.5
China clay	−15.6	4.2	0.9	−10.5	−10.7	0.3	17.0	6.6
Cigar and cheroots	1.2	3.2	0.7	5.2	−17.6	−3.4	5.2	−15.7
Cigar filler, Cuban, stemmed	15.4	−0.5	0.2	15.2	−51.0	16.4	24.6	−10.0
Cigar filler, unstemmed	−1.9	5.7	1.0	4.8	−20.3	5.0	23.5	8.2
Cigar filler, Cuban, unstemmed	−3.9	3.4	2.2	1.7	−25.5	7.4	9.9	−8.3
Cigar leaf	−9.7	−9.2	17.3	−1.6	−20.6	18.4	27.1	24.8
Cigarette paper	−7.4	1.1	0.0	−6.3	−2.6	0.0	0.0	−2.6
Coconuts	0.0	9.6	3.2	12.7	0.0	1.3	10.2	11.4
Dates	0.5	4.0	4.0	8.5	−36.0	−0.3	10.7	−25.6
Diamonds	5.4	0.0	0.0	5.4	4.6	0.0	0.0	4.6
Egg yolk, dried	0.0	0.0	8.6	8.6	0.0	−23.1	245.3	222.1
Egg yolk, other	0.0	38.0	4.5	42.5	0.0	−9.4	101.1	91.7
Feathers, for bed	0.0	0.0	0.0	0.0	0.0	0.0	0.0	0.0
Feathers, ostrich	0.0	0.0	0.0	0.0	0.0	0.0	0.0	0.0
Flaxseed	0.5	9.1	8.8	18.4	−10.1	4.5	33.7	28.0
Matches in boxes	−10.7	3.6	7.1	0.0	−12.3	5.8	46.0	39.6
Mercury	−4.0	3.5	0.8	0.3	−1.0	−22.8	36.5	12.7
Quebracho	−26.0	2.3	0.0	−23.7	−2.1	0.0	0.0	−2.1
Soap, Castille	−4.8	0.9	0.0	−3.9	−1.5	0.0	0.0	−1.5
Sugar, Cuban, 95°	−1.1	55.7	33.0	87.6	−49.1	58.8	82.3	92.0
Sugar, Cuban, 96°	0.5	55.5	31.0	87.0	−52.1	60.1	45.0	53.0

(*Continued*)

Table 3. (*Continued*)

Commodity	Legislative changes 1914	1922	1930	Totals	Price–induced changes 1915–1920	1923–1929	1931–1933	Totals
Sugar, Cuban, 97°	14.6	57.0	2.7	74.3	−58.8	58.9	123.7	123.7
Sugar, Cuban, 100°	0.0	53.3	17.1	70.4	7.0	40.5	47.9	95.3
Toilet water	−12.4	0.0	0.0	−12.4	−7.6	0.0	0.0	−7.6
Tracing cloth	−17.2	0.1	0.3	−16.8	−3.6	−0.3	1.4	−2.5
Vanilla beans	4.6	0.0	−1.8	2.8	10.7	10.7	30.0	51.3
Walnuts, shelled	−7.4	3.2	9.4	5.2	−8.3	−9.7	50.5	2.5

Note: The changes in rates attributed to legislative dates are computed as the difference between the date referenced in the column and the rate prevailing in the previous year. The exception is the year 1922, which uses 1920 as the basis for the change to account for the cumulative effect of the Emergency Tariff Act of 1921 and the Fordney-McCumber Act of 1922. Totals are sums of changes.

of 1914, the Emergency Tariff Act of 1921, the Fordney-McCumber Act of 1922, and the Hawley-Smoot Act of 1930. The intervening periods include World War I inflation from 1915 to 1920, modest deflation from 1923 to 1929, and rapid deflation from 1931 to 1933.

Consistent with the previous discussion, the largest changes in ad valorem equivalent tariff rates are attributable to price movements. Considering only commodities subject to specific duties, the impact of Hawley-Smoot exceeds the deflationary impact of the 1930's in only a single case. In contrast, there are ten cases in which the Underwood Act reduced ad valorem equivalent tariff rates by more than did World War I inflation. However, the magnitude of the inflationary impact is much greater when it does exceed the legislative impact. For 17 of the 32 commodities, the sum of changes due to price changes is greater than the sum of changes due to legislation.

3. Other Implications

Macroeconomists typically use more aggregated tariff data than I have discussed thus far. The tariff index that is almost universally applied in macroeconomics is computed as the ratio of the value of customs duties collected to total dutiable imports (see e.g., Dornbusch and Fisher (1986), Gardner and Kimborough (1989), Ostry and Rose (1989) and Bohara and Kaempfer (1991)). In the discussion that follows, I refer to this index as the aggregate U.S. tariff rate. This index has widely recognized failings: (i) prohibitive tariffs receive a zero weight, leading to a downward bias; (ii) import shares change during the periods between legislative amendments, generating "spurious" movements in the index.

Figure 2 presents three alternative tariff indexes. The organization of this figure follows that for the individual commodities presented earlier. The aggregate U.S. tariff rate is presented in the first row; a variable-import-share-weighted index appears in the second row; and a constant-import-share-weighted index appears in the third row. The latter two indexes are computed from the panel data set. The left-hand panel presents the ad valorem equivalent tariff rate and the legislative component, while the right-hand panel presents the price-level component and the relative-price component.[6]

---

[6]The variable-import-share index is computed from the individual commodity data as follows:

$$\tau_t^* = \sum_{j=1}^{32} s_{jt}\tau_{jt}^* = \sum_{j=1}^{32} s_{jt}(T_{js}^L + T_{jt}^P + T_{jt}^{RP})$$

where

$$s_{jt} = \frac{P_{jt}Q_{jt}}{\sum\limits_{j=1}^{32} P_{jt}Q_{jt}}.$$

The constant-import-share index replaces s_{jt} with

$$s_j = \frac{1}{27}\sum_{t=1914}^{1940} s_{jt}.$$

The decomposition of the aggregate U.S. tariff rate employs a simply regression procedure:

$$\begin{aligned}\tau_t^* &= [d_{14} + d_{21} + d_{22} + d_{30} + d_{34}] \\ &\quad + \left[d_{15}^{20}\frac{1}{P_t} + d_{23}^{29}\frac{1}{P_t} + d_{31}^{33}\frac{1}{P_t} + d_{35}^{40}\frac{1}{P_t}\right] + \varepsilon_t\end{aligned}$$

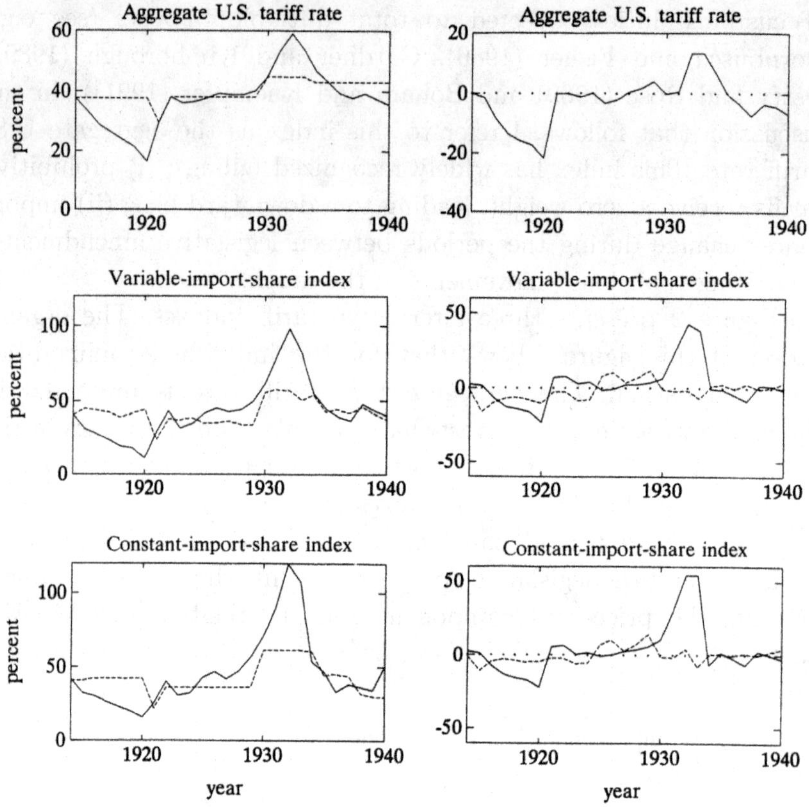

Fig. 2. Aggregate-tariff index decompositions.
Notes: The left-hand panels show the ad valorem equivalent tariff rate (solid line) and the legislative component (dashed line); the right-hand panels show the price-level component (solid line) and the relative-price component (dashed line). For the aggregate U.S. tariff index, no relative-price component is constructed. Construction of the import-share-weighted indexes is described in footnote 6.

---

where, $d_{15} = 1$ in 1915 and zero otherwise, and $d_{15}^{20} = 1$ between 1915 and 1920 and zero otherwise. In this decomposition, the first term in brackets is the legislative component, and the second term in brackets is the import-price-index component.

The legislative component is the ad valorem equivalent rate prevailing in the year the legislation is passed. The interactive dummy variables on the import-price terms account for legislative shifts in the use or magnitude of specific duties relative to pure ad valorem duties. The legislative component is extended through

Three conclusions may be drawn from comparing these alternative indexes. First, as with the individual tariff rates, World War I inflation and deflation in the 1930's explain more of the variation in tariff levels than do legislative amendments. This can be seen by comparing the movements of the dashed lines in the left-hand panels of Fig. 2 with the solid lines in the right-hand panel. The importance of price-level movements carries over to aggregative indexes because this component is common to all commodities subjected to specific duties. Second, the legislative increases that occurred in the early 1920's simply reestablished the ad valorem equivalent rates that existed before World War I. This can be seen in the relatively flat pattern of the legislative component from 1914 to 1929. Finally, changes in the composition of imports in the 1930's cause the variable-import-share index to rise less quickly than the constant-share version, consistent with the view that tariff levels were reaching prohibitive levels in the 1930's. This is apparent in the second and third graphs of the left-hand panel of Fig. 2. The constant-share index reaches about 120 percent in 1932, while the variable-import-share index peaks at about 100 percent. Researchers should make an allowance for the downward bias in the aggregate U.S. tariff rate, due to prohibitive duties, in attempting to quantify the impact of tariffs during the Great Depression.

Razin and Svensson (1983) argue that temporary changes in tariff rates should produce current-account imbalances, while permanent tariff changes have an ambiguous effect. The impact of temporary

---

the years between legislative amendments and subtracted from the import-price component estimated above. Thus, import-price components have a zero mean over each subinterval.

In 1930, the U.S. Tariff Commission produced a "legislative index" quite similar to the one constructed here, for all dutiable imports, but only compared two legislative dates. The commission computed tariff rates that would have prevailed in 1928 under the provisions of the Fordney-McCumber Act and the Hawley-Smoot Act and found that aggregate tariff rates would have been about 34.8 and 41.14, respectively, compared to my regression estimates of 38.1 and 44.7. Thus the average increase in either case is about 3.5 points, though the absolute levels are higher using the regression procedure.

tariff movements on the current account warrants serious consideration in light of the substantial cyclical variation in the aggregate U.S. tariff rate.

The tariff measure appropriate for studying the political economy of commercial policy is also not clear-cut. Tax systems are notorious for containing nominal rigidities. Current examples include nominal interest payments, collection of excise taxes, and imperfect indexation of tax brackets. Treating the ad valorem equivalent tariff rate as the relevant policy variable is analogous to considering taxation of nominal interest as a deliberate inflation tax.

Eichengreen (1989 p. 15), in a rigorous analysis of the political economy of the Hawley-Smoot Tariff Act states that "the effects of price-level trends should be factored out in order to isolate the magnitude of the initial commercial initiative." Under this assumption, the legislative paths in Fig. 2 are the ones relevant for studies of political economy. Judging from this figure, the only interesting commercial initiative during the period is the one studied by Eichengreen. In contrast, Magee *et al.* (1989) and Bohara and Kaempfer (1991) use the aggregate U.S. ad valorem equivalent tariff rate to measure the politically endogenous tariff rate. If the variation in tariff rates between dates of legislative amendment does not represent active tariff policy, then these studies dramatically overstate the variation and cyclicality of endogenous tariffs.

4. Conclusions

The results of this paper provide dramatic evidence that the Hawley-Smoot Tariff Act of 1930 did not have the massive deflationary implications that are widely attributed to it. In fact, the results show convincingly that the opposite is true: the variations in real tariff rates caused by the Hawley-Smoot Tariff Act are quite small relative to the variations in real tariff rates caused by price deflation. This contradicts the "received wisdom" on the subject, which is revived repeatedly in discussions of the connection between Hawley-Smoot and the Great Depression.

The relationship between the nominal price level and real tariff rates suggests a new channel of international transmission of U.S. monetary policy. Deflation and the associated increases in real tariff rates should retard international trade while periods of rising price levels should boost the volume of international trade. As foreign countries also used specific duties, "tariff wars" would result from world-wide deflation, assuming foreign legislators, like their American counterparts, were slow to reduce the nominal levels of specific duties.

Research aimed at exploring the contribution of commercial policy to the severity of the world depression must recognize the strong links among money, prices, and real tariff rates during 1900–1940. Crucini and Kahn (1994) demonstrate that a two-country multisector trade model predicts a collapse of world trade and modest declines in international output and investment, when simulated using aggregate ad valorem equivalent tariff indexes across the United States, Canada, and Europe. While preliminary, this research illustrates the importance of incorporating time-series variation in real tariff rates when attempting to quantify the economic impact of commercial policy.

Acknowledgments

This paper is based on the third chapter of my Ph.D. dissertation. I owe special thanks to my principal adviser, Marianne Baxter. This paper has also benefited from the comments of Stanley Engerman, Ronald Jones, James Kahn, Robert King, and two anonymous referees. I am particularly grateful to the organizers and participants at the NBER Macroeconomic-History Conference, May 1991 for providing a forum for the ideas expressed in this paper. Any errors that remain are the sole responsibility of the author. This research was completed while I was a visiting scholar at the Institute for Empirical Macroeconomics, Federal Reserve Bank of Minneapolis. The views expressed herein are those of the author and not necessarily those of the Federal Reserve Bank of Minneapolis or the Federal Reserve System.

Data Appendix

All data are at the annual frequency. The aggregate tariff rate from 1914 to 1940 is series U20 (ratio of customs duties to dutiable imports) from *The Historical Statistics of the United States: Colonial Times to the Present* (U.S. Bureau of the Census, 1965). The import price index from 1900 to 1940, is series U17, from the same source. The individual commodity data, consisting of quantities, values, and legislated rates of duty, were collected by the author from annual volumes of the *Foreign Trade and Navigation of the United States* (U.S. Department of Commerce, 1903–1940). The dates of legislative amendment and legislated levels of duties are reported in Table A1. The panel data set and plots of the tariff rate decompositions for all 32 commodities are available from the author upon request.

Table A1. Legislated duties.

Date of legislation	1903	1909	1913	1921	1922	1929	1930	1934
Almonds	6¢	—	4¢	—	14¢	—	$16\frac{1}{2}$¢	—
Brazil and cream	free	—	1¢	—	—	—	$4\frac{1}{2}$¢/$1\frac{1}{2}$¢	a
Bristles	$7\frac{1}{2}$¢	—	7¢	—	—	—	3¢	—
Burlap	$\frac{5}{8}+15\%$	$\frac{9}{16}+15\%$	free	—	1¢	—	—	—
Castor beans	25¢	—	15¢	—	25¢	—	—	—
China clay	$2.50	—	$1.25	—	$2.50	—	—	b
Cigar and cheroots	$4.50 + 25%[p]	—	—	—	—	—	—	c
Cigar filler, Cuban, stemmed	50¢[p]	—	—	—	—	—	—	d
Cigar filler, unstemmed	35¢	—	—	—	—	—	—	e
Cigar filler, Cuban, unstemmed	35¢[p]	—	—	—	—	—	$17\frac{1}{2}$¢	f
Cigar leaf wrapper	$1.85	—	—	$2.35	$2.10	—	$2.275	g
Cigarette paper	free	60%	50%	—	60%	—	—	h
Coconuts	free	—	—	—	$\frac{1}{2}$¢	—	—	i
Dates	$\frac{1}{2}$	1¢	—	—	—	—	1¢/2¢	—
Diamonds	10%	—	20%	—	—	—	—	—
Egg yolk, dried	10%	—	—	—	18¢	—	27¢[1931]	—
Egg yolk, other	10%	—	—	—	6¢	$6\frac{1}{2}$¢	$7\frac{1}{2}$¢	—
Feathers, for beds	15%	20%	—	—	—	—	—	—

(*Continued*)

Table A1. (*Continued*)

Date of legislation	1903	1909	1913	1921	1922	1929	1930	1934
Feathers, ostrich	15%	20%	—	—	—	—	—	—
Flaxseed	25¢	—	20¢	30¢	40¢	56¢	65¢	—
Matches in boxes	8¢	6¢	3¢	—	8¢	—	20¢	j
Mercury	7¢	—	10%	—	25¢	—	—	—
Quebracho	$\frac{1}{2}$¢	$\frac{1}{2}$¢/$\frac{3}{4}$¢	free	—	15%	—	—	—
Soap, Castille	$1\frac{1}{4}$¢	—	10%	—	15%	—	—	—
Sugar, Cuban, 95°	1.65¢^{p}	—	1.23¢^{p}	1.96¢^{p}	2.16¢^{p}	—	2.4625¢^{p}	k
Sugar, Cuban, 96°	1.685¢^{p}	—	1.265¢^{p}	2.00¢^{p}	2.206¢^{p}	—	2.50¢^{p}	l
Sugar, Cuban, 97°	1.72¢^{p}	—	1.282¢^{p}	2.04¢^{p}	2.252¢^{p}	—	2.5375¢^{p}	m
Sugar, Cuban, 100°	1.36¢^{p}	—	—	2.16¢^{p}	2.39¢^{p}	—	2.65¢^{p}	n
Toilet water, perfumed	15¢	50%	30%	—	—	—	—	—
Tracing cloth	5¢+ 20%	—	30%	7¢+30%	5¢+ 20%	—	—	—
Vanilla beans	free	—	30¢	—	—	—	—	o
Walnuts	5¢	—	4¢	—	12¢	—	15¢	—

Notes: A superscript p indicates a preference of 20 percent. Key to letter codes in last column: a) $2\frac{1}{4}$¢/$\frac{3}{4}$¢[1936]; b) $1.75 [1939]; c) $2.25 + $12\frac{1}{4}$ percent [1934], $4.50 + 25 percent^{p} [1937]; d) 25¢[1934], 50¢ − 20 percent/25¢[1936], 50¢[1937]; e) 35¢/30¢[1939]; f) $17\frac{1}{2}$¢[1934], 35¢[1936]; g) $1.50 [1937]; h) 45 percent [1937]; i) $\frac{1}{4}$¢[1939]; j) $17\frac{1}{2}$¢[1936]. Notes k–n refer to two-part duties on sugar; Volumes above a certain quota were subject to a higher duty: k) $1.846875 [1934], $0.8865 [1935–1937], $0.9 [1938–1939], $1.37775 [1940]; l) $1.875^{p} [1934], 0.90 [1935–1937], $1.4 [1938], $2.0/$1.5 [1939], $0.9/$1.4 [1940]; m) $1.89936^{p} [1934], $0.9135 [1935–1938], $1.5225/$2.03125 [1939], $0.9135/$1.42225 [1940]; n) $1.9875^{p} [1934], 0.954 [1935–1937], $1,489 [1938], $2.125/$0.954 [1939], $0.954/$1.489 [1940]; o) 15c [1937].
Source: *Foreign Trade and Navigation of the United States* (U.S. Department of Commerce, 1903–1940).

References

Berglund, Abraham. "The Tariff Act of 1922." *American Economic Review,* March 1923, 13(1), pp. 14–33.

Berglund, Abraham. "The Tariff Act of 1930." *American Economic Review,* September 1930, 20(4), pp. 467–79.

Bohara, Alok K. and Kaempfer, William H. "A Test of Tariff Endogeneity in the United States." *American Economic Review,* September 1991, 81(4), pp. 952–60.

Crucini, Mario J. and Kahn, James. "Tariffs and Aggregate Economic Activity: Lessons from the Great Depression." Mimeo, Ohio State University, 1994.

Dornbusch, Rudiger and Fischer, Stanley. "The Open Economy: Implications for Monetary and Fiscal Policy," in Robert J. Gordon, ed., *The American business cycle: Continuity and change.* Chicago: University of Chicago Press, 1986, pp. 459–518.

Eichengreen, Barry. "The Political Economy of the Smoot-Hawley Tariff," in Roger L. Ransom, ed., *Research in Economic History*, Vol. 12. Greenwich, CT: JAI Press, 1989, pp. 1–43.

Gardner, Grant W. and Kimborough, Kent P. "The Behavior of U.S. Tariffs." *American Economic Review*, March 1989, 79(1), pp. 211–18.

Haberler, Gottfried. *The World Economy, Money, and the Great Depression, 1919–1939.* Washington, DC: American Enterprise Institute, 1976.

Jones, Joseph M., Jr. *Tariff Retaliation: Repercussions of the Hawley-Smoot Bill.* Philadelphia: University of Pennsylvania Press, 1934.

Kindleberger, Charles P. *The World in Depression.* London: Allen Lane, 1973.

Magee, Stephen P.; Brock, William A. and Young, Leslie. *Black Hole Tariffs and Endogenous Policy Theory: Political Economy in General Equilibrium.* New York: Cambridge University Press, 1989.

Meltzer, Alan. "Monetary and Other Explanations of the Start of the Great Depression." *Journal of Monetary Economics*, November 1976, 2(4), pp. 455–71.

Ostry, Jonathan D. and Rose, Andrew K. "Tariffs and the Macroeconomy: Some Empirical Evidence." International Monetary Fund Working Paper No. 89–70, September 1989.

Razin, Assaf and Svensson, Lars E. O. "Trade Taxes and the Current Account." *Economics Letters*, 1983, 13(1), pp. 55–57.

Taussig, Frank W. *The Tariff History of the United States.* New York: Putnam's, 1931.

Taussig, Frank W. "The Tariff Act of 1922." *Quarterly Journal of Economics*, November 1922, 37, pp. 1–28.

U.S. Bureau of the Census. *The Historical Statistics of the United States from Colonial Times to the Present.* Stanford, CA: Fair-field, 1965.

U.S. Department of Commerce, Bureau of Foreign and Domestic Commerce. *Foreign Trade and Navigation of the United States.* Washington, DC: U.S. Government Printing Office, annual volumes, 1903–1940.

U.S. Department of Commerce, Bureau of Foreign and Domestic Commerce. *Statistical Abstract of the United States.* Washington, DC: U.S. Government Printing Office, 1932.

U.S. Tariff Commission. *Comparison of Rates of Duty in the Tariff Act of 1930 and in the Tariff Act of 1922.* Washington, DC: U.S. Government Printing Office, 1930.

Chapter 14

Misallocation and Productivity Effects of the Smoot–Hawley Tariff*

Eric W. Bond

Department of Economics, Vanderbilt University, Nashville, TN, USA
eric.bond@vanderbilt.edu

Mario J. Crucini

Department of Economics, Vanderbilt University, Nashville, TN, USA and National Bureau of Economic Research, Cambridge, MA, USA
mario.j.crucini@vanderbilt.edu

Tristan Potter

Department of Economics, Boston College, MA, USA

and

Joel Rodrigue

Department of Economics, Vanderbilt University, Nashville, TN, USA
joel.rodrigue@vanderbilt.edu

Abstract. Using a newly created microeconomic archive of US imports at the tariff line level for 1930–1933, we construct industry-level tariff

*This chapter originally appeared in *Review of Economic Dynamics*, 2013, **16**(1), 120–134.

wedges incorporating the input-output structure of US economy and the heterogeneous role of imports across sectors of the economy. We use these wedges to show that the average tariff rate of 46% in 1933 substantially understated the true impact of the Smoot-Hawley (SH) tariff structure, which we estimate to be equivalent to a uniform tariff rate of 70%. We use these wedges to calculate the impact of the Smoot-Hawley tariffs on total factor productivity and welfare. In our benchmark parameterization, we find that tariff protection reduced TFP by 1.2% relative to free trade prior to the Smoot-Hawley legislation. TFP fell by an additional 0.5% between 1930 and 1933 due to Smoot–Hawley. We also conduct counterfactual policy exercises and examine the sensitivity of our results to changes in the elasticity of substitution and the import share. A doubling of the substitution elasticities yields a TFP decline of almost 5% relative to free trade, with an additional reduction due to SH of 0.4%.

Keywords: Hawley-Smoot tariff; Great depression; Commercial policy; Productivity; Misallocation; Macroeconomic inefficiency

1. Introduction

An emerging literature seeks to understand the quantitative role of microeconomic misallocation of factors of production across uses within a country for macroeconomic efficiency. Restuccia and Rogerson (2008) argue that plants may face different prices for inputs used in production due to idiosyncratic policy distortions. When plants differ in total factor productivity, policy distortions will lower aggregate total factor productivity (TFP) if governments tax more productive plants and subsidize less productive ones. The misallocation literature typically assumes that the parametric form of the neoclassical production function is common across plants up to a constant idiosyncratic total productivity factor and policy distortions are backed out from equilibrium conditions imposed on plant-level data rather than measured directly. The distortions coming out of these exercises are estimated to be large: Hsieh and Klenow (2009) calculate the dispersion of marginal products of capital across firms in India and China and argue that reducing the dispersion in these countries, to the level observed in the US would have the effect of raising productivity by 40–60% in India and 30–50% in China.

This paper seeks to understand the potential for aggregate inefficiency to arise from trade policy. Trade policy seems a very natural candidate for the types of policy distortions modeled in the misallocation literature since the intent of such policies is to favor less efficient domestic producers over their foreign counterparts. We have chosen a historical context when such distortions are likely to be large, namely the high-water mark of protection arising from the passage of the infamous Hawley–Smoot legislation on June 30, 1930. We model tariff distortions as affecting the two margins of choice highlighted in textbook treatments of trade policy. The first is the choice by firms between domestic and imported intermediate inputs. The second is the choice by consumers between domestic and imported final consumption goods. These two margins interact in an important way because imported intermediate inputs are used in different intensities across sectors of the economy. For example, raw sugar imported from Cuba accounted for a substantial fraction of intermediate inputs into food production whereas imported parts were trivial and thus inconsequential for cost of producing US automobiles. Consequently, sugar duties are an example of a production distortion while automobile duties are an example of a consumption distortion.

What makes the study of tariff distortions both interesting and challenging is that they exhibit considerable variation both across time and sectors. Both the mean and standard deviation (across items) increase after the passage of SH, from 30% to 40% in the case of the mean and from 22% to 26% in the case of the standard deviation. This trend continues to 1933 when the mean and standard deviation reach 46% and 35%, respectively. The continued rise in the mean is largely due to the fact that many import duties were specific (e.g., cents per pound). As such the general deflation from 1930 to 1933 increased the mean of the ad valorem equivalent rates in the tariff schedule. Relative price movements, while theoretically ambiguous in their effect on the distribution of tariffs, were such that the dispersion of tariffs across goods also increased from 1930 to 1933.

There are a number of results in the international trade literature which suggest that both the increase in the mean tariff rate and their increased dispersion would have an adverse impact on economic welfare. For example, Hatta (1977) established that tariff reforms which reduce all tariffs proportionally or reduce the highest tariff will be welfare improving under quite general conditions. On the other hand, reductions of tariffs on arbitrary goods will not necessarily be welfare increasing. Anderson and Neary (2005) show that a country's welfare is decreasing in the generalized mean of the tariff rate (if the tariff rate is positive) and decreasing in the generalized variance, where the generalized mean and variance use the normalized substitution matrix of the balance of trade function as a weighting factor. This result suggests that an increase in the "unweighted" variance of tariffs will reduce welfare if the substitution effects are similar across goods, but might not if the substitution effects are asymmetric. Thus, we need to characterize the production structure in order to determine whether the increase in dispersion of tariffs we find is also associated with a decline in welfare.[1]

Turning to the details, we build a microeconomic archive of line-item tariff and trade data and use these data to construct tariff wedges in a structural general equilibrium model of the US economy. The wedges are used to calculate the impact of changes in protection on macroeconomic variables, including employment, consumption, and domestic price indices.[2] We derive two aggregate measures of the welfare impact of tariffs. The first is their effect on total factor productivity, which we define to be the number of units of the composite consumption bundle per unit of domestic productive resources. The second is the consumption equivalent, which is the compensation needed in units of aggregate consumption to make the representative agent indifferent between allocations under free trade and those under the existing tariff structure. In our benchmark parameterization, we find that the pre-Smoot–Hawley tariff legislation had the effect of reducing total factor productivity relative to the free trade level by 1.2%. The increases in tariffs

[1]Harrison *et al.* (1993) show that Turkey could achieve most of the gains from moving to free trade by adopting a uniform tariff structure. Eslava *et al.* (2013) examine the effects of trade reforms in Columbia, where trade liberalization resulted in a substantial reduction in the dispersion of tariffs. They analyze firm level data and find that tariff reforms increase the responsiveness of firms to market fundamentals.

[2]Irwin (1998b) analyzes the effect of the Smoot–Hawley tariffs using aggregate data and a CGE model to estimate sectoral effects, but does not incorporate the extent of sectoral disaggregation that we do.

associated with the Smoot-Hawley and the deflation from 1930–1933 had the effect of reducing TFP by an additional 0.5%. We use a counterfactual exercise to show that if SH had not been passed, the effects of deflation would still have reduced TFP by 0.3% due to the widespread use of specific tariffs. The consumption equivalent measure yields effects of a similar magnitude for the benchmark parameterization. We also show the impact of the dispersion in the tariff structure across goods in the sense that the uniform tariff equivalent of the existing tariff schedule is substantially above the average tariff during this period.

Our analysis abstracts from distortions in factor markets, and focuses on the effect of sectoral tariff wedges. The reductions in total factor productivity we find as a result of sectoral misallocations due to tariff protection are of a much smaller magnitude than those associated with factor market distortions, due in part to the fact that trade accounted for a relatively small fraction of US consumption and intermediate inputs during this period of history. We provide counterfactual exercises to illustrate the sensitivity of our results to changes in the import share of consumption goods and material inputs, as well as to the assumed elasticity of substitution between imports and domestic goods. These exercises provide some perspective on the potential for misallocation effects arising from commercial policy for other time periods and other nations.

We proceed in the following manner. Section 2 presents the multisector general equilibrium model and uses it to construct measures of the effects of tariff rates on aggregate variables. Section 3 describes the construction of the panel data series from line-item tariff rates, compares the sector level panel data to the line-item data and presents model-based estimates of sector level tariff wedges. Section 4 reports the results for the aggregate effects of tariff policy, and Section 5 concludes.

2. The Model

Our goal in this section is to develop a tractable model that can be used in conjunction with our tariff line panel to obtain a measure of the impact of sectoral misallocation on aggregate variables. Our modeling choices are driven by two features of the data from this period. First, 75% of imports are intermediate goods according to the input-output tables for 1929 (Leontief, 1941). Therefore, we want a model that captures the substitution between imported materials and domestically produced materials in the production process. Second, there is substantial variation across tariff lines in the extent to which protection was increased during this period, as well as substantial differences across sectors in the degree to which imported inputs are used in the production process. For example, imports accounted for 75% of intermediate inputs in the sugar, glucose and starch industry, but less than 1% of intermediate inputs into the agricultural industry. This heterogeneity combined with the fact that sugar duties were much higher and varied more over time than most other agricultural duties indicates the different industry-level distortions of these respective duties. This motivates the use of a multisector model that allows for differential effects of tariff protection across the various production sectors.

2.1. *The multisector production model*

We consider a GE production model with N_F sectors producing non-traded final consumption goods and one sector representing exportable goods (sector 0). The N_F final goods sectors correspond to the sectors in the Leontief input-output tables. This model allows us to capture substitution by firms between domestic and imported material inputs, as well substitution by consumers between domestic and imported final consumption goods. Our model also has a block recursive structure that provides simple measures of the effects of the tariff structure on aggregate variables.

Each of the N_F+1 production sectors produces final output using inputs of domestic value added and material inputs, with material inputs produced using domestic value added and imported materials. We assume that domestic capital and labor are used in the same proportions in all sectors, so that value added can be treated as a composite input whose price, p_V, is the same for all sectors. We assume a CES technology in the final goods sector j that can be characterized by the unit cost function $(a_{jV}p_V^{1-\sigma_F} + a_{jM}p_{jM}^{1-\sigma_F})^{\frac{1}{1-\sigma_F}}$, where P_{jM} is the price of materials to sector j and σ_F is the elasticity of substitution between value added and materials in the production of final goods (assumed common across sectors). The unit cost of production for materials in sector j is $(a_{jd}p_V^{1-\sigma_M} + a_{jm}p_{jm}^{1-\sigma_M})^{\frac{1}{1-\sigma_M}}$, where p_{jm} is the cost of a composite of line-item imported inputs used in production in sector j and σ_M is the elasticity of substitution between domestic and imported materials.

Assuming perfect competition in production of final goods and intermediates, the price of materials and final goods will equal their respective unit costs,

$$p_{jF} = \left(a_{jV}p_V^{1-\sigma_F} + a_{jM}\left(a_{jd}p_V^{1-\sigma_M} + a_{jm}p_{jm}^{1-\sigma_M}\right)^{\frac{1-\sigma_F}{1-\sigma_M}} \right)^{\frac{1}{1-\sigma_F}}, \quad j = 0, 1, \ldots, N_F. \tag{1}$$

Letting $\phi_j(p_V, p_{jm})$ denote the unit cost function of the integrated production of final goods and materials in sector j, $\theta_{jm} = (\frac{\partial \phi_j(p_V, p_{jm})}{\partial p_{jm}} \frac{p_{jm}}{p_{jF}})$ is the share of imported inputs and $\theta_{jV} = 1 - \theta_{jm}$ is the cost share of domestic inputs (direct plus indirect) in final goods sector j. The price of imported material inputs to sector j is computed by assuming that the imported material input for sector j is a composite of N_m lines of the import and tariff micro-data. Letting τ_i be one plus the ad valorem tariff rate on good i and q_i the world price of that good, the import price index for materials used by sector j will be

$$p_{jm} = \left[\sum_i^{N_m} b_{ji}(\tau_i q_i)^{1-\sigma_m} \right]^{\frac{1}{1-\sigma_m}}, \quad j = 0, 1, \ldots, N_F, \tag{2}$$

where σ_m is the elasticity of substitution between tariff lines, and the b_{ji} are parameters that reflect the intensity with which good i is used as an input into the production of sector j. The share of imports of tariff line i in the expenditure of activity j on imported inputs is given by $\alpha_{ji} = b_{ji}(\frac{q_i \tau_i}{p_{jm}})^{1-\sigma_m}$. Note that our specification allows for differential impacts of trade policies across sectors due to differences in the intensity of use of imported inputs, as reflected in the $\{a_{jV}, a_{jM}, a_{jm}\}$, as well as to differences in the composition of imports (the b_{ji}). We discuss below how tariff line data and the Leontief input-output tables can be used to construct values for these coefficients.

For a given vector of world prices, $\mathbf{q}$, the system of Eqs. (1) can be solved recursively for a given vector of import tariffs, $\boldsymbol{\tau}$, using (2). The zero profit condition for the exportable sector can be inverted to solve for the return to domestic value added as a function of the price of imported goods used in the exportable sector, $p_V^*(p_{0m})$. This solution for p_V can then be inserted into the remaining zero profit conditions to solve for the prices of the N_F non-traded consumption goods. An increase in tariffs imposed on importables raises the cost of imports to produce exportables, which requires a reduction in p_V to maintain the competitiveness of home exports on world markets. For the non-traded goods, an increase in tariffs has two conflicting effects: the cost of domestic value added rises but the price of imported inputs will rise. Which of these effects dominates depends on the intensity of use of imported inputs relative to the export sector and the extent to which the tariff increases fall on imports used by the sector.[3]

In the case of a small open economy, $\mathbf{q}$ is exogenously given and there will be complete pass-through of tariffs to prices paid by the domestic purchasers of imports. The treatment of the US as a small open economy merits some discussion. This assumption ensures that all of the distorting effects of the tariff are borne by the US, and thus can be thought of as representing an upper bound on the aggregate productivity effects of trade barriers.[4] If the US is a large country, then tariffs will improve the terms of trade by reducing the world price of imports, and some of the cost of the tariff would be borne by

[3]Our assumption of a single export sector is made to be consistent with our assumptions of a single (composite) domestic factor input and exogenously given world prices. The latter assumptions ensure that national income can be maximized by specializing in the traded good that yields the highest return to the domestic factor of production.

[4]We should note however that the effects could be larger in a dynamic model, where tariffs affect capital accumulation.

foreign countries. This could be captured in our analysis by allowing for incomplete pass-through of tariffs to domestic prices. However, there is little evidence of negative effects of tariff rate changes on world prices in our tariff line data.[5] The absence of a significant correlation seems consistent with the fact that US imports were only \$4.4 billion in 1929, which represented approximately 12% of world trade. Also, tariff retaliation by foreign countries would have the effect of mitigating the terms of trade improvements that the US experienced on account of its own tariff rate increases. An equivalent outcome to our assumptions would arise if the US were modeled as a large country with foreign retaliation exactly offsetting the impact of US tariffs on world prices. For the large country case, our results will overstate (understate) the US welfare loss in the case where the net effect of US tariffs and foreign retaliation is to improve (worsen) the US terms of trade.

We conclude our discussion of the production side of the model with the production function for domestic value added,

$$V = AK^{1-\beta}L^{\beta}, \tag{3}$$

where K is the input of capital, L is the input of labor, and A is the productivity level. We will undertake a short run analysis in which the capital stock is assumed to be fixed. The market wage will be determined by the marginal productivity condition,

$$\frac{w}{P_V} = A\beta\left(\frac{K}{L}\right)^{1-\beta}. \tag{4}$$

For a given K/L, protection will lower the wage rate because it lowers $p_V = p_V^*(p_{0m})$. The level of labor input will be determined as part of the household decision problem, to which we now turn.

[5] If US tariffs have a significant effect on world prices, then the world price of goods on which the US imposes higher tariffs should fall relative to other goods. To test this, we regressed changes in world prices on changes in tariff rates, allowing for differential coefficients based on whether goods had ad valorem or specific tariffs. We did not find a significant negative effect of tariff changes on prices for either type of protection.

2.2. *Household decisions and market equilibrium*

The preferences of households are assumed to take the following form:

$$U = \frac{C^{1-s}}{1-s} - \frac{vL^{\gamma}}{\gamma} \tag{5}$$

where

$$C = \left(\sum_{j=1}^{N_F} a_{cj}^{\frac{1}{\sigma_C}} C_j^{\frac{\sigma_C - 1}{\sigma_C}} + a_{cm}^{\frac{1}{\sigma_C}} C_m^{\frac{\sigma_C - 1}{\sigma_C}} \right)^{\frac{\sigma_C}{\sigma_C - 1}},$$

where the intertemporal elasticity of substitution in consumption is given by $\frac{1}{s}$ and the Frisch elasticity of labor supply by $\frac{1}{\gamma-1}$. The consumption levels C_j are demands for the final goods from the production sectors $j = 1, \ldots, N_F, C_m$ is the consumption of imports, and σ_C is the elasticity of substitution between all consumption goods, domestic and imported. Households face a budget constraint given by $\sum_{j=1}^{N_F} p_{jF} C_j + p_{cm} C_m = wL + rK + T$, where T is the amount of tariff revenue transferred to households, with p_{cm} and p_{jF} determined from the production sector by (2) and (1), respectively.

The household consumption allocation between domestic and imported goods can be solved using two stage budgeting. The necessary conditions for choice of C and L yield

$$C^s L^{\gamma - 1} = \frac{w}{vP_C} \tag{6}$$

where

$$P_C = \left(\sum_{j=1}^{N_F} a_{cj} p_{jF}^{1-\sigma_C} + a_{cm} p_{cm}^{1-\sigma_C} \right)^{\frac{1}{1-\sigma_C}}.$$

P_C is the price index for consumption, and we can express the share of expenditure on domestic goods by $\mu_j = a_{cj} (\frac{P_{jF}}{P_C})^{1-\sigma_C}$ for $j = 1, \ldots, N_F$ and the share of consumption on imports by $\mu_m = a_{cm} (\frac{P_{cm}}{P_C})^{1-\sigma_C}$.

In order to determine the level of tariff revenue, we need to derive demands for the imported products at the tariff line level.

The value of imports in tariff line i will be the sum of the value of imports for final consumption, $\alpha_{ci}\mu_m P_C C$, and the value of imports for intermediate use from the various production activities, $\sum_{j=0}^{N_F} \alpha_{ji}\theta_{jm}p_{jF}Y_{jF}$. Using the market clearing conditions for non-traded goods markets and for value added, we obtain an expression for tariff revenue as a function of value added and aggregate consumption:

$$T = \Gamma_V p_V V + \Gamma_C P_C C \tag{7}$$

where

$$\Gamma_V = \sum_{i=1}^{N_m} \left(\frac{\tau_i - 1}{\tau_i}\right) \alpha_{0i} \left(\frac{\theta_{0m}}{\theta_{0V}}\right),$$

$$\Gamma_C = \sum_{i=1}^{N_m} \left(\frac{\tau_i - 1}{\tau_i}\right) \left(\sum_{j=1}^{N_F} \left(\alpha_{ji}\theta_{jm} - \frac{\alpha_{0i}\theta_{0m}\theta_{jV}}{\theta_{0V}}\right)\mu_j + \alpha_{ci}\mu_m\right).$$

The terms Γ_V and Γ_C capture the effect of an increase in value added and consumption on tariff revenue. An increase in V, given C, will result in an increase in production of exportable goods and a corresponding increase in imported inputs for the exportable sector. Γ_V captures the effect of this on tariff revenue, which must be non-negative if $\tau_i \geq 0$ for all i. An increase in C will have two conflicting effects on imports. Higher consumption raises the demand for imports to produce imported consumption goods and non-traded goods, but it will also draw resources from production of the exportable good and reduce the usage of imported inputs in that sector. This leads to an ambiguous effect of an increase in aggregate consumption on tariff revenue, since tariff revenue could actually fall if exports are intensive in the use of intermediate inputs relative to other production and consumption activities and/or tariffs are relatively high on imports to the exportable sector.

Substituting (7) into the budget constraint yields a convenient expression for the level of the C that can be obtained from a given resource bundle V, which can be interpreted as a measure of total factor productivity,

$$\frac{C}{V} = TFP\,(\boldsymbol{\tau}, \mathbf{q}) = \frac{p_V\,(1 + \Gamma_V)}{P_C\,(1 - \Gamma_C)}. \tag{8}$$

The numerator is the social return to value added, which is the market return plus the additional tariff revenue generated from an additional unit of value added. The denominator of this expression is the social cost of consumption, which is the market cost less the tariff revenue generated by additional imports (which could be negative). It can be shown that this expression is maximized at free trade, and that proportional increases in all tariffs will be welfare reducing. The percentage reduction in TFP from the free trade level, $(\frac{TFP(\boldsymbol{\tau},\mathbf{q})}{TFP(1,\,\mathbf{q})} - 1) * 100$, provides a convenient measure of the efficiency loss resulting from tariff protection.

In addition to its impact on the efficiency of resource use, protection will also distort labor supply and consumption decisions. Substituting (6) into (8) and using the fact that $wL = \beta p_V V$, we obtain a solution for the equilibrium level of employment

$$L(\boldsymbol{\tau}, \mathbf{q}) = \left(\frac{\beta}{v}\frac{p_V}{P_C}(AK^{1-\beta})^{1-s}(TFP)^{-s}\right)^{\frac{1}{\beta(s-1)+\gamma}} \tag{9}$$

where $\beta(s-1) + \gamma > 0$ for all $s \geq 0$ since $\gamma \geq 1$. The existence of tariff protection will reduce both $\frac{p_V}{P_C}$ and TFP relative to the free trade level. The former effect reduces the relative price of labor, which is a substitution effect that results in a reduction in L. The latter is a wealth effect, which results in an increase in L. Thus, tariff protection will have an ambiguous effect on employment relative to the free trade level. The equilibrium level of consumption is obtained by substituting from (9) and (4) into (6), which yields

$$C(\boldsymbol{\tau}, \mathbf{q}) = \left(\left(\frac{\beta}{v}\frac{p_V}{P_C}\right)^{\beta}(AK^{1-\beta})^{\gamma}(TFP)^{\gamma-\beta}\right)^{\frac{1}{\beta(s-1)+\gamma}}. \tag{10}$$

Consumption will be increasing in $\frac{p_V}{P_C}$ and *TFP*, so tariff protection will unambiguously reduce consumption relative to the free trade level.

The solutions to (10) and (9) can be substituted into (5) to construct the indirect utility function

$$W(\boldsymbol{\tau}, \mathbf{q}) = \frac{C(\boldsymbol{\tau}, \mathbf{q})^{1-s}}{1-s} - \frac{vL(\boldsymbol{\tau}, \mathbf{q})^{\gamma}}{\gamma}. \tag{11}$$

(11) will be maximized at free trade in the small country case. To calculate the effect of a given tariff structure, $\boldsymbol{\tau}_0$, on welfare we can calculate the level of consumption that would lead to the same welfare as at free trade, given the distorted labor supply. This consumption equivalent value, which we denote C^E, is the solution to

$$U(C^E, L(\boldsymbol{\tau}_0, \mathbf{q})) = W(1, \mathbf{q}). \tag{12}$$

The expressions (8) and (12) can be used to measure the aggregate effects of tariff protection on resource allocation and welfare. If the tariff structure does not affect aggregate employment, then aggregate value added will be constant and the loss in consumption due to tariff protection will coincide with the reduction in TFP. When tariff protection reduces (raises) employment, the loss in consumption will be smaller (larger) than the reduction in TFP.

A second question of interest is the effect of the variance in the tariff structure on welfare. This question can be addressed by solving for the uniform tariff that yields the same welfare level as the existing tariff structure. Letting $\boldsymbol{\tau}_0$ be an initial tariff vector and $\mathbf{q}_0$ the vector of world prices of importable goods, the uniform tariff vector $\boldsymbol{\tau}^U$ that yields the same domestic welfare will be the solution to

$$W(\boldsymbol{\tau}^U, \mathbf{q}_0) = W(\boldsymbol{\tau}_0, \mathbf{q}_0).$$

This measure corresponds to the trade restrictiveness index (TRI) constructed by Anderson and Neary (2005).

3. The Tariff Line Data and Sectoral Price Indices

Three volumes of the FTNUS have been painstakingly converted from the historical text source to an electronic data archive in order to construct a panel consisting of three cross sections. The first cross section records imports during the first six months of 1930 when the Fordney-McCumber tariffs of 1922 were still in effect, which we will refer to as the 1930A cross section. The 1930B cross section covers the last six months of 1930 when the Smoot–Hawley tariffs were first applied to US imports. The third cross section covers the entire year 1933. We chose two post-Smoot–Hawley cross sections to illustrate how the tariff structure changed as a result of the effect of price deflation on sectors with specific tariffs. The year 1933 was chosen for the second post-SH cross section for two reasons. First, it is the trough of the US business cycle and captures the maximum change in imports resulting from the collapse in aggregate demand over the business cycle contraction phase. Second, 1933 also coincides with the price level trough. This is important for our study of the relationship between imports and tariffs because many customs duties were specific. Thus, the price level trough also coincides with the peak ad valorem equivalent rates of duty for many imported goods. As far as we know, this is the only archive of US imports and duties in existence at the line-item level for the 1930s.

Table 1 provides a sense of the scope of our cross sections. The number of line items from the original FTNUS source document increases from 4861 to 5280 and then to 5629 as we move across the

Table 1. Scope of the cross sections (source data).

	Number of observations			Proportion available		
	Pre-SH	Post-SH	1933	Pre-SH	Post-SH	1933
Tariff lines	4861	5280	5629	1.00	1.00	1.00
Value imported	4750	5001	5302	0.98	0.95	0.94
Quantity imported	4388	4685	5007	0.90	0.89	0.88
Price	4290	4422	4690	0.88	0.84	0.83
Duty	4018	4321	4487	0.83	0.82	0.80
Ad valorem rate	3980	4207	4345	0.82	0.80	0.77

three cross sections. The larger increase in 1930, despite the shorter time interval, is largely due to the expansion of the scope and level of detail in the tariff schedules themselves. Relative to these maximums, the fraction of available data varies across the measures of value imported, quantity imported, import price, duty collected and the ad valorem equivalent tariff rate. The value imported is available for more than 95% of the line items. The quantity data are next most abundant, available for about 90% of the line items. The price data are imputed as unit values, taking the ratio of value imported to the physical quantity imported and thus require availability of both measures. As such, they are available for fewer line items than either value or quantity, 85% typically. Since some items are duty free, the duty and tariff columns also have fewer entries than the value column. In sum, the cross sections represent the complete record of US trade flows at the line-item basis.

3.1. *Construction of panel data*

Conducting research in an environment with enormous heterogeneity in the products and the tariff levels across them poses some unique challenges. To measure the change in the quantity imported in response to a good-specific tariff change requires careful control of the quality of the matches of goods across time. Attention must also be paid to the fact that tariff lines are sometimes split or combined. This makes some rudimentary aggregation necessary to avoid excluding a significant number of entry-level items.

To match goods across time, we employed a text-matching algorithm to tariff lines in 1930A with those in the 1930B and 1933 cross sections. Since there was both splitting and aggregation of tariff lines during the period, the text-matching algorithm did not provide one to one matches in many cases. In these cases, we constructed an aggregated line-item series by taking a weighted average of the individual line items using the 1930A import values as weights. This procedure resulted in a balanced panel of 495 line items, accounting for 18% of trade in 1930A and 25% of trade in 1933. The reduction in the number of tariff lines occurs for two reasons. First, aggregation naturally reduces the number of individual tariff lines and due to a

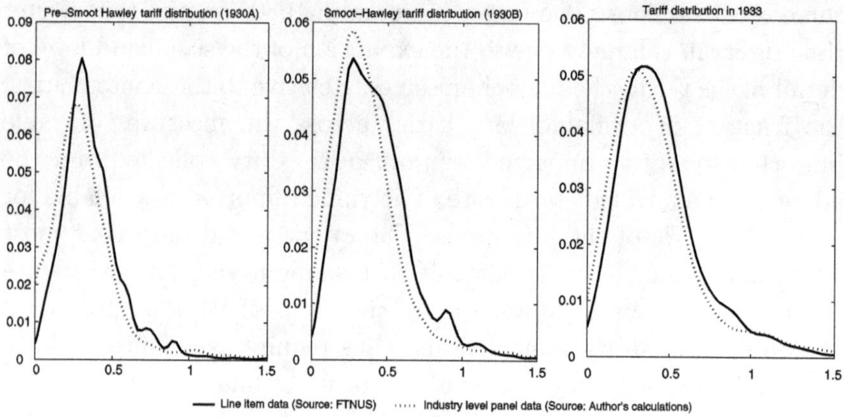

Fig. 1. Ad valorem tariff comparisons. The solid line is density estimate of original ad valorem equivalent tariffs in the FTNUS archive, while the dashed line presents the same estimate from the panel data.

large degree of re-organization between 1930A and 1930B/1933; it is common for two or more line items to be matched to the same line item in a later cross section. Second, aggregation exacerbates missing data issues. Any set of line items which is matched to any individual observation with missing data have to be discarded since the aggregation cannot be performed.[6]

We can provide a sense of how representative our balanced panel is of the underlying cross sections by comparing their distributions and reporting key statistics. Arguably one of the most important distributions is the microeconomic distribution of ad valorem equivalent tariff levels across goods. Figure 1 plots kernel estimates of the distributions of tariffs before Smoot–Hawley was passed, after Smoot–Hawley was passed and in 1933. The solid line is the raw (source) microdata and the dashed line is the balanced panel data. It is quite evident that the balanced panel is representative of the underlying line-item tariff data. The tariff levels are underestimated by the panel, but the differences are quite minor, the largest

[6]A detailed discussion of the quality of the matches from the text-matching algorithm, as well as further discussion of the aggregation procedure, is provided in Appendix A.

difference being the pre-Smoot-Hawley panel where the median ad valorem equivalent rate is 0.31 compared to 0.37 in the full archive. Table A.1 of Appendix A reports additional comparisons of the full cross section and panel.

A second concern about the reliability of our panel data is the extent to which we have successfully matched industries over time. Recall that variation in ad valorem equivalent tariff rates may arise due to changes in tariff rates at dates of legislative amendment or due to changes in import prices that alter the ad valorem equivalent rate associated with a specific duty.

To see this clearly, let $\tilde{\tau}_{it}$ denote one plus the legislated ad valorem tariff and let w_{it} denote the legislated nominal specific tariff, for import i, both recorded based upon the legislated tariff schedule in place at time t. The ad valorem equivalent tariff rate is the sum of the legislated pure ad valorem rate and the ad valorem equivalent of the legislated specific duty:

$$\tau_{it}(q_i) = \tilde{\tau}_{it} + \frac{w_{it}}{q_i}. \tag{13}$$

Clearly, for cases in which the specific duty is not zero, the ad valorem equivalent tariff rate moves inversely with the import price of the good.

The tariff rates under the Fordney–McCumber Act were in effect for the first 6 months of 1930, which is denoted as $t = 0$ (the 1930A cross section). The Smoot–Hawley tariff schedule was in effect for the second 6 months of 1930 (the 1930B ($t = 1$) cross section), and also for the 1933 ($t = 2$) cross section. Note that variation in line-item tariffs between $t = 1$ and $t = 2$ will only arise for imports that are subjected to specific duties. The vector of ad valorem equivalent tariff rates at time t is $\tau_t(q_t)$. We will also use (13) to construct the tariff vector $\tau_0(q_t)$ for $t = 1, 2$ which represents the counterfactual ad valorem equivalent tariff rates that would have been observed if the Smoot–Hawley legislation had not been passed.

If we are not matching industries correctly over time, this will introduce a measurement error into our comparisons of tariff rates over time. Since the tariff legislation did not change between the

1930B and 1933 samples, a crude measure of the quality of a match is the difference between the tariff rate (whether ad valorem or specific) for 1930B and 1933. For ad valorem tariff rates, 75% are within 1% of the base period rate, 77% are within 5% of the base period rate, and 91% are within 25% of the base period rate. The average base period (1930B) tariff rate was 16 percent. For specific tariff rates, 81% are within 1% of the base period duty, 84% are within 5% of the base period duty, and 89% are within 25% of the base period duty. The average base period (1930B) specific duty was 25 cents.

3.2. *Construction of sectoral price indices*

The import price indices defined in (2) represent ideal price indices for the cost of imports to the $N_F + 1$ production sectors and final consumption. Our tariff line panel provides the values of τ_{jt} and q_{jt} required for construction of these indices, but we also need to obtain values for the taste parameters, b_{ji}, and the elasticities of substitution, σ_m.

The expression for the share of imports from tariff line i by activity j, $\alpha_{ji}(\frac{q_i\tau_i}{p_{jm}}) = b_{ji}(\frac{q_i\tau_i}{p_{jm}})^{1-\sigma_m}$, can be used to express the b_{ji} in terms of observables at time t and the elasticity of substitution,

$$b_{ji} = \alpha_{jit}\left(\frac{q_{it}\tau_{it}}{p_{jm}(\mathbf{p}_t)}\right)^{\sigma_m - 1}. \tag{14}$$

Note that since the α_{jit} are homogeneous of degree 0 in the vector of coefficients b_j, the system of Eq. (14) determines the b_{ji} vector only up to a multiplicative constant. We can determine unique values, given σ_m, by choosing a normalization of base period price, $p_{im0}(\mathbf{p}_0) = 1$.

The tariff line data provide the total value of imports in the tariff line i, v_{it}, but not the allocation of these imports across the final goods sectors as required for the α_{jit}. However, we are able to construct a proxy for the budget shares in the base year, α_{ji0}, using the Leontief tables and the tariff line data by making two assumptions. The first assumption is that final good industry i's share of consumption of imports from tariff lines associated with final goods sector k is equal to its share of consumption of domestically produced intermediates from final goods sector k. Letting v_{ij0} denote imports by industry i in tariff line j in the base year, J_k denote the index set of tariff lines associated with industry k, and β_{ki} the share of industry k's output that is sold as intermediate goods to sector i, this assumption implies that $\sum_{j\in J_k} v_{ij0} = \beta_{ki}\sum_{j\in J_k} v_{j0}$. The second assumption is that the imports of final goods sector i from final goods sector j are allocated across tariff lines in proportion to their share in total imports from industry k, which requires $\frac{v_{ij}}{\sum_{j\in J_k} v_{ij}} = (\frac{v_j}{\sum_{j\in J_k} v_j})$. Together these assumptions imply that $v_{ij} = \beta_{ki}v_j$ for all $j \in J_k$, so that the base year budget shares can be expressed as

$$\alpha_{ij0} = \frac{v_{ij0}}{\sum_j v_{ij0}} = \frac{\beta_{ki}v_{j0}}{\sum_k \sum_{j\in J_k} \beta_{ki}v_{j0}},$$
$$i = 1,\ldots,N_c;$$
$$j = 1,\ldots,N_m. \tag{15}$$

The base year budget shares are calculated using Leontief's 1929 input–output tables for the β_{ki} and the 1930 (pre-HS) tariff line data for the v_{j0}.

To complete the construction of the import price indices, we calibrate the values of σ_m and σ_C to match the change in imports between 1930A and 1930B in response to the changes in tariffs and world prices. We can express the demand for imported materials by sector j from tariff line i as $m_{ji} = \alpha_{ji}(\frac{q_i\tau_i}{p_{jm}})\theta_{jm}(p_V, p_{jm})\mu_j(\frac{p_{jF}}{P_c})P_cC$. Totally differentiating this expression and defining $\hat{x} = \frac{dx}{x}$, we have

$$\hat{m}_{ji} = -s^{\tau}_{ji}(\hat{\tau}_i + \hat{q}_i) + s^V_{ji}\hat{p}_V + s^F_{ji}\hat{P}_{iF} + s^V_{ji}\hat{P}_c + \hat{C} \tag{16}$$

where the coefficients s^k_{ji} are functions of the elasticities of substitution, $(\sigma_C, \sigma_F, \sigma_M, \sigma_m)$, and the cost shares. A similar expression can be derived for $\hat{m}_{ci}$, and the model's prediction of the change in imports from tariff line i, $\hat{m}_i$, will be an import share weighted sum of the $\hat{m}_{ji}$. Assuming that $\sigma_F = 1$, $\sigma_m = \sigma_M$, and that

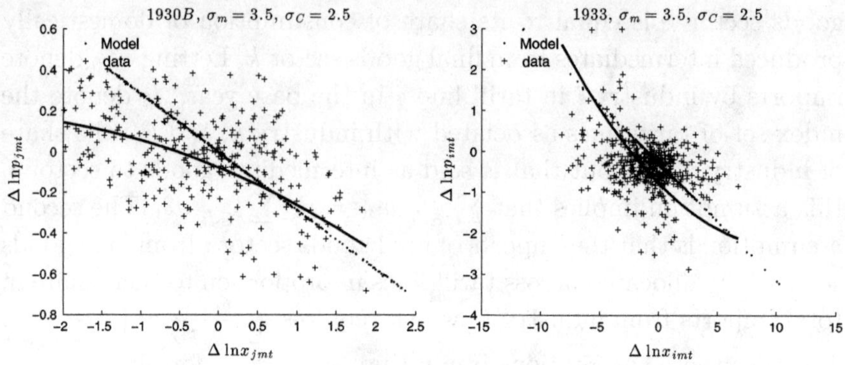

Fig. 2. Predicted vs actual changes in import prices and quantities across line-item goods in the panel data. The crosses represent individual data points. The dotted line is the model's predicted changes, while the solid line is fitted values of a quadratic regression on the actual data.

$\hat{p}_V = \hat{p}_{jF} = \hat{p}_C = \hat{w}$ are given by the rate of change in the GDP deflator, we obtain an expression for the change in imports in tariff line i as a function of σ_C and σ_m. We choose the values σ_C and σ_m to match price and quantity movements in the data between the 1930A and 1930B cross sections. We then compare the change in imports between the 1930A and 1933 cross sections with the predictions based on our calibrated parameters as an out-of-sample check on our parameter choices. The results for the 1930B and 1933 cross sections are displayed in the two panels of Fig. 2.

Figure 2 displays the model predicted data (dots), the actual data (crosses) and a quadratic regression of actual import prices changes on import quantity changes. We observe that the relationship between import price and quantity changes in 1933 is nearly linear. Further, setting $\sigma_m = 3.5$ and $\sigma_C = 2.5$, we find that the model matches the data very closely. In 1930 we observe a less linear relationship between prices and quantities. In particular, there are a number of goods for which we observe large declines in import quantities in response to moderate import price increases. This is arguably reasonable if the legislated tariff increases were foreseen by importers, who were in turn able to increase imports in the first half of 1930 before the tariff changes took effect. Nonetheless, overall the model matches the data relatively well.[7]

Given our benchmark parameterization, we can use our constructed import price indices to measure the impact of the SH policy on the cost of imported goods across industries and over time. Specifically, we calculate the tariff wedges for each industry in year t to be

$$\frac{p_{jm}(\mathbf{p}_t)}{p_{jm}(\mathbf{q}_t)} = \left[\frac{\sum_i^{N_m} \alpha_{ji0}\left(\frac{q_{it}\tau_{it}}{q_{i0}\tau_{i0}}\right)^{1-\sigma_m}}{\sum_i^{N_m} \alpha_{ji0}\left(\frac{q_{it}}{q_{i0}\tau_{i0}}\right)^{1-\sigma_m}}\right]^{\frac{1}{1-\sigma_m}}, \quad j = 0, \ldots, N_F \text{ and } C$$

given the individual tariff line-item data, the Leontief share data and our parameterization of σ_m. The results are presented in Fig. 3 where we have sorted the tariff wedges from lowest to highest based the 1930A, pre-SH tariff wedge.

Figure 3 demonstrates a striking degree of heterogeneity in the tariff wedges across industries and over time. Even before the SH policy was implemented (the solid line) we observe that tariff wedges range from a low of 1.01 (leather shoes) to a high of 1.91 (sugar, glucose, and starch). Both the average tariff wedge and the variance of the wedge across industries increase with the passage of the SH tariff and the propagation of the Great Depression. As expected, after passage of the SH duties (line labeled 1930B) trade barriers increase in 37 of 41 industries, with many of the largest increases occurring in industries that already had large tariff wedges before the change in

[7]These parameter values yield a price elasticity of import demand that averages 3.1. Our estimates of the elasticity parameters are relatively low compared to those presented elsewhere in the trade literature. For instance, Eaton and Kortum (2002) suggest an elasticity of substitution across imports near 8, while Simonovska and Waugh (2011) suggest that an improved estimate would be closer to 4. We note that increasing σ_m from our benchmark estimate results in higher tariff wedges a larger role for tariff policy in determining trade flows. In light of our relatively conservative elasticity estimate, we also consider a counterfactual exercise with larger elasticities.

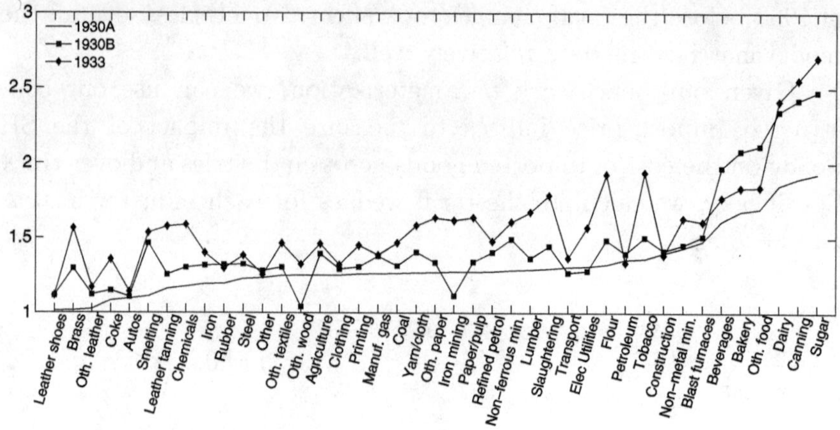

Fig. 3. Industry-specific import tariff wedges in 1930A (solid line), 1930B (squares) and 1933 (diamonds). The import tariff wedges are sorted from lowest to highest based on the 1930A, pre-SH tariff wedge.

policy. By 1933 the wedges range from a low of 1.11 (leather shoes) to a high of 2.73 (sugar, glucose and starch). These are enormous increases in trade barriers. At the low end, the leather shoe industry experiences a 10 percent increase from the pre-SH period, which is not small by historical standards. However, it seems minute relative to the 82 percent increase the sugar, glucose and starch industry over the same period.

Figure 4 shows the decomposition of the change in tariff wedges between the 1930A and 1933 cross sections into a legislated impact and a price-induced effect. The legislated component of the tariff change is the change in ad valorem equivalent tariff rates between 1930A and 1933 that would have occurred if prices remained at the 1930A level, $\log \tau_{i2}(q_{i0}) - \log \tau_{i0}(q_{i0})$. The price-induced change is the impact of the price level changes between 1930A and 1933 on tariff rates, $\log \tau_{i2}(q_{i2}) - \log \tau_{i2}(q_{i0})$. The price-induced changes were of considerable magnitude, and their impact differed significantly across sectors.[8]

[8]The significant role played by price level changes in the effective tariff rate has been emphasized by Crucini (1994) and Irwin (1998a). The correlation between the legislated impact and the price-induced effect is –0.049.

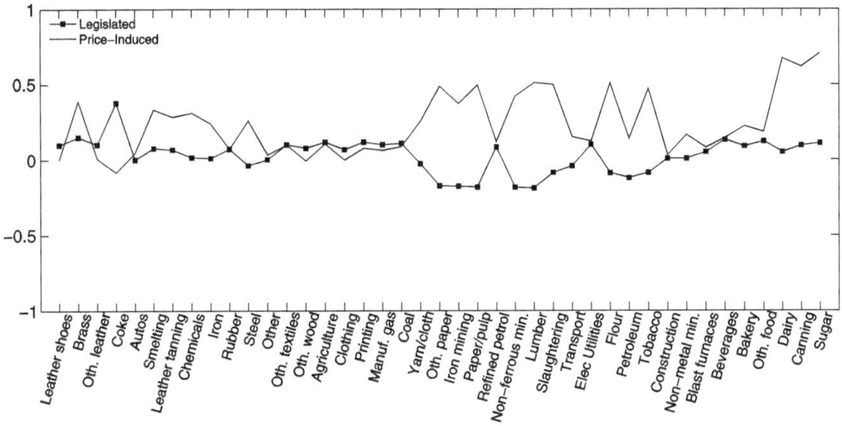

Fig. 4. This figure plots the decomposition of the change in import tariff wedges between 1933 and 1930A. The solid line represents the total change in industry-specific import tariff wedges due to deflation. The line with squares captures the total change due to the change in legislated tariff rates.

Table 2. Tariff wedge moments.

	1930A	1930B	1933
Mean	1.32	1.46	1.59
Variance	0.0486	0.124	0.116
Mean absolute deviation	0	0.156	0.268

Note: The mean absolute deviation is relative to 1930A.

Table 2 provides a summary of the effect of the Smoot–Hawley legislation on the mean and variance of the tariff wedges. The mean tariff wedge prior to SH was equivalent to a 32% tariff on imported inputs. The SH legislative increase combined with deflation during 1930 increased the mean tariff wedge to 46%, and the subsequent deflation further increased it to 59% at the trough of imported prices in 1933. In addition to increasing the mean of the tariff wedges, the SH legislation also raised the cross-sectional variance of tariff rates substantially from 5% prior to SH to 12% in 1933. It should also be noted that the price-induced changes between 1930B and 1933 resulted in a substantial increase in the dispersion of tariff rates relative to the 1930A tariff rates, as indicated by the fact that the mean absolute deviation nearly doubled over the period.

4. Aggregate Effects of the Tariff Structure

The analysis of the previous section documented the wide range of sectoral distortions resulting from the SH tariff legislation and subsequent deflation. In this section we examine the impact of these distortions on aggregate consumption, employment, and welfare using the measures derived in Section 2.

The first exercise we conduct is to calculate the aggregate impact of protection using the tariff rate $\tau_t \equiv \tau_t(q_t)$ in time period t, which is calculated from (13) using the tariff schedule from period t and evaluating the ad valorem equivalent of the specific tariffs using world prices at time t. We thus incorporate both legislated changes in tariff rates and price level induced changes in tariff rates for each period, which results in an increase in the mean tariff rate from 30.8% in 1930A to 45.7% in 1933 and an increase in the variance from 0.052 to 0.125. In order to abstract from terms of trade changes, we solve for the equilibrium values assuming that prices remain constant at the 1930A levels, so that consumers and producers are assumed to be facing the tariff-laden price vector $\tau_t q_0$ at t.[9]

Table 3 reports the values for some of the key the aggregate variables from the model, with each variable reported as a percentage change relative to its free trade variable. Thus, the effect of the pre-SH tariffs is to reduce the return to domestic value added by about 2% relative to the free trade level. This is due to the fact that the pre-SH tariffs increased the price of importables to the production of exports by about 25%, and these imports accounted for approximately 3% of the cost of the exportable good in the base period. Subsequent tariff increases due to SH and deflation had

[9]The cost function parameters (a_{0d}, a_{0V}, a_{0m}) and p_{V0} are the values that satisfy the zero profit condition and match the cost shares $(\theta_{0d}, \theta_{0V}, \theta_{0m})$ from the input-output tables. The (a_{jd}, a_{jV}, a_{jm}) are then solved to match the respective cost shares given p_{V0} for $j = 1, \ldots, N_F$. A similar procedure is used to solve for the a_{cj} from the μ_j in the data.

Table 3. Benchmark case.

	1930A	1930B	1933
Tariff structure			
Mean tariff ($\tau - 1$)	30.8	38.8	45.7
Variance of tariffs	0.052	0.072	0.125
Uniform tariff equivalent ($\tau - 1$)	47.3	55.8	68.2
Percentage change in:			
Value added deflator (p_V)	−2.0	−2.0	−2.6
Consumption deflator (p_C)	0.0	0.1	−0.1
Total factor productivity ($TFP(\boldsymbol{\tau}, \mathbf{q}) = \frac{p_V(1+\Gamma_V)}{p_C(1-\Gamma_C)}$)	−1.2	−1.4	−1.7
Employment (L)	0.1	0.2	0.2
Real consumption (C)	−1.1	−1.3	−1.5
Consumption equivalent ($U(C^E, L(\boldsymbol{\tau}_0, \mathbf{q})) = W(1, \mathbf{q})$)	1.1	1.4	1.6

Note: Parameter values: $s = 2$, $\gamma = 2.5, \beta = 0.667, \sigma_M = \sigma_m = 3.5, \sigma_C = 2.5, \sigma_F = 1$.
Percentage change in is calculated relative to free trade, $\Delta x = 100\left(\frac{x(\tau,q)}{x(1,q)} - 1\right)$.

little impact on the return to value added. Similarly, the cost of the aggregate consumption bundle was unchanged relative to free trade at the pre-SH tariffs, and changed relatively little over the remainder of the period. The aggregate effect of tariff protection on TFP at the peak of tariffs in 1933 was to reduce it by 1.7% relative to the free trade level. Note that more than 2/3 of the effect of tariff protection on TFP was due to the pre-SH tariffs, with SH and the subsequent deflation reducing aggregate productivity by approximately 0.5% compared with the pre-SH level.

In order to calculate the effects on employment and consumption, we choose the utility function parameters $s = 2$ and $\gamma = 2.5$. These choices yield an intertemporal elasticity of substitution of 0.5 and a Frisch elasticity of labor supply of 2/3, which are within the range of values obtained from micro studies.[10] With these parameter choices,

[10]Chetty *et al.* (2011) argue a Frisch elasticity of 0.75 is the upper bound of values that are consistent with micro. Elasticities of intertemporal substitution in the range of 0.5 to 1 are typically obtained in studies using household data on consumption (e.g., Attanasio *et al.*, 2002).

tariff protection leads to a decrease in consumption of about 1.5% and an increase in employment of about 0.2%. As noted in the discussion of (10), tariff protection will decrease consumption relative to free trade because reductions in both *TFP* and $\frac{P_V}{P_C}$ work to reduce consumption. The effects of these two changes on employment are conflicting, and with our chosen parameter values the net effect is a small increase in employment.[11] The equivalent consumption effect indicates that at the peak of tariff protection, consumption would need to be increased by 1.6% to raise welfare to the free trade level. This is essentially equal to the TFP effect due to the minimal effect of protection on the level of employment.[12]

The comparison between the uniform tariff equivalent and the mean tariff shows that although the mean tariff was 45.7% at its peak, the overall effect of the tariff structure was equivalent to that of a uniform tariff of 69.7%. The increase in the variance of tariffs thus had a significant effect in increasing the distortion associated with the protective structure as measured by the uniform tariff equivalent. However, as already noted, the effects on aggregate productivity and welfare were relatively small.

How would the outcome have differed if Smoot–Hawley had never been passed? We can address this question by solving the model using the effective tariff rates associated with the pre-SH tariff legislation for all three periods of the panel, $\boldsymbol{\tau}_0(q_t)$. This exercise captures the effect of the decline in world prices on the ad valorem equivalent tariff rates for goods that had specific tariffs under the pre-SH legislation. As in the benchmark case, we assume world prices remain fixed at the initial level. The results for this counterfactual exercise on the aggregate measures are reported in Table 4. Since the pre-SH tariff included a number of specific tariff rates, the decline in prices still yielded an increase in the mean tariff rate for the 1930B and

[11]If we choose $s = 1$ and $\gamma = 1$, we obtain a small reduction in employment as a result of tariffs. However, the consumption equivalent is similar in this case.

[12]It can be shown that the measures reported in Table 3 are independent of the parameters v, A, and K.

Table 4. No Smoot–Hawley.

	1930A	1930B	1933
Tariff structure			
Mean tariff ($\tau - 1$)	30.8	33.1	38.4
Variance of tariffs	0.052	0.072	0.125
Uniform tariff equivalent ($\tau - 1$)	49.0	55.0	61.6
Percentage change in:			
Value added deflator (p_V)	−2.0	−2.1	−2.1
Consumption deflator (p_C)	0.0	0.1	0.1
Total factor productivity ($TFP(\boldsymbol{\tau}, \mathbf{q}) = \frac{p_V(1+\Gamma_V)}{p_C(1-\Gamma_C)}$)	−1.2	−1.3	−1.5
Employment (L)	0.1	0.2	0.2
Real consumption (C)	−1.2	−1.2	−1.3
Consumption equivalent ($U(C^E, L(\boldsymbol{\tau}_0, \mathbf{q})) = W(1, \mathbf{q})$)	1.2	1.3	1.5

Note: See Table 3.

1933 cross sections that was about half that arising from the Smoot-Hawley legislation. Interestingly, the variance of tariffs in 1933 would have been comparable to that under SH. This is consistent with the observation from Fig. 4 that deflation was a major factor in the rise in dispersion of tariff rates over the period. As a result, the increase in the uniform tariff equivalent is almost 2/3 of that occurring with SH. The decline in TFP in the absence of SH would have been 1.5% relative to the free trade level, and the required consumption increase to compensate for the decline in tariff protection would have been 1.5% as well. These results indicate that if Smoot–Hawley had not been passed, the increase in the tariff distortion would have been more than half of that which occurred under SH, because deflation would have been responsible for a substantial increase in both the mean and dispersion of tariff rates.

In order to test the sensitivity of these results to our parametric assumptions, we also consider a case where we double the elasticities to $\sigma_m = \sigma_M = 7$ and $\sigma_C = 5$. In competitive trade models, the change in welfare resulting from a change in tariffs is proportional to the tariff weighted change in import volumes. This occurs because the marginal social benefit of importing a good exceeds its marginal

Table 5. Double substitution elasticities.

	1930A	1930B	1933
Uniform tariff equivalent $(\tau - 1)$	65.3	71.9	84.5
Percentage change in:			
Value added deflator (P_V)	−6.8	−6.3	−6.9
Consumption deflator (p_C)	2.7	3.2	2.9
Total factor productivity $(TFP(\boldsymbol{\tau}, \mathbf{q}) = \frac{p_V(1+\Gamma_V)}{p_C(1-\Gamma_C)})$	−7.4	−7.7	−8.1
Employment (L)	2.2	2.4	2.5
Real consumption (C)	−6.2	−6.3	−6.6
Consumption equivalent $(U(C^E, L(\boldsymbol{\tau}_0, \mathbf{q})) = W(1, \mathbf{q}))$	8.1	8.4	8.9

Notes: Parameter values: $\sigma_C = 5, \sigma_m = \sigma_M = 7$, rest as in benchmark.

social cost in the presence of a tariff, so decreases in imports of tariff-laden goods will reduce welfare. Since the responsiveness of import flows is larger when elasticities of substitution are higher, these parameter values are likely to affect the magnitude of the welfare effects. In addition, it seems likely that import volumes would be more responsive to increases in the dispersion of tariffs (as occurred in our sample) when the elasticity of substitution between types of imports are higher. In order to keep our exercise consistent with the data, we also adjust the taste parameters in the model so that they generate the observed trade flows at the higher elasticity values. This has the effect of increasing the taste for imports as the elasticity of substitution rise.

The results for this exercise are reported in Table 5. TFP now declines by 7.4% relative to free trade with the pre-SH tariffs with the higher substitution elasticities, which is almost 6 times that in the benchmark case. A higher substitution elasticity results in a greater change in import volumes, both because of the increased responsiveness of imports to trade barriers and because of the correspondingly higher taste for imports required to match the trade data at higher substitution elasticities. The greater change in import volumes exacerbates the productivity loss.[13] In addition

[13]The importance of the role of the endogenous taste parameters can be seen by considering a symmetric two country endowment model, where each country has

to a larger effect on productivity, the higher elasticity also results in a substantially larger impact on employment, which now rises by 2.2%. As a result of the increase in employment, the amount of consumption required to reach the free trade level (8.1%) exceeds the TFP effect (6.8%) in magnitude. The subsequent SH tariffs and deflation (1933) reduce TFP by an additional 0.7% relative to the free trade level. Finally, we note that increasing the elasticity of substitution between importables also has the effect of increasing the uniform tariff equivalent of the tariff structure. The greater substitution elasticities raise the distortion associated with variance in the tariff structure, and thus tends to raise the uniform tariff equivalent.[14]

These results suggest that the aggregate cost of tariff protection can be sensitive to the assumptions made regarding the elasticities of substitution. Figure 5 elaborates on this point by showing how the loss in TFP varies with the value of the substitution elasticities for

---

an endowment of a single good and preferences are CES. If taste parameters are held constant, the distorting effects of tariffs go to 0 as $\sigma \to \infty$, because domestic goods become a perfect substitute for imports. This yields a non-monotonic relationship between the elasticity of substitution and the welfare loss from tariffs. If the taste parameter is adjusted to maintain a constant import share, as in our counterfactual, the distorting effects of tariffs are increasing in σ and approach a positive upper bound as $\sigma \to \infty$. In the latter case, the preferences parameter for domestic goods becomes arbitrarily small in the limit in order to match a finite import share.

[14]To provide further insight about the role of the elasticities in our model, we did two additional exercises. The first was to double σ_C and σ_M while holding σ_m constant at the benchmark level. This exercise increases the substitutability between domestic and imported goods (both as final consumption goods and as material inputs), while holding the substitutability between different categories of imported inputs constant. This exercise had an effect that was approximately half of that obtained when all 3 of the elasticities are doubled. We then considered a doubling of the elasticity between imported goods, σ_m, while holding the other elasticities constant at the benchmark levels. This exercise emphasizes substitutability between different types of imports, while holding substitution between imports and domestic goods constant. The impact of this change was approximately one fourth of that obtained by doubling all elasticities. These exercises illustrate that all three of the elasticities play a role in the amount of deadweight loss, and that their impacts are complementary.

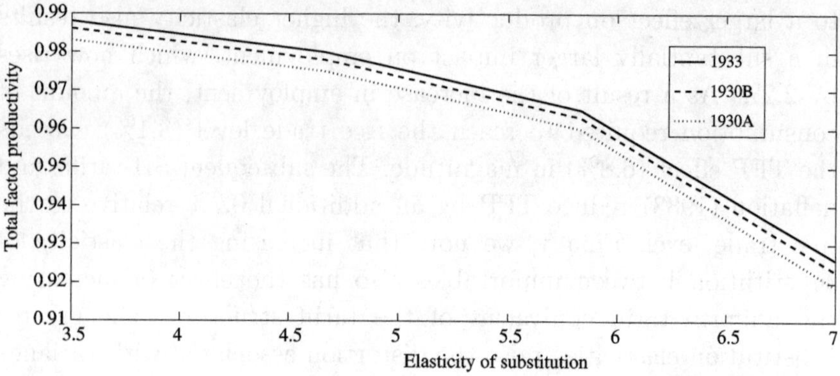

Fig. 5. This figure plots the losses in TFP due to tariffs in each cross section. TFP is maximized under free trade at 1. The vertical axis measures losses (relative to free trade) from tariffs as we vary substitution elasticities along the horizontal axis.

each of the cross sections, with elasticities $(\sigma_m, \sigma_M, \sigma_C)$ evaluated at 1, 4/3, 5/3 and 2 times their benchmark values. For each cross section, the magnitude of the total loss from tariff protection relative to free trade is non-linear in the substitution elasticity. Interestingly, however, the incremental loss moving from 1930A to 1933 due to the SH tariffs is in the 0.5–0.7% range for all of the elasticity values. This indicates that the biggest impact of elasticity differences is occurring for tariff distortions below those associated with the initial 1930A tariff levels, so that much of the substitution away from imported goods is occurring at relatively lower tariff levels.

Our results can be compared with two recent papers that consider the relationship between trade costs and welfare. Arkolakis *et al.* (2012) consider models where trade costs take the form of real resource costs, and show that knowledge of the elasticity of imports with respect to trade costs and the change in market share of domestic producers will be sufficient to calculate the welfare effects of changes in trade barriers for a variety of different trade models. A key difference between our results and theirs is that when trade barriers represent real resource costs, the impact of changes in trade barriers on welfare in competitive models is determined by the volume of imports. In contrast, the impact of tariff changes on welfare at constant terms of trade is determined by the tariff weighted change in import volumes. Thus, although the elasticity of imports with respect to trade costs plays a role in our model as well, the channel through which it operates is different. In particular, the existence of dispersion in tariff rates means that it is important to know the change in composition of imports in order to obtain the change in welfare. The change in domestic market share will not be sufficient to capture the welfare effect of trade cost changes. Atkeson and Burstein (2010) also consider the effect of changes in trade costs using a model of monopolistically competitive firms and an R&D sector, and find that the magnitude of firm level responses has little impact on the aggregate welfare change. Their model differs from ours in significant ways. They consider trade costs that are real resource costs, as in the case of Arkolakis *et al.*, so the first order effect of changes in trade costs on welfare operates through a different channel. In addition, the elasticity of substitution in their model identifies substitution between all brands, rather than the substitutability between domestic and imported goods.

As a final exercise, we consider the impact of a doubling of the US import share using the benchmark elasticity assumptions. That imports were a small fraction of GDP is one factor in explaining why the aggregate impact of tariff protection is relatively small in our benchmark case. This raises the question of how large import shares must be in order to have significant effects on aggregate productivity and welfare. Table 6 considers a counterfactual exercise of doubling the US import share from its 1930 levels. This change has the effect of doubling the impact of tariffs on the price of value added. The effect of the pre-SH tariffs on TFP is approximately double that in the benchmark case, since TFP now decreases by 2.4% from the pre-SH tariffs. Doubling the import share more than doubles the percentage increase in consumption required to compensate for the effect of the tariff structure relative to free trade, because the employment effects are somewhat larger in this case. Note that although the aggregate effects are increased substantially in this counterfactual, there is only a minor effect on the uniform tariff equivalent. This is because the uniform tariff equivalent captures the effect of tariffs on one import

Table 6. Double all import shares.

	1930A	1930B	1933
Uniform tariff equivalent	44.7	52.8	65.6
Percentage change in:			
Value added deflator (p_v)	−4.3	−4.4	−5.5
Consumption deflator (p_c)	−0.3	−0.1	−0.7
Total factor productivity ($TFP(\boldsymbol{\tau}, \mathbf{q}) = \frac{p_V(1+\Gamma_V)}{p_C(1-\Gamma_C)}$)	−2.4	−2.9	−3.4
Employment (L)	0.3	0.4	0.6
Real consumption (C)	−1.9	−2.2	−2.6
Consumption equivalent ($U(C^E, L(\boldsymbol{\tau}_0, \mathbf{q})) = W(1, \mathbf{q})$)	2.5	2.9	3.5

Note: See Table 3.

category relative to another. Doubling the import volume increases the effects on all import categories proportionally, and thus has a minimal effect on this aggregate measure.

5. Conclusions

We have constructed a panel of tariff lines to quantify the effect of the Smoot–Hawley legislation on the mean and dispersion of tariff rates. The panel shows that the mean effective tariff rate increased from 31% to 46% between 1930 and 1933, and that the variance of tariff rates at the tariff line level more than doubled over the same period. We used this panel to construct industry tariff wedges reflecting the increased price of imported materials used for domestic production. The mean of these wedges increased by more than the mean tariff, from 32% to 59%, and the variance across industries more than doubled. The role of dispersion on tariff rates was captured by the fact that the uniform tariff rate equivalent exceeded the average tariff rate by 18% under the pre-SH tariffs in 1930, and this differential increased to 24% by 1933. Thus, the tariff structure was substantially more distorting than suggested by the average tariff rate, and the increased variance in tariff rates from SH raised the differential between the uniform tariff equivalent and the average tariff.

Although our tariff line analysis indicated the existence of substantial sectoral distortions, our general equilibrium model indicated that the impact of these distortions at the aggregate level was relatively modest in the benchmark parameterization. The pre-SH tariff protection reduced TFP by 1.2% relative to free trade, and the SH legislation was responsible for a further 0.5% decline in TFP. We also showed that if SH had not been passed, the presence of specific tariffs in the existing tariff legislation would have reduced TFP by 0.3% between 1930 and 1933 due to declining world prices. This conclusion is consistent with previous findings of Crucini (1994) and Irwin (1998a) that deflation was responsible for a significant portion of the increase in ad valorem equivalent tariff rates that occurred following the passage of the SH legislation.

Two caveats should be kept in mind in interpreting our results on the aggregate effects of the SH tariffs. First, the aggregate effects could be larger if the true substitution elasticities are larger than the ones used in our benchmark analysis. Our counterfactual exercise showed that a doubling of the elasticities of substitution led to a six-fold increase in the effect of pre-SH tariffs on TFP. In addition, larger elasticities resulted in more significant effects on labor markets. Note however, that the incremental effect of the SH legislation and decline in world prices on TFP from 1930–1933 was quite robust across the different elasticity assumptions. This suggests the value of investigating the tariff policies over the entire interwar era to better capture the aggregate impacts of commercial policy during the Great Depression.

Second, we assume that tariffs have no effect on world prices. Such an assumption is appropriate when the country in question is a small country, or when retaliation by foreign countries offsets any effects of tariffs on the terms of trade. The existence of a favorable terms of trade effect for the tariff imposing country would reduce the magnitude of the loss in productivity, or could even lead to a higher productivity level. However, our data did not suggest the presence of significant reductions in world prices as a result of the Smoot–Hawley tariffs.

Our analysis could be extended to incorporate additional effects of tariff protection. Our analysis does not incorporate the additional negative effects of tariff protection on aggregate capital accumulation emphasized by Crucini and Kahn (1996). Tariff protection could also lead to larger effects on productivity if it leads firms to increase markups. Such an outcome could occur if firms are imperfectly competitive and tariffs make firm demand curves less elastic, or if protection facilitates the formation of cartels. These represent important areas for future work.

Acknowledgments

We thank Cem Karayalcin, Diego Restuccia, and Richard Rogerson for comments that substantively improved our paper. We also thank conference participants at the SED Mini-Conference on Misallocation held in Ghent, Belgium in 2011, the Conference on Macroeconomics Policy, hosted by Bilgi University in Istanbul, Turkey in 2011, and the International Trade Workshop at Florida International University in 2012. We thank David Schenck for excellent research assistance.

Appendix A

The matching algorithm takes two arrays of text descriptions as inputs. The output is a matrix of scores in which the ijth element is a number between zero and 1 for the quality of a match between row i from the first data set and row j from the second. A score of 1 means that the text descriptions are identical and a score of zero means they have no characters in common. For example, in the 1930A and 1930B cross sections (pre- and post-SH) a minimum threshold of 0.8, yields 1800 matches and the number of matches falls to about 1690 where the match is for all intents and purposes ‘perfect,’ a matching score of 0.97.

While the matching algorithm is an invaluable tool, it does not resolve the issue of eight scenarios involving line-item splitting, aggregation or re-organization across periods. For example, our matching procedure does not rule out more than one 1930A line item being matched to the same 1930B (or 1933) line item. We

Table A.1. Moments of source data and balanced panel.

	Pre-smoot-hawley		Post-smoot-hawley		1933	
	Source	Panel	Source	Panel	Source	Panel
			Value imported			
Mean	359	723	282	784	276	918
Median	6	47	6	22	5	29
Std. dev.	3292	3404	3066	5426	2926	6578
			Quantity imported			
Mean	3842	9109	3352	9720	5437	10,233
Median	6	69	7	47	9	67
Std. dev.	51,787	82,835	47,230	99,545	75,885	84,489
			Price (unit value)			
Mean	23.85	2.05	40.25	1.98	19.17	1.55
Median	0.89	0.44	0.81	0.40	0.50	0.31
Std. dev.	367.48	9.84	833.04	10.34	323.62	8.87

must account for this type of aggregation in the data. To do this we collect the set all best matches which are connected to each other through one or more line-item aggregations. We then construct an aggregated line-item series by creating a weighted average of the individual line items where the 1930A import values are used as weights. After completing the construction of a balanced panel, the size of our cross section shrinks to 495 line items. This occurs for two reasons. First, aggregation naturally reduces the number of individual tariff lines and due to a large degree of re-organization between 1930A and 1930B/1933; it is common for two or line items to be matched to the same line item in a later cross section. Second, aggregation exacerbates missing data issues. Any set of line items which is matched to any individual observation with missing data have to be discarded since the aggregation cannot be performed.

References

Anderson, James, Neary, Peter, 2005. *Measuring the Restrictiveness of International Trade Policy.* MIT Press, Cambridge.

Arkolakis, Costas, Costinot, Arnaud, Rodriguez-Clare, Andres, 2012. New trade models, same old gains.*American Economic Review* 102 (1), 94–130.

Atkeson, Andrew, Burstein, Ariel, 2010. Innovation, firm dynamics, and international trade. *Journal of Political Economy* 118 (5), 433–483.

Attanasio, Orazio, Banks, James, Tanner, Sarah, 2002. Asset holding and consumption volatility. *Journal of Political Economy* 110, 771–792.

Chetty, Raj, Guren, Adam, Manoli, Day, Weber, Andrea, 2011. Are micro and macro labor elasticities consistent? A review of the evidence on intensive and extensive margins. *American Economic Review* 101 (3), 471–475.

Crucini, Mario J., 1994. Sources of variation in real tariff rates: The United States, 1900–1940. *American Economic Review* 84 (3), 732–743.

Crucini, Mario J., Kahn, James, 1996. Tariffs and aggregate economic activity: Lessons from the Great Depression. *Journal of Monetary Economics* 38 (3), 427–467.

Eaton, Jonathan, Kortum, Samuel, 2002. Technology, geography, and trade. *Econometrica* 70 (5), 1741–1779.

Eslava, Marcela, Haltiwanger, John, Kugler, Adriana, Kugler, Maurice, 2013. Trade and market selection: Evidence from manufacturing plants in Colombia. *Review of Economic Dynamics* 16 (1), 135–158. http://dx.doi.org/10.1016Zj.red.2012.10.009.

Harrison, Glenn, Rutherford, Thomas, Tarr, David, 1993. Trade reform in the partially liberalized economy of Turkey. *The World Bank Economic Review* 7 (2), 191–217.

Hatta, Tatsuo, 1977. A theory of piecemeal policy recommendations. *Review of Economic Studies* 44, 1–21.

Hsieh, Chiang-ti, Klenow, Peter, 2009. Misallocation and manufacturing TFP in India and China. *Quarterly Journal of Economics* 124 (4), 1403–1448.

Irwin, Douglas, 1998a. Changes in US tariffs: The role of import prices and commercial policy. *American Economic Review* 88 (4), 1015–1026.

Irwin, Douglas, 1998b. The Smoot Hawley Tariff: A quantitative assessment. *Review of Economics and Statistics* 89, 326–334.

Leontief, Wassily W., 1941. *The Structure of the American Economy.* Oxford University Press.

Restuccia, Diego, Rogerson, Richard, 2008. Policy distortions and aggregate productivity with heterogeneous establishments. *Review of Economic Dynamics* 11, 707–720.

Simonovska, Ina, Waugh, Michael, 2011. The elasticity of trade: Evidence and estimates. CESifo Working Paper Series No. 3356.

Chapter 15

Tariffs and the Great Depression Revisited*

Mario J. Crucini

Department of Economics, Vanderbilt University, Nashville, TN, USA and National Bureau of Economic Research, Cambridge, MA, USA
mario.j.crucini@vanderbilt.edu

and

James A. Kahn

Research Department, Federal Reserve Bank of New York, New York, NY, USA

In our 1996 *Journal of Monetary Economics* paper, we made the following arguments:

1. Effective tariff rates during the 1930s were higher than their apparent nominal rates because of deflation.
2. Because of the importance of material inputs in traded goods, the impact of a given tariff rate could be magnified due to the impact on productive efficiency.

*This chapter originally appeared in *Great Depressions of the Twentieth Century*, Timothy Kehoe and Edward Prescott (eds.), Federal Reserve Bank of Minneapolis, 2007, pp. 305–334.

3. There was substantial retaliation from foreign countries in their tariff rates.
4. Consequently, even a neoclassical equilibrium model with flexible prices and no other distortions suggests that tariff increases of the order of magnitude that took place in the 1930s could have resulted in a substantial decline in output.
5. Though large enough to look like a modest recession, these model-calibrated output declines are only on the order of one-tenth the magnitude of the actual declines that occurred during the Great Depression.

Since this 1996 paper appeared in print, some new tools for business cycle analysis have emerged. In a series of papers (Hall 1997; Mulligan 2002a, 2002b; Chari, Kehoe, and McGrattan 2002; and Galí, Gertler, and López-Salido 2001), movements in output and employment have been decomposed into three sources, which amount to deviations from equilibrium conditions in the one-sector neoclassical growth model. The three conditions are an aggregate resource constraint, a static optimality condition relating consumption and leisure, and an intertemporal condition relating capital accumulation and expected consumption growth. It should be emphasized that this decomposition is really just an accounting framework. It does not offer a deeper explanation of the fundamental causes of fluctuations, but the results of the accounting exercise may shed some light on what the causes could and could not be, and provide a set of stylized facts with which theories must be consistent. Thus, for example, Hall (1997) finds that most employment fluctuations in postwar U.S. data appear to be accounted for by deviations in the static optimality condition relating the marginal product of labor (MPL) with the marginal rate of substitution (MRS) between consumption and leisure. This fact is consistent with any number of theories, and proposed candidates include preference shocks, distortions in labor markets resulting from taxes, unionization, and rigid prices and wages, among others. It is not consistent with theories of employment fluctuations that result in no change in the "wedge" between the MRS and MPL. On the other hand, both Hall (1997) and Chari, Kehoe, and McGrattan (2002) find that output fluctuations are composed of a mix of movements in both the MRS-MPL (or "labor") and efficiency wedges.

Similar analysis applied to the interwar period has generated more debate concerning the relative importance of the labor and efficiency wedges. Mulligan (2002a, 2002b) argues that the employment declines during this period were almost entirely attributable to an increase in the labor wedge, whereas Chari, Kehoe, and McGrattan (2002) show total factor productivity in substantial decline — at least from 1929 to 1933. Mulligan asserts that tariffs in the sort of model we proposed would result primarily in reductions in labor productivity, which in the accounting framework described earlier amounts to a distortion in the resource constraint, or an efficiency wedge. The claim is that the production inefficiency that results from the tariffs would show up as a decline in total factor productivity (TFP), and in the context of standard modeling assumptions would lead to very little change in aggregate employment.

In light of these more recent developments, we return here to the argument in our 1996 paper. We will show, first, that tariff increases in our model do indeed correspond to an increased efficiency wedge in a prototype one-sector model. This would seem to support Mulligan's view that tariffs were not an important factor in the Great Depression. His argument is problematic for two reasons, however. First, the source of the wedge in the trade model is due to the production inefficiencies that arise when the domestic (and foreign) country imposes a tariff on imported intermediate goods. Since the production possibilities of each final goods sector are not altered by the imposition of the tariffs, a standard Solow accounting exercise should not generate measurable fluctuations in total factor productivity as measured by Chari, Kehoe, and McGrattan. Thus, the magnitude of measured TFP movements has little bearing on the validity of our estimates of the contribution of tariffs to the Great Depression.

Mulligan's (2002a, 2002b) second argument — that productivity did not decline in the 1930s — is debatable. Mulligan makes his argument on the basis of wage data. This is a reasonable thing to do under the null hypothesis of a flexible price equilibrium. If the production technology is Cobb-Douglas with constant share parameters, then the wage, which must equal the marginal product of labor in equilibrium, is also proportional to the average product of labor. Since real wages did not show any decline in the 1930s, it follows that the average product of labor did not decline either. The more relevant measure of productivity in discussing the efficiency wedge is total factor productivity. Total factor productivity actually shows substantial declines — at least from 1929 to 1933 — according to Chari, Kehoe, and McGrattan (2002). Using aggregate wage data to infer total factor productivity is problematic on two counts. First, there are distribution effects — to the extent that lower wage workers are disproportionately affected by unemployment, the average wage may not be affected. Of course, this problem presumably affects measured labor productivity as well. The second problem is that for whatever reason (sticky wages, labor hoarding), labor's share of income is typically countercyclical, and indeed rose substantially during the 1929–33 period. According to Mulligan's calculations, for example, labor's share of national income (excluding proprietors' income) rose from 0.71 in 1929 to 0.83 in 1933.

We conclude from our reading of the interwar productivity literature that a decline in TFP follows the peak-to-trough movements in output fairly well, with the quantitative magnitude of the swing and underlying economic reasons for the movement remaining the subject of ongoing debate. The Chari, Kehoe, and McGrattan (2002) business cycle accounting approach for measuring wedges appears to be ill-suited for characterizing the inefficiencies generated by our tariff model. More generally, the quantitative contribution of various shocks and their propagation mechanisms remain the subject of active business cycle research.

The plan of this paper is as follows. In the next section we will review the historical evidence. Then we will present the model of tariffs and economic activity from our 1996 paper, examining both the steady-state implications of permanent tariff increases and business cycle implications for cyclical variation in tariffs. Next we will use the one-sector stochastic growth model as a prototype (as suggested in Chari, Kehoe, and McGrattan 2002) to show how tariffs in our three-sector two-country model translate into wedges in the prototype model. We will then compare the implied wedges with the historical ones, and discuss the implications of our results for future research.

1. The Historical Context

Our 1996 paper identified three historical facts that are essential to understanding why the macroeconomic effects of tariffs in the Great Depression were potentially much larger than had previously been thought. First, tariff levels increased both at home and abroad by a factor of at least three from 1928 to 1933, not just from statutory changes but also from the interaction of deflation and specific (as opposed to ad valorem) tariffs. The magnitude of the tariff increases was such that they were too large to be "optimal tariffs," even for a large economy such as the United States. Further, foreign retaliation tends to wipe out such gains, leaving the United States and its major trading partners worse off. Second, the majority of imports into the United States were material inputs; as a result, tariffs introduced production distortions. Third, the tariff changes were persistent so their effects were propagated through changes in the stock of capital.

1.1. *Interwar trading patterns*

In this section we review U.S. trading patterns and present a brief tariff history. We begin with an examination of the volume and composition of trade between the United States and some of its major trading partners: Canada and Europe (consisting of France, Germany, Italy, and the United Kingdom).

The pattern of U.S. trade was quite different during the interwar period than observed today. As Table 1 indicates, U.S. trade was heavily skewed toward nonmanufactured goods. For every dollar of nonmanufactures exported, the United States exported less than fifty cents of manufactures (imports were even more skewed). Thus, the U.S. trade balance shows no obvious pattern of specialization across manufactured versus nonmanufactured goods. In contrast, France and Germany exported more than two dollars of manufactures for every dollar of nonmanufactures exported. Imports are even more skewed in the opposite direction, favoring raw materials. Thus, the industrialized countries of Europe had a distinctive pattern of specialization that favored manufactured goods. Canada's exports were reasonably balanced across categories, but imports favored manufactures very strongly. In terms of trading partners, Canada and the United Kingdom

Table 1. Trade composition and U.S. trading patterns in 1925.

	Trade ratio: Manufactures to nonmanufactures		Fraction of U.S.	
	Exports	Imports	Exports	Imports
United States	0.48	0.29	—	—
Canada	0.78	1.31	15.6	11.0
France	2.30	0.27	5.7	4.1
Germany	2.54	0.18	9.6	3.9
Italy	NA	NA	4.2	2.4
United Kingdom	NA	NA	21.0	9.7

were the two most important sources and destinations for U.S. products. Canada's geographic proximity was probably important, as was the United Kingdom's dominant position in world trade.

1.2. *A brief tariff history*

Much of the historical tariff literature has focused on questions of political economy, most prominently in the U.S. case, by Frank Taussig (1931) and more recently in studies that focus on the Hawley-Smoot tariffs by Eichengreen (1989) and Irwin and Kroszner (1996): Why was such a bill passed at such a crucial time? Who benefited (ex ante) and who lost? While the political origins of interwar tariffs are by now fairly well understood (as classic examples of political log-rolling), their macroeconomic impact is not, and this is the question on which we focus.

Many countries passed legislative increases just after World War I and again during the period from 1927 to 1932. Historians emphasize internal reasons for the escalation of tariff levels following the war and emphasize international retaliation in the wake of the infamous Hawley-Smoot Tariff Act during the 1930s.[1]

Table 2 reports summary statistics for international tariff indexes computed as the ratio of customs duties to total imports (except for the United States, where the ratio of customs duties to dutiable imports is also presented). Using total imports (to be consistent with

[1] Jones (1934) discusses the question of retaliation in detail.

Table 2. International tariff levels.

Countries	Average ad valorem equivalent tariffs 1920–29	1930–40
United States		
Total imports	13.0	16.6
Dutiable imports	35.1	44.5
Other countries		
Trade-weighted average	9.9	19.9
Canada	13.4	15.2
France	7.1	21.0
Germany	7.2	26.1
Italy	4.5	16.8
United Kingdom	9.8	23.2

data available from other countries), tariffs in the United States rose from the level of 13 percent during the 1920s to 16.6 percent during the 1930s, while those in most European countries more than tripled. Comparing these numbers gives the impression that the United States bore the brunt of the tariff escalation. On a U.S. trade-weighted basis, however, things look more symmetric with foreign tariffs rates rising from 9.9 percent to 19.9. These numbers reflect the more modest increases in tariffs imposed by Canada and the United Kingdom (from all sources) and the fact that these two countries account for a considerable fraction of U.S. exports. Although these estimates provide a useful starting point, there are reasons to interpret them with caution.

First, as is well-known, revenue-based tax measures tend to be downward biased as individuals substitute from high-tax goods to low-tax goods. At the extreme, prohibitive tariffs receive no weight at all. Using a constant import share-weighted tariff index for thirty-two major U.S. imports, Crucini (1994) estimates that the average tariff level increases from 15 percent in 1920 to 120 percent in 1932, compared to an increase from 11 percent to a tariff level of 98 percent for the variable import share index. By this metric, the variable import share index understates the level of tariffs by about 20 percent in 1932.

Second, the tariffs are computed using imports from all locations, yet countries tend to levy country-specific rates, which is particularly relevant before the General Agreement on Tariffs and Trade (GATT). We know that one reaction to Hawley-Smoot during the early 1930s was for Canada and the United Kingdom to increase duties on goods imported from the United States while maintaining Commonwealth preference. Aggregative bilateral tariff indexes are available for Canada and show exactly this type of pattern. The average duty on Canadian imports from the United States rose by 27 percent from 14.1 in 1929 to 17.9 percent in 1932, while the average duty on Canadian imports from the United Kingdom rose by only 6 percent from 20.6 to 21.9 during the same period.[2] As a result, the increase in the Canadian tariff index reported in Table 2 understates the tariff increases on U.S. exports to Canada. Given the large increases in tariff rates by France, Germany, and the United Kingdom, it would be interesting to investigate if the increases were even greater for imports from the United States.

Finally, the tariff levels are often quite heterogeneous across goods, which may make the averages of dubious value in assessing commercial policy. The heterogeneity in tariff levels is evident in comparing the implied ad valorem rate on total imports and dutiable imports. We see that for the United States, items subject to duty were taxed at rates closer to 35 to 45 percent, not the 15 percent suggested by the rates computed using total imports.

2. The Model

With the preceding historical analysis as background, we would argue that an empirically plausible model must (a) incorporate the fact that tariff changes were persistent and volatile, (b) include an important role for trade in intermediate inputs, and (c) incorporate the fact that the countries involved in the trade war were large enough to affect world prices. We incorporate each of these features

[2]The details of the political economy of the Canadian tariff increases have recently been studied by McDonald, O'Brien, and Callahan (1997).

into a tractable aggregative model, drawing from two strands of quantitative equilibrium theory.

The first strand of the literature is real business cycle research, which has focused on economic fluctuations over time with particular attention given to the process of intertemporal choice under rational expectations. The dynamic features of real business cycle (RBC) models allow us to capture the effects of both temporary and permanent tariff changes on investment and labor supply decisions. As we shall see, endogenous capital and labor supply decisions are essential in generating plausible aggregative effects of tariffs. Our modeling approach has also been heavily influenced by the computable general equilibrium (CGE) literature, which has long emphasized the economic significance of the large volume of trade in intermediate goods and the production inefficiencies that arise when these trade flows are taxed. At the macroeconomic level, we will additionally want to incorporate the fact that the nontraded consumption goods sector is large relative to the traded goods sector.

To match these observations and modeling considerations, each country must produce three goods: (a) a nontraded consumption-investment good, (b) a traded consumption good, and (c) materials. We adopt the Armington (1969) assumption common in the trade literature, treating the traded final goods as imperfect substitutes in consumption and the traded material inputs as imperfect substitutes in production.

Consumers in each country choose consumption of the home nontradable C_{1t}, consumption of the home export C_{2t}, consumption of the foreign export C_{3t}, and leisure L_t to maximize

$$E(U) = E_0 \sum_{t=0}^{\infty} \beta^t U(C_{1t}, C_{2t}, C_{3t}, L_t) = E_0 \sum_{t=0}^{\infty} \beta^t \log C_t + \kappa L_t \quad (1)$$

in the case of the home country and

$$E(U) = E_0 \sum_{t=0}^{\infty} \beta^t U(C^*_{1t}, C^*_{2t}, C^*_{3t}, L^*_t) = E_0 \sum_{t=0}^{\infty} \beta^t \log C^*_t + \kappa L^*_t \quad (2)$$

in the case of the foreign country. The relationship between aggregate consumption and leisure follows Rogerson (1988), who considers environments in which nonconvexities in the labor-leisure choice at the individual level result in "representative agent" preferences that are linear in leisure. The variable C is a composite variable representing constant elasticity of substitution (CES) aggregation of individual consumption components:

$$C \equiv [b_1 C_1^{-\gamma} + b_2 C_2^{-\gamma} + b_3 C_3^{-\gamma}]^{-\frac{1}{\gamma}} \tag{3}$$

The CES function for consumption goods captures the idea that domestic and foreign goods are imperfect substitutes. The weights b_1, b_2, and b_3 influence how consumption expenditure is allocated across goods.

A single representative agent (in each country) allocates market time across the three sectors of the domestic economy and leisure subject to the constraint that these activities exhaust total hours available (which we normalize to unity).

$$1 - L_t - N_{1t} - N_{2t} - N_{4t} \geq 0 \tag{4}$$

The foreign country faces an analogous constraint:

$$1 - L_t^* - N_{1t}^* - N_{3t}^* - N_{4t}^* \geq 0 \tag{5}$$

Implicit in these constraints is the fact that labor is completely mobile across sectors within the period, yet immobile across countries.

The functional forms that describe our production sectors are given by Eqs. (6) and (7). Domestic output in each sector is produced with capital, labor, and a fixed proportion of intermediate inputs. Letting Y_{it} denote gross output in sector i, and for the moment ignoring the intermediate input requirement, we have

$$Y_{it} = F(K_{it}, N_{it}) = K_{it}^{\alpha_i} N_{it}^{1-\alpha_i}, \quad i = 1, 2, 4 \tag{6}$$

for the home country, while the foreign country produces the goods according to

$$Y_{it}^* = F(K_{it}^*, N_{it}^*) = K_{it}^{*\alpha_i} N_{it}^{*1-\alpha_i}, \quad i = 1, 3, 4. \tag{7}$$

Note that production occurs in sectors 1, 2, and 4 in the home country, and in sectors 1, 3, and 4 of the foreign country.

Each sector of the economy requires intermediate goods as a Leontief input into production (Leontief 1941). The fixed intermediate input requirement for the production of good i is $\theta_i Y_{it}$. The input requirements are themselves combinations of domestic and foreign raw materials, denoted m_{hht} and m_{fht}, where the first subscript indicates the location of production of the raw material and the second indicates where that material is being combined for use in final production. The home composite intermediate good is given by

$$\begin{aligned} M_t &= G(m_{hht}, m_{fht}) = [\psi m_{hht}^{-\sigma} + (1-\psi) m_{fht}^{-\sigma}]^{-1/\sigma} \\ &= \theta_1 Y_{1t} + \theta_2 Y_{2t} + \theta_4 Y_{4t}, \end{aligned} \tag{8}$$

while the foreign composite is

$$\begin{aligned} M_t^* &= G(m_{fft}, m_{hft}) = [\psi m_{fft}^{-\sigma} + (1-\psi) m_{hft}^{-\sigma}]^{-1/\sigma} \\ &= \theta_1 Y_{1t}^* + \theta_3 Y_{3t}^* + \theta_4 Y_{4t}^*. \end{aligned} \tag{9}$$

The parameters ψ and $1 - \psi$ influence the fraction of domestic materials that are used in production of domestic intermediate inputs. The second line in Eqs. (8) and (9) indicates that composite materials produced in the current period, by a particular country, are completely exhausted by their uses across the three sectors operating within the economy.

Capital is a nontraded good and hence is produced in sector 1 of each country. Despite being immobile across countries, it is assumed to be perfectly mobile across sectors within a country. For the home country, capital obeys the standard accumulation equation

$$K_{t+1} = (1-\delta)K_t + I_t = K_{1t+1} + K_{2t+1} + K_{4t+1} \tag{10}$$

and

$$K_{t+1}^* = (1-\delta)K_t^* + I_t^* = K_{1t+1}^* + K_{3t+1}^* + K_{4t+1}^* \tag{11}$$

for the foreign country.

We assume that markets are complete, to simplify the solution to this model. As a result, market-clearing conditions are imposed by individual sector rather than by individual budget constraint. The resource constraints are

$$\begin{aligned} Y_{1t} &= C_{1t} + I_t & Y_{1t}^* &= C_{1t}^* + I_t^* \\ Y_{2t} &= C_{2t} + C_{2t}^* & Y_{3t}^* &= C_{3t} + C_{3t}^* \\ Y_{4t} &= m_{hht} + m_{hft} & Y_{4t}^* &= m_{fft} + m_{fht} \end{aligned} \tag{12}$$

Tariff revenue equals transfers back to individuals, when combined with complete markets means the production possibilities of the distorted world economy are the same as in the undistorted economy. However, the tariffs are distortionary (i.e., they will affect consumption and production decisions) as individuals equate marginal rates of substitution and transformation to distorted equilibrium prices, and this is how allocations are affected by the presence of tariffs.

2.1. *Calibration*

Providing a quantitative estimate of the impact of the tariff war requires that we calibrate the twenty-eight parameters that describe preferences and technology in our model of the world economy. Fortunately, our macroeconomic focus rationalizes two convenient symmetry restrictions that together reduce the number of parameters to just ten.

Our first symmetry assumption is that the two regions, which we treat as the United States and an aggregate of its major trading partners, are completely symmetric in terms of the parameters of taste and technology. These cross-country restrictions create a natural, and easily understandable, benchmark model in which symmetric retaliation leads to the same quantitative changes in economic variables in both countries. The number of parameters is reduced from twenty-eight to fourteen with these restrictions imposed.

Table 3. Model calibration.

Panel A: Aggregate parameters	
$r = \beta^{-1} - 1$	0.05
$\bar{N}$	0.27
α	0.3
δ	0.10
Panel B: Sectoral parameters	
θ	0.2
ψ	0.8
b_1	0.98
b_2, b_3	0.01
Panel C: Elasticity parameters	
γ	0
σ	0.6
Panel D: Great ratios	
Consumption	0.80
Investment	0.20
Exports	0.07
Imports	0.07
Tariff revenue	0.007

The second set of symmetry assumptions is made at the sector level. We assume that the factor and material intensities are equal across sectors. In terms of the notation of our model, this requires that $\alpha_i = \alpha$ and $\theta_i = \theta$. These two assumptions have the implication that the equilibrium response to an increase in the tariff on intermediate inputs is an inward shift in the aggregate production function at unchanged marginal rates of transformation across goods within each country.

The ten parameters that remain are reported in Table 3. The first four parameters listed are often found in real business cycle models of closed economies: the discount factor, β determines the steady-state real interest rate, r, which is set to 5 percent; the parameter κ is determined such that the fraction of hours spent in the workplace, $\bar{N}$, matches the value of 0.27, approximately a 6.5 hour workday; the historical average share of value added accounted for by rental payments to physical capital 0.30 determines α; and the depreciation rate of capital, δ, is set at 10 percent per annum.

Parameters introduced by our multisector analysis are of two basic types. First we have parameters that determine additional "shares": (a) the cost share of intermediate inputs relative to value added, θ; (b) the share of domestic raw materials that are combined with foreign raw materials to produce the domestic intermediate good, ψ; and (c) the share of nontraded goods in aggregate consumption, b_1. Second we have the elasticities of substitution: (a) across domestic and foreign consumption goods, γ; and (b) across domestic and foreign materials in the production of intermediate inputs used in domestic production, σ.

We set the cost share for intermediate inputs at 0.20, which is in the lower range of values reported in Leontief's (1941) classic input-output study of the interwar U.S. economy. Later we will consider the importance of tariffs on materials by setting $\theta = 0$ so that the sensitivity of the model's predictions to the existence of materials will be transparent.

Leontief's study also indicates that about 80 percent of U.S. imports during the interwar period were intermediate factors of production.[3] We capture the importance of imported materials while minding the constraint on the total import share, setting $1-\psi$ equal to 0.20. When the tariff levels are 10 percent, as in our initial steady state, the ratio of domestic to foreign materials is 2.5 to 1.

The weight on imported goods in the utility function, b_3, makes up the remainder of domestic imports, such that we match the historical average of the trade shares for the United States of about 7 percent. As Table 3 indicates, this requires a weight of 0.98 on nontraded goods in the CES function for aggregate consumption services. Our symmetry assumptions require that the remainder of consumption be equally divided between imports and consumption of the domestic export. This means that the weights on the remaining consumption goods, b_2 and b_3, each equal 0.01.

[3]Note that this is approximately the same as the fraction of U.S. imports categorized as nonmanufactured in Table 1, which is not nearly as precise a disaggregation of commodities as in Leontief's input-output analysis.

Our baseline parameterization of preferences across consumption goods is Cobb-Douglas, in which case the parameter setting $b_1 = 0.98$ means that 98 percent of aggregate consumption is accounted for by nontraded goods. When we consider the model without intermediate goods, nontraded consumption drops to 82 percent of total consumption. Thus, we will also have results that indicate the consequences of changing the quantity of consumption imports.

Finally, we must determine the values of the elasticities of substitution across domestic and foreign goods. Our baseline choice of the parameter $\gamma = 0$ is consistent with a large number of empirical studies that report elasticities of substitution between domestic and foreign goods of about unity (note that the elasticity of substitution is $1/(1+\gamma)$). However, we consider as wide a range of estimates of this parameter, as reported in Whalley (1985). We look at less substitution, setting γ equal to unity, then at more substitution by setting γ equal to $-1/3$. We employ a similar range of estimates for the substitutability of domestic and foreign materials but keep the baseline elasticity of substitution somewhat lower, setting σ at 0.6.

The investment-to-output ratio is 20 percent, having been determined by parameters that have already been set. The consumption-to-output ratio is 80 percent, given our decision to constrain the trade balance to be zero in the initial steady state. As mentioned earlier, the export share is set at 7 percent, approximately the U.S. average over this period of time. Tariff revenue as a fraction of output is 0.7 percent, which is simply the import share of 7 percent times the baseline tariff rate, which we set at 10 percent (the trade-weighted average of foreign tariff levels reported in Table 2 for the period 1920–1929).

3. The Results

Economists are confronted with two important and difficult tasks in any attempt to estimate the contribution of the collapse of world trade to the Depression in the United States. The first is identification: What fraction of the decline in exports should be attributed to the tariff war versus other domestic or international disturbances? The second issue is: How do we translate the change in exports into a change in aggregate activity? What is the "export multiplier"?

That the answers to these questions are important in the context of the Great Depression should be obvious. Real exports declined by almost 50 percent between 1929 and 1933, while real GNP declined by about 30 percent over the same period. Attributing the entire decline in exports to the tariff, we would explain about 10 percent of the peak-to-trough decline in GNP if the export multiplier was equal to one, and one-third of the swing if the multiplier equaled three.

Our approach is to let the calibrated model and estimates of tariff levels determine both the value of export multipliers and the quantitative decline in exports. Discussion can then be focused on the plausibility of the economic mechanisms that give rise to multipliers of different size rather than debate over ad hoc specifications of the multipliers. We also avoid the temptation to parameterize the model in such a way that it matches the quantitative decline in exports that is observed during the Depression years, since to do so would rule out any possibility of declines in international trade originating from disturbances other than the tariff war.

3.1. *Steady-state implications*

We begin our quantitative analysis with the steady-state implications of a symmetric tariff war that involves permanent tariff increases. While somewhat counterfactual in the sense that the tariff increases were persistent, not literally permanent, the steady-state analysis helps us understand the key structural issues that translate tariff changes into significant macroeconomic effects even when the trade share is small.

We examine tariff wars with tariff levels rising from 10 percent to either 30 percent or 60 percent. Recall that most tariff indexes using the ratio of customs revenue to total imports moved from a low of about 10 percent in the early 1920s to highs approaching 30 percent in the 1930s. The first case is intended to match these observations. The second case deals with the problem that tariff indexes are increasingly downwardly biased as customs duties escalate toward prohibitive levels. For example, we saw that the U.S. tariff index that used only dutiable imports rose from about 15 percent in 1920 to a high of about 60 percent in 1932.

We will begin summarizing the quantitative findings and then provide the economic intuition for the results. It will be useful to define some terminology at the outset. Let us define an "export multiplier" as the ratio of the change in output to the change in exports times the export share. For example, if after an escalation of tariff levels, exports fall by 10 percent and the export share is 7 percent, an export multiplier of 1 would mean output is predicted to fall by 0.7 percent.

Table 4 presents the main results of our steady-state analysis. We consider three radically different parameterizations: (a) a baseline model that we calibrate to match the interwar period; (b) a case that holds the aggregate capital stock fixed; and (c) a model without intermediate inputs.

The first panel of Table 4 presents the results with parameters set as in Table 3. As is evident, the tariff war causes all macroeconomic aggregates except tariff revenue to decline. When tariffs rise from 10 percent to 30 percent, the largest decline occurs in exports at 9.7 percent, followed by investment at 3.1 percent, output at 2.1 percent, consumption at 1.8 percent, and effort at 1.5 percent. Tariff revenue rises by 171 percent. The export multiplier for the baseline case is 3.1.

To put these results in perspective, suppose we had ignored our tariff measures and increased tariff levels in the model until we produced the 50 percent real decline observed in U.S. exports from 1929 to 1933. Our model would be capable of explaining one-third of the real decline in output over this period! However, tariff increases required to generate such a large drop in world trade are implausible given our empirical estimates of international tariff levels, even allowing for a generous view of their inherent downward bias. Applying this empirical discipline, the model predicts export declines of between 10 and 20 percent in the baseline version (see Table 4). These export declines translate into output declines of between 2 and 5 percent, which amount to between 7 and 16 percent of the decline in output observed in the United States from 1929 to 1933.

Table 4. Steady-state results with symmetric retaliation: The role of capital, materials, and tariff measurement.

	Steady-state level	Case I	Case II
Panel A: Baseline parameterization			
Output	100	−2.1	−4.9
Consumption	80	−1.8	−4.3
Investment	20	−3.1	−7.2
Effort	0.27	−1.5	−3.4
Exports	7	−9.7	−20.3
Export multiplier	—	3.1	3.4
Tariff revenue	0.7	+171	+377
Panel B: Fixed world capital			
Output	100	−0.8	1.9
Consumption	80	−1.0	−2.4
Investment	20	0.0	0.0
Effort	0.27	−1.0	−2.3
Exports	7	−8.5	−17.9
Export multiplier	—	1.3	1.5
Tariff revenue	1.2	+174	+391
Panel C: No materials			
Output	100	−1.4	−2.8
Consumption	80	−1.4	−2.9
Investment	20	−1.3	−2.6
Effort	0.27	−1.3	−2.6
Exports	7	−15.4	−31.2
Export multiplier	—	1.3	1.3
Tariff revenue	0.7	+151	+303

Note: Baseline refers to the parameterization described in Table 3, except that for $\theta = 0$, the consumption share parameters (b_i) are altered to keep the export/GNP ratio approximately at 0.07. The values are $b_1 = 0.82, b_2 = b_3 = 0.09$. Steady-state levels are normalized such that output equals 100. Case I has tariffs rising from 10% to 30% both at home and abroad, and Case II has tariffs rising from 10% to 60% both at home and abroad. Results are identical across countries due to the symmetry of the model and the assumption of symmetric retaliation.

The substantive declines in output that our model predicts can be traced to the interaction of capital accumulation and production distortions introduced by tariffs on intermediate goods. The second panel of Table 4 holds capital fixed, as is assumed in many of the early CGE exercises. We see that while the impact of the tariff war has a similar impact on exports, the export multiplier is only 1.3, so the aggregative effects are modest. Output falls by 0.8 percent, about two-thirds less than in the baseline case.

Similar results obtain when capital is allowed to vary but intermediate inputs are dropped from the model. While the export multiplier is again about 1.3 in this case, exports decline by more, so the output effects are somewhat larger here compared to the fixed capital case. However, output still falls by only 1.4 percent, one-third less than in the baseline.

The impact of tariffs on effort is determined by three factors. First, the tariff distortion lowers the value marginal product of labor in precisely the same way that it has lowered the value marginal product of capital. Second, a lower steady-state capital stock lowers the marginal product of labor. Both of these effects operate to reduce the equilibrium wages and the level of effort. Third, individuals have suffered a negative wealth effect associated with the increase in global tariff levels, which increases the equilibrium amount of effort. The substitution effect of a lower wage dominates the wealth effect in our model, so effort falls.

We can use similar reasoning to explain the consequence of holding capital fixed. With capital held fixed, the tariff on materials no longer results in a lower steady-state capital stock. The wage is reduced by the higher price of materials as before, but this is not reinforced by a decline in capital. Consequently, effort declines by only 1.0 percent when capital is held fixed, compared to 1.5 percent when capital is allowed to vary. The output effects are dramatically reduced when capital is held fixed, first, by eliminating the direct effect of a lower steady-state capital stock and, second, by mitigating the reduction of the decline in effort. As we see in Table 4, the result is to reduce the export multiplier from 3.1 to 1.3.

The consequences of ignoring tariffs on intermediate inputs is easy to understand given the interpretation of this tariff as a distortion to the value marginal product of each factor of production. Our previous discussion indicated that this will reduce the aggregate effect of tariffs. Another interesting feature of the last panel of Table 4 is that the effects of a consumption tariff are basically uniform across output, consumption, investment, and effort. Absent the production distortion, there is little to change real wages in equilibrium. At a constant wage-rental ratio, capital and labor must fall by the same proportion, and this carries over directly to output. Thus, tariffs on intermediate inputs not only increase the magnitude of changes in aggregate variables like output, but also call forth very different quantitative responses from the components of national income.

Before concluding the steady-state results and moving on to time series simulations, we investigate the sensitivity of the baseline model to alterations in the degree of substitutability between domestic and foreign goods.[4] Table 5 reports the results of these experiments. The first column repeats the steady state of the world economy and the baseline results, from Table 4, for comparison purposes. Columns 2 and 3 examine the sensitivity of the results to substitutability across consumption goods for the range of empirical estimates documented by Whalley (1985). Except for exports, the quantitative effects are larger the lower the elasticity of substitution in consumption, but for a wide range of elasticities, the predicted impacts on output, investment, consumption, and employment are basically identical.

The results for the material inputs are only slightly more sensitive to the elasticity of substitution parameter with the volume of trade now declining by 25.6 in the case of higher elasticity of substitution, and by only 16 percent in the case of lower substitution. As one would expect, the less substitutable the domestic and foreign materials, the greater the impact of a tariff on the supply side. We see this in the larger declines in investment, effort, and output in column 4 relative

[4]In these experiments we are careful to alter the share parameters for domestic and foreign goods as we vary the elasticity of substitution. To see why this is necessary, consider the condition for the choice of domestic versus foreign materials: $m_{hh}/m_{fh} = [(\psi/(1-\psi))(1+\tau)]^{1/(1+\sigma)}$. From this equation we see that reducing the elasticity of substitution has the effect of reducing the use of domestic materials relative to foreign materials for given values of ψ and τ. Since the left side of this expression is pinned down by a steady-state ratio (the ratio of domestic materials to imported materials used in production of intermediate products), we hold it fixed as we alter the elasticity of substitution, σ, by adjusting the parameter ψ.

Table 5. Steady-state results with symmetric retaliation: Sensitivity analysis.

		Elasticity of substitution in:			
		Consumption $1/(1+\gamma)$		Materials $1/(1+\sigma)$	
	Baseline (1, 0.625)	0.5	1.5	0.4	0.9
Aggregate	(1)	(2)	(3)	(4)	(5)
Output	−4.9	−4.9	−4.8	−5.1	−4.7
Consumption	−4.3	−4.3	−4.2	−4.4	−4.2
Investment	−7.2	−7.3	−7.2	−7.6	−6.9
Effort	−3.4	−3.5	−3.2	−3.7	−3.1
Exports	−20.3	−18.9	−21.5	−16.0	−25.6
Export multipliers	3.4	3.7	3.2	−4.5	2.6
Tariff revenue	377	385	370	402	345

Note: Baseline refers to the parameterization described in Table 3. The weighting parameters in the aggregator functions for consumption and materials are altered across cases to keep the share of exports approximately equal across cases.

to column 5. Again, however, the quantitative impact of the tariff increase on these variables is broadly similar across a wide range of parameter values.

The general lesson here is that the key elements of the model that generate significant macroeconomic effects of tariffs are the presence of material inputs and endogenous capital accumulation. The results are insensitive to the choice of parameters once these features of the model are present. While the tariff war results in a collapse of world trade independently of whether trade and tariffs involve final goods or intermediate imports, the macroeconomic repercussions stem from the interaction of distorted material prices and the dynamic propagation of these effects through capital accumulation and labor supply decisions.

3.2. *Implications for business cycles*

The fact that tariffs varied in a cyclical fashion is readily apparent in Fig. 1, which plots three tariff indexes annually from 1920 to 1940 in percentage deviations from their sample means. The figure presents

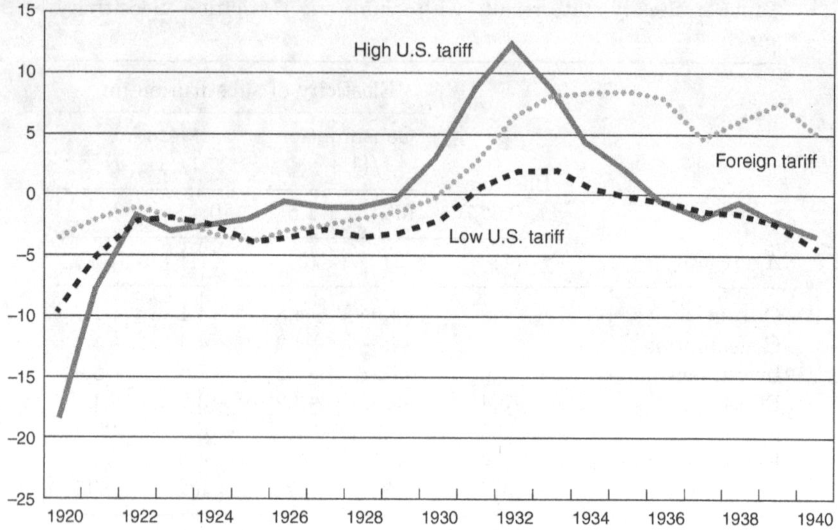

Fig. 1. Ad valorem equivalent tariff levels expressed as percentage deviations from their sample averages.

two estimates of the aggregate tariff level for the United States and one for its major trading partners. The first of the U.S. estimates takes tariff revenue and divides by total imports, while the second takes tariff revenue and divides by dutiable imports. In our model we treat all imports as dutiable so that if we utilize the index that incorporates only dutiable imports, we are applying the tariff rate to a greater volume of imports than were actually subject to tariffs. Using the index computed from total imports, we are applying a downward-biased tariff to all imports. In the case of the European countries, we only have tariff indexes computed as tariff revenue divided by total imports.

The source of the cyclicality is largely due to the use of specific duties during this period of history. Specific duties are tariff levies assessed in nominal currency per physical unit imported. This fact, combined with considerable nominal price variation and few (though sometimes dramatic) legislative adjustments, imparts a strong negative correlation between the ad valorem equivalent tariff rates and the price level. In fact, Crucini (1994) finds that most of the interwar variation in U.S. tariff levels originated from this source.

We see in Fig. 1 that the U.S. index using only dutiable imports is much more variable than the index constructed using total U.S. imports. Note that in addition to the notorious increases of the early 1930s, there was a comparable increase in tariff rates in 1920–21. Just as the tariff increases in the early 1930s were a mix of legislative changes (Hawley-Smoot) and price deflation, the increases in the early 1920s reflected both legislated increases (the Emergency Tariff Act and the Fordney-McCumber Tariff Act) and the effect of postwar price deflation.

Viewing the U.S. tariff indexes along with their foreign counterparts paints a classic picture of the global escalation of tariff levels during the interwar period. The figure also shows that foreign tariff levels did not rise abruptly following the passage of the Hawley-Smoot Tariff Act in 1930, but increased gradually throughout much of the period.

Our earlier paper conducted a simulation exercise in which the tariff sequences were fed into the dynamic equilibrium model to produce simulated paths of U.S. and foreign aggregates. The exact index used influenced the quantitative results, but the qualitative picture was close to one involving a symmetric tariff war, with tariffs escalating in tandem over time. Because there is a tendency for tariff levels estimated using tariff revenue data to systematically understate actual legislated tariff levels, and to ensure that we convey the gist of our results, we focus on a case in which the U.S. and foreign tariff levels both follow the path of the U.S. tariff rate computed as the ratio of customs duties to dutiable imports (the solid line in Fig. 1).

Figure 2 presents the paths of output, consumption, and effort from 1928 to 1940. We see that the model predicts about a 2 percent drop in output and effort relative to the steady state between 1928 and the trough in 1932. Moreover, output does not recover to its steady-state level until 1937, so that output is below the steady state for seven years. We know of no other quantitative exercise that produces such a large and sustained decline in U.S. output as

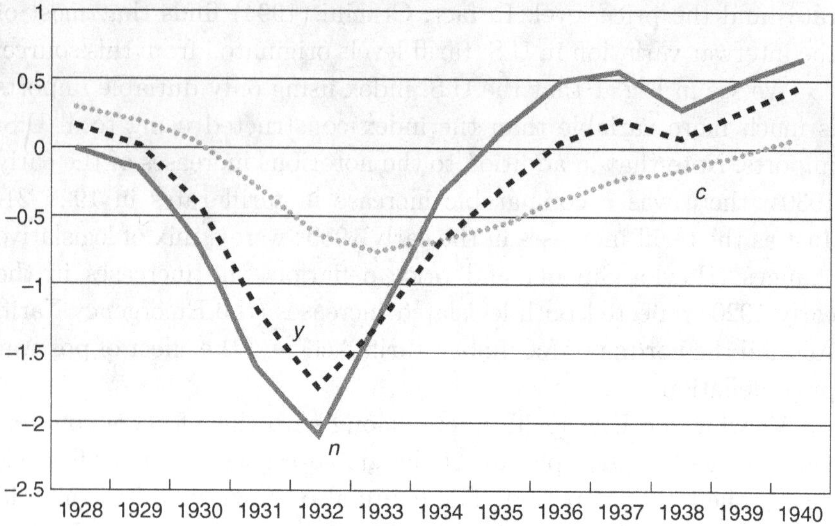

Fig. 2. Simulation of a symmetric tariff war.

a result of commercial policy. Of course, in the context of the Great Depression, the quantitative decline is small and its duration too short. We turn to these issues in the next section, which examines the cyclical impact of tariffs in the context of efficiency effects and labor market distortions.

4. The Prototype Economy

Here we undertake to show how our model, notwithstanding its complexity — two countries, three types of output in each country, three consumption goods, material inputs — can be represented by a "prototype economy" of the sort that Chari, Kehoe, and McGrattan (2002) use for business cycle accounting. For illustrative purposes, and to reduce somewhat the complexity of the calculations, we will focus on the symmetric case in which both countries impose the same tariffs at the same time. In this case the prototype is a one-sector *closed economy* neoclassical growth model with two relatively straightforward distortions represented by linear taxes.

In the prototype model, a representative consumer solves

$$\max E_{t-1}\left\{\sum\nolimits_{s=t}^{\infty}\beta^{s-t}[\log(C_s)+\nu(1-N_s)]\right. \tag{13}$$

subject to a budget constraint

$$C_t+K_{t+1}\leq K_t(1-\delta)+w_tN_t(1-\tau_{Nt})+r_tK_t(1-\tau_{Kt})+T_t. \tag{14}$$

The representative firm chooses K_{t+1} and N_t to maximize

$$\sum\nolimits_{s=t}^{\infty}Z_{ts}[A_sF(K_s,N_s)-w_sN_s-r_sK_s], \tag{15}$$

where $Z_{ts}=\Pi_{j=t+1}^{s}(1+r_j)^{-1}(s\geq t+1), Z_{tt}=1$. The corresponding economy-wide resource constraints are

$$A_tF(K_tN_t)-C_t-\Delta K_{t+1}-\delta K_t\geq 0 \tag{16}$$

$$\tau_{Kt}K_t+\tau_{Nt}N_t=T_t. \tag{17}$$

We will show how the macroeconomic effects of the changes in tariff levels during the Great Depression may be represented as a combination of an efficiency effect (decreasing A) and a wage tax (increasing τ_N).

4.1. *Productivity disturbances and efficiency wedges*

Consider the analogous problem solved by a representative firm in one of our production sectors, but with intermediate inputs into production and no productivity variation. Keep in mind that we assume that $\theta_i=\theta$ and $\alpha_i=\alpha$ and that factor inputs are freely mobile across sectors within countries, so it must be the case that the capital-labor ratios are identical across sectors. The implication is that the prices of sectoral goods move in lockstep, though they may change relative to p_{mt} (which is the price of materials produced via the Armington aggregator). That being the case, we may drop the i subscript and normalize nominal wages by the common final goods price:

$$\sum_{s=t}^{\infty} Z_{ts}[F(K_s, N_s, M_s) - w_s N_s - r_s K_s - p_{ms} M_s], \tag{18}$$

where Z_{ts} is the discount factor from t to s as defined in Eq. (15).

There are two differences between this problem and the previous one-sector planner's problem: the output concept in this maximization problem is gross output, and there are three inputs into production, the new one being materials. This is where the Leontief (1941) assumption for materials is convenient, as may be seen by imposing $M_s = \theta Y_s$ at the outset:

$$\sum_{s=t}^{\infty} Z_{ts}[(1 - \theta p_{ms})F(K_s, N_s) - w_s N_s - r_s K_s]. \tag{19}$$

From the point of view of the decision problem of an atomistic firm, p_{mt} is exogenous and shifts the labor and investment demand schedules of the firm in exactly the same way as a total factor productivity change would in the basic neoclassical model.

To see this more clearly, consider the first-order conditions for labor N_t and capital K_t in our trade model:

$$(1 - \theta p_{mt})D_2 F(K_t, N_t) = w_t \tag{20}$$

$$(1 - \theta p_{mt})D_1 F(K_t, N_t) = r_t \tag{21}$$

and the analogous conditions for the prototype economy:

$$A_t D_2 F(K_t, N_t) = w_t \tag{22}$$

$$A_t D_1 F(K_t, N_t) = r_t. \tag{23}$$

Thus, the efficiency wedge implied by the trade model is the level of productivity (common to all sectors) that would give rise to the same input choices by the firm, namely,

$$A_t = (1 - \theta p_{mt}), \tag{24}$$

where it is understood that p_{mt} is the price of materials relative to the price of final goods.

Suppose that we were modeling the United States as a small open economy. In that environment, we would take the foreign price of materials as given (as we did in the firm-level problem) and the domestic price would be $p_{mt} = (1 + \tau_t)p_m^*$, where τ_t is the ad valorem equivalent tariffs on imports of foreign materials and p_m^* is the foreign ("world") price of materials, which we normalize to unity in the steady state. The magnitude of the change in the efficiency wedge in the prototype model that would produce the same marginal effects on the productivity of capital and labor (holding fixed the world price of materials) as the tariff changes would be

$$A_t = (1 - \theta(1 + \tau_t)) \tag{25}$$

$$\hat{A}_t \equiv -\varphi\hat{\Omega}_t \tag{26}$$

$$\varphi \equiv \frac{\theta(1+\tau)}{(1 - \theta(1+\tau))},$$

where $\Omega_t \equiv 1 + \tau_t$. For an initial tariff level of zero, φ is the ratio of materials cost to value added, which equals 0.25 in our baseline calibration. Combined with an initial tariff level of 10 percent gives us $\varphi = 0.282$. Thus, an increase in tariffs from 10 percent to 60 percent (the trough-to-peak movement in the U.S. tariffs as measured by customs duties relative to dutiable imports) would be equivalent to a productivity drop of 12.8 percent, which would translate into a 18.7 percent drop in output (in the calibrated prototype model) if the tariff increase was viewed as permanent. Unfortunately, this estimate is problematic because it ignores foreign tariff retaliation and the fact that the countries imposing the tariffs are large enough to affect world prices.

In our general equilibrium model, the prices of domestic and foreign materials are endogenous, which complicates the intuition somewhat and alters the quantitative implications. The wedge in our general equilibrium model is

$$A_t = 1 - \theta\frac{(1 + \tau_{4t})}{D_2G(m_{hht}, m_{fht})}, \tag{27}$$

where the materials price is substituted out using the first-order condition for the choice of imported materials used by the home country (i.e., $p_{mt}D_2G(m_{hht}, m_{fht}) = (1+\tau_t)p^*_{4t}$) and we have incorporated the fact that within-country final goods prices are equal in our model (both in the steady state and over time). The only difference between this wedge and that in the small open economy is the appearance of $D_2G(m_{hht},m_{fht})$ in the denominator, which is the marginal product of foreign materials in the provision of the domestic aggregate material input.

Two factors work to mitigate the impact of tariffs on aggregate economic activity relative to the small open economy benchmark. First, there is a terms-of-trade effect such that when the home country raises its tariffs, it tends to reduce the world relative price of materials. Thus, the new equilibrium relative price of materials rises by less than the increase in the tariff. In a symmetric tariff war, however, this effect is inoperative. The second factor absent in the partial equilibrium model is the presence of domestic producers of material inputs. The quantitative response of domestic producers will depend to a significant extent on the elasticity of substitution between domestic and foreign materials. The implication, though, is that an expansion of domestic materials production mitigates the materials price increase and reduces the aggregative impact of the tariff war. This effect is operative even in a symmetric tariff war, since both countries have domestic materials producing sectors. As it turns out, the peak-to-trough movement in the efficiency wedge is just over 1 percent once these general equilibrium effects are taken into account — approximately one-tenth of what the partial equilibrium analysis suggested.

4.2. *Labor wedge*

Next consider the impact of τ_3 on domestic consumption decisions. There are two dimensions on which to consider this impact: static and intertemporal. The static impact of τ_3 is reflected by the marginal rate of substitution between goods 1 and 3:

$$\frac{b_3}{b_1}\left(\frac{C_{3t}}{C_{1t}}\right)^{-(1+\gamma)} = \frac{p^*_{3t}(1+\tau_{3t})}{p_{1t}} \tag{28}$$

Substituting this and first-order conditions involving C_1 and C_2 into the definition of C, $C \equiv [b_1 C_1^{-\gamma} + b_2 C_2^{-\gamma} + b_3 C_3^{-\gamma}]^{-(1/\gamma)}$, and one can show that

$$C_t \equiv \left[b_1^{\frac{1}{1+\gamma}} p_{1t}^{\frac{1}{1+\gamma}} + b_2^{\frac{1}{1+\gamma}} p_{2t}^{\frac{1}{1+\gamma}} + b_3^{\frac{1}{1+\gamma}} [p_{3t}^*(1+\tau_{3t})]^{\frac{\gamma}{1+\gamma}} \right]^{-\frac{1+\gamma}{\gamma}}. \quad (29)$$

The first-order condition for C_t and N_t in the prototype economy is

$$\frac{1/C_t}{\nu'(1-N_t)} = \frac{1}{w_t(1-\tau_{N_t})}. \quad (30)$$

This suggests that we could set

$$1 - \tau_{Nt} = \left[\frac{b_1^{\frac{1}{1+\gamma}} p_{1t}^{\frac{\gamma}{1+\gamma}} + b_2^{\frac{1}{1+\gamma}} p_{2t}^{\frac{\gamma}{1+\gamma}} + b_3^{\frac{1}{1+\gamma}} [p_{3t}^*(1+\tau_{3t})]^{\frac{\gamma}{1+\gamma}}}{b_1^{\frac{1}{1+\gamma}} p_{1t}^{\frac{\gamma}{1+\gamma}} + b_2^{\frac{1}{1+\gamma}} p_{2t}^{\frac{\gamma}{1+\gamma}} + b_3^{\frac{1}{1+\gamma}} [p_{3t}^*]^{\frac{\gamma}{1+\gamma}}} \right]^{-\frac{1+\gamma}{\gamma}}, \quad (31)$$

which of course equals 1 if $\tau_{3t} = 0$, and is decreasing in τ_{3t} for $\gamma > -1$. This reflects the fact that the tariff in effect reduces real wages by making the preferred consumption bundle more expensive.

4.3. *Comparing the tariff and historical wedges*

We next compute the implied wedges, given our baseline parameterization, for the symmetric case, based on the high tariff series shown earlier in Fig. 1. While these are not strictly comparable to the historical experience (because we have not incorporated in the prototype model the asymmetric behavior of foreign tariffs), they nonetheless provide a close approximation of the tariffs' impact. This may be verified by comparing the simulations reported here with the asymmetric tariff simulations in our earlier paper.

We see in Fig. 3 that what is needed in the prototype model to match the path of output predicted by the tariff-driven trade model is mostly an efficiency wedge. In comparison to the wedges measured by Chari, Kehoe, and McGrattan (2002) in Fig. 4, the

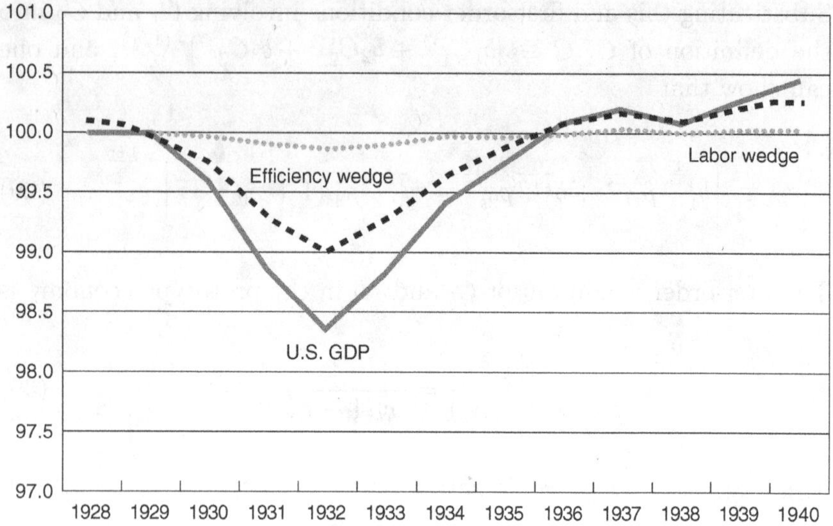

Fig. 3. U.S. GDP and the labor and efficiency wedges implied by the trade model viewed through the lens of the prototype aggregate neoclassical model. All series are normalized to 100 in 1929.

efficiency wedge correlates very strongly with the model simulation during the entire sample period. The small labor wedge produced by the consumption tariff in our model declines at the same time as the empirical labor wedge from 1929 to 1993, but we predict a rising labor wedge (declining distortion) as the tariff levels fall from 1933 onward. Both empirical wedges are at least an order of magnitude larger than those produced by our simulation, which simply reflects the fact that our model can only account for, at most, 10 percent of the swing in output during the Great Depression.

Care should be taken in interpreting the estimated labor and efficiency wedges coming from the trade model and those estimated by Chari, Kehoe, and McGrattan. Although tariffs in our model produce distortions resulting in lower real output, they do not directly imply either reductions in total factor productivity (TFP) or failures of the first-order condition linking the marginal rate of substitution of consumption and leisure to the marginal product of labor to hold. The fact that researchers find such "wedges" using

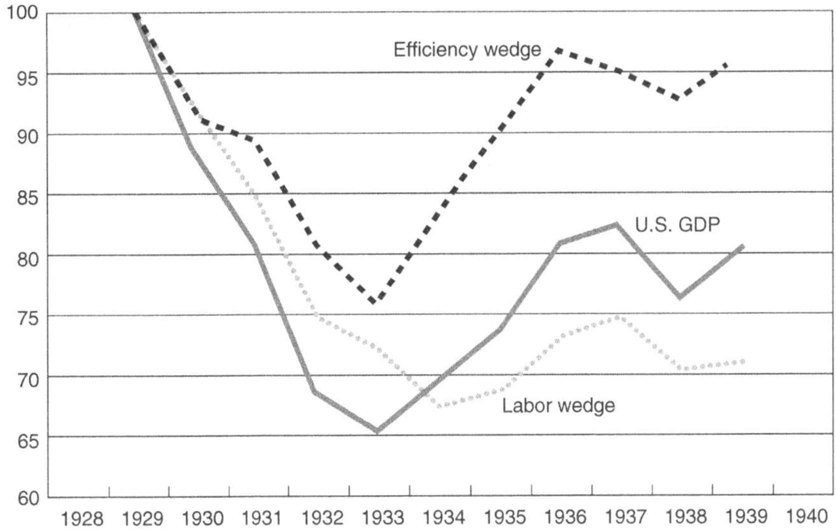

Fig. 4. U.S. GDP and the labor and efficiency wedges estimated by Chari, Kehoe and McGrattan (2002). All series are normalized to 100 in 1929.

the measures and aggregation methods of the basic neoclassical model raises some interesting questions in the context of quantitative business cycle analysis. Specifically, under what circumstances could the tariff-induced distortions as described by our model lead to empirical efficiency or labor wedges? For example, a model in which changes in labor inputs are correlated with reductions in (unobservable) work effort (i.e., labor hoarding) could have such an impact. A second question concerns the Chari, Kehoe, and McGrattan business cycle accounting framework. If the distortions induced by our tariffs do not yield observable wedges in their methodology, then where do they show up? It would seem that the Chari, Kehoe, and McGrattan framework is not well suited to account for these distortions.

5. Conclusions

In this paper we have revisited the issues addressed in Crucini and Kahn (1996) in light of recent research on the Great Depression. In that paper we had argued that particular features of the Hawley-Smoot tariffs could have provided them with a stronger impact than conventional wisdom had held, and we described the magnitudes in a calibrated general equilibrium model. We suggested that while the tariffs could directly account for only a small part of the Great Depression, they nonetheless had a significant, recession-sized impact — "small" only in the context of the Great Depression.

Here we have reformulated our arguments in the context of the business cycle accounting framework of Chari, Kehoe, and McGrattan (2002). We have shown that tariff increases in our model surface mostly as variation in aggregate efficiency with a small role for the labor wedge. Although the implied efficiency wedges from tariffs do not translate into measured TFP declines, their correlation with the Chari, Kehoe, and McGrattan efficiency wedges during the Great Depression suggests the possibility of a connection, either through measurement issues or through some propagation mechanism. In any case, the methodology allowed us to discuss the quantitative impact and aggregate channels by which tariffs affect macroeconomic aggregates in a manner that may be easily understood by economists familiar with the inner workings of the one-sector stochastic growth model.

We regard our findings as only the beginning of an effort to understand the role of tariffs in the Depression. In a sense we have argued that the shocks were larger than might have been previously thought, but with conventional propagation the contribution was modest relative to the scale of the Depression. If wages are sticky above market-clearing levels, then a decline in aggregate efficiency (from whatever source) should result in a larger quantitative impact than under flexible prices. In fact, in their paper in this volume, Perri and Quadrini use wage rigidities to amplify the impact of tariffs in their study of the Great Depression in Italy. Moreover, for any event of such magnitude, it is likely that there were many contributing factors. Any effort to account for the Depression will likely have to look for both large shocks and nonstandard propagation mechanisms before a sufficient understanding is reached.

Data Appendix

The macroeconomic aggregates — output, prices, investment, merchandise exports, merchandise imports, and consumption for Canada, Italy, the United Kingdom, and the United States — were generously provided by David Backus. They are described in detail in Backus and Kehoe (1992).

The trade data reported in Table 1 are taken from the League of Nations. II. Economic and Financial, 1931, columns 1–2 Table X, columns 3–9 Table XI, except Canada. Canadian data in columns 1 and 2 are from the Canada Yearbook External Trade Table XI (fully manufactured and aggregate of raw materials and partly manufactured).

The tariff indexes for Germany, Italy, Sweden, and the United Kingdom were computed as the ratio of customs revenue to total imports and are from *European Historical Statistics 1750–1970.*

The tariff indexes for Canada are from *Canada Year Book*, selected years.

The tariff indexes for the United States and imports by country of origin are from *The Statistical History of the United States, from Colonial Times to the Present.*

The trade-weighted tariff levels (in Table 2) use the shares of U.S. imports from each country in 1929 normalized to total 100. The countries included in the calculation were Canada, France, Germany, Italy, and the United Kingdom. U. S. export shares are used because we are assuming that the world consists of the United States and these countries, and we are ignoring imports of these countries from countries other than the United States. Thus, we are also assuming that tariffs were imposed on imports independent of the country of origin. To the extent that countries were retaliating directly against the United States, we are understating the magnitude of the tariff increases.

For the business cycle simulations, the tariff levels are transformed to log deviations from their sample means to correspond to the units of the linearized model, which measures aggregate variables in log deviations from their steady-state growth path. The U.S. tariff and rest-of-the-world tariff levels correspond to the U.S. index using dutiable imports.

Acknowledgments

We are grateful to Rick Bond, Timothy Kehoe, Andrea Maneschi, and Ananth Ramanarayanan for helpful comments. The views expressed herein are those of the authors and not necessarily those of the Federal Reserve Bank of New York or the Federal Reserve System. Portions of this paper were reprinted from "Tariffs and Aggregate Economic Activity: Lessons from the Great Depression," *Journal of Monetary Economics* 38, no. 3 (1996): 427–67.

References

Armington, Paul S. 1969. A theory of demand for products distinguished by the place of production. *International Monetary Fund Staff Papers* 16 (March): 159–78.

Backus, David K., and Patrick J. Kehoe. 1992. International evidence on the historical properties of business cycles. *American Economic Review* 82 (September): 864–88.

Chari, V. V.; Patrick J. Kehoe; and Ellen R. McGrattan. 2002. Business cycle accounting. Working Paper 625. Federal Reserve Bank of Minneapolis.

Crucini, Mario J. 1994. Sources of variation in real tariff rates: The United States, 1900 to 1940. *American Economic Review* 84 (June): 732–43.

Crucini, Mario J., and James Kahn. 1996. Tariffs and aggregate economic activity: Lessons from the Great Depression. *Journal of Monetary Economics* 38 (December): 427–67.

Eichengreen, Barry. 1989. The political economy of the Smoot-Hawley Tariff. *Research in Economic History* 12: 1–43.

Galí, Jordi; Mark Gertler; and David López-Salido. 2001. Markups, gaps, and the welfare costs of fluctuations. Manuscript.

Hall, Robert E. 1997. Macroeconomic fluctuations and the allocation of time. *Journal of Labor Economics* 15 (January): 223–50.

Irwin, Douglas A., and Randall S. Kroszner. 1996. Log-rolling and economic interests in the passage of the Smoot-Hawley Tariff. *Carnegie-Rochester Series on Public Policy* 45 (December): 173–200.

Jones, Joseph M. 1934. *Tariff retaliation: Repercussions of the Hawley-Smoot bill.* Ph.D. dissertation. University of Pennsylvania.

Leontief, Wassily. 1941. *The structure of the American economy, 1919–1939: An empirical application of equilibrium analysis.* Cambridge, MA: Harvard University Press.

McDonald, Judith A.; Anthony P. O'Brien; and Colleen M. Callahan. 1997. Trade wars: Canada's reaction to the Smoot-Hawley Tariff. *Journal of Economic History* 57 (December): 802–26.

Mulligan, Casey B. 2002a. A dual method of empirically evaluating dynamic competitive equilibrium models with market distortions, applied to the Great Depression and World War II. Working Paper 8775. National Bureau of Economic Research.

Mulligan, Casey B. 2002b. A century of labor-leisure distortions. Working Paper 8774. National Bureau of Economic Research.

Rogerson, Richard. 1988. Indivisible labor, lotteries, and equilibrium. *Journal of Monetary Economics* 21 (January): 3–16.

Taussig, Frank W. 1931. *The tariff history of the United States*, 8th ed. New York: Putnam & Sons.

Whalley, John. 1985. *Trade liberalization among major world trading areas.* Cambridge, MA: MIT Press.

CPSIA information can be obtained
at www.ICGtesting.com
Printed in the USA
BVHW040923160320
575132BV00002B/9

9 789811 20823